PSYCHOLOGY IN PROGRESS

Readings from
SCIENTIFIC
AMERICAN

PSYCHOLOGY
IN PROGRESS

With Introductions by
Richard C. Atkinson
Stanford University

and

Study Guides by
John P. J. Pinel
University of British Columbia

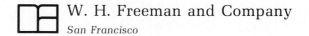 W. H. Freeman and Company
San Francisco

All of the SCIENTIFIC AMERICAN articles in
PSYCHOLOGY IN PROGRESS are available as separate
Offprints. For a complete list of more than 950 articles
now available as Offprints, write to W. H. Freeman and
Company, 660 Market Street, San Francisco, California
94104.

Library of Congress Cataloging in Publication Data

Atkinson, Richard C   comp.
  Psychology in progress.

  Published in 1971 under title: Contemporary psychology.
  Includes bibliographies and index.
  1. Psychology—Addresses, essays, lectures.
I. Scientific American. II. Title. [DNLM: 1. Psychology—
Collected works. BF21 A877p]
BF149.A8 1975   150′.8   74-23602
ISBN 0-7167-0517-6
ISBN 0-7167-0516-8 pbk.

9 8 7 6 5 4 3 2 1

PREFACE

Each article in this book presents intriguing new discoveries in the search for an understanding of the psychological processes that govern human behavior. Although most of the articles are written by psychologists, research by other specialists—neurologists, psychiatrists, and anthropologists—is also included. The very diversity of topics covered in this book points up the scope of psychology as both a scientific and applied discipline. It is indeed a long step from the topic of the first article (how the brain changes in response to environmental experiences) to that of the last article (how cultural factors influence perception). For the layman this book will serve as an introduction to the rapidly expanding field of psychology. For the psychology student it will present a variety of possibilities for future study and research. For either it should provide fascinating reading.

The 39 articles in this volume have been selected from more than 250 articles on psychology and related topics published in *Scientific American* during the past two decades. *Scientific American* has gained wide recognition for its excellence in scientific reporting; significant discoveries are presented clearly and accurately, but with a minimum of technical detail. To select from such a large number of outstanding articles has been a difficult task. Three criteria were used in making a final selection: (1) that the collected articles acquaint the reader with the frontiers of research in psychology; (2) that they cover a broad range of psychological topics; and (3) that they stimulate the interest of the reader. In some instances an older article on a given topic was chosen if it was more interesting or more comprehensive than more recent articles. Although an older article may not precisely reflect the author's current thinking, it may still be an excellent introduction to the topic under discussion.

The articles are organized into five sections. Section I, "Biological and Developmental Determiners of Behavior," deals with how the brain and nervous system are related to psychological processes and how these processes change as the organism matures. It focuses particularly on the influence of early experiences on development. Section II, "Perception and Awareness," discusses the sensory mechanisms that make it possible for us to be aware of events around us and how sensory inputs are organized into perceptions. Because vision is our predominant sense, most of the articles are concerned with visual perception. Section III, "Memory, Learning and Thinking," examines a wide range of cognitive processes—from memory and forgetting to language and problem-solving. Section IV, "Personality and Behavior Disorders," deals with a few of the many aspects of personality, the ways in which normal personality development may go awry, and recent techniques used to modify behavior disorders. The content of Section V is best described by its title: "Social Influences on Behavior."

The organization of the articles into sections was necessarily somewhat arbitrary. For example, "Social Deprivation in Monkeys" would have been just as suitable in Sections I or V as Section IV. Similarly, "Pictorial Perception and Culture," could equally well have been placed in Section II rather than in Section V. The order of the sections need not be followed (the reader primarily interested in social problems could start with Section V). The later articles do not depend on earlier ones.

Students will find the study guides extremely valuable. These include, for each article, a brief summary of the article, a glossary, and a set of questions. This supplementary material can be used in a number of ways. One possibility is to first read the summary in the study guide, then read the article itself, and finally, for review, examine the glossary and answer the study questions in the study guide. This approach should be particularly effective in mastering the concepts and facts presented in each article. The study guides should also prove helpful in preparing for examinations.

February 1975   *Richard C. Atkinson*

CONTENTS

Note on cross-references: References to articles included in this book are noted by the title of the article and the page on which it begins; references to articles that are available as Offprints, but are not included here, are noted by the article's title and Offprint number; references to articles published by SCIENTIFIC AMERICAN, but which are not available as Offprints, are noted by the title of the article and the month and year of its publication.

PSYCHOLOGY IN PROGRESS

BIOLOGICAL AND DEVELOPMENTAL DETERMINERS OF BEHAVIOR

I

I

BIOLOGICAL AND DEVELOPMENTAL DETERMINERS OF BEHAVIOR

INTRODUCTION

An understanding of psychological processes often can be amplified by studying both the physiological mechanisms underlying the processes and the development of those processes as the organism grows from infancy to adulthood. The human brain with its twelve billion nerve cells and virtually infinite number of interconnections and pathways may well be the most complex structure in the universe. In principle, all psychological events are related to activities of the brain and nervous system in conjunction with other body systems, but recent discoveries have dramatized this relationship. Emotional reactions, such as fear and rage, have been produced in animals and humans by mild electrical stimulation of specific areas in the brain. Electrical stimulation of certain areas in the human brain will produce sensations of pleasure and pain and even vivid memories of past experience. Thus, an understanding of psychology requires at least a familiarity with neurobiology; it also requires some understanding of developmental processes. The saying "The child is the father to the man" points up the importance of early experience in determining adult behavior. Since the time of Sigmund Freud, psychologists have been aware that the events of infancy are of great significance for personality development. Recent research indicates that early experiences may be even more crucial than was previously believed. The articles in this section present some of the research relating psychological phenomena to neurobiological and developmental processes.

Mark Rosenzweig, Edward Bennett, and Marian Diamond ("Brain Changes in Response to Experience") describe research that is concerned with evaluating experiences in infancy as they relate to the adult brain and neural mechanisms. Placing young rats in an "enriched" environment for as little as 30 days caused measurable changes in brain anatomy and chemistry. Rats in the enriched environment lived together in a large cage furnished with a variety of objects that they could play with; a new set of playthings was placed in the cage each day. Rats in an "impoverished" environment lived alone in bare cages. When these animals were later sacrificed, analyses indicated among other things that the weight of the brain cortex of the enriched animals was significantly greater than for the impoverished animals.

Seymour Levine in his article "Stimulation in Infancy" concludes that stimulation, or even stress, in infancy may be necessary for optimal development of the organism. Infant rats that had been given mild electric shock, or removed from their nests and handled for a few minutes each day, developed more rapidly than rats that had been left alone in their nests. The stimulated rats opened their eyes sooner, grew larger, gained more weight, and were also more capable of coping with stress in adult life. Although it is not clear to what extent these results can be generalized to the treatment of human infants, a number of studies have shown that an infant provided with a stimulating environment during the early months of life—one who is handled, talked to, and exposed to many different things to see and hear—develops more rapidly than one who spends most of the time lying alone in a crib with a minimum of stimulation.

In "The Visual Cortex of the Brain" David Hubel describes how nerve cells in the visual system are organized to respond to stimuli. Using microelectrodes, he and his colleagues record the responses of individual nerve cells in the cat to various visual patterns; recordings have been made starting with cells in the retina and progressing up the optic nerve to the visual cells of the cortex. They found that at each successive level in the system more complex stimuli are required to activate the cells. Thus, whereas nerve cells in the retina respond to almost any pattern of light, cells of the visual cortex (the area where vision is represented in the brain) are more discriminating, responding only to very specific patterns of stimulation. For example, some cortical cells fire only when stimulated by a narrow slit of light oriented in a horizontal direction; others are activated only by a vertical slit; and yet others by stimuli moving in only one direction or forming a certain angle. Thus, for the cat at least, the perception of certain stimuli appears to be a fixed characteristic of the nerve cells.

Much about the localization of brain functions has been learned from studying behavior following specific brain injuries. Using a different method of investigation, James Olds ("Pleasure Centers in the Brain") discovered a region near the midline of the brain associated not with specific behavior but with emotions and motivation—feelings of pleasure and pain. His technique was to stimulate specific areas of a rat's brain with mild electric current. He found that stimulation of a certain area (the hypothalamus) resulted in feelings of pleasure, judging from the fact that the animal would press a lever hour after hour to receive electrical stimulation in this brain area, and preferred such stimulation to a food reward, even when hungry. Adjacent areas were found to be "pain" rather than "pleasure" centers; the rat would press a bar to *avoid* stimulation in these areas. Olds' theory is that electrical stimulation in the pleasure centers excites some of the nerve cells that would normally be excited by satisfaction of such basic drives as hunger, thirst, and sex.

The complex behaviors of various animal species—the nest-building of birds, swarming of bees, migration of birds and fishes, mating rituals, caring for the young—have defied any simple explantion. The word "instinct" was widely used in the past to refer to any unlearned, patterned, goal-directed behavior characteristic of a species. The word was often used to describe human behavior as well—a mother's love illustrating a "parental instinct," warfare an "aggressive instinct," social behavior a "herd instinct," and so on. The presence or absence of instincts in man was a source of intense controversy in the 1920s. The argument became part of a larger controversy over the relative contributions of heredity and environment to development. Those who believed in instincts considered heredity the major developmental influence. Those who did not believe in them won out in the end because the believers failed to agree with one another on either the number or the kinds of instincts man possessed. Because of man's relatively prolonged infancy and the great importance of learning in all that he does, the concept of instinct has not proved helpful in studying or understanding human behavior.

The problems raised by the study of instincts in animals other than man have taken on renewed interest as a result of the work of a group of psychologists and zoologists known as ethologists. Their studies have called attention to the study of organisms in their natural environments. *Imprinting*, one of their concepts, is a kind of learning that capitalizes on an inherited tendency appearing when the time is ripe. The clearest example is the tendency of a young duckling to follow its "mother" shortly after it is hatched, and then to follow only this particular female duck. Incubator-hatched ducklings can be imprinted on artificial models, both inanimate and human. For example, mallard ducklings exposed to a moving model for ten minutes between twelve and seventeen hours after hatching will continue to treat the model as though it were the "mother" and remain with it even against the attraction of live mallard ducks. Once imprinting has occurred, "following" will be elicited only by the imprinted object. Eckhard Hess in his article "Imprinting in a Natural Laboratory" reviews recent research on imprinting and examines the implications for psychological theory. These findings bear on the age-old question of the role of instincts in human affairs.

The last two articles in this section are concerned with developmental processes, specifically the development of visual perception. A question long debated by philosophers and psychologists is whether man's ability to perceive the world is an innate capacity, or whether it is learned. Does a newborn infant, like the adult, see a world of stable objects, or is the infant confronted by a constantly changing array of shapes, sizes, and edges that he must learn to identify as stable objects? The problem exists because the image projected on the retina of the eye does not faithfully represent what we "see." For example, the retinal image of a dinner plate seen lying on a table is quite different in shape from the retinal image of the same plate seen full face. Yet, in both instances we "see" the same unchanging object, a "dinner plate." Similarly, the retinal image of a person standing across the room is much larger than the image of the same person viewed from across the street, yet we "see" the person as the same size.

The question of man's innate perceptual abilities was a subject of great debate among philosophers in the seventeenth century. The *navtivists* (Descartes and Kant, for example) maintained that we are born with the ability to see the world as it is seen in adulthood. The *empiricists* (Berkeley and Locke, for example) claimed that our perceptions are learned through experience with a specific environment. In the centuries that followed scientists have been divided on the problem.

Because an infant cannot describe what he sees, the question is not easily answered. T. G. R. Bower ("The Object in the World of the Infant") used a series of ingenious experimental procedures to investigate various aspects of infants' perception of stationary and moving objects. He concludes that infants are far more capable of making certain types of perceptual responses than had previously been supposed (supporting the nativist view), but that other perceptual processes clearly improve over time and depend upon the infant's experiences (giving some support to the empiricists' view). Presumably, through maturation, humans develop the *capacity to integrate* sensory information into a meaningful framework, thus allowing us to cope with the physical world in a predictable way.

In another series of experiments, Gibson and Walk ("The Visual Cliff") demonstrate that the perception of depth is largely innate—at least it is evident as soon as the organism is able to move about. When human infants old enough to crawl are placed at the brink of a "visual cliff" (a solid glass surface with the visual impression of sudden depth in the middle), they will refuse to cross the "cliff" to their mother on the opposite side. Parents may be reassured to know that their infant's propensity to fall off tables and out of the crib does not indicate an inability to appreciate height, but rather, a lack of the motor control required to keep from falling.

The seven articles in this section provide only a sample of the many research topics currently being explored by physiological and developmental psychologists. They do, however, indicate the broad range of topics and the variety of research in these areas.

Brain Changes in Response to Experience

by Mark R. Rosenzweig, Edward L. Bennett
and Marian Cleeves Diamond
February 1972

*Rats kept in a lively environment for 30 days show
distinct changes in brain anatomy and chemistry
compared with animals kept in a dull environment.
The implications of these effects for man are assessed*

Does experience produce any observable change in the brain? The hypothesis that changes occur in brain anatomy as a result of experience is an old one, but convincing evidence of such changes has been found only in the past decade. It has now been shown that placing an experimental animal in enriched or impoverished environments causes measurable changes in brain anatomy and chemistry. How these changes are related to learning and memory mechanisms is currently being studied by an interdisciplinary approach that involves neurochemical, neuroanatomical and behavioral techniques.

The earliest scientific account of brain changes as a result of experience that we have been able to find was written in the 1780's by an Italian anatomist, Michele Gaetano Malacarne. His experimental design is worth describing briefly, since it resembles the one we are using in our laboratory at the University of California at Berkeley. He worked with two dogs from the same litter and with two parrots, two goldfinches and two blackbirds, each pair of birds from the same clutch of eggs. He trained one member of each pair for a long period; the other member of the pair was left untrained. He then killed the animals and examined their brains. He reported that there were more folds in the cerebellum of the trained animals than in that of the untrained ones. Although his study was noted by some of his contemporaries, we have not found any evidence that others attempted to carry out similar experiments. Knowledge of Malacarne's experiment quickly faded away.

During the 19th century there was considerable interest in the relation between the size of the human head and intellectual ability and training. In the 1870's Paul Broca, a famous French physician and anthropologist, compared the head circumference of medical students and male nurses and found that the students had larger heads. Since he believed the two sets of young men were equal in ability, he concluded that the differences in head size must have been due to the differences in training. Clearly Broca's logic was not impeccable, and there are other possible explanations for the differences he found. His critics pointed to the lack of correspondence between skull size and brain volume, the important roles of age and body size in determining brain size and the relative stability of the size of the brain in comparison with the size of most other organs. By the beginning of the 20th century not only had experimenters failed to prove that training resulted in changes in the gross anatomy of the brain but also a consensus had developed that such changes could not be detected, and so the search was generally abandoned.

With the development of new biochemical tools and techniques in the 1950's, some investigators began to ask if chemical changes in the brain following training could be detected. They looked for changes at the synapses that transmit impulses from one nerve cell to another or for changes in the nucleic acids (RNA and DNA) of nerve cells. The techniques used to find chemical or anatomical changes in the brain following experience are not difficult in principle but they must be carried out with precision because many of the changes that occur are not large. Here is how a basic experiment is conducted with laboratory rats of a given strain. (In our experiments we have worked with several strains of rats and with laboratory mice and gerbils; we have observed similar effects in all these animals.) At a given age, often at weaning, sets of three males are taken from each litter. Usually

a dozen sets of three males are used in an experiment. This yields stabler and more reliable results than working with a single set, as Malacarne did.

The use of rodents for these studies is convenient for several reasons. Brain dissection is simpler in rodents than it is in carnivores or primates because the cerebral cortex of rodents is smooth and not convoluted like the cortex of higher mammals. The gray cortex can be stripped away from the underlying white matter more readily in rodents than it can in higher mammals. Rodents are small, inexpensive and bear large litters, so that littermates with the same genetic background can be assigned to different conditions. In addition, geneticists have developed inbred lines of rats and mice, and working with these inbred lines gives us further control over the genetic background.

The three male rats from each litter are assigned at random so that one rat remains in the standard laboratory colony cage, one rat is placed in an enriched environment and the third is put in an impoverished environment. It should be noted that "enriched" and "impoverished" are not used in an absolute sense but only in relation to the standard laboratory colony environment that is the usual baseline for studies in anatomy, biochemistry, physiology, nutrition and behavior.

In the standard laboratory conditions a few rats live in a cage of adequate size with food and water always present [*see illustration on following page*]. In the enriched environment several rats live in a large cage furnished with a variety of objects they can play with. A new set of playthings, drawn out of a pool of 25 objects, is placed in the cage every day. In the impoverished environment each rat lives alone in a cage. Originally the isolated rats were kept in a separate quiet room, but this turned out to be unnecessary.

At the end of a predetermined experimental period, which can be from a few days to several months, the rats are sacrificed and their brains are removed. The brain dissection and analysis of each set of three littermates are done in immediate succession but in a random order and identified only by code number so that the person doing the dissection does not know which cage the rat comes from. With practice a skillful worker can do dissections with considerable precision and reliability. To delineate the various cortical regions a small plastic calibrated T square is used [*see illustration on page 8*]. Samples removed from a cortical region are weighed to the nearest tenth of a milligram and then placed on dry ice. The samples are kept frozen until chemical analysis is performed to determine the activity of the neurotransmitter enzymes in them.

If the rat brains are to be used for anatomical studies, the animal is anesthetized and perfused with a fixative solution. Later sections of the brain are prepared for microscopy.

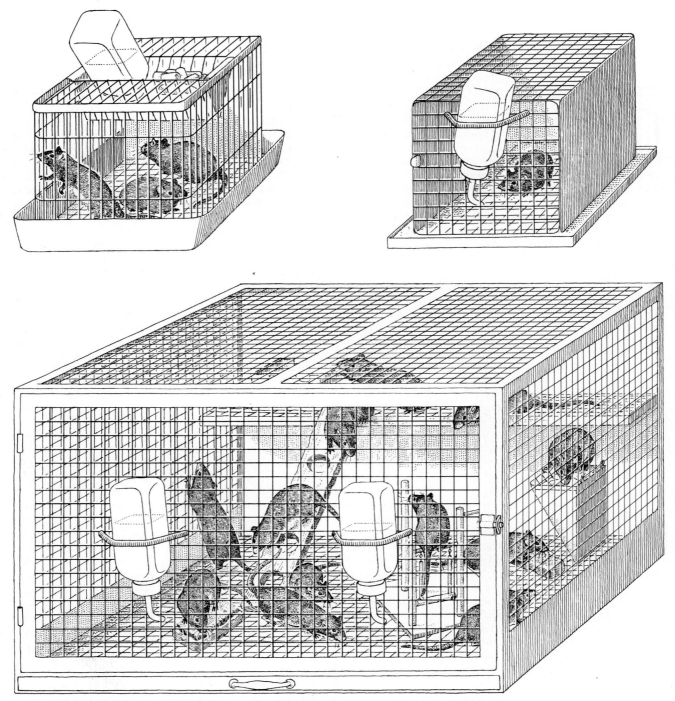

THREE LABORATORY ENVIRONMENTS that produce differences in brain anatomy of littermate rats are depicted. In the standard laboratory colony there are usually three rats in a cage (*upper left*). In the impoverished environment (*upper right*) a rat is kept alone in a cage. In the enriched environment 12 rats live together in a large cage furnished with playthings that are changed daily. Food and water are freely available in all three environments. The rats typically remain in the same environment for 30 days or more.

In the 1950's we had been attempting to relate individual differences in the problem-solving behavior of rats to individual differences in the amount of the enzyme acetylcholinesterase in the brain. (At the time and until 1966 the psychologist David Krech was a member of the research group.) The enzyme rapidly breaks down acetylcholine, a substance that acts as a transmitter between nerve cells. The excess transmitter must be neutralized quickly because nerve impulses can follow each other at a rate of hundreds per second. This enzymatic activity is often measured in terms of tissue weight, and so in our early experiments we recorded the weight of each sample of brain tissue we took for chemical analysis. We found indications that the level of brain acetylcholinesterase was altered by problem-solving tests, and this led us to look for effects of more extensive experience. To our surprise we found that different experiences not only affected the enzymatic activity but also altered the weight of the brain samples.

By 1964 we had found that rats that had spent from four to 10 weeks in the enriched or the impoverished environments differed in the following ways: rats with enriched experience had a greater weight of cerebral cortex, a greater thickness of cortex and a greater total activity of acetylcholinesterase but less activity of the enzyme per unit of tissue weight. Moreover, rats with enriched experience had considerably greater activity of another enzyme: cholinesterase, which is found in the glial cells and blood capillaries that surround the nerve cells. Glial cells (named from the Greek word for "glue") perform a variety of functions, including transportation of materials between capillaries and nerve cells, formation of the fatty insulating sheath around the neural axons and removal of dead neural tissue.

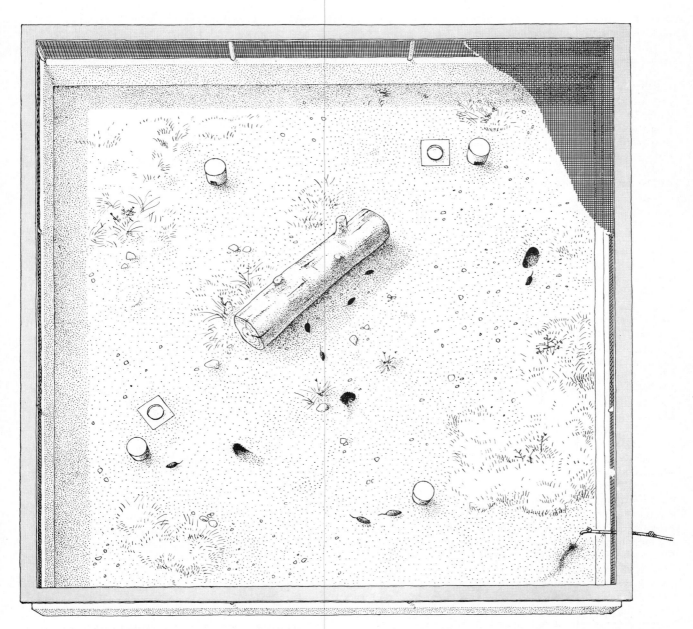

SEMINATURAL ENVIRONMENT for studying the effects of experience on the brain is provided by outdoor enclosures at the Field Station for Research in Animal Behavior at the University of California at Berkeley. The enclosures have a concrete base 30 feet by 30 feet with a screen over the top. Inbred laboratory rats thrive in the outdoor setting when food and water are provided. The rats revert to burrowing, something that their ancestors, which had lived in laboratory cages, had not done for more than 100 generations.

We later found that there were more glial cells in rats from the enriched environment than there were in rats from the impoverished one, and this may account for the increased activity of cholinesterase. Although differences in experience did not change the number of nerve cells per unit of tissue, the enriched environment produced larger cell bodies and nuclei. These larger cell bodies indicate higher metabolic activity. Further chemical measures involving RNA and DNA pointed in the same direction. The amount of DNA per milligram of tissue decreased, presumably because the bulk of the cortex increased as the number of neurons, whose nuclei contain a fixed amount of DNA, remained relatively constant. The amount of RNA per milligram remained virtually unchanged, yielding a significant increase in the ratio of RNA to DNA, and this suggests a higher metabolic activity. In most of the experiments the greatest differences between enriched and impoverished experience were found in the occipital cortex, which is roughly the rear third of the cortical surface.

We do not know why the occipital region of the cortex is affected by enriched experience more than other regions. At first we thought that differences in visual stimulation might be responsible, but when we used blinded rats, the occipital cortex still showed significant differences between littermates from the enriched and the impoverished environments. We found the same effects when normal rats were placed in the different environments and kept in darkness for the entire period. This is not to say that deprivation of vision did not have an effect on the anatomy and chemistry of the brain. The occipital cortex of rats that were blinded or kept totally in the dark gained less weight than the occipital cortex of littermates that were raised in standard colony conditions with a normal light-dark cycle, but this did not prevent the occurrence of the enrichment-impoverishment effect.

Although the brain differences induced by environment are not large, we are confident that they are genuine. When the experiments are replicated, the same pattern of differences is found repeatedly. For example, in 16 replications between 1960 and 1969 of the basic enriched-environment-v.-impoverished-environment experiment, using the same strain of rat exposed to the experimental conditions from the age of 25 to 105 days, each experiment resulted in a greater occipital-cortex weight for the rats in the enriched environment. Twelve

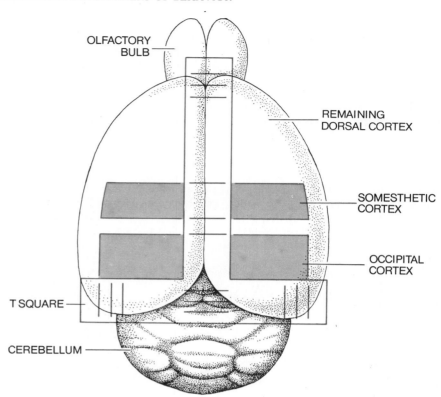

CORTICAL AREAS of a rat brain are located for dissection with the aid of a calibrated plastic T square to ensure uniform samples. The desired sections are removed, weighed and stored on dry ice. The remaining cortex and the subcortex also are weighed and frozen.

of the 16 replications were significantly at better than the .05 level, that is, for each of the 12 experiments there was less than one chance in 20 that the difference was due simply to chance or biological variability. For weight of the total cortex, 13 of the 16 experiments showed significant differences [see top illustration on opposite page].

The most consistent effect of experience on the brain that we found was the ratio of the weight of the cortex to the weight of the rest of the brain: the subcortex. It appears that the cortex increases in weight quite readily in response to an enriched environment, whereas the weight of the rest of the brain changes little. Moreover, since rats with larger bodies tend to have both a heavier cortex and a heavier subcortex than smaller rats, the ratio of the cortex to the rest of the brain tends to cancel the influence of body weight. For animals of a given strain, sex, age and environment the cortex/subcortex ratio tends to be the same even if the animals differ in body weight. When the environment is such that the cortex grows, the cortex/subcortex ratio shows the change very clearly and reliably. On this measure 14 of the 16 experiments were significant at the .01 level.

One of the major problems for measuring the effects of experience on the brain is finding an appropriate baseline. Initially we took the standard laboratory colony condition as the baseline, as most other investigators have. The cortex/subcortex-weight ratio in rats from the enriched environment is greater than the ratio in rats from the standard colony environment, and this ratio in turn is greater than the ratio in rats from the impoverished environment. Where thickness of cortex is concerned, both environmental enrichment and impoverishment are effective but on different regions of the cortex.

Suppose that the natural environment in which the animals evolved were taken as the baseline. Compared with the laboratory environments, even the enriched one, a natural environment may be much richer in learning experiences. For inbred laboratory animals, however, it is no longer clear what the natural environment is. Laboratory rats and mice have been kept for more than 100 generations in protected environments, and inbreeding has made their gene pool different from the natural one. For this reason we have begun to study wild deer mice (Peromyscus). The mice are trapped in the San Francisco area and brought to our laboratory; some are kept in almost

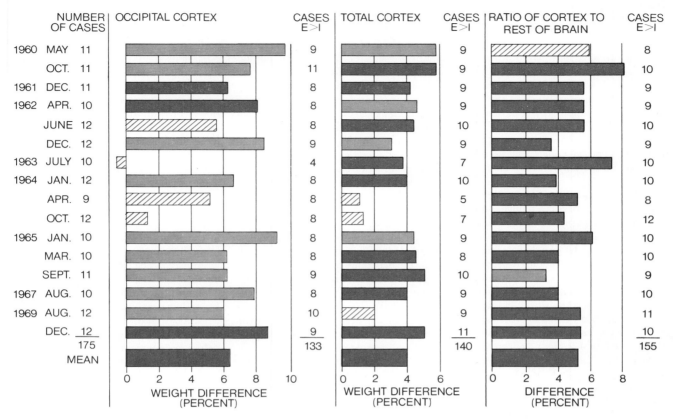

BRAIN-WEIGHT DIFFERENCES between rats from enriched environments and their littermates from impoverished environments were replicated in 16 successive experiments between 1960 and 1969 involving an 80-day period and the same strain of rat. For the occipital cortex, weight differences in three of the replications were significant at the probability level of .01 or better (*dark colored bars*), nine were significant at the .05 level (*light colored bars*) and four were not significant (*hatched bars*). The ratio of the weight of the cortex to the rest of the brain proved to be the most reliable measure, with 14 of the 16 replications significant at the .01 level.

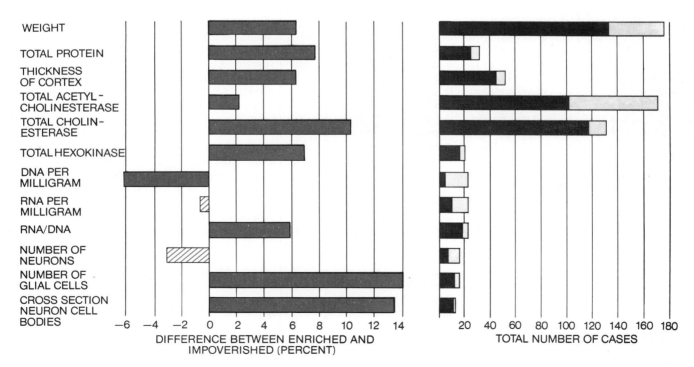

OCCIPITAL CORTEX of rats kept in enriched or impoverished environments from 25 to 105 days showed the effects of the different experiences. The occipital cortex of rats from the enriched environment, compared with that of rats from the impoverished one, was 6.4 percent heavier. This was significant at the .01 level or better, as were most other measures (*dark colored bars*). Only two measures were not significant (*hatched bars*). The dark gray bars on the right show the number of cases in which the rat from the enriched environment exceeded its littermate from the impoverished environment in each of the measures that are listed.

natural conditions at an outdoor station and others are put into laboratory cages. The work with deer mice is still in progress, but we have also placed laboratory rats in the outdoor setting. We found that when food is provided, laboratory rats can thrive in an outdoor enclosure even in a wet winter when the temperature drops to the freezing point. When the ground was not too wet, the rats dug burrows, something their ancestors had not done for more than 100 generations. In each of eight experiments the rats kept for one month in the outdoor setting showed a greater brain development than their littermates that had been kept in enriched laboratory cages. This indicates that even the enriched laboratory environment is indeed impoverished in comparison with a natural environment.

It is possible that the brain changes we found are not the result of learning and memory but are due to other aspects of the experimental situation, such as the amount of handling and stress, or perhaps an altered rate of maturation. For example, simply handling rats, particularly young ones, is known to increase the weight of their adrenal glands. Rats in the enriched environment are handled each day when they are removed from their cage while their playthings are being changed, whereas rats in the impoverished environment are handled only once a week for weighing. We tested the effects of handling on brain changes some years ago. Some rats were handled for several minutes a day for either 30 or 60 days; their littermates were never handled. There were no differences between the handled rats and the nonhandled ones in brain weight or brain-enzyme activity. More recently rats from both the enriched and the impoverished environments were handled once a day and the usual brain differences developed.

Stress was another possible cause of the cerebral effects. Rats from the impoverished environment might have suffered from "isolation stress" and rats from the enriched environment may have been stressed by "information overload." To test this notion Walter H. Riege subjected rats to a daily routine of stress. The rats were briefly tumbled in a revolving drum or given a mild electric shock. The stress produced a significant increase in the weight of the adrenal glands but did not give rise to changes in the brain measures that we use. It seems clear that stress is not responsible for the cerebral changes we have found.

It was also possible, since some of the brain changes we have found go in the same direction as changes that occur in normal maturation, that enriched experience simply accelerates maturation or that isolation retards it. Changes in the depth of the cerebral cortex and certain other changes resulting from an enriched environment go in the opposite direction to what is found in normal growth. The cortical thickness of standard colony rats reaches a maximum at 25 days after birth and then decreases slightly with age, whereas enriched experience causes cortical thickness to increase even in year-old rats. In fact, Riege has found that an enriched environment will produce as great an increase in brain weight in fully mature rats as it does in young rats, although the adult rats require a longer period of environmental stimulation to show the maximum effect.

The effect of enriched environment on very young rats has been tested by Dennis Malkasian. He puts sets of three litters of six-day-old rat pups and their mother either into an unfurnished cage or into a cage containing play objects. Brains were taken for anatomical analysis at 14, 19 and 28 days of age. At each age pups from the enriched environment showed a greater thickness of cerebral cortex, and in some parts of the cortex the differences were larger than those found in experiments with rats examined after weaning.

When we first reported our results other investigators were understandably skeptical, since the effect of experience on the brain had not been previously demonstrated. After our findings had been replicated, some investigators began to think that the brain may be so plastic that almost any treatment can modify it, for example merely placing a rat for 15 minutes a day in any apparatus other than its home cage. This does not happen; although cerebral changes are easier to induce than we had supposed at first, a moderate amount of experience is still necessary. We recently demonstrated that two hours of daily enriched experience over a 30-day period is sufficient to produce the typical changes in brain weight. On the other hand, placing a group of 12 rats in a large unfurnished cage for two hours a day for 30 days did not bring about significant changes in our usual brain measures. Moreover, putting rats alone in large cages with play objects for two hours a day is not very effective, probably because a single rat does not play with the objects much and tends to rest or to groom itself. The enriched environment will produce cerebral changes in a single rat if the rat is stimulated to interact with the objects. This can be done by giving the rat a moderate dose of an excitant drug or by putting it into the enriched environment during the dark part of its daily cycle (rats are nocturnal animals). A recent experiment indicates that cerebral changes can also be achieved by putting the rat into the enriched environment after several hours of food deprivation and placing tiny pellets of food on and in the play objects.

There can now be no doubt that many aspects of brain anatomy and brain chemistry are changed by experience. Some of our most recent efforts have been directed toward determining the changes that occur at the synaptic level in the occipital cortex, a region of the brain that shows relatively large changes with experience in enriched environments. Over the past few years Albert Globus of the University of California at Irvine has been counting the number of dendritic spines in brain sections from rats that have been exposed to an enriched environment or an impoverished one in our laboratory. Most of the synaptic contacts between nerve cells in the cortex are made on the branchlike dendrites of the receiving cell or on the dendritic spines, which are small projections from the dendrites. Globus made his counts on the cortical neuron called a pyramidal cell [see top illustration on opposite page]. He found more spines, particularly on the basal dendrites, in rats exposed to an enriched environment than in littermates from the impoverished environment.

An even more detailed view of changes in the synaptic junctions has come out of a study we have done in collaboration with Kjeld Møllgaard of the University of Copenhagen, who spent a year in our laboratory. He prepared electron micrographs of brain sections from the third layer of the occipital cortex of rats. Measurement of the synaptic junctions revealed that rats from enriched environments had junctions that averaged approximately 50 percent larger in cross section than similar junctions in littermates from impoverished environments. The latter, however, had more synapses per unit area [see illustration on page 12].

William T. Greenough, Roger West and T. Blaise Fleischmann of the University of Illinois have also found that there is increased synaptic contact in enriched-experience rats. Some other workers have reported that increased size of synapse is associated with a decreased number of synapses, whereas decreased size of synapse is associated with an increased number. It seems that memory

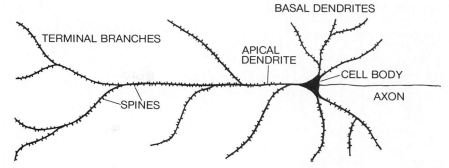

DENDRITIC SPINES, tiny "thorns," or projections, from the dendrites of a nerve cell, serve as receivers in many of the synaptic contacts between neurons. The drawing is of a type of cortical neuron known as the pyramidal cell. Rats from an enriched environment have more spines on these cells than their littermates from an impoverished environment.

or learning may be encoded in the brain either by the selective addition of contacts between nerve cells or by the selective removal of contacts, and that both processes may go on at the same time.

Does an enriched environment or an impoverished environment alter learning ability? Although some studies suggest that experience in an enriched environment usually improves subsequent learning, the effects are often short-lived. The result depends on many factors, for example the measure of learning that is used, the age at which the enriched experience is provided and the type of task that is learned. Early enrichment may improve subsequent learning of one task, have no effect on another task and actually impair learning in a third. Perhaps we should not expect much transfer of capacity among entirely different kinds of behavior. Nor should we expect experience in an enriched environment to lead to an increase in "general ability"; every environment is specific and so are abilities. Harry F. Harlow of the University of Wisconsin has shown that early problem-solving in monkeys may have the deleterious effect of fixating infantile behavior patterns; such monkeys may never reach the efficient adult performance that they would have attained without the early training. Again, this result is specific and should be generalized only with caution.

Formal training of rats, such as teaching them to press a lever in response to a signal or to run a maze, produces changes in brain anatomy and chemistry, but the type of training seems to determine the kind of changes. Victor Fedorov and his associates at the Pavlov Institute of Physiology near Leningrad found changes in brain weight and in the activity of acetylcholinesterase and cholinesterase after prolonged training of rats, but the pattern of changes is different from what we found with enriched and impoverished environments. In our laboratory we have given rats daily formal training in either operant-conditioning devices or in a series of mazes for a month or more and have found changes in brain weight and brain enzymes. These changes, however, were rather small and also had a pattern different from the changes induced by environmental experience. This is clearly a problem that requires more research.

The effect of experimental environments on the brains of animals has sometimes been cited as bearing on problems of human education. We should like to sound a cautionary note in this regard. It is difficult to extrapolate from an experiment with rats under one set of conditions to the behavior of rats under another set of conditions, and it is much riskier to extrapolate from a rat to a mouse to a monkey to a human. We have found generally similar brain changes as a result of experience in several species of rodents, and this appears to have fostered the assumption that similar results may be found with carnivores and with primates, including man. Only further research will show whether or not this is so. Animal research raises questions and allows us to test concepts and techniques, some of which may later prove useful in research with human subjects.

If this research leads to knowledge of how memories are stored in the brain, it will have obvious implications for the study of conditions that favor learning and memory and also of conditions that impair learning and the laying down of memories. Among the unfavorable conditions that are of great social concern are mental retardation and senile decline in ability to form new memories. Clues to the prevention or amelioration of these conditions could be of great social value. Let us also consider two other areas into which such research on brain plasticity may extend.

One of these areas concerns the effects of malnutrition on the development of the brain and of intelligence. Some investigators, such as R. H. Barnes and David A. Levitsky of the Cornell University Graduate School of Nutrition, have proposed that certain effects of malnutrition may actually be secondary effects of environmental impoverishment. That is,

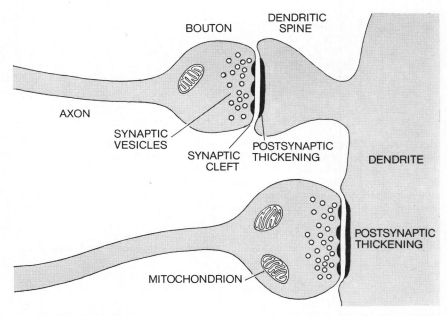

SYNAPTIC JUNCTIONS between nerve cells can be between axon and dendritic spine or between axon and the dendrite itself. The vesicles contain a chemical transmitter that is released when an electrical signal from the axon reaches the end bouton. The transmitter moves across the synaptic cleft and stimulates the postsynaptic receptor sites in the dendrite. The size of the postsynaptic membrane is thought to be an indicator of synaptic activity.

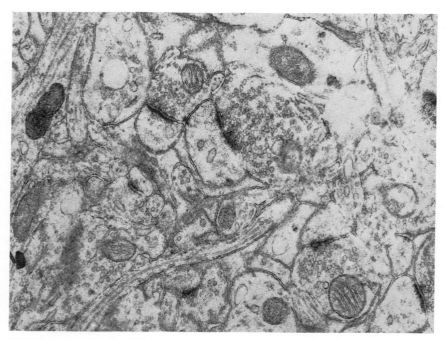

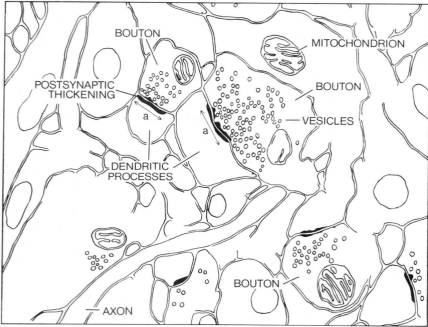

BRAIN SECTION from the occipital cortex of a rat is enlarged 37,000 times in this electron micrograph by Kjeld Møllgaard. The map identifies some of the components. Measurement of the postsynaptic thickening is shown in the map of the section by the arrow (a). The number of synaptic junctions was also counted. It was found that rats reared in an enriched environment had junctions approximately 50 percent larger than littermates from an impoverished environment, and the latter had more junctions, although smaller ones, per unit area.

cation on the postmortem examination of the brain of a blind deaf-mute, Laura Bridgman. It was found that the parts of her cortex that were involved in vision and hearing were thin and lacked the pattern of folding found in the normal human brain. In contrast, the region of her cortex devoted to touch had a normal appearance. It would be of interest to see if such results could be generalized by a large-scale modern postmortem study of brains of people who had been deprived of one or more senses. It would be even more interesting to find out if heightened employment of a sense leads to supranormal development of the associated brain region. Would musicians as a group, for example, show an enhanced development of the auditory cortex?

The human brain, because of the specialization of the two cerebral hemispheres, is more likely to provide answers to such questions than animal brains. Spoken words are analyzed in the auditory region of the left cerebral hemisphere, whereas music is analyzed in the auditory region of the right hemisphere. (These hemispheric functions are reversed in a few people.) The relative development of different regions in the same brain could be measured, so that the subjects would be their own control. In recent investigations Norman Geschwind and Walter Levitsky of the Harvard Medical School have found that 65 percent of the human brains they examined showed a greater anatomical development of the auditory area in the left hemisphere, 11 percent showed a greater auditory development in the right hemisphere and 24 percent showed equal development on the two sides. On the other hand, behavioral and physiological tests indicate that 96 percent of the people tested have left-hemisphere speech dominance and presumably have a greater development of the auditory area on that side. Is it possible that people with musical training account for most of the cases in which size of the right auditory area equals or exceeds the size of the left? In order to find out investigators will have to measure sufficient numbers of brains of individuals whose major abilities and disabilities are known. In fact, such a program was proposed 100 years ago by Broca, but the techniques available then were not adequate to carrying out the project. Today the results of our animal studies can serve as a guide, and investigators can look more penetratingly for the anatomical and chemical changes in the human brain that are correlated with experience and learning.

since a prominent effect of malnutrition is to make the person or animal apathetic and unresponsive to the environment, the individual then suffers from lack of stimulation, and this may be the direct cause of some of the symptoms usually associated with malnutrition. Current research suggests that some of the effects of malnutrition may be offset by programs of environmental stimula-

tion or increased by environmental impoverishment.

Another possibly beneficial result of our research findings would be to stimulate a resurgence of attempts to determine relations between experience and brain anatomy in man. This was a topic of some interest late in the 19th century, and a number of reports were published. For example, in 1892 there was a publi-

Stress and Behavior

2

January 1971

The chain of pituitary and adrenal hormones that regulates responses to stress plays a major role in learning and other behaviors. It may be that effective behavior depends on some optimum level of stress

Hans Selye's concept of the general "stress syndrome" has surely been one of the fruitful ideas of this era in biological and medical research. He showed that in response to stress the body of a mammal mobilizes a system of defensive reactions involving the pituitary and adrenal glands. The discovery illuminated the causes and symptoms of a number of diseases and disorders. More than that, it has opened a new outlook on the functions of the pituitary-adrenal system. One can readily understand how the hormones of this system may defend the body against physiological insult, for example by suppressing inflammation and thus preventing tissue damage. It is a striking fact, however, that the system's activity can be evoked by all kinds of stresses, not only by severe somatic stresses such as disease, burns, bone fractures, temperature extremes, surgery and drugs but also by a wide range of psychological conditions: fear, apprehension, anxiety, a loud noise, crowding, even mere exposure to a novel environment. Indeed, most of the situations that activate the pituitary-adrenal system do not involve tissue damage. It appears, therefore, that these hormones in animals, including man, may have many functions in addition to the defense of tissue integrity, and as a psychologist I have been investigating possible roles of the pituitary-adrenal system in the regulation of behavior.

The essentials of the system's operation in response to stress are as follows. Information concerning the stress (coming either from external sources through the sensory system or from internal sources such as a change in body temperature or in the blood's composition) is received and integrated by the central nervous system and is presumably delivered to the hypothalamus, the basal area of the brain. The hypothalamus secretes a substance called the corticotropin-releasing factor (CRF), which stimulates the pituitary to secrete the hormone ACTH. This in turn stimulates the cortex of the adrenal gland to step up its synthesis and secretion of hormones, particularly those known as glucocorticoids. In man the glucocorticoid is predominantly hydrocortisone; in many lower animals such as the rat it is corticosterone.

The entire mechanism is exquisitely controlled by a feedback system. When the glucocorticoid level in the circulating blood is elevated, the central nervous system, receiving the message, shuts off the process that leads to secretion of the stimulating hormone ACTH. Two experimental demonstrations have most clearly verified the existence of this feedback process. If the adrenal gland is removed from an animal, the pituitary puts out abnormal amounts of ACTH, presumably because the absence of the adrenal hormone frees it from restriction of this secretion. On the other hand, if crystals of glucocorticoid are implanted in the hypothalamus, the animal's secretion of ACTH stops almost completely, just as if the adrenal cortex were releasing large quantities of the glucocorticoid.

Now, it is well known that a high level of either of these hormones (ACTH or glucocorticoid) in the circulating blood can have dramatic effects on the brain. Patients who have received glucocorticoids for treatment of an illness have on occasion suffered severe mental changes, sometimes leading to psychosis. And patients with a diseased condition of the adrenal gland that caused it to secrete an abnormal amount of cortical hormone have also shown effects on the brain, including changes in the pattern of electrical activity and convulsions.

Two long-term studies of my own, previously reported in SCIENTIFIC AMERICAN [see "Stimulation in Infancy," Offprint 436, and Sex Differences in the Brain," Offprint 498], strongly indicated that hormones play an important part in the development of behavior. One study showed that rats subjected to shocks and other stresses in early life developed normally and were able to cope well with stresses later, whereas animals that received no stimulation in infancy grew up to be timid and deviant in behavior. At the adult stage the two groups differed sharply in the response of the pituitary-adrenal system to stress: the animals that had been stimulated in infancy showed a prompt and effective hormonal response; those that had not been stimulated responded slowly and ineffectively. The other study, based on the administration or deprivation of sex hormones at a critical early stage of development in male and female rats, indicated that these treatments markedly affected the animals' later behavior, nonsexual as well as sexual. It is noteworthy that the sex hormones are steroids rather similar to those produced by the adrenal cortex.

Direct evidence of the involvement of the pituitary-adrenal system in overt behavior was reported by two groups of experimenters some 15 years ago. Mortimer H. Appley, now at the University of Massachusetts, and his co-workers were investigating the learning of an avoidance response in rats. The animals were placed in a "shuttle box" divided into two compartments by a barrier. An electric shock was applied, and if the animals crossed the barrier, they could avoid or terminate the shock. The avoidance response consisted in making the move across the barrier when a conditioned stimulus, a buzzer signaling the onset of the shock, was sounded. Appley found that when the pituitary gland was removed surgically from rats, their learning of the avoidance response was severely retarded. It turned out that an injection of ACTH in pituitary-deprived rats could restore the learning ability to normal. At about the same time Robert E. Miller and Robert Murphy of the University of Pittsburgh reported experiments showing that ACTH could affect extinction of the avoidance response. Normally if the shocks are discontinued, so that the animal receives no shock when it fails to react to the conditioned stimulus (the buzzer in this case), the avoidance response to the buzzer is gradually extinguished. Miller and Murphy found that when they injected ACTH in animals during the learning period, the animals continued to make the avoidance response anyway, long after it was extinguished in animals that had not received the ACTH injection. In short, ACTH inhibited the extinction process.

These findings were not immediately followed up, perhaps mainly because little was known at the time about the details of the pituitary-adrenal system and only rudimentary techniques were available for studying it. Since then purified preparations of the hormones involved and new techniques for accurate measurement of these substances in the circulating blood have been developed, and the system is now under intensive study. Most of the experimental investigation is being conducted at three centers: in the Institute of Pharmacology at the University of Utrecht under David de Wied, in the Institute of Physiology at the University of Pecs in Hungary under Elemér Endroczi and in our own laboratories in the department of psychiatry at Stanford University.

The new explorations of the pituitary-adrenal system began where the ground had already been broken: in studies of the learning and extinction of the avoidance response, primarily by use of the shuttle box. De Wied verified the role of ACTH both in avoidance learning and in inhibiting extinction of the response. He did this in physiological terms by means of several experiments. He verified the fact that removal of the pituitary gland severely retards the learning of a conditioned avoidance response. He also removed the adrenal gland from rats and found that the response was then not extinguished, presumably because adrenal hormones were no longer present to re-

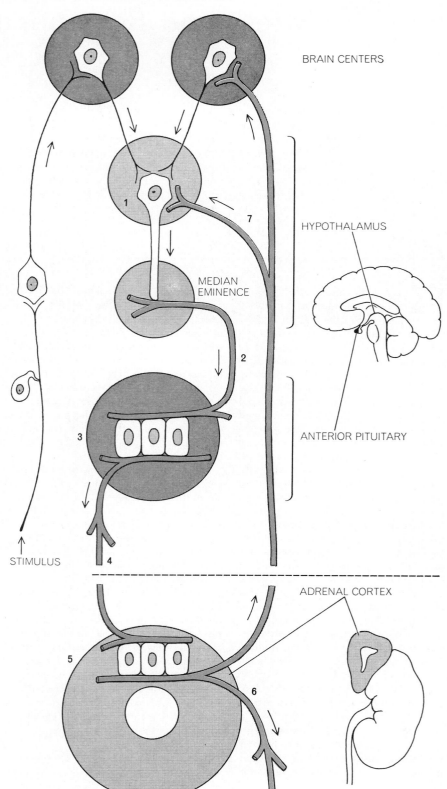

PITUITARY-ADRENAL SYSTEM involves nerve cells and hormones in a feedback loop. A stress stimulus reaching neurosecretory cells of the hypothalamus in the base of the brain (1) stimulates them to release corticotropin-releasing factor (CRF), which moves through short blood vessels (2) to the anterior lobe of the pituitary gland (3). Pituitary cells thereupon release adrenocorticotrophic hormone (ACTH) into the circulation (4). The ACTH stimulates cells of the adrenal cortex (5) to secrete glucocorticoid hormones (primarily hydrocortisone in man) into the circulation (6). When glucocorticoids reach neurosecretory cells or other brain cells (it is not clear which), they modulate CRF production (7).

strict the pituitary's output of ACTH. When he excised the pituitary, thus eliminating the secretion of ACTH, the animals returned to near-normal behavior in the extinction of the avoidance response.

In further experiments De Wied injected glucocorticoids, including corticosterone, the principal steroid hormone of the rat's adrenal cortex, into animals that had had the adrenal gland, but not the pituitary, removed; as expected, this had the effect of speeding up the extinction of the avoidance response. Similarly, the administration to such animals of dexamethasone, a synthetic glucocorticoid that is known to be a potent inhibitor of ACTH, resulted in rapid extinction of the avoidance response; the larger the dose, the more rapid the extinction. Curiously, De Wied found that corticosterone and dexamethasone promoted extinction even in animals that lacked the pituitary gland, the source of ACTH. This indicated that the glucocorticoid can produce its effect not only through suppression of ACTH but also, in some way, by acting directly on the central nervous system. It has recently been found, on the other hand, that there may be secretions from the pituitary other than ACTH that can affect learning and

inhibit extinction of the avoidance response. The inhibition can be produced, for example, by a truncated portion of the ACTH molecule consisting of the first 10 amino acids in the sequence of 39 in the rat's ACTH—a molecular fragment that has no influence on the adrenal cortex. The same fragment, along with other smaller peptides recently isolated by De Wied, can also overcome the deficit in avoidance learning that is produced by ablation of the pituitary.

With an apparatus somewhat different from the shuttle box we obtained further light in our laboratory on ACTH's effects on behavior. We first train the animals to press a bar to obtain water. After this learning has been established the animal is given an electric shock on pressing the bar. This causes the animal to avoid approaching the bar (called "passive avoidance") for a time, but after several days the animal will usually return to it in the effort to get water and then will quickly lose its fear of the bar if it is not shocked. We found, however, that if the animal was given doses of ACTH after the shock, it generally failed to return to the bar at all, even though it was very thirsty. That is to say, ACTH suppressed the bar-pressing response, or, to put it another way, it strengthened the

passive-avoidance response. In animals with the pituitary gland removed, injections of ACTH suppressed a return to bar-pressing after a shock but injections of hydrocortisone did not have this effect.

The experiments I have described so far have involved behavior under the stress of fear and anxiety. Our investigations with the bar-pressing device go on to reveal that the pituitary-adrenal system also comes into play in the regulation of behavior based on "appetitive" responses (as opposed to avoidance responses). Suppose we eliminate the electric shock factor and simply arrange that after the animal has learned to press the bar for water it fails to obtain water on later trials. Normally the animal's bar-pressing behavior is then quickly extinguished. We found, however, that when we injected ACTH in the animals in these circumstances, the extinction of bar-pressing was delayed; the rats went on pressing the bar for some time although they received no water as reinforcement. Following up this finding, we measured the corticosterone levels in the blood of normal, untreated rats both when they were reinforced and when they were not reinforced on pressing the

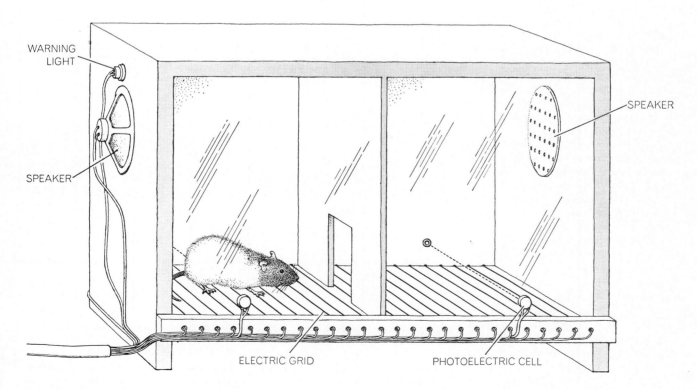

WARNING LIGHT

SPEAKER

SPEAKER

ELECTRIC GRID

PHOTOELECTRIC CELL

"SHUTTLE BOX" used for studying avoidance behavior is a two-compartment cage. The floor can be electrically charged. A shock is delivered on the side occupied by the rat (detected by the photo-cell). The rat can avoid the shock by learning to respond to the conditioned stimulus: a light and noise delivered briefly before the shock. The avoidance response, once learned, is slowly "extinguished" if the conditioned stimulus is no longer accompanied by a shock. Injections of ACTH inhibited the extinction process.

bar. The animals that received no water reinforcement, with the result of rapid extinction of bar-pressing, showed a marked rise in activity of the pituitary-adrenal system during this period, whereas in animals that received water each time they pressed the bar there was no change in the hormonal output. In short, the extinction of appetitive behavior in this case clearly involved the pituitary-adrenal system.

Further investigations have now shown that the system affects a much wider range of behavior than learning and extinction. One of the areas that has been studied is habituation: the gradual subsidence of reactions that had appeared on first exposure to a novel stimulus when the stimulus is repeated. An organism presented with an unexpected stimulus usually exhibits what Ivan Pavlov called an orientation reflex, which includes increased electrical activity in the brain, a reduction of blood flow to the extremities, changes in the electrical resistance of the skin, a rise in the level of adrenal-steroid hormones in the blood and some overt motor activity of the body.

If the stimulus is repeated frequently, these reactions eventually disappear; the organism is then said to be habituated to the stimulus. Endroczi and his co-workers recently examined the influence of ACTH on habituation of one of the reactions in human subjects—the increase of electrical activity in the brain, as indicated by electroencephalography. The electrical activity evoked in the human brain by a novel sound or a flickering light generally subsides, after repetition of the stimulus, into a pattern known as electroencephalogram (EEG) synchronization, which is taken to be a sign of habituation. Endroczi's group found that treatment of their subjects with ACTH or the 10-amino-acid fragment of ACTH produced a marked delay in the appearance of the synchronization pattern, indicating that the hormone inhibits the process of habituation.

Experiments with animals in our laboratory support that finding. The stimulus we used was a sudden sound that produces a "startle" response in rats, which is evidenced by vigorous body movements. After a number of repetitions of the sound stimulus the startle response fades. It turned out that rats deprived of the adrenal gland (and consequently with a high level of ACTH in their circulation) took significantly longer than intact animals to habituate to the sound stimulus. An implant of the adrenal hormone hydrocortisone in the hy-

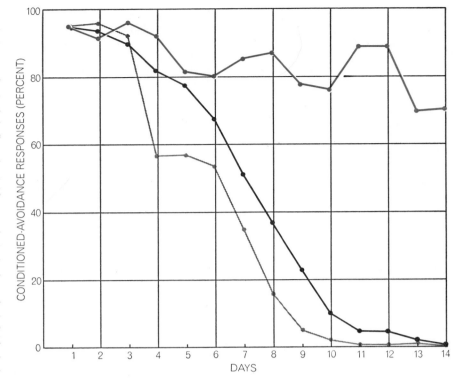

EXTINCTION of the avoidance response was studied by David de Wied of the University of Utrecht. Removal of the adrenal gland inhibited extinction (*color*); the rats responded to the conditioned stimulus in the absence of shock, presumably because adrenal hormones were not available to restrict ACTH output. When the pituitary was removed, the rate of extinction (*gray*) was about the same as in rats given only a sham operation (*black*).

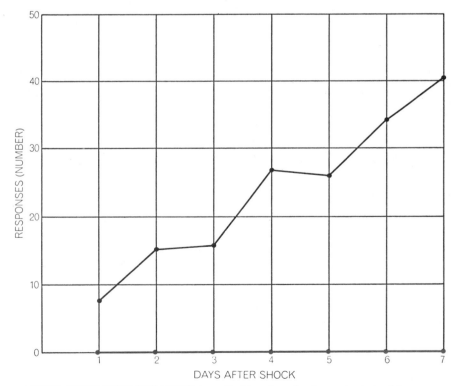

PASSIVE AVOIDANCE BEHAVIOR is studied by observing how rats, trained to press a bar for water, avoid the bar after they get a shock on pressing it. Before being shocked rats pressed the bar about 75 times a day. After the shock the control animals returned to the bar and, finding they were not shocked, gradually increased their responses (*black curve*). Rats injected with ACTH stayed away (*color*): ACTH strengthens the avoidance response.

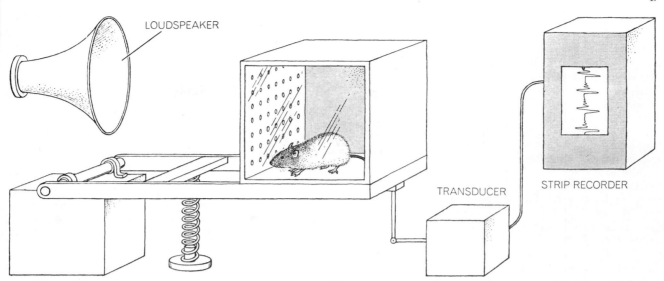

"STARTLE" RESPONSE is measured by placing a rat in a cage with a movable floor and exposing it to a sudden, loud noise. The rat tenses or jumps, and the resulting movement of the floor is transduced into movement of a pen on recording paper. After a number of repetitions of the noise the rat becomes habituated to it and the magnitude of the animal's startle response diminishes.

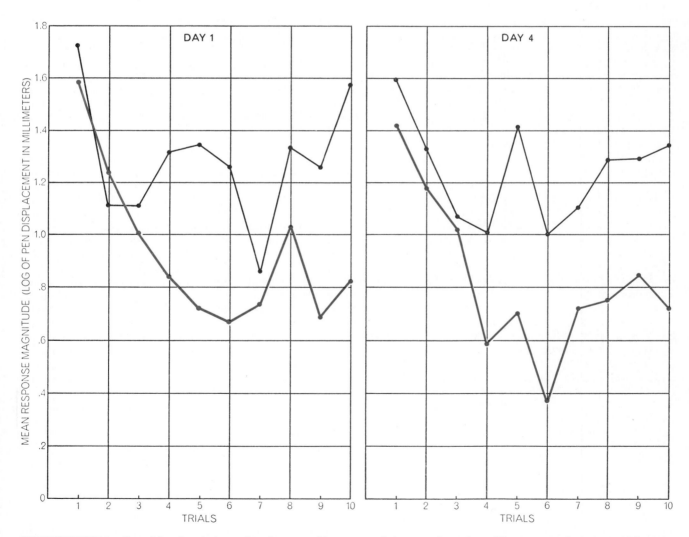

HABITUATION is affected by the pituitary-adrenal system. If a crystal of the adrenal hormone hydrocortisone is implanted in a rat's hypothalamus, preventing ACTH secretion, habituation is speeded up, as shown here. The mean startle response (shown as the logarithm of the recording pen's movement) falls away more rapidly in implanted rats (*color*) than in control animals (*black*).

pothalamus, on the other hand, speeded up habituation.

A series of studies by Robert I. Henkin of the National Heart Institute has demonstrated that hormones of the adrenal cortex play a crucial role in the sensory functions in man. Patients whose adrenal gland has been removed surgically or is functioning poorly show a marked increase in the ability to detect sensory signals, particularly in the senses of taste, smell, hearing and proprioception (sensing of internal signals). On the other hand, patients with Cushing's syndrome, marked by excessive secretion from the adrenal cortex, suffer a considerable dulling of the senses. Henkin showed that sensory detection and the integration of sensory signals are regulated by a complex feedback system involving interactions of the endocrine system and the nervous system. Although patients with a deficiency of adrenal cortex hormones are extraordinarily sensitive in the detection of sensory signals, they have difficulty integrating the signals, so that they cannot evaluate variations in properties such as loudness and tonal qualities and have some difficulty understanding speech. Proper treatment with steroid hormones of the adrenal gland can restore normal sensory detection and perception in such patients.

Henkin has been able to detect the effects of the adrenal corticosteroids on sensory perception even in normal subjects. There is a daily cycle of secretion of these steroid hormones by the adrenal cortex. Henkin finds that when adrenocortical secretion is at its highest level, taste detection and recognition is at its lowest, and vice versa.

In our laboratory we have found that the adrenal's steroid hormones can have a truly remarkable effect on the ability of animals to judge the passage of time. Some years ago Murray Sidman of the Harvard Medical School devised an experiment to test this capability. The animal is placed in an experimental chamber and every 20 seconds an electric shock is applied. By pressing a bar in the chamber the animal can prevent the shock from occurring, because the bar resets the triggering clock to postpone the shock for another 20 seconds. Thus the animal can avoid the shock altogether by appropriate timing of its presses on the bar. Adopting this device, we found that rats learned to press the bar at intervals averaging between 12 and 15 seconds. This prevented a majority of the shocks. We then gave the animals glucocorticoids and found that they became significantly more efficient!

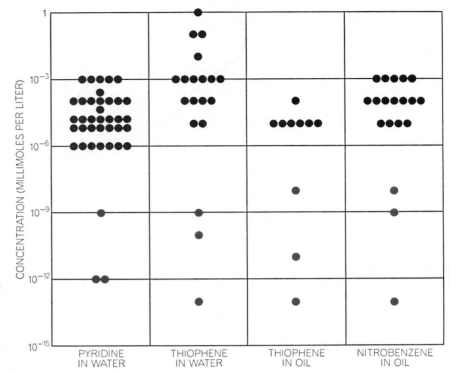

SENSORY FUNCTION is also affected by adrenocortical hormones. Robert I. Henkin of the National Heart Institute found that patients whose adrenal-hormone function is poor are much more sensitive to odor. Placing various chemicals in solution, he measured the detection threshold: the concentration at which an odor could be detected in the vapor. The threshold was much lower in the patients (*color*) than in normal volunteers (*black*).

They lengthened the interval between bar presses and took fewer shocks. Evidently under the influence of the hormones the rats were able to make finer discriminations concerning the passage of time. Monkeys also showed improvement in timing performance in response to treatment with ACTH.

The mechanism by which the pituitary-adrenal hormones act to regulate or influence behavior is still almost completely unknown. Obviously they must do so by acting on the brain. It is well known that hormones in general are targeted to specific sites and that the body tissues have a remarkable selectivity for them. The uterus, for instance, picks up and responds selectively to estrogen and progesterone among all the hormones circulating in the blood, and the seminal vesicles and prostate gland of the male select testosterone. There is now much evidence that organs of the brain may be similarly selective. Bruce Sherman McEwen of Rockefeller University has recently reported that the hippocampus, just below the cerebral cortex, appears to be a specific receptor site for hormones of the adrenal cortex, and other studies indicate that the lateral portion

of the hypothalamus may be a receptor site for gonadal hormones. We have the inviting prospect, therefore, that exploration of the brain to locate the receptor sites for the hormones of the pituitary-adrenal system, and studies of the hormones' action on the cells of these sites, may yield important information on how the system regulates behavior. Bela Bohun in Hungary has already demonstrated that implantation of small quantities of glucocorticoids in the reticular formation in the brain stem facilitates extinction of an avoidance response.

Since this system plays a key role in learning, habituation to novel stimuli, sensing and perception, it obviously has a high adaptive significance for mammals, including man. Its reactions to moderate stress may contribute greatly to the behavioral effectiveness and stability of the organism. Just as the studies of young animals showed, contrary to expectations, that some degree of stress in infancy is necessary for the development of normal, adaptive behavior, so the information we now have on the operations of the pituitary-adrenal system indicates that in many situations effective behavior in adult life may depend on exposure to some optimum level of stress.

The Visual Cortex
of the Brain

by David H. Hubel
November 1963

*A start toward understanding how it analyzes images
on the retina can be made through studies of the
responses that individual cells in the visual system
of the cat give to varying patterns of light*

An image of the outside world striking the retina of the eye activates a most intricate process that results in vision: the transformation of the retinal image into a perception. The transformation occurs partly in the retina but mostly in the brain, and it is, as one can recognize instantly by considering how modest in comparison is the achievement of a camera, a task of impressive magnitude.

The process begins with the responses of some 130 million light-sensitive receptor cells in each retina. From these cells messages are transmitted to other retinal cells and then sent on to the brain, where they must be analyzed and interpreted. To get an idea of the magnitude of the task, think what is involved in watching a moving animal, such as a horse. At a glance one takes in its size, form, color and rate of movement. From tiny differences in the two retinal images there results a three-dimensional picture. Somehow the brain manages to compare this picture with previous impressions; recognition occurs and then any appropriate action can be taken.

The organization of the visual system —a large, intricately connected population of nerve cells in the retina and brain —is still poorly understood. In recent years, however, various studies have begun to reveal something of the arrangement and function of these cells. A decade ago Stephen W. Kuffler, working with cats at the Johns Hopkins Hospital, discovered that some analysis of visual patterns takes place outside the brain, in the nerve cells of the retina. My colleague Torsten N. Wiesel and I at the Harvard Medical School, exploring the first stages of the processing that occurs in the brain of the cat, have mapped the visual pathway a little further: to what appears to be the sixth step from the retina to the cortex of the cerebrum. This kind of work falls far short of providing a full understanding of vision, but it does convey some idea of the mechanisms and circuitry of the visual system.

In broad outline the visual pathway is clearly defined [*see bottom illustration on following page*]. From the retina of each eye visual messages travel along the optic nerve, which consists of about a million nerve fibers. At the junction known as the chiasm about half of the nerves cross over into opposite hemispheres of the brain, the other nerves remaining on the same side. The optic nerve fibers lead to the first way stations in the brain: a pair of cell clusters called the lateral geniculate bodies. From here new fibers course back through the brain to the visual area of the cerebral cortex. It is convenient, although admittedly a gross oversimplification, to think of the pathway from retina to cortex as consisting of six types of nerve cells, of which three are in the retina, one is in the geniculate body and two are in the cortex.

Nerve cells, or neurons, transmit messages in the form of brief electrochemical impulses. These travel along the outer membrane of the cell, notably along the membrane of its long principal fiber, the axon. It is possible to obtain an electrical record of impulses of a single nerve cell by placing a fine electrode near the cell body or one of its fibers. Such measurements have shown that impulses travel along the nerves at velocities of between half a meter and 100 meters per second. The impulses in a given fiber all have about the same amplitude; the strength of the stimuli that give rise to them is reflected not in amplitude but in frequency.

At its terminus the fiber of a nerve cell makes contact with another nerve cell (or with a muscle cell or gland cell), forming the junction called the synapse. At most synapses an impulse on reaching the end of a fiber causes the release of a small amount of a specific substance, which diffuses outward to the membrane of the next cell. There the substance either excites the cell or inhibits it. In excitation the substance acts to bring the cell into a state in which it is more likely to "fire"; in inhibition the substance acts to prevent firing. For most synapses the substances that act as transmitters are unknown. Moreover, there is no sure way to determine from microscopic appearances alone whether a synapse is excitatory or inhibitory.

It is at the synapses that the modification and analysis of nerve messages take place. The kind of analysis depends partly on the nature of the synapse: on how many nerve fibers converge on a single cell and on how the excitatory and inhibitory endings distribute themselves. In most parts of the nervous system the anatomy is too intricate to reveal much about function. One way to circumvent this difficulty is to record impulses with microelectrodes in anesthetized animals, first from the fibers coming into a structure of neurons and then from the neurons themselves, or from the fibers they send onward. Comparison of the behavior of incoming and outgoing fibers provides a basis for learning what the structure does. Through such exploration of the different parts of the brain concerned with vision one can hope to build up some idea of how the entire visual system works.

That is what Wiesel and I have undertaken, mainly through studies of the visual system of the cat. In our experiments the anesthetized animal faces a wide screen 1.5 meters away, and we shine various patterns of white light on the screen with a projector. Simultane-

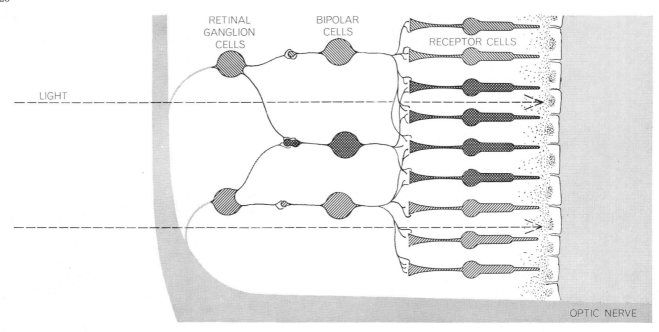

STRUCTURE OF RETINA is depicted schematically. Images fall on the receptor cells, of which there are about 130 million in each retina. Some analysis of an image occurs as the receptors transmit messages to the retinal ganglion cells via the bipolar cells. A group of receptors funnels into a particular ganglion cell, as indicated by the shading; that group forms the ganglion cell's receptive field. Inasmuch as the fields of several ganglion cells overlap, one receptor may send messages to several ganglion cells.

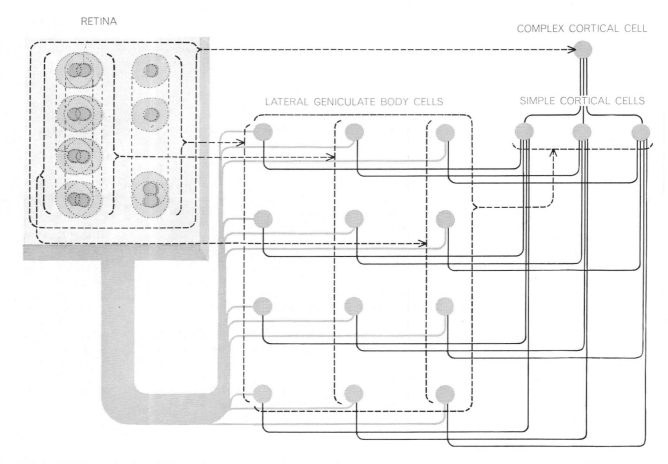

VISUAL PROCESSING BY BRAIN begins in the lateral geniculate body, which continues the analysis made by retinal cells. In the cortex "simple" cells respond strongly to line stimuli, provided that the position and orientation of the line are suitable for a particular cell. "Complex" cells respond well to line stimuli, but the position of the line is not critical and the cell continues to respond even if a properly oriented stimulus is moved, as long as it remains in the cell's receptive field. Broken lines indicate how receptive fields of all these cells overlap on the retina; solid lines, how several cells at one stage affect a single cell at the next stage.

ously we penetrate the visual portion of the cortex with microelectrodes. In that way we can record the responses of individual cells to the light patterns. Sometimes it takes many hours to find the region of the retina with which a particular visual cell is linked and to work out the optimum stimuli for that cell. The reader should bear in mind the relation between each visual cell—no matter how far along the visual pathway it may be—and the retina. It requires an image on the retina to evoke a meaningful response in any visual cell, however indirect and complex the linkage may be.

The retina is a complicated structure, in both its anatomy and its physiology, and the description I shall give is highly simplified. Light coming through the lens of the eye falls on the mosaic of receptor cells in the retina. The receptor cells do not send impulses directly through the optic nerve but instead connect with a set of retinal cells called bipolar cells. These in turn connect with retinal ganglion cells, and it is the latter set of cells, the third in the visual pathway, that sends its fibers—the optic nerve fibers—to the brain.

This series of cells and synapses is no simple bucket brigade for impulses: a receptor may send nerve endings to more than one bipolar cell, and several receptors may converge on one bipolar cell. The same holds for the synapses between the bipolar cells and the retinal ganglion cells. Stimulating a single receptor by light might therefore be expected to have an influence on many bipolar or ganglion cells; conversely, it should be possible to influence one bipolar or retinal ganglion cell from a number of receptors and hence from a substantial area of the retina.

The area of receptor mosaic in the retina feeding into a single visual cell is called the receptive field of the cell. This term is applied to any cell in the visual system to refer to the area of retina with which the cell is connected—the retinal area that on stimulation produces a response from the cell.

Any of the synapses with a particular cell may be excitatory or inhibitory, so that stimulation of a particular point on the retina may either increase or decrease the cell's firing rate. Moreover, a single cell may receive several excitatory and inhibitory impulses at once, with the result that it will respond according to the net effect of these inputs. In considering the behavior of a single cell an observer should remember that it is just one of a huge popu-

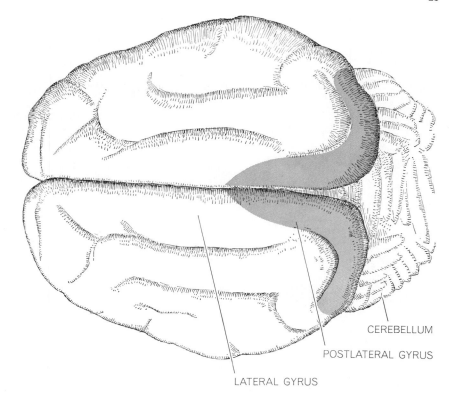

CORTEX OF CAT'S BRAIN is depicted as it would be seen from the top. The colored region indicates the cortical area that deals at least in a preliminary way with vision.

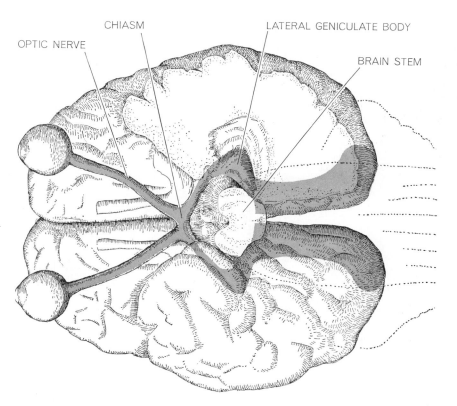

VISUAL SYSTEM appears in this representation of the human brain as viewed from below. Visual pathway from retinas to cortex via the lateral geniculate body is shown in color.

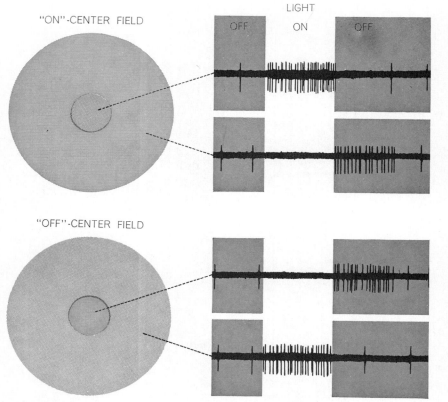

CONCENTRIC FIELDS are characteristic of retinal ganglion cells and of geniculate cells. At top an oscilloscope recording shows strong firing by an "on"-center type of cell when a spot of light strikes the field center; if the spot hits an "Off" area, the firing is suppressed until the light goes off. At bottom are responses of another cell of the "off"-center type.

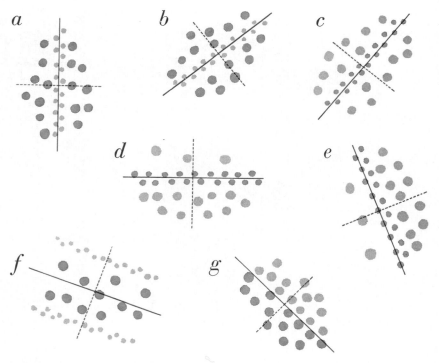

SIMPLE CORTICAL CELLS have receptive fields of various types. In all of them the "on" and "off" areas, represented by colored and gray dots respectively, are separated by straight boundaries. Orientations of fields vary, as indicated particularly at *a* and *b*. In the cat's visual system such fields are generally one millimeter or less in diameter.

lation of cells: a stimulus that excites one cell will undoubtedly excite many others, meanwhile inhibiting yet another array of cells and leaving others entirely unaffected.

For many years it has been known that retinal ganglion cells fire at a fairly steady rate even in the absence of any stimulation. Kuffler was the first to observe how the retinal ganglion cells of mammals are influenced by small spots of light. He found that the resting discharges of a cell were intensified or diminished by light in a small and more or less circular region of the retina. That region was of course the cell's receptive field. Depending on where in the field a spot of light fell, either of two responses could be produced. One was an "on" response, in which the cell's firing rate increased under the stimulus of light. The other was an "off" response, in which the stimulus of light decreased the cell's firing rate. Moreover, turning the light off usually evoked a burst of impulses from the cell. Kuffler called the retinal regions from which these responses could be evoked "on" regions and "off" regions.

On mapping the receptive fields of a large number of retinal ganglion cells into "on" and "off" regions, Kuffler discovered that there were two distinct cell types. In one the receptive field consisted of a small circular "on" area and a surrounding zone that gave "off" responses. Kuffler termed this an "on"-center cell. The second type, which he called "off"-center, had just the reverse form of field—an "off" center and an "on" periphery [*see top illustration on this page*]. For a given cell the effects of light varied markedly according to the place in which the light struck the receptive field. Two spots of light shone on separate parts of an "on" area produced a more vigorous "on" response than either spot alone, whereas if one spot was shone on an "on" area and the other on an "off" area, the two effects tended to neutralize each other, resulting in a very weak "on" or "off" response. In an "on"-center cell, illuminating the entire central "on" region evoked a maximum response; a smaller or larger spot of light was less effective.

Lighting up the whole retina diffusely, even though it may affect every receptor in the retina, does not affect a retinal ganglion cell nearly so strongly as a small circular spot of exactly the right size placed so as to cover precisely the receptive-field center. The main concern of these cells seems to be the contrast in illumination between one retinal region and surrounding regions.

Retinal ganglion cells differ greatly in the size of their receptive-field centers. Cells near the fovea (the part of the retina serving the center of gaze) are specialized for precise discrimination; in the monkey the field centers of these cells may be about the same size as a single cone—an area subtending a few minutes of arc at the cornea. On the other hand, some cells far out in the retinal periphery have field centers up to a millimeter or so in diameter. (In man one millimeter of retina corresponds to an arc of about three degrees in the 180-degree visual field.) Cells with such large receptive-field centers are probably specialized for work in very dim light, since they can sum up messages from a large number of receptors.

Given this knowledge of the kind of visual information brought to the brain by the optic nerve, our first problem was to learn how the messages were handled at the first central way station, the lateral geniculate body. Compared with the retina, the geniculate body is a relatively simple structure. In a sense there is only one synapse involved, since the incoming optic nerve fibers end in cells that send their fibers directly to the visual cortex. Yet in the cat many optic nerve fibers converge on each geniculate cell, and it is reasonable to expect some change in the visual messages from the optic nerve to the geniculate cells.

When we came to study the geniculate body, we found that the cells have many of the characteristics Kuffler described for retinal ganglion cells. Each geniculate cell is driven from a circumscribed retinal region (the receptive field) and has either an "on" center or an "off" center, with an opposing periphery. There are, however, differences between geniculate cells and retinal ganglion cells, the most important of which is the greatly enhanced capacity of the periphery of a geniculate cell's receptive field to cancel the effects of the center. This means that the lateral geniculate cells must be even more specialized than retinal ganglion cells in responding to spatial differences in retinal illumination rather than to the illumination itself. The lateral geniculate body, in short, has the function of increasing the disparity—already present in retinal ganglion cells—between responses to a small, centered spot and to diffuse light.

In contrast to the comparatively simple lateral geniculate body, the cerebral cortex is a structure of stupendous complexity. The cells of this great plate of

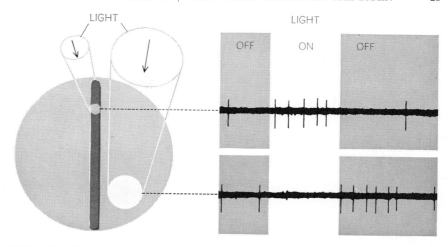

RESPONSE IS WEAK when a circular spot of light is shone on receptive field of a simple cortical cell. Such spots get a vigorous response from retinal and geniculate cells. This cell has a receptive field of type shown at *a* in bottom illustration on opposite page.

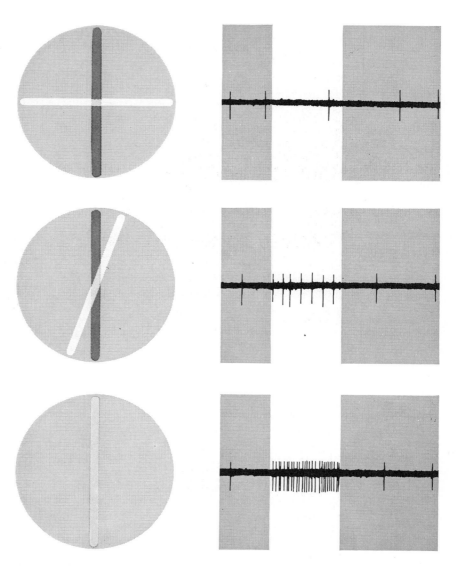

IMPORTANCE OF ORIENTATION to simply cortical cells is indicated by varying responses to a slit of light from a cell preferring a vertical orientation. Horizontal slit (*top*) produces no response, slight tilt a weak response, vertical slit a strong response.

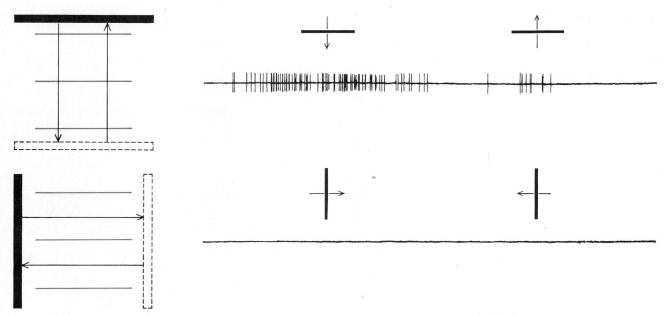

COMPLEX CORTICAL CELL responded vigorously to slow downward movement of a dark, horizontal bar. Upward movement of bar produced a weak response and horizontal movement of a vertical bar produced no response. For other shapes, orientations and movements there are other complex cells showing maximum response. Such cells may figure in perception of form and movement.

gray matter—a structure that would be about 20 square feet in area and a tenth of an inch thick if flattened out— are arranged in a number of more or less distinct layers. The millions of fibers that come in from the lateral geniculate body connect with cortical cells in the layer that is fourth from the top. From here the information is sooner or later disseminated to all layers of the cortex by rich interconnections between them. Many of the cells, particularly those of the third and fifth layers, send their fibers out of the cortex, projecting to centers deep in the brain or passing over to nearby cortical areas for further processing of the visual messages. Our problem was to learn how the information the visual cortex sends out differs from what it takes in.

Most connections between cortical cells are in a direction perpendicular to the surface· side-to-side connections are generally quite short. One might therefore predict that impulses arriving at a particular area of the cortex would exert their effects quite locally. Moreover, the retinas project to the visual cortex (via the lateral geniculate body) in a systematic topologic manner; that is, a given area of cortex gets its input ultimately from a circumscribed area of retina. These two observations suggest that a given cortical cell should have a small receptive field; it should be influenced from a circumscribed retinal region only, just as a geniculate or retinal ganglion cell is. Beyond this the anatomy provides no hint of what the cortex does

with the information it receives about an image on the retina.

In the face of the anatomical complexity of the cortex, it would have been surprising if the cells had proved to have the concentric receptive fields characteristic of cells in the retina and the lateral geniculate body. Indeed, in the cat we have observed no cortical cells with concentric receptive fields; instead there are many different cell types, with fields markedly different from anything seen in the retinal and geniculate cells.

The many varieties of cortical cells may, however, be classified by function into two large groups. One we have called "simple"; the function of these cells is to respond to line stimuli—such shapes as slits, which we define as light lines on a dark background; dark bars (dark lines on a light background), and edges (straight-line boundaries between light and dark regions). Whether or not a given cell responds depends on the orientation of the shape and its position on the cell's receptive field. A bar shone vertically on the screen may activate a given cell, whereas the same cell will fail to respond (but others will respond) if the bar is displaced to one side or moved appreciably out of the vertical. The second group of cortical cells we have called "complex"; they too respond best to bars, slits or edges, provided that, as with simple cells, the shape is suitably oriented for the particular cell under observation. Complex cells, how-

ever, are not so discriminating as to the exact position of the stimulus, provided that it is properly oriented. Moreover, unlike simple cells, they respond with sustained firing to moving lines.

From the preference of simple and complex cells for specific orientation of light stimuli, it follows that there must be a multiplicity of cell types to handle the great number of possible positions and orientations. Wiesel and I have found a large variety of cortical cell responses, even though the number of individual cells we have studied runs only into the hundreds compared with the millions that exist. Among simple cells, the retinal region over which a cell can be influenced—the receptive field—is, like the fields of retinal and geniculate cells, divided into "on" and "off" areas. In simple cells, however, these areas are far from being circularly symmetrical. In a typical example the receptive field consists of a very long and narrow "on" area, which is adjoined on each side by larger "off" regions. The magnitude of an "on" response depends, as with retinal and geniculate cells, on how much either type of region is covered by the stimulating light. A long, narrow slit that just fills the elongated "on" region produces a powerful "on" response. Stimulation with the slit in a different orientation produces a much weaker effect, because the slit is now no longer illuminating all the "on" region but instead includes some of the antagonistic "off" region. A slit at right angles to the optimum orientation for a cell of this type is usually completely ineffective.

In the simple cortical cells the process of pitting these two antagonistic parts of a receptive field against each other is carried still further than it is in the lateral geniculate body. As a rule a large spot of light—or what amounts to the same thing, diffuse light covering the whole retina—evokes no response at all in simple cortical cells. Here the "on" and "off" effects apparently balance out with great precision.

Some other common types of simple receptive fields include an "on" center with a large "off" area to one side and a small one to the other; an "on" and an "off" area side by side; a narrow "off" center with "on" sides; a wide "on" center with narrow "off" sides. All these fields have in common that the border or borders separating "on" and "off" regions are straight and parallel rather than circular [see bottom illustration on page 22]. The most efficient stimuli—slits, edges or dark bars—all involve straight lines. Each cell responds best to a particular orientation of line; other orientations produce less vigorous responses, and usually the orientation perpendicular to the optimum evokes no response at all. A particular cell's optimum, which we term the receptive-field orientation, is thus a property built into the cell by its connections. In general the receptive-field orientation differs from one cell to the next, and it may be vertical, horizontal or oblique. We have no evidence that any one orientation, such as vertical or horizontal, is more common than any other.

How can one explain this specificity of simple cortical cells? We are inclined to think they receive their input directly from the incoming lateral geniculate fibers. We suppose a typical simple cell has for its input a large number of lateral geniculate cells whose "on" centers are arranged along a straight line; a spot of light shone anywhere along that line will activate some of the geniculate cells and lead to activation of the cortical cell. A light shone over the entire area will activate all the geniculate cells and have a tremendous final impact on the cortical cell [see bottom illustration on page 20].

One can now begin to grasp the significance of the great number of cells in the visual cortex. Each cell seems to have its own specific duties; it takes care of one restricted part of the retina, responds best to one particular shape of stimulus and to one particular orientation. To look at the problem from the

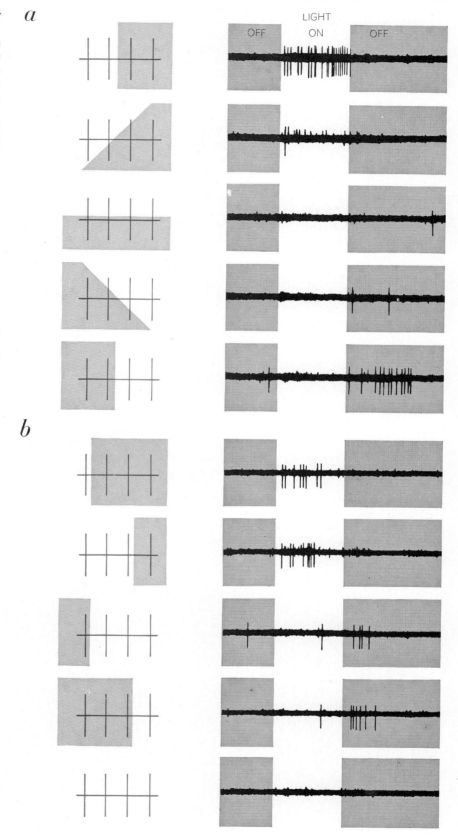

SINGLE COMPLEX CELL showed varying responses to an edge projected on the cell's receptive field in the retina. In group *a* the stimulus was presented in differing orientations. In group *b* all the edges were vertical and all but the last evoked responses regardless of where in the receptive field the light struck. When a large rectangle of light covered entire receptive field, however, as shown at bottom, cell failed to respond.

opposite direction, for each stimulus—each area of the retina stimulated, each type of line (edge, slit or bar) and each orientation of stimulus—there is a particular set of simple cortical cells that will respond; changing any of the stimulus arrangements will cause a whole new population of cells to respond. The number of populations responding successively as the eye watches a slowly rotating propeller is scarcely imaginable.

Such a profound rearrangement and analysis of the incoming messages might seem enough of a task for a single structure, but it turns out to be only part of what happens in the cortex. The next major transformation involves the cortical cells that occupy what is probably the sixth step in the visual pathway: the complex cells, which are also present in this cortical region and to some extent intermixed with the simple cells.

Complex cells are like simple ones in several ways. A cell responds to a stimulus only within a restricted region of retina: the receptive field. It responds best to the line stimuli (slits, edges or dark bars) and the stimulus must be oriented to suit the cell. But complex fields, unlike the simple ones, cannot be mapped into antagonistic "on" and "off" regions.

A typical complex cell we studied happened to fire to a vertical edge, and it gave "on" or "off" responses depending on whether light was to the left or to the right. Other orientations were almost completely without effect [see illustration on preceding page]. These re-sponses are just what could be expected from a simple cell with a receptive field consisting of an excitatory area separated from an inhibitory one by a vertical boundary. In this case, however, the cell had an additional property that could not be explained by such an arrangement. A vertical edge evoked responses anywhere within the receptive field, "on" responses with light to the left, "off" responses with light to the right. Such behavior cannot be understood in terms of antagonistic "on" and "off" subdivisions of the receptive field, and when we explored the field with small spots we found no such regions. Instead the spot either produced responses at both "on" and "off" or evoked no responses at all.

Complex cells, then, respond like simple cells to one particular aspect of the stimulus, namely its orientation. But when the stimulus is moved, without changing the orientation, a complex cell differs from its simple counterpart chiefly in responding with sustained firing. The firing continues as the stimulus is moved over a substantial retinal area, usually the entire receptive field of the cell, whereas a simple cell will respond to movement only as the stimulus crosses a very narrow boundary separating "on" and "off" regions.

It is difficult to explain this behavior by any scheme in which geniculate cells project directly to complex cells. On the other hand, the findings can be explained fairly well by the supposition that a complex cell receives its input from a large number of simple cells. This supposition requires only that the simple cells have the same field orientation and be all of the same general type. A complex cell responding to vertical edges, for example, would thus receive fibers from simple cells that have vertically oriented receptive fields. All such a scheme needs to have added is the requirement that the retinal positions of these simple fields be arranged throughout the area occupied by the complex field.

The main difficulty with such a scheme is that it presupposes an enormous degree of cortical organization. What a vast network of connections must be needed if a single complex cell is to receive fibers from just the right simple cells, all with the appropriate field arrangements, tilts and positions! Yet there is unexpected and compelling evidence that such a system of connections exists. It comes from a study of what can be called the functional architecture of the cortex. By penetrating with a microelectrode through the cortex in many directions, perhaps many times in a single tiny region of the brain, we learned that the cells are arranged not in a haphazard manner but with a high degree of order. The physiological results show that functionally the cortex is subdivided like a beehive into tiny columns, or segments [see illustration on next page], each of which extends from the surface to the white matter lower in the brain. A column is de-

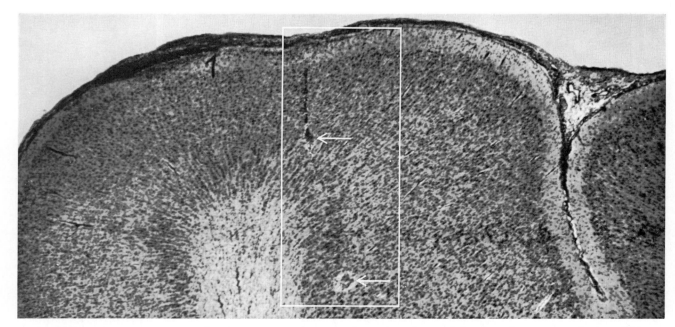

SECTION OF CAT'S VISUAL CORTEX shows track of micro-electrode penetration and, at arrows, two points along the track where lesions were made so that it would be possible to ascertain later where the tip of the electrode was at certain times. This section of cortex is from a single gyrus, or fold of the brain; it was six millimeters wide and is shown here enlarged 30 diameters.

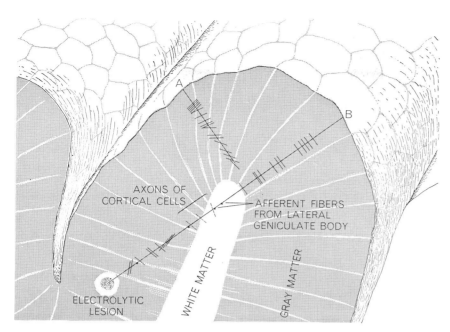

FUNCTIONAL ARRANGEMENT of cells in visual cortex resembled columns, although columnar structure is not apparent under a microscope. Lines *A* and *B* show paths of two microelectrode penetrations; colored lines show receptive-field orientations encountered. Cells in a single column had same orientation; change of orientation showed new column.

fined not by any anatomically obvious wall—no columns are visible under the microscope—but by the fact that the thousands of cells it contains all have the same receptive-field orientation. The evidence for this is that in a typical microelectrode penetration through the cortex the cells—recorded in sequence as the electrode is pushed ahead—all have the same field orientation, provided that the penetration is made in a direction perpendicular to the surface of the cortical segment. If the penetration is oblique, as we pass from column to column we record several cells with one field orientation, then a new sequence of cells with a new orientation, and then still another.

The columns are irregular in cross-sectional shape, and on the average they are about half a millimeter across. In respects other than receptive-field orientation the cells in a particular column tend to differ; some are simple, others complex; some respond to slits, others prefer dark bars or edges.

Returning to the proposed scheme for explaining the properties of complex cells, one sees that gathered together in a single column are the very cells one should expect to be interconnected: cells whose fields have the same orientation and the same general retinal position, although not the same position. Furthermore, it is known from

the anatomy that there are rich interconnections between neighboring cells, and the preponderance of these connections in a vertical direction fits well with the long, narrow, more or less cylindrical shape of the columns. This means that a column may be looked on as an independent functional unit of cortex, in which simple cells receive connections from lateral geniculate cells and send projections to complex cells.

It is possible to get an inkling of the part these different cell types play in vision by considering what must be happening in the brain when one looks at a form, such as, to take a relatively simple example, a black square on a white background. Suppose the eyes fix on some arbitrary point to the left of the square. On the reasonably safe assumption that the human visual cortex works something like the cat's and the monkey's, it can be predicted that the near edge of the square will activate a particular group of simple cells, namely cells that prefer edges with light to the left and dark to the right and whose fields are oriented vertically and are so placed on the retina that the boundary between "on" and "off" regions falls exactly along the image of the near edge of the square. Other populations of cells will obviously be called into action by the other three edges of the square. All the cell populations will change if the eye strays from the point fixed on, or if

the square is moved while the eye remains stationary, or if the square is rotated.

In the same way each edge will activate a population of complex cells, again cells that prefer edges in a specific orientation. But a given complex cell, unlike a simple cell, will continue to be activated when the eye moves or when the form moves, if the movement is not so large that the edge passes entirely outside the receptive field of the cell, and if there is no rotation. This means that the populations of complex cells affected by the whole square will be to some extent independent of the exact position of the image of the square on the retina.

Each of the cortical columns contains thousands of cells, some with simple fields and some with complex. Evidently the visual cortex analyzes an enormous amount of information, with each small region of visual field represented over and over again in column after column, first for one receptive-field orientation and then for another.

In sum, the visual cortex appears to have a rich assortment of functions. It rearranges the input from the lateral geniculate body in a way that makes lines and contours the most important stimuli. What appears to be a first step in perceptual generalization results from the response of cortical cells to the orientation of a stimulus, apart from its exact retinal position. Movement is also an important stimulus factor; its rate and direction must both be specified if a cell is to be effectively driven.

One cannot expect to "explain" vision, however, from a knowledge of the behavior of a single set of cells, geniculate or cortical, any more than one could understand a wood-pulp mill from an examination of the machine that cuts the logs into chips. We are now studying how still "higher" structures build on the information they receive from these cortical cells, rearranging it to produce an even greater complexity of response.

In all of this work we have been particularly encouraged to find that the areas we study can be understood in terms of comparatively simple concepts such as the nerve impulse, convergence of many nerves on a single cell, excitation and inhibition. Moreover, if the connections suggested by these studies are remotely close to reality, one can conclude that at least some parts of the brain can be followed relatively easily, without necessarily requiring higher mathematics, computers or a knowledge of network theories.

4 Pleasure centers in the Brain

by James Olds
October 1956

Rats can be made to gratify the drives of hunger, thirst and sex by self-stimulation of their brains with electricity. It appears that motivation, like sensation, has local centers in the brain

The brain has been mapped in various ways by modern physiologists. They have located the sensory and motor systems and the seats of many kinds of behavior—centers where messages of sight, sound, touch and action are received and interpreted. Where, then, dwell the "higher feelings," such as love, fear, pain and pleasure? Up to three years ago the notion that the emotions had specific seats in the brain might have been dismissed as naive—akin perhaps to medieval anatomy or phrenology. But recent research has brought a surprising turn of affairs. The brain does seem to have definite loci of pleasure and pain, and we shall review here the experiments which have led to this conclusion.

The classical mapping exploration of the brain ranged mainly over its broad, fissured roof—the cortex—and there localized the sensory and motor systems and other areas which seemed to control most overt behavior. Other areas of the brain remained mostly unexplored, and comparatively little was known about their functions. Particularly mysterious was the series of structures lying along the mid-line of the brain from the roof down to the spinal cord, structures which include the hypothalamus and parts of the thalamus [*see diagram on page 30*]. It was believed that general functions of the brain might reside in these structures. But they were difficult

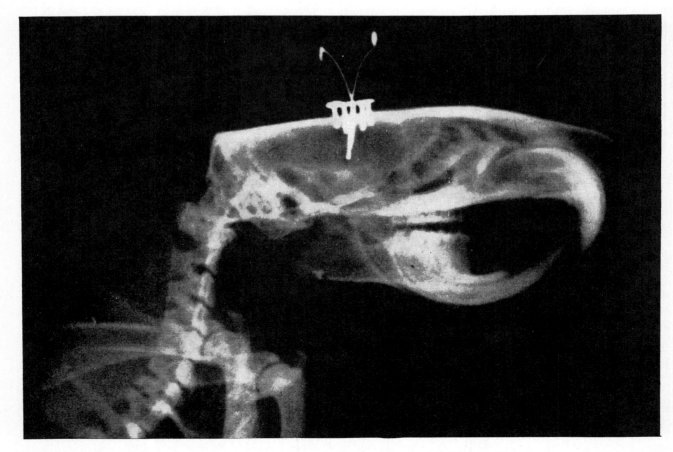

IMPLANTED ELECTRODES in the brain of a rat are shown in this X-ray photograph. The electrodes are held in a plastic carrier screwed to the skull. They can be used to give an electrical stimulus to the brain or to record electrical impulses generated by the brain.

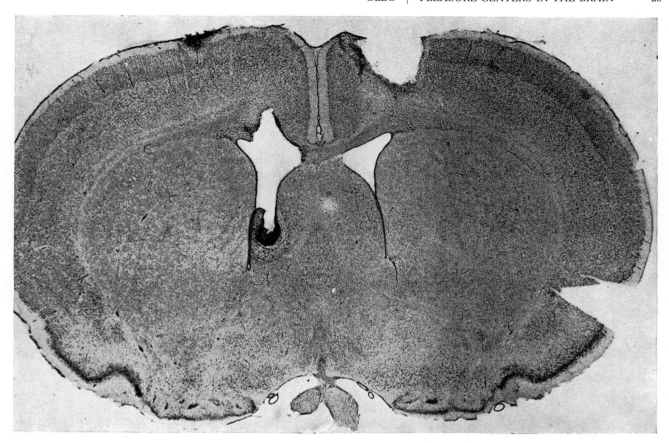

RAT'S BRAIN in a photomicrographic cross section shows a black spot to left of center, marking the point where electrical stimulus was applied. Such cross sections make it possible to tell exactly which center in the brain was involved in the animal's response.

to investigate, for two reasons. First, the structures were hard to get at. Most of them lie deep in the brain and could not be reached without damaging the brain, whereas the cortex could be explored by electrical stimulators and recording instruments touching the surface. Secondly, there was a lack of psychological tools for measuring the more general responses of an animal. It is easy to test an animal's reaction to stimulation of a motor center in the brain, for it takes the simple form of flexing a muscle, but how is one to measure an animal's feeling of pleasure?

The first difficulty was overcome by the development of an instrument for probing the brain. Basically the instrument is a very fine needle electrode which can be inserted to any point of the brain without damage. In the early experiments the brain of an animal could be probed only with some of its skull removed and while it was under anesthesia. But W. R. Hess in Zurich developed a method of studying the brain for longer periods and under more normal circumstances. The electrodes were inserted through the skull, fixed in position

and left there; after the skin healed over the wound, the animal could be studied in its ordinary activities.

Using the earlier technique, H. W. Magoun and his collaborators at Northwestern University explored the region known as the "reticular system" in the lower part of the mid-brain [see page 30]. They showed that this system controls the sleep and wakefulness of animals. Stimulation of the system produced an "alert" electrical pattern, even from an anesthetized animal, and injury to nerve cells there produced more or less continuous sleep.

Hess, with his new technique, examined the hypothalamus and the region around the septum (the dividing membrane at the mid-line), which lie forward of the reticular system. He found that these parts of the brain play an important part in an animal's automatic protective behavior. In the rear section of the hypothalamus is a system which controls emergency responses that prepare the animal for fight or flight. Another system in the front part of the hypothalamus and in the septal area apparently controls rest, recovery, diges-

tion and elimination. In short, these studies seemed to localize the animal's brain responses in situations provoking fear, rage, escape or certain needs.

There remained an important part of the mid-line region of the brain which had not been explored and whose functions were still almost completely unknown. This area, comprising the upper portion of the middle system, seemed to be connected with smell, and to this day it is called the rhinencephalon, or "smell-brain." But the area appeared to receive messages from many organs of the body, and there were various other reasons to believe it was not concerned exclusively or even primarily with smell. As early as 1937 James W. Papez of Cornell University suggested that the rhinencephalon might control emotional experience and behavior. He based this speculation partly on the observation that rabies, which produces profound emotional upset, seems to attack parts of the rhinencephalon.

Such observations, then, constituted our knowledge of the areas of the brain until recently. Certain areas had

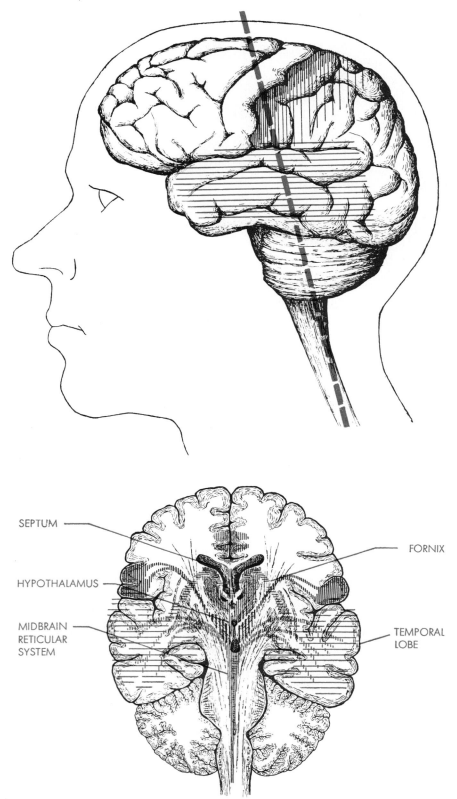

LOCATIONS OF FUNCTION in the human brain are mapped in these two diagrams. The white areas in both diagrams comprise the motor system; the black crosshatched areas, the sensory system. Crosshatched in color are the "nonspecific" regions now found to be involved in motivation of behavior. The diagram at bottom shows the brain from behind, dissected along the heavy dashed line at top. The labels here identify the centers which correspond to those investigated in the rat. The fornix and parts of the temporal lobes, plus associated structures not labeled, together constitute the rhinencephalon or "smell-brain."

been found to be involved in various kinds of emotional behavior, but the evidence was only of a general nature. The prevailing view still held that the basic motivations—pain, pleasure and so on—probably involved excitation or activity of the whole brain.

Investigation of these matters in more detail became possible only after psychologists had developed methods for detecting and measuring positive emotional behavior—pleasure and the satisfaction of specific "wants." It was B. F. Skinner, the Harvard University experimental psychologist, who produced the needed refinement. He worked out a technique for measuring the rewarding effect of a stimulus (or the degree of satisfaction) in terms of the frequency with which an animal would perform an act which led to the reward. For example, the animal was placed in a bare box containing a lever it could manipulate. If it received no reward when it pressed the lever, the animal might perform this act perhaps five to 10 times an hour. But if it was rewarded with a pellet of food every time it worked the lever, then its rate of performing the act would rise to 100 or more times per hour. This increase in response frequency from five or 10 to 100 per hour provided a measure of the rewarding effect of the food. Other stimuli produce different response rates, and in each case the rise in rate seems to be a quite accurate measure of the reward value of the given stimulus.

With the help of Hess's technique for probing the brain and Skinner's for measuring motivation, we have been engaged in a series of experiments which began three years ago under the guidance of the psychologist D. O. Hebb at McGill University. At the beginning we planned to explore particularly the midbrain reticular system—the sleep-control area that had been investigated by Magoun.

Just before we began our own work, H. R. Delgado, W. W. Roberts and N. E. Miller at Yale University had undertaken a similar study. They had located an area in the lower part of the mid-line system where stimulation caused the animal to avoid the behavior that provoked the electrical stimulus. We wished to investigate positive as well as negative effects—that is, to learn whether stimulation of some areas might be sought rather than avoided by the animal.

We were not at first concerned to hit very specific points in the brain, and in fact in our early tests the electrodes did not always go to the particular areas in the mid-line system at which they were aimed. Our lack of aim turned out to be a fortunate happening for us. In one animal the electrode missed its target and landed not in the mid-brain reticular system but in a nerve pathway from the rhinencephalon. This led to an unexpected discovery.

In the test experiment we were using, the animal was placed in a large box with corners labeled A, B, C and D. Whenever the animal went to corner A, its brain was given a mild electric shock by the experimenter. When the test was performed on the animal with the electrode in the rhinencephalic nerve, it kept returning to corner A. After several such returns on the first day, it finally went to a different place and fell asleep. The next day, however, it seemed even more interested in corner A.

At this point we assumed that the stimulus must provoke curiosity; we did not yet think of it as a reward. Further experimentation on the same animal soon indicated, to our surprise, that its response to the stimulus was more than curiosity. On the second day, after the animal had acquired the habit of returning to corner A to be stimulated, we began trying to draw it away to corner B, giving it an electric shock whenever it took a step in that direction. Within a matter of five minutes the animal was in corner B. After this, the animal could be directed to almost any spot in the box at the will of the experimenter. Every step in the right direction was paid with a small shock; on arrival at the appointed place the animal received a longer series of shocks.

Next the animal was put on a T-shaped platform and stimulated if it turned right at the crossing of the T but not if it turned left. It soon learned to turn right every time. At this point we reversed the procedure, and the animal had to turn left in order to get a shock. With some guidance from the experimenter it eventually switched from the right to the left. We followed up with a test of the animal's response when it was hungry. Food was withheld for 24 hours. Then the animal was placed in a T both arms of which were baited with mash. The animal would receive the electric stimulus at a point halfway down the right arm. It learned to go there, and it always stopped at this point, never going on to the food at all!

After confirming this powerful effect of stimulation of brain areas by experiments with a series of animals, we set out to map the places in the brain where

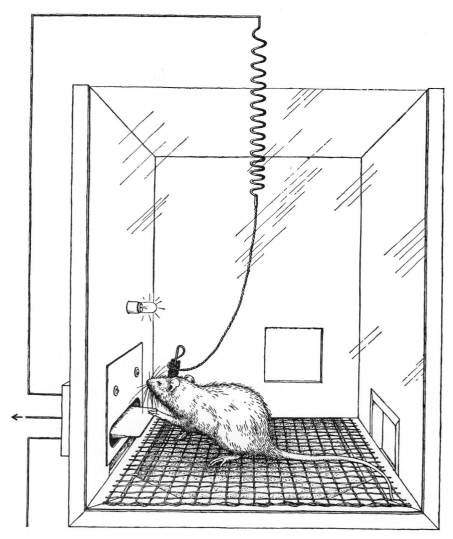

SELF-STIMULATION CIRCUIT is diagrammed here. When the rat presses on treadle it triggers an electric stimulus to its brain and simultaneously records action via wire at left.

such an effect could be obtained. We wanted to measure the strength of the effect in each place. Here Skinner's technique provided the means. By putting the animal in the "do-it-yourself" situation (*i.e.*, pressing a lever to stimulate its own brain) we could translate the animal's strength of "desire" into response frequency, which can be seen and measured.

The first animal in the Skinner box ended all doubts in our minds that electric stimulation applied to some parts of the brain could indeed provide reward for behavior. The test displayed the phenomenon in bold relief where anyone who wanted to look could see it. Left to itself in the apparatus, the animal (after about two to five minutes of learning) stimulated its own brain regularly about once every five seconds, taking a stimulus of a second or so every time. After 30 minutes the experimenter turned off the current, so that the animal's pressing of the lever no longer stimulated the brain. Under these conditions the animal pressed it about seven times and then went to sleep. We found that the test was repeatable as often as we cared to apply it. When the current was turned on and the animal was given one shock as an *hors d'oeuvre*, it would begin stimulating its brain again. When the electricity was turned off, it would try a few times and then go to sleep.

The current used to stimulate was ordinary house current reduced by a small transformer and then regulated between one and five volts by means of a potentiometer (a radio volume control). As the resistance in the brain was approximately 12,000 ohms, the current ranged from about .000083 to .000420 of an ampere. The shock lasted up to about a second, and the animal had to release the lever and press again to get more.

We now started to localize and quantify the rewarding effect in the brain by planting electrodes in all parts of the brain in large numbers of rats. Each rat had a pair of electrodes consisting of insulated silver wires a hundredth of an inch in diameter. The two stimulating tips were only about one 500th of an inch apart. During a test the animal was placed in a Skinner box designed to produce a chance response rate of about 10 to 25 bar-presses per hour. Each animal was given about six hours of testing with the electric current turned on and one hour with the current off. All responses were recorded automatically, and the animal was given a score on the basis of the amount of time it spent stimulating its brain.

When electrodes were implanted in the classical sensory and motor systems, response rates stayed at the chance level of 10 to 25 an hour. In most parts of the mid-line system, the response rates rose to levels of from 200 to 5,000 an hour, definitely indicative of a rewarding effect of the electric stimulus. But in some of the lower parts of the mid-line system there was an opposite effect: the animal would press the lever once and never go back. This indicated a punishing effect in those areas. They appeared to be the same areas where Delgado, Roberts and Miller at Yale also had discovered the avoidance effect—and where Hess and others had found responses of rage and escape.

The animals seemed to experience the strongest reward, or pleasure, from stimulation of areas of the hypothalamus and certain mid-brain nuclei—regions which Hess and others had found to be centers for control of digestive, sexual, excretory and similar processes. Animals with electrodes in these areas would stimulate themselves from 500 to 5,000 times per hour. In the rhinencephalon the effects were milder, producing self-stimulation at rates around 200 times per hour.

Electric stimulation in some of these regions actually appeared to be far more rewarding to the animals than an ordinary satisfier such as food. For example, hungry rats ran faster to reach an electric stimulator than they did to reach food. Indeed, a hungry animal often ignored available food in favor of the pleasure of stimulating itself electrically. Some rats with electrodes in these places stimulated their brains more than 2,000 times per hour for 24 consecutive hours!

Why is the electric stimulation so rewarding? We are currently exploring this question, working on the hypothesis that brain stimulation in these regions must excite some of the nerve cells that would be excited by satisfaction of the basic drives—hunger, sex, thirst and so forth. We have looked to see whether some parts of the "reward system" of the brain are specialized; that is, there may be one part for the hunger drive, another for the sex drive, etc.

In experiments on hunger, we have found that an animal's appetite for electric stimulation in some brain regions increases as hunger increases: the animal will respond much faster when hungry than when full. We are performing similar tests in other places in the brain with variations of thirst and sex hormones. We have already found that there are areas where the rewarding effects of a brain stimulus can be abolished by castration and restored by injections of testosterone.

Our present tentative conclusion is that emotional and motivational mechanisms can indeed be localized in the brain; that certain portions of the brain are sensitive to each of the basic drives. Strong electrical stimulation of these areas seems to be even more satisfying than the usual rewards of food, etc. This finding contradicts the long-held theory that strong excitation in the brain means punishment. In some areas of the brain it means reward.

The main question for future research is to determine how the excited "reward" cells act upon the specific sensory-motor systems to intensify the rewarded

RAT IS CONNECTED to electrical circuit by a plug which can be disconnected to free the animal during rest periods. Presence of electrodes does not pain or discommode the rat.

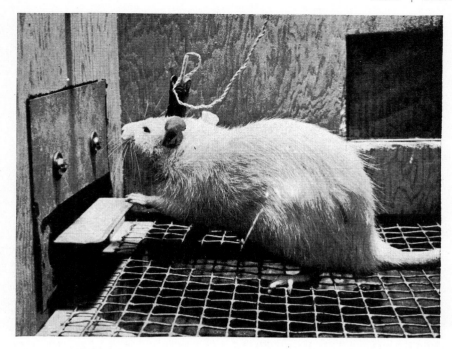

RAT SEEKS STIMULUS as it places its paw on the treadle. Some of the animals have been seen to stimulate themselves for 24 hours without rest and as often as 5,000 times an hour.

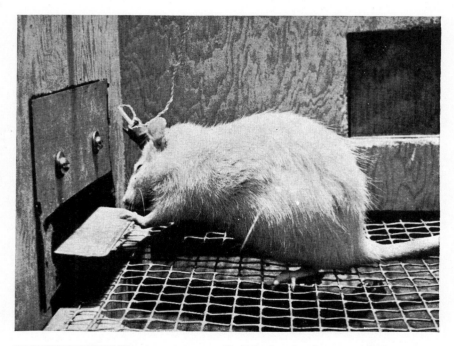

RAT FEELS STIMULUS as it presses on treadle. Pulse lasts less than a second; the current is less than .0005 ampere. The animal must release lever and press again to renew the stimulus.

behavior.

At the moment we are using the self-stimulating technique to learn whether drugs will selectively affect the various motivational centers of the brain. We hope, for example, that we may eventually find one drug that will raise or lower thresholds in the hunger system, another for the sex-drive system, and so forth. Such drugs would allow control of psychological disorders caused by surfeits or deficits in motivational conditions.

Enough of the brain-stimulating work has been repeated on monkeys by J. V. Brady and J. C. Lilly (who work in different laboratories in Washington, D. C.) to indicate that our general conclusions can very likely be generalized eventually to human beings—with modifications, of course.

5

"Imprinting" in a Natural Laboratory

by Eckhard H. Hess
August 1972

*A synthesis of laboratory and field techniques has led
to some interesting discoveries about imprinting,
the process by which newly hatched birds rapidly
form a permanent bond to the parent*

In a marsh on the Eastern Shore of Maryland, a few hundred feet from my laboratory building, a female wild mallard sits on a dozen infertile eggs. She has been incubating the eggs for almost four weeks. Periodically she hears the faint peeping sounds that are emitted by hatching mallard eggs, and she clucks softly in response. Since these eggs are infertile, however, they are not about to hatch and they do not emit peeping sounds. The sounds come from a small loudspeaker hidden in the nest under the eggs. The loudspeaker is connected to a microphone next to some hatching mallard eggs inside an incubator in my laboratory. The female mallard can hear any sounds coming from the laboratory eggs, and a microphone beside her relays the sounds she makes to a loudspeaker next to those eggs.

The reason for complicating the life of an expectant duck in such a way is to further our understanding of the phenomenon known as imprinting. It was through the work of the Austrian zoologist Konrad Z. Lorenz that imprinting became widely known. In the 1930's Lorenz observed that newly hatched goslings would follow him rather than their mother if the goslings saw him before they saw her. Since naturally reared geese show a strong attachment for their parent, Lorenz concluded that some animals have the capacity to learn rapidly and permanently at a very early age, and in particular to learn the characteristics of the parent. He called this process of acquiring an attachment to the parent *Prägung*, which in German means "stamping" or "coinage" but in English has been rendered as "imprinting." Lorenz regarded the phenomenon as being different from the usual kind of learning because of its rapidity and apparent permanence. In fact, he was hesitant at first to regard imprinting as a form of learn-

ing at all. Some child psychologists and some psychiatrists nevertheless perceived a similarity between the evidence of imprinting in animals and the early behavior of the human infant, and it is not surprising that interest in imprinting spread quickly.

From about the beginning of the 1950's many investigators have intensively studied imprinting in the laboratory. Unlike Lorenz, the majority of them have regarded imprinting as a form of learning and have used methods much the same as those followed in the study of associative learning processes. In every case efforts were made to manipulate or stringently control the imprinting process. Usually the subjects are incuba-

CLUCKS emitted by a female wild mallard in the fourth week of incubating eggs are shown in the sound spectrogram (*upper illustration*). Each cluck lasts for about 150 milliseconds

tor-hatched birds that are reared in the laboratory. The birds are typically kept isolated until the time of the laboratory imprinting experience to prevent interaction of early social experience and the imprinting experience. Various objects have been used as artificial parents: duck decoys, stuffed hens, dolls, milk bottles, toilet floats, boxes, balls, flashing lights and rotating disks. Several investigators have constructed an automatic imprinting apparatus into which the newly hatched bird can be put. In this kind of work the investigator does not observe the young bird directly; all the bird's movements with respect to the imprinting object are recorded automatically.

Much of my own research during the past two decades has not differed substantially from this approach. The birds I have used for laboratory imprinting studies have all been incubated, hatched and reared without the normal social and environmental conditions and have then been tested in an artificial situation. It is therefore possible that the behavior observed under such conditions is not relevant to what actually happens in nature.

It is perhaps not surprising that studies of "unnatural" imprinting have produced conflicting results. Lorenz' original statements on the permanence of natural imprinting have been disputed. In many instances laboratory imprinting experiences do not produce permanent and exclusive attachment to the object selected as an artificial parent. For example, a duckling can spend a considerable amount of time following the object to which it is to be imprinted, and immediately after the experience it will follow a completely different object.

In one experiment in our laboratory we attempted to imprint ducklings to ourselves, as Lorenz did. For 20 continuous hours newly hatched ducklings were exposed to us. Before long they followed us whenever we moved about. Then they were given to a female mallard that had hatched a clutch of ducklings several hours before. After only an hour and a half of exposure to the female mallard and other ducklings the human-imprinted ducklings followed the female on the first exodus from the nest. Weeks later the behavior of the human-imprinted ducks was no different from the behavior of the ducks that had been hatched in the nest. Clearly laboratory imprinting is reversible.

We also took wild ducklings from their natural mother 16 hours after hatching and tried to imprint them to humans. On the first day we spent many hours with the ducklings, and during the next two months we made lengthy attempts every day to overcome the ducklings' fear of us. We finally gave up. From the beginning to the end the ducks remained wild and afraid. They were released, and when they had matured, they were observed to be as wary of humans as normal wild ducks are. This result suggests that natural imprinting, unlike artificial laboratory imprinting, is permanent and irreversible. I have had to conclude that the usual laboratory imprinting has only a limited resemblance to natural imprinting.

It seems obvious that if the effects of natural imprinting are to be understood, the phenomenon must be studied as it

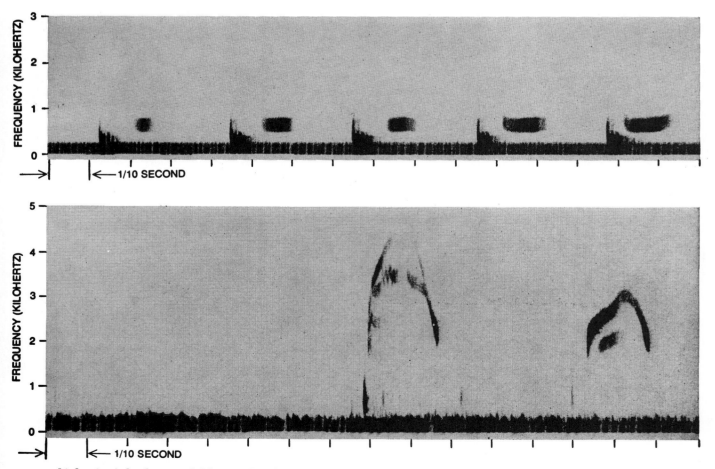

and is low in pitch: about one kilohertz or less. Sounds emitted by ducklings inside the eggs are high-pitched, rising to about four kilohertz (*lower illustration*). Records of natural, undisturbed imprinting events in the nest provide a control for later experiments.

operates in nature. The value of such studies was stressed as long ago as 1914 by the pioneer American psychologist John B. Watson. He emphasized that field observations must always be made to test whether or not conclusions drawn from laboratory studies conform to what actually happens in nature. The disparity between laboratory results and what happens in nature often arises from the failure of the investigator to really look at the animal's behavior. For years I have cautioned my students against shutting their experimental animals in

"black boxes" with automatic recording devices and never directly observing how the animals behave.

This does not mean that objective laboratory methods for studying the behavior of animals must be abandoned. With laboratory investigations large strides have been made in the development of instruments for the recording of behavior. In the study of imprinting it is not necessary to revert to imprecise naturalistic observations in the field. We can now go far beyond the limitations of traditional field studies. It is possible to

set up modern laboratory equipment in actual field conditions and in ways that do not disturb or interact with the behavior being studied, in other words, to achieve a synthesis of laboratory and field techniques.

The first step in the field-laboratory method is to observe and record the undisturbed natural behavior of the animal in the situation being studied. In our work on imprinting we photographed the behavior of the female mallard during incubation and hatching. We photographed the behavior of the ducklings

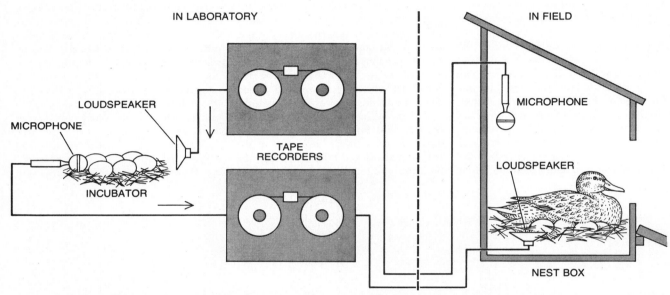

FEMALE MALLARD sitting on infertile eggs hears sounds transmitted from mallard eggs in a laboratory incubator. Any sounds she makes are transmitted to a loudspeaker beside the eggs in the laboratory. Such a combination of field and laboratory techniques permits recording of events without disturbing the nesting mallard and provides the hatching eggs with nearly natural conditions.

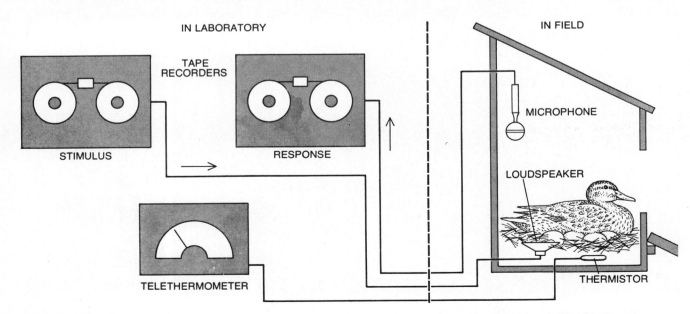

REMOTE MANIPULATION of prehatching sounds is accomplished by placing a sensitive microphone and a loudspeaker in the nest of a female wild mallard who is sitting on her own eggs. Prerecorded hatching-duckling sounds are played at specified times through the loudspeaker and the female mallard's responses to this stimulus are recorded. A thermistor probe transmits the temperature in the nest to a telethermometer and chart recorder. The thermistor records provide data about when females are on nest.

during and after hatching. We recorded all sounds from the nest before and after hatching. Other factors, such as air temperature and nest temperature, were also recorded.

A detailed inventory of the actual events in natural imprinting is essential for providing a reference point in the assessment of experimental manipulations of the imprinting process. That is, the undisturbed natural imprinting events form the control situation for assessing the effects of the experimental manipulations. This is quite different from the "controlled" laboratory setting, in which the ducklings are reared in isolation and then tested in unnatural conditions. The controlled laboratory study not only introduces new variables (environmental and social deprivation) into the imprinting situation but also it can prevent the investigator from observing factors that are relevant in wild conditions.

My Maryland research station is well suited for the study of natural imprinting in ducks. The station, near a national game refuge, has 250 acres of marsh and forest on a peninsula on which there are many wild and semiwild mallards. Through the sharp eyes of my technical assistant Elihu Abbott, a native of the Eastern Shore, I have learned to see much I might otherwise have missed. Initially we looked at and listened to the undisturbed parent-offspring interaction of female mallards that hatched their own eggs both in nests on the ground and in specially constructed nest boxes. From our records we noticed that the incubation time required for different clutches of eggs decreased progressively between March and June. Both the average air temperature and the number of daylight hours increase during those months; both are correlated with the incubation time of mallard eggs. It is likely, however, that temperature rather than photoperiod directly influences the duration of incubation. In one experiment mallard eggs from an incubator were slowly cooled for two hours a day in a room with a temperature of seven degrees Celsius, and another set of eggs was cooled in a room at 27 degrees C. These temperatures respectively correspond to the mean noon temperatures at the research station in March and in June. The eggs that were placed in the cooler room took longer to hatch, indicating that temperature affects the incubation time directly. Factors such as humidity and barometric pressure may also play a role.

We noticed that all the eggs in a wild

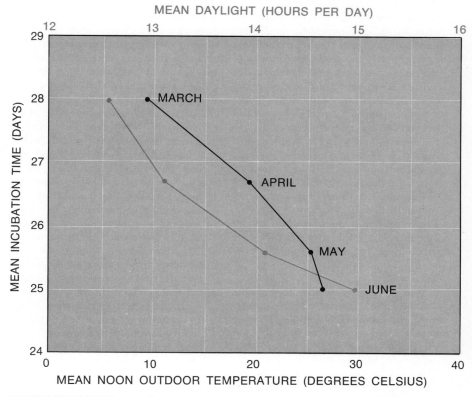

INCUBATION TIME of mallard eggs hatched naturally in a feral setting at Lake Cove, Md., decreased steadily from March to June. The incubation period correlated with both the outdoor temperature (*black curve*) and the daily photoperiod (*colored curve*).

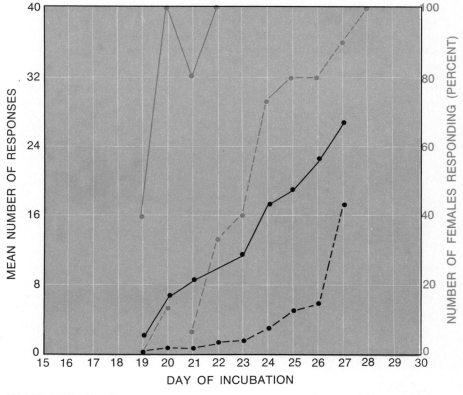

VOCAL RESPONSES to hatching-duckling sounds of 15 female wild mallards (*broken curves*) and five human-imprinted mallards (*solid curves*), which were later released to the wild, followed the same pattern, although the human-imprinted mallards began responding sooner and more frequently. A tape recording of the sounds of a hatching duckling was played daily throughout the incubation period to each female mallard while she was on her nest. Responses began on the 19th day of incubation and rose steadily until hatching.

nest usually hatch between three and eight hours of one another. As a result all the ducklings in the same clutch are approximately the same age in terms of the number of hours since hatching. Yet when mallard eggs are placed in a mechanical incubator, they will hatch over a two- or three-day period even when precautions are taken to ensure that all the eggs begin developing simultaneously. The synchronous hatching observed in nature obviously has some survival value. At the time of the exodus from the nest, which usually takes place between 16 and 32 hours after hatching, all the ducklings would be of a similar age and thus would have equal motor capabilities and similar social experiences.

Over the years our laboratory studies and actual observations of how a female mallard interacts with her offspring have pointed to the conclusion that imprinting is related to the age after hatching rather than the age from the beginning of incubation. Many other workers, however, have accepted the claim that age from the beginning of incubation determines the critical period for maximum effectiveness of imprinting. They base their belief on the findings of Gilbert Gottlieb of the Dorothea Dix Hospital in Raleigh, N.C., who in a 1961 paper described experiments that apparently showed that maximum imprint-

ing in ducklings occurs in the period between 27 and 27½ days after the beginning of incubation. To make sure that all the eggs he was working with started incubation at the same time he first chilled the eggs so that any partially developed embryos would be killed. Yet the 27th day after the beginning of incubation can hardly be the period of maximum imprinting for wild ducklings that hatch in March under natural conditions, because such ducklings take on the average 28 days to hatch. Moreover, if the age of a duckling is measured from the beginning of incubation, it is hard to explain why eggs laid at different times in a hot month in the same nest will hatch within six to eight hours of one another under natural conditions.

Periodic cooling of the eggs seems to affect the synchronization of hatching. The mallard eggs from an incubator that were placed in a room at seven degrees C. hatched over a period of a day and a half, whereas eggs placed in the room at 27 degrees hatched over a period of two and a half days (which is about normal for artificially incubated eggs). Cooling cannot, however, play a major role. In June the temperature in the outdoor nest boxes averages close to the normal brooding temperature while the female mallard is absent. Therefore an egg laid on June 1 has a head start in incubation over those laid a week later. Yet we have observed that all the eggs in clutches

laid in June hatch in a period lasting between six and eight hours.

We found another clue to how the synchronization of hatching may be achieved in the vocalization pattern of the brooding female mallard. As many others have noted, the female mallard vocalizes regularly as she sits on her eggs during the latter part of the incubation period. It seemed possible that she was vocalizing to the eggs, perhaps in response to sounds from the eggs themselves. Other workers had observed that ducklings make sounds before they hatch, and the prehatching behavior of ducklings in response to maternal calls has been extensively reported by Gottlieb.

We placed a highly sensitive microphone next to some mallard eggs that were nearly ready to hatch. We found that the ducklings indeed make sounds while they are still inside the egg. We made a one-minute tape recording of the sounds emitted by a duckling that had pipped its shell and was going to hatch within the next few hours. Then we made a seven-minute recording that would enable us to play the duckling sounds three times for one minute interspersed with one-minute silences. We played the recording once each to 37 female mallards at various stages of incubation. There were no positive responses from the female mallards during

NEST EXODUS takes place about 16 to 32 hours after hatching. The female mallard begins to make about 40 to 65 calls per minute and continues while the ducklings leave the nest to follow her. The ducklings are capable of walking and swimming from hatching.

the first and second week of incubation. In fact, during the first days of incubation some female mallards responded with threat behavior: a fluffing of the feathers and a panting sound. In the third week some females responded to the recorded duckling sounds with a few clucks. In the fourth week maternal clucks were frequent and were observed in all ducks tested.

We found the same general pattern of response whether the female mallards were tested once or, as in a subsequent experiment, tested daily during incubation. Mallards sitting on infertile eggs responded just as much to the recorded duckling sounds as mallards sitting on fertile eggs did. Apparently after sitting on a clutch of eggs for two or three weeks a female mallard becomes ready to respond to the sounds of a hatching duckling. There is some evidence that the parental behavior of the female mallard is primed by certain neuroendocrine mechanisms. We have begun a study of the neuroendocrine changes that might accompany imprinting and filial behavior in mallards.

To what extent do unhatched ducklings respond to the vocalization of the female mallard? In order to find out we played a recording of a female mallard's vocalizations to ducklings in eggs that had just been pipped and were scheduled to hatch within the next 24 hours. As before, the sounds were interspersed with periods of silence. We then recorded all the sounds made by the ducklings during the recorded female mallard vocalizations and also during the silent periods on the tape. Twenty-four hours before the scheduled hatching the ducklings emitted 34 percent of their sounds during the silent periods, which suggests that at this stage they initiate most of the auditory interaction. As hatching time approaches the ducklings emit fewer and fewer sounds during the silent periods. The total number of sounds they make, however, increases steadily. At the time of hatching only 9 percent of the sounds they make are emitted during the silent periods. One hour after hatching, in response to the same type of recording, the ducklings gave 37 percent of their vocalizations during the silent periods, a level similar to the level at 24 hours before hatching.

During the hatching period, which lasts about an hour, the female mallard generally vocalizes at the rate of from zero to four calls per one-minute interval. Occasionally there is an interval in which she emits as many as 10 calls. When the duckling actually hatches, the female mallard's vocalization increases

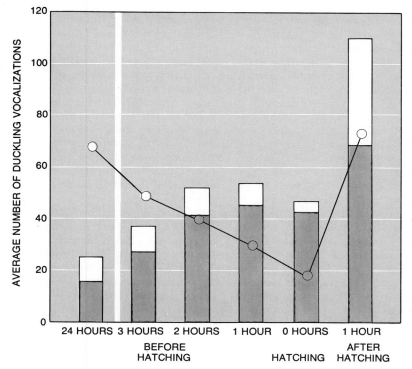

NUMBER OF SOUNDS from ducklings before and after hatching are shown. The ducklings heard a recording consisting of five one-minute segments of a female mallard's clucking sounds interspersed with five one-minute segments of silence. The recording was played to six mallard eggs and the number of vocal responses by the ducklings to the clucking segments (gray bars) and to the silent segments (white bars) were counted. Twenty-four hours before hatching 34 percent of the duckling sounds were made during the silent interval, indicating the ducklings initiated a substantial portion of the early auditory interaction. As hatching time approached the ducklings initiated fewer and fewer of the sounds and at hatching vocalized most in response to the clucks of the female mallard.

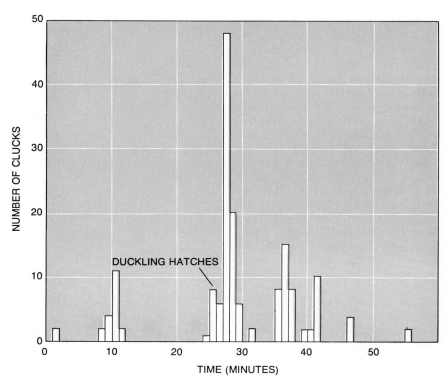

CLUCKING RATE of a wild, ground-nesting female mallard rose dramatically for about two minutes while a duckling hatched and then slowly declined to the prehatching rate. Each bar depicts the number of clucks emitted by the female during a one-minute period.

dramatically to between 45 and 68 calls per minute for one or two minutes.

Thus the sounds made by the female mallard and by her offspring are complementary. The female mallard vocalizes most when a duckling has just hatched. A hatching duckling emits its cries primarily when the female is vocalizing.

After all the ducklings have hatched the female mallard tends to be relatively quiet for long intervals, giving between zero and four calls per minute. This continues for 16 to 32 hours until it is time for the exodus from the nest. As the exodus begins the female mallard quickly builds up to a crescendo of between 40 and 65 calls per minute; on rare occasions we have observed between 70 and 95 calls per minute. The duration of the high-calling-rate period depends on how quickly the ducklings leave the nest to follow her. There is now a change in the sounds made by the female mallard. Up to this point she has been making clucking sounds. By the time the exodus from the nest takes place some of her sounds are more like quacks.

The auditory interaction of the female mallard and the duckling can begin well before the hatching period. As I have indicated, the female mallard responds to unhatched-duckling sounds during the third and fourth week of incubation. Normally ducklings penetrate a membrane to reach an air space inside the eggshell two days before hatching. We have not found any female mallard that vocalized to her clutch before the duckling in the egg reached the air space. We have found that as soon as the duckling penetrates the air space the female begins to cluck at a rate of between zero and four times per minute. Typically she continues to vocalize at this rate until the ducklings begin to pip their eggs (which is about 24 hours after they have entered the air space). As the eggs are being pipped the female clucks at the rate of between 10 and 15 times per minute. When the pipping is completed, she drops back to between zero and four calls per minute. In the next 24 hours there is a great deal of auditory interaction between the female and her unhatched offspring; this intense interaction may facilitate the rapid formation of the filial bond after hatching, although it is quite possible that synchrony of hatching is the main effect. Already we have found that a combination of cooling the eggs daily, placing them together so that they touch one another and transmitting parent-young vocal responses through the microphone-loudspeaker hookup between the female's nest and the laboratory incubator causes

the eggs in the incubator to hatch as synchronously as eggs in nature do. In fact, the two times we did this we found that all the eggs in the clutches hatched within four hours of one another. It has been shown in many studies of imprinting, including laboratory studies, that auditory stimuli have an important effect on the development of filial attachment. Auditory stimulation, before and after hatching, together with tactile stimulation in the nest after hatching results in ducklings that are thoroughly imprinted to the female mallard that is present.

Furthermore, it appears that auditory interaction before hatching may play an important role in promoting the synchronization of hatching. As our experiments showed, not only does the female mallard respond to sounds from her eggs but also the ducklings respond to her clucks. Perhaps the daily cooling of the eggs when the female mallard leaves the nest to feed serves to broadly synchronize embryonic and behavioral development, whereas the auditory interaction of the mother with the ducklings and of one duckling with another serves to provide finer synchronization. Margaret Vince of

the University of Cambridge has shown that the synchronization of hatching in quail is promoted by the mutual auditory interaction of the young birds in the eggs.

Listening to the female mallards vocalize to their eggs or to their newly hatched offspring, we were struck by the fact that we could tell which mallard was vocalizing, even when we could not see her. Some female mallards regularly emit single clucks at one-second intervals, some cluck in triple or quadruple clusters and others cluck in clusters of different lengths. The individual differences in the vocalization styles of female mallards may enable young ducklings to identify their mother. We can also speculate that the characteristics of a female mallard's voice are learned by her female offspring, which may then adopt a similar style when they are hatching eggs of their own.

The female mallards not only differ from one another in vocalization styles but also emit different calls in different situations. We have recorded variations in pitch and duration from the same mallard in various nesting situations. It

SOUND SPECTROGRAM of the calls of newly hatched ducklings in the nest and the mother's responses is shown at right. The high-pitched peeps of the ducklings are in the

DISTRESS CALLS of ducklings in the nest evoke a quacklike response from the female mallard. The cessation of the distress calls and the onset of normal duckling peeping sounds

seems likely that such variations in the female mallard call are an important factor in the imprinting process.

Studies of imprinting in the laboratory have shown that the more effort a duckling has to expend in following the imprinting object, the more strongly it prefers that object in later testing. At first it would seem that this is not the case in natural imprinting; young ducklings raised by their mother have little difficulty following her during the exodus from the nest. Closer observation of many nests over several seasons showed, however, that ducklings make a considerable effort to be near their parent. They may suffer for such efforts, since they can be accidentally stepped on, squeezed or scratched by the female adult. The combination of effort and punishment may actually strengthen imprinting. Work in my laboratory showed that chicks given an electric shock while they were following the imprinting object later showed stronger attachment to the object than unshocked chicks did. It is reasonable to expect similar results with ducklings.

Slobodan Petrovich of the University of Maryland (Baltimore County) and I have begun a study to determine the relative contributions of prehatching and posthatching auditory experience on imprinting and filial attachment. The auditory stimuli consist of either natural mallard maternal clucks or a human voice saying "Come, come, come." Our results indicate that prehatching stimulation by natural maternal clucks may to a degree facilitate the later recognition of the characteristic call of the mallard. Ducklings lacking any experience with a maternal call imprint as well to a duck decoy that utters "Come, come, come" as to a decoy that emits normal mallard clucks. Ducklings that had been exposed to a maternal call before hatching imprinted better to decoys that emitted the mallard clucks. We found, however, that the immediate posthatching experiences, in this case with a female mallard on the nest, can highly determine the degree of filial attachment and make imprinting to a human sound virtually impossible.

It is important to recognize that almost all laboratory imprinting experiments, including my own, have been deprivation experiments. The justification for such experiments has been the ostensible need for controlling the variables of the phenomenon, but the deprivation may have interfered with the normal behavioral development of the young ducklings. Whatever imprinting experiences the experimenter allows therefore do not produce the maximum effect.

Although our findings are far from complete, we have already determined enough to demonstrate the great value of studying imprinting under natural conditions. The natural laboratory can be profitably used to study questions about imprinting that have been raised but not answered by traditional laboratory experiments. We must move away from the in vitro, or test-tube, approach to the study of behavior and move toward the in vivo method that allows interaction with normal environmental factors. Some of the questions are: What is the optimal age for imprinting? How long must the imprinting experience last for it to have the maximum effect? Which has the greater effect on behavior: first experience or the most recent experience? Whatever kind of behavior is being studied, the most fruitful approach may well be to study the behavior in its natural context.

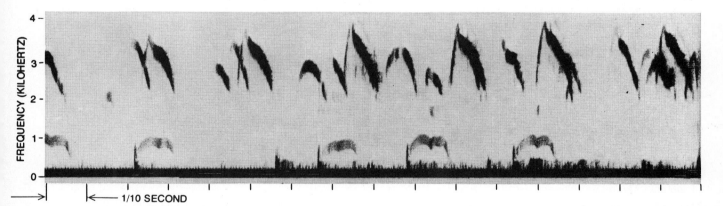

two-to-four-kilohertz range. They normally have the shape of an inverted V. The female mallard's clucks are about one kilohertz and last about 130 milliseconds. After the eggs hatch the vocalization of the female changes both in quantity and in quality of sound.

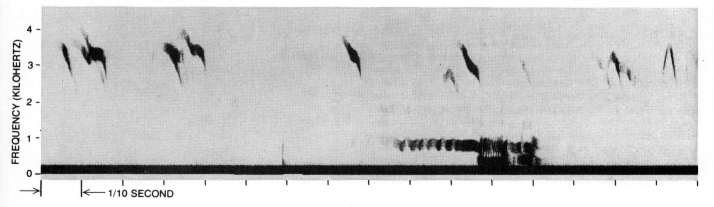

is almost immediate, as can be seen in this sound spectrogram. The female mallard's quacklike call is about one kilohertz in pitch and has a duration of approximately 450 milliseconds. The call is emitted about once every two seconds in response to distress cries.

6

The Object in the World of the Infant

by T. G. R. Bower
October 1971

At what stage of development does an infant begin to associate qualities such as solidity with objects that he sees? Experiments with infants reveal that this occurs much earlier than expected

According to most traditional theories of how we come to perceive the world around us, the quality of solidity belongs to the sense of touch in the same way that the quality of color belongs to the sense of vision or the quality of pitch to the sense of hearing. Only the sense of touch has the intrinsic ability to distinguish solids from nonsolids. The ability to identify solid objects visually is the result of learning to associate visual clues with tactile impressions, or so the traditional arguments have asserted. The classic version of the theory was presented by Bishop Berkeley. It was espoused in the 19th century by Hermann von Helmholtz and more recently by J. McV. Hunt, Burton White and Richard L. Gregory.

If the ability to associate touch and sight is learned, then at what stage of human development does the learning occur? Since young children clearly exhibit a unity of the senses, such learning must take place at some early stage of infancy. The infant who has not yet made the association must therefore live in a world of clouds, smoke puffs and insubstantial images of objects rather than in a world of solid, stable objects.

A similar situation holds when we observe an object move behind another object and disappear from sight. An adult knows that the object is still there, that it has not ceased to exist. This can be verified simply by removing the obstructing object or looking around it. It is hard to understand how an infant could know that the object is still there by using vision alone; how can vision provide information about the location of an invisible object? Touch must play a critical role in the development of the ability to deal with hidden objects. The hand can go around obstacles to reach such objects, and only as a result of such

explorations can an infant come to know that the object is still there. So, again, goes the traditional argument, and very plausible it seems.

These aspects of objects—solidity and permanence—present deep problems to the student of human development. Not the least formidable of the problems is finding ways to measure a naïve infant's response to objects. The infant, with his limited repertory of responses, is a refractory subject for psychological investigation. Recent advances in techniques of studying space perception and pattern recognition in infants are inherently unsuitable. These methods mostly determine whether or not the infant discriminates between two presentations, for example a regular pattern and an irregular one. One could present a solid object and, say, a bounded air space with the same external contour to an infant. Undoubtedly an infant of any age could discriminate between the two objects. The mere fact of discrimination would not tell us that the infant knew the object was solid, tangible and would offer resistance to his touch. There are visual differences between solids and nonsolids, and the infant could pick up these differences without realizing that they signify solidity. Indeed, according to some theories there must be such a stage, where the infant does perceive differences but is not aware of their significance.

The methods I adopted to measure the infant's expectation of solidity involve the element of surprise and the use of an optical illusion. The illusion is produced with a binocular shadow-caster, a device consisting of two light projectors with polarizing filters and a rear-projection screen. The object, made of translucent plastic, is suspended be-

tween the lights and the screen so that it casts a double shadow on the rear of the screen. The small subject sits in front of the screen and views the shadows through polarizing goggles that have the effect of making only one shadow visible to each eye. The two retinal images are combined by the normal processes of binocular vision to yield a stereoscopic percept of the object. This virtual object appears in front of the screen and looks very real and solid. It is nonetheless an illusion and is therefore intangible. When the infant attempts to grasp it, his hand closes on empty air. To reach out for a seemingly solid object and come in contact with nothing is startling for anyone. The surprise clearly is a consequence of the nonfulfillment of the expectation that the seen object will be tangible.

Since even very young infants display the startle response, it can serve as an indicator of surprise. If the infant is startled by the absence of solidity in the virtual object, that can be taken as an index of an expectation that the seen object will be tangible. In contrast, a startle response on contact with the real object could be taken as an indication that the seen object is not expected to be tangible.

In the first experiment the infant sat before a screen and was presented with the virtual object or the real object. The two situations were presented several times, always beginning with the virtual object. We looked for evidence of startle behavior. The startle response can be measured in numerous ways, some of which are sophisticated and expensive, but in this experiment we used very simple indicators: facial expression and crying. These measures, so simple as to seem unscientific, are in fact as reliable as the more complex ones we used later.

Our subjects were infants between 16 and 24 weeks old. The results were quite unambiguous. None of the infants showed any sign of surprise when he touched the real object in front of him. Every infant showed marked surprise when his hand failed to make contact with the perceived virtual object. Whenever the infant's hand reached the place where the virtual object seemed to be, within a fraction of a second he emitted a coo, a whoop or a cry, accompanied by a change in facial expression so marked as to seem a caricature. The older infants reacted even more: they stared at their hand, rubbed their hands together or banged their hand on the chair before reaching again for the virtual object. All of this supports the idea that the infants expected to be able to touch a seen object and were very surprised when their attempts to do so produced no tactile feedback.

Although these results are interesting, they do not resolve the problem under investigation. They merely indicate that learning to coordinate vision and touch must take place, if it takes place at all, before the age of 16 weeks. We therefore attempted to study coordination between vision and touch in even younger infants, hoping to find a period of noncoordination. The communication problem is intensified in very young infants, since their behavioral repertory is even more limited than that of older infants.

Some investigators have reported that an infant less than six weeks old will not show defensive or avoidance behavior when an object approaches him. Other studies, however, have shown that an infant can discriminate changes in the position of objects in space well before the age of six weeks [see "The Visual World of Infants," by T. G. R. Bower; SCIENTIFIC AMERICAN Offprint 502]. The lack of defensive behavior may indicate the absence of the expectation that the seen object would produce tactile consequences, and it seemed to us that the infant's response to approaching objects would be a promising area to investigate.

Our preliminary investigations were highly encouraging. We took infants in their second week of life, placed them on their back and moved objects toward their face. We used objects of a wide variety of sizes and a wide variety of speeds. Some objects were moved noisily, some silently. All of this was to no avail. The infants, more than 40 of them, did not even blink. These two-week-old infants certainly did not seem to expect a seen object to have tactile consequences. It appeared that we had indeed found a period when vision and touch were not coordinated.

At this point in the research I became aware of the work of Heinz Prechtl, who

INTANGIBLE OBJECT is produced by a shadow-caster, in which two oppositely polarized beams of light cast a double shadow of an object on a rear-projection screen. An infant views the double shadows through polarizing goggles that make a different shadow visible to each eye. The innate processes of stereopsis fuse the two images to make the infant think he is seeing a solid object in front of the screen. When the infant tries to grasp the virtual image, he is startled when his hand closes on empty air; within a fraction of a second he cries and his face expresses marked surprise. When a real object is placed in front of the screen, none of the infants show any signs of surprise when they touch it. These results indicate that the infants expect a seen object to be solid and tangible.

had gathered evidence that implied infants under two weeks old are never fully awake while they are lying on their back. Since one could not expect defensive behavior from infants who were half-asleep, we repeated the experiment with infants of the same age who were held in an upright or semiupright position. With this modification the results were totally different. The infants clearly showed a defensive response to an approaching object. They pulled their head back and put their hands between their face and the object. These responses were accompanied by distress and crying so intense that the experiment had to be terminated earlier than had been planned. We were nonetheless able to try a few variations. We found that the defensive behavior was specific to an approaching object; if an object moved away, it produced neither defensive behavior nor crying. Moreover, the response was specific to a seen object. A moving solid object displaces air, which presumably causes pressure changes at the surface of the skin. In order to rule out the possibility that such pressure changes were the effective stimulus, we had a group of infants view an approaching virtual object produced by a shadow-caster. An object behind a translucent screen was moved away from the infant toward a projector. When the infant is placed at the same distance in front of the screen as the projectors are behind it, a shadow on the screen produces an image on the infant's retina that is identical with the image produced by a real object moving toward the baby, without the displacement of air and other nonvisual changes that accompany the movement of a real object.

The results were that seven out of seven infants in their second week of life exhibited defensive behavior when they saw the approaching virtual object. In our study the intensity of the infant's response to the virtual object seems somewhat less than the response to the real object, but a replication of the experiment by E. Tronick and C. Ball of Harvard University showed that the two responses are not that different. As a further check on the role of air movement another group of infants was presented with air displacement alone (produced by an air hose) with no object in the field of vision. None of these infants exhibited any defensive behavior or marked distress.

Taken together, these results suggest that by the second week of life an infant expects a seen object to have tactile consequences. The precocity of this expectation is quite surprising from the traditional point of view. Indeed, it seems to me that these findings are fatal to traditional theories of human development. In our culture it is unlikely that an infant less than two weeks old has been hit in the face by an approaching object, so that none of the infants in the study could have been exposed to situations where they could have learned to fear an approaching object and expect it to have tactile qualities. We can only conclude that in man there is a primitive unity of the senses, with visual variables specifying tactile consequences, and that this primitive unity is built into the structure of the human nervous system.

In an effort to further test this hypothesis we repeated the original virtual-object experiment with a group of newborn infants. It was not easy to do this, since the infants had to meet the criterion that they would wear the polarizing goggles without fussing. Newborn infants do not reach for objects in the same way that older infants do. They will, however, reach out and grasp ob-

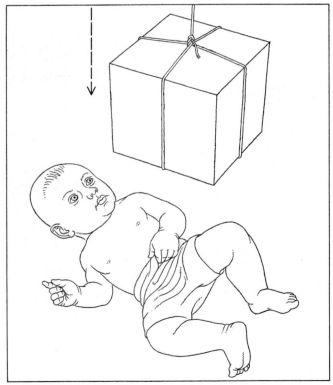

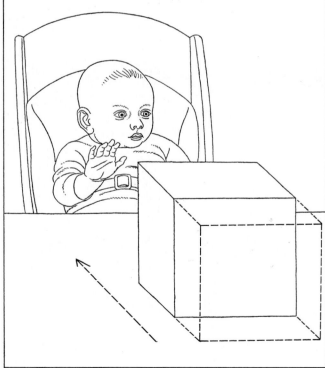

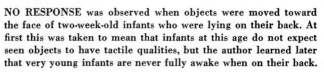

NO RESPONSE was observed when objects were moved toward the face of two-week-old infants who were lying on their back. At first this was taken to mean that infants at this age do not expect seen objects to have tactile qualities, but the author learned later that very young infants are never fully awake when on their back.

DEFENSIVE RESPONSE and marked distress to an approaching object was exhibited by upright two-week-old infants, even when the approaching object was an illusion produced by a shadow-caster. This evidence contradicts the theory that the perception of solidity is learned by associating tactile impressions and vision.

jects if they are supported so that their hands and arms are free to move to the objects in front of them. (They also reach out and grasp at empty air, but that does not affect the argument.)

We found that all the newborn infants touched and grasped real objects without any sign of being disturbed. The virtual object, however, produced a howl as soon as the infant's hand went to the intangible object's location. Here too, then, in dealing with the absence of tactile input in a situation where it normally would be expected, we have evidence of a primitive unity of the senses. This unity is unlikely to have been learned, given the early age and the history of the infants studied.

These results were surprising and interesting. They showed that at least one aspect of the eye-and-hand interaction is built into the nervous system. If it is built in, might not a more complex aspect of objects, namely permanence, also be built in? Is it possible that inborn structural properties ensure that an infant knows an object moving out of sight behind another object is still there? In order to find out we again used the startle response as an indicator of surprise. We sat an infant in front of an object. A screen moved in from one side and covered the object. After various intervals (1.5, 3, 7.5 or 15 seconds) the screen moved away. In half of the trials the object was still there when the screen moved away. In the other trials the object was no longer there when the screen moved away. If the infant knew that the object was still there behind the screen, its absence when the screen moved should have surprised him. If, on the other hand, the infant thought the object had ceased to exist when it was covered by the screen, its reappearance when the screen moved away should have been surprising.

In this experiment surprise was determined by a more quantitative index: a change in the heart rate. It is well known that the heart rate of an adult changes when he is surprised, and the same is true of infants. We measured the change in the heart rate of an infant by comparing his average heart rate over the 10 seconds after the moment of revelation with the average heart rate over the 10 seconds before the object was covered with the screen. Our subjects were infants who were 20, 40, 80 and 100 days old.

The results revealed an interesting pattern. When the object had been occluded for 1.5 seconds, all the infants manifested greater surprise at its nonreappearance than at its reappearance.

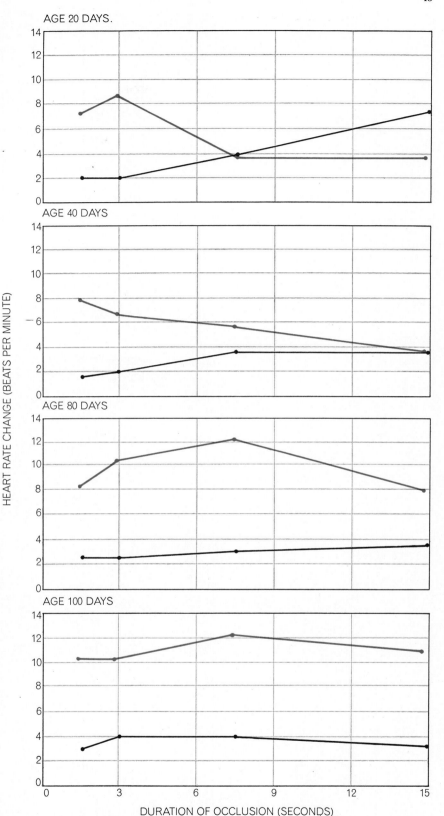

CHANGES IN HEART RATE reveal the degree of surprise in infants at the reappearance or disappearance of an object after it has been covered by a moving screen for various periods of time. Older infants are not surprised at the reappearance (*black curves*) of the object when the screen moves on, regardless of the duration of occlusion, and show little change in their heart rate. They are surprised when the object does not reappear (*colored curves*) from behind the moving screen. The youngest infants also are surprised by the object's failure to reappear when the occluding period is brief; when the time is increased to 15 seconds, they seem to forget about the object and show surprise at its reappearance.

46

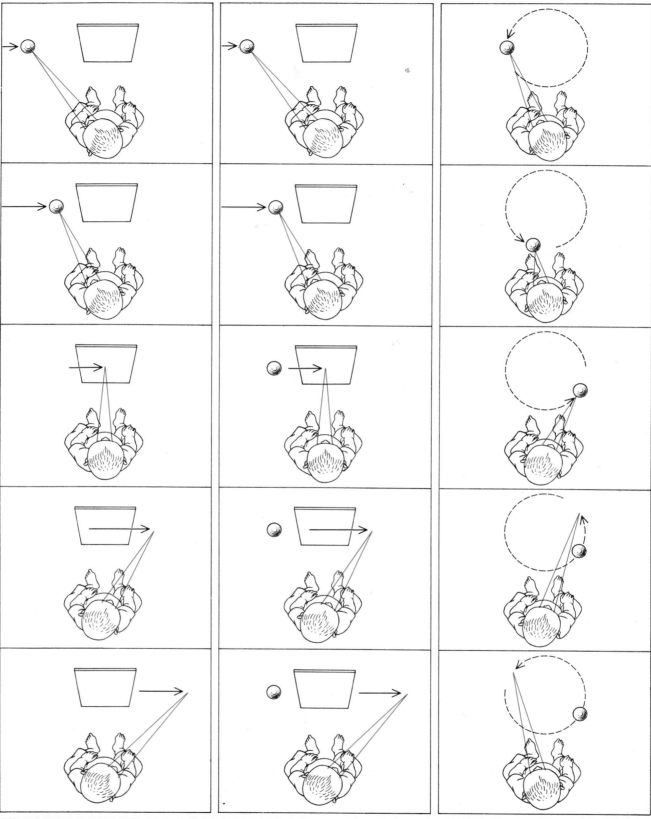

INFANT'S ANTICIPATION of the reappearance of an object that moves behind a screen and stops (*left*) seems to prove that the infant knew the object was still behind the screen. When the object stops before it reaches the screen, however, the infant continues to track the path of motion as if he could not arrest his head movement (*middle*). Next the infant was shown an object moving in a circle. If inability to arrest head movement were responsible for the continuation of tracking, then when the object stops halfway up the arc (*right*), the infant's gaze should continue tangentially to the circular path. Instead the infant's gaze paused on the stopped object for half a second and then continued along the circular path. It seems that the eight- and 16-week-old infants did not identify an object as being the same object when it was moving and when it was stationary and so they continued to look for the moving object.

In short, they expected the object to still be there. When the object failed to reappear, the change in the heart rate was about seven beats per minute; when the object did reappear, the change was very slight.

The oldest infants expected the object to reappear even after the longest occlusion period; when the object did not reappear, the change in their heart rate was 11 beats per minute. Curiously, the youngest infants exhibited a reverse effect after the longest occlusion period. They showed more surprise at the object's reappearance than at its nonreappearance. It seems that even very young infants know that an object is still there after it has been hidden, but if the time of occlusion is prolonged, they forget the object altogether. The early age of the infants and the novelty of the testing situation make it unlikely that such a response has been learned.

If object permanence is a built-in property of the nervous system, then it should show up in other situations. If the object was moved behind a stationary screen instead of the screen's moving to cover a stationary object, the same neural process should inform the infant that the object was behind the screen. We tested this assumption by having an eight-week-old infant watch an object that could be moved from side to side in front of him. A screen hid the center segment of the object's path. We reasoned that if the infant knew that the object had gone behind the screen rather than disappearing into some kind of limbo, he should be able to anticipate its reappearance on the other side of the screen. On the other hand, if the infant did not know that the object was behind the screen, he should not look over to the place where it would reappear; his eye movement should be arrested at the point of disappearance.

Two television cameras were lined up with the infant's face in order to record what side of the screen the infant was looking at. In the first part of the experiment the object would begin at one side, move slowly toward the screen, go behind it, emerge and continue to move for some distance. Then on random trials the object stopped behind the screen. Would such eight-week-old infants look over to the side where the object was due to emerge, or would they halt their gaze at the point of disappearance? The answer was quite straightforward: all the infants anticipated the reappearance of the object. Their behavior supported the hypothesis that a built-in neural process had informed them the object was behind the screen.

Unfortunately this result might have been an artifact of the experiment. Perhaps the infant following the object could not stop the movement of his head and the movement simply continued after it had begun. In order to test this possibility we ran a comparison series of experiments in which the object stopped in full view before it reached the screen. We reasoned that if the infant's apparent anticipation of the object's reappearance had been the result of the continuing movement of his head, the movement should continue after the object had stopped. On the other hand, if the infant had been genuinely anticipating the reappearance of the object, he would not look at the other side of the screen for an object he had just seen stop before reaching the screen. To our great disappointment the infants all looked over to the other side of the screen. This result seemed to rule out the hypothesis that eight-week-old infants seeing an object go behind a screen know that the object is still there and will reappear. Further studies indicated that infants up to 16 weeks old also were likely to look for the object to reappear in both experimental situations.

The inability to arrest head movement is an intrinsically unsatisfying explanation, particularly since it does not explain the results from the experiment with the stationary object and the moving screen. We therefore tried a variety of other experiments. In one test infants were presented with an object that moved in a circular trajectory at right angles to their line of sight. After a time the object stopped in full view at a point halfway up the arc. If the continuation of tracking was the result of an inability to arrest ongoing movement, a pause in the object's movement on a circular path should have produced head movements tangential to the path. Every infant, however, continued to look along the circular trajectory. Furthermore, frame-by-frame analysis of motion pictures of the head movements and eye movements revealed that the infant's fixation on the object was held for about half a second before the tracking movement continued. This bizarre behavior, continuing to track a moving object after seeing it stop, cannot be the result of an inability to arrest head movement. Every infant was able to momentarily hold his gaze on the object when it stopped. Therefore the infants must at least have noticed that the object had stopped. Yet they continued to track the path the object would have taken had it continued to move.

The explanation of this behavior was not, and is not, obvious. Superficially the infant's behavior appears to reflect an inability to identify a stationary object with the same object when it is moving. It was as if the infants had been tracking a moving object, had noticed the stationary object that the moving object had become, had looked at it for a while and then had looked farther on to find the moving object again. It seems that they had not been aware that the stationary object was in fact the same as the moving object.

Could the converse be true? Would infants look for an object in the place where it had been stationary after seeing it move off to a new location? In order to find out we seated an infant in front of a toy railroad track that had a train on it. The train carried flashing lights to attract the infant's attention. At the beginning of the experiment the train was stationary in the middle of the track. After 10 seconds the train moved slowly to the left and stopped at a new position, where it remained for 10 seconds, and then returned to its original position. The cycle was repeated 10 times.

How would this simple to-and-fro movement be seen by a three-month-old infant? Our hypothesis was that an infant of this age fails to recognize the identity of a moving object and the same object standing still. Initially the infant should see a stationary object in a particular place. Then the object would disappear and a new moving object would appear. Then the moving object would disappear and a stationary object would appear in a new place. After a time that too would disappear and a new moving object would appear, which in turn would give way to the original object in the original place again. To the infant the cycle would seem to involve perhaps four objects, whereas in reality there is only one. An infant quickly learns to look from one place to another as an object moves between them. If our hypothesis is correct, the infant is not following an object from place to place; rather he is applying a rule in the form, "Object disappears at A, object will reappear at B."

Suppose now that after the 10th cycle the train moves to the right to an entirely new position instead of moving to the left as usual. A subject who was following a single object would have no trouble. If an infant is applying the rule above, he should make an error. Specifically, when the stationary object moves to the right for the first time, thereby disappearing at the middle, the infant should look for the stationary object to the left in the place where it has reappeared before. When we tested three-month-old infants, every infant made the error predicted by our hypothesis. That is, when the train moved to the right, the infant looked to the left and

stared at the empty space where the train had stopped before. Meanwhile the train with its flashing lights was in full view in its new place to the right.

This last result, together with those from our earlier studies, confirms the hypothesis that three-month-old infants do not recognize the identity of an object at a standstill and the same object in motion, and vice versa. Note that I am using "identity" in a rather special

sense, meaning to recognize an object as being the same object rather than another identical object. If an infant does not identify a stationary object with a moving object when they are the same object, how does he identify a stationary object with itself when it is stationary in the same place later? How does he identify a moving object with itself when it is moving along a continuous trajectory? We began a new series of experiments to answer this fundamental question. The most obvious features of an object are its size, shape and color. These seem to serve as identification elements for adults. For an infant their role would seem to be somewhat different.

We presented infants with four situations: (1) An object (a small white mannikin) moved along a track, went behind a screen, emerged on the other side, moved on for a short distance, stopped and then returned to its original position. (2) The object moved along the track, went behind a screen and at the moment when the object should have emerged on the other side of the screen a totally different object (a stylized red lion) emerged, moved on for a short distance before reversing and repeating the entire cycle in the opposite direction. In this sequence there were differences of size, shape and color between the two objects, but there was only one kind of movement in any one direction. (3) The object moved along a track as before, except that at a time when, according to its speed before occlusion, it should still have been behind the screen, an identical object moved out. Here the objects were identical but there were two kinds of movement and evidence that there were two different objects since a single object could not have moved quickly enough to get across the screen in such a short time. (4) The object moved along a track as before, and at a time when it still should have been behind the screen a totally different object moved out. Here there were two kinds of difference in movement and features to indicate that there were two different objects. In all the situations only one object was visible at a time.

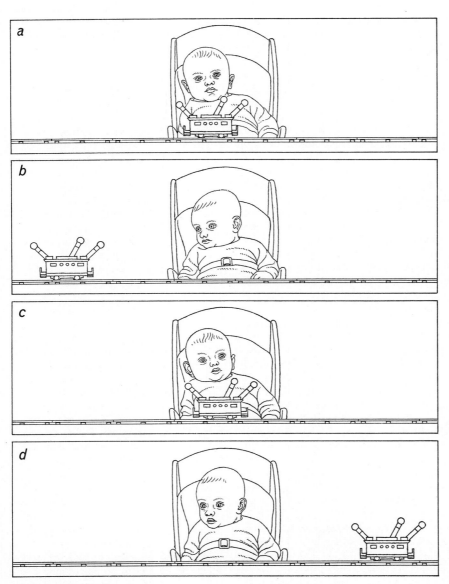

DISAPPEARING TRAIN confirms the hypothesis that infants 12 weeks old do not watch a single object when the object is at first stationary, then moves and stops. They do not follow the moving object from place to place but rather apply a cognitive rule that can be stated: "Object disappears at *A*; object reappears at *B*." In the experimental test the infant sat watching a toy train with flashing lights at rest in the middle of the track (*a*). After 10 seconds the train moved to the left and stopped (*b*) and remained there for 10 seconds before returning to the center again. The cycle was repeated 10 times. On the next cycle (*c*, *d*) the train moved slowly to the right and stopped. If the infant had been following the moving object, he would have looked to the right, but if he had been following the hypothesized cognitive rule, he would have looked to the left in the place where the train had stopped before. Every 12-week-old infant tested made the error predicted by the hypothesis.

We conducted the experiment with groups of infants between six and 22 weeks old. The older infants tracked the moving object in Situation 1 quite happily; when the object stopped, they stopped tracking it. In Situation 2, where a different object emerged, they also followed the object in motion, although some glancing back and forth between the sides of the screen was noticeable. When the object stopped, at least 25 percent of the time they looked to the other side of the screen as if they were looking for the object that had disappeared. Their responses in Situation 3 and Situation 4 were similar, with the difference that when the object stopped, on every trial the infants looked to the other half of the track in apparent anticipation of the appearance of the other object.

Infants less than 16 weeks old showed a complete contrast in behavior. In Situation 1 they followed the moving object with no sign of being disturbed. When the object stopped, they continued to follow its path of movement. In Situation 2, when a different object emerged, they also continued to track it with no sign of being disturbed. When the object stopped, they continued to track it. In Situation 3, however, where the object came out from behind the screen sooner than it should have, they were upset and refused to look any more. They also refused to look in Situation 4. In both cases when the object stopped, the infants did not continue to follow its path as they had in the first two situations. This was largely due to their refusal to track at all.

These results show that younger infants are not affected by feature differences. For them movement is predominant. They respond to a change in motion but not to a change in size, shape or color. They ignore features to such an extent that I would suggest they respond not to moving objects but to movements. Similarly, I would suggest that they respond not to stationary objects but to places. In contrast, older infants have learned to define an object as something that can go from place to place along pathways of movement. They identify an object by its features rather than by its place or movement. For them different features imply different objects that can move independently, so that the stopping of one does not imply the stopping of the other.

This attainment is obviously one of tremendous significance. It transforms the perceptual world of the infant at one stroke into something very close to the perceptual world of the adult. According to these studies it seems that infants less than 16 weeks old live in a world articulated in terms of solids that are stably arranged in space according to their location, with a constancy of existence when they occlude one another. It is, however, a grossly overpopulated

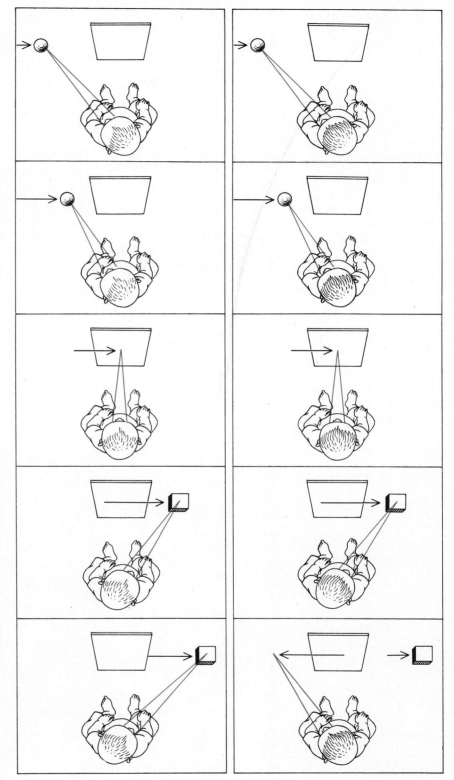

MOVEMENT AND FEATURES mean different things in the perceptual worlds of young and older infants. Infants less than 16 weeks old tracked a moving object (*left*) until it went behind a screen and anticipated its reappearance; when a different object emerged, they continued to track its motion with no sign of surprise. Older infants also tracked the object in motion when a different object emerged from behind the screen (*right*), but when the object stopped, the older infants often glanced to the other side of the screen as if they were looking for the first object. This indicates that the younger infants do not respond to moving objects but to movements, and not to stationary objects but to places. Older infants have learned to recognize an object by its features rather than by its place or movement.

world. An object becomes a different object as soon as it moves to a new location. In this world every object is unique. The infant must cope with a large number of objects when only one is really there.

In the last experiment I shall describe infants sat in front of an arrangement of mirrors that produced two or three images of a person. In some instances the infant was presented with two or three images of his mother; in others he would see his mother and one or two strangers who were seated so that they were in a position identical with the earlier additional images of his mother.

In the multiple-mother presentation infants less than 20 weeks old happily responded with smiles, coos and arm-waving to each mother in turn. In the mother-stranger presentation the infants were also quite happy and interacted with their mother, and they normally ignored the strangers. This demonstrates that young infants can recognize features in recognizing their mother, but they recognize the mother as one of many identical mothers. They do not recognize the identity of the multi-

ple mothers in the special sense in which I have used the word "identity," that is, they do not identify the multiple images of the mother as belonging to one and the same person.

Infants more than 20 weeks old also ignored the strangers and interacted with their mothers. In the multiple-mother situation, however, the older infants became quite upset at the sight of more than one mother. This shows, I would argue, that the younger infants do identify objects with places and hence think they have a multiplicity of mothers. Because the older infants identify objects by features, they know that they have only one mother, and this is why they are upset by the sight of multiple mothers.

The discovery of the object concept must simplify the world of the infant more than almost any subsequent intellectual advance. Two pressing questions arise from this research. We do not know why the object concept must be discovered rather than being built into the neural system (as so many other kinds of perceptual knowledge are), nor

do we know how the discovery is made. There are indications that built-in analyzers are limited to the initial input areas of the brain and their cross-connections. It is known that place and movement are separately coded in the visual system. Moreover, errors of the kind made by young infants persist in adults in some form. The late Baron Albert Michotte of the University of Louvain found that adults who are shown an impossible sequence such as the one described in Situation 3, where an object reappears from behind the screen sooner than it should, will say something like, "It looks as if it is the same object, but I know...." This kind of response indicates that the infant's error persists in the adult's perceptual system and is overcome by a cognitive rule. We do know that particular environments can speed or slow the acquisition of such conceptual behavior. In line with this fact there is evidence that nonhuman primates never overcome perceptual errors and remain much like the young infants we studied. The object concept may thus be outside the limits of intrinsic neural specification.

MULTIPLE MOTHERS were presented to infants by an arrangement of mirrors. In other instances the infant would see his mother and two unfamiliar women seated in the same position as the mirror images of the mother. Infants less than 20 weeks old waved their arms, smiled and called to each of the mother images in turn. Older infants, however, became quite disturbed by the sight of more than one mother. All the infants ignored the strangers and interacted only with the mother. It seems that the younger infants think they have a multiplicity of mothers because they identify objects with places. Older infants identify objects by features and know they have only one mother. Learning to identify objects by features is one of the major intellectual advances made by infants.

The "Visual Cliff"

by Eleanor Gibson and Richard D. Walk
April 1960

*This simple apparatus is used to investigate depth
perception in different animals. All species thus far
tested seem able to perceive and avoid a sharp
drop as soon as they can move about*

Human infants at the creeping and toddling stage are notoriously prone to falls from more or less high places. They must be kept from going over the brink by side panels on their cribs, gates on stairways and the vigilance of adults. As their muscular coordination matures they begin to avoid such accidents on their own. Common sense might suggest that the child learns to recognize falling-off places by experience—that is, by falling and hurting himself. But is experience really the teacher? Or is the ability to perceive and avoid a brink part of the child's original endowment?

Answers to these questions will throw light on the genesis of space perception in general. Height perception is a special case of distance perception: information in the light reaching the eye provides stimuli that can be utilized for the discrimination both of depth and of receding distance on the level. At what stage of development can an animal respond effectively to these stimuli? Does the onset of such response vary with animals of different species and habitats?

At Cornell University we have been investigating these problems by means of a simple experimental setup that we call a visual cliff. The cliff is a simulated one and hence makes it possible not only to control the optical and other stimuli (auditory and tactual, for instance) but also to protect the experimental subjects. It consists of a board laid across a large sheet of heavy glass which is supported a foot or more above the floor. On one side of the board a sheet of patterned material is placed flush against the undersurface of the glass, giving the glass the appearance as well as the substance of solidity. On the other side a sheet of the same material is laid upon the floor; this side of the board thus becomes the visual cliff.

We tested 36 infants ranging in age from six months to 14 months on the visual cliff. Each child was placed upon the center board, and his mother called him to her from the cliff side and the shallow side successively. All of the 27 infants who moved off the board crawled out on the shallow side at least once; only three of them crept off the brink onto the glass suspended above the pattern on the floor. Many of the infants crawled away from the mother when she called to them from the cliff side; others cried when she stood there, because they could not come to her without crossing an apparent chasm. The experiment thus demonstrated that most human infants can discriminate depth as soon as they can crawl.

The behavior of the children in this situation gave clear evidence of their dependence on vision. Often they would peer down through the glass on the deep side and then back away. Others would pat the glass with their hands, yet despite this tactual assurance of solidity would refuse to cross. It was equally clear that their perception of depth had matured more rapidly than had their locomotor abilities. Many supported themselves on the glass over the deep side as they maneuvered awkwardly on the board; some even backed out onto the glass as they started toward the mother on the shallow side. Were it not for the glass some of the children would have fallen off the board. Evidently infants should not be left close to a brink, no matter how well they may discriminate depth.

This experiment does not prove that the human infant's perception and avoidance of the cliff are innate. Such an interpretation is supported, however, by the experiments with nonhuman infants. On the visual cliff we have observed the behavior of chicks, turtles, rats, lambs, kids, pigs, kittens and dogs. These animals showed various reactions, each of which proved to be characteristic of their species. In each case the reaction is plainly related to the role of vision in the survival of the species, and the varied patterns of behavior suggest something about the role of vision in evolution.

In the chick, for example, depth perception manifests itself with special rapidity. At an age of less than 24 hours the chick can be tested on the visual cliff. It never makes a "mistake" and always hops off the board on the shallow side. Without doubt this finding is related to the fact that the chick, unlike many other young birds, must scratch for itself a few hours after it is hatched.

Kids and lambs, like chicks, can be tested on the visual cliff as soon as they can stand. The response of these animals is equally predictable. No goat or lamb ever stepped onto the glass of the deep side, even at one day of age. When one of these animals was placed upon the glass on the deep side, it displayed characteristic stereotyped behavior. It would refuse to put its feet down and would back up into a posture of defense, its front legs rigid and its hind legs limp. In this state of immobility it could be pushed forward across the glass until its head and field of vision crossed the edge of the surrounding solid surface, whereupon it would relax and spring forward upon the surface.

At the Cornell Behavior Farm a group of experimenters has carried these experiments with kids and goats a step further. They fixed the patterned material to a sheet of plywood and were thus able to adjust the "depth" of the deep side. With the pattern held immediately be-

52

CHILD'S DEPTH PERCEPTION is tested on the visual cliff. The apparatus consists of a board laid across a sheet of heavy glass, with a patterned material directly beneath the glass on one side and several feet below it on the other. Placed on the center board (*top left*), the child crawls to its mother across the "shallow" side (*top right*). Called from the "deep" side, he pats the glass (*bottom left*), but despite this tactual evidence that the "cliff" is in fact a solid surface he refuses to cross over to the mother (*bottom right*).

neath the glass, the animal would move about the glass freely. With the optical floor dropped more than a foot below the glass, the animal would immediately freeze into its defensive posture. Despite repeated experience of the tactual solidity of the glass, the animals never learned to function without optical support. Their sense of security or danger continued to depend upon the visual cues that give them their perception of depth.

The rat, in contrast, does not depend predominantly upon visual cues. Its nocturnal habits lead it to seek food largely by smell, when moving about in the dark, it responds to tactual cues from the stiff whiskers (vibrissae) on its snout. Hooded rats tested on the visual cliff show little preference for the shallow side so long as they can feel the glass with their vibrissae. Placed upon the

KITTEN'S DEPTH PERCEPTION also manifests itself at an early age. Though the animal displays no alarm on the shallow side (*top*), it "freezes" when placed on the glass over the deep side (*bottom*); in some cases it will crawl aimlessly backward in a circle.

GOATS SHOW DEPTH PERCEPTION at an age of only one day. A kid walks freely on the shallow side (*top*); on the deep side (*middle*) it leaps the "chasm" to safety (*bottom*).

glass over the deep side, they move about normally. But when we raise the center board several inches, so that the glass is out of reach of their whiskers, they evince good visual depth-discrimination: 95 to 100 per cent of them descend on the shallow side.

Cats, like rats, are nocturnal animals, sensitive to tactual cues from their vibrissae. But the cat, as a predator, must rely more strongly on its sight. Kittens proved to have excellent depth-discrimination. At four weeks—about the earliest age that a kitten can move about with any facility—they invariably choose the shallow side of the cliff. On the glass over the deep side, they either freeze or circle aimlessly backward until they reach the center board [*see illustrations on preceding page*].

The animals that showed the poorest performance in our series were the turtles. The late Robert M. Yerkes of Harvard University found in 1904 that aquatic turtles have somewhat poorer depth-discrimination than land turtles. On the visual cliff one might expect an aquatic turtle to respond to the reflections from the glass as it might to water and so prefer the deep side. They showed no such preference: 76 per cent of the aquatic turtles crawled off the board on the shallow side. The relatively large minority that choose the deep side suggests either that this turtle has poorer depth-discrimination than other animals, or that its natural habitat gives it less occasion to "fear" a fall.

All of these observations square with what is known about the life history and ecological niche of each of the animals tested. The survival of a species requires that its members develop discrimination of depth by the time they take up independent locomotion, whether at one day (the chick and the goat), three to four weeks (the rat and the cat) or six to 10 months (the human infant). That such a vital capacity does not depend on possibly fatal accidents of learning in the lives of individuals is consistent with evolutionary theory.

To make sure that no hidden bias was concealed in the design of the visual cliff we conducted a number of control experiments. In one of them we eliminated reflections from the glass by lighting the patterned surfaces from below the glass (to accomplish this we dropped the pattern below the glass on both sides, but more on one side than on the other). The animals—hooded rats—still consistently chose the shallow side. As a test of the role of the patterned surface we

55

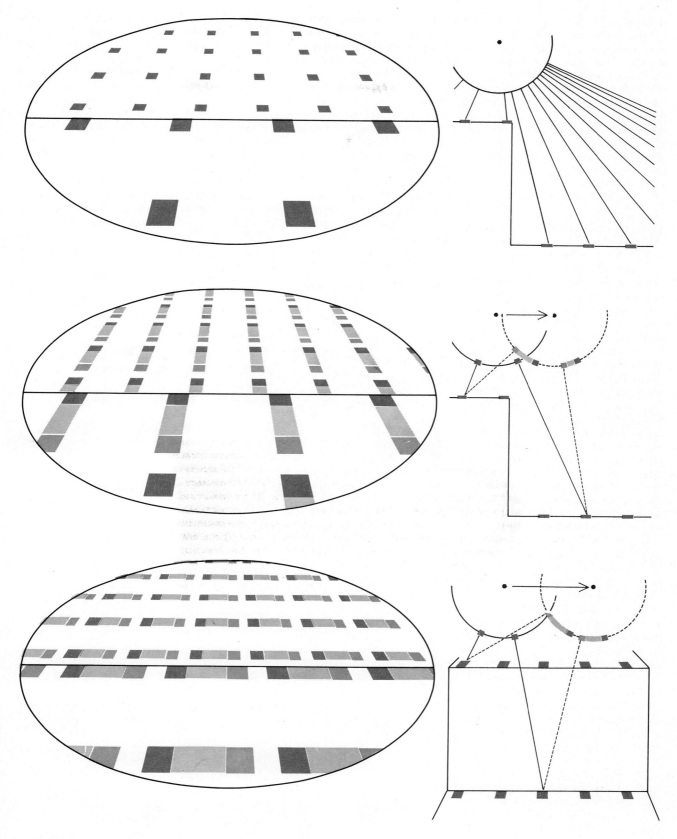

TWO TYPES OF VISUAL DEPTH-CUE are diagrammed schematically on this page. Ellipses approximate the visual field of an animal standing near the edge of the cliff and looking toward it; diagrams at right give the geometrical explanation of differences in the fields. The spacing of the pattern elements (*solid color*) decreases sharply beyond the edge of the cliff (*top*). The optical motion (*shaded color*) of the elements as the animal moves forward (*center*) or sideways (*bottom*) shows a similar drop-off.

replaced it on either side of the centerboard with a homogeneous gray surface. Confronted with this choice, the rats showed no preference for either the shallow or the deep side. We also eliminated the optical difference between the two sides of the board by placing the patterned surface directly against the undersurface of the glass on each side. The rats then descended without preference to either side. When we lowered the pattern 10 inches below the glass on each side, they stayed on the board.

We set out next to determine which of two visual cues plays the decisive role in depth perception. To an eye above the center board the optical pattern on the two sides differs in at least two important respects. On the deep side distance decreases the size and spacing of the pattern elements projected on the retina. "Motion parallax," on the other hand, causes the pattern elements on the shallow side to move more rapidly across the field of vision when the animal moves its position on the board or moves its head, just as nearby objects seen from a moving car appear to pass by more quickly than distant ones [see illustration on preceding page]. To eliminate the potential distance cue provided by pattern density we increased the size and spacing of the pattern elements on the deep side in proportion to its distance from the eye [see top illustration at right]. With only the cue of motion parallax to guide them, adult rats still preferred the shallow side, though not so strongly as in the standard experiment. Infant rats chose the shallow side nearly 100 per cent of the time under both conditions, as did day-old chicks. Evidently both species can discriminate depth by differential motion alone, with no aid from texture density and probably little help from other cues. The perception of distance by binocular parallax, which doubtless plays an important part in human behavior, would not seem to have a significant role, for example, in the depth perception of chicks and rats.

To eliminate the cue of motion parallax we placed the patterned material directly against the glass on either side of the board but used smaller and more densely spaced pattern-elements on the cliff side. Both young and adult hooded rats preferred the side with the larger pattern, which evidently "signified" a nearer surface. Day-old chicks, however, showed no preference for the larger pattern. It may be that learning plays some part in the preference exhibited by the

rats, since the young rats were tested at a somewhat older age than the chicks. This supposition is supported by the results of our experiments with animals reared in the dark.

The effects of early experience and of such deprivations as dark-rearing represent important clues to the relative roles of maturation and learning in animal behavior. The first experiments along this line were performed by K. S. Lashley and James T. Russell at the University of Chicago in 1934. They tested light-reared and dark-reared rats on a "jumping stand" from which they induced animals to leap toward a platform placed at varying distances. Upon finding that both groups of animals jumped with a force closely correlated with distance, they concluded that depth perception in rats is innate. Other investi-

gators have pointed out, however, that the dark-reared rats required a certain amount of "pretraining" in the light before they could be made to jump. Since the visual-cliff technique requires no pretraining, we employed it to test groups of light-reared and dark-reared hooded rats. At the age of 90 days both groups showed the same preference for the shallow side of the apparatus, confirming Lashley's and Russell's conclusion.

Recalling our findings in the young rat, we then took up the question of whether the dark-reared rats relied upon motion parallax or upon contrast in texture density to discriminate depth. When the animals were confronted with the visual cliff, cued only by motion parallax, they preferred the shallow side, as had the light-reared animals. When the

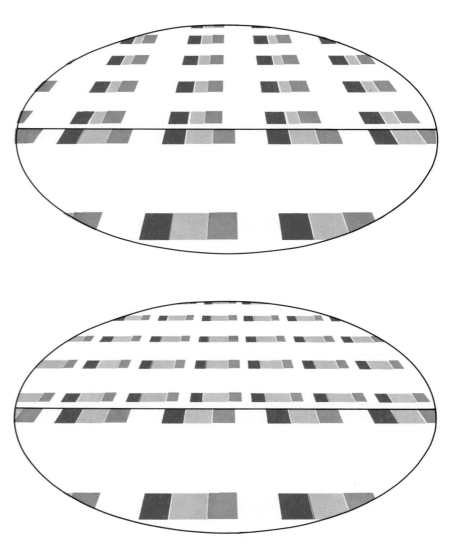

SEPARATION OF VISUAL CUES is shown in these diagrams. Pattern density is held constant (*top*) by using a larger pattern on the low side of the cliff; the drop in optical motion (motion parallax) remains. Motion parallax is equalized (*bottom*) by placing patterns at same level; the smaller pattern on one side preserves difference in spacing.

IMPORTANCE OF PATTERN in depth perception is shown in these photographs. Of two patterns set at the same depth, normal rats almost invariably preferred the larger (*top row and bottom left*), presumably because it "signified" a nearer and therefore safer surface. Confronted with two patternless surfaces set at different depths, the animals displayed no preference (*bottom right*).

choice was cued by pattern density, however, they departed from the pattern of the normal animals and showed no significant preference [*see bottom illustration at left*]. The behavior of dark-reared rats thus resembles that of the day-old chicks, which also lack visual experience. It seems likely, therefore, that of the two cues only motion parallax is an innate cue for depth discrimination. Responses to differential pattern-density may be learned later.

One cannot automatically extrapolate these results to other species. But experiments with dark-reared kittens indicate that in these animals, too, depth perception matures independently of trial and error learning. In the kitten, however, light is necessary for normal visual maturation. Kittens reared in the dark to the age of 27 days at first crawled or fell off the center board equally often on the deep and shallow sides. Placed upon the glass over the deep side, they did not back in a circle like normal kittens but showed the same behavior that they had exhibited on the shallow side. Other investigators have observed equivalent behavior in dark-reared kittens; they bump into obstacles, lack normal eye movement and appear to "stare" straight ahead. These difficulties pass after a few days in the light. We accordingly tested the kittens every day. By the end of a week they were performing in every respect like normal kittens. They showed the same unanimous preference for the shallow side. Placed upon the glass over the deep side, they balked and circled backward to a visually secure surface. Repeated descents to the deep side, and placement upon the glass during their "blind" period, had not taught them that the deep side was "safe." Instead they avoided it more and more consistently. The initial blindness of dark-reared kittens makes them ideal subjects for studying the maturation of depth perception. With further study it should be possible to determine which cues they respond to first and what kinds of visual experience accelerate or retard the process of maturation.

From our first few years of work with the visual cliff we are ready to venture the rather broad conclusion that a seeing animal will be able to discriminate depth when its locomotion is adequate, even when locomotion begins at birth. But many experiments remain to be done, especially on the role of different cues and on the effects of different kinds of early visual experience.

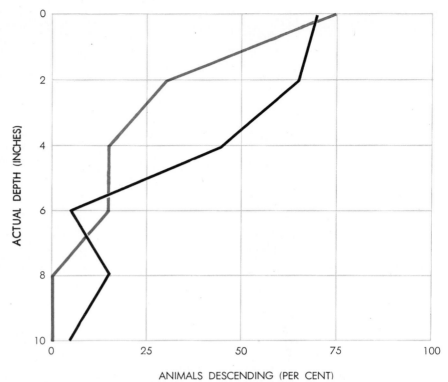

CONTROL EXPERIMENT measured the effect on rats of reflections on the glass of the apparatus. The percentage of animals leaving the center board decreased with increasing depth in much the same way, whether glass was present (*black curve*) or not (*colored curve*).

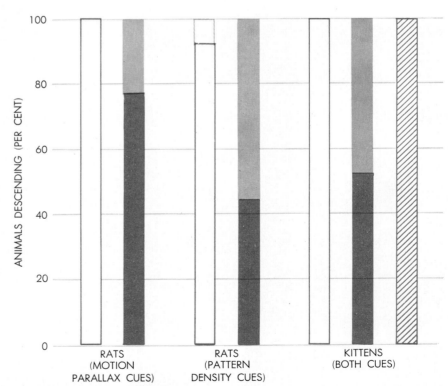

DARK-REARING EXPERIMENTS reveal the order in which different depth-cues are utilized as animals mature. Animals reared in the light (*open bars*) all strongly preferred the shallow side (*color*) to the deep side (*gray*). Dark-reared rats (*solid bars*), utilizing motion parallax alone, still preferred the shallow side; pattern density alone elicited no preference. Dark-reared kittens also showed no preference, because of temporary blindness. After seven days in the light all of them chose the shallow side (*hatched bar*).

PERCEPTION AND AWARENESS

II   PERCEPTION AND AWARENESS

INTRODUCTION

Awareness of the environment depends upon the ability of our sense organs to change various forms of physical energy into nerve impulses. Complex structures in the ear transduce the mechanical energy of sound waves into the electrical energy of nerve impulses. Certain specialized cells on the skin's surface change the mechanical energy of pressure into nerve impulses that convey the sensation of touch. Receptor cells in the eye transform the electromagnetic energy of light into nerve impulses. But the activation and transmission of nerve impulses by the sensory systems is only the first step in awareness. Our brain integrates these messages with messages from other parts of the body, and then interprets the total information in the light of experience. Perception thus requires interaction between sensory mechanisms and those parts of the brain that are concerned with storage and retrieval of past experiences.

The mechanisms by which different perceptual systems receive, transduce, and interpret a stimulus input are complex and varied. We could not possibly survey the variety of research in all the senses in one section on perception. Therefore, this section is concerned primarily with visual perception—the perceptual system that normally dominates our awareness of the world, and the one that has been most thoroughly investigated.

The fine discriminations of the visual system are possible only because the eyes are constantly in motion. Even though you think you are staring fixedly at an object, your eyes make many tiny oscillating movements every second. This involuntary tremor, which insures that the visual cells receive changing stimulation, is necessary for normal vision. It is not possible to prevent these involuntary movements without damaging the eye, but Roy Pritchard in his article "Stabilized Images on the Retina" describes a clever technique that stabilizes the retinal image, so that light from a viewed object always falls on the same retinal cells. Under this condition the visual image fades and disappears within a matter of seconds. Although the physiological basis of this phenomenon is not completely understood, it may have something to do with sensory adaptation—the fact that in vision, as in other senses, a receptor that receives continual stimulation eventually decreases its response. But adaptation cannot be the complete answer. The organized or meaningful parts of an image stabilized on the retina remain visible longer than the unorganized parts, suggesting the importance of learning in visual perception.

As we noted earlier, perception involves more than the transmission of nerve impulses by the sensory systems. The brain must interpret the information it receives. The image projected on the retina is not a faithful representation of all that we perceive. We normally perceive a coin as unvarying in size—whether it is in our hand or lying on a table across the room—even though the retinal image is actually quite different in the two instances. As Ulric Neisser points out in "The Processes of Vision," our visual world is not a photographic copy of the retinal image. What we perceive is somehow constructed by the brain from a composite of information—information that is extracted from rapidly changing retinal patterns as our eyes move about, as well as information from past visual inputs that is retrieved from memory. Neisser discusses the properties of stimuli that determine what we perceive and then considers visual imagery, the memory of visual events not immediately present.

An unusual type of visual imagery is discussed by Ralph Haber in his article "Eidetic Images." Eidetic imagery is another name for "photographic memory"—the ability to visualize in great detail a scene or object viewed in the past. This ability occurs in some form in about 10 percent of school children, but it is fairly rare after puberty. Haber describes some interesting techniques for investigating eidetic imagery, and discusses the relation of this visual memory to other types of memory.

Even when our sense receptors function properly and we receive adequate sensory feedback, our perceptions may not accurately depict reality—we may experience an illusion. In "Visual Illusions" Richard Gregory describes some of the most common optical illusions and offers one explanation of why such illusions occur. Perception may be a search for the best interpretation of sensory information, based on our knowledge of object characteristics. In other words, a perceived object may be a *hypothesis* suggested by the sensory data. The notion of hypothesis-testing suggests that the perceptual system is *active* rather than passive; the perceptual system does not merely receive inputs, but searches for the percept that is most consistent with the sensory data. In most situations there is only one reasonable interpretation of the sensory data, and the search for the correct percept proceeds so quickly and automatically that we are unaware of it. Only under unusual conditions, as when viewing an illusion or ambiguous figure, does the hypothesis-testing nature of perception become apparent.

Employing a similar approach, Fred Attneave in "Multistability in Perception" examines various kinds of pictures and geometric forms that spontaneously shift in their principal aspect when looked at steadily. Some of the most striking of these are pictures that can be seen as either of two familiar objects, for example a figure that may look like a duck one moment and a rabbit the next. Attneave's analysis of this phenomenon elaborates on the hypothesis-testing view of perception and suggests that the perceptual machinery is "motivated" to represent the outside world as economically as possible, within the constraints of the input received and the limitations of its encoding capabilities.

In the article by Irvin Rock ("The Perception of Distorted Figures") additional evidence is brought to bear on the active, cognitive, nature of perception. He argues persuasively that perception of form cannot be reduced to the detection of a set of component features. Although, as noted in the earlier article by Hubel, the detection of features does play an important role in perception, features themselves do not constitute form. Rock's findings suggest that the perception of form is based to a much greater extent on cognitive processes than most current theories maintain. This direction of theorizing is pursued in another article by Rock and Charles Harris ("Vision and Touch"), in which the authors examine the interrelationship of vision and touch in the perceptual ·process. A series of experiments demonstrates that when vision and touch provide contradictory information, one's perception of an object is dominated by the visual information.

The last article in this section ("Sources of Ambiguity in the Prints of Maurits C. Escher") is quite different from the others. It is not concerned with psychological research but rather the work of the Dutch graphic artist Escher, considered one of the great artists of this century. The author, Marianne Teuber, discusses Escher's use of visual ambiguity in his prints—the ambiguity of figure and ground, of two and three dimensions on a flat surface, and of the reversible cube. Escher's novel use of ambiguity illustrates several aspects of perception. This is not surprising since, as Teuber shows, Escher was greatly influenced by psychological research on perception. There is little doubt that he was familiar with the early experiments of the Gestalt psychologists, in particular with Kurt Koffka's 1935 book *Principles of Gestalt Psychology*.

The significance of stimulus patterns in producing a perceptual experience was recognized by proponents of *Gestalt psychology*, a school of psychology that arose in Austria and Germany near the end of the nineteenth century. "Gestalt" is a German word that has no exact English translation, though "form," "configuration," or "pattern" come close. The word itself helps to emphasize the idea that properties of the whole affect the way in which parts are perceived. Perception "draws together" (*gestalten*) the sensory data into a *holistic* pattern; for this reason it is sometimes said that "the whole is different from the sum of its parts"—a favorite phrase of Gestalt psychologists. Escher's work not only illustrates many of the principles of Gestalt psychology, but his use of psychological research and writings helps us appreciate his unusual contribution to modern art.

Stabilized Images on the Retina

by Roy M. Pritchard
June 1961

*When the involuntary movements of an image across
the retina are prevented, the image fades and
reappears in a manner that provides new information
on two major theories of perception*

In normal vision the eye is constantly in motion. Small involuntary movements persist even when the eye is "fixed" on a stationary object. As a result the image of the object on the retina of the eye is kept in constant motion. One movement of the eyeball makes the image drift slowly away from the center of the fovea, the region of maximum visual acuity in which the cone receptor cells are most densely concentrated. The drifting motion terminates in a flick that brings the image back toward the center of the fovea. Superimposed on the drift motion is a tremor with frequencies up to 150 cycles per second and an amplitude of about half the diameter of a single cone receptor.

These three involuntary movements of the eyeball, all much smaller than the voluntary movements involved in looking at the visual world or in reading, have been known to physiologists for many years. During the past decade Lorrin A. Riggs of Brown University and R. W. Ditchburn of the University of Reading in England succeeded in measuring them with great accuracy. Though the movements cannot be stopped without incapacitating the subject or endangering the eye, Ditchburn and Riggs found ways to circumvent them and so make an image stand still on the retina. They were thereby able to show that the motion of the image plays a significant role in the sensory function of the eye. When an image is stabilized on the retina by one means or another, it soon fades and disappears. Just how this happens is not yet completely understood.

It was also observed, however, that the stabilized image regenerates after a time and again becomes visible to the subject in whole or in part. The image—or fragments of it—alternately fades and regenerates over prolonged periods of observation. This finding has attracted the attention of psychologists interested in the perceptual aspects of vision, those aspects which involve the functioning of the brain as well as the cells of the retina. At McGill University, D. O. Hebb, Woodburn Heron and I have been investigating the stabilized visual image as a source of data for the formulation of a comprehensive theory of visual perception. We have found that the fragmentation, or the alternate partial fading and partial regeneration, of the image is related to the character and content of the image itself.

Our evidence supports to some extent the "cell assembly" idea that experience is needed to develop the innate potential of perception: a pattern is perceived through the combination in the brain of separate neural impressions that have been established there and correspond to various learned elements. But the evidence also sustains the Gestalt, or holistic, theory, which holds that perception is innately determined: a pattern is perceived directly as a whole and without synthesis of parts, a product of unlearned capacity to perceive "form," "wholeness" and "organization." It is becoming apparent that the complete explanation of perception must be sought in a resolution of these opposing views.

We stabilize the image by attaching the target to be viewed to the eyeball itself. The device we use for this purpose consists of a tight-fitting contact lens on which is mounted a tiny, self-contained optical projector [*see illustration on following page*]. With the subject lying on a couch, the device is set in place on the cornea and focused to project an image on the retina. The experimenter changes the tar-get film from time to time, and he keeps a continuous record of the subject's report of what he sees.

What the subject sees, before fading sets in, is an image located at apparent infinity and subtending a visual angle of two degrees in a patch of light that subtends an angle of five degrees in the surrounding darkness. Provided that the contact lens does not slip on the cornea, the image remains fixed on the retina and does not move with movement of the eyeball.

After a few seconds of viewing, the image disappears progressively and bit by bit, leaving a structureless gray field of light. Later this gray field may darken, and with complete loss of sensation of light the field becomes intensely black. When the image disappears or reappears the uninitiated subject at first rotates his eyes in an effort to bring the image or a center of interest in the image back to the center of the fovea. These movements are, of course, futile because they cannot change the geometrical relationship between the target, the lens of the eye and the retina. Soon the subject learns to view the image passively and discovers that he can still transfer his attention from point to point over the limited visual field.

In general we have found that the image of a simple figure, such as a single line, vanishes rapidly and then reappears as a complete image. A more complex target, such as the profile of a face or a pattern of curlicues, may similarly disappear and reappear as a whole; on the other hand, it may vanish in fragments, with one or more of its parts fading independently. We have found in addition that the length of time an image persists is also a function of its complexity. A single line may be visible for only 10 per cent of the aggregate view-

64

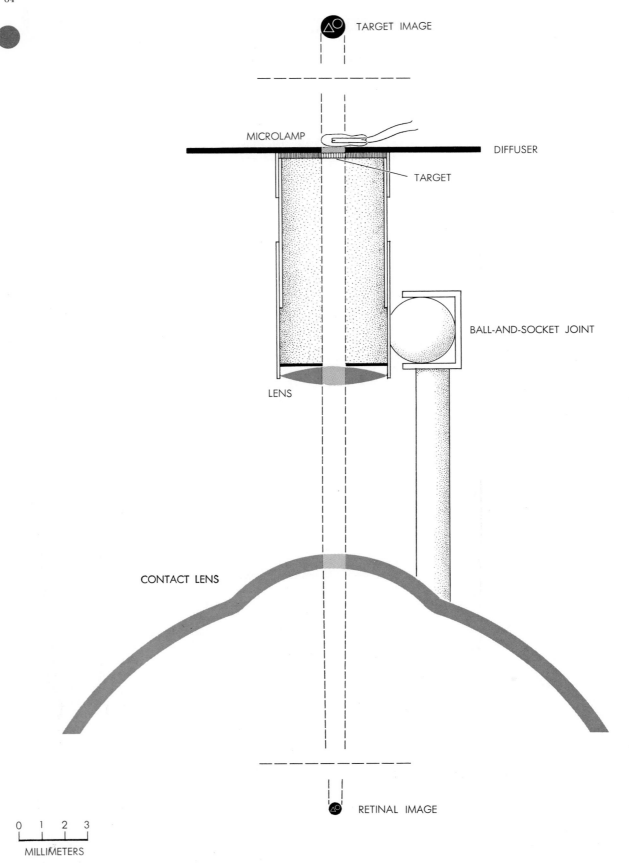

TARGET IMAGE

MICROLAMP

DIFFUSER

TARGET

BALL-AND-SOCKET JOINT

LENS

CONTACT LENS

RETINAL IMAGE

0 1 2 3
MILLIMETERS

STABILIZED-IMAGE DEVICE is a tiny projector mounted on a contact lens worn by the subject. The contact lens moves with every movement of the eyeball; so, therefore, does the projector, and as a result the target image (*at top of illustration*) is kept **fixed at one point on the retina (*as suggested at bottom of illustration*). The convex lens focuses parallel rays of light on the retina, so the target is viewed by the subject as if it were at an infinite distance. The entire optical system weighs only .25 gram.**

ing time, whereas a more complex figure may remain visible in whole or in part for as much as 80 per cent of the time.

The contrasting manner in which complex images fade and regenerate lends support to the role of learning in perception. For example, the figure of the human profile invariably fades and regenerates in meaningful units. The front of the face, the top of the head, the eye and the ear come and go as recognizable entities, separately and in various combinations. In contrast, on first presentation a meaningless pattern of curlicues is described as extremely "active"; the individual elements fade and regenerate rapidly, and the subject sees almost every configuration that can be derived from the original figure. After prolonged viewing, however, certain combinations of curlicues become dominant and these then disappear and reappear as units. The newly formed groupings persist for longer periods than other combinations, and the figure can no longer be considered unorganized and meaningless.

In the cell-assembly approach to a theory of perception these observations are explained in terms of "perceptual elements," as opposed to purely sensory elements. The "organized," "meaningful" or "recognizable" parts of the image correspond to perceptual elements previously learned or established by experience. The parts of the human profile would thus function as perceptual elements at the outset in the behavior of the stabilized image. Given time for learning, parts of the originally meaningless curlicue pattern become recognizable in turn and operate as perceptual elements. These elements may be excited, it is argued, by the minimum retinal stimulation provided by the stabilized image. To evoke and maintain the image of the entire figure would require the additional information normally supplied by the movement of the image across the retinal receptors.

This interpretation gains additional support from what subjects report about the stabilized images of monograms that combine such symbols as the letters *H* and *B*. One or the other letter, or a fragment such as *P*, constitutes the unit that is perceived from one period to the next, with periods of complete fadeout intervening. When entire words are presented, the partial fragmentation of letters can cause different words to be perceived [*see bottom illustration on following page*]. In a figure that presents a meaningful symbol such as *B* obscured by hatching lines, the subject sees either

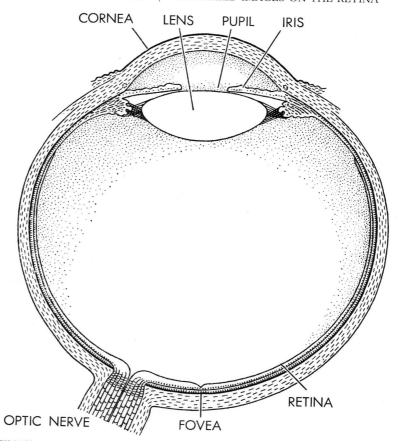

HUMAN EYE, seen here in horizontal cross section, works much like a camera. Light entering through the pupil is focused by the lens upon the retina's light-sensitive receptor cells, from which impulses travel via the optic nerve to the brain. The fovea, the area of most acute vision, is 1.5 millimeters in diameter and subtends a visual angle of five degrees.

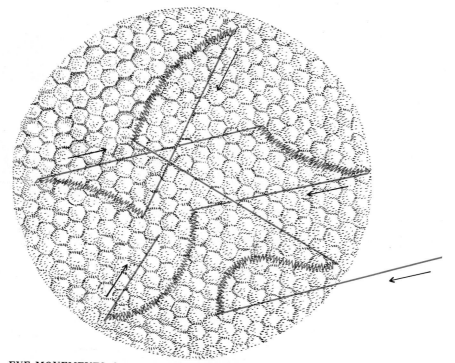

EYE MOVEMENTS that are halted in stabilized vision normally carry an image across the receptors of the retina as shown here. The three movements are a drift (*curved lines*) away from the center of vision, a faster flick (*straight lines*) back toward the center and a high-frequency tremor superimposed on the drift. The magnitude of all these movements is very small; the diameter of the patch of the fovea shown above is only .05 millimeter.

the intact *B* or the hatching lines independently. He may also on occasion see the two elements together, but then the *B* appears to float in a plane in front of the one containing the hatching lines. There is nothing haphazard about the fading of such figures, and these effects cannot be attributed to random fluctuation of threshold in various parts of the retina. Even if such fluctuation is thought to occur in the retinal system, the organized or meaningful unit remains visible longer than the unorganized one, in keeping with the presumed importance of learning in visual perception.

But the Gestalt psychologist can argue that it is unnecessary to bring learning and experience into the explanation of these effects. The same effects show up in experiments with meaningless or only semimeaningful figures and can be explained in terms of the Gestalt concept of perception as a process that works by "the whole." If an irregular shape, like that of an amoeba, is obscured by hatching lines, for example, the subject may report the same unitary and separate fading of the amoeba shape and of the hatching lines that he reports in the case of a letter of the alphabet. The two parts of the complete figure may also appear separated in different planes. More commonly in this case, however, parts of both the amoeba shape and the obscuring lines disappear together, and the remaining elements amalgamate to form a new composite figure. The hybrid is a more compact, tidy figure, with fewer disrupting elements.

When the amoeba shape is presented alone, parts of the figure tend to disappear. One or more of the bulges in the figure fade from view, and a line or lines are hallucinated to seal off the gaps produced by their disappearance. The limb or limbs that fade are invariably the grosser or more distorted features of the figure, and their disappearance, together with the closures, produces a "better" or more rounded figure. Any other comparatively irregular or jagged figure similarly appears unstable on first

STABILIZED IMAGES typically fade as in the illustrations on this and the following two pages. The parts of a profile drawing that stay visible are invariably specific features or groups of features, such as the front of the face or the top of the head.

MEANINGLESS CURLICUES first come and go in random sequence. But after a while small groups of curlicues organized in recognizable patterns start to behave as units. This suggests that they have themselves become meaningful perceptual elements.

MONOGRAM formed of the letters *H* and *B* also seems to illustrate the importance of elements that are meaningful because of past experience. When the monogram breaks up it is the recognizable letters and numbers within it that come successively into view.

WORDS containing other words behave in much the same manner as the monogram. Here, for example, the subject sees new words made up of letters and parts of letters in the original. He is far less likely to report seeing meaningless groups of letters such as *EER*.

viewing. Its individual elements come and go until the holistic "editing" process reduces it to a more rounded configuration. A smooth, rounded figure, in contrast, appears more stable at the outset and tends to operate more as a whole in the alternate process of fading and regeneration.

As Gestalt theory would predict, contiguity and similarity strongly determine the functioning of the groups as entities isolated from the total figure. A target consisting of rows of small squares usually fades to leave one whole row—horizontal, diagonal or vertical—visible. Similarly a random collection of dots will fade to leave only those dots which lie approximately in a line, and it is the

disappearance of the remainder that reveals this linear association. At the same time it must be emphasized that the original figure as well as each configuration that can be derived from it may function as a single unit, disappearing and reappearing as a whole.

Our experiments with stabilized images have thus produced evidence to sustain both of the major theoretical approaches to visual perception, which have for so long been considered mutually exclusive. It may be, however, that the two concepts are really complementary. As in the historic clash of the wave and the particle concepts in physics, the apparent opposition may arise solely from

a difference in approach to the same problem. We have performed a number of experiments that conform equally well to both interpretations. This supports our expectation that a modern theory of perception will eventually result from a mating of the two systems.

In experiments with simple straight-line figures the cell-assembly approach is supported by the observation that the line is the apparent unit of perception just as the line is the unit of structure in the figure. It is always the whole line that fades or reappears, independently or in association with others, and the breaking, when fading occurs, is always at the intersection of lines. In fact, the overwhelmingly independent action of

OBSCURING LINES drawn over a figure act in various ways. In the case of the B, the lines often drop into a plane behind the meaningful letter. But lines over a less meaningful amoeba shape usually combine with the amoeba to form a more compact figure.

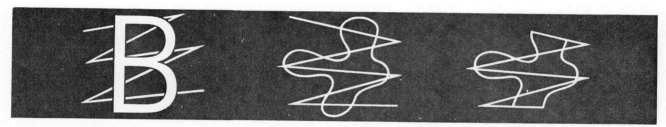

AMOEBA SHAPE standing alone usually fades by losing one or more bulges. What fades, as in this case, is always the most distorted feature, and it is replaced by a new closure "ghosted" by the subject and tending to form a more symmetrical and rounded figure.

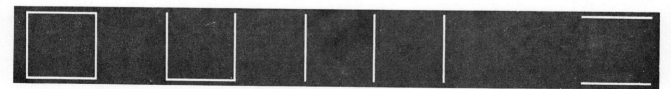

LINES act independently in stabilized vision, with breakage in the fading figure always at an intersection of lines. Adjacent or parallel lines may operate as units. This independent action of lines tends to support the cell-assembly theory of perception.

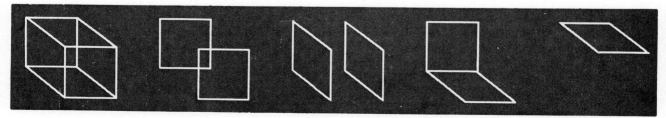

PLANES operate as units in three-dimensional figures. In this Necker cube (which gives an illusion of reversing in stabilized as well as in normal vision) a line may act alone. But usually lines defining a plane operate together, leaving parallel planes.

lines makes inevitable the inclusion of some cell-assembly concepts in any complete theory of perception.

In a figure composed of a circle and a triangle, either the circle or the triangle may fade to leave the other visible. One could take this independent action of meaningful figures as evidence for the role of learning in perception. On the other hand, the Gestalt psychologist can just as readily explain the unitary action of the circle or triangle as evidence of the behavior of wholes.

But the fading process may also dissect the figure in other ways—for example, it may leave only one side of the triangle and the segment of the circle closest or most nearly parallel to it in view. Gestalt theory explains this report by the so-called field effect. The minimal sensory stimulus provided by the stabilized image is said to excite a perceptual response that goes well beyond the region of actual stimulation. In straight-line figures, furthermore, there is a tendency for noncontiguous parallel lines to operate together, and lines of the Necker cube [see bottom illustration on preceding page] usually vanish to leave parallel planes visible in space, with one of the planes in advance of the other. These observations can also be advanced as evidence of a field effect.

Most figures are seen as three-dimensional when viewed as a stabilized image. Most line drawings appear at some stage as "wires" suspended in space. The small squares in a repetitive pattern are perceived as protrusions or depressions. And a simple hexagon has been reported to be the outline of a cube in three dimensions that "reverses" in the same manner as the Necker cube.

In the case of figures drawn in solid tones as distinguished from those drawn in outline, the behavior of the stabilized image seems more consistent with cell-assembly theory. The corner now replaces the line as the unit of independent action. A solid square will fade from its center, and the fading will obliterate first one and then another corner, leaving the remaining corners sharply outlined and isolated in space. Regeneration

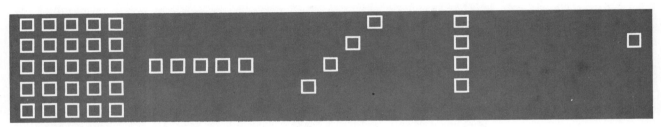

LINEAR ORGANIZATION is emphasized by the fading of this target composed of rows of squares. The figure usually fades to leave one whole row visible: horizontal, diagonal or vertical. In some cases a three-dimensional "waffle" effect is also noted.

CIRCLE AND TRIANGLE may fade as units, leaving one or the other in view. When there is partial fading, a side of the triangle may remain in view along with a parallel segment of the circle, suggesting the "field effect" postulated in Gestalt visual theory.

CORNERS are the basic units when solid-tone figures are used. The fading starts in the center and the sharply defined corners disappear one by one. This target, like the others in the series, was presented to subjects both in white-on-black and black-on-white.

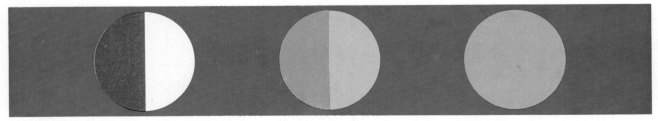

SENSE OF COLOR is lost with particular speed. A two-color field like this fades almost immediately when stabilized, to leave two values of gray; then the brightness difference disappears. The stabilized technique promises to be useful for studying color vision.

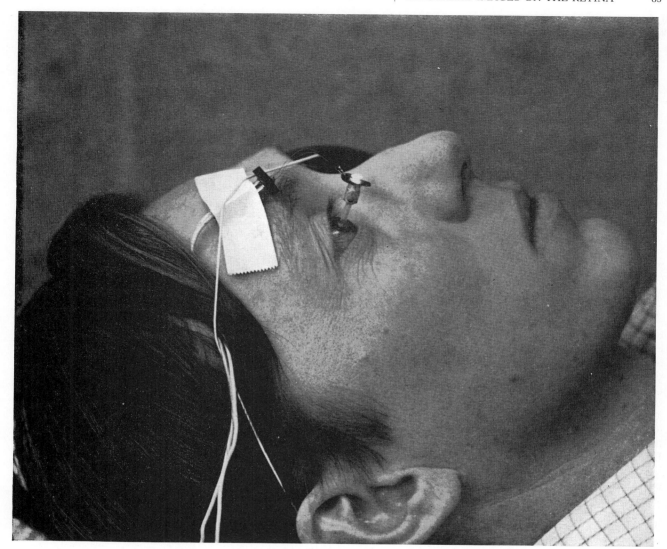

TAKING TURN AS SUBJECT in a stabilized-vision experiment, the author wears on his right eye a contact lens on which the projector is mounted. The other eye is occluded by a patch. Wires lead from the small projector lamp to a battery through a connecting jack taped to his forehead. The experimenter inserts a target film under the diffuser. At first the image is clear to the subject, but it soon fades and then regenerates. The subject makes a continuous report of what he sees, and the experimenter records his comments.

correspondingly begins with the reappearance of first one and then another corner, yielding a complete or partial figure with the corners again sharply outlined.

The basic concepts of Gestalt theory receive strong support in our experiments from the observed importance of field effects, from the dominance of "good" figures and from the action of whole figures and of groups of design elements as perceptual entities. But it is the independent action of the parts and not the whole of a figure that is paramount in stabilized vision. This observation agrees with cell-assembly theory and the perceptual elements it postulates. On the other hand, the perceptual elements themselves appear as organized entities and so conform to Gestalt concepts. Perhaps the Gestalt perception-by-the-whole theory can best be used in interpreting perception in a broad sense, while the cell-assembly idea of perception by parts may turn out to be most useful for analysis of perception in detail.

Meanwhile stabilized images have opened up a promising approach to another significant problem in the field of perception: color vision. Color disappears quickly in the stabilized image of a colored figure. In a field composed of the three primary colors, the red, green and blue hues disappear to leave a colorless field of three different brightnesses. These brightness differences also disappear with time, but it is the color that goes first. This supports the suggestion that the hue of a color is produced by radiation of a given wavelength on the retina and that the perception of hue is maintained by continuous changes in the luminosity of the radiation falling on a receptor cell or cells. Movement of the edges of a patch of color across the retina, produced by normal eye movements, would therefore be necessary for continuous perception of color. We are now making an investigation of the amplitude, frequency and form of movement necessary to sustain or regenerate a particular color.

9   The Processes of Vision

by Ulric Neisser
September 1968

Light enables us to see, but optical images on the retina are only the starting point of the complex activities of visual perception and visual memory

It was Johannes Kepler who first compared the eye to a "camera" (a darkened chamber) with an image in focus on its rear surface. "Vision is brought about by pictures of the thing seen being formed on the white concave surface of the retina," he wrote in 1604. A generation later René Descartes tried to clinch this argument by direct observation. In a hole in a window shutter he set the eye of an ox, just in the position it would have had if the ox had been peering out. Looking at the back of the eye (which he had scraped to make it transparent), he could see a small inverted image of the scene outside the window.

Since the 17th century the analogy between eye and camera has been elaborated in numerous textbooks. As an account of functional anatomy the analogy is not bad, but it carries some unfortunate implications for the study of vision. It suggests all too readily that the perceiver is in the position of Descartes and is in effect looking through the back of his own retina at the pictures that appear there. We use the same word—"image"—for both the optical pattern thrown on the retina by an object and the mental experience of seeing the object. It has been all too easy to treat this inner image as a copy of the outer one, to think of perceptual experiences as images formed by the nervous system acting as an optical instrument of extraordinarily ingenious design. Although this theory encounters insurmountable difficulties as soon as it is seriously considered, it has dominated philosophy and psychology for many years.

Not only perception but also memory has often been explained in terms of an image theory. Having looked at the retinal picture, the perceiver supposedly files it away somehow, as one might put a photograph in an album. Later, if he is lucky, he can take it out again in the form of a "memory image" and look at it a second time. The widespread notion that some people have a "photographic memory" reflects this analogy in a particularly literal way, but in a weaker form it is usually applied even to ordinary remembering. The analogy suggests that the mechanism of visual memory is a natural extension of the mechanisms of vision. Although there is some truth to this proposition, as we shall see below, it is not because both perception and memory are copying processes. Rather it is because *neither* perception *nor* memory is a copying process.

The fact is that one does not see the retinal image; one sees with the aid of the retinal image. The incoming pattern of light provides information that the nervous system is well adapted to pick up. This information is used by the perceiver to guide his movements, to anticipate events and to construct the internal representations of objects and of space called "conscious experience." These internal representations are not, however, at all like the corresponding optical images on the back of the eye. The retinal images of specific objects are at the mercy of every irrelevant change of position; their size, shape and location are hardly constant for a moment. Nevertheless, perception is usually accurate: real objects appear rigid and stable and appropriately located in three-dimensional space.

The first problem in the study of visual perception is therefore the discovery of the stimulus. What properties of the incoming optic array are informative for vision? In the entire distribution of light, over the retina and over a period of time, what determines the way things look? (Actually the light is distributed over two retinas, but the binocularity of vision has no relevance to the variables considered here. Although depth perception is more accurate with two eyes than with one, it is not fundamentally different. The world looks much the same with one eye closed as it does with both open; congenitally monocular people have more or less the same visual experiences as the rest of us.)

As a first step we can consider the patterns of reflected light that are formed when real objects and surfaces are illuminated in the ordinary way by

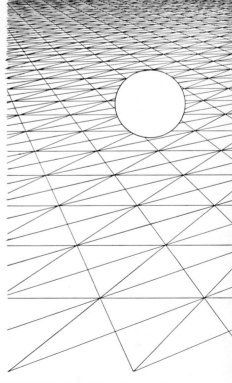

PERCEPTION OF SIZE relies heavily on cues provided by a textured surface. These five disks, if seen alone, would appear to lie

sunshine or lamplight. J. J. Gibson of Cornell University, who has contributed much to our understanding of perception, calls this inquiry "ecological optics." It is an optics in which point sources, homogeneous fields and the other basic elements of classical optics rarely appear. Instead the world we ordinarily look at consists mostly of *surfaces,* at various angles and in various relations to one another. This has significant consequences for the visual input.

One of these consequences (the only one we shall examine here) is to give the visual field a microstructure. Most surfaces have some kind of texture, such as the grain in wood, the individual stalks of grass in a field or the weave in a fabric. These textures structure the light reaching the eye in a way that carries vital information about the layout of environmental objects. In accordance with the principles of perspective the texture elements of more distant surfaces are represented closer to one another on the retina than the elements of surfaces nearby. Thus the microstructure of a surface that slants away from the observer is represented on the retina as a gradient of density—a gradient that carries information about the orientation of the surface.

Consider now an ordinary scene in which discrete figures are superposed on textured surfaces. The gradient of increasing texture density on the retina, corresponding to increasing distance from the observer, gives a kind of "scale" for object sizes. In the ideal case when the texture units are identical, two figures of the same real size will always occlude the same number of texture units, regardless of how far away either one may be. That is, the relation between the retinal texture-size and the dimensions of the object's retinal image is invariant, in spite of changes of distance. This relation is a potentially valuable source of information about the real size of the object—more valuable than the retinal image of the object considered alone. That image, of course, changes in dimension whenever the distance between the object and the observer is altered.

Psychologists have long been interested in what is called "size constancy": the fact that the sizes of real objects are almost always perceived accurately in spite of the linear dependence of retinal-image size on distance. It must not be supposed that this phenomenon is fully explained by the scaling of size with respect to texture elements. There are a great many other sources of relevant information: binocular parallax, shifts of retinal position as the observer moves, relative position in the visual field, linear perspective and so on. It was once traditional to regard these sources of information as "cues" secondary to the size of the object's own retinal image. That is, they were thought to help the observer "correct" the size of the retinal image in the direction of accuracy. Perhaps this is not a bad description of Descartes's situation as he looked at the image on the back of the ox's eye: he may have tried to "correct" his perception of the size of the objects revealed to him on the ox's retina. Since one does not see one's own retina, however, nothing similar need be involved in normal perceiving. Instead the apparent size of an object is determined by information from the entire incoming light pattern, particularly by certain properties of the input that remain invariant with changes of the object's location.

The interrelation of textures, distances and relative retinal sizes is only one example of ecological optics. The example may be a misleadingly simple one, because it assumes a stationary eye, an eye fixed in space and stably oriented in a particular direction. This is by no means a characteristic of human vision. In normal use the eyes are rarely still for long. Apart from small tremors, their

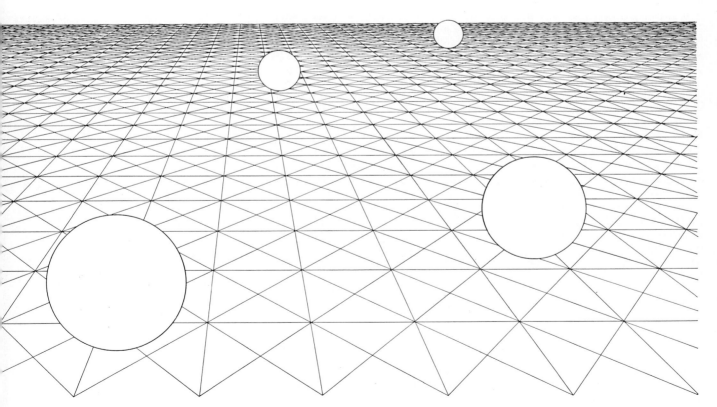

in one plane and be of different sizes. Against this apparently receding surface, however, they seem to lie in five different planes. Since each disk masks the same amount of surface texture, there is a tendency to see them as being equal in size. This illustration, the one at the bottom of the next two pages and the one on page 128 are based on the work of J. J. Gibson of Cornell University.

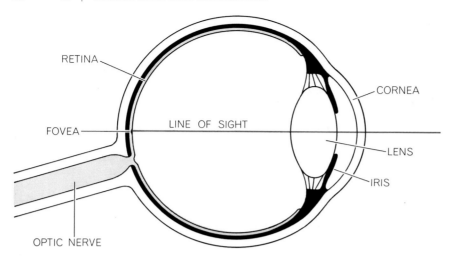

RETINA

FOVEA

LINE OF SIGHT

OPTIC NERVE

CORNEA

LENS

IRIS

SITE OF OPTICAL IMAGE is the retina, which contains the terminations of the optic nerve. In the tiny retinal depression known as the fovea the cone nerve endings are clustered. Their organization and dense packing make possible a high degree of visual acuity.

most common movement is the flick from one position to another called a "saccade." Saccades usually take less than a twentieth of a second, but they happen several times each second in reading and may be just as frequent when a picture or an actual scene is being inspected. This means that there is a new retinal image every few hundred milliseconds.

Such eye movements are necessary because the area of clear vision available to the stationary eye is severely limited. To see this for oneself it is only necessary to fixate on a point in some unfamiliar picture or on an unread printed page. Only a small region around the fixation point will be clear. Most of the page is seen peripherally, which means that it is hazily visible at best. Only in the fovea, the small central part of the retina, are the receptor cells packed close enough together (and appropriately organized) to make a high degree of visual acuity possible. This is the reason one must turn one's eyes (or head) to look directly at objects in which one is particularly interested. (Animals with non-foveated eyes, such as the horse, do not find this necessary.) It is also the reason why the eye must make several fixations on each line in reading, and why it roves widely over pictures.

Although it is easy to understand the function of saccadic movements, it is difficult or impossible to reconcile them with an image theory of perception. As long as we think of the perceiver as a homunculus looking at his retinal image, we must expect his experience to be one of almost constant interruption and change. Clearly this is not the case; one sees the page or the scene as a whole without any apparent discontinuity in

space or time. Most people are either unaware of their own eye movements or have erroneous notions about them. Far from being a copy of the retinal display, the visual world is somehow *constructed* on the basis of information taken in during many different fixations.

The same conclusion follows, perhaps even more compellingly, if we consider the motions of external objects rather than the motions of the eyes. If the analogy between eye and camera were valid, the thing one looked at would have to hold still like a photographer's model in order to be seen clearly. The opposite is true: far from obscuring the shapes and spatial relations of things, movement generally clarifies them. Consider the visual problem presented by a distant arrow-shaped weather vane. As long as the weather vane and the observer remain motionless, there is no way to tell whether it is a short arrow oriented at right angles to the line of sight or a longer arrow slanting toward (or away from) the observer. Let it begin to turn in the wind, however, and its true shape and orientation will become visible immediately. The reason lies in the systematic distortions of the retinal image produced by the object's rotation. Such distortions provide information that the nervous system can use. On the basis of a fluidly changing retinal pattern the perceiver comes to experience a rigid object. (An interesting aspect of this example is that the input information is ambiguous. The same retinal changes could be produced by either a clockwise or a counterclockwise rotation of the weather vane. As a result the perceiver may alternate between two perceptual experiences, one of which is illusory.)

Some years ago Hans Wallach and D. N. O'Connell of Swarthmore College showed that such motion-produced changes in the input are indeed used as a source of information in perceiving; in fact this kind of information seems to be a more potent determiner of what we see than the traditionally emphasized cues for depth are. In their experiment the subject watched the shadow of a wire form cast on a translucent screen. He could not see the object itself. So long as the object remained stationary the subject saw only a two-dimensional shadow on a two-dimensional screen, as might be expected. The form was mounted in such a way, however, that it could be swiveled back and forth by a small electric motor. When the motor was turned on, the true three-dimensional shape of the form appeared at once, even though the only stimulation reaching the subject's eyes came from a distorting shadow on a flat screen. Here the kinetic depth effect, as it has been called, overrode binocular stereoscopic information that continued to indicate that all the movement was taking place in a flat plane.

In the kinetic depth effect the constructive nature of perception is particularly apparent. What one sees is somehow a composite based on information accumulated over a period of time. The same is true in reading or in any instance where eye movements are involved: information from past fixations is used together with information from the present fixation to determine what is seen. But if perception is a temporally extended act, some storage of information, some kind of memory, must be involved in it. How shall we conceive of this storage? How is it organized? How

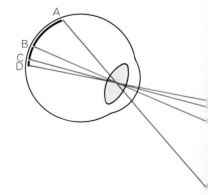

A
B
C
D

CONTRACTION OF IMAGE takes place as the distance between the viewer and the

long does it last? What other functions might it serve?

With questions like these, we have moved beyond the problem of specifying the visual stimulus. In addition to identifying the sources of information for vision, we want to know how that information is processed. In the long run, perhaps, questions about processes should be answered in neurological terms. However, no such answers can be given at present: The neurophysiology of vision has recently made great strides, but it is still not ready to deal with the constructive processes that are central to perception. We shall have to be content with a relatively abstract account, one that does not specify the neural locus of the implicated mechanisms.

Although seeing requires storage of information, this memory cannot be thought of as a sequence of superposed retinal images. Superposition would give rise only to a sort of smear in which all detail is lost. Nor can we assume that the perceiver keeps careful track of his eye movements and thus is able to set each new retinal image in just the right place in relation to the older stored ones. Such an alignment would require a much finer monitoring of eye motion than is actually available. Moreover, the similar synthesis of information that is involved in the kinetic depth effect could not possibly be explained that way. It seems, therefore, that perceiving involves a memory that is not representational but schematic. During a series of fixations the perceiver synthesizes a model or schema of the scene before him, using information from each successive fixation to add detail or to extend the construction. This constructed whole is what guides his

movements (including further eye movements in many cases) and it is what he describes when he is being introspective. In short, it is what he sees.

Interestingly enough, although the memory involved in visual synthesis cannot consist simply of stored retinal afterimages, recent experiments indicate that storage of this kind does exist under certain circumstances. After a momentary exposure (too short for eye movement) that is followed by a blank field the viewer preserves an iconic image of the input pattern for some fraction of a second. George Sperling of the Bell Telephone Laboratories has shown that a signal given during this postexposure period can serve to direct a viewer's attention to any arbitrary part of the field, just as if it were still present.

The displays used in Sperling's experiments consisted of several rows of letters—too many to be reported from a single glance. Nevertheless, subjects were able to report any *single row*, indicated by the postexposure signal, rather well. Such a signal must come quickly; letters to which the observer does not attend before the brief iconic memory has faded are lost. That is why the observer cannot report the entire display: the icon disappears before he can read it all.

Even under these unusual conditions, then, people display selectivity in their use of the information that reaches the eye. The selection is made from material presented in a single brief exposure, but only because the experimental arrangements precluded a second glance. Normally selection and construction take place over a series of glances; no iconic memory for individual "snapshots" can survive. Indeed, the presentation of a

second stimulus figure shortly after the first in a brief-exposure experiment tends to destroy the iconic replica. The viewer may see a fusion of the two figures, only the second, or an apparent motion of the figures, depending on their temporal and spatial relations. He does not see them separately.

So far we have considered two kinds of short-term memory for visual information: the iconic replica of a brief and isolated stimulus, and the cumulative schema of the visible world that is constructed in the course of ordinary perception. Both of these processes (which may well be different manifestations of a single underlying mechanism) involve the storage of information over a period of time. Neither of them, however, is what the average man has in mind when he speaks of memory. Everyday experience testifies that visual information can be stored over long periods. Things seen yesterday can be recalled today; for that matter they may conceivably be recalled 20 years from now. Such recall may take many forms, but perhaps the most interesting is the phenomenon called visual imagery. In a certain sense one can see again what one has seen before. Are these mental images like optical ones? Are they revived copies of earlier stimulation? Indeed, does it make any sense at all to speak of "seeing" things that are not present? Can there be visual experience when there is no stimulation by light?

To deal with these problems effectively we must distinguish two issues: first, the degree to which the mechanisms involved in visual memory are like those involved in visual perception and, second, the degree to which the perceiver

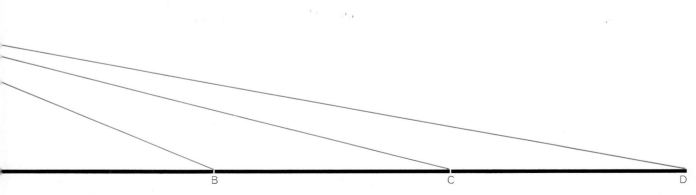

object in view increases. The texture elements of a distant surface are also projected closer together than similar elements nearby.

Thus a textured surface slanting away from the viewer is represented optically as a density gradient (*see illustration on next page*).

is willing to say his images look real, that is, like external things seen. Although the first issue is perhaps the more fundamental—and the most relevant here—the second has always attracted the most attention.

One reason for the perennial interest in the "realness" of images is the wide range of differences in imaging capacity from person to person and from time to time. When Francis Galton conducted the first empirical study of mental im-

agery (published in 1883), he found some of his associates skeptical of the very existence of imagery. They assumed that only poetic fancy allowed one to speak of "seeing" in connection with what one remembered; remembering consisted simply in a knowledge of facts. Other people, however, were quite ready to describe their mental imagery in terms normally applied to perception. Asked in the afternoon about their breakfast table, they said they could see it clearly, with

colors bright (although perhaps a little dimmer than in the original experience) and objects suitably arranged.

These differences seem to matter less when one is asleep; many people who report little or no lifelike imagery while awake may have visual dreams and believe in the reality of what they see. On the other hand, some psychopathological states can endow images with such a compelling quality that they dominate the patient's experience. Students of per-

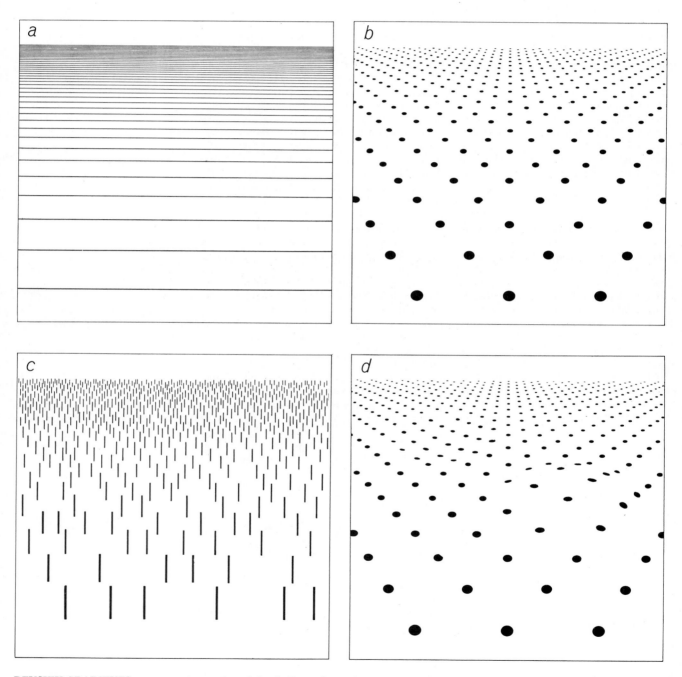

DENSITY GRADIENTS convey an impression of depth. Depending on the size, shape and spacing of its textural elements, the gradient may create the impression of a smooth flat surface (a, b), a rough flat surface (c) or a surface broken by an elevation and a depression (d). Like the gradients depicted, the textured surfaces of the visual world (by structuring the light that falls on the retina) convey information concerning the orientation of the surface. Textured surfaces also provide a scale for gauging the size of objects.

ception have often disregarded dreams and phantasms, considering them "hallucinatory" and thus irrelevant to normal seeing. However, this is a difficult position to defend either logically or empirically. Logically a sharp distinction between perception and hallucination would be easy enough if perceptions were copies of the retinal image; hallucinations would then be experiences that do *not* copy that image. But since perception does more than mirror the stimulus (and since hallucinations often incorporate stimulus information), this distinction is not clear-cut. Moreover, a number of recent findings seem to point up very specific relations between the processes of seeing and of imagining.

Perhaps the most unexpected of these findings has emerged from studies of sleep and dreams. The dreaming phase of sleep, which occurs several times each night, is regularly accompanied by bursts of rapid eye movements. In several studies William C. Dement and his collaborators have awakened experimental subjects immediately after a period of eye motion and asked them to report their just-preceding dream. Later the eye-movement records were compared with a transcript of the dream report to see if any relation between the two could be detected. Of course this was not possible in every case. (Indeed, we can be fairly sure that many of the eye movements of sleep have no visual significance; similar motions occur in the sleep of newborn babies, decorticated cats and congenitally blind adults.) Nevertheless, there was appreciably more correspondence between the two kinds of record than could be attributed to chance. The parallel between the eye movements of the dreamer and the content of the dream was sometimes striking. In one case five distinct upward deflections of the eyes were recorded just before the subject awoke and reported a dream of climbing five steps!

Another recent line of research has also implicated eye movements in the processes of visual memory. Ralph Norman Haber and his co-workers at Yale University reopened the study of eidetic imagery, which for a generation had remained untouched by psychological research. An eidetic image is an imaginative production that seems to be external to the viewer and to have a location in perceived space; it has a clarity comparable to that of genuinely perceived objects; it can be examined by the "*Eidetiker*," who may report details that he did not notice in the original presentation of the stimulus. Most *Eidetikers*

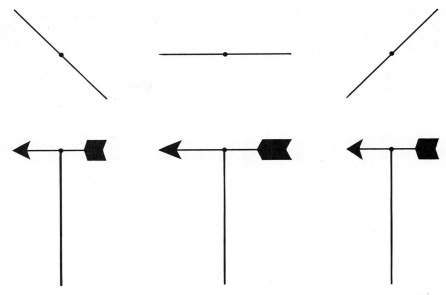

AMBIGUOUS VISUAL INPUT can arise from a stationary weather vane. The weather vane in three different orientations is shown as it would be seen from above (*top*) and in side view (*bottom*). If the vane begins to rotate, its real length will become apparent.

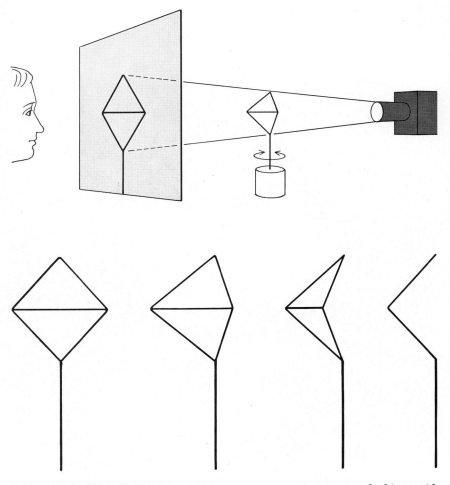

KINETIC DEPTH EFFECT shows how movement can endow perceived objects with three-dimensional shape. The shadow of a bent wire form (*shown at bottom in four different orientations*) looks as flat as the screen on which it is cast so long as the form remains stationary. When it is swiveled back and forth, the changing shadow is seen as a rigid rotating object with the appropriate three-dimensionality. The direction of rotation remains ambiguous, as in the case of the weather vane in the illustration at top of the page.

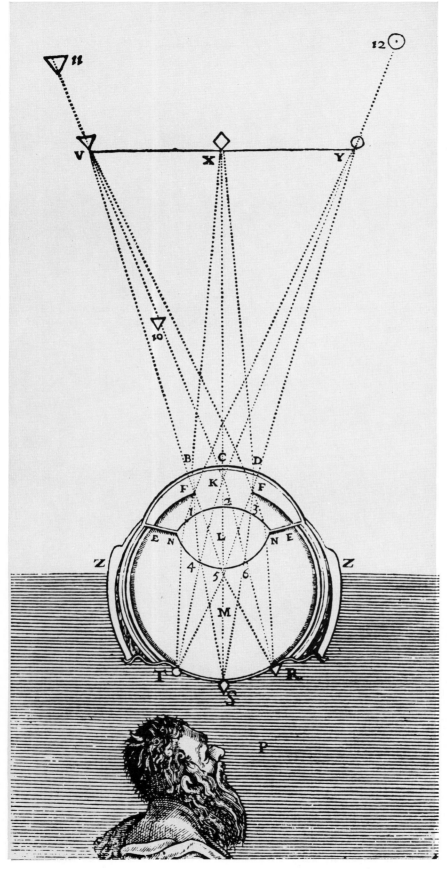

are children, but the developmental course of this rather rare ability is not well understood. What is most interesting about these images for the present argument is that the *Eidetiker* scans them with his eyes. Asked about a detail in one or another corner of the image, he moves his eyes to look at the appropriate part of the blank wall on which he has "projected" it. That is, he does just what anyone would do who was really looking at something.

Are these esoteric phenomena really relevant to the study of vision? It might be argued that they do not provide a safe basis for inference; dreaming is a very special physiological state and eidetic imagery is restricted to very special types of people. It is not difficult, however, to show that similar processes occur in persons who do not have vivid visual imagery at all. A simple demonstration suggested by Julian Hochberg of New York University helps to make this point: Try to remember how many windows there are in your own house or apartment.

If you have never considered this question before, it will be hard to find the answer without actively looking and counting. However, you will probably not need to look at the windows themselves. Most people, even those who say they have no visual imagery, can easily form and scan an *internal representation* of the walls, counting off the windows as they appear in them. This process evidently uses stored visual information. It seems to involve mechanisms much like those used for seeing and counting real windows.

We can draw three conclusions from this demonstration. First, seeing and imagining employ similar—perhaps the same—mechanisms. Second, images can be useful, even when they are not vivid or lifelike, even for people who do not have "good imagery." Third, mental images are constructs and not copies. This last point may have been obvious in any case—you might just as well have been asked to imagine a gryphon and to count its claws—but it bears further emphasis. All the windows could not have been optically imaged on the retina simultaneously, and they may not even have appeared there in rapid succession. The image (or series of images) developed in solving this problem is new; it is not a replica of any previous stimulus.

The first two of these points have received additional confirmation in a recent experiment by Lee R. Brooks of McMaster University, whose method puts imagery and visual perception in di-

OPTICAL ANALYSIS BY DESCARTES included an experiment in which he removed the eye of an ox, scraped the back of the eye to make it transparent and observed on the retina the inverted image of a scene. The illustration is from Descartes's essay *La Dioptrique*.

rect competition. In one of his studies the subjects were shown a large block F and told to remember what it looked like. After the F was removed from view they were asked to describe the succession of corner points that would be encountered as one moved around it, responding "Yes" for each point that was either on the extreme top or the bottom of the F, and "No" for each point in between. This visual-memory task proved to be more difficult when the responses were made by *pointing* to a printed series of yeses and noes than when a spoken "Yes" or "No" was allowed. However, the difficulty was not intrinsic to the act of pointing; it resulted from the conflict between pointing and simultaneously visualizing the F. In another of Brooks's tasks the subjects had to respond "Yes" for each noun and "No" for each non-noun in a memorized sentence.

In this case they tended to rely on verbal-auditory memory rather than visual memory. As a result spoken response was the more difficult of the two.

We would not have been surprised to find a conflict between visually guided pointing and corner-counting on an F the viewer was *looking at*. After all, he could not be expected to look in two places at once. Even if the F had appeared on the same sheet of paper with the yeses and noes, interference would have been easy to understand: the succession of glances required to examine the corners of the F would have conflicted with the visual organization needed to point at the right succession of responses. What Brooks has shown, rather surprisingly, is that this conflict exists even when the F is merely imagined. Visual images are apparently produced by the same integrative processes that

make ordinary perception possible.

In short, the reaction of the nervous system to stimulation by light is far from passive. The eye and brain do not act as a camera or a recording instrument. Neither in perceiving nor in remembering is there any enduring copy of the optical input. In perceiving, complex patterns are extracted from that input and fed into the constructive processes of vision, so that the movements and the inner experience of the perceiver are usually in good correspondence with his environment. Visual memory differs from perception because it is based primarily on stored rather than on current information, but it involves the same kind of synthesis. Although the eyes have been called the windows of the soul, they are not so much peepholes as entry ports, supplying raw material for the constructive activity of the visual system.

10   Eidetic Images

by Ralph Norman Haber
April 1969

Certain individuals report that they briefly retain an almost photographic image of something they have seen. Experiments with children suggest that such images are a real phenomenon

Many people believe they can retain a vivid image of something they have seen. When such people undertake to describe this ability, it usually turns out that the images are fleeting and lacking in true visual quality; the person describing the images is not quite sure that he is not merely remembering or imagining them. Certain individuals, however, report something rather different: a sharp visual image that persists for many seconds or even minutes. They speak of the image being localized in space in front of their eyes, usually in the same plane as the original stimulus. They maintain that it is so well defined that they can describe it in far more detail than they could from memory alone. They report that the image can be formed when their eyes simply flick over the original scene without fixating it, and also that the image can be scanned as it remains stationary in space.

Such reported images have been named eidetic, after the Greek *eidētikos,* meaning pertaining to images. Eidetic imagery was once the subject of considerable investigation; more than 200 experiments and studies on it have been published, most of them before 1935. This work indicated that whereas eidetic ability is relatively rare after puberty, it is common in young children (an average of 50 percent of the elementary-school-age children who were studied appeared to possess it). These findings were based, however, on widely divergent and often inconsistent methods. In spite of the seeming prevalence of eidetic imagery, the poor methods and an inability to explain the phenomenon tended to lead psychologists to ignore eidetic images, along with most of the other mental states that depend so heavily on subjective reports.

The past decade has witnessed a renewed interest in visual imagery of all kinds, particularly in connection with how images facilitate perceptual memory. It seemed only natural to look again at eidetic imagery, the most enduring and complete kind of imagery. Does it really exist? Can children (or adults) with this ability be found, and if so, in what other ways might their visual perception and perceptual memory be different? Exactly how do eidetic images differ from the ordinary visual memories reported by most adults? How does a child with eidetic imagery prevent his visual experiences from becoming a hopeless muddle? Is eidetic imagery a more primitive or developmentally earlier mode of perception and memory?

To answer some of these questions my colleagues and I (including from the beginning my wife and more recently Jan Leask Fentress) launched a large-scale effort to find eidetic children and examine aspects of their imagery and other perceptual abilities. Because of the elusive nature of the phenomenon, and because of the difficulty of finding a large number of eidetic children, we have conducted comparatively few formal experiments. Even so, we have found answers to a few of the questions listed above (although more questions have been raised). I shall describe how we conducted our search for eidetic children and some of the more outstanding results of the project. I shall also discuss, as I present the evidence, the visual character of eidetic imagery.

The basic procedures we followed in order to locate eidetic children were adapted from research of 40 years ago. Children from four elementary schools were tested individually, and as it became clear that eidetic imagery was going to be a rare phenomenon, we found it necessary to test large numbers of them. Our results are based on about 20 eidetic children, although more than 500 children have been screened in all.

The screening began with a test designed to elicit afterimages, which are a common phenomenon not to be confused with eidetic images. The subject sat before a table on which an easel of a neutral gray color was placed. His eyes were about two feet from the middle of the easel [*see illustration on page 82*]. A tape recorder transcribed the voices of the subject and the experimenter.

The first stimulus placed on the easel was a four-by-four-inch square of red paper mounted on a board of the same material as the easel. After 10 seconds the board was removed, and the subject then reported what he saw on the easel. At the beginning of this test he was instructed to stare at the center of the colored square as hard as he could, trying not to move his eyes. He was told: "After the square is removed, you will still be able to see something there. It is very much like when you stare hard at a light bulb and then look away. You can still see something out there in front of your eyes." If a child acted as if he was unfamiliar with this phenomenon, he was told to try it out with one of the overhead lights in the room. He was also encouraged to report, without waiting to be asked, what he saw after the square was removed and he continued to stare at the place where it had been.

During the exposure the experimenter watched carefully to be sure that the subject did not move his eyes. If, when the square was taken away, the subject said he saw nothing, he was encouraged by being assured that it was all right to see something. If he still said he saw nothing, he was reminded to stare hard and not move his eyes at all, and he was

TEST PICTURE was shown for half a minute to elementary school children; a few then reported eidetic images of it. For example, one boy saw in his image "about 16" stripes in the cat's tail. The picture, painted by Marjorie Torrey, appears in an edition of Lewis Carroll's *Alice in Wonderland* abridged by Josette Frank and is reproduced with the kind permission of Random House.

COMPOSITE PICTURES, closely resembling each other, provided a test of eidetic imagery. A child capable of maintaining eidetic images of both pictures would presumably be better equipped to distinguish between them accurately than would a child without such images who relied solely on his memory of the pictures. The montages were made by Leonard W. Doob of Yale University.

questioned about whether he knew what these instructions meant.

If the subject said he did see something, he was allowed to report spontaneously. Then he was questioned about items he had not reported. Was the image still visible? What was its color and shape? When the subject moved his eyes (he had been asked to try to look slowly toward the top of the easel), did the image move? How did it disappear? After the image had faded completely the experimenter repeated the initial instructions and another square, a blue one, was placed on the easel. The same procedure was followed with a black square and then a yellow one.

After the last square had been reported on, the test for eidetic imagery began. Four pictures were shown: two silhouettes of black paper pasted on a gray board (one showing a family scene and one an Indian hunter) and two illustrations in color taken from books for children. Each picture was presented for 30 seconds. For this test the subject was given the instructions: "Now I am going to show you some pictures. For these, however, I do not want you to stare in one place, but to move your eyes around so that you can be sure you can see all of the details. When I take the picture away, I want you to continue to look hard at the easel where the picture was, and tell me what you can still see after I take it away. After I take it away, you also can move your eyes all over where it was on the easel. And be sure, while the picture is on the easel, that you move your eyes around it to see all of the parts."

During the viewing period the experimenter watched to be sure that the picture was scanned and not fixated. After the first picture was removed the subject was reminded to continue looking at the easel and report whatever he could still see. He was also reminded that he could move his eyes. If a subject reported seeing something, the experimenter asked if he was actually seeing it then or remembering it from when the picture was still on the easel. The subject was frequently asked if he was still seeing something, since subjects would often fail to say that the image had faded and would continue reporting it from memory. The experimenter probed for further description of all objects still visible in the image. He noted the relation between the direction of the subject's gaze and details of his report. This process was repeated for all four pictures. The average time for testing varied from four or five minutes for a young subject with no visual imagery to more than 30 minutes for an older subject with extensive imagery.

The tests were scored by encoding the tape recordings on data sheets. A different coding sheet was set up for each stimulus. The reliability of this condensation of the data was nearly perfect because there were categories for every object in the picture and most of their attributes. The coder rarely had to make a scoring decision.

We have introduced a number of variations in the screening, but these represent the main procedures. When a child was considered to be eidetic, further tests, demonstrations and examinations usually followed. I shall not present them in chronological or systematic order here, since most of the sessions did not constitute formal experiments.

Before discussing specific characteristics of eidetic imagery, let me make a few general comments. About half of the children screened said they saw something on the easel after the picture was removed, but nearly all these reports were of afterimages and the like, that is, the images were fleeting and indistinct. Between 5 and 10 percent of the children, however, reported images that lasted much longer (a half-minute or more) and that possessed some sharp detail. Without committing ourselves, we labeled these children eidetic and observed them further. Hereafter I shall refer to this group as eidetic, although you can judge for yourself whether they can be differentiated from the rest, and whether they have any visual imagery of noteworthy quality. I feel that the answer to both questions is clearly yes.

Let me start by offering an example (taken directly from a tape recording) of a report of an eidetic image. Not all eidetic reports are like this one; on the other hand, it is not atypical. The subject, a 10-year-old boy, was seated before a blank easel from which a picture from *Alice in Wonderland* had just been removed.

Experimenter: Do you see something there?

Subject: I see the tree, gray tree with three limbs. I see the cat with stripes around its tail.

Experimenter: Can you count those stripes?

Subject: Yes (*pause*). There's about 16.

Experimenter: You're counting what? Black, white or both?

Subject: Both.

Experimenter: Tell me what else you see.

Subject: And I can see the flowers on the bottom. There's about three stems, but you can see two pairs of flowers. One on the right has green leaves, red flower on bottom with yellow on top. And I can see the girl with a green dress. She's got blonde hair and a red hair band and there are some leaves in the upper left-hand corner where the tree is.

Experimenter: Can you tell me about the roots of the tree?

Subject: Well, there's two of them going down here (*points*) and there's one that cuts off on the left-hand side of the picture.

Experimenter: What is the cat doing with its paws?

Subject: Well, one of them he's holding out and the other one is on the tree.

Experimenter: What color is the sky?

Subject: Can't tell.

Experimenter: Can't tell at all?

Subject: No. I can see the yellowish ground, though.

Experimenter: Tell me if any of the parts go away or change at all as I'm talking to you. What color is the girl's dress?

Subject: Green. It has some white on it.

Experimenter: How about her legs and feet?

(*The subject looks away from the easel and then back again.*)

Experimenter: Is the image gone?

Subject: Yes, except for the tree.

Experimenter: Tell me when it goes away.

Subject: (*pause*) It went away.

The fact that only about 5 percent of the children reported images as prolonged and vivid as this one raised our immediate concern about the validity of eidetic imagery. How could it shrink in frequency so much in the 35 years since the early investigations? Perhaps it did not exist at all. The children might be faking or be strongly suggestible, giving us answers we led them to expect we want. Or could we as psychologists be fooled into thinking that these few children are describing their imagery when they are only telling us about their vivid memories? All of these have been difficult questions to answer or even to investigate. Furthermore, some of the most convincing evidence in support of visual images comes not from experiments but from incidental observations or comments made by the children that suggest the visual characteristics rather than the memory characteristics of the reports. Instead of listing such evidence out of context I shall consider it in relation to some of the properties of eidetic imagery we measured.

First, who are the eidetic children? Those we labeled as such were distributed fairly evenly over the five grades from the second through the sixth. The absence of eidetics from the first grade and kindergarten (which were also tested) seemed due to the verbal demands of the task that was set, so that we have no way of being sure that younger children are less likely to be eidetic. The sex and racial makeup of the eidetic group mirrored the school populations as closely as such a small sample can. We tested I.Q., reading achievement and aspects of personality, but we could find nothing that differentiated the eidetic group from comparable noneidetic children.

The rather unsuccessful attempt to find some distinguishing characteristic of eidetic children has given us concern, although without further enlightenment. There is no question about the reliability of the testing for eidetic imagery, however. Once labeled this way, an eidetic child always produces such images. We have tested a few of the children four times over a five-year period, and have found no loss in the quality of their imagery.

One aspect of eidetic imagery we measured was the length of exposure time required for the formation of an image. For nearly all the eidetic children a five-second viewing of a picture will lead to an image of at least parts of it (the parts examined during that time). The better eidetic children (those who could more easily report long-lived and complete images) could occasionally form an image after only three seconds. Although we did not make careful measurements, it appears that three to five seconds of central viewing is needed to produce an image, and that the size of such an image is two or three degrees of visual angle. This is roughly the size covered by the fovea, the area of the retina that provides sharp vision. Thus to have a complete image of a typical picture measuring five degrees by five degrees at least four separate fixations would be needed. The children report that they do not have an image of parts of the picture they did not look at long enough, even though they may know and be able to remember what the parts contain. Moreover, the relation between duration of exposure and the production of an eidetic image holds even if the picture is totally familiar to the child. Hence his memory of it could be essentially perfect and complete and yet whether or not he has an image depends on how long his eyes dwell on the picture in the most recent viewing. Observations of this kind further suggest the visual character of eidetic images.

We wondered why eidetic children were not confused by the continual bombardment of images. The children described several ways they controlled the production of images. One way, of course, is not to look at anything too long. Moreover, most of the children indicated that exaggerated eye blinks could serve to "erase" an image. Nearly all the children said that if they moved their eyes from the original surface on which the picture was viewed, the image would disappear. This would further reduce the possibility of an eidetic child's picking up random images as he looks about the world.

By far the most intriguing method of control reported to us (again by most of the children) was based on naming the items in the picture. That is, if while the child is looking at the picture, he names, labels, rehearses or otherwise actively attends to the items, he will not have an image. After several children mentioned this spontaneously, we examined it more explicitly. In viewing some pictures a child would be asked to name each part; for other pictures the experimenter named the parts but the child was not asked to do so. We found a clear difference: no image or only a poor, brief image would form of those pictures for which the child had named the parts.

We have not yet been able to pursue

SUBJECT WAS TIMED as he inspected the picture; he was also watched to see whether he examined every part of it. After the picture was removed from view he reported to the experimenter what (if anything) he saw on the blank easel. His words were recorded.

this finding further. It seems to imply at one level that eidetic children retain information either in the form of an image or in the form of a verbal memory or another kind of memory more similar to that in adults. The children do not seem to be able to do both at once. This can help to explain an earlier finding of ours. In one screening test, after an eidetic child had completed a description of his eidetic image and had said it had faded completely, he was asked to describe the stimulus from memory. Noneidetic children who had no images at all were also asked to describe the stimulus from memory. We expected the eidetic child to have a far superior memory, because he had had the opportunity to view not only the picture but also his enduring image, but we found that eidetic children were only slightly better than the others, and in some cases no better at all. It was as if the eidetic child paid no attention to his image in organizing his memory. Interpreting this behavior in the light of the later observations, it seems that if an eidetic child wishes to get an image, he can pay no attention to the picture in composing his memory, because trying to do so interferes with the image. The child asked to produce images sacrifices the memory. I shall return to this point. Let me note that here again we can make a distinction between the visual character and the memory character of the child's report, suggesting that the visual nature of eidetic imagery has some validity.

Can an eidetic child prolong his image or bring it back after it has disappeared? Does he have any control over its disappearance? Can he change the size or orientation of his image, or move it to another surface? The answer to each of these questions is in general negative. Few eidetic children seem to have any control over the images once they are formed.

The group of eidetic children we studied differed substantially among themselves with respect to the quality of their images. For example, the child with the most enduring images consistently reported them as lasting 10 minutes or more. Some eidetic children had good images that lasted no more than a minute. There was also variation among children in the completeness of the image, particularly for nonpictorial material such as printed letters. Some children could regularly see in their image all the letters of a very long nonsense word. Other children could see only some of the letters, still others just a few letter fragments. There were eidetic children

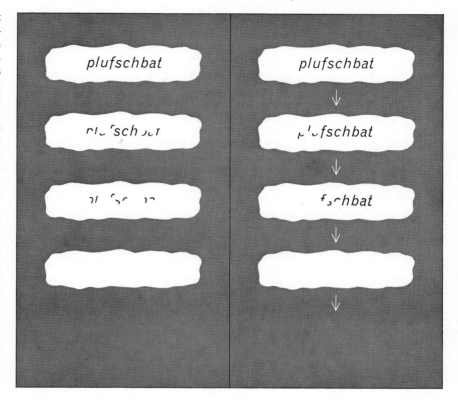

QUALITY OF EIDETIC IMAGES (reconstructed from verbal reports) varied from child to child. At left is the range of image completeness (of a nonsense word) for all the children with eidetic ability. Each reconstruction characterizes a different child most of the time. At right is the sequence of fading of all eidetic images. A perfect "image" is used as a model.

who could get images of pictures easily but could rarely see any print in an image. What is interesting about this is that the pattern of fading for a particular eidetic child seems to reproduce the spectrum of image completeness of the group as a whole [see illustration above]. All the eidetic children reported that their images ended in the same manner each time, the image fading part by part in a comparatively independent fashion. As a good image begins to fade, first some fragments disappear and then more of them go until just a gray streak is left and finally nothing remains. The parallel between completeness and fading suggests that the mechanism responsible for the completeness of an eidetic image is similar to the one for its subsequent fading.

None of our eidetic children maintained that he could by any action prolong his image. One girl reported the ability to bring an image back after it had faded. She was asked to do this over periods of several weeks and reported being able to do so.

We explored somewhat more fully whether the eidetic child can move his image or change its size or orientation. The apparent size of an afterimage varies with the distance of the surface on which the image is projected (an effect known as Emmert's law). No such effect can be tested with eidetic imagery because the eidetic child cannot move his image off the original surface without losing it. The image could be moved over the surface, but nearly all the children said that when they tried moving the image over the edge, it "falls off." Only the girl who was able to bring her images back could move her image off the surface. (She said she could move it anywhere and even turn it upside down.) With this one exception the image seems to be related in specific ways to the picture that produced it. It has the same size, orientation and shape. It moves on its "own" surface but not into space or onto a "foreign" surface.

We had used pictures selected to be interesting to children in our screening procedures, because the older studies suggested that these elicited better eidetic images. We were also most interested in images of letters and how much information was maintained in these images. This was significant in its own right and also because eidetic imagery might facilitate or hinder reading. Although all the eidetic children were able to develop images of print (we used long nonsense words, strings of digits or misspelled words), these images were in general poorer than images of pictures. They were less complete and distinct, and did not last as long. The quality of the image did not differ according to the kind of printed material. The duration of exposure also seemed to be irrelevant. An eidetic child with only a partial image of print would not get a better one if he looked longer.

One procedure we followed was to show a subject letters or digits one at a time through a small viewing window in a screen. The most striking result was the nearly uniform statement by the children that as each new item appeared in the window they moved their image of the preceding one along the surface to the left [see illustration below]. When the image of the first letter exposed reached the left margin of the surface, it would (if it had not yet faded with the passage of time) "fall off" the edge and disappear. Note again the visual character of this description given by nearly every eidetic child.

Regardless of whether the child scanned a group of letters from left to right or from right to left, the items seen last exerted a strong effect. This was clearly due to the fact that the images of the first items scanned were fading before the last ones were scanned. Since in a task of this kind the first items viewed would normally be remembered better, the finding again seems to indicate that the children are seeing something rather than just remembering it.

We were disappointed in how few letters (or digits) can be maintained in a visual image. For a relatively good eidetic child an average of only about eight of 10 letters (one presented every three seconds) remained in an image after the 30 seconds of total exposure, and this held only under optimum conditions. A few of the children could probably have done better had we given them more letters, but for most of the children items of this kind do not persist in images for nearly as long as parts of pictures. Although we did not try to use a page of printed words as a stimulus, it was clear that none of the children would have had an eidetic image of even part of it.

In an attempt to learn the amount of information retained in an image, we tried two tests utilizing pictorial items. For one test we designed a "rogues' gallery," showing a group of letters and a series of digits in conjunction with the shoulders and head of the "wanted" man [see illustration on opposite page]. Only four of the eidetic children could develop an image of even part of the gallery, and these images were so incomplete that the children were unable to report much information. None of the children felt he could have maintained better images with longer exposures. (The exposure time was about three seconds per rogue.)

In the second test montages made up of familiar objects were presented to the children. The montages were in pairs, one member of the pair rather closely resembling the other [see illustration on page 80]. We expected (and showed) that from memory alone children and adults often tended to confuse which element belonged in which picture of the pair, assuming that they could remember all the elements to start with. An eidetic child, however, if he could have a good image of both members of a pair, should have no trouble describing them accurately. Unfortunately when first one and then the other montage was shown to the eidetic group, only one child was able to maintain an image of the two pictures side by side. Several children could retain images of the second montage shown, but the first image would disappear. None of the eidetic children could report any more detail or accurate positioning of detail than noneidetic children could.

We therefore have been unable to determine how much information an eidetic image can contain, because eidetic children do not achieve satisfactory images of either high-information stimuli or even simple nonpictorial stimuli. One

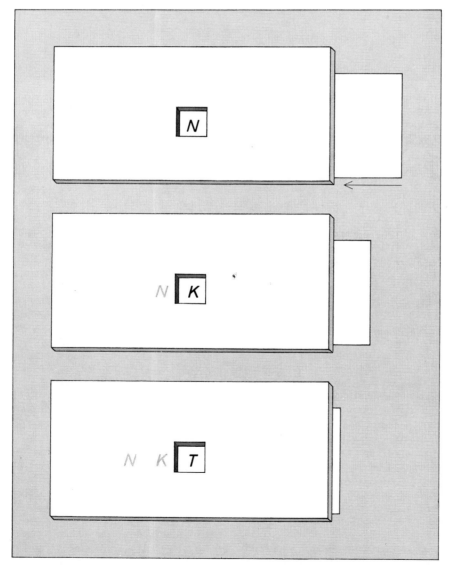

SEQUENCE OF LETTERS appeared one at a time in an aperture of a screen as children who had previously displayed eidetic ability watched. They reported that the image they formed of a letter (gray letter) moved to the left as a new letter appeared in the window.

00-6114   84-9270   53-0624   79-3516   90-4265

"ROGUES' GALLERY" STIMULUS was designed to provide a basis for estimating the amount of information contained in an eidetic image. In addition to the name and the number associated with a rogue there are binary dimensions that could be used descriptively, for example the presence or absence of hair or a hat. The rogues (together with 20 others) were shown as a group to the children.

reason for the poor response to letters may have been the tendency to name them, which we already know interferes with the formation of a good image. These results are somewhat in contrast with the seemingly better images from complex but cohesive pictures.

We have also tried to elicit eidetic imagery with a few three-dimensional objects. Three of the eight children so tested reported images of everyday objects, at which they looked for 30 seconds. They were able to move their images and reported that they had clear three-dimensional qualities. The children were also shown the visual illusion known as the Necker cube, a line figure that spontaneously reverses in apparent depth [*see top illustration on next page*]. During the 30 seconds of scanning time all the children reported reversals of depth; only three (the same three mentioned above) could report reversals in their image. The number of reversals in the image was about four per 30 seconds compared with seven per 30 seconds during the viewing of the drawing of the cube. Since (barring deliberate faking) a report of a reversal requires a three-dimensional view, a few of the eidetic children seem to be capable of forming three-dimensional eidetic images. A reversal also requires a visual experience. There is nothing in the memory of a Necker cube that would cause its orientation to alternate.

At several points in this article I have raised the question of whether eidetic imagery could merely be vivid memory. This is a crucial aspect of the research. Some criticisms of the earlier studies of eidetic imagery focused on the lack of evidence that the eidetic children were reporting a visual image rather than just describing their memory of the stimulus. Whereas many in-

credibly detailed reports of eidetic images have been described in these studies, there is no reason to doubt that some children may have superb memories and be quite capable of the same feats from memory alone.

I believe that resting the case for eidetic imagery on the fidelity of reports is the wrong approach. Our own evidence suggests that the amount of detail an eidetic child can report from his image is in general not phenomenally good (although we have had some amazing exceptions). I see no reason to assert that an eidetic image has to be complete or contain all the content of the original stimulus, or that it must last long enough to enable the eidetic child to describe all the content before it fades.

If we are not to depend on the criterion of accuracy, then what does differentiate eidetic images from other kinds of images or from memory? The only distinction with respect to other images is in their location. Afterimages seem to be the result of differential adaptation of retinal receptors and neural units. The image, once formed, is "burned on" the retina and cannot be moved in relation to the retina. Moreover, during the formation of an afterimage reasonably stable fixation is required to produce the differential adaptation. The likelihood of an afterimage's being produced should thus vary inversely with the amount of scanning during inspection and with the degree to which the image itself can be scanned once it is formed. Since in all our work with eidetic images we demand scanning during inspection of the stimulus and check further to be sure the child moves his eyes during his report of his image, it seems almost certain that this image cannot simply be retinal in origin.

We still leave open the possibility that an eidetic image is not an image at

all. The child may not be seeing anything in front of his eyes. It is always possible that these children are trying to fool us when they say they see the image; that our questions effectively structure their answers to be as if they saw images; that since they think we want them to talk about images, they do; that they are so suggestible they "think" they see images even if they do not, or that the distinction between seeing and remembering is so difficult for a child (let alone an adult) that he is innocently confused. All of these are possible explanations and are likely to be true for perhaps one or two children most of the time and for many of the children occasionally.

Still, sufficient evidence is available to support the argument that these are images that are visual in nature and not dependent on memory in any way (except perhaps negatively). Whereas this argument cannot be settled to the degree we would wish, let me repeat some of the observations or comments that support the visual character of eidetic imagery: (1) An eidetic child can remember parts of the picture he cannot see in his image, and he says he did not have an image of those parts because he did not look at them long enough. (2) A conscious attempt to label the content of the stimulus interferes with the formation of an image. (3) Nearly all the eidetic children report the same pattern of fading in their images, even though that is only one of a number of possible sequences. (4) When asked to move their image from one surface to another, eidetic children report spontaneously that when it reaches the edge it falls off. (5) When the child forms an image of letters exposed individually in a window, he moves his image to the left as a new letter appears in the window. Furthermore, when the image reaches the edge of the

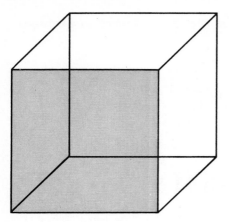

VISUAL ILLUSION was presented to children to explore their ability to form three-dimensional images. The area of the cube in color can appear as a front surface or as a rear surface, producing (in some children's images) a reversal in the cube's orientation.

surface, it too falls off. (6) Children are most capable of seeing details that they scanned most recently, a result contrary to normal organization in memory. (7) At least some of the eidetic children are able to develop three-dimensional images. This was particularly true with the Necker cube, for which reversals cannot be the result of anything other than a visual three-dimensional image.

This list should be longer, and there are certainly a large number of other observations that could be made to help verify the distinction proposed here. At present this represents the nature and amount of evidence we have.

We have tried only one direct test of the visual character of eidetic imagery. This has been very difficult to work out, and our first step is only a beginning. We wanted a test for the screening of eidetic imagery that did not depend on verbal facility and could not be biased by memory. The best solution we have found so far is to use a sequence of pictures that together form another picture [*see illustration below*]. The first picture shown to the child is designed in such a way that, although it is cohesive in its own right, if it is superimposed on a second picture, a third picture (a face) is formed by the combination. Assuming that the combination picture is unpredictable from either picture alone, the only way the eidetic child could know what the combination is would be if he could superimpose one picture on the other visually. If he viewed the pictures separately, this could be accomplished only by maintaining an image of the first picture long enough to superimpose it on the second one.

We have given this test to 20 eidetic children. Only four (who were among the best four in other criteria as well) were able to "see" the combination face picture. The reaction of one child was quite impressive to us. After developing a good image of the first picture, he superimposed his eidetic image of it on the second and at first persisted in reporting the various separate elements of each picture. Suddenly, with obvious surprise, he reported the composite face and exclaimed that the experimenter was pretty "tricky" to have fooled him that way.

Although a few adults appear able to see the outline of the face in the first picture alone, children do not seem able to. Nevertheless, many more versions of the test need to be tried. It is a stringent test, since not only does it require a fairly complete image of the first picture lasting long enough for it to be superimposed on a second picture but also it assumes that the first image will not be erased and can be lined up with the second picture. The instance mentioned above seems to be one where an initially poor alignment stood in the way of a meaningful result. The child suddenly saw the composite after nearly a minute of viewing, when presumably he achieved a better alignment of image and picture.

This test cannot be faked, nor does it depend on memory or on any distinction between memory and imagery. All the child has to do is describe what he can see when the second picture is presented. The test could in fact be used with very young and preverbal children (and could be adapted for animals, if anyone thought they might be eidetic).

Much more work needs to be done with eidetic imagery. We know very little about eidetic children as individuals and have only an inkling of what their imagery is like, but the shunning of an interesting psychological phenomenon for 35 years should be ended. Imagery is an important characteristic of many cognitive tasks, and it should be further opened to serious scientific investigation.

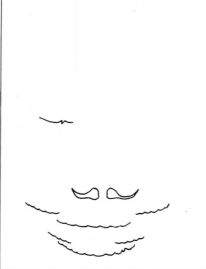

RECOGNITION TEST posed the problem of visually superimposing an image of a picture on another picture. The eidetic children first were shown the picture at left; it was then removed and the middle picture was exposed to view. Some children then "saw" a face. At right is the picture formed by combining the other two pictures. None of the children saw a face in the picture at left.

Visual Illusions

by Richard L. Gregory
November 1968

*Why do simple figures sometimes appear distorted
or ambiguous? Perhaps because the visual system
has to make sense of a world in which everyday
objects are normally distorted by perspective*

A satisfactory theory of visual perception must explain how the fleeting patterns of light reaching the retina of the eye convey knowledge of external objects. The problem of how the brain "reads" reality from the eye's images is an acute one because objects are so very different from images, which directly represent only a few of the important characteristics of objects. At any instant the retinal image represents the color of an object and its shape from a single position, but color and shape are in themselves trivial. Color is dependent on the quality of the illumination, and on the more subtle factors of contrast and retinal fatigue. Shape, as we all know, can be strongly distorted by various illusions. Since it is obviously not in the best interests of the possessor of an eye to be tricked by visual illusions, one would like to know how the illusions occur. Can it be that illusions arise from information-processing mechanisms that under normal circumstances make the visible world easier to comprehend? This is the main proposition I shall examine here.

Illusions of various kinds can occur in any of the senses, and they can cross over between the senses. For example, small objects feel considerably heavier than larger objects of exactly the same weight. This can be easily demonstrated by filling a small can with sand and then putting enough sand in a much larger can until the two cans are in balance. The smaller can will feel up to 50 percent heavier than the larger can of precisely the same weight. Evidently weight is perceived not only according to the pressure and muscle senses but also according to the expected weight of the object, as indicated by its visually judged size. When the density is unexpected, vision produces the illusion of weight. I believe all systematic-distor-

tion illusions are essentially similar to this size-weight illusion.

Although several visual illusions were known to the ancient Greeks, they have been studied experimentally for only a little more than a century. The first scientific description in modern times is in a letter to the Scottish physicist Sir David Brewster from a Swiss naturalist, L. A. Necker, who wrote in 1832 that a drawing of a transparent rhomboid reverses in depth: sometimes one face appears to be in front and sometimes the other. Necker noted that although changes of eye fixation could induce this change in perception, it would also occur quite spontaneously. This celebrated effect is generally illustrated with an isometric cube rather than with Necker's original figure [see top illustration on page 89].

Somewhat later W. J. Sinsteden reported an equally striking effect that must have long been familiar to Netherlanders. If the rotating vanes of a windmill are viewed obliquely or directly from the side, they spontaneously reverse direction if there are no strong clues to the direction of rotation. This effect can be well demonstrated by projecting on a screen the shadow, seen in perspective, of a slowly rotating vane. In the absence of all clues to the direction of rotation the vane will seem to reverse direction spontaneously and the shadow will also at times appear to expand and contract on the plane of the screen. It is important to note that these effects are not perceptual distortions of the retinal image; they are alternative interpretations of the image in terms of possible objects. It is as though the brain entertains alternative hypotheses of what object the eye's image may be representing. When sensory data are inadequate, alternative hypotheses are entertained and the brain never "makes up its mind."

The most puzzling visual illusions are systematic distortions of size or shape. These distortions occur in many quite simple figures. The distortion takes the same direction and occurs to much the same extent in virtually all human observers and probably also in many animals. To psychologists such distortions present an important challenge because they must be explained by a satisfactory theory of normal perception and because they could be important clues to basic perceptual processes.

Distortion Illusions

The simplest distortion illusion was also the first to be studied. This is the horizontal-vertical illusion, which was described by Wilhelm Wundt, assistant to Hermann von Helmholtz at Heidelberg and regarded as the father of experimental psychology. The illusion is simply that a vertical line looks longer than a horizontal line of equal length. Wundt attributed the distortion to asymmetry in the system that moves the eye. Although this explanation has been invoked many times since then, it must be ruled out because the distortions occur in afterimages on the retina and also in normal images artificially stabilized so as to remain stationary on the retina. In addition, distortions can occur in several directions at the same time, which could hardly be owing to eye movements. It is also difficult to see how curvature distortions could be related to eye movements. All the evidence suggests that the distortions originate not in the eyes but in the brain.

Interest in the illusions became general on the publication of several figures showing distortions that could produce errors in the use of optical instruments. These errors were an important concern to physicists and astronomers a centu-

ZÖLLNER ILLUSION was published in 1860 by Johann Zöllner; the first of the special distortion illusions.

ry ago, when photographic and other means of avoiding visual errors were still uncommon. The first of the special distortion figures was the illusion published by Johann Zöllner in 1860 [*see illustration above*]. The same year Johann Poggendorff published his line-displacement illusion [*see middle illustration on page 89*]. A year later Ewald Hering presented the now familiar illusion in which parallel lines appear bowed; the converse illusion was conceived in 1896 by Wundt [*see illustrations on page 91*].

Perhaps the most famous of all distortion illusions is the double-headed-arrow figure devised by Franz Müller-Lyer

and presented in 15 variations in 1889 [*see illustration, page 92*]. This figure is so simple and the distortion is so compelling that it was immediately accepted as a primary target for theory and experiment. All kinds of theories were advanced. Wundt again invoked his eye-movement theory. It was also proposed that the "wings" of the arrowheads drew attention away from the ends of the central line, thus making it expand or contract; that the heads induced a state of empathy in the observer, making him feel as if the central line were being either stretched or compressed; that the distortion is a special case of a supposed general principle that acute angles tend

to be overestimated and obtuse angles underestimated, although why this should be so was left unexplained.

All these theories had a common feature: they were attempts to explain the distortions in terms of the stimulus pattern, without reference to its significance in terms of the perception of objects. There was, however, one quite different suggestion. In 1896 A. Thiery proposed that the distortions are related to the way the eye and brain utilize perspective to judge distances or depths. Thiery regarded the Müller-Lyer arrows as drawings of an object such as a sawhorse, seen in three dimensions; the legs would be going away from the observer

89

in the acute-angled figure and toward him in the obtuse-angled figure. Except for a brief discussion of the "perspective theory" by Robert S. Woodworth in 1938, Thiery's suggestion has seldom been considered until recently.

Woodworth wrote: "In the Müller-Lyer figure the obliques readily suggest perspective and if this is followed one of the vertical lines appears farther away and therefore objectively longer than the other." This quotation brings out the immediate difficulties of developing an adequate theory along such lines. The distortion occurs even when the perspective suggestion is not followed up, because the arrows generally appear flat and yet are still distorted. Moreover, no hint is given of a mechanism responsible for the size changes. An adequate theory based on Thiery's suggestion must show how distortion occurs even though the figures appear flat. It should also indicate the kind of brain mechanisms responsible.

The notion that geometric perspective—the apparent convergence of parallel lines with distance—has a bearing on the problem is borne out by the occurrence of these distortions in photographs of actual scenes in which perspective is pronounced. Two rectangles of equal size look markedly unequal if they are superposed on a photograph of converging railroad tracks [see illustration on page 90]. The upper rectangle in the illustration, which would be the more distant if it were a real object lying between the tracks, looks larger than the lower (and apparently nearer) one. This corresponds to the Ponzo illusion [see bottom illustration on this page].

Similarly, the eye tends to expand the inside corner of a room, as it is seen in a photograph, and to shrink the outside corners of structures [see illustration on page 97]. The effect is just the same as the one in the Müller-Lyer figures, which in fact resemble outline drawings of corners seen in perspective. In both cases the regions indicated by perspective as being distant are expanded, whereas those indicated as being closer are shrunk. The distortions are opposite to the normal shrinking of the retinal image when the distance to an object is increased. Is this effect merely fortuitous, or is it a clue to the origin of the illusions?

Paradoxical Pictures

Before we come to grips with the problem of trying to develop an adequate theory of perspective it will be helpful to consider some curious fea-

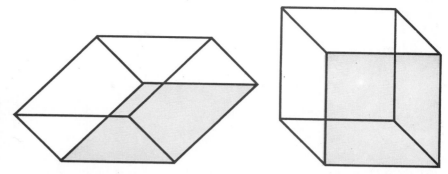

NECKER ILLUSION was devised in 1832 by L. A. Necker, a Swiss naturalist. He noticed that a transparent rhomboid (left) spontaneously reverses in depth. The area lightly tinted in color can appear either as an outer surface or as an inner surface of a transparent box. The illusion is now more usually presented as a transparent cube (right), known as a Necker cube.

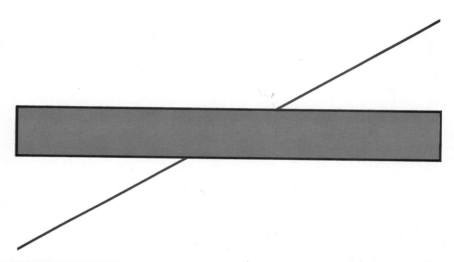

POGGENDORFF ILLUSION was proposed by Johann Poggendorff in 1860, the same year that Johann Zöllner proposed the figure shown on page 88. In Poggendorff's figure the two segments of the diagonal line seem to be offset.

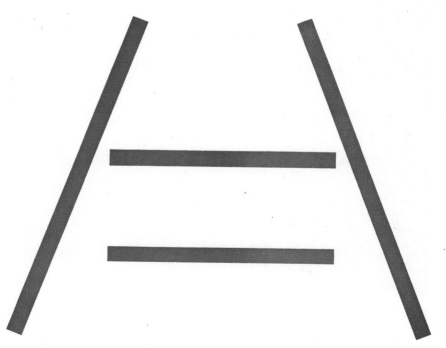

PONZO ILLUSION, also known as the railway lines illusion, was proposed by Mario Ponzo in 1913. It is the prototype of the illusion depicted in the photograph on the following page.

90

ILLUSION INVOLVING PERSPECTIVE is remarkably constant for all human observers. The two rectangles superposed on this photograph of railroad tracks are precisely the same size, yet the top rectangle looks distinctly larger. The author regards this illusion as the prototype of visual distortions in which the perceptual mechanism, involving the brain, attempts to maintain a rough size constancy for similar objects placed at different distances. Since we know that the distant railroad ties are as large as the nearest ones, any object lying between the rails in the middle distance (the upper rectangle) is unconsciously enlarged. Indeed, if the rectangles were real objects lying between the rails, we would know immediately that the more distant was larger.

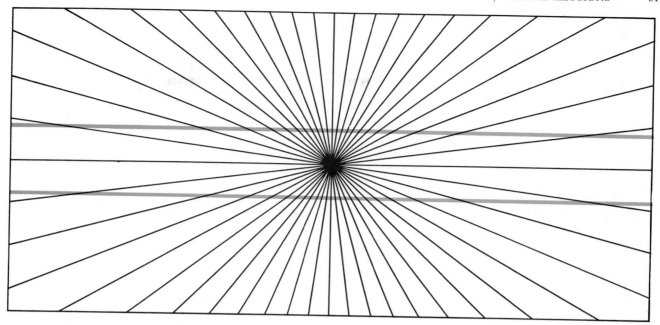

HERING ILLUSION was published in 1861 by Ewald Hering. The horizontal lines are of course straight. Physicists and astron- omers of that period took a lively interest in illusions, being concerned that visual observations might sometimes prove unreliable.

tures of ordinary pictures. Pictures are the traditional material of perceptual research, but all pictures are highly artificial and present special problems to the perceiving brain. In a sense all pictures are impossible because they have a dual reality. They are seen both as patterns of lines lying on a flat background and as objects depicted in a quite different three-dimensional space. No actual object can be both two-dimensional and three-dimensional, yet pictures come close to it. Viewed as patterns they are seen as being two-dimensional; viewed as representing other objects they are seen in a quasi-three-dimensional space. Pictures therefore provide a paradoxical visual input. They are also ambiguous, because the third dimension is never precisely defined.

The Necker cube is an example of a picture in which the depth ambiguity is so great that the brain never settles for a single answer. The fact is, however, that any perspective projection could represent an infinity of three-dimensional shapes. One would think that the perceptual system has an impossible task! Fortunately for us the world of objects does not have infinite variety; there is usually a best bet, and we generally interpret our flat images more or less correctly in terms of the world of objects.

The difficulty of the problem of seeing the third dimension from the two dimensions of a picture, or from the

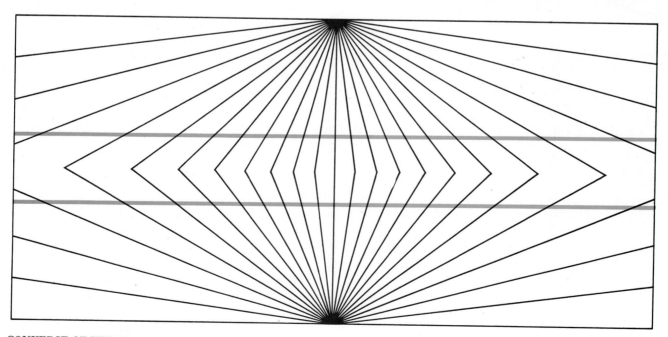

CONVERSE OF HERING ILLUSION was conceived in 1896 by Wilhelm Wundt, who introduced experimentation into psychology. Wundt earlier described the simplest of the visual illusions: that a vertical line looks longer than a horizontal line of equal length.

retinal images of normal objects, is ingeniously brought out by special "impossible pictures" and "impossible objects." They show what happens when clearly incompatible distance information is presented to the eye. The impossible triangle devised by Lionel S. Penrose and R. Penrose cannot be perceptually interpreted as an object in normal three-dimensional space [*see illustration on page 93*]. It is, however, perfectly possible to make actual three-dimensional objects, not mere pictures, that give rise to the same perceptual confusion—provided that they are viewed with only one eye. For example, the Penrose triangle can be built as an open three-dimensional structure [*see top illustration on page 95*] that looks like an impossible closed structure when it is viewed with one eye (or photographed) from exactly the right position [*see bottom illustration on page 95*].

Ordinary pictures are not so very different from obviously impossible pictures. All pictures showing depth are paradoxical: we see them both as being flat (which they really are) and as having a kind of artificial depth that is not quite right. We are not tempted to touch objects shown in a picture through the surface of the picture or in front of it. What happens, however, if we remove the sur-

face? Does the depth paradox of pictures remain?

The Removal of Background

To remove the background for laboratory experiments we make the pictures luminous so that they glow in the dark. In order to deprive the brain of stereoscopic information that would reveal that the pictures are actually flat the pictures are viewed with one eye. They may be wire figures coated with luminous paint or photographic transparencies back-illuminated with an electroluminescent panel. In either case there is no visible background, so that we can discover how much the background is responsible for the depth paradox of pictures, including the illusion figures.

Under these conditions the Müller-Lyer arrows usually look like true corners according to their perspective. They may even be indistinguishable from actual luminous corners. The figures are not entirely stable: they sometimes reverse spontaneously in depth. Nonetheless, they usually appear according to their perspective and without the paradoxical depth of pictures with a background. The distortions are still present. The figure that resembles a dou-

ble-headed arrow looks like an outside corner and seems shrunk, whereas the figure with the arrowheads pointing the wrong way looks like an inside corner and is expanded. Now, however, the paradox has disappeared and the figures look like true corners. With a suitable apparatus one can point out their depth as if they were normal three-dimensional objects.

Having removed the paradox, it is possible to measure, by quite direct means, the apparent distance of any selected part of the figures. This we do by using the two eyes to serve as a range finder for indicating the apparent depth of the figure, which is visible to only one eye. The back-illuminated picture is placed behind a polarizing filter so that one eye is prevented from seeing the picture by a second polarizing filter oriented at right angles to the first. Both eyes, however, are allowed to see one or more small movable reference lights that are optically introduced into the picture by means of a half-silvered mirror set at 45 degrees to the line of sight. The distance of these lights is given by stereoscopic vision, that is, by the convergence angle of the eyes; by moving the lights so that they seem to coincide with the apparent distance of selected parts of the picture we can plot the visual space of the observer in three dimensions [*see top illustration on page 94*].

When this plotting is done for various angles of the "fin," or arrowhead line, in the Müller-Lyer illusion figure, it becomes clear that the figures are perceived as inside and outside corners. The illusion of depth conforms closely to the results obtained when the magnitude of the illusion is independently measured by asking subjects to select comparison lines that match the apparent length of the central line between two kinds of arrowhead [*see bottom illustration on page 94*]. In the latter experiment the figures are drawn on a normally textured background, so that they appear flat.

The two experiments show that when the background is removed, depth very closely follows the illusion for the various fin angles. The similarity of the plotted results provides evidence of a remarkably close connection between the illusion as it occurs when depth is not seen and the depth that is seen when the background is removed. This suggests that Thiery was essentially correct: perspective can somehow create distortions. What is odd is that perspective produces the distortions according to *indicated* perspective depth even when depth is *not* consciously seen.

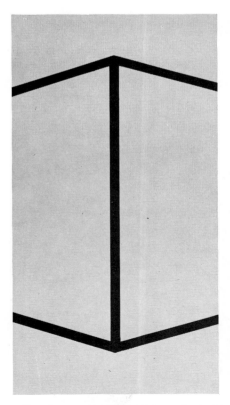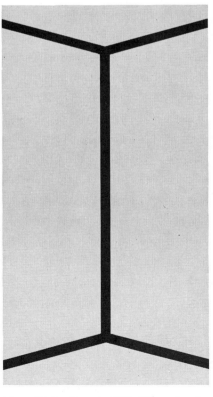

MÜLLER-LYER ILLUSION was devised by Franz Müller-Lyer in 1889. Many theories were subsequently invoked in an attempt to explain why reversed arrowheads (*right*) seem to lengthen a connecting shaft whereas normal arrowheads seem to shrink the shaft (*left*).

Size Constancy

The next step is to look for some perceptual mechanism that could produce this relation between perspective and apparent size. A candidate that should have been obvious many years ago is size constancy. This phenomenon was clearly described in 1637 by René Descartes in his *Dioptrics*. "It is not the absolute size of images [in the eyes] that counts," he wrote. "Clearly they are 100 times bigger [in area] when objects are very close than when they are 10 times farther away, but they do not make us see the objects 100 times bigger. On the contrary, they seem almost the same size, at any rate as we are not deceived by too great a distance."

We know from many experiments that Descartes is quite right. What happens, however, when distance information, such as perspective, is presented to the eye but two components of the scene, one of which should be shrunk by dis-tance, are the same size? Could it be that perspective presented on a flat plane triggers the brain to compensate for the expected shrinking of the images with distance even though there is no shrinking for which to compensate? If some such thing happens, it is easy to see why figures that suggest perspective can give rise to distortions. This would provide the start of a reasonable theory of illusions. Features indicated as being distant would be expanded, which is just what we find, at least for the Müller-Lyer and the Ponzo figures.

It is likely that this approach to the problem was not developed until recently because, although size constancy was quite well known, it has always been assumed that it simply follows apparent distance in all circumstances. Moreover, it has not been sufficiently realized how very odd pictures are as visual inputs. They are highly atypical and should be studied as a special case, being both paradoxical and ambiguous.

Size constancy is traditionally identified with an effect known as Emmert's law. This effect can be explained by a simple experiment involving the apparent size of afterimages in vision. If one can obtain a good afterimage (preferably by briefly illuminating a test figure with an electronic flash lamp), one can "project" it on screens or walls located at various distances. The afterimage will appear almost twice as large with each doubling of distance, even though the size of the image from the flash remains constant. It is important to note, however, that there *is* a change in retinal stimulation for each screen or wall lying at a different distance; their images *do* vary. It is possible that the size change of the afterimage is due not so much to a brain mechanism that changes its scale as to its size on the retina with respect to the size of the screen on which it appears to lie. Before we go any further, it is essential to discover whether Emmert's law is due merely to the relation between the areas covered by the afterimage and the screen, or whether the visual information of distance changes the size of the afterimage by some kind of internal scaling. This presents us with a tricky experimental problem.

As it turns out, there is a simple solution. We can use the ambiguous depth phenomenon of the Necker cube to establish whether Emmert's law is due to a central scaling by the brain or is merely an effect of relative areas of stimulation of the retina. When we see a Necker cube that is drawn on paper reverse in depth, there is no appreciable size change. When the cube is presented on a textured background, it occupies the paradoxical depth of all pictures with visible backgrounds; it does not change in size when it reverses in pseudo-depth.

What happens, however, if we remove the cube's background? The effect is dramatic and entirely repeatable: with each reversal in depth the cube changes its apparent shape, even though there is no change in the retinal image. Whichever face appears to be more distant always appears to be the larger. The use of depth-ambiguous figures in this way makes it possible to separate what happens when the pattern of stimulation of the retina is changed. The answer is that at least part of size constancy, and of Emmert's law, is due to a central size-scaling mechanism in the brain that responds to changes in apparent distance although the retinal stimulation is unchanged.

Apparent size, then, is evidently established in two ways. It can be estab-

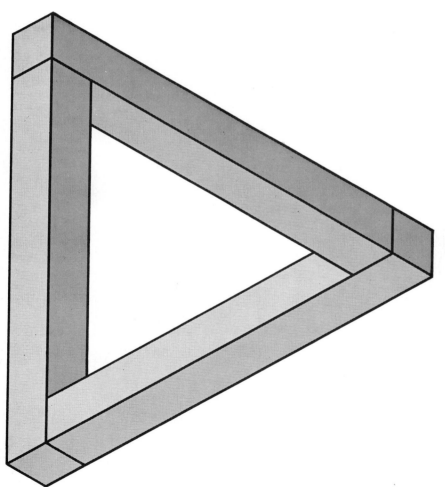

IMPOSSIBLE TRIANGLE was devised by Lionel S. Penrose and R. Penrose of University College London. It is logically consistent over restricted regions but is nonsensical overall. The author sees a certain similarity between such impossible figures and ordinary photographs, which provide the illusion of a third dimension even though they are flat.

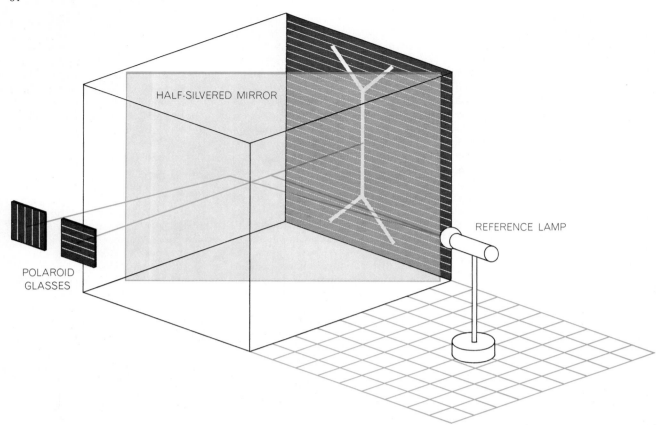

APPARATUS FOR STUDYING ILLUSIONS was devised by the author. The objective is to present figures such as the Müller-Lyer arrows with the background removed so that the figures seem suspended in space. Under these conditions the Müller-Lyer arrows generally look like true corners. The subject can adjust a small light so that it appears to lie at the same depth as any part of the figure. The light, which the subject sees in three-dimensional space with both eyes, is superposed on the illuminated figure by means of a half-silvered mirror. A polarizing filter is placed over the figure and the subject wears polarizing glasses that allow him to see the figure with only one eye. Thus he has no way of telling whether the figure is really two-dimensional or three-dimensional.

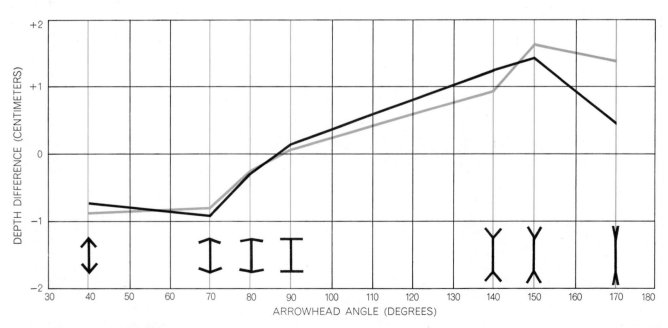

QUANTITATIVE MEASUREMENT OF ILLUSION produced the results plotted here for Müller-Lyer arrows. The black curve shows the average results for 20 subjects who were asked to select a comparison line that matched the length of a central shaft to which were attached arrowheads set at the angles indicated. When arrowheads were set at less than 90 degrees, the comparison lines were as much as one centimeter shorter. When the arrowhead was set at 150 degrees, the comparison line was more than 1.5 centimeters longer. The colored curve shows the maximum depth difference perceived for the same set of arrows when displayed, with the background removed, in the apparatus shown in the illustration at the top of the page. The two curves match quite closely except at the extreme setting of 170 degrees, when the figure no longer resembles a true corner when presented in the light box.

lished purely by apparent distance. It can also be established directly by visual depth features, such as perspective in two-dimensional pictures, even though depth is not seen because it is countermanded by competing depth information such as a visible background. When atypical depth features are present, size scaling is established inappropriately and we have a corresponding distortion illusion.

The size scaling established directly by depth features (giving systematic distortions when it is established inappropriately) we may call "depth-cue scaling." It is remarkably consistent and independent of the observer's perceptual "set." The other system is quite different and more subtle, being only indirectly related to the prevailing retinal information. It is evidently linked to the interpretation of the retinal image in terms of what object it represents. When it appears as a different object, the scaling changes at once to suit the alternative object. If we regard the seeing of an object as a hypothesis, suggested (but never strictly proved) by the image, we may call the system "depth-hypothesis scaling," because it changes with each change of the hypothesis of what object is represented by the image. When the hypothesis is wrong, we have an illusion that may be dramatic. Such alternations in hypotheses underlie the changes in direction, and even size, that occur when one watches the shadow of a rotating vane.

Observers in Motion

The traditional distortion illusions can be attributed to errors in the setting of the depth-cue scaling system, which arise when figures or objects have misleading depth cues, particularly perspective on a flat plane. Although these illusions might occasionally bother investigators making visual measurements, they are seldom a serious hazard. The other kind of illusion—incorrect size-scaling due to an error in the prevailing perceptual hypothesis—can be serious in unfamiliar conditions or when there is little visual information available, as in space flight. It can also be important in driving a car at night or in landing an airplane under conditions of poor visibility. Illusions are most hazardous when the observer is in rapid motion, because then even a momentary error may lead to disaster.

So far little work has been done on the measurement of illusions experienced by observers who are in motion with respect to their surroundings. The ex-

ACTUAL IMPOSSIBLE TRIANGLE was constructed by the author and his colleagues. The only requirement is that it be viewed with one eye (or photographed) from exactly the right position. The top photograph shows that two arms do not actually meet. When viewed in a certain way (*bottom*), they seem to come together and the illusion is complete.

perimental difficulties involved in making such measurements are severe; nevertheless, we have been tackling the problem with support from the U.S. Air Force. The equipment, which is fairly elaborate, can move the observer with controlled velocity and acceleration through various visual environments, including the blackness of space (with or without artificial stars presented optically at infinite distance).

We measure the observer's visual sense of size constancy as he is moving by having him look at a projected display that changes size as he approaches or recedes from it. As he moves away from it, the display is made to expand in size; as he approaches it, the display is made to shrink. The change in size is adjusted until, to the moving observer, the display appears fixed in size. If there were no perceptual mechanism for constancy scaling, the size of the display would have to be adjusted so that its image on the observer's retina would be the same size regardless of his distance from it. If, at the other extreme, the size-

constancy effect were complete, we could leave the display unchanged and it would still appear to be the same size regardless of its actual distance from the observer. In practice some size change between these limits provides the illusion of an unchanging display, and this gives us a measure of the size-constancy effect as the observer is moved about.

We find that when the observer is in complete darkness, watching a display that is projected from the back onto a large screen, there is no measurable size constancy when the observer is moving at a fixed speed. When he is accelerated, size constancy does appear but it may be wildly wrong. In particular, if he interprets his movement incorrectly, either in direction or in amount, size constancy usually fails and can even work in reverse. This is rather similar to the reversal of size constancy with reversal of the depth of the luminous Necker cube. In the conditions of space, perception may be dominated by the prevailing hypothesis of distance and velocity. If either is wrong, as it may well be for

lack of reliable visual information, the astronaut may suffer visual illusions that could be serious.

The Nonvisual in Vision

Visual perception involves "reading" from retinal images a host of characteristics of objects that are not represented directly by the images in the eyes. The image does not convey directly many important characteristics of objects: whether they are hard or soft, heavy or light, hot or cold. Nonvisual characteristics must somehow be associated with the visual image, by individual learning or conceivably through heredity, for objects to be recognized from their images. Psychologists now believe individual perceptual learning is very important for associating the nonoptical properties of objects with their retinal images. Such learning is essential for perception; without it one would have mere stimulus-response behavior.

Perception seems to be a matter of looking up information that has been stored about objects and how they behave in various situations. The retinal image does little more than select the relevant stored data. This selection is rather like looking up entries in an encyclopedia: behavior is determined by the contents of the entry rather than by the stimulus that provoked the search. We can think of perception as being essentially the selection of the most appropriate stored hypothesis according to current sensory data.

Now, a look-up system of this kind has great advantages over a control system that responds simply to current input. If stored information is used, behavior can continue in the temporary absence of relevant information, or when there is inadequate information to provide precise control of behavior directly. This advantage has important implications for any possible perceptual system, including any future "seeing machine": a robot equipped with artificial eyes and a computer and designed to control vehicles or handle objects by means of artificial limbs. Even when enough direct sensory information is available for determining the important characteristics of surrounding objects (which is seldom the case), it would require a rate of data transmission in excess of that provided by the human nervous system (or current computers) to enable a robot to behave appropriately. Hence there are strong general design reasons for supposing that any effective seeing system—whether biological or man-made—should use current sensory

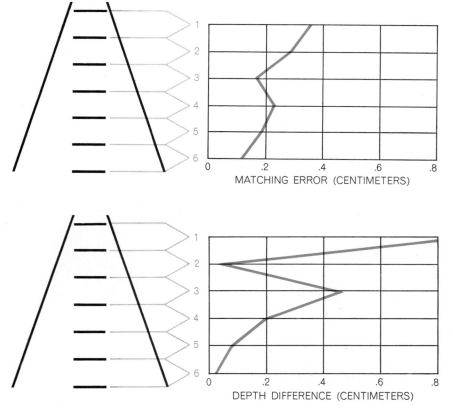

RAILWAY LINES ILLUSION can also be studied quantitatively. The methods are the same as those described in the bottom illustration on page 94. Subjects were presented with a horizontal line at one of the indicated positions and asked to select a second line that seemed to match it in length. The matching error for different pairs is plotted in the top curve. Pairs of lines were then presented in the apparatus shown at the top of page 94 and the subjects adjusted the light to match the apparent depth of each line. Under these conditions (*bottom curve*) the illusion of depth is much more dependent on where a given pair of lines is located with respect to the "rails," but the trend of the top curve is preserved.

THEORY OF MÜLLER-LYER ILLUSION favored by the author suggests that the eye unconsciously interprets the arrow-like figures as three-dimensional skeleton structures, resembling either an outside (*left*) or inside corner (*right*) of a physical structure. A perceptual mechanism evidently shrinks the former and enlarges the latter to compensate for distortion caused by perspective.

information for selecting preformed hypotheses, or models, representing important features of the external world of objects as opposed to controlling behavior directly from sensory inputs.

If we consider the problems of storing information about objects, it soon becomes clear that it would be most uneconomical to store an independent model of each object for every distance and orientation it might occupy in surrounding space. It would be far more economical to store only typical characteristics of objects and to use current sensory information to adjust the selected model to fit the prevailing situation.

The model must be continually scaled for distance and orientation if the owner of the perceptual system is to interact with the object.

We might guess that depth-cue scaling represents this adjustment of the selected model in the light of the available depth information. When the available information is inappropriate (as in the case of perspective features on a flat plane), it will scale the perceptual model wrongly. There will be a systematic error: a distortion illusion due to inappropriate depth-cue scaling. There will also be errors—possibly very large ones— whenever a wrong model is selected. We

see this happening in a repeatable way in the ambiguous figures, such as the luminous Necker cube, that change shape with each depth reversal even though the sensory input is unchanged.

If this general account of perception as essentially a look-up system is correct, we should expect illusions similar to our own to arise in any effective perceptual system, including future robots. Illusions are not caused by any limitation of our brain. They are the result of the imperfect solutions available to any data-handling system faced with the problem of establishing the reality of objects from ambiguous images.

Multistability in Perception

by Fred Attneave
December 1971

*Some kinds of pictures and geometric forms
spontaneously shift in their principal aspect
when they are looked at steadily. The reason
probably lies in the physical organization
of the perceptual system*

Pictures and geometric figures that spontaneously change in appearance have a peculiar fascination. A classic example is the line drawing of a transparent cube on this page. When you first look at the cube, one of its faces seems to be at the front and the other at the back. Then if you look steadily at the drawing for a while, it will suddenly reverse in depth and what was the back face now is the front one. The two orientations will alternate spontaneously; sometimes one is seen, sometimes the other, but never both at once.

When we look steadily at a picture or a geometric figure, the information received by the retina of the eye is relatively constant and what the brain perceives usually does not change. If the figure we are viewing happens to be an ambiguous figure, what the brain perceives may change swiftly without any change in the message it is receiving from the eye. The psychologist is interested in these perceptual alternations not as a curiosity but for what they can tell us about the nature of the perceptual system.

It is the business of the brain to represent the outside world. Perceiving is not just sensing but rather an effect of sensory input on the representational system. An ambiguous figure provides the viewer with an input for which there are two or more possible representations

that are quite different and about equally good, by whatever criteria the perceptual system employs. When alternative representations or descriptions of the input are equally good, the perceptual system will sometimes adopt one and sometimes another. In other words, the perception is multistable. There are a number of physical systems that have the same kind of multistable characteristics, and a comparison of multistability in physical and perceptual situations may yield some significant clues to the basic processes of perception. First, however, let us consider several kinds of situations that produce perceptual multistability.

Figure-ground reversal has long been used in puzzle pictures. It is often illustrated by a drawing that can be seen as either a goblet or a pair of faces [*see top illustration on next page*]. This figure was introduced by the Danish psychologist Edgar Rubin. Many of the drawings and etchings of the Dutch artist Maurits C. Escher are particularly elegant examples of figure-ground reversal [*see bottom illustration on next page*]. These examples are somewhat misleading because they suggest that the components of a figure-ground reversal must be familiar objects. Actually you can make a perfectly good reversing figure by scribbling a meaningless line down the middle of a circle. The line will be seen as a contour or a boundary, and its appearance is quite different depending on which side of the contour is seen as the inside and which as the outside [*see top illustration on page 101*]. The difference is so fundamental that if a person first sees one side of the contour as the object or figure, the probability of his recognizing the same contour when it is shown as part of the other half of the field is little better than if he had never seen it at all; this was demonstrated by Rubin in a

classic study of the figure-ground dichotomy.

Note that it is quite impossible to see both sides of the contour as figures at the same time. Trying to think of the halves as two pieces of a jigsaw puzzle that fit together does not help; the pieces are still seen alternately and not simultaneously. What seems to be involved here is an attribution of surface properties to some parts of a field but not to others. This kind of distinction is of central importance in the problem of scene analysis that Marvin Lee Minsky of the Massachusetts Institute of Technology and other investigators of computer simulation have been grappling with lately. The figure made by drawing a line through a circle is actually tristable rather than bistable; the third possibility is being able to see the line as a thing in itself, as a twisted wire rather than the boundary of a figure.

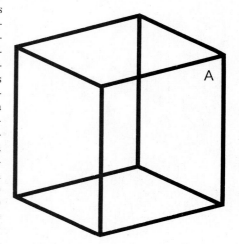

NECKER CUBE, a classic example of perspective reversal, is named after Louis Albert Necker, who in 1832 reported that line drawings of crystals appeared to reverse in depth spontaneously. Corner *A* alternates from front to back when gazed at steadily.

PAINTING BY SALVADOR DALI on the opposite page is an example of the use of ambiguous figures by a serious artist. The illustration is a portion of "Slave Market with Apparition of the Invisible Bust of Voltaire." It is reproduced with the permission of the Dali Museum in Cleveland. When viewed at close range, the figures of people predominate; when viewed at a distance, bust of Voltaire becomes apparent.

REVERSIBLE GOBLET was introduced by Edgar Rubin in 1915 and is still a favorite demonstration of figure-ground reversal. Either a goblet or a pair of silhouetted faces is seen.

WOODCUT by Maurits C. Escher titled "Circle Limit IV (Heaven and Hell)" is a striking example of both figure-ground reversal and competition between rival-object schemata. Devils and angels alternate repeatedly but neither seems to be able to overpower the other.

The point of basic interest in figure-ground reversal is that one line can have two shapes. Since an artist's line drawing is readily identifiable with the object it is supposed to portray, and since a shape has much the same appearance whether it is white on black, black on white or otherwise colored, many workers have suggested that the visual system represents or encodes objects primarily in terms of their contours. As we have seen, however, a contour can be part of two shapes. The perceptual representation of a contour is specific to which side is regarded as the figure and which as the ground. Shape may be invariant over a black-white reversal, but it is not invariant over an inside-outside reversal.

Under natural conditions many factors cooperate to determine the figure-ground relationship, and ambiguity is rare. For example, if one area encloses another, the enclosed area is likely to be seen as the figure. If a figure is divided into two areas, the smaller of the areas is favored as the figure [see middle illustration on opposite page].

The visual field usually consists of many objects that overlap and occlude one another. The perceptual system has an impressive ability to segregate and sort such objects from one another. Along with distinguishing figure from ground, the system must group the fragments of visual information it receives into separate sets that correspond to real objects. Elements that are close to one another or alike or homogeneous in certain respects tend to be grouped together. When alternative groupings are about equally good, ambiguity results.

For example, if a set of dots are aligned, the perceptual system tends to group them on the basis of this regularity. When the dots are in regular rows and columns, they will be seen as rows if the vertical distance between the dots is greater than the horizontal distance, and they will seem to be in columns if the horizontal distance is greater than the vertical distance. When the spacing both ways is the same, the two groupings—rows and columns—tend to alternate. What is interesting and rather puzzling about the situation is that vertical and horizontal groupings are competitive at all. Geometrically the dots form both rows and columns; why, then, does seeing them in rows preclude seeing them in columns at the same moment? Whatever the reason is in terms of perceptual mechanisms, the principle involved appears to be a general one: When elements are grouped perceptually, they are partitioned; they are not simultaneously cross-classified.

A related case of multistability involves apparent movement. Four lights are arranged in a square so that the diagonally opposite pairs of lights flash simultaneously. If the two diagonal pairs of lights are flashed alternately, it will appear to an observer as if the lights are moving. The apparent motion can take either of two forms: the observer will see motion along the vertical sides of the square, with two pairs of lights, one on the left and the other on the right, moving in opposite directions up and down, or he will see two sets of lights moving back and forth horizontally in opposite directions. If he continues to watch for a while, the motion will switch from vertical to horizontal and vice versa. When one apparent motion gives way to the other, the two perceptions are subjectively so different that the unsuspecting observer is likely to believe there has been some physical change. Apparent movement involves the grouping of events that are separated in both space and time, but the events so grouped are represented as having a common identity; specifically it appears that the same light has moved to a new place. The rivalry between the horizontal and the vertical movement is thus easier to comprehend than the rivalry between rows and columns of dots: if the representational system reflects the laws of the world it represents, the same object cannot traverse two different paths simultaneously or occupy two different places at once.

Ambiguities of grouping are also evident in fields of repetitive elements such as a floor with hexagonal tiles or even a matrix of squares drawn on paper [*see top illustration on page 105*]. If one stares at the matrix for a while, certain subsets of the squares will spontaneously organize themselves into simple figures. With voluntary effort one can attain fairly stable perceptions of rather complex figures. The most readily seen figures, however, tend to be simple, compact and symmetrical.

Some of the most striking and amusing ambiguous figures are pictures (which may or may not involve figure-ground reversal) that can be seen as either of two familiar objects, for example a duck or a rabbit, a young girl or an old woman, and a man or a girl [*see illustrations on next two pages*]. What is meant by "familiar" in this context is that the visual inputs can be matched to some acquired or learned schemata of classes of objects. Just what such class

REVERSING FIGURE can be made by scribbling a line through a circle. The shape of the contour formed depends on which side of the line is regarded as part of the figure.

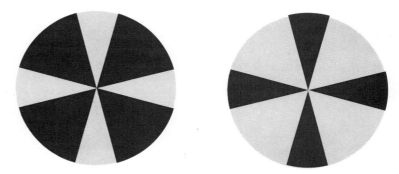

LARGER AREA of a figure is more likely to be seen as the background. Either the large crosses or the small ones may be seen as the figure, but the small crosses have the advantage.

REVERSAL AND ROTATION occur simultaneously in this ingenious design. When the stylized maple-leaf pattern alternates between black and white, it also rotates 90 degrees.

RABBIT-DUCK FIGURE was used in 1900 by psychologist Joseph Jastrow as an example of rival-schemata ambiguity. When it is a rabbit, the face looks to the right; when it is a duck, the face looks to the left. It is difficult to see both duck and rabbit at the same time.

YOUNG GIRL–OLD WOMAN was brought to the attention of psychologists by Edwin G. Boring in 1930. Created by cartoonist W. E. Hill, it was originally published in *Puck* in 1915 as "My Wife and My Mother-in-law." The young woman's chin is the old woman's nose.

schemata consist of—whether they are like composite photographs or like lists of properties—remains a matter of controversy. In any case the process of identification must involve some kind of matching between the visual input and a stored schema. If two schemata match the visual input about equally well, they compete for its perceptual interpretation; sometimes one of the objects is seen and sometimes the other. Therefore one reason ambiguity exists is that a single input can be matched to different schemata.

In certain ambiguous figures we can clearly see the nature of the positive feedback loop that accounts for the "locking in," or stabilization, of one or another aspect of the figure at any given time. For example, if in the young girl–old woman figure a certain line is tentatively identified as a nose, then a line below it must be the mouth and the shapes above must be the eyes. These partial identifications mutually support one another to form a stable perception of an old woman. If, however, the line we started with is seen as a chin instead of as a nose, then the perception formed is that of a young woman. The identification of wholes and of parts will likewise be reciprocally supportive, contributing further to the locking-in process.

Why one aspect of an ambiguous figure, once it is locked in, should ever give way to the other is a fundamental question. Indeed, a person can look for quite a long time at an ambiguous figure and see only one aspect of it. Robert Leeper of the University of Oregon showed that if a subject was first exposed to a version of the figure that was biased in favor of one of the interpretations, he would almost always see only that aspect in the ambiguous version. Not until the other aspect was pointed out would the figure spontaneously alternate. It is only after the input has made contact with both schemata that they become competitive. Making the initial contact and the associated organization must entail a type of learning.

Ambiguities of depth characterize a large class of multistable figures, of which the cube on page 99 is the most familiar. In 1832 a Swiss geologist, Louis Albert Necker, pointed out that a drawing of a transparent rhomboid crystal could be seen in either of two different ways, that the viewer often experiences "a sudden and involuntary change in the apparent position of a crystal or solid represented by an engraved figure." Necker concluded that the aspect seen depends entirely on the point of

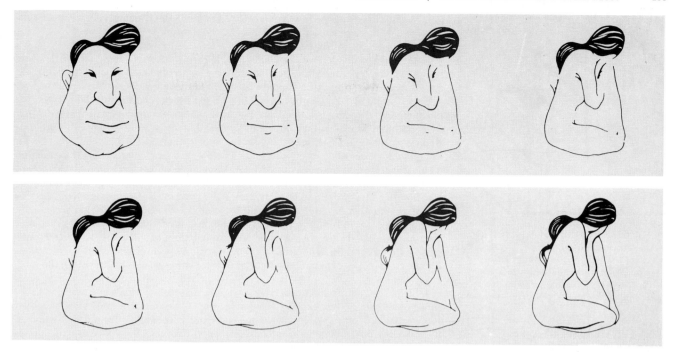

MAN-GIRL FIGURES are part of a series of progressively modified drawings devised by Gerald Fisher in 1967. He found that the last drawing in the top row has equal probability of being seen as a man or as a girl. Perception of middle pictures can be biased toward the man by viewing series in sequence beginning from top left and can be biased toward the girl by starting from bottom right.

fixation, "the point of distinct vision" being perceived as the closer. Although the fixation point is indeed important, it has been shown that depth reversal will readily occur without eye movement.

If we want to understand how depth relationships can be multistable, we must first consider the more general question of how the perceptual system can derive a three-dimensional representation from a two-dimensional drawing. A straight line in the outside world casts a straight line on the retina. A given straight line on the retina, however, could be the image of any one of an infinite number of external lines, and not necessarily straight lines, that lie in a common plane with one another and the eye. The image on a single retina is always two-dimensional, exactly as a photograph is. We should not be surprised, therefore, that depth is sometimes ambiguous; it is far more remarkable that the perceptual system is able to select a particular orientation for a line segment (or at worst to vacillate between two or three orientations) out of the infinite number of legitimate possibilities that exist.

On what basis does the system perform this feat? According to the Gestalt psychologists the answer is to be found in a principle of *Prägnanz:* one perceives the "best" figure that is consistent with a given image. For most practical purposes "best" may be taken to mean "simplest." The advantage of this interpretation is that it is easier to find objective standards for complexity than for such qualities as being "best." One observes a particular configuration of lines on paper, such as the Necker cube, and assigns a three-dimensional orientation to the lines such that the whole becomes a cube (although an infinite number of noncubical forms could project the same form) because a cube is the simplest of the possibilities. In a cube the lines (edges) are all the same length; they take only three directions, and the angles they form are all equal and right

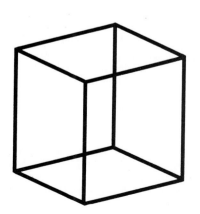
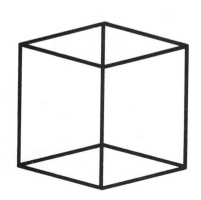
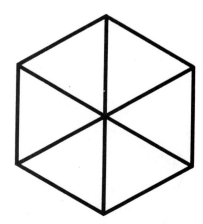

PROJECTIONS OF A CUBE onto a two-dimensional surface are nearly always seen in depth when they resemble the Necker cube (*left*). As the projection becomes simpler and more regular it is more likely to be seen as a flat figure, such as a hexagon (*right*).

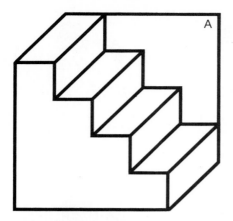

SCHRÖDER STAIRS line drawing is another classic example of perspective reversal. Corner *A* is part of the rear wall when the staircase goes up to the left; when reversal occurs, corner *A* becomes part of the front wall and the bottom of the stairway is seen.

angles. No other interpretation of the figure, including the two-dimensional aspect itself, is as simple and regular. In cases of reversible perspective two maximally simple tridimensional constructions are permissible, each being symmetrical with the other in depth.

If this reasoning is correct, simple projections of a given solid should be perceived as being flat more often than complex projections of the same solid. Julian Hochberg and his colleagues at Cornell University studied various two-dimensional projections of a cube and other regular solids [*see bottom illustra-*

tion on preceding page]. Relatively complex projections are nearly always perceived in depth. A figure such as a regular hexagon divided into equilateral triangles, which is simple and regular in two dimensions, stays two-dimensional because seeing it as a cube does not make it any simpler. Intermediate figures become tristable; they are sometimes seen as being flat and sometimes as being one or another aspect of a cube. The measure of complexity devised by Hochberg and Virginia Brooks involved the number of continuous lines in the figure, the number of interior angles and the number of different angles. This measure predicted with considerable accuracy the proportion of the time that a figure was seen in depth rather than as being flat.

I have been emphasizing the importance of simplicity, but it is obvious that familiarity also plays an important role in instances of ambiguous depth. The two factors are hard to disentangle. Simple structures are experienced with great frequency, particularly in man-made environments. As Alvin G. Goldstein of the University of Missouri has shown by experiment, within limits a nonsense shape is judged to be simpler the more often it is experienced. In my view familiarity and simplicity become functionally equivalent in the perceptual system when a given input corresponds closely to a schema that is already well established by experience and can therefore be encoded or described (in the lan-

guage of the nervous system) most simply in terms of that schema.

Depth reversal does not occur only with two-dimensional pictures. As the Austrian physicist and philosopher Ernst Mach pointed out, the perspective of many real objects will reverse when the object is viewed steadily with one eye. A transparent glass half-filled with water is a particularly dramatic example, but it requires considerable effort to achieve the reversal and the stability of the reversal is precarious. Mach discovered an easier reversal that is actually more instructive. Take a white card or a small piece of stiff paper and fold it once along its longitudinal axis [*see bottom illustration on this page*]. Place the folded card or paper in front of you on a table so that it makes a rooflike structure. Close one eye and view the card steadily for a while from directly above. It will reverse (or you can make it reverse) so that it appears as if the fold is at the bottom instead of the top. Now view the card with one eye from above at about a 45-degree angle so that the front of the folded card can be seen. After a few seconds the card will reverse and stand up on end like an open book with the inside toward you. If the card is asymmetrically illuminated and is seen in correct perspective, it will appear to be more or less white all over, as it is in reality, in spite of the fact that the illuminated plane reflects more light than the shadowed one. When the reversal occurs, the shadowed plane looks gray instead of white and the illuminated plane may appear luminous. In the perspective reversal the perceptual mechanism that preserves the constancy of reflectance is fooled; in order to maintain the relation between light source and the surfaces the perceptual system makes corrections that are erroneous because they are based on incorrect information.

Another remarkable phenomenon involving the folded card seems to have escaped Mach's notice. Recently Murray Eden of the Massachusetts Institute of Technology found that if after you make the folded card reverse you move your head slowly from side to side, the card will appear to rock back and forth quite as convincingly as if it were physically in motion. The explanation, very roughly, is that the mechanism that makes allowance for head movements, so that still objects appear still even though the head moves, is operating properly but on erroneous premises when the perspective is reversed. The perceived rocking of the card is exactly what would

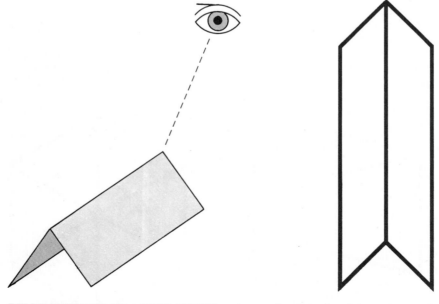

DEPTH REVERSAL OF A REAL OBJECT can occur when it is viewed from above with one eye, an effect discovered by Ernst Mach. When a folded card is viewed from above and the front, it will appear to stand on end like an open book when it reverses. The same kind of depth reversal occurs with a simple line drawing of a folded card (*above right*).

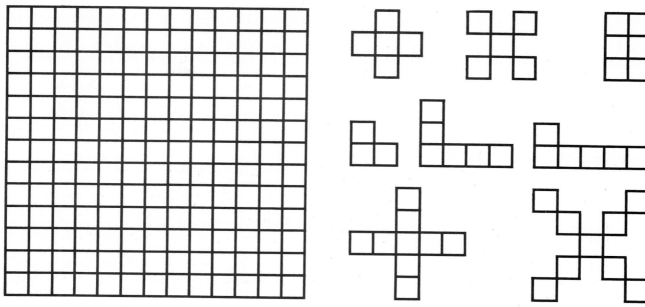

FIGURAL GROUPINGS occur when one stares at a matrix of squares. The simple figures organize themselves spontaneously and with effort more complex figures can be perceived. Some figures, however, are so complex that they are difficult to maintain.

ALIGNED DOTS fall into a regular pattern when viewed. Depending on the spacing, dots can be seen as columns (*left*) or as rows (*middle*). When vertical and horizontal spacing are equal, dots can be seen as rows or columns but not as both at the same time.

EQUILATERAL TRIANGLES appear in one of three orientations depending on the dominant axis of symmetry (*left*). Usually all point in the same direction at one time, although the direction can change spontaneously. The scalene triangles (*middle*) fluctuate in orientation even though they are asymmetrical because they can also appear as isosceles or right triangles that point down or up. The same shape can be seen as either diamonds or tilted squares (*right*) depending on the orientation of the local reference system.

have to happen objectively if the card were really reversed to account for the sequence of retinal images accompanying head movement. What is remarkable about this is not that the mechanism can be wrong but rather that it can function so efficiently as a "lightning calculator" of complex problems in projective geometry and compensate so completely to maintain the perceived orientation. It seems to me that this capacity is a good argument for the existence of some kind of working model of three-dimensional space within the nervous system that solves problems of this type by analogue operations. Indeed, the basic concept of *Prägnanz*, of a system that finds its way to stable states that are simple by tri-dimensional criteria, is difficult to explain without also postulating a neural analogue model of three-dimensional space. We have no good theory at present of the nature of the neural organization that might subserve such a model.

A few years ago I stumbled on a principle of ambiguity that is different from any we have been considering. While planning an experiment on perceptual grouping I drew a number of equilateral triangles. After looking at them for a time I noticed that they kept changing in their orientation, sometimes pointing one way, sometimes another and sometimes a third way [*see bottom illustration on preceding page*]. The basis for this tristable ambiguity seems to be that the perceptual system can represent symmetry about only one axis at a time, even though an equilateral triangle is objectively symmetrical about three axes. In other words, an equilateral triangle is always perceived as being merely an isosceles triangle in some particular orientation. Compare any two sides or any two angles of an equilateral triangle and you will find that the triangle immediately points in the direction around which the sides and angles are symmetrical. When a group of equilateral triangles points upward, the triangles cease to fluctuate; the perceptual system strongly prefers the vertical axis of symmetry. Indeed, any perceived axis of symmetry seems to have the character of a locally rotated vertical.

When scalene triangles (triangles with three unequal sides) are grouped together with their corresponding sides parallel, they also appear to fluctuate in orientation after a brief inspection [*see bottom illustration on preceding page*]. This is at first puzzling since they have no axes of symmetry at all. The answer to the puzzle involves the third dimension: When the triangles are seen to point in a given direction, they simultaneously go into depth in such a way that they look like isosceles triangles seen at an angle. Perspective reversal doubles the possibilities, so that there are six ways the scalene triangles can be seen as isosceles. The same triangles may also be seen as right triangles in depth, with the obtuse angles most easily becoming the right angles.

These observations begin to make sense if we suppose the perceptual system employs something quite like a Cartesian coordinate system to locate and describe things in space. (To call the system Cartesian is really putting the issue backward, since Descartes clearly took the primary perceptual directions of up-down, left-right and front-back as his reference axes.) The multistable states of triangles thus appear to involve simple relations between the figure and the reference system. The reference system may be tilted or rotated locally by the perceptual system and produce the apparent depth or orientation of the triangles.

In the same way we can explain how the same shape can appear to be so different when it is seen as a square or as a diamond. The square is perceived as having horizontal and vertical axes along its sides; the diamond is perceived as being symmetrical about a vertical axis running through opposite corners. Yet in certain kinds of grouping the perceptual axes can be locally rotated and the diamond can look like a tilted square [*see bottom illustration on preceding page*].

It should be evident by now that some principle of *Prägnanz*, or minimum complexity, runs as a common thread through most of the cases. It seems likely that the perceptual machinery is a teleological system that is "motivated" to represent the outside world as economically as possible, within the constraints of the input received and the limitations of its encoding capabilities.

A good reason for invoking the concept of multistability to characterize figural ambiguity is that we know a great deal about multistable physical and electronic systems and may hope to apply some of this knowledge to the perceptual processes. The multistable behavior of the perceptual system displays two notable characteristics. The first is that at any one moment only one aspect of the ambiguous figure can be seen; mixtures or intermediate states occur fleetingly if at all. The second is that the different percepts alternate periodically. What accounts for this spontaneous alternation? Once the perceptual system locks into one aspect of the figure, why does it not remain in that state? An analogous physical system is a trapdoor that is stable only when it is either open or closed.

As Necker pointed out, changing the point of visual fixation may cause perspective to reverse. In the instances where the input is being matched against more than one schema visual fixation on a feature that is more critical to one representation than the other may lock perception into only one aspect of the ambiguous figure. Since the percepts can alternate without a change in the point of fixation, however, some additional explanation is needed. The most likely is that the alternative aspects of the figure are represented by activity in different neural structures, and that when one such structure becomes "fatigued," or satiated or adapted, it gives way to another that is fresher and more excitable. Several investigators have noted that a reversing figure alternates more rapidly the longer it is looked at, presumably because both alternative neural structures build up some kind of fatigue. In some respects the neural structures behave like a multistable electronic circuit. A common example of multistability in electronic circuitry is the multivibrator flip-flop circuit, which can incorporate either vacuum tubes or transistors. In the vacuum tube version [*see illustration on opposite page*] when one tube is conducting a current, the other tube is prevented from conducting by the low voltage on its grid. The plates and the grids of the two tubes are cross-coupled through capacitors, and one tube continues to conduct until the charge leaks from the coupling capacitor sufficiently for the other tube to start conducting. Once this tube begins to conduct, the positive feedback loop quickly makes it fully conducting and the other tube is cut off and becomes

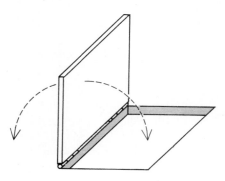

PHYSICAL SYSTEM that exhibits a simple form of multistability is a trapdoor that is stable only when it is either open or shut.

nonconducting. The process reverses and the system flip-flops between one state and the other.

What is "fatigued" in the multivibrator is the suppressive linkage. In other words, the inhibition of the nonconducting tube slowly weakens until it is no longer strong enough to prevent conduction. The possibility of an analogous neural process, in which the inhibition of the alternative neural structure progressively weakens, is worth considering.

Brain lesions may affect the perception of ambiguous figures. The finding most generally reported is that in people who have suffered brain damage the rate of alternation is lower, more or less independently of the locus of the lesion. On the other hand, a study of a group of brain-damaged war veterans conducted by Leonard Cohen at New York University indicated that damage to both frontal lobes increases the rate of alternation of a reversible figure, whereas damage to only one frontal lobe decreases the rate. The theoretical implications of these neurological findings are quite obscure and will doubtless remain so until we have some fundamental picture of the way the nervous system represents form and space.

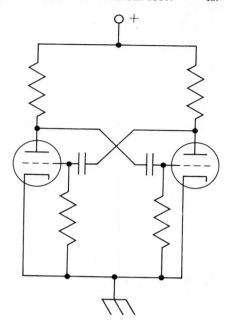

MULTIVIBRATOR CIRCUIT spontaneously alternates between two states. When one vacuum tube is conducting, the other is inhibited. A charge leaking from the coupling capacitor eventually starts the inhibited tube conducting. The positive feedback loop quickly makes it fully conducting and cuts off conduction in the first tube. The entire process is repeated in reverse, and the circuit flops from one state to the other.

13

The Perception of Disoriented Figures

by Irvin Rock
January 1974

*Many familiar things do not look the same when their
orientation is changed. The reason appears to be that
the perception of form embodies the automatic assignment
of a top, a bottom and sides*

Many common experiences of everyday life that we take for granted present challenging scientific problems. In the field of visual perception one such problem is why things look different when they are upside down or tilted. Consider the inverted photograph on the opposite page. Although the face is familiar to most Americans, it is difficult to recognize when it is inverted. Even when one succeeds in identifying the face, it continues to look strange and the specific facial expression is hard to make out.

Consider also what happens when printed words and words written in longhand are turned upside down. With effort the printed words can be read, but it is all but impossible to read the longhand words [*see top illustration on page 110*]. Try it with a sample of your own handwriting. One obvious explanation of why it is hard to read inverted words is that we have acquired the habit of moving our eyes from left to right, and that when we look at inverted words our eyes tend to move in the wrong direction. This may be one source of the difficulty, but it can hardly be the major one. It is just as hard to read even a single inverted word when we look at it without moving our eyes at all. It is probable that the same factor interfering with the recognition of disoriented faces and other figures is also interfering with word recognition.

The partial rotation of even a simple figure can also prevent its recognition, provided that the observer is unaware of the rotation. A familiar figure viewed in a novel orientation no longer appears to have the same shape [*see bottom illustration on page 110*]. As Ernst Mach pointed out late in the 19th century, the appearance of a square is quite different when it is rotated 45 degrees. In fact, we call it a diamond.

Some may protest that a familiar shape looks different in a novel orientation for the simple reason that we rarely see it that way. But even a figure we have not seen before will look different in different orientations [*see top illustration on page 111*]. The fact is that orientation affects perceived shape, and that the failure to recognize a familiar figure when it is in a novel orientation is based on the change in its perceived shape.

On the other hand, a figure can be changed in various ways without any effect on its perceived shape. For example, a triangle can be altered in size, color and various other ways without any change in its perceived shape [*see middle illustration on page 111*]. Psychologists, drawing an analogy with a similar phenomenon in music, call such changes transpositions. A melody can be transposed to a new key, and although all the notes then are different, there is no change in the melody. In fact, we generally remain unaware of the transposition. Clearly the melody derives from the relation of the notes to one another, which is not altered when the melody is transposed. In much the same way a visual form is based primarily on how parts of a figure are related to one another geometrically. For example, one could describe a square as being a four-sided figure having parallel opposite sides, four right angles and four sides of equal length. These features remain unchanged when a square is transposed in size or position; that is why it continues to look like a square. We owe a debt to the Gestalt psychologists for emphasizing the importance in perception of relations rather than absolute features.

Since a transposition based on rotation also does not alter the internal geometric relations of a figure, then why does it look different in an altered orientation? At this point we should consider the meaning of the term orientation. What changes are introduced by altering orientation? One obvious change is that rotating a figure would result in a change in the orientation of its image on the retina of the eye. Perhaps, therefore, we should ask why different retinal orientations of the same figure should give rise to different perceived shapes. That might lead us into speculations about how the brain processes information about form, and why differently oriented projections of a retinal image should lead to different percepts of form.

Before we go further in this direction we should consider another meaning of the term orientation. The inverted and rotated figures in the illustrations for this article are in different orientations with respect to the vertical and horizontal directions in their environment. That part of the figure which is normally pointed upward in relation to gravity, to the sky or to the ceiling is now pointed downward or sideways on the page. Perhaps it is this kind of orientation that is responsible for altered perception of shape when a figure is disoriented.

It is not difficult to separate the retinal and the environmental factors in an experiment. Cut out a paper square and tape it to the wall so that the bottom of the square is parallel to the floor. Compare the appearance of the square first with your head upright and then with your head tilted 45 degrees. You will see that the square continues to look like a square when your head is tilted. Yet when your head is tilted 45 degrees, the retinal image of the square is the same as the image of a diamond when the diamond is viewed with the head upright. Thus it is not the retinal image that is responsible for the altered appearance of a square when the square is rotated 45 degrees. The converse experiment points to the same conclusion. Rotate the square on the wall so that it becomes a diamond. The diamond viewed with your head tilted 45 degrees produces a retinal image of a square, but the diamond still looks like a diamond. Needless to say, in these simple demonstrations one continues to perceive correctly where the top, bottom and sides of the figures are even when one's posture changes. It is therefore the change of a figure's perceived orientation in the environment that affects its apparent shape and not the change of orientation of its retinal image.

These conclusions have been substantiated in experiments Walter I. Heimer and I and other colleagues have conducted with numerous subjects. In one series of experiments the subjects were shown unfamiliar figures. In the first part of the experiment a subject sat at a table and simply looked at several figures shown briefly in succession. Then some of the subjects were asked to tilt their head 90 degrees by turning it to the side and resting it on the table. In this position the subject viewed a series of figures. Most of the figures were new, but among them were some figures the subject had seen earlier. These figures were shown in either of two orientations: upright with respect to the room (as they had been in the first viewing) or rotated 90 degrees so that the "top" of the figure corresponded to the top of the subject's tilted head. The subject was asked to say whether or not he had seen each figure in the first session. He did not know that the orientation of the figures seen previously might be different. Other subjects viewed the test figures while sitting upright.

When we compared the scores of subjects who tilted their head with subjects who sat upright for the test, the results were clear. Tilted-head subjects recognized the environmentally upright (but retinally tilted) figures about as well as the upright observers did. They also failed to recognize the environmentally tilted (but retinally upright) figures about as often as the upright subjects did. In other words, the experiments confirmed that it is rotation with respect to the up-down and left-right coordinates in the environment that produces the change in the perceived shape of the figure. It is not rotation of the retinal image that produces the change, since altering the image's orientation does not adversely affect recognition and preserving it does not improve recognition.

In another experiment subjects viewed an ambiguous or reversible figure that could be perceived in one of two ways depending on its orientation. For example, when one figure that looked like a map of the U.S. was rotated 90 degrees, it looked like the profile of a bearded man. Subjects were asked to rest their head on the table when viewing the ambiguous figures. The question we asked ourselves was: Which "upright" would dominate, the retinal upright or the environmental upright? The results were decisive. About 80 percent of the subjects reported seeing only the aspect of the ambiguous figure that was environmentally upright, even though the alternative was upright on their retina [see bottom illustration on page 112].

Why does the orientation of a figure with respect to the directional coordinates of the environment have such a profound effect on the perceived shape of the figure? The answer I propose is that perceived shape is based on a cognitive process in which the characteristics of the figure are implicitly described by the perceptual system. For example, the colored figure at the left in the top illustration on page 111 could be described as a closed figure resting on a horizontal base with a protrusion on the figure's left side and an indentation on its right side. The colored figure to the right of it, although it is identical and only rotated 90 degrees, would be described quite differently, as being symmetrical with two bumps on the bottom and with left and right sides more or less straight and identical with each other. I am not suggesting that such a description is conscious or verbal; obviously we would be aware of the descriptive process if it were either. Furthermore, animals and infants who are nonverbal perceive shape much as we do. I am proposing that a process analogous to such a description does take place and that it is not only based on the internal geometry of a figure but also takes into account the location of the figure's top, bottom and sides. In such a description orienta-

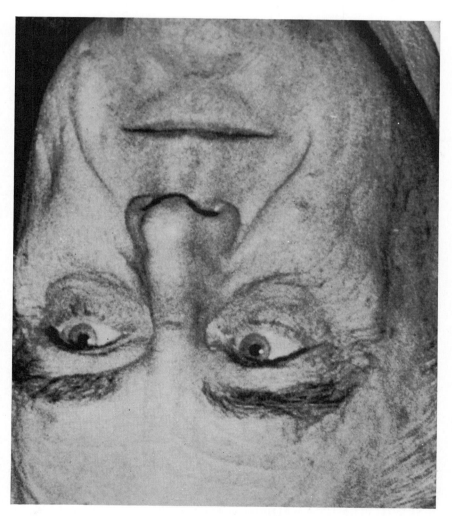

INVERTED PHOTOGRAPH of a famous American demonstrates how difficult it is to recognize a familiar face when it is presented upside down. Even after one succeeds in identifying the inverted face as that of Franklin D. Roosevelt, it continues to look strange.

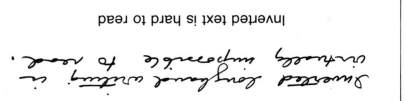

Inverted text is hard to read

INVERTED WORDS are difficult to read when they are set in type, and words written in longhand are virtually impossible to decipher. The difficulty applies to one's own inverted handwriting in spite of a lifetime of experience reading it in the normal upright orientation.

tion is therefore a major factor in the shape that is finally perceived.

From experiments I have done in collaboration with Phyllis Olshansky it appears that certain shifts in orientation have a marked effect on perceived shape. In particular, creating symmetry around a vertical axis where no symmetry had existed before (or vice versa), shifting the long axis from vertical to horizontal (or vice versa) and changing the bottom of a figure from a broad horizontal base to a pointed angle (or vice versa) seemed to have a strong effect on perceived shape. Such changes of shape can result from only a moderate angular change of

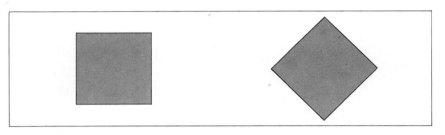

SQUARE AND DIAMOND are two familiar shapes. The two figures shown here are identical; their appearance is so different, however, that we call one a square and the other a diamond. With the diamond the angles do not spontaneously appear as right angles.

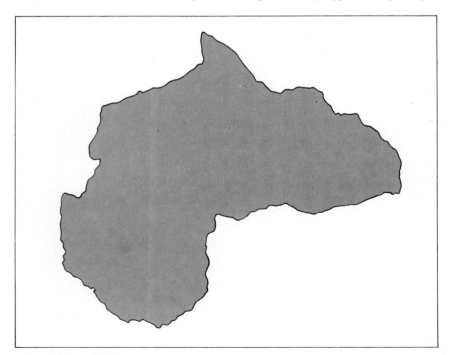

"UNFAMILIAR" SHAPE shown here becomes a familiar shape when it is rotated clockwise 90 degrees. In a classroom experiment, when the rotated figure was drawn on the blackboard, it was not recognized as an outline of the continent of Africa until the teacher told the class at the end of the lecture that the figure was rotated out of its customary orientation.

orientation, say 45 or 90 degrees. Interestingly enough, inversions or rotations of 180 degrees often have only a slight effect on perceived shape, perhaps because such changes will usually not alter perceived symmetry or the perceived orientation of the long axis of the figure.

There is one kind of orientation change that has virtually no effect on perceived shape: a mirror-image reversal. This is particularly true for the novel figures we used in our experiments. How can this be explained? It seems that although the "sides" of visual space are essentially interchangeable, the up-and-down directions in the environment are not. "Up" and "down" are distinctly different directions in the world we live in. Thus a figure can be said to have three main perceptual boundaries: top, bottom and sides. As a result the description of a figure will not be much affected by whether a certain feature is on the left side or the right. Young children and animals have great difficulty learning to discriminate between a figure and its mirror image, but they can easily distinguish between a figure and its inverted counterpart.

Related to this analysis is a fact observed by Mach and tested by Erich Goldmeier: A figure that is symmetrical around one axis will generally appear to be symmetrical only if that axis is vertical. Robin Leaman and I have demonstrated that it is the perceived vertical axis of the figure and not the vertical axis of the figure's retinal image that produces this effect. An observer who tilts his head will continue to perceive a figure as being symmetrical if that figure is symmetrical around an environmental vertical axis. This suggests that perceived symmetry results only when the two equivalent halves of a figure are located on the two equivalent sides of perceptual space.

If, as I have suggested, the description of a figure is based on the location of its top, bottom and sides, the question arises: How are these directions assigned in a figure? One might suppose that the top of a figure is ordinarily the area uppermost in relation to the ceiling, the sky or the top of a page. In a dark room an observer may have to rely on his sense of gravity to inform him which way is up.

Numerous experiments by psychologists have confirmed that there are indeed two major sources of information for perceiving the vertical and the horizontal: gravity (as it is sensed by the vestibular apparatus in the inner ear, by the pressure of the ground on the body and by feedback from the muscles) and information from the scene itself. We have been able to demonstrate that either can affect the perceived shape of a figure. A luminous figure in a dark room will not be recognized readily when it is rotated to a new orientation even if the observer is tilted by exactly the same amount. Here the only source of information about directions in space is gravity. In a lighted room an observer will often fail to recognize a figure when he and the figure are upright but the room is tilted. The tilted room creates a strong impression of where the up-down axis should be, and this leads to an incorrect attribution of the top and bottom of the figure [see "The Perception of the Upright," [by Herman A. Witkin; SCIENTIFIC AMERICAN Offprint 410].

Merely informing an observer that a figure is tilted will often enable him to perceive the figure correctly. This may explain why some readers will not perceive certain of the rotated figures shown here as being strange or different. The converse situation, misinforming an observer about the figures, produces impressive results. If a subject is told that the top of a figure he is about to see is somewhere other than in the region uppermost in the environment, he is likely not to recognize the figure when it is presented with the orientation in which he first saw it. The figure is not disoriented and the observer incorrectly assigns the directions top, bottom and sides on the basis of instructions.

Since such knowledge about orientation will enable the observer to shift the directions he assigns to a figure, and since it is this assignment that affects the perception of shape, it is absolutely essential to employ naïve subjects in perception experiments involving orientation. That is, the subject must not realize that the experiment is concerned with figural orientation, so that he does not examine the figures with the intent of finding the regions that had been top, bottom and sides in previous viewings of it. There are, however, some figures that seem to have intrinsic orientation in that regardless of how they are presented a certain region will be perceived as the top [see top illustration on next page]. It is therefore difficult or impossible to adversely affect the recognition of such figures by disorienting them.

In the absence of other clues a subject will assign top-bottom coordinates according to his subjective or egocentric reference system. Consider a figure drawn on a circular sheet of paper that is lying on the ground. Neither gravity nor visual clues indicate where the top

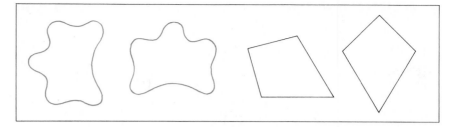

NOVEL OR UNFAMILIAR FIGURES look different in different orientations, provided that we view them naïvely and do not mentally rotate them. The reason may be the way in which a figure is "described" by the perceptual system. The colored figure at left could be described as a closed shape resting on a horizontal base with a protrusion on its left side and an indentation on its right side. The colored figure adjacent to it, although identical, would be described as a symmetrical shape resting on a curved base with a protrusion at the top. The first black figure could be described as a quadrilateral resting on a side. The black figure at right would be described as a diamondlike shape standing on end.

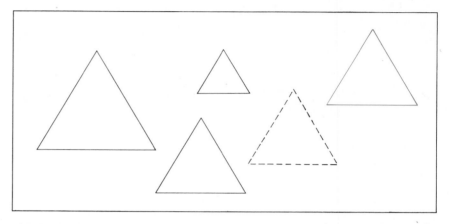

ALTERATION IN SIZE, color or type of contour does not change the perceived shape of a triangle. Even varying the location of the triangle's retinal image (by looking out of the corner of your eyes or fixating on different points) does not change perceived shape.

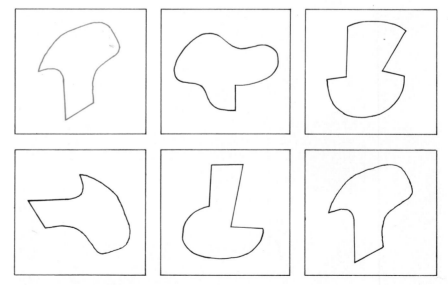

ROTATION OF RETINAL IMAGE by tilting the head 90 degrees does not appreciably affect recognition of a novel figure (color). Subjects first viewed several novel targets while sitting upright. Then they were shown a series of test figures (black) and were asked to identify those they had seen before. Some subjects tilted their head 90 degrees; others viewed the test figures with their head upright. Tilted-head subjects failed to recognize figures that were retinally "upright" (for example figure at bottom left) about as much as upright viewers did (to whom such figures were not retinally upright). Tilted-head subjects recognized environmentally upright figures (bottom right) as often as upright viewers did.

FIGURES WITH INTRINSIC ORIENTATION appear to have a natural vertical axis regardless of their physical orientation. A region at one end of the axis is perceived as top.

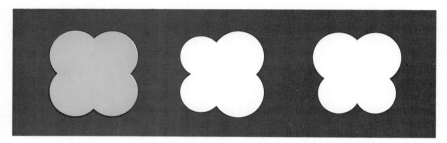

IMPRESSION OF SYMMETRY is spontaneous only when a figure is symmetrical around a vertical axis. Subjects were asked to indicate which of two figures (*middle and right*) was most like the target figure (*left*). The figure at right was selected most frequently, presumably because it is symmetrical around its vertical axis. If the page is tilted 90 degrees, the figure in the middle will now be selected as being more similar to the target figure. Now if the page is held vertically and the figures are viewed with the head tilted 90 degrees, the figure at right is likely to be seen as being the most similar. This suggests that it is not the symmetry around the egocentric vertical axis on the retina but rather the symmetry around the environmental axis of the figure that determines perceived symmetry.

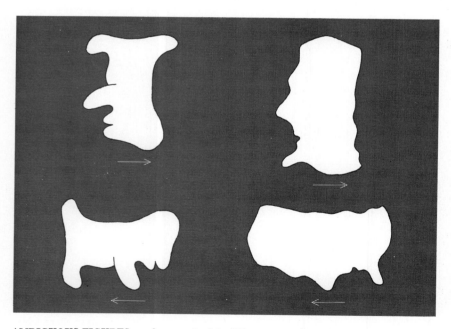

AMBIGUOUS FIGURES can be perceived in different ways depending on the orientation assigned to them. Figure at left can look like the profile of a man's head with a chef's hat (*top left*) or, when rotated 90 degrees, like a dog (*bottom left*). Figure at right can look like the profile of a bearded man's head (*top right*) or like a map of the U.S. (*bottom right*). When subjects with their head tilted 90 degrees to one side viewed these ambiguous figures (*direction of subject's head is shown by arrow*), they preferentially recognized the figure that was upright in the environment instead of the figure that was upright on the retina.

and bottom are. Nevertheless, an observer will assign a top to that region of the figure which is uppermost with respect to his egocentric coordinate reference system. The vertical axis of the figure is seen as being aligned with the long axis of the observer's head and body. The upward direction corresponds to the position of his head. We have been able to demonstrate that such assignment of direction has the same effect on the recognition that other bases of assigning direction do. A figure first seen in one orientation on the circular sheet will generally not be recognized if its egocentric orientation is altered.

Now we come to an observation that seems to be at variance with much of what I have described. When a person lies on his side in bed to read, he does not hold the book upright (in the environmental sense) but tilts it. If the book is not tilted, the retinal image is disoriented and reading is quite difficult. Similarly, if a reader views printed matter or photographs of faces that are environmentally upright with his head between his legs, they will be just as difficult to recognize as they are when they are upside down and the viewer's head is upright. The upright pictures, however, are still perceived as being upright even when the viewer's head is inverted. Conversely, if the pictures are upside down in the environment and are viewed with the head inverted between the legs, there is no difficulty in recognizing them. Yet the observer perceives the pictures as being inverted. Therefore in these cases it is the orientation of the retinal image and not the environmental assignment of direction that seems to be responsible for recognition or failure of recognition.

Experiments with ambiguous figures conducted by Robert Thouless, G. Kanizsa and G. Tampieri support the notion that retinal orientation plays a role in recognition of a figure [*see illustration on page 115*]. Moreover, as George Steinfeld and I have demonstrated, the recognition of upright words and faces falls off in direct proportion to the degree of body tilt [*see illustration on opposite page*]. With such visual material recognition is an inverse function of the degree of disorientation of the retinal image. As we have seen, the relation between degree of disorientation and recognizability does not hold in cases where the assignment of direction has been altered. In such cases the greatest effect is not with a 180-degree change but with a 45- or 90-degree change.

The results of all these experiments

have led me to conclude that there are two distinct factors involved in the perception of disoriented figures: an assignment-of-direction factor and a retinal factor. I believe that when we view a figure with our head tilted, we automatically compensate for the tilt in much the same way that we compensate for the size of distant objects. An object at a moderate distance from us does not appear small in spite of the fact that its retinal image is much smaller than it is when the object is close by. This effect usually is explained by saying that the information supplied by the retinal image is somehow corrected by allowing for the distance of the object from us. Similarly, when a vertical luminous line in a dark room is viewed by a tilted observer, it will still look vertical or almost vertical in spite of the fact that the retinal image in the observer's eye is tilted. Thus the tilt of the body must be taken into account by the perceptual system. The tilted retinal image is then corrected, with the result that the line is perceived as being vertical. Just as the correction for size at a distance is called size constancy, so can correction for the vertical be called orientation constancy.

When we view an upright figure with our head tilted, before we have made any correction, we begin with the information provided by an image of the figure in a particular retinal orientation. The first thing that must happen is that the perceptual system processes the retinal image on the basis of an egocentrically assigned top, bottom and sides, perhaps because of a primitive sense of orientation derived from retinal orientation. For example, when we view an upright square with our head tilted, which yields a diamondlike retinal image, we may perceive a diamond for a fleeting moment before the correction goes into operation. Head orientation is then automatically taken into account to correct the perception. Thus the true top of the figure is seen to be one of the sides of the square rather than a corner. The figure is then "described" correctly as one whose sides are horizontal and vertical in the environment, in short as a "square." This correction is made quickly and usually without effort. In order to describe a figure the viewer probably must visualize or imagine it in terms of its true top, bottom and sides rather than in terms of its retinal top, bottom and sides.

If the figure is relatively simple, the correction is not too difficult to achieve. If we view an upright letter with our head tilted, we recognize it easily; it is of interest, however, that there is still

something strange about it. I believe the dual aspect of the perception of orientation is responsible for this strangeness. There is an uncorrected perception of the letter based on its retinal-egocentric orientation and a corrected perception of it based on its environmental orientation. The first perception produces an unfamiliar shape, which accounts for the strangeness of the letter in spite of its subsequent recognition. In our experiments many of the figures we employed were structurally speaking equivalent to letters, and in some cases we actually used letters from unfamiliar alphabets.

With a more complex figure, such as an inverted word or an upright word

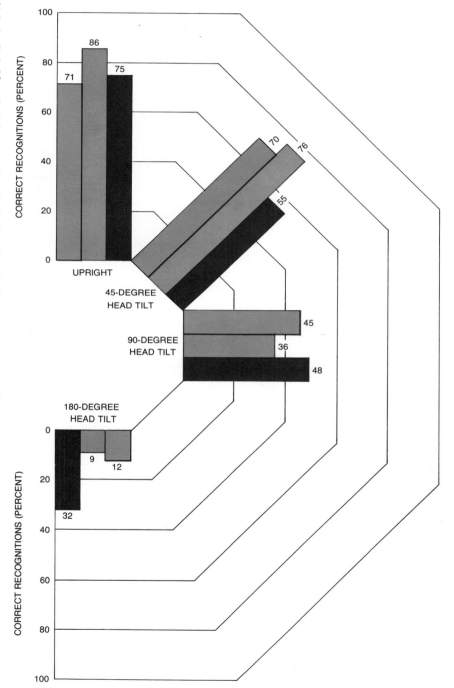

RECOGNITION OF CERTAIN KINDS OF VISUAL MATERIAL decreases almost in direct proportion to the degree of head tilt of the observer. In a series of experiments the number of correct recognitions of faces (*colored bars*), written words (*gray*) and fragmented figures (*black*) were recorded for various degrees of head tilt. Subject saw several examples of each type of test material in each of the head positions. For this visual material recognition is an inverse function of the degree of disorientation of the retinal image.

SINGLE LETTER that is tilted can be easily identified once it is realized how it is oriented. A strangeness in its appearance, however, remains because the percept arising from the uncorrected retinal image continues to exist simultaneously with the corrected percept.

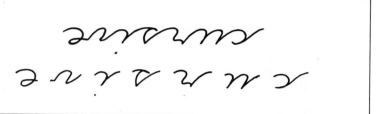

INVERTED LONGHAND WRITING is difficult to decipher because many inverted units resemble written upright letters. For example, an inverted *u* will look like an *n* and an inverted *c* like an *s*. Moreover, the connection between letters leads to uncertainty about where a letter begins and ends. Several inverted units can be grouped together and misperceived as an upright letter. Separating the inverted letters makes them easier to decipher.

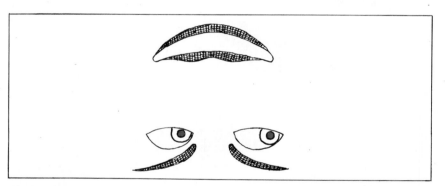

INVERTED FACIAL FEATURES are difficult to interpret because while attention is focused on correcting one feature other features remain uncorrected. For example, one might succeed in correcting the eyes shown here so that they are perceived as gazing downward and leftward, but at that very moment the mouth is uncorrected and expresses sorrow rather than pleasure. Conversely, one might correct the mouth and misperceive the eyes.

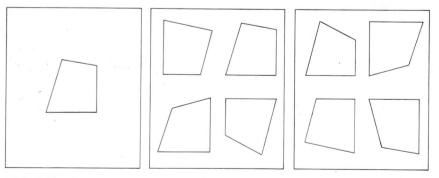

MULTIPLE ITEMS were found to have an adverse effect on recognition of even simple figures. Subjects sitting upright viewed the target (*left*). Then they were briefly shown test cards, some of which contained the target figure (*middle*) and some of which did not (*right*). The subjects were to indicate when they saw a figure that was identical with the target figure. Half of the test cards were viewed with the head upright and half with the head inverted. Recognition was poor when inverted subjects viewed the test cards. In other experiments with a single test figure head inversion did not significantly affect recognition.

viewed by an inverted observer, the corrective mechanism may be entirely overtaxed. Each letter of the word must be corrected separately, and the corrective mechanism apparently cannot cope simultaneously with multiple components. It is true that if an observer is given enough time, an inverted word can be deciphered, but it will never look the same as it does when it is upright. While one letter is being corrected the others continue to be perceived in their uncorrected form. There is a further difficulty: letter order is crucial for word recognition, and inverting a word reverses the normal left-to-right order.

The recognition of inverted longhand writing is even more difficult. When such writing is turned upside down, many of the inverted "units" strongly resemble normal upright longhand letters. Moreover, since the letters are connected, it is difficult to tell where one letter ends and another begins. Separating the letters of the inverted word makes recognition easier. Even so, it is all too easy to confuse a *u* and an *n*. This type of confusion is also encountered with certain printed letters, namely, *b* and *q*, *d* and *p* and *n* and *u*, although not as frequently. In other words, if a figure is recognized on the basis of its upright retinal-egocentric orientation, this may tend to stabilize the perception and block the correction process. The dominance of the retinally upright faces in the illustration on the opposite page probably is an effect of just this kind.

There may be a similar overtaxing of the corrective mechanism when we view an inverted face. It may be that the face contains a number of features each of which must be properly perceived if the whole is to be recognized [see "The Recognition of Faces," by Leon D. Harmon; SCIENTIFIC AMERICAN Offprint 555]. While attention is focused on correcting one feature, say the mouth, other features remain uncorrected and continue to be perceived on the basis of the image they form on the retina. Of course, the relation of features is also important in the recognition of a face, but here too there are a great number of such relations and the corrective mechanism may again be overtaxed.

Charles C. Bebber, Douglas Blewett and I conducted an experiment to test the hypothesis that it is the presence of multiple components that creates the difficulty of correcting figures. Subjects were briefly shown a quadrilateral figure and asked to study it. They viewed the target figure with their head upright. Then they were shown a series of test

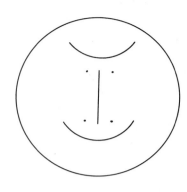

AMBIGUOUS FACES are perceived differently when their images on the retina of the observer are inverted. If you hold the illustration upright and view it from between your legs with your head inverted, the alternative faces will be perceived even though they are upside down in terms of the environment. The same effect occurs when the illustration is inverted and viewed from an upright position. Such tests provide evidence that figures such as faces are recognized on the basis of their upright retinal orientation.

cards each of which had four quadrilateral figures. The test cards were viewed for one second, and the subjects were required to indicate if the target figure was on the card.

The subjects understood that they were to respond affirmatively only when they saw a figure that was identical with the target figure both in shape and in orientation. (Some of the test figures were similar to the target figure but were rotated by 180 degrees.) Half of the test cards were seen with the subject's head upright and half with the subject's head inverted. It was assumed that the subject would not be able to correct all four test figures in the brief time that was allowed him while he was viewing them with his head down. He had to perceive just as many units in the same brief time while he was viewing them with his head upright, but he did not have to correct any of the units. We expected that target figures would often not be recognized and that incorrect figures would be mistakenly identified as the target when the subjects viewed the test cards with their head inverted.

The results bore out our prediction. When multiple components have to be corrected, retinal disorientation has an adverse effect on recognition. The observer responded to twice as many test cards correctly when he was upright than he did when he was inverted.

As I have noted, when we look at figures that are difficult to recognize when they are retinally disoriented, the difficulty increases as the degree of disorientation increases. Why this happens may also be related to the nature of the correction process. I suggested that the observer must suppress the retinally (egocentrically) upright percept and substitute a corrected percept. To do this, however, he must visualize or imagine

how the figure would look if it were rotated until it was upright with respect to himself or, what amounts to the same thing, how it would look if he rotated himself into alignment with the figure. The process of mental rotation requires visualizing the entire sequence of angular change, and therefore the greater the angular change, the greater the difficulty.

As every parent knows, children between the ages of two and five seem to be quite indifferent to how a picture is oriented. They often hold a book upside down and seem not at all disturbed by it. On the basis of such observations and the results of some early experiments, many psychologists concluded that the orientation of a figure did not enter into its recognition by young children. More recent laboratory experiments, however, do not confirm the fact that children recognize figures equally well in any orientation. They have as much difficulty as, or more difficulty than, adults in recognizing previously seen figures when the figure is shown in a new orientation. Why then do young children often spontaneously look at pictures upside down in everyday situations? Perhaps they have not yet learned to pay attention to orientation, and do not realize that their recognition would improve if they did so. When children learn to read after the age of six, they are forced to pay attention to orientation because certain letters differ only in their orientation.

In summary, the central fact we have learned about orientation is that the perceived shape of a figure is not simply a function of its internal geometry. The perceived shape is also very much a function of the up, down and side directions we assign to the figure. If there is a change in the assigned directions, the figure will take on a different per-

ceptual shape. I have speculated that the change in perceived shape is based on a new "description" of the figure by the perceptual system. The directions assigned are based on information of various kinds about where the top, bottom and sides of a figure are and usually do not depend on the retinal orientation of the image of the figure. When the image is not retinally upright, a process of correction is necessary in order to arrive at the correct description, and this correction is difficult or impossible to achieve in the case of visual material that has multiple components.

All of this implies that form perception in general is based to a much greater extent on cognitive processes than any current theory maintains. A prevailing view among psychologists and sensory physiologists is that form perception can be reduced to the perception of contours and that contour perception in turn can be reduced to abrupt differences in light intensity that cause certain neural units in the retina and brain to fire. If this is true, then perceiving form results from the specific concatenation of perceived contours. Although the work I have described does not deny the possible importance of contour detection as a basis of form perception, it does suggest that such an explanation is far from sufficient, and that the perception of form depends on certain mental processes such as description and correction. These processes in turn are necessary to account for the further step of recognition of a figure. A physically unchanged retinal image often will not lead to recognition if there has been a shift in the assigned directions. Conversely, if there has been no shift in the assigned directions, even a very different retinal image will still allow recognition.

14   Vision and Touch

by Irvin Rock and Charles S. Harris
May 1967

*It has been held that human beings must learn how to
see, and that they are taught by the sense of touch. New
experiments demonstrate, however, that vision completely
dominates touch and even shapes it*

A visual perception is not simply a copy of the image on the retina. The image has two dimensions, the perceived object three. The image is upside down, but the object is seen right-side up. An image of a given size can be projected on the retina either from a small object that is nearby or from a large object that is distant, and yet one usually perceives the actual size of the object quite accurately. The image is received by millions of separate light-sensitive cells in the retina, but one sees a unified object with a definite shape.

The striking differences between the retinal image and perception have led many philosophers and psychologists to assume that one must learn how to see. If the retinal image supplies only distorted and incomplete information, one must at first make use of some other source of information about the properties of objects. The most likely source has been considered the sense of touch. In the 18th century the philosopher George Berkeley proposed that an infant discovers by touching an object that it is a distinct, three-dimensional body of a certain size and shape in a certain location and orientation. Thus touch presumably educates vision, adding meaning to the initially meaningless jumble of retinal images.

We have investigated this assumption and have concluded on the basis of several experiments that it is wrong. The sense of touch does not educate vision; vision is totally dominant over touch. As an example, one of our experiments shows that if a subject looks at his hand through a prism, so that the hand appears to be several inches to the right of where it really is, he soon comes to believe the hand is where it appears to be, in spite of nerve messages to the contrary that must be traveling from

the hand to his brain. Indeed, one can now turn the traditional argument around and suggest that vision shapes the sense of touch.

We should emphasize that in referring to the sense of touch we mean more than the sensations of contact with the skin that one experiences when touching an object. Touch includes several other components, of which the one most significant for this discussion is the position sense: the sense that enables us to know the position of our body parts when our eyes are closed. It is touch in this broad definition that has been so widely believed to educate vision.

The arguments for the belief rest not only on the recognition of the differences between a retinal image and a visual perception but also on observable evidence. For instance, people who gain sight after having been blind since birth seem at first to have trouble seeing correctly. The phenomenon has been interpreted as suggesting that they must learn to see on the basis of information from touch.

Similar implications have been drawn from experiments by a number of psychologists. A classic experiment was conducted in 1895 by George M. Stratton of the University of California. He spent several days wearing lenses that turned everything upside down. Ivo Kohler of the University of Innsbruck has conducted similar experiments and has also used prisms that reverse right and left. Experiments with prisms that displace the retinal image to one side were carried out in the 19th century by Hermann von Helmholtz and more recently by Richard Held of the Massachusetts Institute of Technology [see the article "Plasticity in Sensory-Motor Systems," by Richard Held, page 150].

In these studies the subject at first saw

the world upside down, reversed or displaced, and he acted accordingly. He tried to duck under objects he should have climbed over, he made wrong turns, he missed when he reached for things. After a while, however, he adapted: he behaved normally again, reacting appropriately in spite of the abnormal retinal image.

Such adaptations create the impression that they involve radical adjustments in vision so that the subject again sees the world as normal. Indeed, the adaptations would not be surprising if visual perception is derived from touch. If an infant must learn how to see, an adult could be expected to relearn how to see when his sense of touch tells him that his eyes are deceiving him.

Let us now, however, consider some arguments against the proposition that visual perception is based on touch. In the first place, the same reasoning that seems to rule out innate visual perception also argues against any innate sense of touch on which to build visual perception. Why should one assume that the separate tactile and position components of touch are innately organized into an impression of a solid object with a particular shape? Second, the sense of touch seems far too imprecise to be the source of the accurate perception of form and space that is achieved through vision.

Third, a considerable body of recent evidence suggests that vision is well developed at birth or very soon thereafter. Eleanor J. Gibson of Cornell University and Richard D. Walk of George Washington University found, for example, that babies, chicks and other infant animals have good depth perception before they have had any opportunity to learn it in any way [see the article "The 'Visual Cliff,'" by Eleanor J. Gibson and Richard D. Walk, page 51]. T. G. R. Bower of Harvard University found that human infants see the size and shape of things in the same way adults do [see "The Visual World of Infants," by T. G. R. Bower; SCIENTIFIC AMERICAN Offprint 502].

A fourth argument is provided by our own experiments. Even though we have worked separately and have used somewhat different techniques, we have both arrived at essentially the same conclusion, namely that when vision and touch provide contradictory information, perception is dominated by the information from vision. (Similar experiments by Charles R. Hamilton at the California Institute of Technology and by Julian Hochberg, John C. Hay and Herbert Pick, Jr., at Cornell have led them to similar conclusions.)

One of us (Rock) has been investigating perception of size and shape in collaboration with Jack Victor, a graduate student at Yeshiva University. By using a lens that reduces the size of an object's retinal image we can present a subject with contradictory information from vision and from touch [see illustration at right]. If he grasps an object while viewing it through the reducing lens, vision should tell him the object is a certain size and touch should tell him it is much larger.

We wanted to find out what the subject would experience under these conditions. Would he be aware that he was seeing an object of one size and feeling an object of another size? Or would he somehow reconcile the conflicting sensory information to achieve a unified perception or impression? If the latter were the case, which sense would have the most influence—vision or touch?

We considered it essential that the subject remain ignorant of the actual situation, otherwise the experiment might be reduced to a conscious decision about which sense to rely on. Because the subject would know that vision can be optically distorted but touch cannot, he would undoubtedly judge the size of the object in terms of what he felt. Accordingly we did not tell the subject that he was looking through a reducing lens. Moreover, we arranged matters so that he saw nothing through the lens except a one-inch white square made of hard plastic.

The subject grasped the square from below through a cloth so that he could not see his own hand; if he could have seen it, he might have deduced that he was looking through a reducing lens, since he would be familiar with the visual size of his hand. To be certain that the subject would not make measurements, such as laying off the side of the square against his finger, we did not ask him anything until after he had been exposed to the conflicting information for five seconds. Each subject was exposed to such a situation only once.

In assessing the subject's perception we could not ask him what was the size of the object he saw or what was the size of the object he felt; either question would prejudice the outcome. Instead we asked him to give his impression of the size of the square. We measured the impression in several ways [see illustration on page 119]. Some subjects were asked to draw the size of the square as accurately as they could; drawing involves both vision and touch. We asked others to pick out a matching square from a series of squares presented only visually. Still others were asked to choose a matching square from a series of squares that could be grasped but not seen.

The results of all the tests were clear. Most of the subjects were not even aware that they were receiving conflicting sensory information. This in itself is a most interesting fact. The subjects had a definite unitary experience of the size of the square, and the experience agreed closely with the illusory visual appearance of the square. The average size drawn or matched was about the same when the square was both seen and felt as when, in a control experiment, it was only seen. That size was consistently smaller than the size in another control experiment in which the square was only touched. Thus touch had almost no effect on the perceived size.

We then performed an experiment on the perception of shape. For this test we used a cylindrical optical device that made things seem narrower, so that a square looked like a rectangle with sides in the proportion of two to one. What would happen when the subject simultaneously saw and touched an object that looked like a rectangle but felt like a square?

The result was again quite clear. Vision was completely dominant. In fact, it was so dominant that most subjects said the square actually felt the way it looked. If subjects closed their eyes while grasping the object, they often thought they felt it changing its shape from a rectangle to a square.

A similar domination of touch by vision has been found by Hay, Pick and

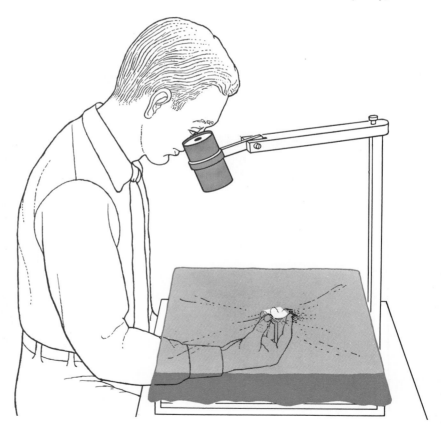

EXPERIMENTAL ARRANGEMENT used to test the effect of a reducing lens on a subject's impression of size included the lens, a cloth over the subject's hand so that he would not deduce from the small appearance of his hand that he was looking through a reducing lens, and a square made of hard plastic. In this test he looked at square and simultaneously grasped it.

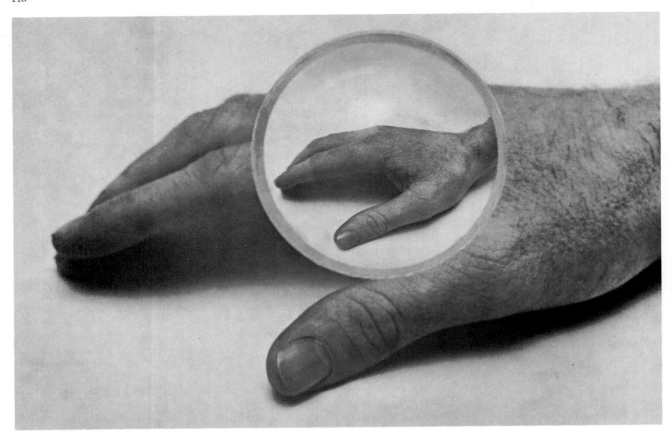

OPTICAL DEVICES were used in experiments to determine whether vision or touch would have the stronger effect on a subject to whom they were providing conflicting information. A reducing lens (*top*) made an object look half its actual size; a prism (*bottom*) reversed left and right. When subjects looked through such a lens or prism and also used touch, they received conflicting sensory data.

Karren Ikeda, working at Smith College. They had each subject rest one hand on a table and look at it through wedge prisms that displaced its visual image to one side. When the subject was asked to reach under the table and make a mark directly below the forefinger of his upper hand, a task he could perform quite accurately when blindfolded, he marked a location about as far from the finger's actual location as the prism-displaced image. Subjects did the same even when they were urged to rely entirely on where they felt the fingertip to be and to ignore its visual appearance. The investigators used for this effect of vision on touch the vivid term "visual capture."

Visual capture had also been observed 30 years earlier by James J. Gibson (then also at Smith but now at Cornell). He noted that when subjects ran their hand along a straight rod while looking through prisms that made the rod look curved, the rod felt curved. Torsten Nielsen of the University of Copenhagen recently demonstrated a similar form of visual capture without using any prisms. His subjects inserted one arm into a box and ran a pencil along a straight line while looking through a peephole. What they actually saw, however, was not their own hand but the experimenter's, reflected in a mirror so that it appeared to be in the same location as theirs. At first both the subject and the experimenter moved their hand back and forth along the line in time to a metronome. Then the experimenter started veering off the line. Strangely enough, few of Nielsen's subjects realized even then that the hand was not their own. They felt that their own hand was uncontrollably moving in a curve in spite of their efforts to stay on the line.

All these experiments show that when vision and touch provide conflicting information, the visual information dominates. Still, this is an immediate effect. Those who believe vision is originally educated by touch are thinking about the long-term result of continuous experience with the two senses. Perhaps, therefore, the experiments we have described are not crucial to the argument. A more pertinent question is: What happens after a period of exposure that is long enough to allow a genuine change in perception to take place?

In the experiments we have cited it could be that vision suppresses touch only temporarily, with the result that as soon as a person closes his eyes his touch perceptions return to normal. It could even be that although vision is at first

dominant, it eventually changes to match touch. On the other hand, the converse could be true: with sufficient exposure the sense of touch may be altered so that misperceptions by touch persist even after vision is blocked. With this issue in mind, we shall now consider

experiments in which changes in perception might be expected to occur because the exposure to the conflict is continued over a period of time.

Experiments by Helmholtz, Held and others using goggles fitted with sideways-displacing prisms do demonstrate

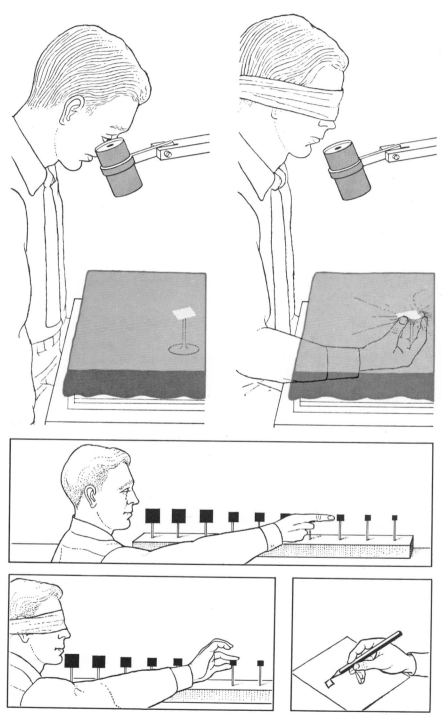

VARIETY OF TESTS determined what size a subject perceived a square to be when he was receiving conflicting data from vision and touch. In control tests he looked at the square without touching it (*top left*) and touched it without seeing it (*top right*). Then he matched it against squares shown only visually (*center*), matched it by touch alone (*bottom left*) and drew it (*bottom right*). In the tests the illusory visual size of the square predominated.

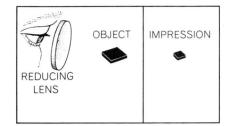

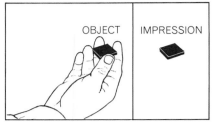

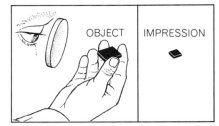

SUBJECT'S IMPRESSIONS in various experiments involving the reducing lens are indicated. In some cases (*left*) he merely saw an object through the lens; in some (*center*) he only felt the object, and in others (*right*) he simultaneously saw an object and felt it.

that appropriate exposure to a conflict between vision and touch produces aftereffects. When an observer first puts on the prisms and tries to point rapidly at an object, he misses. After several minutes of looking at his moving hand through the prisms, however, he points much more accurately even though his retinal images are still displaced. This adaptation is evident even if the subject's view of his hand is blocked during the pointing tests, thus preventing him from steering his seen hand to the seen target.

What does this adaptation show? It could be that the subject's visual perception has changed. He may be pointing more accurately because he is now seeing the object's location more accurately in spite of the displaced retinal image. If so, it could be contended that touch, which remained correct, had educated vision.

Conversely, it could just as well be that the subject is still seeing the object as displaced but now mistakenly feels that his hand is displaced when it is actually pointing straight ahead. This would mean that the adaptive change is in the sense of touch, specifically the sense of where one part of the body is with respect to the rest—the position sense. With continued exposure to the prisms the sensation of where the hand is may more closely approximate its observed location. The subject's misperception of his hand would compensate for his visual misperception of the object, enabling him to point fairly accurately.

To find out which explanation of the adaptation to sideways displacement is correct, one of us (Harris) carried out a series of experiments (some in collaboration with his wife, Judith R. Harris). The apparatus we used consisted of a glass surface that was just below the eye level of a seated subject and had as targets a row of lettered rods standing upright on the glass [*see illustration below*]. The experiments had three parts: pretest, adaptation and retest. In the pretest a black cloth was thrown over the glass surface so that the subject could see the targets but not his hand below the glass, and he was asked to

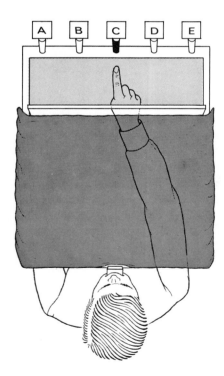

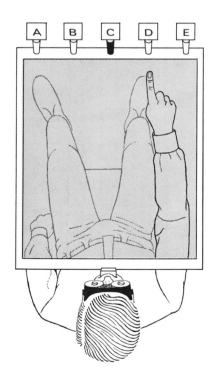

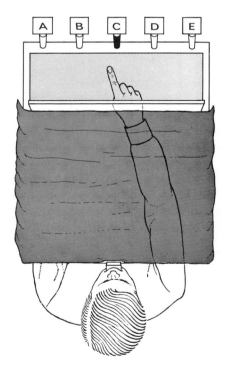

DISPLACED VISION was tested with this apparatus. First (*left*) the subject pointed at lettered rods without being able to see his hand; this pretest determined his normal responses. Then (*center*) he wore prism goggles that displaced his vision about four inches to one side, in this case to the right; while wearing them he was asked to point repeatedly at the center target with one hand. He usually missed at first because of the goggles. Finally (*right*) with the goggles off he was asked to point at various targets. Subjects typically showed an adaptation, or shift in pointing, with the hand used while wearing goggles but little or none with the other hand. Experiment suggested that his sense of the position of the adapted arm had changed. Biting device kept the subject's head steady.

point at various targets from below the glass. The pretest determined the subject's normal responses to the tests he would be given after adapting.

During adaptation the subject wore prism goggles for three minutes. The prisms shifted his visual field 11 degrees to the right or the left; the shift amounted to about four inches at arm's length. The subject's task was to point repeatedly with one hand at the center target. The cloth was removed during this phase so that the subject could see his hand through the glass. At first, because of the prisms, he tended to miss the target, but he quickly became more accurate.

For the retest we needed more than one kind of measurement in order to decide between the alternative explanations for the adaptive change in pointing by the subjects. The tests we chose were (1) pointing at visual targets seen without prisms, (2) pointing in the direction of sounds and (3) pointing in whatever direction the subject thought was straight ahead. During the nonvisual tests, of course, the subject kept his eyes closed.

We found that the subjects showed a large shift in pointing with the adapted hand on all three retests [see bottom illustration at right]. In contrast, there was little or no adaptive shift when a subject pointed with his unadapted hand —the one he had not seen through prisms. Each of these results has been obtained in at least one other laboratory, although there are still some unanswered questions about the effects of changing certain details of the experimental procedure.

This pattern of results is consistent with the conclusion that the adaptation involved a change in the position sense of the adapted arm. If the adapted subject feels that he is pointing straight ahead when he is actually pointing about five degrees to one side, he will make the same error no matter what he is pointing at: a visual object, a sound source or the straight-ahead direction. With his unadapted hand, however, he will show no error in pointing.

The findings clearly rule out the possibility that the adaptation is a change in visual perception. First, if the subject had learned to perceive the visual target in a new location, he should point at that new place with either hand. What actually happened was that when our subjects were asked to point at a target, they pointed in one direction with one hand and in a different direction with the other. Second, if adaptation were

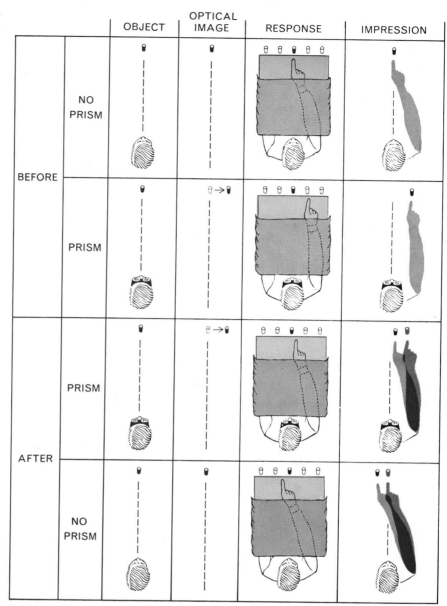

RESULTS OF TESTS with displacing prisms are charted before and after adaptation. "Object" column shows actual location of a target viewed by the subject; "image" column, how prisms displaced the target; "response," how the subject pointed. His impression of where the object was and where he was pointing is in last column. Experiment sought to find if pointing change after adaptation arose because he saw target differently (gray) or because he felt the position of his arm differently (color). Results showed that it was the latter.

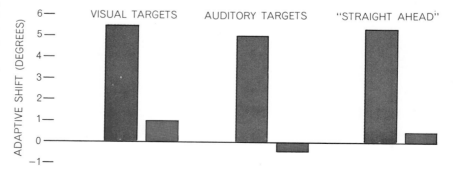

SHIFT IN RESPONSE was made by eight subjects after they had pointed at an object with one hand while wearing prisms that displaced vision to the side. Their shifts in subsequent pointing without prisms are shown for adapted hand (color) and unadapted hand (gray).

PROLONGED EXPOSURE to conflicting data from vision and touch was achieved with this apparatus. The revolving wheel held squares of various sizes. For 30 minutes the subject looked through the reducing lens while grasping one square after another through a cloth that prevented him from seeing his hand. Tests were given before and after the 30-minute exposure. Aim of experiment was to find if visual perception or touch perception changed.

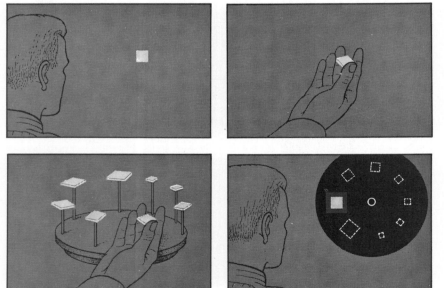

MATCHING TESTS given before and after 30-minute exposure to conflicting data included asking a subject to look at a square in a dark room (*top left*) and to match it by touch from a set of squares he could not see (*bottom left*). He was also asked to feel a square (*top right*) and to match it from a set displayed visually (*bottom right*). Use of reducing lens made subjects choose by touch a larger square than before as matching the visual standard; by vision they chose a smaller square than before as matching a square they had touched.

only a change in visual perception, it should have no effect on tests performed with the subject's eyes closed. Yet we found large adaptive shifts in pointing in the direction of a sound or in the straight-ahead direction—about as large as in pointing at visual targets. Third, if the adaptation is a change in visual perception, it should be revealed by tests of visual localization in which pointing is not involved, but no such effect has been found in this type of experiment.

Another potential explanation of adaptation to prisms (and it is a popular one among psychologists) is that adaptation is the learning of new motor responses: the subject simply learns to make movements appropriate to the altered visual stimulus. A person could correct his movements without any changes in perception. In fact, it may be that in some earlier experiments this is what happened. For example, it is quite clear that Stratton, who wore lenses that inverted the retinal image, did gradually learn to avoid the motor errors he initially made so often. The improvement does not, however, in itself demonstrate that he underwent any perceptual changes, such as learning to see normally through the inverting lenses. In our experiments too it could be that the adaptive shifts in pointing indicate only changes in motor response rather than in perception of where the arm is located.

To find out whether the change is in the subject's position sense or just in the movements he makes, we need a condition in which he judges the location of his hand without moving it. In one such test we had the subject estimate the distance between his hands while he was blindfolded. He made these judgments before and after one arm had been adapted. The adaptation procedure was the same as in the earlier experiment: the subject undertook to point repeatedly with his right hand at a visual target seen through prisms. During the pretest and retest, however, he was blindfolded and his right hand was moved by the experimenter to a predetermined location on the table in front of him. The subject was asked to place his unadapted left hand at a specified distance from his right hand. The right hand was then moved by the experimenter to a new location and the process was repeated.

We knew from the earlier results that the unadapted left hand had not been affected by the adaptation procedure, and during this test the adapted right hand was given no opportunity to execute any new responses it might have learned. Thus the subjects were forced to rely on their position sense in judging how far apart their hands felt. Their judgments indicated that after their right hand had been adapted to prisms that shifted the visual field to the right, the subjects felt that, at a given physical distance, their hands were farther apart than before. After adapting to a visual shift to the left, they felt that their hands were closer together. The results show that the subject's position sense had indeed been altered to the point that he misperceived the location of his adapted hand with respect to the location of his other hand.

The observations with the reducing lens mentioned earlier at first seem to contradict this finding. Although vision was dominant over touch when both senses were active, in that experiment touch returned to normal as soon as the subject closed his eyes. Would the change in touch outlast the conflict situation if the conflict situation were continued for a longer time? This question was investigated in experiments by one of us (Rock) in collaboration with Arien Mack, A. Lewis Hill and Laurence Adams. Over a 30-minute period the subject handled squares of various sizes while looking at them through a reducing lens [*see top illustration on preceding page*]. A cloth prevented the subject from seeing his hand during this time.

Two matching tests administered before and after the 30-minute period showed that the subject's perception of size had changed. In one test we showed him a standard square that he could see but not touch and asked him to select by touch a matching square from a set he could touch but not see. After the 30-minute period with the reducing lens subjects typically selected by touch a larger square than before as matching the visual standard. When they were given a standard square to touch without being able to see it, they typically chose a smaller matching square from a set that was displayed visually. (In both tests the squares were coated with luminous paint and presented in the dark so that there would be no familiar objects to which a square could be compared.)

Both results demonstrate that after exposure to the conflicting information the subject matches felt size with seen size differently than he did before. For a felt object and a seen object to seem equal to him the visual object has to be smaller than before. These results do not reveal, however, which sense has

changed to yield the new match. Did the subject pick a smaller seen square because seen objects now looked larger or because felt objects now felt smaller? Although the immediate result of the conflict between vision and touch is a dominance of vision, the correct information provided by touch may still be having an effect, even if it does not enter the consciousness. In that case the square might look larger after adaptation, perhaps ultimately reaching its true size. If, on the other hand, the visual size of the square were to serve as the crucial information and the square were to come to feel smaller than it is, we would have an example consistent with all our other findings.

To determine whether it was vision or touch that had changed, we used a "remembered standard" test. In the test of visual size we first had the subject practice looking at a one-inch square and then matching it visually from immediate memory. Then, after the 30 minutes

of looking through the reducing lens, we asked him to select visually a square the same size as he remembered the standard square to be. The selection was again done in the dark with luminous squares.

If visual size has undergone a change, the subject should now (without the reducing lens) select a smaller square as matching the standard one than he did before the exposure to the conflict situation; the smaller square should now look larger than it is. The result, however, was that the subject selected a square that was the same size on the average as the one he chose before exposure to the conflict situation. In other words, there was no change in the visual perception of size.

We used a similar procedure to find out if touch had changed. Before exposure to the conflict the subject practiced feeling the standard square and matching it by touch from immediate recollection. After exposure to the conflict situa-

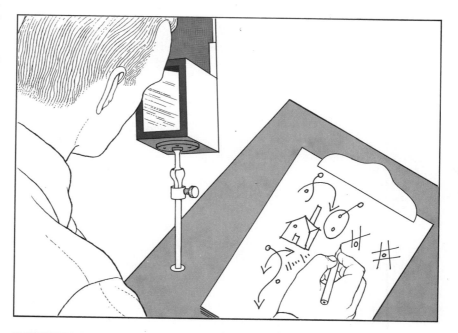

REVERSING-PRISM EXPERIMENTS called for a subject to doodle (*top*) while looking through a prism that reversed right and left. Before exposure to the prisms every subject wrote numbers and letters as shown at bottom left; after use of the prisms the subjects often wrote as shown at bottom right. Vision was blocked in writing tests. Subjects often thought the letters they had written backward were normal and normal letters were backward.

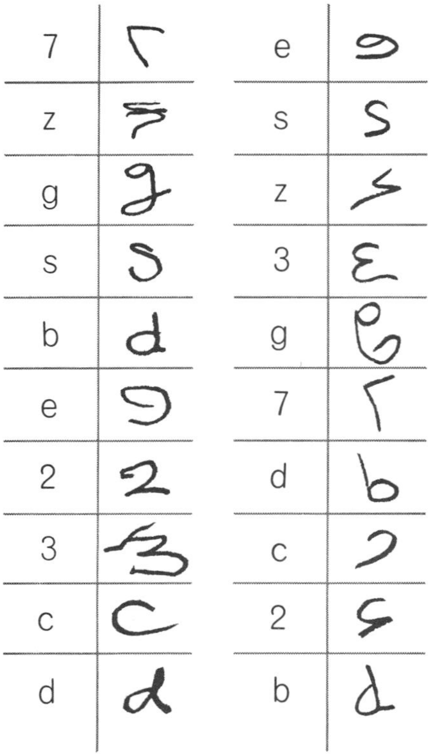

7	*(handwritten)*	e	*(handwritten)*
z	*(handwritten)*	s	*(handwritten)*
g	*(handwritten)*	z	*(handwritten)*
s	*(handwritten)*	3	*(handwritten)*
b	*(handwritten)*	g	*(handwritten)*
e	*(handwritten)*	7	*(handwritten)*
2	*(handwritten)*	d	*(handwritten)*
3	*(handwritten)*	c	*(handwritten)*
c	*(handwritten)*	2	*(handwritten)*
d	*(handwritten)*	b	*(handwritten)*

WRITING ABERRATIONS of two subjects after exposure to reversing prisms are represented. The letters and numbers they were asked to write are at left; what they wrote is at right. In the second sample only the *S* is normal; that was the only letter the subject thought she had written backward.

tion he selected by touch alone a square that he felt was the same size as the previously experienced one-inch square. The great majority of subjects chose a larger square as matching the standard than they had before. The larger square now felt smaller than it was.

What would happen if there were a more dramatic conflict between vision and touch, as in experiments on inversion or reversal of the retinal image? If a subject looks through reversing prisms, for example, while moving his hand from left to right, could he be misled into feeling it as moving right to left? An experiment undertaken by one of us (Harris) and Judith Harris showed that vision is powerful enough to accomplish even this radical a misperception.

We had the subject look through a right-angle prism, which acts like a mirror, reversing the visual field right for left [*see illustration on preceding page*]. The prism was attached to a rigid frame. The subject watched his hand through the prism, while drawing and doodling, for 15 minutes a day on four different days. For reasons that will soon become evident, he was not allowed to write or see any letters or numbers while looking through the prism.

For most subjects there was no immediate visual capture. When they felt their hand move in one direction, they saw it stubbornly going in the opposite direction. The felt hand and the seen hand seemed to be separate things.

Within a matter of minutes, however, visual capture took over. Most subjects no longer experienced any discrepancy between how they saw their hands move and how they felt them move. They no longer had trouble drawing or doodling or reaching for locations indicated by the experimenter.

In order to determine if there was an aftereffect of this visual capture, we hit on the following simple procedure. At the end of each prism period we slid a metal plate in front of the prism, blocking the subject's view. We then asked him to quickly write 10 letters and numbers as we dictated them. We had previously told the subjects that the adaptation procedure might make them write an occasional letter backward and that they must be sure to tell us whenever they thought they had done so.

Actually a subject could have two kinds of misperception. He could believe a letter was normal when it was really backward, and he could believe a letter was backward when it was really normal. We found that both kinds of misperception occurred; every one of our eight subjects made at least one such error. In fact, immediately after looking through the prism the subjects misperceived fully 30 percent of the letters and numbers they wrote. (In the pretests given before the use of the prism, of course, no subject ever misperceived what he was writing.) The results, some of which are shown in the illustration on this page, are particularly surprising in view of the fact that writing normal letters and numbers is such a highly practiced skill.

Our experiments all show, then, that when a subject's sense of touch conveys information that disagrees with what he is seeing, the visual information determines his perception. What happens during such a conflict to the information the sense of touch is providing? Is it blocked before it reaches the brain, is it ignored or is it transformed? After sufficient exposure to an intersensory disagreement there is a change in the sense of touch itself. Since the subject continues to misperceive by touch even with his eyes closed, he cannot be blocking or ignoring the information provided by touch. It is therefore a **reasonable** guess that the information is not blocked or ignored when his eyes are open either. Instead it must be transformed into new touch perceptions that are consistent with visual perception.

The further implications of our experiments are less clear, particularly for situations that are more normal than the restricted conditions under which our subjects worked. What kind of adaptation to altered retinal images takes place when a subject can move about freely and can see much more of his environment than our subjects saw? The experimental data are still fragmentary enough to allow us to disagree on this point.

One of us (Rock) believes visual perception can change if a person subjected to optical distortion has adequate visual information about the distortion. For example, the world might look upside down through reversing prisms, but if the subject can see his own body—the image of which would also be inverted—he realizes that the world is not upside down in relation to himself. Similarly, if a seated subject looks at a straight vertical line through prisms that at first make it appear curved and he then stands up, the appearance of the line will change in a way that would not be the case if the line were really curved. Hence he may come to see that the line is straight. This argument maintains that a change in visual perception can occur but acknowledges that information from touch alone is insufficient to cause such a change.

The other of us (Harris) thinks all substantial adaptation to optical distortions probably results from changes in the sense of the position of the limbs, the head or the eyes. If a person felt that his arms and legs were where he saw them through inverting or reversing prisms, he would make responses like those reported by Stratton and Kohler. If he felt that his eyes were pointing directly ahead or tracing a straight path when they were actually pointing somewhat to one side or tracing a curved path, he would show the kind of adaptation to displacement or curvature that is found in some other experiments.

Our disagreement does not affect the basic points demonstrated by our separate experiments. Those points are that there is no convincing evidence for the time-honored theory that touch educates vision and that there is strong evidence for the contrary theory. Further experiments along these lines can be expected to clarify the points that remain obscure.

Sources of Ambiguity in the Prints of Maurits C. Escher

by Marianne L. Teuber
July 1974

The fascinating graphic inventions of the late Dutch artist reflect a strong mathematical and crystallographic influence. Their original inspiration, however, came from experiments on visual perception

If ambiguity is a sign of our time, the late Dutch graphic artist Maurits C. Escher managed to represent it in striking visual terms. In Escher's art there is the ambiguity of figure and ground; the ambiguity of two and three dimensions on the flat surface; the ambiguity of the reversible cube; the ambiguous limits of the infinitely small and the infinitely large. In his prints visual ambiguity goes hand in hand with ambiguity of meaning. Good and evil are contemplated in the figure-ground reversal of black devils and white angels. Day changes into night; sky becomes water; fish metamorphose into fowl.

Escher's regular subdivisions of the surface have been compared to the packed periodic structures of crystals and to the mathematical transformations of topology and non-Euclidean geometry [see "Mathematical Games," SCIENTIFIC AMERICAN, April, 1961, and April, 1966]. The original inspiration for his unusual ambiguous patterns, however, can be traced to contemporary sources more familiar to the student of psychology and visual perception. Psychological studies of the relation of figure and ground—in turn encouraged by the positive and negative forms of Art Nouveau —were for Escher the primary stimulus. Only after he had mastered reversible figure-ground constructions of his own invention did he recognize their similarity to certain principles of crystallography, and his interest in mathematics was aroused.

Figure-ground designs appear at an early stage in Escher's work—as early as 1921, when he was only 23 years old. It was not until the late 1930's, however, when Escher "rediscovered" the style that made him famous, that the figure-ground ambiguity clearly became the dominant feature of his art. The well-known woodcuts *Development I, Day and Night* and *Sky and Water I,* among others, date from this period.

From Escher's own commentary on these prints in *The Graphic Work of M. C. Escher* one must conclude that he knew the pertinent psychological literature. In particular he seems to have been familiar with the early experiments on figure and ground by the Danish psychologist Edgar Rubin, with Kurt Koffka's 1935 book *Principles of Gestalt Psychology,* where Rubin's results are summarized, and with the studies of Molly R. Harrower, a student of Koffka's. Patterns related to crystallography and geometry turn out to be a later development.

One of Rubin's best-known patterns, presented in his 1915 monograph dealing with visually perceived form as a function of the relation of figure to ground, can be seen either as a vase in the center or as two profiles facing each other [*see illustration at left*]. When the profiles are seen, the vase becomes ground, and vice versa. It is impossible, as Rubin points out, to see vase and profiles simultaneously as figures.

Rubin's book was published in a German translation in Copenhagen in 1921. The following year, when the young Escher was completing his training at the School of Architecture and Ornamental Design in Haarlem, he carved a

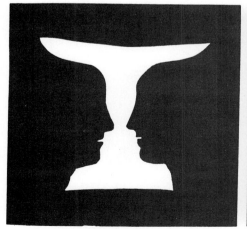

REVERSIBLE PATTERNS published originally in 1915 by the Danish psychologist Edgar Rubin in a study of the role of the figure-ground relation in visual perception were presumably familiar to Escher at an early stage. The pattern at left can be seen either as a vase in the center or as two profiles facing each other. The more abstract pattern at right can be seen either as a black figure against a white background or vice versa. In each case it is impossible, said Rubin, to see both the black and the white areas simultaneously as figures.

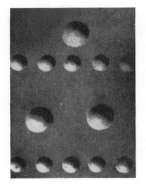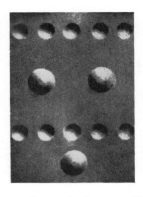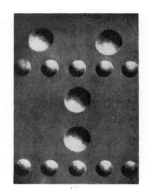

EXPERIMENTAL PATTERNS designed to study the crater illusion were published by the Finnish psychologist Kai von Fieandt in 1938. The patterns test the changes in depth perception from concave to convex, depending on the direction of the illumination.

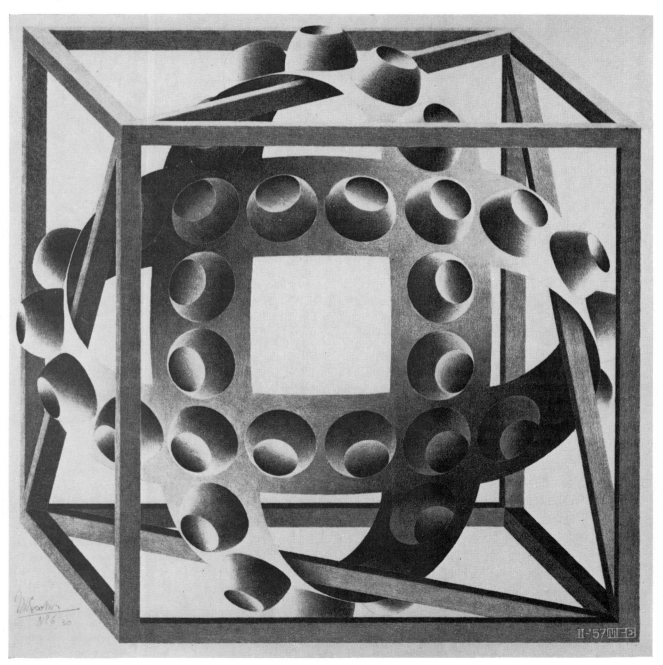

"CUBE WITH MAGIC RIBBONS," a 1957 Escher lithograph in the Roosevelt collection at the National Gallery, uses strips of small "buttonlike protuberances" just like those illustrated in the von Fieandt study to explore "inversions" of concave and convex.

woodcut called *Eight Heads* [*see illustration below*]. Each head fills exactly the space left between neighboring heads and acts alternately as figure and ground, depending on the viewer's attitude. Escher is quite explicit about his purpose. In *The Graphic Work of M. C. Escher* the artist himself provides an introduction and comments on his prints. These explanations reflect the technical language of his scientific sources. The wording here leaves no doubt about the

specific psychological studies that contributed to the formation of his unique style.

One can easily discern the link with Rubin's experiments when Escher classifies *Eight Heads* and his later reversible patterns of fish and bird in *Sky and Water I* or *Day and Night* under the heading "The Function of Figures as a Background." Escher comments: "Our eyes are accustomed to fixing on a specific object. The moment this happens every-

thing round about becomes reduced to background." This description is in keeping with Rubin's analysis of his ambiguous vase-profile pattern.

Whereas Escher insisted on meaningful, if fantastic, creatures for his basic reversible units, Rubin, in his attempt to find general principles of figure formation, actually preferred more abstract designs. In his 1915 book Rubin even cites Wassily Kandinsky's contemporary abstract paintings as good examples of the

"EIGHT HEADS," a woodcut carved by Escher in 1922, the year he finished his training at the School of Architecture and Ornamental Design at Haarlem in the Netherlands, bears a strong resemblance to Rubin's diagrams. Each of the four male and four female heads can act alternately as figure or ground. *Eight Heads* was Escher's first attempt at an infinitely repeating subdivision of a plane surface. This reproduction is from a print in the Escher Foundation collection in the Haags Gemeentemuseum at The Hague.

MAJOLICA TILES at the Alhambra in Spain were sketched by Escher during a trip in 1936. The internal symmetry and the am-biguous contours of the Moorish designs appear to have helped revive Escher's early fascination with the figure-ground problem.

equivalence of color fields. By means of abstract test patterns Rubin hoped to isolate basic characteristics of form perception without the distractions caused by figurative images. As he points out, it is always the form with the greater realistic or emotional appeal that tends to attract our attention; in the vase-profile pattern, for instance, the profiles will win out when the reversals are observed over prolonged periods.

To avoid these pitfalls Rubin derived the main principles of what makes for figure and what for ground from his abstract patterns. According to Rubin, one usually sees the smaller enclosed form as figure by contrast with the larger surrounding expanse of the ground. The figure has "solid-object quality," whereas the ground takes on a "film quality." The figure protrudes; the ground recedes and stretches behind the figure. The contour is seen as belonging to the figure and not to the ground.

In ambiguous patterns, however, the one-sided function of the contour is challenged. Rubin's analysis of contours can be recognized in Escher's description of the difficulties he encountered in drawing his ambiguous creatures. In discussing the borderline between two adjacent shapes having a double function Escher notes that "the act of tracing such a line is a complicated business. On either side of it, simultaneously, a recognizability takes shape. But the human eye and mind cannot be busy with two things at the same moment, and so there must be a quick and continual jumping from one side to the other.... This difficulty is perhaps the very moving-spring of my perseverance."

After his early exposure to Rubin's work in 1921 and 1922, Escher left his native Netherlands to live in Italy until

"METAMORPHOSIS I," a woodcut designed by Escher in 1937, represents an abrupt change in his style from the flat periodic sub-divisions he had invented up to 1936 to the development of forms from flat to plastic on the two-dimensional plane. This new ap-

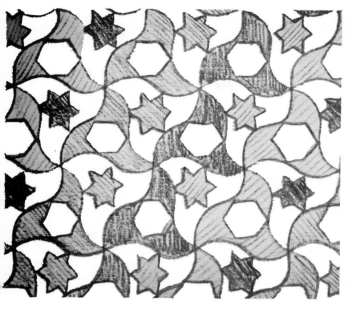

Unlike the Moorish artists, however, Escher continued to design his flat tessellations with contiguous human and animal forms.

Escher's original color drawings of the Alhambra tiles are part of the Escher Foundation collection in the Haags Gemeentemuseum.

1934. An extraordinarily skillful craftsman, he created a large series of woodcuts and lithographs; they represent landscapes, architecture and portraiture in brilliantly realistic style, in which the traditional Renaissance picture space prevails. Only once during his Italian period did the figure-ground problem return: in 1926 he designed some interlocking animal shapes, very similar to his later periodic structures on the picture surface. Escher claims that the departure from Italy in 1934 was responsible for his change in style. He felt that landscape in the North did not attract him as

it had in Italy; instead, he writes, "I concentrated...on personal ideas...and inner visions." He lived for more than a year in Switzerland and for five years in Belgium before settling in 1941 at Baarn in the Netherlands, where he remained until his death in 1972, except for brief visits to Britain, the U.S. and Canada.

As I have noted, the major turning point in Escher's style came in the late 1930's after he left Italy. What caused that change? It is evident that at some time between 1935 and 1938 Escher became acquainted with Koffka's *Princi-*

ples of Gestalt Psychology. That Escher was indebted to Koffka can be documented from his graphic work and written comments. Koffka, one of the three chief proponents of Gestalt psychology (with Max Wertheimer and Wolfgang Köhler), relied heavily on Rubin's work, although Rubin never counted himself among the Gestalt psychologists. In *Principles of Gestalt Psychology* an entire chapter is devoted to the topic of figure and ground. Thus, through Koffka, an old and fascinating preoccupation of Escher's was revived.

Escher's development can be appre-

proach appears to have been influenced by his reading of Kurt Koffka's 1935 book *Principles of Gestalt Psychology*. The design is

reproduced here from an original print in the National Gallery of Art in Washington, D.C. (gift of Cornelius Van Schaak Roosevelt).

ciated by considering drawings the artist made in 1936 on a trip to Spain when he copied majolica tiles at the Alhambra [*see top illustration on preceding two pages*]. These examples of Moorish art with their internal symmetry and obviously ambiguous contours must have attracted him precisely because he had been familiar with the figure-ground problem since 1921. He looked at the Alhambra tiles with eyes trained by Rubin's experiments. As in the case of Rubin's abstract patterns, however, he regretted that the Moorish artists were not allowed to make "graven images" and "always restricted themselves... to designs of an abstract geometrical type. Not one single Moorish artist... ever made so bold... as to use concrete, recognizable, naturalistically conceived figures of fish, birds, reptiles or human beings as elements in their surface coverage."

Instead Escher preferred to design his flat tessellations with contiguous human and animal forms. In the course of the next year or so, however, he abruptly transformed this flat motif into three-dimensional cubes and an entire town in his woodcut *Metamorphosis I* [*see bottom illustration on preceding two pages*]. One of the new aspects noticeable in Escher's post-1937 work, in contrast with the flat periodic subdivisions he had invented up to 1936, is the development of forms from flat to plastic on the two-dimensional plane. In *Principles of Gestalt Psychology* Koffka demonstrates the compelling three-dimensional organization of two-dimensional lines and planes under certain conditions. He shows, among other examples, how a hexagon, depending on the internal arrangement of its lines, can change from a flat pattern to a cube, just as in Escher's *Metamorphosis I*. In summarizing experiments by Hertha Kopfermann and himself, Koffka points out that it is the intrinsic tendency toward simplicity of organization that makes one see one array of forms as two-dimensional and a slightly altered one as three-dimensional.

Many of Escher's prints of the following years are based on just such a change of forms from flat to plastic. A noteworthy example is the lithograph *Reptiles*, designed in 1943 [*see illustration below*]. Escher describes this series of prints in words that echo Koffka's text: "The chief characteristics of these prints is the transition from flat to spatial and vice versa." Escher goes on to show how in such designs the individual creatures free themselves from the flat ground in which they are rigidly embedded. He writes: "We can think in terms of an interplay between the stiff, crystallized two-dimensional figures of a regular pattern and the individual freedom of three-dimensional creatures capable of moving about in space without hindrance. On the one hand, the members of the planes of collectivity come to life in space; on the other, the free individuals sink back and lose themselves in the community."

In the same manner Koffka speaks in the last chapter of his book of the embracing ground and the protruding figure as paradigms for the relation between personality and "behavioral social field." The reptiles in Escher's lithograph thus free themselves from the contiguous design on the flat page to venture into three-dimensional space, only to return to the flat surface where their individuality is again submerged. On their way they pass the paraphernalia of smoking and other ephemeral artifacts drawn in hard illusionistic style; they crawl over one of the Platonic solids (a dodecahedron). These forms fascinated Escher because, as he said, geometric shapes were timeless and not man-made.

During the same period (1936–1938) Escher also became aware of an experimental study by Harrower, who in April, 1936, published an article titled "Some Factors Determining Figure-Ground Articulation" in the *British Journal of Psychology*. She varied Rubin's pattern in the following manner. Several test cards emphasized the outline of the vase and let the profiles recede into the background; other cards emphasized the profiles and allowed the vase to become ground; the center card showed the vase and profiles as being equivalent. Two years later, in 1938, Escher created two of his most striking woodcuts, *Sky and Water I* [*see illustration at top right on opposite page*] and *Day and Night* [*see bottom illustration on opposite page*], according to the same principle; in these works the ground slowly becomes figure and the figure becomes ground; the forms in the center, however, remain equivalent. In his interpretation of *Sky and Water I* Escher employs Harrower's terminology when he says: "In the horizontal central strip there are birds and fish equivalent to each other."

This principle of equivalence, first discussed by Rubin and emphasized by Harrower, is an important ingredient of Escher's many inventive preparatory drawings for his woodcuts. When explaining his compositions, Escher would frequently refer to the fact that his forms had to be "equivalent." The crystallographic terms "distinct" and "equivalent" should not, of course, be confused with the simple notion of equivalence Escher (and Harrower) had in mind. The ingenious basic drawing of *Fish and*

"REPTILES," a lithograph designed in 1943, is a notable example of Escher's increasing preoccupation after 1937 with the transformation of forms from flat to plastic. This reproduction is from a print in the Lessing J. Rosenwald collection at the National Gallery.

"FISH AND FOWL," a preliminary drawing for the woodcut *Sky and Water I*, is a good example of Escher's interest in the "equivalence" of visual forms, a notion he adapted from Molly R. Harrower, a student of Koffka's. The original is in the Gemeentemuseum.

"SKY AND WATER I," carved in 1938, is one of Escher's best-known woodcuts. Unlike the preliminary watercolor drawing at left, the forms of the birds and the fish are equivalent only in the center. This reproduction is from a print in the Gemeentemuseum.

Fowl for *Sky and Water I* is a good example of equivalence; the surfaces of the individual birds and fish are approximately equal in extent, internal design, light-dark contrast and simplicity of contour [see illustration at top left on this page]. Such equivalence makes the figures ambiguous, and a rapid reversal is the result.

In her 1936 article Harrower tested the relation of figure to ground by introducing a number of variables, among them increasing and decreasing brightness contrast (or graded grays). Escher's woodcut *Development I*, made in 1937, shows how faint gray squares arranged along the periphery gain in black-and-white contrast as well as distinctness of shape until they become four black and white reptiles in the center [see top illustration on next page]. The two "factors"

"DAY AND NIGHT," another 1938 woodcut, represents the same slow transformation of ground into figure and figure into ground, with only the forms in the center remaining equivalent. The principle of transformation is the same as that discussed by Harrower in her 1936 article in the *British Journal of Psychology*. The original print is in the Rosenwald collection at the National Gallery.

"DEVELOPMENT I," a 1937 Escher woodcut, incorporates two basic variables from Harrower's experiments: brightness gradient and development from shapeless ground to distinct figure. This print is in the John D. Merriam collection at the Boston Public Library.

from Harrower's experiments, brightness gradient and development from shapeless ground to distinct figure, are the basic compositional principles of this impressive work. Escher's comment on the print is again couched in the technical language of Harrower's study. He writes: "Scarcely visible gray squares at the edges evolve in form and contrast toward the center."

Escher groups several additional prints under the category "Development of Form and Contrast," in keeping with Harrower's analysis. One of these is the lithograph *Liberation,* designed in 1955 [*see illustration on opposite page*]. He describes this print in terms that are reminiscent of Harrower's test cards and Koffka's text: "On the uniformly gray strip of paper that is being unrolled, a simultaneous development in form and contrast is taking place. Triangles—at first scarcely visible—change into more complicated figures, whilst the color contrast between them increases. In the middle they are transformed into white and black birds, and from there fly off into the world as independent creatures, and so the strip of paper on which they are drawn disappears."

In *Liberation* Escher presents us with a surrealist situation; the birds freed from the gray scroll are caught, nevertheless, on the surface on which the lithograph is printed. The artist reflects here on the visual absurdity of his own craft, as he had implicitly in *Reptiles.*

To summarize this important phase in Escher's artistic development, starting in 1937, he transforms his ambiguous figurative patterns in three ways: (1) from flat to plastic, derived from Koffka's *Principles of Gestalt Psychology* of 1935; (2) from shaped form to shapeless ground, derived from Harrower's study of 1936; (3) from strong black-and-white contrast to gray, also derived from Harrower.

Sky and Water I and *Day and Night,* both done in 1938, exhibit these categories of transformation of shape. In *Day and Night* the square gray fields in the foreground gain in articulation of shape and contrast; they become an equivalent pattern of distinct black birds and white birds in the upper center and from there develop into three-dimensional creatures flying off into the "real" world of day or night. In *Sky and Water I* the strongly articulated plastic single bird and single fish, above and below, evolve from the flat equivalent strip in the middle. What was bird becomes watery ground and what was fish becomes sky. Here Escher enhances the individuality, or object quality, of the figure compared with the film quality of the ground, features already emphasized by Rubin in 1915.

It is difficult to reconstruct by what route Escher came in such close contact with the technical aspects of figure-ground experiments. He may have had a mentor. The artist himself belonged to a family where professional and intellectual achievement were the rule, and he may have come across Koffka's and Harrower's experiments because of his own strong interests. The year in the French-speaking part of Switzerland (1936), near the universities of Geneva and Lau-

"SWANS," a 1956 woodcut, is a good example of how, in experimenting with space-filling tessellations on a flat surface, Escher often relied on crystallographic rules of transformation. He himself classified this print under the heading "Glide Reflexion." The print used to make this reproduction is in the Roosevelt collection at the National Gallery.

sanne, and the five years in Ukkel, not far from the University of Brussels (1937–1941), were the period of his "conversion," when he made the figure-ground problem a permanent feature of his style. Whatever his contacts may have been, by the 1930's not only was the impact of Gestalt psychology widespread at European universities but also it had become fashionable among intellectuals.

The figure-ground studies of the Gestalt psychologists were not, however, Escher's only source of inspiration. He varied his fantastic tessellations on the picture plane by following the structural principles of periodic packing in crystals. Caroline H. MacGillavry analyzed Escher's inventions in these terms in her 1965 monograph *Symmetry Aspects of M. C. Escher's Periodic Drawings*. In *Color and Symmetry*, published in 1971, A. L. Loeb selects striking instances of form and color symmetry from Escher's work to accompany his text. Escher himself recognized the similarities of his regular subdivisions on the plane to principles of crystallography. They had been pointed out to him by his brother, B. G. Escher, professor of geology at the University of Leyden. By that time, however, the artist had created his own figure-ground patterns based on Rubin's visual analyses and the Moorish tiles at the Alhambra. As the mathematician H. S. M. Coxeter has remarked, the Moors had already made use of all 17 crystallographic groups of symmetry structures, subsequently established by E. S. Fedorov in 1891.

In experimenting with space-filling creatures on the flat surface, Escher arrived at many intriguing compositions that follow crystallographic rules of transformation; a good example is his woodcut *Swans*, designed in 1956 [*see bottom illustration on opposite page*]. Again Escher writes a commentary, as he had done for his figure-ground inventions. He groups these prints under the heading "Glide Reflexion" and acknowledges the "three fundamental principles of crystallography"; they are, in his words, "repeated shifting (translation), turning about axes (rotation) and glide mirror image (reflexion)." Among

"LIBERATION," a lithograph designed in 1955, was classified by Escher under the heading "Development of Form and Contrast," in keeping with the technical terms of Harrower's analysis. This print is in Merriam collection at Boston Public Library.

scientists this aspect of Escher's graphic work is probably the best known.

Yet the origin of his compositions from playful manipulations of the figure-ground ambiguity has so far been noted only once before—by the art historian E. H. Gombrich in his article "Illusions and Visual Deadlock" (reprinted in his 1963 book *Meditations on a Hobby Horse*). This oversight is understandable, since Escher's later prints suggest mathematical prototypes as a primary source for his work. Such an interpretation is offered, for example, by Coxeter. In his essay "The Mathematical Implications of Escher's Prints" (reprinted in *The World of M. C. Escher*) Coxeter marvels at Escher's ability to extend the theory of crystallographic groups beyond Fedorov's original 17 by anticipating "through artistic intuition" the added principle of color symmetry.

Escher, however, was led to these extensions by his earlier sources from the psychological literature. Thus he knew how to combine both the figurative reversals and the crystallographic rules of regular and semiregular tessellations in one and the same composition on the flat picture surface. In *Reptiles* and in many other drawings he achieved such a feat. The fundamental region of a tessellation is a polygon (triangle, square or hexagon) or a combination of polygons; they must meet corner to corner. In *Reptiles* three heads, three elbows and three toes abut exactly at the corners of a hexagon, which forms the fundamental region of this regular tessellation on the plane. Escher looked at these solutions, some more difficult than others, with a great deal of pride.

A similar close association between crystallographic principles and the design of densely packed surfaces was recognized by Paul Klee and later by Victor Vasarely. Both painters based certain pictures and diagrams on Johannes Kepler's humorous treatise *De Nive Sexangula* (*The Six-cornered Snowflake*), published in 1611. Kepler's neo-Platonic concept of an underlying order or harmony—the belief in a mathematical structure of the universe—was shared by Escher. Occasionally one or another of his graphic works illustrates that idea, for example *Reptiles* or *Stars*, a 1948 wood engraving in the style of the early 17th century, Kepler's period [*see illustration on this page*]. This work depicts a star-studded sky in which the stellar bodies are composed of the Platonic solids cherished by Kepler. In such prints Escher intends to draw a contrast between the permanent laws of mathematics and the incidentals of debris or the changing colors of chameleons. "There is something in such laws that takes the breath away," Escher wrote in his essay "Approaches to Infinity." He continued: "They are not discoveries or inventions of the human mind but exist independently of us." Thus had Socrates explained the intrinsic beauty of geometric forms in Plato's *Philebus*. The abstract laws or principles of simplicity of form that attracted Escher to the perceptual analyses of the Gestalt psychologists were also essentially Platonic in concept.

Through his new interest in mathematics and contact with mathematicians, Escher expanded his vocabulary of ambiguous forms. He used the Möbius strip, the Klein bottle, knots and various forms of polygons. *Circle Limit I*, a hyperbolic (non-Euclidian) construction, was developed in 1958 in an exchange of letters with Coxeter [*see illustration at top left on opposite page*]. It gave Escher a chance to represent "the limits of infinite smallness," as he termed it. *Heaven and Hell*, done in 1960, belongs to the same series [*see illustration at top right on opposite page*].

In the 1950's Escher returned to sources from the psychology of visual perception in a group of prints dealing with reversible perspectives. The 1957 lithograph *Cube with Magic Ribbons* combines the reversible Necker cube (a discovery of the 19th-century Swiss mineralogist L. A. Necker) with the crater illusion [*see bottom illustration on page 126*]. In 1938 the Finnish psychologist Kai von Fieandt published a study on apparent changes in depth perception from concave to convex depending on different directions of light. For his experiments he used small knobs shaped

"STARS," a 1948 wood engraving done in the style of the early 17th century, celebrates Escher's identification with Johannes Kepler's neo-Platonic belief in an underlying mathematical order in the universe. The print is in Roosevelt collection at the National Gallery.

"CIRCLE LIMIT I," a woodcut designed by Escher in 1958, was based on a non-Euclidean mathematical construction developed in an exchange of letters with the mathematician H. S. M. Coxeter. The reproduction is made from a print in the Gemeentemuseum.

"HEAVEN AND HELL," a 1960 Escher woodcut in which the figure-ground ambiguity mirrors an ambiguity of meaning (good and evil), belongs to the same series of mathematically derived designs. The reproduction is from a print in the Gemeentemuseum.

just like those appearing on Escher's band [*see top illustration on next page*]. Escher must have known von Fieandt's experiments. The artist explains: "If we follow...the strips of buttonlike protuberances...with the eye, then these nodules surreptitiously change from convex to concave."

Concave and Convex [*see top illustra-* *tion on page 136*] belongs to the same group of prints where reversible perspectives, or "inversions," as Escher called them, are the topic. The cluster of cubes on the flag announces the basic visual motif of the composition. In this 1955 lithograph Escher plays with the ambiguity of volumes on the flat picture plane; they switch from solid to hollow,

from inward to outward, from roof to ceiling—like the symbol on the flag.

In 1958 Escher created *Belvedere,* an impossible building, also based on the reversible Necker cube [*see bottom illustration on page 137*]. By the end of the 19th century the Necker cube had become one of the most popular and most frequently debated optical illusions

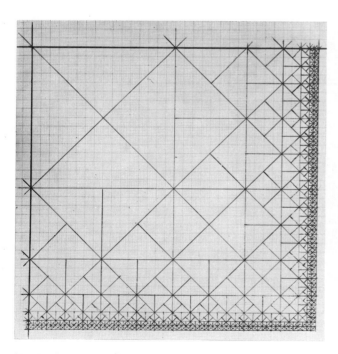

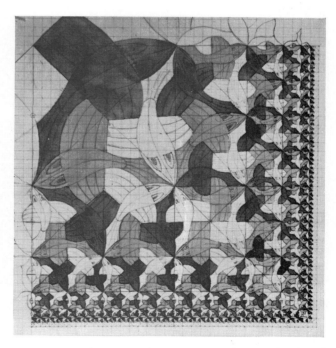

STUDIES for Escher's 1964 woodcut *Square Limit* reveal that this design was carried out by simply dividing surface after surface in half, up to the limit of visibility at the outer edge. This reproduction is from the original drawing in the Gemeentemuseum.

"CONCAVE AND CONVEX," a lithograph designed by Escher in 1955, also makes use of reversible perspectives to bring out the ambiguity of volumes portrayed on the flat picture plane. The original print is in the Rosenwald collection at the National Gallery.

EIGHTEENTH-CENTURY ENGRAVING by Giovanni Battista Piranesi, one of a series titled *Carceri (Prisons)*, is distinguished by perspective aberrations of a type similar to those in Escher's prints. Escher actually owned a set of Piranesi's *Carceri*, but he discounted their influence on his own work, pointing out that he was much more inspired by experiments on visual perception. This detail of a print catalogued Plate XI, 2nd State is reproduced here by courtesy of the Museum of Fine Arts in Boston (gift of Miss Ellen Bullard).

in the psychological literature. To emphasize the theme of the fantastic piece of architecture, the boy on the bench contemplates the reversible cube in his hands and on paper. The corners that are flipping forward and backward during reversals are connected by diagonals, just as in Necker's original 1832 drawing [*see top illustration on next page*]. In *Belvedere*, however, Escher not only uses reversible perspective but also introduces perceptual impossibility, which obstructs the two perceptual interpretations of the cube simultaneously. This technique resembles the constructions of impossible figures published in 1958 by L. S. Penrose and R. Penrose in the *British Journal of Psychology*, acknowledged by Escher as a source for his 1960 lithograph *Ascending and Descending*.

The Schröder stairs, another 19th-century reversible-perspective illusion, first published by H. Schröder in 1858 [*see top illustration on page 138*], is the theme of Escher's 1953 lithograph *Relativity* [*see middle illustration on page 138*]. The stairs show the characteristic shading that facilitates reversals, so that they look either like a staircase going up or an overhang of wall coming down. For the inhabitants of this structure the stairs lead up and down at the same time.

These compositions resemble certain 18th-century engravings, particularly Giovanni Battista Piranesi's *Carceri (Prisons)*, with their obsessional repetitions and their shifting viewpoints that break up the unity of Renaissance perspective, thus giving a hallucinatory quality to these architectural dreams [*see bottom illustration at left*]. Note in the distance in the upper left quadrant of Piranesi's print a light-shaded underside of an arch. Or is it a walkway leading to a set of stairs? In *Concave and Convex* Escher employs the same motif in both orientations. Escher actually owned a set of Piranesi's engravings, according to his son, George A. Escher, who relates the following revealing story about his father and *Belvedere*:

"One evening, it must have been late 1958, we were looking at the *Carceri* by Piranesi, which he greatly admired and of which he owned a posthumously printed set. We had been hunting for the many perspective aberrations of the same nature as occur in *Belvedere* and I asked him whether these had inspired him to make that print. No, he said, he had been aware of these oddities since long, but had always considered them as carelessness due to the reputed furious pace at which Piranesi had produced the prints during an illness. They had never awakened the particular twist of fantasy which gave birth to *Belvedere*. That, he said, was the direct consequence of noting somewhere…a picture of the reversible…cube."

Nothing could confirm more closely the essentials of Escher's art. As I have tried to show, the artist was fascinated by certain phenomena from experimental work on vision. These were the intellectual starting points for his inventions. Once gripped by one of his "visual ideas" he would spend sleepless nights, writes his son, "trying to bring some vague concept to clarity…. For weeks he would refuse to talk about what he was doing and lock his studio, whether he was there or not." The perspective displacements in Piranesi's *Carceri* or the ambiguities in the reversible patterns of the tiles of the Alhambra were exciting to him because he felt a kinship with these works reaching back over the centuries, but they were not his primary sources.

It is quite apparent that Escher's use of principles derived from the contemporary psychology of visual perception meant much more to him than a new set of themes or artistic techniques. Escher himself described the profound change that occurred in his style between 1936 and 1938 as if it had been the result of a religious conversion: "There came a moment when it seemed as though scales fell from my eyes…I became gripped by a desire the existence of which I had never suspected. Ideas came into my head quite unrelated to graphic art, notions which so fascinated me that I longed to communicate them to other people." It is no contradiction that this sudden revelation had been foreshadowed in Escher's much earlier application of Rubin's original ideas in the beginning of the 1920's. Artistic ideas, like scientific ideas, have a way of going underground only to reemerge with full force at a later stage.

Once gained, Escher's insights stayed with him into his final years. Even 30 years after his first contact with Koffka's work, when Escher was 70 years old, he expressed himself entirely in Koffka's terms (in his 1968 essay "Approaches to Infinity"): "No one can draw a line that is not a boundary line; every line splits a singularity into a plurality. Every closed contour, no matter what its shape, whether a perfect circle or an irregular random form, evokes in addition the notions of 'inside' and 'outside' and the suggestion of 'near' and 'far away,' of 'object' and 'background.' "

Here Escher refers not only to the

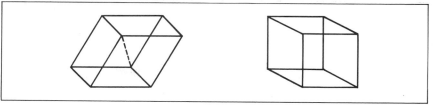

NECKER CUBE, a famous reversible-perspective illusion, was first described in 1832 by the Swiss mineralogist L. A. Necker, who noticed the reversals in his drawings of crystals.

"BELVEDERE," a 1958 lithograph by Escher, is also based on the ambiguous geometry of the Necker cube. The reversible cube, in which the corners that flip forward and backward during reversals are connected by diagonals, appears in three different forms in this print: in the impossible architecture of the building itself, in the model held by the boy sitting on the bench in front of the building and in the drawing on the piece of paper lying on the floor. The reproduction is from a print in the Roosevelt collection at the National Gallery.

SCHRÖDER STAIRS, another 19th-century reversible-perspective diagram, was first published in 1858 by H. Schröder, who pointed out that the shading facilitates the reversals.

"RELATIVITY," a 1953 Escher lithograph, shows reversals similar to those in the diagram at top. The reproduction is from a print in the Rosenwald collection at the National Gallery.

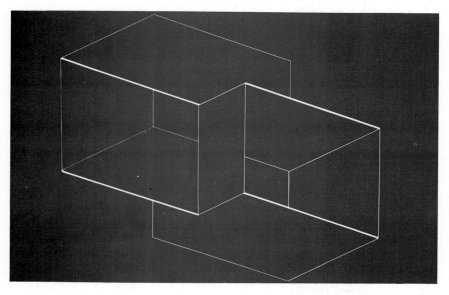

"STRUCTURAL CONSTELLATION," a laminated-plastic construction by Josef Albers, can also be traced to certain reversible-perspective diagrams in the psychological literature.

principle of protruding figure and receding ground, and the double function of contours, but also to well-known Gestalt investigations on closed-contour figures and the problem of *"unum* and *duo* organization" of surface subdivisions analyzed by Wertheimer and Koffka. Regular subdivisions, as in Escher's studies for *Square Limit* of 1964 [*see bottom illustration on page 135*], could be carried out by simply dividing surface after surface in half, up to the limit of visibility at the outer edge. Therefore Escher could say with Koffka: "Every line splits a singularity into a plurality."

The figure-ground ambiguity of Rubin, Koffka and Harrower provided the decisive impetus for Escher to give up the traditional Renaissance picture space. Although he held on to the recognizable image of beast or man for his reversible units, he arrived at a new—sometimes surreal—emphasis on the flat picture surface, a development that the great innovators of 20th-century art had reached at a much earlier date. Picasso and Braque painted their first Cubist pictures between 1907 and 1909; Kandinsky's first abstract color compositions date from 1911. The interdigitation of shapes and their symbolic interpretation in Escher's graphic work, however, can be traced to a trend antedating the modern movement, namely the flat positive and negative patterns of Art Nouveau—often equally charged with meaning and in vogue just before and after the turn of the century.

Escher's contact with the visual experiments of the Gestalt psychologists is not an isolated instance. Joseph Albers' striking constructions on laminated plastic and many of his drawings can be traced to similar prototypes from the psychological literature [*see bottom illustration at right*]. Such ambiguous forms had become a focus of renewed interest at the Bauhaus in Dessau, Germany, in 1929 and 1930, when lectures on Gestalt psychology were offered at this influential school of design. Albers, first a student and then a teacher at the Bauhaus from 1920 until its closing by the Nazis in 1933, became fascinated by reversible perspectives. Beginning in 1931, abstract reversible-line constructions have continued to fascinate him throughout his artistic career.

In the 1930's (almost contemporaneously with Escher) Albers and Vasarely, both precursors of the "Op art" movement (which Albers prefers to call "perceptual art"), created paintings and woodcuts displaying the ambiguity of figure and ground. Yet it is apparent that the intellectual stimulation provided by Gestalt theory manifests itself in very different ways, depending on the artist's choice and predisposition. Albers and Vasarely continue the abstract tradition of modern art by giving it a new direction through insights gained from investigations on vision and visual perception. Escher instead extended the decorative tradition of Art Nouveau coupled with the Symbolist movement. It is perhaps no accident that Art Nouveau patterns are similarly repetitive and crowd the flat surface, just as Escher's inventions do.

Uncovering Escher's sources does not diminish the fascination of his work. Indeed, it underscores how directly the awe we experience before his compositions derives from the perplexing ambiguity of his scientific prototypes. By employing motifs from contemporary attempts at the scientific analysis of form perception, the artist plays with stripped-down mechanisms of perception and reflects on his own visual means.

Similarly, the abstract perceptual artist of the 1960's reflects on the presumed functional property of our visual apparatus by making his patterns vibrate with repetitive line and color stimuli. It is remarkable that such art culminated at the very time when physiologists of the brain began to demonstrate mechanisms for primitive "feature detection" in the cerebral visual pathways [see the article "The Visual Cortex of the Brain," by D. H. Hubel, beginning on page 19]. As the British information theorist D. M. MacKay has pointed out, complementary mechanisms of form perception (similar to complementary color perception) play a role in these scintillating patterns [see top illustration at right]. These effects were adopted by the Op-art painters in their provocative arrays of lines. Without any other visual clues to guide us, these patterns make the feature-extracting machinery in the human visual system reverberate in vacuo.

Escher instead clings tenaciously to meaningful, if fantastic, patterns and invites the viewer to repeat the basic figure-ground experiments of the Gestalt school. This can best be seen in the four-color woodcut Sun and Moon, which combines the Symbolist yearnings of the turn of the century with demonstrations of ambiguity in the perceptual process [see bottom illustration at right]. If you focus on the light birds, the crescent of the moon appears and night prevails; if you focus on the dark birds, the sun will shine.

"RAY PATTERN," published originally in *Nature* in 1957 by the British information theorist D. M. MacKay, influenced the work of the Op artists of the 1960's. A scintillating pattern of fine lines appears to run at right angles to the rays, indicating that a line-detecting mechanism of form perception complementary to the ray pattern has been stimulated.

"SUN AND MOON," a four-color woodcut designed by Escher in 1948, epitomizes, in the author's view, "the symbolist yearnings of the turn of the century with ... demonstrations of ambiguity in the visual process." Reproduction is from a print in the Gemeentemuseum.

III

MEMORY, LEARNING, AND THINKING

III

MEMORY, LEARNING, AND THINKING

INTRODUCTION

This section covers a wide range of cognitive activities—learning, memory, language, and problem-solving. In its broadest sense learning refers to a relatively permanent change in behavior that occurs as a result of experience—organisms "learn" when they adapt their behavior in response to changes in the environment. Learning capacity is thus an important factor in an organism's ability to survive. Learning entails memory; if nothing were retained from experience, there could be no learning. Higher organisms, with complex nervous systems, can store memories from events long past and use such memories to think about and solve present problems. Thinking requires the ability to use symbols to represent objects and events. Symbolization permits man to represent the past in his consciousness, and thus to seek solutions to unsolved problems.

In the first article in this section ("The Control of Short-Term Memory") Richard Atkinson and Richard Shiffrin offer a theory of how new information is acquired by humans and how that information is retained over time. They propose two types of memory mechanisms: one for immediate information (a telephone number just looked up) and one for repeated information (your own telephone number). These two storage mechanisms are labeled "short-term" and "long-term" memory. Long-term memory stores such items as your name, the words and grammar of language, addition and multiplication tables, and important events in your life. Except for occasional mental blocking on a word or the name of an acquaintance, these memories are relatively permanent. In contrast, the telephone number you have just looked up, the definition the instructor has just given in class, or the name of a stranger to whom you have just been introduced remain with you in short-term memory only; unless you make a conscious effort to focus your attention on such information, it is quickly lost. Using this distinction between short- and long-term memory, the authors formulate a theory of memory and learning, and use the theory to account for a range of psychological data.

In "How We Remember What We See" Ralph Haber breaks down even further the memory process for visual information. He suggests that a visual display generates an iconic (visual) image in the brain that precedes its representation in short-term memory. Although the iconic image lasts for less than a second, during this time information is extracted from it and transferred to short-term memory. A brief visual presentation of a word, for example, will generate an icon that can be scanned, appropriately coded, and operated upon by the subject, even after the stimulus has disappeared. The coding operation might involve transforming the printed word into spoken form. The spoken form will be stored in short-term memory, whence it may be forgotten; if it receives additional attention in the form of rehearsal or further coding, it may be transferred to long-term memory for more permanent storage. Haber describes some interesting experiments that indicate that pictorial and linguistic information may be stored differently.

If the reader has an animal at home that he wishes to train, the article by B. F. Skinner ("How to Teach Animals") will prove interesting. Skinner gives a step-by-step description of a procedure for modifying behavior, called *operant conditioning*. The principle is to provide immediate reinforcement, in the form of food or praise, for any act that approaches desired behavior (the same principle, of course, is applicable to the social training of children). By requiring progressively closer approximations of the desired behavior, it is possible to "shape" the animal's behavior in a relatively short period of time. The principles of operant conditioning have been applied extensively in a variety of learning situations, adding much to our understanding of the conditions that produce optimal learning. A later article in this volume ("Behavioral Psychotherapy," by Albert Bandura, Section IV) describes the use of operant conditioning techniques in treating human subjects with psychological disorders.

Like other parts of the body that exhibit bilateral symmetry, the brain has two halves that are essentially mirror images of each other; these are connected by a broad band of nerve fibers called the corpus callosum. In his article "The Split Brain in Man" Michael Gazzaniga describes what happens when the corpus callosum is severed. "Brain-splitting" is sometimes conducted for medical reasons; the operation is quite successful in treating epilepsy, for example, and produces no noticeable changes in personality or general intelligence. Under certain circumstances, however, the patient behaves as though he had two brains. Once the corpus collosum is severed, information that goes to only one hemisphere may not be communicated to the other, so that in some cases the left hand actually does not know what the right hand is doing. Evidence indicates that separation of the hemispheres literally creates two independent spheres of consciousness; each is able to learn and think without influencing the other, but each has a somewhat different expertise. As Gazzaniga points out, this conclusion may be disturbing to those who view consciousness and learning as an indivisible property of the human brain.

Using the principles of operant conditioning, Ann and David Premack ("Teaching Language to an Ape") attempted to teach a form of human language to a young chimpanzee named Sarah. The outcome of their work is quite remarkable. Sarah easily mastered a vocabulary of about 130 "words," but her understanding goes beyond the meaning of individual words and includes class concepts and sentence structure. In assessing the results of the experiment one must be careful not to expect that Sarah should be able to match the ability of a human adult; compared with a two-year-old child, however, Sarah holds her own in language ability. And it seems likely that enough has been learned from this project about the most effective procedure for teaching language to chimpanzees that future efforts may be even more successful. How such work will contribute to understanding the psychology of language is hard to specify at this time, but obviously an important and exciting field of research has been defined.

Research on language perception and production in humans is described by Victoria Fromkin in "Slips of the Tongue." The author believes that an idea generated in one's mind must undergo a series of specific transformations before it is spoken. Examining speech errors (slips of the tongue) provides important clues to the nature of these transformations and to how language may be organized in the brain. Such study also provides good data for testing some speculations on the psychological nature of language.

In "Bilingualism and Information-Processing" Paul Kolers studies people who are proficient in the use of two languages in order to investigate how symbols are used in thinking. A person who speaks two languages fluently uses two distinct sets of symbols. Because languages differ in grammatical rules, word meanings, and sound structures, switching from one language to another is a complicated psychological task—but one that bilingual persons perform almost automatically. Kolers' experiments with bilingual subjects provide valuable information about the coding and storage of verbal symbols.

In problem-solving, man utilizes his experiences to aid in coping with new situations. Martin Scheerer in his article "Problem-Solving" describes the history of research on this topic. He contrasts the trial-and-error approach of the stimulus-response psychologists with the Gestalt approach, which emphasizes the perception of the total situation and the capacity for insight. Scheerer adheres to the Gestalt viewpoint, and examines a number of experimental problems where "fixation" on inappropriate strategies prevents the subject from perceiving relationships that might lead to a rapid solution.

The Control of Short-Term Memory

16

August 1971

Memory has two components: short-term and long-term. Control processes such as "rehearsal" are essential to the transfer of information from the short-term store to the long-term one

The notion that the system by which information is stored in memory and retrieved from it can be divided into two components dates back to the 19th century. Theories distinguishing between two different kinds of memory were proposed by the English associationists James Mill and John Stuart Mill and by such early experimental psychologists as Wilhelm Wundt and Ernst Meumann in Germany and William James in the U.S. Reflecting on their own mental processes, they discerned a clear difference between thoughts currently in consciousness and thoughts that could be brought to consciousness only after a search of memory that was often laborious. (For example, the sentence you are reading is in your current awareness; the name of the baseball team that won the 1968 World Series may be in your memory, but to retrieve it takes some effort, and you may not be able to retrieve it at all.)

The two-component concept of memory was intuitively attractive, and yet it was largely discarded when psychology turned to behaviorism, which emphasized research on animals rather than humans. The distinction between short-term memory and long-term memory received little further consideration until the 1950's, when such psychologists as Donald E. Broadbent in England, D. O. Hebb in Canada and George A. Miller in the U.S. reintroduced it [see "Information and Memory," by George A. Miller; Scientific American Offprint 419]. The concurrent development of computer models of behavior and of mathematical psychology accelerated the growth of interest in the two-process viewpoint, which is now undergoing considerable theoretical development and is the subject of a large research effort. In particular, the short-term memory system, or short-term store (STS), has been given a position of pivotal importance. That is because the processes carried out in the short-term store are under the immediate control of the subject and govern the flow of information in the memory system; they can be called into play at the subject's discretion, with enormous consequences for performance.

Some control processes are used in many situations by everyone and others are used only in special circumstances. "Rehearsal" is an overt or covert repetition of information—as in remembering a telephone number until it can be writ-

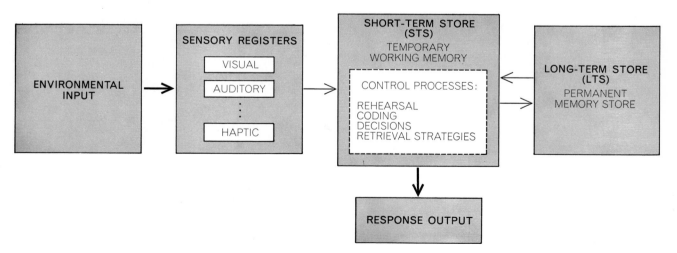

INFORMATION FLOW through the memory system is conceived of as beginning with the processing of environmental inputs in sensory registers (receptors plus internal elements) and entry into the short-term store (STS). While it remains there the information may be copied into the long-term store (LTS), and associated information that is in the long-term store may be activated and entered into the short-term store. If a triangle is seen, for example, the name "triangle" may be called up. Control processes in the short-term store affect these transfers into and out of the long-term store and govern learning, retrieval of information and forgetting.

ten down, remembering the names of a group of people to whom one has just been introduced or copying a passage from a book. "Coding" refers to a class of control processes in which the information to be remembered is put in a context of additional, easily retrievable information, such as a mnemonic phrase or sentence. "Imaging" is a control process in which verbal information is remembered through visual images; for example, Cicero suggested learning long lists (or speeches) by placing each member of the list in a visual representation of successive rooms of a well-known building. There are other control processes, including decision rules, organizational schemes, retrieval strategies and problem-solving techniques; some of them will be encountered in this article. The point to keep in mind is the optional nature of control processes. In contrast to permanent structural components of the memory system, the control processes are selected at the subject's discretion; they may vary not only with different tasks but also from one encounter with the same task to the next.

We believe that the overall memory system is best described in terms of the flow of information into and out of short-term storage and the subject's control of that flow, and this conception has been central to our experimental and theoretical investigation of memory. All phases of memory are assumed to consist of small units of information that are associatively related. A set of closely interrelated information units is termed an image or a trace. Note that "image" does not necessarily imply a visual representation; if the letter-number pair *TKM–4* is presented for memory, the image that is stored might include the size of the card on which the pair is printed, the type of print, the sound of the various symbols, the semantic codes and numerous other units of information.

Information from the environment is accepted and processed by the various sensory systems and is entered into the short-term store, where it remains for a period of time that is usually under the control of the subject. By rehearsing one or more items the subject can keep them in the short-term store, but the number that can be maintained in this way is strictly limited; most people can maintain seven to nine digits, for example. Once an image is lost from the short-term store it cannot thereafter be recovered from it. While information resides in short-term storage it may be copied into

the long-term store (LTS), which is assumed to be a relatively permanent memory from which information is not lost. While an image is in short-term storage, closely related information in the long-term store is activated and entered in the short-term store too. Information entering the short-term store from the sensory systems comes from a specific modality—visual, auditory or whatever—but associations from the long-term store in all modalities are activated to join it. For instance, an item may be presented visually, but immediately after input its verbal "name" and associated meanings will be activated from the long-term store and placed in the short-term one [*see illustration on opposite page*].

Our account of short-term and long-term storage does not require that the two stores necessarily be in different parts of the brain or involve different physiological structures. One might consider the short-term store simply as being a temporary activation of some portion of the long-term store. In our thinking we tend to equate the short-term store with "consciousness," that is, the thoughts and information of which we are currently aware can be considered part of the contents of the short-term store. (Such a statement lies in the realm of phenomenology and cannot be verified scientifically, but thinking of the short-term store in this way may help the reader to conceptualize the system.) Because consciousness is equated with the short-term store and because control processes are centered in and act through it, the short-term store is considered a working memory: a system in which decisions are made, problems are solved and information flow is directed. Retrieval of information from short-term storage is quite fast and accurate. Experiments by Saul Sternberg of the Bell Telephone Laboratories and by others have shown that the retrieval time for information in short-term storage such as letters and numbers ranges from 10 to 30 milliseconds per character.

The retrieval of information from long-term storage is considerably more complicated. So much information is contained in the long-term store that the major problem is finding access to some small subset of the information that contains the desired image, just as one must find a particular book in a library before it can be scanned for the desired information. We propose that the subject activates a likely subset of information, places it in the short-term store and then scans that store for the desired image. The image may not be present in the

current subset, and so the retrieval process becomes a search in which various subsets are successively activated and scanned [*see illustration below*]. On the basis of the information presented to him the subject selects the appropriate "probe information" and places it in the short-term store. A "search set," or subset of information in the long-term store closely associated with the probe, is then activated and put in the short-term store. The subject selects from the search set some image, which is then examined. The information extracted from the selected image is utilized for a decision: has the desired information

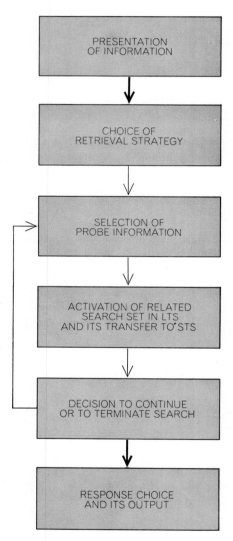

RETRIEVAL from the long-term store requires a choice of strategy and selection of certain information as a "probe" that is placed in the short-term store. The probe activates a "search set" of information in the long-term store. The search set is placed in the short-term store and is examined for the desired information. If it is not found, search is halted or recycled with new probe.

been found? If so, the search is terminated.

If the information has not been found, the subject may decide that continuation is unlikely to be productive or he may decide to continue. If he does, he begins the next cycle of the search by again selecting a probe, which may or may not be the same probe used in the preceding cycle depending on the subject's strategy. For example, a subject asked to search for states of the U.S. starting with the letter *M* may do so by generating states at random and checking their first letter (in which case the same probe information can be used in each search cycle), or he may generate successive states in a regular geographic order (in which case the probe information is systematically changed from one cycle to the next). It can be shown that strategies in which the probe information is systematically changed will result more often in successful retrieval but will take longer than alternative "random" strategies. (Note that the Freudian concept of repressed memories can be considered as being an inability of the subject to generate an appropriate probe.)

This portrayal of the memory system almost entirely in terms of the operations of the short-term store is quite intentional. In our view information storage and retrieval are best described in terms of the flow of information through the short-term store and in terms of the subject's control of the flow. One of the most important of these control processes is rehearsal. Through overt or covert repetition of information, rehearsal either increases the momentary strength of information in the short-term store or otherwise delays its loss. Rehearsal can be shown not only to maintain information in short-term storage but also to control transfer from the short-term store to the long-term one. We shall present several experiments concerned with an analysis of the rehearsal process.

The research in question involves a memory paradigm known as "free recall," which is similar to the task you face when you are asked to name the people present at the last large party you went to. In the typical experimental procedure a list of random items, usually common English words, is presented to the subject one at a time. Later the subject attempts to recall as many words as possible in any order. Many psychologists have worked on free recall, with major research efforts carried out by

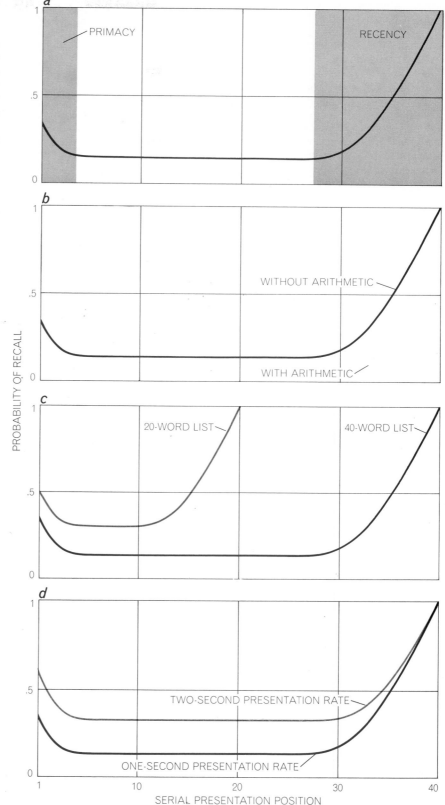

PROBABILITY OF RECALL in free-recall experiments varies in a characteristic way with an item's serial position in a list: a "primacy effect" and a "recency effect" are apparent (*a*). If an arithmetic task is interpolated between presentation and recall, the recency effect disappears (*b*). Words in long lists are recalled less well than words in short lists (*c*). Slower presentation also results in better recall (*d*). The curves are idealized ones based on experiments by James W. Deese Bennet Murdock, Leo Postman and Murray Glanzer.

Bennet Murdock of the University of Toronto, Endel Tulving of Yale University and Murray Glanzer of New York University. The result of principal interest is the probability of recalling each item in a list as a function of its place in the list, or "serial-presentation position." Plotting this function yields a *U*-shaped curve [*see "a" in illustration on preceding page*]. The increased probability of recall for the first few words in the list is called the primacy effect; the large increase for the last eight to 12 words is called the recency effect. There is considerable evidence that the recency effect is due to retrieval from short-term storage and that the earlier portions of the serial-position curve reflect retrieval from long-term storage only. In one experimental procedure the subject is required to carry out a difficult arithmetic task for 30 seconds immediately following presentation of the list and then is asked to recall. One can assume that the arithmetic task causes the loss of all the words in short-term storage, so that recall reflects retrieval from long-term storage only. The recency effect is eliminated when this experiment is performed; the earlier portions of the serial-position curve are unaffected [*b*]. If variables that influence the long-term store but not the short-term one are manipulated, the recency portion of the serial-position curve should be relatively unaffected, whereas the earlier portions of the curve should show changes. One such variable is the number of words in the presented list. A word in a longer list is less likely to be recalled, but the recency effect is quite unaffected by list length [*c*]. Similarly, increases in the rate of presentation decrease the likelihood of recalling words preceding the recency region but leave the recency effect largely unchanged [*d*].

In free-recall experiments many lists are usually presented in a session. If the subject is asked at the end of the session to recall all the words presented during the session, we would expect his recall to reflect retrieval from long-term storage only. The probability of recalling words as a function of their serial position within each list can be plotted for end-of-session recall and compared with the serial-position curve for recall immediately following presentation [*see illustration on this page*]. For the delayed-recall curve the primacy effect remains, but the recency effect is eliminated, as predicted. In summary, the recency region appears to reflect retrieval from both short-term and long-term storage whereas the serial-position curve preced-

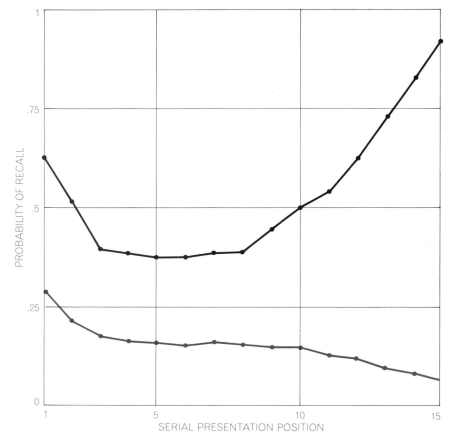

EFFECT OF DELAY is tested by asking subjects to recall at the end of a session all words from the entire session, and then plotting probability of recall against serial position within each list. An experiment by Fergus Craik compares immediate recall (*black*) with delayed recall (*color*). The delayed-recall curve emphasizes transitory nature of recency effect.

ing the recency region reflects retrieval from long-term storage only.

In 1965, at a conference sponsored by the New York Academy of Sciences, we put forward a mathematical model explaining these and other effects in terms of a rehearsal process. The model assumed that in a free-recall task the subject sets up a rehearsal buffer in the short-term store that can hold only a fixed number of items. At the start of the presentation of a list the buffer is empty; successive items are entered until the buffer is filled. Thereafter, as each new item enters the rehearsal buffer it replaces one of the items already there. (Which item is replaced depends on a number of psychological factors, but in the model the decision is approximated by a random process.) The items that are still being rehearsed in the short-term store when the last item is presented are the ones that are immediately recalled by the subject, giving rise to the recency effect. The transfer of information from the short-term to the long-term store is

postulated to be a function of the length of time an item resides in the rehearsal buffer; the longer the time period, the more rehearsal the item receives and therefore the greater the transfer of information to long-term storage. Since items presented first in a list enter an empty or partly empty rehearsal buffer, they remain longer than later items and consequently receive additional rehearsal. This extra rehearsal causes more transfer of information to long-term storage for the first items, giving rise to the primacy effect.

This rehearsal model was given a formal mathematical statement and was fitted to a wide array of experiments, and it provided an excellent quantitative account of a great many results in free recall, including those discussed in this article. A more direct confirmation of the model has recently been provided by Dewey Rundus of Stanford University. He carried out free-recall experiments in which subjects rehearsed aloud during list presentation. This overt rehearsal was tape-recorded and was compared with the recall results. The number of different words contained in the "rehearsal set" (the items overtly rehearsed between successive presentations) was one after the first word was presented and then rose until the fourth word; from the fourth word on the number of different words in the rehearsal set remained fairly constant (averaging about 3.3) until the end of the list. The subjects almost always reported the members of the most recent rehearsal set when the list ended and recall began. A close correspondence is evident between the number of rehearsals and the recall probability for words preceding the recency effect; in the recency region, however, a sharp disparity occurs [see illustrations below]. The hypothesis that

long-term storage is a function of the number of rehearsals can be checked in other ways. The recall probability for a word preceding the recency region was plotted as a function of the number of rehearsals received by that word; the result was an almost linear, sharply increasing function. And words presented in the middle of the list given the same number of rehearsals as the first item presented had the same recall probability as that first item.

With efficacy of rehearsal established both for storing information in the long-term store and for maintaining information in the short-term store, we did an experiment in which the subjects' rehearsal was manipulated directly. Our subjects were trained to engage in one

of two types of rehearsal. In the first (a one-item rehearsal set) the most recently presented item was rehearsed exactly three times before presentation of the next item; no other items were rehearsed. In the second (a three-item rehearsal set) the subject rehearsed the three most recently presented items once each before presentation of the next item, so that the first rehearsal set contained three rehearsals of the first word, the second rehearsal set contained two rehearsals of the second word and one rehearsal of the first word, and all subsequent sets contained one rehearsal of each of the three most recent items [see illustration on following page].

When only one item is rehearsed at a time, each item receives an identical number of rehearsals and the primacy effect disappears, as predicted. Note that the recency effect appears for items preceding the last item even though the last item is the only one in the last rehearsal set. This indicates that even when items are dropped from rehearsal, it takes an additional period of time for them to be completely lost from short-term storage. The curve for the three-item rehearsal condition shows the effect also. The last rehearsal set contains the last three items presented and these are recalled perfectly, but a recency effect is still seen for items preceding these three. It should also be noted that a primacy effect occurs in the three-rehearsal condition. This was predicted because the first item received a total of five rehearsals rather than three. A delayed-recall test for all words was given at the end of the experimental session. The data confirmed that long-term-store retrieval closely parallels the number of rehearsals given an item during presentation, for both rehearsal schemes.

These results strongly implicate rehearsal in the maintenance of information in the short-term store and the transfer of that information to the long-term system. The question then arises: What are the forgetting and transfer characteristics of the short-term store in the absence of rehearsal? One can control rehearsal experimentally by blocking it with a difficult verbal task such as arithmetic. For example, Lloyd R. Peterson and Margaret Peterson of Indiana University [see "Short-Term Memory," by Lloyd R. Peterson; SCIENTIFIC AMERICAN Offprint 499] presented a set of three letters (a trigram) to be remembered; the subject next engaged in a period of arithmetic and then was asked to recall as many letters of the trigram

ITEM PRESENTED	ITEMS REHEARSED (REHEARSAL SET)
1 REACTION	REACTION, REACTION, REACTION, REACTION
2 HOOF	HOOF, REACTION, HOOF, REACTION
3 BLESSING	BLESSING, HOOF, REACTION
4 RESEARCH	RESEARCH, REACTION, HOOF, RESEARCH
5 CANDY	CANDY, HOOF, RESEARCH, REACTION
6 HARDSHIP	HARDSHIP, HOOF, HARDSHIP, HOOF
7 KINDNESS	KINDNESS, CANDY, HARDSHIP, HOOF
8 NONSENSE	NONSENSE, KINDNESS, CANDY, HARDSHIP
⋮	⋮
20 CELLAR	CELLAR, ALCOHOL, MISERY, CELLAR

OVERT-REHEARSAL experiment by Dewey Rundus shows the effect of rehearsal on transfer into long-term storage. The subject rehearses aloud. A partial listing of items rehearsed in one instance shows typical result: early items receive more rehearsals than later items.

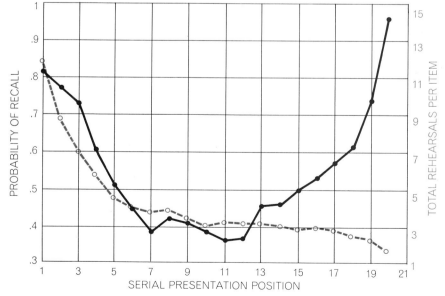

EFFECT OF REHEARSAL is demonstrated by comparison of an item's probability of recall (*black*) with the total number of rehearsals item receives (*color*). The two are related in regions reflecting retrieval from long-term storage (preceding recency region). That is, long-term storage efficacy depends on number of rehearsals and is reflected in retrieval.

ONE-ITEM REHEARSAL SCHEME

SERIAL POSITION	ITEM PRESENTED	ITEMS REHEARSED	TOTAL REHEARSALS PER ITEM
1	A	AAA	3
2	B	BBB	3
3	C	CCC	3
4	D	DDD	3
5	E	EEE	3
6	F	FFF	3
.	.	.	.
.	.	.	.
.	.	.	.
14	N	NNN	3
15	O	OOO	3
16	P	PPP	3

THREE-ITEM REHEARSAL SCHEME

SERIAL POSITION	ITEM PRESENTED	ITEMS REHEARSED	TOTAL REHEARSALS PER ITEM
1	A	AAA	5
2	B	BBA	4
3	C	CBA	3
4	D	DCB	3
5	E	EDC	3
6	F	FED	3
.	.	.	.
.	.	.	.
.	.	.	.
14	N	NML	3
15	O	ONM	2
16	P	PON	1

NUMBER OF REHEARSALS is controlled with two schemes. In one (*top*) only the current item is rehearsed and all items have three rehearsals. In the other (*bottom*) the latest three items are rehearsed; early ones have extra rehearsals. (Letters represent words.)

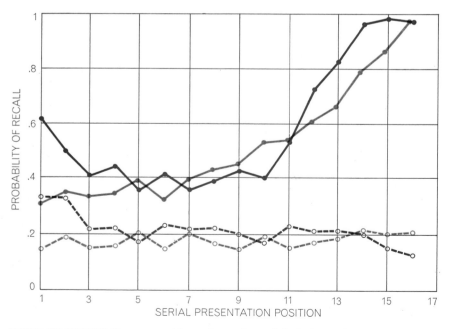

PRIMACY EFFECT disappears with one-item rehearsal (*color*), in which all items have equal rehearsal, but remains with three-item rehearsal (*black*). Recency effect is pronounced for both schemes in immediate recall (*solid lines*). Curves for delayed recall (*broken lines*), which reflect only retrieval from long-term storage, parallel the number of rehearsals.

as possible. When the probability of recall is plotted as a function of the duration of the arithmetic task, the loss observed over time is similar to that of the recency effect in free recall [*see top illustration on next page*]. Short-term-store loss caused by an arithmetic task, then, is similar to loss from short-term storage caused by a series of intervening words to be remembered. The flat portion of the curve reflects the retrieval of the trigram from long-term storage alone and the earlier portions of the curve represent retrieval from both short-term and long-term storage; the loss of the trigram from short-term storage is represented by the decreasing probability of recall prior to the asymptote.

Does the forgetting observed during arithmetic reflect an automatic decay of short-term storage that occurs inevitably in the absence of rehearsal or is the intervening activity the cause of the loss? There is evidence that the amount of new material introduced between presentation and test is a much more important determinant of loss from short-term storage than simply the elapsed time between presentation and test. This finding is subject to at least two explanations. The first holds that the activity intervening between presentation and test is the *direct* cause of an item's loss from short-term storage. The second explanation proposes that the rate of intervening activity merely affects the number of rehearsals that can be given the item to be remembered and thus *indirectly* determines the rate of loss.

It has recently become possible to choose between these two explanations of loss from the short-term store. Judith Reitman of the University of Michigan substituted a signal-detection task for the arithmetic task in the Petersons' procedure. The task consisted in responding whenever a weak tone was heard against a continuous background of "white" noise. Surprisingly, no loss from short-term storage was observed after 15 seconds of the task, even though subjects reported no rehearsal during the signal detection. This suggests that loss from the short-term store is due to the type of interference during the intervening interval: signal detection does not cause loss but verbal arithmetic does. Another important issue that could potentially be resolved with the Reitman procedure concerns the transfer of information from the short-term to the long-term store: Does transfer occur only at initial presentation and at subsequent rehearsals, or does it occur throughout the period during which the information resides in the short-term store, regardless of rehearsals?

To answer these questions, the following experiment was carried out. A consonant pentagram (a set of five consonants, such as *QJXFK*) was presented for 2.5 seconds for the subject to memorize. This was followed by a signal-detection task in which pure tones were presented at random intervals against a continuous background of white noise. The subjects pressed a key whenever they thought they detected a tone. (The task proved to be difficult; only about three-fourths of the tones presented were correctly detected.) The signal-detection period lasted for either one second, eight seconds or 40 seconds, with tones sounded on the average every 2.5 seconds. In conditions 1, 2 and 3 the subjects were tested on the consonant pentagram immediately after the signal detection; in conditions 4, 5 and 6, however, they were required to carry out 30 seconds of difficult arithmetic following the signal detection before being tested [see *middle illustration at right*]. In order to increase the likelihood that rehearsal would not occur, we paid the subjects for performing well on signal detection and for doing their arithmetic accurately but not for their success in remembering letters. In addition they were instructed not to rehearse letters during signal detection or arithmetic. They reported afterward that they were not consciously aware of rehearsing. Because the question of rehearsal is quite important, we nevertheless went on to do an additional control experiment in which all the same conditions applied but the subjects were told to rehearse the pentagram aloud following each detection of a tone.

The results indicate that arithmetic causes the pentagram information to be lost from the short-term store but that in the absence of the arithmetic the signal-detection task alone causes no loss [see *bottom illustration at right*]. What then does produce forgetting from the short-term store? It is not just the analysis of any information input, since signal detection is a difficult information-processing task but causes no forgetting. And time alone causes no noticeable forgetting. Yet verbal information (arithmetic) does cause a large loss. Mrs. Reitman's conclusion appears to be correct: forgetting is caused by the entry into the short-term store of other, similar information.

What about the effect of rehearsal? In the arithmetic situation performance improves if subjects rehearse overtly

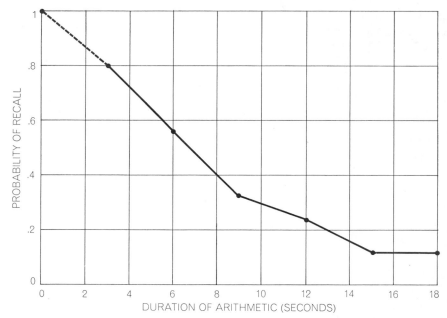

ARITHMETIC TASK before recall reduces the probability of recall. Lloyd R. Peterson and Margaret Peterson charted recall probability against duration of arithmetic. The probability falls off with duration until it levels off when recall reflects retrieval from long-term storage alone. Does curve reflect only lack of rehearsal or also nature of intervening task?

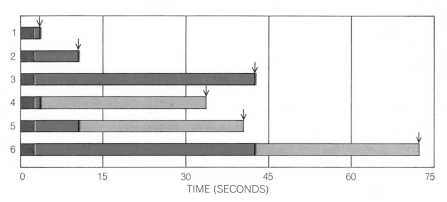

TWO TASKS were combined in an experiment with these six conditions. Five consonants were presented for 2.5 seconds (*dark gray*), followed by a signal-detection task for one second, eight seconds or 40 seconds (*color*), followed in three cases by arithmetic (*light gray*). Then came the test (*arrows*). Rehearsal during detection was included in a control version.

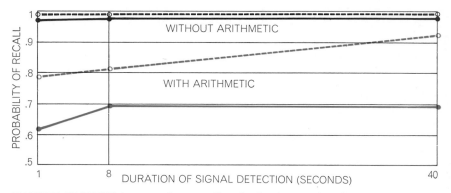

NATURE OF TASKS is seen to have an effect. In the absence of arithmetic, signal detection leaves the short-term store virtually unaffected, with rehearsal (*broken black curve*) or without (*solid black*). Arithmetic, however, causes loss from the short-term store (*color*); decreased recall shown reflects retrieval from long-term store only. Retrieval improves with duration of signal detection if there is rehearsal, which increases transfer to the long-term store (*broken colored curve*) but not in the absence of rehearsal (*solid color*).

during the signal-detection period. Presumably the rehearsal transfers information about the pentagram to the long-term store; the additional transfer during the long signal-detection period is reflected in the retrieval scores, and the rehearsal curve rises. The no-rehearsal curve is horizontal over the last 32 seconds of signal detection, however, confirming that no rehearsal was occurring during that period. The fact that the lowest curve is flat over the last 32 seconds has important implications for transfer from the short-term store to the long-term. It indicates that essentially no transfer occurred during this period even though, as the results in the absence of arithmetic show, the trace remained in the short-term store. Hence the presence of a trace in the short-term store is alone not enough to result in transfer to the long-term store. Apparently transfer to the long-term system occurs primarily during or shortly after rehearsals. (The rise in the lowest curve over the first eight seconds may indicate that the transfer effects of a presentation or rehearsal take at least a few seconds to reach completion.)

The emphasis we have given to rote rehearsal should not imply that other control processes are of lesser importance. Although much evidence indicates that transfer from short-term storage to long-term is strongly dependent on rehearsals, effective later retrieval from long-term storage can be shown to be highly dependent on the type of information rehearsed. Coding is really the choosing of particular information to be rehearsed in the short-term store. In general, coding strategies consist in adding appropriately chosen information from long-term storage to a trace to be remembered and then rehearsing the entire complex in the short-term store. Suppose you are given (as is typical in memory experiments) the stimulus-response pair HRM–4; later HRM will be presented alone and you will be expected to respond "4." If you simply rehearse HRM–4 several times, your ability to respond correctly later will probably not be high. Suppose, however, HRM reminds you of "homeroom" and you think of various aspects of your fourth-grade classroom. Your retrieval performance will be greatly enhanced. Why? First of all, the amount and range of information stored appears to be greater with coding than with rote rehearsal. Moreover, the coding operation provides a straightforward means by which you can gain access to an appropriate and small region of memory

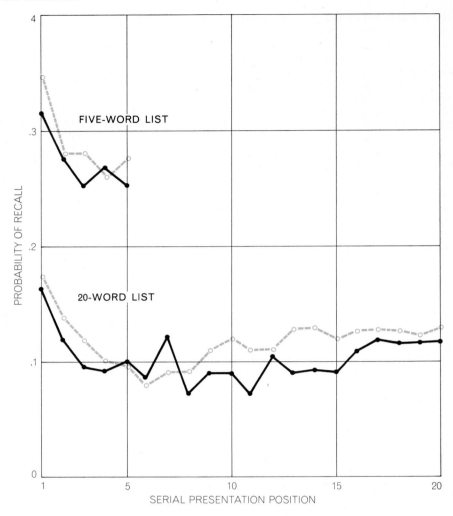

LENGTH OF LIST rather than amount of "interference" governs recall probability. Subjects were asked to recall the list before the one just studied. Five-word lists (*top*) were recalled better than 20-word lists (*bottom*) whether they were followed by intervening lists of five words (*black*) or of 20 words (*color*). The data are averages from three experiments.

during retrieval. In the above example, when HRM is presented at the moment of test, you are likely to notice, just as during the initial presentation, that HRM is similar to "homeroom." You can then use "homeroom" (and the current temporal context) as a further probe and would almost certainly access "fourth grade" and so generate the correct response.

As the discussion of coding suggests, the key to retrieval is the selection of probe information that will activate an appropriate search set from the long-term store. Since in our view the long-term store is a relatively permanent repository, forgetting is assumed to result from an inadequate selection of probe information and a consequent failure of the retrieval process. There are two basic ways in which the probe selection

may prove inadequate. First, the wrong probe may be selected. For instance, you might be asked to name the star of a particular motion picture. The name actually begins with T but you decide that it begins with A and include A in the probe information used to access the long-term store. As a result the correct name may not be included in the search set that is drawn into the short-term store and retrieval will not succeed.

Second, if the probe is such that an extremely large region of memory is accessed, then retrieval may fail even though the desired trace is included in the search set. For example, if you are asked to name a fruit that sounds like a word meaning "to look at," you might say "pear." If you are asked to name a living thing that sounds like a word meaning "to look at," the probability of your coming up with "pear" will be greatly reduced. Again, you are more likely to remember a "John Smith" if you met him at a party with five other people than if there had been 20 people at the party. This effect can be explained on grounds other than a failure of memory search, however. It could be argued that more attention was given to "John Smith" at the smaller party. Or if the permanence of long-term storage is not accepted, it could be argued that the names of the many other people met at the larger party erode or destroy the memory trace for "John Smith." Are these objections reasonable? The John Smith example is analogous to the situation in free recall where words in long lists are less well recalled from long-term storage than words in short lists.

The problem, then, is to show that the list-length effect in free recall is dependent on the choice of probe information rather than on either the number of words intervening between presentation and recall or the differential storage given words in lists of different size. The second issue is disposed of rather easily: in many free-recall experiments that vary list length, the subjects do not know at the beginning of the list what the length of the list will be. It is therefore unlikely that they store different amounts of information for the first several words in lists of differing length. Nevertheless, as we pointed out, the first several words are recalled at different levels.

To dispose of the "interference" explanation, which implicates the number of words between presentation and recall, is more difficult. Until fairly recently, as a matter of fact, interference theories of forgetting have been predominant [see "Forgetting," by Benton J. Underwood, SCIENTIFIC AMERICAN Offprint 482, and "The Interference Theory of Forgetting," by John Ceraso, Offprint 509]. In these theories forgetting has often been seen as a matter of erosion of the memory trace, usually by items presented following the item to be remembered but also by items preceding the item to be remembered. (The list-length effect might be explained in these terms, since the average item in a long list is preceded and followed by more items than the average item in a short list.) On the other hand, the retrieval model presented in this article assumes long-term storage to be permanent; it maintains that the strength of long-term traces is independent of list length and that forgetting results from the fact that the temporal-contextual probe cues used to access any given list tend to elicit a larger search set for longer lists, thereby producing less efficient retrieval.

In order to distinguish between the retrieval and the interference explanations, we presented lists of varying lengths and had the subject attempt to recall not the list just studied (as in the typical free-recall procedure) but the list before the last. This procedure makes it possible to separate the effect of the size of the list being recalled from the effect of the number of words intervening between presentation and recall. A large or a small list to be recalled can be followed by either a large or a small intervening list. The retrieval model predicts that recall probability will be dependent on the size of the list being recalled. The interference model predicts that performance will be largely determined by the number of words in the intervening list.

We used lists of five and of 20 words and presented them in four combina-tions: 5–5, 5–20, 20–5, 20–20; the first number gives the size of the list being recalled and the second number the size of the intervening list. One result is that there is no recency effect [see illustration on preceding page]. This would be expected since there is another list and another recall intervening between presentation and recall; the intervening activity causes the words in the tested list to be lost from short-term storage and so the curves represent retrieval from long-term storage only. The significant finding is that words in lists five words long are recalled much better than words in lists 20 words long, and the length of the intervening list has little, if any, effect. The retrieval model can predict these results only if a probe is available to access the requested list. It seems likely in this experiment that the subject has available at test appropriate cues (probably temporal in nature) to enable him to select probe information pertaining to the desired list. If the experimental procedure were changed so that the subject was asked to recall the 10th preceding list, then selection of an adequate probe would no longer be possible. The results demonstrate the importance of probe selection, a control process of the short-term store.

The model of memory we have described, which integrates the system around the operations of the short-term store, is not in any sense a final theory. As experimental techniques and mathematical models have become increasingly sophisticated, memory theory has undergone progressive changes, and there is no doubt that this trend will continue. We nevertheless think it is likely that the short-term store and its control processes will be found to be central.

How We Remember What We See

by Ralph Norman Haber
May 1970

It depends on whether what we see is pictorial (scenes, photographs and so forth) or linguistic (words, numbers and so on). Experiments indicate that the linguistic memory is different from the pictorial

Visual perception is as much concerned with remembering what we have seen as with the act of seeing itself. When I look at a picture, I am aware that I am seeing it, and I can describe the experience of seeing. I can also remember what I saw after the picture is no longer there. How does this kind of perceptual memory work? Is it perhaps a process involving several steps in sequence, or one involving only one step during which many processes occur in parallel? Are scenes, faces and pictures remembered differently from linguistic material such as words and numbers?

In seeking to answer such questions my colleagues and I at the University of Rochester and workers in other laboratories have been studying the process of visual memory in human subjects. Our tools include tachistoscopes (devices that can display a series of images in rapid succession), slide projectors and screens, instruments for following eye movements, instruments for measuring the time needed to respond to stimuli, and various kinds of pictorial and linguistic material. These experiments are beginning to reveal several important characteristics of the visual memory process. Among the most significant of these findings is the suggestion that there is one kind of memory for pictorial material and another for linguistic.

The capacity of memory for pictures may be unlimited. Common experience suggests that this is so. For example, almost everyone has had the experience of recognizing a face he saw only briefly years before. (It is significant, as we shall see, that the name is usually harder to recall.) The reality of such experiences is supported by experiment. In one such experiment subjects were able to recognize as many as 600 pictures they had seen for only a short period of time.

More recently Lionel G. Standing and I have conducted an experiment showing that at least four times this amount of material can be recognized.

In our test of visual memory capacity subjects were shown 2,560 photographic slides at the rate of one every 10 seconds during viewing sessions held on consecutive days. Suspecting that fatigue might have some effect on performance, we had some of our volunteers follow a rigorous viewing schedule that consisted in looking at 1,280 pictures a day during four-hour sessions on two consecutive days. The rest of the subjects viewed only 640 pictures a day during two-hour sessions on four consecutive days.

One hour after a subject had seen the last of the slides he was shown 280 pairs of pictures. One member of each pair was a picture from the series the subject had already seen. The other was from a similar set, but it had never been shown to the subject. When the subjects were asked to say which of the two pictures they had seen before, 85 to 95 percent of their choices were correct. Surprisingly, subjects whose endurance had been pressed did as well as subjects who had followed a more leisurely viewing schedule. In another version of the experiment the high scores were maintained even when the pictures were shown as their mirror image during the identification sessions, so that the right-hand side became the left-hand side. The scores diminished only slightly when the subjects were asked if the pictures had been reversed [*see illustration on page 156*].

Although a person may remember almost any picture he has ever seen, he frequently is unable to recall details from a specific image when asked to do so. In another experiment Matthew H. Erdelyi and I attempted to find out what

happens to these omitted details. Are they never seen in the first place? Are they seen but then forgotten, or are they seen and remembered but in such a way that they are not retrievable under normal circumstances? In order to find out each subject was briefly shown a very detailed picture and then was asked to recall both in words and in a drawing all of the picture he could remember seeing. When he said he could remember no more, we asked him nondirective questions until his ability to recall all further details seemed exhausted. (For example: "You drew a man standing here; can you describe his clothing?" "You left the lower right-hand corner of the drawing blank; can you remember anything in the picture down there?")

After this initial questioning half of the subjects were individually engaged in a 30-minute game of darts, described as an unrelated experiment. Each of the remaining subjects was asked to lean back in his chair, stare at a projection screen, relax and report whatever words came to his mind. The first 10 words spoken by the subject were written down on separate cards. Each card was then handed one at a time to the subject, who was asked first to associate more words to it, and then to express any thoughts that came to his mind in relation to the word. The entire association exercise usually lasted about 30 minutes.

Following either the dart game or the word-association task, each subject was asked again to try to recall the picture by talking about it and redrawing it. The same kinds of probing questions were asked. All the subjects were given a rationale for the interpolated task. The dart-throwers were told that we expected their memory to improve because they had spent 30 minutes thinking about something unrelated, and the word-associators were told that we expected their memory to improve because they had just spent 30 minutes intensively exercising it.

We found that the dart-throwers' ability to recall more pictorial detail neither improved nor deteriorated. Each word-associator, however, recovered a number of details he had left out of his earlier recall. We also analyzed the content of the associations themselves, and we found that if a previously unrecalled detail was prominent in the associations, it was more likely to be recovered on the subsequent recall. These results, in addition to those from other parts of the experiment, indicate that some information about fine details is maintained in memory even though it may not normally be available for report. If this were not so, even the most intense memory-jogging and free association would have

failed to yield more detail than was originally reported.

Another conclusion can be drawn from this experiment. It would appear that the pictures were not originally stored in the form of words. If they had been, the details would have been recalled during the first questioning. Instead a period of intense associative activity was required during which the subject was able to attach words to the pictorial images so that the individual details of the picture could be recalled.

The first of these experiments with pictorial stimuli suggests that recognition of pictures is essentially perfect. The results would probably have been the same if we had used 25,000 pictures instead of 2,500. The second experiment indicates that such recognition is based

on some type of representation in memory that is maintained without labels, words, names or the need for rehearsal. If the representation were linguistic, subjects asked to recall the details of a picture in words or other symbols should remember much more than they actually do. The test results also suggest that since the pictures are not stored in words they cannot be recalled in words either, at least not in much detail, unless the memory is stirred by an activity such as the free-association exercise.

One implication of these findings is that if techniques could be found to facilitate an attaching of words to visual images, recall might dramatically improve. Some people believe they have this ability, for example politicians who seem to be able to associate a name with every face they ever saw. Freud argued

VISUAL MEMORY EXPERIMENT required a test subject to look at 280 pairs of photographic slides. Each pair consisted of one slide that had been shown to subject before in a series of 2,560 viewed at the rate of one every 10 seconds. Subject presses button that signals that he thinks slide on left was one he had seen. Subjects remembered nearly all the slides they had been shown.

a

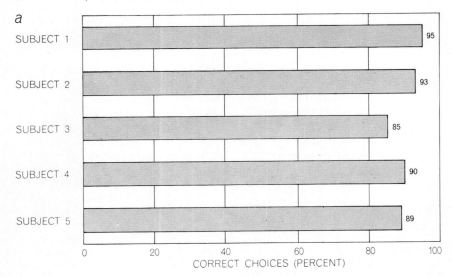

b

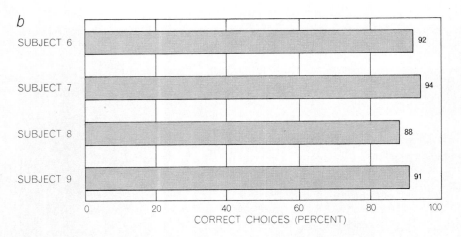

c

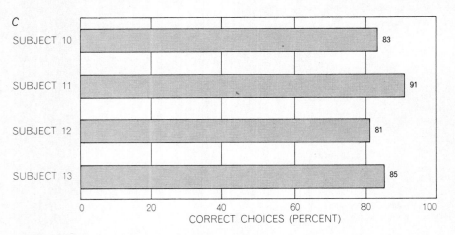

RESULTS OF VISUAL MEMORY EXPERIMENT indicate that the capacity for remembering pictures may be unlimited. Subjects in *a* recognized between 85 and 95 percent of the 2,560 slides they had previously viewed. In order to determine whether fatigue would reduce memory capacity, subjects No. 4 and No. 5 viewed 1,280 slides a day on each of two days, whereas subjects No. 1, No. 2 and No. 3 viewed only 640 slides a day on each of four days. Surprisingly, there was no significant difference between the scores of the two groups. Subjects in *b* looked at slides shown in mirror-image orientation, so that left became right, yet they were still able to identify slides as accurately as the subjects in *a* did. Subjects in *c* were also shown slides that had been reversed. When they were asked if the orientation of each photograph had been changed, the subjects responded correctly in most instances.

strongly that free association was an ideal way to recover irretrievable memories. Although Freud was concerned with repressed memories rather than with merely irretrievable ones, a more general statement is possible: The recall of previous stimulation may fail because we do not use words to remember pictures or feelings, and therefore we have difficulty using words to describe the memory later.

When the pictorial memory process is compared with the process by which words, numbers and other symbols are remembered, it becomes clear that the two systems are probably very different. Each kind of memory handles material that is perceived when light stimulates the retina, generating impulses that are then coded, organized and sent to the brain. In the case of pictures the image is received and stored permanently in pictorial form. Where words or other symbols are concerned the first step of memory is to take the stimulus out of its visual, pictorial form, code the items and extract their meaning. The collection of letters making up a printed word is not remembered as an image of distinct letters on a page; they are stored and recalled as the word itself. And words are remembered as ideas, not as a literal collection of words. A road sign is not remembered as a brightly colored panel with an arrow or a warning on it but as a message to stop, slow down or turn.

This particular memory process accounts for the ease with which a reader may overlook spelling errors in printed text. Instead of visualizing the word as it actually appears in physical reality, the reader tends almost immediately to extract the word itself from the printed characters and thus does not see the error. By the same token an unskilled proofreader may overlook the fact that a single letter in a word is printed in a typeface different from the face of the rest of the letters because he sees not the physical character but the spelling of the word.

The process of extracting linguistic material from its representational form and storing it conceptually appears to consist of several steps [*see top illustration, page 158*]. The first step is a brief moment of "iconic," or visual, storage. As we shall see, this storage lasts less than a second after perception. During this time the image may be scanned and coded. (For instance, a word may be taken out of the form of a collection of letters and translated into spoken form.) This item is then stored in the short-term memory. From the short-term memory the item is passed on to the long-term memory.

The short-term memory can probably hold from four to six unrelated items without decay, but beyond that number some kind of rehearsal is needed to prevent loss. A common example of rehearsal is our need to repeat a telephone number we have just looked up or heard as we hurry to the telephone to dial it. The seven digits cannot survive in the memory for more than a few seconds without some repetition. Another strategy for increasing the capacity of the short-term memory consists in recoding the item to be remembered. A long series of letters can be more easily held in the short-term memory, for instance, if they are made into an acronym or a word. In this case the word rather than the individual letters is remembered.

How does the material move from the short-term memory to the long-term one? Recoding from the names of the items to their meanings, a semantic coding, probably underlies this transition. No further maintenance is needed to hold

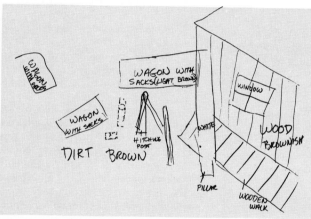
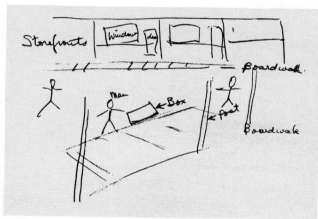

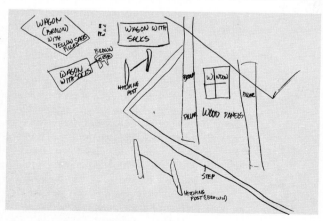
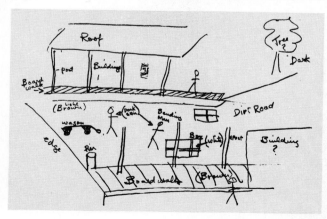

RECALL OF DETAIL indicates that pictures, faces and other pictorial material are stored in the memory as images. In this experiment two subjects were shown the same photograph of a rural scene (*pictures at top*) and each was asked to recall as much of the picture as he could by describing and drawing it (*middle picture*). At this point both subjects displayed similar levels of recall. One subject then threw darts for half an hour while the other tried to recall more details by thinking about the picture and speaking whatever words came to mind. Afterward both subjects were asked to redraw the picture. Drawing at lower left by dart-thrower indicates that his memory was relatively unchanged by his activity. Drawing at right by other subject contains much detail not present in his earlier drawing, indicating that the memory exercise helped him to attach words to the pictorial detail in his memory. If such details had been stored in the form of words rather than pictures, both subjects should have remembered all of them at first recall.

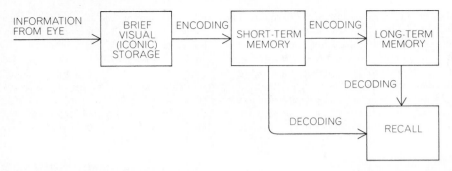

MEMORY PROCESS for words, numbers and other linguistic material has several stages. At left information such as a printed word seen by the eye is briefly stored as it actually looks. While this visual image lasts the word can be scanned, even if the original stimulus has disappeared. At center, during scanning, the word is encoded into its name (the letters *c*, *a* and *t* may become the word "cat") and is then entered in the short-term memory. At right the word enters the long-term memory, perhaps by being encoded again, this time from its name into its meaning. At lower right word is recalled by being decoded into its name.

the information in recallable form at this point, although the information may have to be coded back into names if it is to be recalled. The evidence does not yet indicate whether awareness of seeing the stimulus is synonymous with the iconic storage or short-term memory, or is something that happens with or after semantic coding.

This model of the linguistic memory process is a rather generalized one. Many specific models have been proposed, and the experimental evidence is not yet complete enough to choose between them. Nevertheless, several recent experiments have clarified what happens in the early stages. One problem that was investigated was the source of the

errors that are made when an individual is asked to recall several items in a large display. Do such omissions indicate a limited memory capacity or are they due to a failure to perceive some of the items?

It is known that only four to six items can be remembered without the aid of rehearsal or recoding. Thus it seems possible that whereas all the objects might have been perceived at first, some were simply lost because there was no room for them in the short-term memory. Items might also be lost at later stages in the memory process.

How could these hypotheses be tested? How, in other words, could failure to perceive be experimentally distinguished

from some limitation of memory capacity? One cannot solve the problem merely by asking the subject if he saw every item in the display when it was first perceived. If a subject's memory capacity is too limited to contain all the items in a display, he will not be able to recall whether or not he perceived each of them initially.

An experimental approach to this problem, developed a century ago by N. Baxt, was rediscovered by George Sperling of the Bell Telephone Laboratories. In one of Sperling's experiments based on Baxt's method the subject was presented with an array of letters in a tachistoscope. The array remained visible for about 50 milliseconds. Once the display ended, the subject was asked to remember all the letters until a marker appeared that indicated the position of from one to four of the letters that he was to report. If there was no delay, that is, if the indicator came on immediately after the termination of the display, the subject made virtually no errors. This period of error-free reporting lasted for approximately 250 milliseconds (a quarter of a second). As the delay between the end of the display and the appearance of the indicator increased, however, so did the frequency of the subject's errors.

Some important conclusions about the memory process and the source of the errors can be drawn from these results. If recall is perfect at the instant after the tachistoscopic flash of the array ends, it follows that nearly all the information in the display has probably been stored in the memory. If the storage were not virtually complete, the subject would be unable to recall some items because those indicated for report are selected randomly. There is accordingly no way for the subject to remember only those items to be selected for recall.

It can also be concluded from the highly accurate recall that the initial perception, that is, the image conveyed by the visual system to the memory system, must itself be accurate. If perception were not detailed and inclusive, the iconic image in the memory would contain errors and so would the recall. The initial perception, then, cannot be the source of the errors.

Since the subject is never asked to report more than four items, a quantity within the capacity of the short-term memory, the errors and omissions subjects make when they try to recall items from a large display must apparently originate in the later processing stages of the memory, not in the initial iconic-

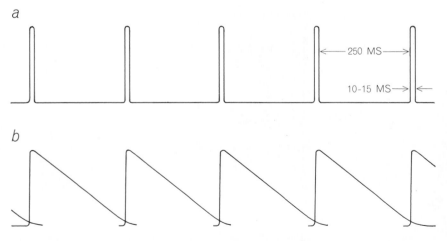

VISUAL IMAGE in an observer's memory makes a flash of light appear to persist after it has actually faded. In one experiment demonstrating such persistence a subject watched a train of flashes, each lasting between 10 and 15 milliseconds and spaced 250 milliseconds apart. In *a* flashes are represented by peaks. In *b* the images excited by the flashes are represented by curves indicating how the flashes looked to subject. The curves show that a visual image is excited by each flash (*sharply rising phase*). This image persists in the memory, fading gradually over 250 milliseconds so that it outlasts the flash itself. Because one image is still perceptible when the next image begins (*intersections of falling and rising curves*) flashes appear to subject to blend into each other, forming a flickering train.

storage stage or in a limitation on reporting by the subject.

These experiments suggested, but did not directly confirm, that the iconic image persists in the memory for about a quarter of a second. Standing and I devised two further experiments that provided this confirmation. Our results also confirm that the iconic image is visual. We argued that if a visual representation actually persisted for 250 milliseconds or so after the termination of the flash, it should be possible to have a subject estimate this persistence directly. We knew that it is not possible, however, to ask him to provide a judgment of absolute duration. With suitable adjustment in intensity, flashes lasting from one nanosecond (10^{-9} second) to 10 milliseconds (10^{-2} second) seem equal. We have tried two other procedures, both considerably more direct than Sperling's estimates.

Our first experiment tested the assumption that a brief flash of light creates an iconic image that persists in the memory for perhaps 250 milliseconds after the stimulus has ended. If this were so, it could be predicted that when the interval between flashes is equal to or slightly shorter than the duration of the iconic image, the subject should report that no flash completely faded away before the next one began. The train of flashes might appear to be flickering, but there should be no completely dark intervals between the flashes. We tested this prediction by recycling a briefly presented small black-on-white circle in one channel of a two-channel tachistoscope. The other channel was set at the same luminance as the one with the circle, in order to keep the subject's eyes adapted to light. The flash presenting the circle lasted from 10 to 15 milliseconds. A number of trains of flashes were presented, each with a different interval between flashes. After the subject had viewed a particular train of flashes he was asked to indicate if the circle completely faded away each time before it reappeared. As long as the interval between flashes did not exceed about 250 milliseconds all the subjects reported that the form never completely faded away. Intervals longer than 250 milliseconds produced reports of complete fading.

What effect, if any, did the length of the flash itself have on the duration of the iconic image? We found that for relatively short presentation times ranging between four and 200 milliseconds (well above threshold) the iconic image still persisted for about 250 milliseconds. In other words, the duration of the iconic image seemed to be independent of

TACHISTOSCOPE (*tall box at right*) is a viewing chamber in which an experimental subject watches rapidly changing stimuli such as images or light flashes. Apparatus at left controls timing and presentation of the stimuli. The subject also wears earphones through which he hears clicking sounds. He controls the tone generator that produces the clicks so that one coincides with the onset of an image and the other with the termination. Such experiments reveal how the memory processes letters, numbers and similar material.

the duration of the original stimulus, at least for very brief stimuli.

Our evidence for the existence of an iconic image seemed to be falling very neatly into place. None of the tests we had conducted so far, however, excluded the possibility that we were measuring the properties of a retinal image rather than an image formed during the first stages of the memory process. In order to eliminate this possibility—or to substantiate it—we devised another procedure. In this variation of the experiment the first flash of a train was presented to the right eye while the left eye's vision was blocked; then the right eye's vision would be blocked while the next flash was delivered to the left eye, and so forth. Under these conditions subjects

still needed about 250 milliseconds between flashes. This result clearly indicates that although there may be some persistence at the retinal level, the iconic image exists centrally, after the information from the two eyes has been combined. If this were not so, the flashes would have had to be only 125 milliseconds apart (250 milliseconds to each eye separately).

In our next experiment we attempted to refine and extend our earlier results. Following a plan suggested by Sperling, we used a three-channel tachistoscope. One channel was a blank illuminated field, the second displayed the target whose duration was to be estimated by the subject and the third presented random designs (the visual equivalent of "noise"). The subject wore earphones through which he heard a brief click at about the time the target was presented in the tachistoscope. His task was to turn a knob so that he judged the click and the beginning of the flash to come at exactly the same time. There was a click-flash presentation every few seconds. When the subject was satisfied with the match between the click and the beginning of the display, he had to repeat the procedure, but this time he had to match the click to the end of the display. The difference in the timing of the clicks thus represented the subject's estimate of the duration of the display.

As we expected, the second click followed the actual termination of the very brief display by about 200 milliseconds, indicating that the iconic image is of that duration. It will be recalled that in the preceding experiment the duration of the iconic image was independent of the duration of a flash less than 200 milliseconds long. In this experiment the persistence of the image decreased, however, as the stimulus's duration increased. When the display lasted for 500 milliseconds, the image persisted for less than 50 milliseconds. The iconic image associated with a one-second flash is less than 30 milliseconds. An iconic image lasts longer than about 250 milliseconds—for 400 milliseconds, in fact—only when the subject is dark-adapted.

Both of these studies are in close agreement with the more cumbersome estimates in the literature. They confirm the fact that the memory process seems to increase the effective length of all brief flashes to at least 200 milliseconds. If the flashes are already that long, further increases are minimized. The studies also clearly demonstrate that the brief storage Sperling postulated is in fact visual, since subjects describe the iconically stored image as if they were talking about the flash itself.

What other factors determine the length of this visual storage? Can it be lengthened or shortened under normal as well as experimental circumstances? What role does it play in the extraction of information from visual stimuli? It should be obvious that a brief period of visual storage, effectively extending a stimulus for less than a second, will be useful only when that extension provides some critical advantage. Are perceivers only asked to describe the effects of brief flashes when experimental psychologists present such flashes? Have we perhaps invented a concept of visual storage that serves no function in nature (except perhaps to read in the dark during a lightning storm)? I believe quite the contrary. There are many rapidly presented visual stimuli encountered in the environment. For literate adults the most important and continuing visual experience is reading, and reading if nothing else is a task of viewing a rapid succession of brief visual exposures containing large amounts of information.

Evidence that the persistent iconic image aids in reading and therefore in similar visual tasks has been suggested by many workers. These investigators have found that a slow reader or someone reading slowly fixes his eyes on each word for about a quarter of a second. A faster reader also fixes his eyes for about the same amount of time. Such a fast reader attains his higher speed by reducing the number of fixations, that is, he looks at and processes several words instead of one word during each fixation. Both kinds of reader need from 30 to 50 milliseconds to shift their eyes from one fixation point to the next.

It would seem, then, that both fast and slow readers need about a quarter of a second to perceive and extract the information contained in any word. Since the length of this interval is under the reader's control, the conclusion can be drawn that the interval constitutes the adequate minimum processing time for encoding linguistic material into the memory. If this is true, it follows that a visual storage medium might serve the purpose of prolonging a stimulus that does not last long enough to be recognized otherwise. It should not be regarded as mere coincidence that the duration of iconic storage and the minimum fixation time in reading are both about a quarter of a second.

Evidence supporting this line of reasoning is beginning to accumulate, but it is still by no means adequate. Part of the evidence concerns how an iconic image is erased and what effect erasure has on information processing. If a persistent iconic image helps the viewer to process information, there should also be a way to erase the iconic image when it has served its purpose. If there were no erasing process, a reader or someone rapidly scanning the faces in a crowd might be hampered by the persistence of an iconic image from the last stimulus as he tried to assimilate a new one.

A large number of experiments show that superimposing a new visual pattern or a visual noise field over the old one will in fact wipe out the iconic image, thereby interfering with or actually stopping the processing of information contained in the pattern. This will normally

ADAPTATION CHANNEL

IMAGE CHANNEL

SOUND

DURATION OF VISUAL IMAGE is measured. In an experiment shown schematically the subject was asked to match a clicking sound (bottom) to the onset of a repeated stimulus consisting of a black circle on a

ADAPTATION CHANNEL

IMAGE CHANNEL

SOUND

LONG-LASTING STIMULUS in the tachistoscope produces a brief visual image in the memory. In a subject has already adjusted

ADAPTATION CHANNEL

VISUAL NOISE CHANNEL

IMAGE CHANNEL

SOUND

VISUAL IMAGE IS ERASED by the appearance of a new stimulus. In a black circle is presented for 50 milliseconds, an interval normally long enough to produce a

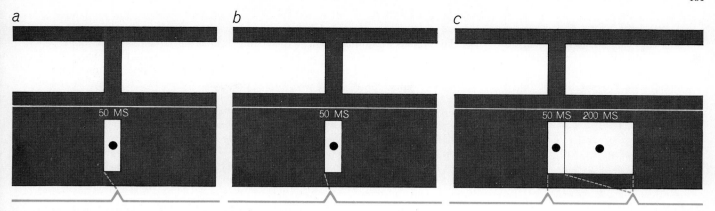

a *b* *c*

white field displayed in the tachistoscope. Adaptation field in the tachistoscope (*top*) keeps the subject's eyes adjusted to a given light level. In *a* the subject hears a click after he sees the stimulus. In *b* subject has begun to make the click coincide with the onset of the next image. In *c* adjustment has been made and subject has

also matched a second click with what he perceives as the end of the stimulus. Actually the click marks the end of the visual image in the subject's memory rather than the end of the stimulus itself, which has faded out 200 milliseconds earlier. This interval from fade-out to click therefore represents duration of the visual image.

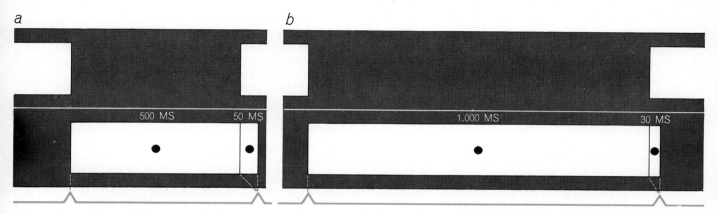

a *b*

one click so that it coincides with the beginning of the stimulus and another so that it coincides with the perceived end. The stimulus actually lasts for 500 milliseconds. The interval between clicks,

however, is about 550 milliseconds, an indication that the visual image lasts 50 milliseconds. In *b*, when stimulus lasts twice as long as in *a*, visual image it excites is still shorter, about 30 milliseconds.

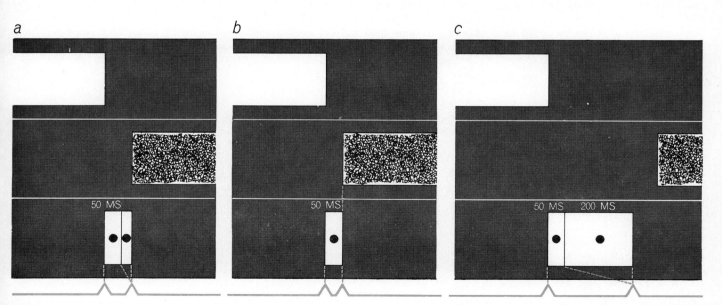

a *b* *c*

200-millisecond visual image. In this instance, however, visual noise (a random pattern of letters) appears. This new stimulus ends the visual image of the black circle after only a few milliseconds. Therefore interval between clicks is only slightly longer

than the duration of the stimulus. In *b* noise begins as circle vanishes, so that interval between clicks equals the duration of stimulus, indicating that there is no visual image at all. In *c* the noise has no effect on image because it begins after the image has faded.

happen in reading when the eyes focus on a new portion of print. The new stimulus wipes out the iconic image of the old, so that the way is cleared for the processing of new material.

The experiment of the click-flash pairings is relevant to this issue. The third channel of the tachistoscope in another condition of that study presented visual noise in the form of random patterns. At various times after the flash this visual noise channel was turned on. If the new stimulus (visual noise) erased the image of the old stimulus, as we expected, then the time interval between the two clicks should be reduced if visual noise arrives before the iconic image has had time to fade. Specifically, if the visual noise coincides with the end of the flash, the time interval between the clicks should be no longer than the flash itself. Conversely, if the visual noise were delayed beyond the normal persistence of the iconic image, the subject's performance should not be affected. This is exactly what was found.

This task did not require the subject to extract information; he was asked only to estimate how much time he would need to extract the information. The results provide fairly direct support for the erasive and therefore process-stopping effect of visual noise.

Even more convincing, however, is the fact that when one display is removed and another is presented to the subject before he has time to process the image, he reports that he was aware of seeing the first stimulus but did not have enough time to recognize it. This result can be obtained whether the display is followed by visual noise or by more information. It can be concluded that the visual noise reduces a subject's

time for extracting information, not the time available for perceiving the stimulus; the quarter-second occupied by the iconic image is not needed for seeing a display but for processing its content.

This effect was most clearly shown in a sequential word-recognition experiment. As the subject watched, each letter of a word appeared in succession on the screen of an electroluminescent panel, each in the same location so that the second letter should destroy the persistence of the first, the third letter the persistence of the second and so on. In this way the rate of presentation effectively controlled the time the subject had for processing each letter. The rate was varied from 20 milliseconds per letter to 300 milliseconds per letter. It was not surprising that the probability of recognizing each letter was higher for the slower rates of presentation. More important (and more relevant to this argument) was the finding that for each rate it did not matter whether the time from the onset of one letter to the onset of the next was used entirely for presenting the letter or whether the letter was presented for just a few milliseconds. Once a letter is seen, further viewing time is irrelevant as long as its persistence is unimpaired. The extra time is used to process the information that is already secured.

Finally, several experiments dating back to an earlier one of Sperling's have shown that when the interval between the onset of the stimulus and the arrival of visual noise is varied so that the time available for processing the content of the stimulus is also varied, a nearly linear function is revealed between processing time and the number of items the perceiver can recognize. In

an experiment conducted in my laboratory we have shown that this relationship is much more apparent in subjects without practice in this particular task; it is attenuated after they acquire more experience. In the first few days of the experiment it appears that the perceiver needs about 10 milliseconds of processing time to recognize each letter after having some time to perceive all the letters and set up the iconic storage. For the particular displays we used, this perception and setup time was about 50 milliseconds. Thus a four-letter word requires about 90 milliseconds of time before the visual noise arrives in order for each of its letters to be correctly recognized. After several days, however, four letters require little more time than one does. This suggests that perceivers are developing more efficient strategies for processing information as they become familiar with the task and the items to be recognized.

Clearly much is happening in the first few milliseconds after the onset of a visual stimulus that is to be encoded into verbal memory. It can also be seen that the memory process can be regarded as a system concerned with information processing that consists of several stages and has its own time constants for extraction, decay, mode of persistence, susceptibility to interference or erasure, and the like. Viewing the memory process in this way is likely to lead investigators to design still other experiments that will yield a basic understanding of visual perception. Such knowledge is important for its own sake, but I hope it is also clear how much our knowledge of reading and other visual skills is ultimately related to our understanding of visual perception and information processing.

How to Teach Animals

by B. F. Skinner
December 1951

*Some simple techniques of the psychological
laboratory can also be used in the home. They
can train a dog to dance, a pigeon to play a toy
piano and will illuminate the learning process in man*

TEACHING, it is often said, is an art, but we have increasing reason to hope that it may eventually become a science. We have already discovered enough about the nature of learning to devise training techniques which are much more effective and give more reliable results than the rule-of-thumb methods of the past. Tested on animals, the new techniques have proved superior to traditional methods of professional animal trainers; they yield more remarkable results with much less effort.

It takes rather subtle laboratory conditions to test an animal's full learning capacity, but the reader will be surprised at how much he can accomplish even under informal circumstances at home. Since nearly everyone at some time or other has tried, or wished he knew how, to train a dog, a cat or some other animal, perhaps the most useful way to explain the learning process is to describe some simple experiments which the reader can perform himself.

"Catch your rabbit" is the first item in a well-known recipe for rabbit stew. Your first move, of course, is to choose an experimental subject. Any available animal—a cat, a dog, a pigeon, a mouse, a parrot, a chicken, a pig—will do. (Children or other members of your family may also be available, but it is suggested that you save them until you have had practice with less valuable material.) Suppose you choose a dog.

The second thing you will need is something your subject wants, say food. This serves as a reward or—to use a term which is less likely to be misunderstood—a "reinforcement" for the desired behavior. Many things besides food are reinforcing—for example, simply letting the dog out for a run—but food is usually the easiest to administer in the kind of experiment to be described here. If you use food, you must of course perform the experiment when the dog is hungry, perhaps just before his dinnertime.

The reinforcement gives you a means of control over the behavior of the animal. It rests on the simple principle that whenever something reinforces a particular activity of an organism, it increases the chances that the organism will repeat that behavior. This makes it possible to shape an animal's behavior almost as a sculptor shapes a lump of clay. There is, of course, nothing new in this principle. What is new is a better understanding

PIGEON can be taught to choose one card rather than another and even apparently to read. This is done by "reinforcing" the animal when it pecks the right card and turning out the light when it pecks the wrong one.

of the conditions under which reinforcement works best.

To be effective a reinforcement must be given almost simultaneously with the desired behavior; a delay of even one second destroys much of the effect. This means that the offer of food in the usual way is likely to be ineffective; it is not fast enough. The best way to reinforce the behavior with the necessary speed is to use a "conditioned" reinforcer. This is a signal which the animal is conditioned to associate with food. The animal is always given food immediately after the signal, and the signal itself then becomes the reinforcer. The better the association between the two events, the better the result.

For the conditioned reinforcer you need a clear signal which can be given instantly and to which the subject is sure to respond. It may be a noise or a flash of-light. A whistle is not effective because of the time it takes to draw a breath before blowing it. A visual signal like a wave of the arm may not always be seen by the animal. A convenient signal is a rap on a table with a small hard object or the noise of a high-pitched device such as a "cricket."

YOU are now ready to start the experiment with your dog. Work in a convenient place as free as possible from distraction. Let us say that you have chosen a "cricket" as your conditioned reinforcer. To build up the effect of the reinforcer begin by tossing a few scraps of food, one at a time and not oftener than once or twice a minute, where the dog may eat them. Use scraps of food so small that 30 or 40 will not greatly reduce the animal's hunger. As soon as the dog eats each scrap readily and without delay, begin to pair the cricket with the food. Sound the cricket and then toss a piece of food. Wait half a minute or so and repeat. Sound the cricket suddenly, without any preparatory movements such as reaching for food.

At this stage your subject will probably show well-marked begging behavior. It may watch you intently, perhaps jump on you, and so on. You must break up this behavior, because it will interfere with other parts of the experiment. Never sound the cricket or give food when the dog is close to you or facing you. Wait until it turns away, then reinforce. Your conditioned reinforcer is working properly when your subject turns immediately and approaches the spot where it receives food. Test this several times. Wait until the dog is in a fairly unusual position, then sound the signal. Time spent in making sure the dog immediately approaches the food will later be saved manyfold.

Now, having established the noise as the reinforcer, you may begin teaching the dog. To get the feel of the technique start with some simple task, such as getting the dog to approach the handle on a low cupboard door and touch it with its nose. At first you reinforce any activity which would be part of the final completed act of approaching and touching the handle of the cupboard. The only permissible contact between you and the dog is *via* the cricket and the food. Do not touch the dog, talk to it, coax it, "draw its attention" or interfere in any other way with the experiment. If your subject just sits, you may have to begin by reinforcing any movement, however slight. As soon as the dog moves, sound the cricket and give food. Remember that your reaction time is important. Try to reinforce as nearly simultaneously with the movement as possible.

After your subject is moving freely about, reinforce any turn toward the cupboard. Almost immediately you will notice a change in its behavior. It will begin to face toward the cupboard most of the time. Then begin to reinforce only when the dog moves nearer the cupboard. (If you withhold reinforcement too long at this stage, you may lose the facing response. If so, go back and pick it up.) In a very short time—perhaps a minute or two—you should have the dog standing close to the cupboard. Now begin to pay attention to its head. Reinforce any movement that brings the nose close to the handle. You will have to make special efforts now to reduce the time between the movement and the reinforcement to the very minimum. Presently the dog will touch the handle with its nose, and after reinforcement it will repeat this behavior so long as it remains hungry.

DOG can easily be trained to touch its nose to the handle of a cupboard with the aid of a mechanical "cricket." The experimenter holds the cricket in one hand and a bit of food in the other. When the dog makes any move-

Usually it takes no more than five minutes, even for a beginner, to teach a dog this behavior. Moreover, the dog does not have to be particularly smart to learn it; contrary to the usual view, all normal dogs will learn with about equal facility by this conditioning technique.

Before going on with other experiments test the effect of your conditioned reinforcer again two or three times. If the dog responds quickly and eats without delay you may safely continue. You should "extinguish" the response the dog has already learned, however, before teaching it another. Stop reinforcing the act of touching the cupboard handle until the dog abandons this activity.

As a second test, let us say, you want to teach the dog to lift its head in the air and turn around to the right. The general procedure is the same, but you may need some help in sharpening your observation of the behavior to be reinforced. As a guide to the height to which the dog's head is to be raised, sight some horizontal line on the wall across the room. Whenever the dog, in its random movements, lifts its head above this line, reinforce immediately. You will soon see the head rising above the line more and more frequently. Now raise your sights slightly and reinforce only when the dog's head rises above the new level. By a series of gradual steps you can get the dog to hold its head much higher than usual. After this you can begin to emphasize any turning movement in a clockwise direction while the

head is high. Eventually the dog should execute a kind of dance step. If you use available food carefully, a single session should suffice for setting up this behavior.

HAVING tested your ability to produce these simple responses, you may feel confident enough to approach a more complex assignment. This time suppose you try working with a pigeon. Pigeons do not tame easily. You will probably want a cage to help control the bird, and for this you can rig up a large cardboard carton with a screen or lattice top and windows cut in the side for observing the bird. It is much less disturbing to the bird if you watch it from below its line of vision than if you peer at it from above. In general keep yourself out of the experimental situation as much as possible. You may still use a cricket as a conditioned reinforcer, and feed the bird by dropping a few grains of pigeon feed into a small dish through a hole in the wall. It may take several daily feedings to get the bird to eat readily and to respond quickly to the cricket.

Your assignment is to teach the pigeon to identify the visual patterns on playing cards. To begin with, hang a single card on a nail on the wall of the cage a few inches above the floor so that the pigeon can easily peck it. After you have trained the bird to peck the card by reinforcing the movements that lead to that end, change the card and again reinforce the

peck. If you shuffle the cards and present them at random, the pigeon will learn to peck any card offered.

Now begin to teach it to discriminate among the cards. Let us say you are using diamonds and clubs (excluding face cards and aces) and want the bird to select diamonds. Reinforce only when the card presented is a diamond, never when it is a club. Almost immediately the bird will begin to show a preference for diamonds. You can speed up its progress toward complete rejection of clubs by discontinuing the experiment for a moment (a mild form of punishment) whenever it pecks a club. A good conditioned punishment is simply to turn off the light or cover or remove the card. After half a minute replace the card or turn on the light and continue the experiment. Under these conditions the response which is positively reinforced with food remains part of the repertoire of the bird, while the response that leads to a blackout quickly disappears.

There is an amusing variation of this experiment by which you can make it appear that a pigeon can be taught to read. You simply use two printed cards bearing the words PECK and DON'T PECK, respectively. By reinforcing responses to PECK and blacking out when the bird pecks DON'T PECK, it is quite easy to train the bird to obey the commands on the cards.

The pigeon can also be taught the somewhat more "intellectual" performance of matching a sample object. Let us

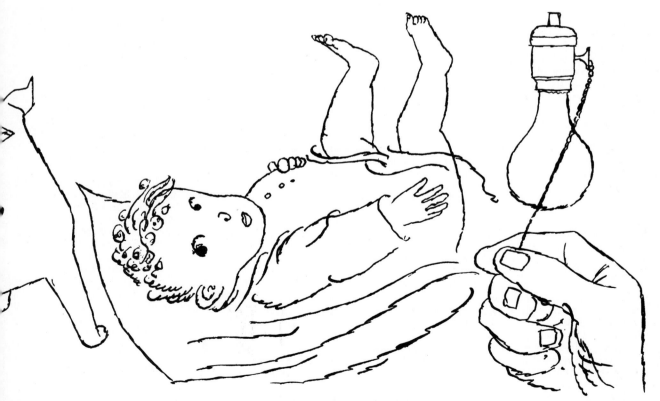

ment toward the handle, the experimenter sounds the cricket and tosses the food. Babies are just as smart as dogs in learning such tricks. At right a baby is taught to lift its arm when a lamp is turned off and on.

say the sample to be matched is a certain card. Fasten three cards to a board, with one above and the two others side by side just below it. The board is placed so that the bird can reach all the cards through windows cut in the side of the cage. After training the bird to peck a card of any kind impartially in all three positions, present the three chosen cards. The sample to be matched, say the three of diamonds, is at the top, and below it put a three of diamonds and a three of clubs. If the bird pecks the sample three of diamonds at the top, do nothing. If it pecks the matching three of diamonds below, reinforce it; if it pecks the three of clubs, black out. After each correct response and reinforcement, switch the positions of the two lower cards. The pigeon should soon match the sample each time. Conversely, it can also be taught to select the card that does not match the sample. It is important to reinforce correct choices immediately. Your own behavior must be letter-perfect if you are to expect perfection from your subject. The task can be made easier if the pigeon is conditioned to peck the sample card before you begin to train it to match the sample.

IN A MORE elaborate variation of this experiment we have found it possible to make a pigeon choose among four words so that it appears to "name the suit" of the sample card. You prepare four cards about the size of small calling cards, each bearing in block letters the name of a suit: SPADES, HEARTS, DIAMONDS and CLUBS. Fasten these side by side in a row and teach the pigeon to peck them by reinforcing in the usual way. Now arrange a sample playing card just above them. Cover the name cards and reinforce the pigeon a few times for pecking the sample. Now present, say, the three of diamonds as the sample. When the pigeon pecks it, immediately uncover the name cards. If the pigeon pecks DIAMONDS, reinforce instantly. If it pecks a wrong name instead, black out for half a minute and then resume the experiment with the three of diamonds still in place and the name cards covered. After a correct choice, change the sample card to a different suit while the pigeon is eating. Always keep the names covered until the sample card has been pecked. Within a short time you should have the bird following the full sequence of pecking the sample and then the appropriate name card. As time passes the correct name will be pecked more and more frequently and, if you do not too often reinforce wrong responses or neglect to reinforce right ones, the pigeon should soon become letter-perfect.

A toy piano offers interesting possibilities for performances of a more artistic nature. Reinforce any movement of the pigeon that leads toward its pressing a key. Then, by using reinforcements and blackouts appropriately, narrow the response to a given key. Then build up a two-note sequence by reinforcing only when the sequence has been completed and by blacking out when any other combination of keys is struck. The two-note sequence will quickly emerge. Other notes may then be added. Pigeons, chickens, small dogs and cats have been taught in this way to play tunes of four or five notes. The situation soon becomes too complicated, however, for the casual experimenter. You will find it difficult to control the tempo, and the reinforcing contingencies become very complex. The limit of such an experiment is determined as much by the experimenter's skill as by that of the animal. In the laboratory we have been able to provide assistance to the experimenter by setting up complicated devices which always reinforce consistently and avoid exhaustion of the experimenter's patience.

The increased precision of the laboratory also makes it possible to guarantee performance up to the point of almost complete certainty. When relevant conditions have been controlled, the behavior of the organism is fully determined. Behavior may be sustained in full strength for many hours by utilizing different schedules of reinforcement. Some of these correspond to the contingencies established in industry in daily wages or in piece-work pay; others resemble the subtle but powerful contingencies of gambling devices, which are notorious for their ability to command sustained behavior.

THE human baby is an excellent subject in experiments of the kind described here. You will not need to interfere with feeding schedules or create any other state of deprivation, because the human infant can be reinforced by very trivial environmental events; it does not need such a reward as food. Almost any "feed-back" from the environment is reinforcing if it is not too intense. A crumpled newspaper, a pan and a spoon, or any convenient noisemaker quickly generates appropriate behavior, often amusing in its violence. The baby's rattle is based upon this principle.

One reinforcer to which babies often respond is the flashing on and off of a table lamp. Select some arbitrary response—for example, lifting the hand. Whenever the baby lifts its hand, flash the light. In a short time a well-defined response will be generated. (Human babies are just as "smart" as dogs or pigeons in this respect.) Incidentally, the baby will enjoy the experiment.

The same principle is at work in the behavior of older children and adults. Important among human reinforcements are those aspects of the behavior of others, often very subtle, that we call "attention," "approval" and "affection."

Behavior which is successful in achieving these reinforcements may come to dominate the repertoire of the individual.

All this may be easily used—and just as easily misused—in our relations with other people. To the reader who is anxious to advance to the human subject a word of caution is in order. Reinforcement is only one of the procedures through which we alter behavior. To use it, we must build up some degree of deprivation or at least permit a deprivation to prevail which it is within our power to reduce. We must embark upon a program in which we sometimes apply relevant reinforcement and sometimes withhold it. In doing this, we are quite likely to generate emotional effects. Unfortunately the science of behavior is not yet as successful in controlling emotion as it is in shaping practical behavior.

A scientific analysis can, however, bring about a better understanding of personal relations. We are almost always reinforcing the behavior of others, whether we mean to or not. A familiar problem is that of the child who seems to take an almost pathological delight in annoying its parents. In many cases this is the result of conditioning which is very similar to the animal training we have discussed. The attention, approval and affection that a mother gives a child are all extremely powerful reinforcements. Any behavior of the child that produces these consequences is likely to be strengthened. The mother may unwittingly promote the very behavior she does not want. For example, when she is busy she is likely not to respond to a call or request made in a quiet tone of voice. She may answer the child only when it raises its voice. The average intensity of the child's vocal behavior therefore moves up to another level—precisely as the head of the dog in our experiment was raised to a new height. Eventually the mother gets used to this level and again reinforces only louder instances. This vicious circle brings about louder and louder behavior. The child's voice may also vary in intonation, and any change in the direction of unpleasantness is more likely to get the attention of the mother and is therefore strengthened. One might even say that "annoying" behavior is just that behavior which is especially effective in arousing another person to action. The mother behaves, in fact, as if she had been given the assignment to teach the child to be annoying! The remedy in such a case is simply for the mother to make sure that she responds with attention and affection to most if not all the responses of the child which are of acceptable intensity and tone of voice and that she never reinforces the annoying forms of behavior.

The Split Brain in Man

by Michael S. Gazzaniga
August 1967

The human brain is actually two brains, each capable of advanced mental functions. When the cerebrum is divided surgically, it is as if the cranium contained two separate spheres of consciousness

The brain of the higher animals, including man, is a double organ, consisting of right and left hemispheres connected by an isthmus of nerve tissue called the corpus callosum. Some 15 years ago Ronald E. Myers and R. W. Sperry, then at the University of Chicago, made a surprising discovery: When this connection between the two halves of the cerebrum was cut, each hemisphere functioned independently as if it were a complete brain. The phenomenon was first investigated in a cat in which not only the brain but also the optic chiasm, the crossover of the optic nerves, was divided, so that visual information from the left eye was dispatched only to the left brain and information from the right eye only to the right brain. Working on a problem with one eye, the animal could respond normally and learn to perform a task; when that eye was covered and the same problem was presented to the other eye, the animal evinced no recognition of the problem and had to learn it again from the beginning with the other half of the brain.

The finding introduced entirely new questions in the study of brain mechanisms. Was the corpus callosum responsible for integration of the operations of the two cerebral hemispheres in the intact brain? Did it serve to keep each hemisphere informed about what was going on in the other? To put the question another way, would cutting the corpus callosum literally result in the right hand not knowing what the left was doing? To what extent were the two half-brains actually independent when they were separated? Could they have separate thoughts, even separate emotions?

Such questions have been pursued by Sperry and his co-workers in a wide-ranging series of animal studies at the California Institute of Technology over the past decade [see "The Great Cerebral Commissure," by R. W. Sperry; SCIENTIFIC AMERICAN Offprint 174. Recently these questions have been investigated in human patients who underwent the brain-splitting operation for medical reasons. The demonstration in experimental animals that sectioning of the corpus callosum did not seriously impair mental faculties had encouraged surgeons to resort to this operation for people afflicted with uncontrollable epilepsy. The hope was to confine a seizure to one hemisphere. The operation proved to be remarkably successful; curiously there is an almost total elimination of all attacks, including unilateral ones. It is as if the intact callosum had served in these patients to facilitate seizure activity.

This article is a brief survey of investigations Sperry and I have carried out at Cal Tech over the past five years with some of these patients. The operations were performed by P. J. Vogel and J. E. Bogen of the California College of Medicine. Our studies date back to 1961, when the first patient, a 48-year-old war veteran, underwent the operation: cutting of the corpus callosum and other commissure structures connecting the two halves of the cerebral cortex [see *illustration, page 169*]. As of today 10 patients have had the operation, and we have examined four thoroughly over a long period with many tests.

From the beginning one of the most striking observations was that the operation produced no noticeable change in the patients' temperament, personality or general intelligence. In the first case the patient could not speak for 30 days after the operation, but he then recovered his speech. More typical was the third case: on awaking from the surgery the patient quipped that he had a "split-ting headache," and in his still drowsy state he was able to repeat the tongue twister "Peter Piper picked a peck of pickled peppers."

Close observation, however, soon revealed some changes in the patients' everyday behavior. For example, it could be seen that in moving about and responding to sensory stimuli the patients favored the right side of the body, which is controlled by the dominant left half of the brain. For a considerable period after the operation the left side of the body rarely showed spontaneous activity, and the patient generally did not respond to stimulation of that side: when he brushed against something with his left side he did not notice that he had done so, and when an object was placed in his left hand he generally denied its presence.

More specific tests identified the main features of the bisected-brain syndrome. One of these tests examined responses to visual stimulation. While the patient fixed his gaze on a central point on a board, spots of light were flashed (for a tenth of a second) in a row across the board that spanned both the left and the right half of his visual field. The patient was asked to tell what he had seen. Each patient reported that lights had been flashed in the right half of the visual field. When lights were flashed only in the left half of the field, however, the patients generally denied having seen any lights. Since the right side of the visual field is normally projected to the left hemisphere of the brain and the left field to the right hemisphere, one might have concluded that in these patients with divided brains the right hemisphere was in effect blind. We found, however, that this was not the case when the patients were directed to point to the lights that had flashed instead of giving a verbal report. With this manual response they were able to indicate when lights had

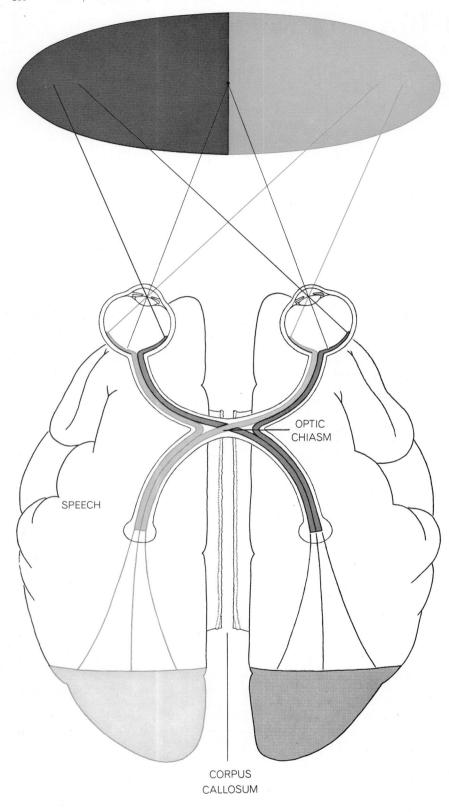

SPEECH

OPTIC
CHIASM

CORPUS
CALLOSUM

**VISUAL INPUT to bisected brain was limited to one hemisphere by presenting infor-
mation only in one visual field. The right and left fields of view are projected, via the
optic chiasm, to the left and right hemispheres of the brain respectively. If a person fixes
his gaze on a point, therefore, information to the left of the point goes only to the right
hemisphere and information to the right of the point goes to the left hemisphere. Stimuli in
the left visual field cannot be described by a split-brain patient because of the disconnec-
tion between the right hemisphere and the speech center, which is in the left hemisphere.**

been flashed in the left visual field, and
perception with the brain's right hemisphere proved to be almost equal to perception with the left. Clearly, then, the
patients' failure to report the right hemisphere's perception verbally was due to
the fact that the speech centers of the
brain are located in the left hemisphere.

Our tests of the patients' ability to
recognize objects by touch at first resulted in the same general finding. When
the object was held in the right hand,
from which sensory information is sent to
the left hemisphere, the patient was able
to name and describe the object. When
it was held in the left hand (from which
information goes primarily to the right
hemisphere), the patient could not describe the object verbally but was able to
identify it in a nonverbal test—matching
it, for example, to the same object in a
varied collection of things. We soon realized, however, that each hemisphere receives, in addition to the main input
from the opposite side of the body, some
input from the same side. This "ipsilateral" input is crude; it is apparently good
mainly for "cuing in" the hemisphere as
to the presence or absence of stimulation
and relaying fairly gross information
about the location of a stimulus on the
surface of the body. It is unable, as a
rule, to relay information concerning the
qualitative nature of an object.

Tests of motor control in these split-
brain patients revealed that the left
hemisphere of the brain exercised normal control over the right hand but had
less than full control of the left hand (for
instance, it was poor at directing individual movements of the fingers). Similarly,
the right hemisphere had full control of
the left hand but not of the right hand.
When the two hemispheres were in conflict, dictating different movements for
the same hand, the hemisphere on the
side opposite the hand generally took
charge and overruled the orders of the
side of the brain with the weaker control. In general the motor findings in the
human patients were much the same as
those in split-brain monkeys.

We come now to the main question
on which we centered our studies,
namely how the separation of the hemispheres affects the mental capacities of
the human brain. For these psychological tests we used two different devices.
One was visual: a picture or written information was flashed (for a tenth of a
second) in either the right or the left
visual field, so that the information was
transmitted only to the left or to the right
brain hemisphere [see illustration on
page 170]. The other type of test was

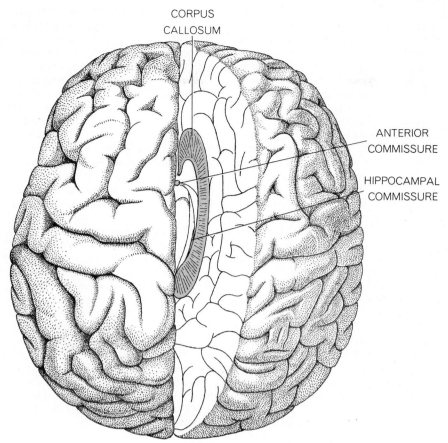

CORPUS
CALLOSUM

ANTERIOR
COMMISSURE

HIPPOCAMPAL
COMMISSURE

TWO HEMISPHERES of the human brain are divided by neurosurgeons to control epileptic seizures. In this top view of the brain the right hemisphere is retracted and the corpus callosum and other commissures, or connectors, that are generally cut are shown in color.

tactile: an object was placed out of view in the patient's right or left hand, again for the purpose of conveying the information to just one hemisphere—the hemisphere on the side opposite the hand.

When the information (visual or tactile) was presented to the dominant left hemisphere, the patients were able to deal with and describe it quite normally, both orally and in writing. For example, when a picture of a spoon was shown in the right visual field or a spoon was placed in the right hand, all the patients readily identified and described it. They were able to read out written messages and to perform problems in calculation that were presented to the left hemisphere.

In contrast, when the same information was presented to the right hemisphere, it failed to elicit such spoken or written responses. A picture transmitted to the right hemisphere evoked either a haphazard guess or no verbal response at all. Similarly, a pencil placed in the left hand (behind a screen that cut off vision) might be called a can opener or a cigarette lighter, or the patient might not

even attempt to describe it. The verbal guesses presumably came not from the right hemisphere but from the left, which had no perception of the object but might attempt to identify it from indirect clues.

Did this impotence of the right hemisphere mean that its surgical separation from the left had reduced its mental powers to an imbecilic level? The earlier tests of its nonverbal capacities suggested that this was almost certainly not so. Indeed, when we switched to asking for nonverbal answers to the visual and tactile information presented in our new psychological tests, the right hemisphere in several patients showed considerable capacity for accurate performance. For example, when a picture of a spoon was presented to the right hemisphere, the patients were able to feel around with the left hand among a varied group of objects (screened from sight) and select a spoon as a match for the picture. Furthermore, when they were shown a picture of a cigarette they

succeeded in selecting an ashtray, from a group of 10 objects that did not include a cigarette, as the article most closely related to the picture. Oddly enough, however, even after their correct response, and while they were holding the spoon or the ashtray in their left hand, they were unable to name or describe the object or the picture. Evidently the left hemisphere was completely divorced, in perception and knowledge, from the right.

Other tests showed that the right hemisphere did possess a certain amount of language comprehension. For example, when the word "pencil" was flashed to the right hemisphere, the patients were able to pick out a pencil from a group of unseen objects with the left hand. And when a patient held an object in the left hand (out of view), although he could not say its name or describe it, he was later able to point to a card on which the name of the object was written.

In one particularly interesting test the word "heart" was flashed across the center of the visual field, with the "he" portion to the left of the center and "art" to the right. Asked to tell what the word was, the patients would say they had seen "art"—the portion projected to the left brain hemisphere (which is responsible for speech). Curiously when, after "heart" had been flashed in the same way, the patients were asked to point with the left hand to one of two cards— "art" or "he"—to identify the word they had seen, they invariably pointed to "he." The experiment showed clearly that both hemispheres had simultaneously observed the portions of the word available to them and that in this particular case the right hemisphere, when it had had the opportunity to express itself, had prevailed over the left.

Because an auditory input to one ear goes to both sides of the brain, we conducted tests for the comprehension of words presented audibly to the right hemisphere not by trying to limit the original input but by limiting the ability to answer to the right hemisphere. This was done most easily by having a patient use his left hand to retrieve, from a grab bag held out of view, an object named by the examiner. We found that the patients could easily retrieve such objects as a watch, comb, marble or coin. The object to be retrieved did not even have to be named; it might simply be described or alluded to. For example, the command "Retrieve the fruit monkeys like best" results in the patients' pulling out a banana from a grab bag full of plastic fruit; at the command "Sunkist sells a lot of them" the patients retrieve an orange. We knew that touch information from the left hand was going exclusively to the right hemisphere because moments later, when the patients were asked to name various pieces of fruit placed in the left hand, they were unable to score above a chance level.

The upper limit of linguistic abilities in each hemisphere varies from subject to subject. In one case there was little or no evidence for language abilities in the right hemisphere, whereas in the other three the amount and extent of the capacities varied. The most adept patient showed some evidence of even being able to spell simple words by placing plastic letters on a table with his left hand. The subject was told to spell a word such as "pie," and the examiner then placed the three appropriate letters, one at a time in a random order, in his left hand to be arranged on the table. The patient was able to spell even more abstract words such as "how," "what" and "the." In another test three or four letters were placed in a pile, again out of view, to be felt with the left hand. The letters available in each trial would spell only one word, and the instructions to the subject were "Spell a word." The patient was able to spell such words as "cup" and "love." Yet after he had completed this task, the patient was unable to name the word he had just spelled!

The possibility that the right hemisphere has not only some language but even some speech capabilities cannot be ruled out, although at present there is no firm evidence for this. It would not be surprising to discover that the patients are capable of a few simple exclamatory remarks, particularly when under emotional stress. The possibility also remains, of course, that speech of some type could be trained into the right hemisphere. Tests aimed at this question, however, would have to be closely scrutinized and controlled.

The reason is that here, as in many of the tests, "cross-cuing" from one hemisphere to the other could be held responsible for any positive findings. We had a case of such cross-cuing during a series of tests of whether the right hemisphere could respond verbally to simple red or green stimuli. At first, after either a red or a green light was flashed to the right hemisphere, the patient would guess the color at a chance level, as might be expected if the speech mechanism is solely represented in the left hemisphere. After a few trials, however, the score improved whenever the examiner allowed a second guess.

We soon caught on to the strategy the patient used. If a red light was flashed and the patient by chance guessed red, he would stick with that answer. If the flashed light was red and the patient by chance guessed green, he would frown,

shake his head and then say, "Oh no, I meant red." What was happening was that the right hemisphere saw the red light and heard the left hemisphere make the guess "green." Knowing that the answer was wrong, the right hemisphere precipitated a frown and a shake of the head, which in turn cued in the left hemisphere to the fact that the answer was wrong and that it had better correct itself! We have learned that this cross-cuing mechanism can become extremely refined. The realization that the neurological patient has various strategies at his command emphasizes how difficult it is to obtain a clear neurological description of a human being with brain damage.

Is the language comprehension by the right hemisphere that the patients exhibited in these tests a normal capability of that hemisphere or was it acquired by learning after their operation, perhaps during the course of the experiments themselves? The issue is difficult to decide. We must remember that we are examining a half of the human brain, a system easily capable of learning from a single trial in a test. We do know that the right hemisphere is decidedly inferior to the left in its overall command of language. We have established, for instance, that although the right hemisphere can respond to a concrete noun such as "pencil," it cannot do as well with verbs; patients are unable to re-

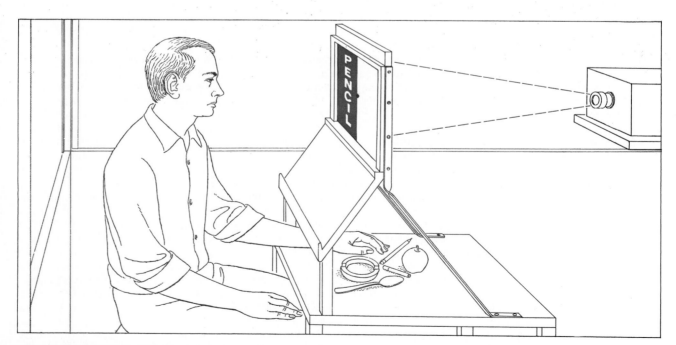

RESPONSE TO VISUAL STIMULUS is tested by flashing a word or a picture of an object on a translucent screen. The examiner first checks the subject's gaze to be sure it is fixed on a dot that marks the center of the visual field. The examiner may call for a verbal response—reading the flashed word, for example—or for a nonverbal one, such as picking up the object that is named from among a number of things spread on the table. The objects are hidden from the subject's view so that they can be identified only by touch.

spond appropriately to simple printed instructions, such as "smile" or "frown," when these words are flashed to the right hemisphere, nor can they point to a picture that corresponds to a flashed verb. Some of our recent studies at the University of California at Santa Barbara also indicate that the right hemisphere has a very poorly developed grammar; it seems to be incapable of forming the plural of a given word, for example.

In general, then, the extent of language present in the adult right hemisphere in no way compares with that present in the left hemisphere or, for that matter, with the extent of language present in the child's right hemisphere. Up to the age of four or so, it would appear from a variety of neurological observations, the right hemisphere is about as proficient in handling language as the left. Moreover, studies of the child's development of language, particularly with respect to grammar, strongly suggest that the foundations of grammar—a ground plan for language, so to speak—are somehow inherent in the human organism and are fully realized between the ages of two and three. In other words, in the young child each hemisphere is about equally developed with respect to language and speech function. We are thus faced with the interesting question of why the right hemisphere at an early age and stage of development possesses substantial language capacity whereas at a more adult stage it possesses a rather poor capacity. It is difficult indeed to conceive of the underlying neurological mechanism that would allow for the establishment of a capacity of a high order in a particular hemisphere on a temporary basis. The implication is that during maturation the processes and systems active in making this capacity manifest are somehow inhibited and dismantled in the right hemisphere and allowed to reside only in the dominant left hemisphere.

Yet the right hemisphere is not in all respects inferior or subordinate to the left. Tests have demonstrated that it excels the left in some specialized functions. As an example, tests by us and by Bogen have shown that in these patients the left hand is capable of arranging blocks to match a pictured design and of drawing a cube in three dimensions, whereas the right hand, deprived of instructions from the right hemisphere, could not perform either of these tasks. It is of interest to note, however, that although the patients (our first subject in particular) could not execute such tasks

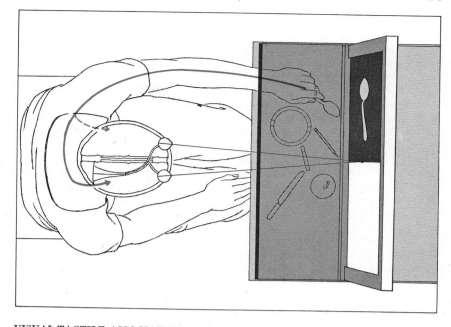

VISUAL-TACTILE ASSOCIATION is performed by a split-brain patient. A picture of a spoon is flashed to the right hemisphere; with the left hand he retrieves a spoon from behind the screen. The touch information from the left hand projects (*color*) mainly to the right hemisphere, but a weak "ipsilateral" component goes to the left hemisphere. This is usually not enough to enable him to say (using the left hemisphere) what he has picked up.

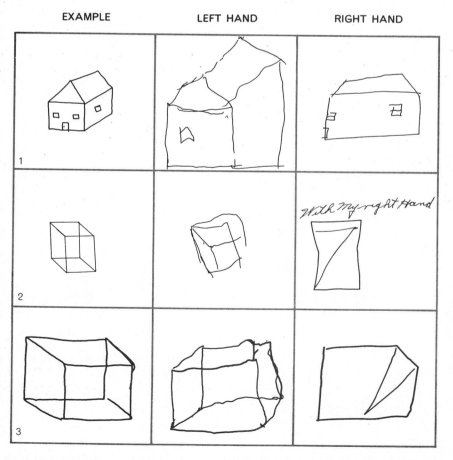

"VISUAL-CONSTRUCTIONAL" tasks are handled better by the right hemisphere. This was seen most clearly in the first patient, who had poor ipsilateral control of his right hand. Although right-handed, he could copy the examples only with his left hand.

with the right hand, they were capable of matching a test stimulus to the correct design when it appeared among five related patterns presented in their right visual field. This showed that the dominant left hemisphere is capable of discriminating between correct and incorrect stimuli. Since it is also true that the patients have no motor problems with their right hand, the patients' inability to perform these tasks must reflect a breakdown of an integrative process somewhere between the sensory system and the motor system.

We found that in certain other mental processes the right hemisphere is on a par with the left. In particular, it can independently generate an emotional reaction. In one of our experiments exploring the matter we would present a series of ordinary objects and then suddenly flash a picture of a nude woman. This evoked an amused reaction regardless of whether the picture was presented to the left hemisphere or to the right. When the picture was flashed to the left hemisphere of a female patient, she laughed and verbally identified the picture as a nude. When it was later presented to the right hemisphere, she said in reply to a question that she saw nothing, but almost immediately a sly smile spread over her face and she began to chuckle. Asked what she was laughing at, she said: "I don't know... nothing... oh—that funny machine." Although the right hemisphere could not describe what it had seen, the sight nevertheless elicited an emotional response like the one evoked from the left hemisphere.

Taken together, our studies seem to demonstrate conclusively that in a split-brain situation we are really dealing with two brains, each separately capable of mental functions of a high order. This implies that the two brains should have twice as large a span of attention—that is, should be able to handle twice as much information—as a normal whole brain. We have not yet tested this precisely in human patients, but E. D. Young and I have found that a split-brain monkey can indeed deal with nearly twice as much information as a normal animal [see illustration below]. We have so far determined also that brain-bisected patients can carry out two tasks as fast as a normal person can do one.

Just how does the corpus callosum of the intact brain combine and integrate the perceptions and knowledge of the two cerebral hemispheres? This has been investigated recently by Giovanni Berlucchi, Giacomo Rizzolati and me at the Istituto di Fisiologia Umana in Pisa. We made recordings of neural activity in the posterior part of the callosum of the cat with the hope of relating the responses of that structure to stimulation of the animal's visual fields. The kinds of responses recorded turned out to be similar to those observed in the visual cortex of the cat. In other words, the results suggest that visual pattern information can be transmitted through the callosum. This finding militates against the notion that learning and memory are transferred across the callosum, as has usually been suggested. Instead, it looks as though in animals with an intact callosum a copy of the visual world as seen in one hemisphere is sent over to the other, with the result that both hemispheres can learn together a discrimination presented to just one hemisphere. In the split-brain animal this extension of the visual pathway is cut off; this would explain rather simply why no learning proceeds in the visually isolated hemisphere and why it has to learn the discrimination from scratch.

Curiously, however, the neural activity in the callosum came only in response to stimuli at the midline of the visual field. This finding raises difficult questions. How can it be reconciled with the well-established observation that the left hemisphere of a normal person can give a running description of all the visual information presented throughout the entire half-field projected to the right hemisphere? For this reason alone one is wearily driven back to the conclusion that somewhere and somehow all or part of the callosum transmits not only a visual scene but also a complicated neural code of a higher order.

All the evidence indicates that separation of the hemispheres creates two independent spheres of consciousness within a single cranium, that is to say, within a single organism. This conclusion is disturbing to some people who view consciousness as an indivisible property of the human brain. It seems premature to others, who insist that the capacities revealed thus far for the right hemisphere are at the level of an automaton. There is, to be sure, hemispheric inequality in the present cases, but it may well be a characteristic of the individuals we have studied. It is entirely possible that if a human brain were divided in a very young person, both hemispheres could as a result separately and independently develop mental functions of a high order at the level attained only in the left hemisphere of normal individuals.

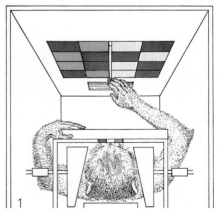 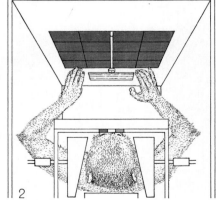 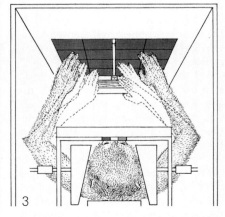

SPLIT-BRAIN MONKEYS can handle more visual information than normal animals. When the monkey pulls a knob (1), eight of the 16 panels light momentarily. The monkey must then start at the bottom and punch the lights that were lit and no others (2). With the panels lit for 600 milliseconds normal monkeys get up to the third row from the bottom before forgetting which panels were lit (3). Split-brain monkeys complete the entire task with the panels lit only 200 milliseconds. The monkeys look at the panels through filters; since the optic chiasm is cut in these animals, the filters allow each hemisphere to see the colored panels on one side only.

Teaching Language to an Ape

by Ann James Premack and David Premack
October 1972

Sarah, a young chimpanzee, has a reading and writing vocabulary of about 130 "words." Her understanding goes beyond the meaning of words and includes the concepts of class and sentence structure

Over the past 40 years several efforts have been made to teach a chimpanzee human language. In the early 1930's Winthrop and Luella Kellogg raised a female chimpanzee named Gua along with their infant son; at the age of 16 months Gua could understand about 100 words, but she never did try to speak them. In the 1940's Keith and Cathy Hayes raised a chimpanzee named Vicki in their home; she learned a large number of words and with some difficulty could mouth the words "mama," "papa" and "cup." More recently Allen and Beatrice Gardner have taught their chimpanzee Washoe to communicate in the American Sign Language with her fingers and hands. Since 1966 in our laboratory at the University of California at Santa Barbara we have been teaching Sarah to read and write with variously shaped and colored pieces of plastic, each representing a word; Sarah has a vocabulary of about 130 terms that she uses with a reliability of between 75 and 80 percent.

Why try to teach human language to an ape? In our own case the motive was to better define the fundamental nature of language. It is often said that language is unique to the human species. Yet it is now well known that many other animals have elaborate communication systems of their own. It seems clear that language is a general system of which human language is a particular, albeit remarkably refined, form. Indeed, it is possible that certain features of human language that are considered to be uniquely human belong to the more general system, and that these features can be distinguished from those that are unique to the human information-processing regime. If, for example, an ape can be taught the rudiments of human language, it should clarify the dividing line between the general system and the human one.

There was much evidence that the chimpanzee was a good candidate for the acquisition of language before we began our project. In their natural environment chimpanzees have an extensive vocal "call system." In captivity the chimpanzee has been taught to sort pictures into classes: animate and inanimate, old and young, male and female. Moreover, the animal can classify the same item in different ways depending

SARAH, after reading the message "Sarah insert apple pail banana dish" on the magnetic board, performed the appropriate actions. To be able to make the correct interpretation that she should put the apple in the pail and the banana in the dish (not the apple, pail and banana in the dish) the chimpanzee had to understand sentence structure rather than just word order. In actual tests most symbols were colored (*see illustration on following page*).

174

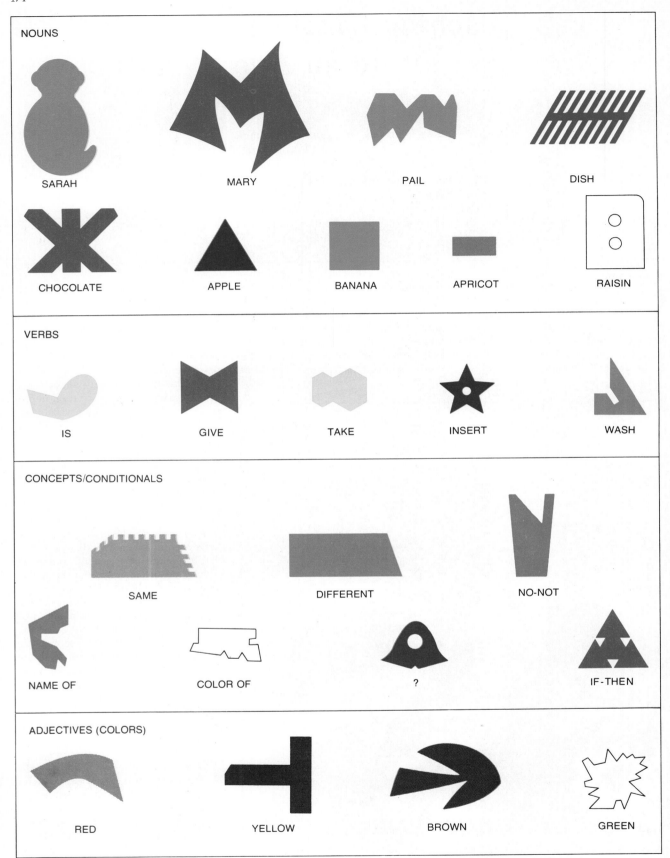

NOUNS

SARAH

MARY

PAIL

DISH

CHOCOLATE

APPLE

BANANA

APRICOT

RAISIN

VERBS

IS

GIVE

TAKE

INSERT

WASH

CONCEPTS/CONDITIONALS

SAME

DIFFERENT

NO-NOT

NAME OF

COLOR OF

?

IF-THEN

ADJECTIVES (COLORS)

RED

YELLOW

BROWN

GREEN

PLASTIC SYMBOLS that varied in color, shape and size were chosen as the language units to be taught to Sarah. The plastic pieces were backed with metal so that they would adhere to a magnetic board. Each plastic symbol stood for a specific word or concept. A "Chinese" convention of writing sentences vertically from top to bottom was adopted because at the beginning of her training Sarah seemed to prefer it. Sarah had to put the words in proper sequence but the orientation of the word symbols was not important.

on the alternatives offered. Watermelon is classified as fruit in one set of alternatives, as food in another set and as big in a third set. On the basis of these demonstrated conceptual abilities we made the assumption that the chimpanzee could be taught not only the names of specific members of a class but also the names for the classes themselves.

It is not necessary for the names to be vocal. They can just as well be based on gestures, written letters or colored stones. The important thing is to shape the language to fit the information-processing capacities of the chimpanzee. To a large extent teaching language to an animal is simply mapping out the conceptual structures the animal already possesses. By using a system of naming that suits the chimpanzee we hope to find out more about its conceptual world. Ultimately the benefit of language experiments with animals will be realized in an understanding of intelligence in terms not of scores on tests but of the underlying brain mechanisms. Only then can cognitive mechanisms for classifying stimuli, for storing and retrieving information and for problem-solving be studied in a comparative way.

The first step in teaching language is to exploit knowledge that is already present. In teaching Sarah we first mapped the simple social transaction of giving, which is something the chimpanzee does both in nature and in the laboratory. Considered in terms of cognitive and perceptual elements, the verb "give" involves a relation between two individuals and one object, that is, between the donor, the recipient and the object being transferred. In order to carry out the act of giving an animal must recognize the difference between individuals (between "Mary" and "Randy") and must perceive the difference between donors and recipients (between "Mary gives Randy" and "Randy gives Mary"). In order to be able to map out the entire transaction of giving the animal has to distinguish agents from objects, agents from one another, objects from one another and itself from others.

The trainer began the process of mapping the social transaction by placing a slice of banana between himself and Sarah. The chimpanzee, which was then about five years old, was allowed to eat the tasty morsel while the trainer looked on affectionately. After the transaction had become routine, a language element consisting of a pink plastic square was placed close to Sarah while the slice of banana was moved beyond her reach. To obtain the fruit Sarah now had to put the plastic piece on a "language board" on the side of her cage. (The board was magnetic and the plastic square was backed with a thin piece of steel so that it would stick.) After Sarah had learned this routine the fruit was changed to an apple and she had to place a blue plastic word for apple on the board. Later several other fruits, the verb "give" and the plastic words that named each of them were introduced.

To be certain that Sarah knew the meaning of "give" it was necessary to contrast "give" with other verbs, such as "wash," "cut" and "insert." When Sarah indicated "Give apple," she was given a piece of apple. When she put "Wash apple" on the board, the apple was placed in a bowl of water and washed. In that way Sarah learned what action went with what verb.

In the first stage Sarah was required to put only one word on the board; the name of the fruit was a sufficient indicator of the social transaction. When names for different actions—verbs—were introduced, Sarah had to place two words on the board in vertical sequence. In order to be given an apple she had to write "Give apple." When recipients were named, two-word sentences were not accepted by the trainer; Sarah had to use three words. There were several trainers, and Sarah had to learn the name of each one. To facilitate the teaching of personal names, both the chimpanzees and the trainers wore their plastic-word names on a string necklace. Sarah learned the names of some of the recipients the hard way. Once she wrote "Give apple Gussie," and the trainer promptly gave the apple to another chimpanzee named Gussie. Sarah never repeated the sentence. At every stage she was required to observe the proper word sequence. "Give apple" was accepted but "Apple give" was not. When donors were to be named, Sarah had to identify all the members of the social transaction: "Mary give apple Sarah."

The interrogative was introduced with the help of the concepts "same" and "different." Sarah was given a cup and a spoon. When another cup was added, she was taught to put the two cups together. Other sets of three objects were given to her, and she had to pair the two objects that were alike. Then she was taught to place the plastic word for "same" between any two similar objects and the plastic word for "different" between unlike objects. Next what amounted to a question mark was placed between pairs of objects. This plastic shape (which bore no resemblance to the usual kind of question mark) made the question explicit rather than implicit, as it had been in the simple matching tests. When the interrogative element was placed between a pair of cups, it meant: "What is the relation between cup A and cup B?" The choices provided Sarah were the plastic words "same" and "different." She learned to remove the interrogative particle and substitute the correct word [see top illustration on following page]. Sarah was able to transfer what she had learned and apply the word "same" or "different" to numerous pairs of objects that had not been used in her training.

Any construction is potentially a question. From the viewpoint of structural linguistics any construction where one or more elements are deleted becomes a question. The constructions we used with Sarah were "A same A" and "A different B." Elements in these constructions were removed and the deletion was marked with the interrogative symbol; Sarah was then supplied with a choice of missing elements with which she could restore the construction to its familiar form. In principle interrogation can be taught either by removing an element from a familiar situation in the animal's world or by removing the element from a language that maps the animal's world. It is probable that one can induce questions by purposively removing key elements from a familiar situation. Suppose a chimpanzee received its daily ration of food at a specific time and place, and then one day the food was not there. A chimpanzee trained in the interrogative might inquire "Where is my food?" or, in Sarah's case, "My food is?" Sarah was never put in a situation that might induce such interrogation because for our purposes it was easier to teach Sarah to answer questions.

At first Sarah learned all her words in the context of social exchange. Later, when she had learned the concepts "name of" and "not name of," it was possible to introduce new words in a more direct way. To teach her that objects had names, the plastic word for "apple" and a real apple were placed on the table and Sarah was required to put the plastic word for "name of" between them. The same procedure was repeated for banana. After she had responded correctly several times, the symbol for "apple" and a real banana were placed on the table and Sarah had to put "not

CONCEPTS "SAME" AND "DIFFERENT" were introduced into Sarah's vocabulary by teaching her to pair objects that were alike (*top illustration*). Then two identical objects, for example apples, were placed before her and she was given plastic word for "same" and induced to place word between the two objects. She was also taught to place the word for "different" between unlike objects.

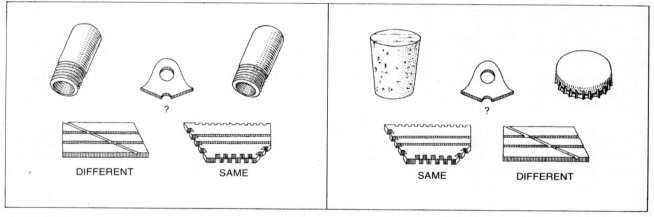

THE INTERROGATIVE was introduced with the help of the concepts "same" and "different." A plastic piece that meant "question mark" was placed between two objects and Sarah had to replace it with either the word for "same" or the word for "different."

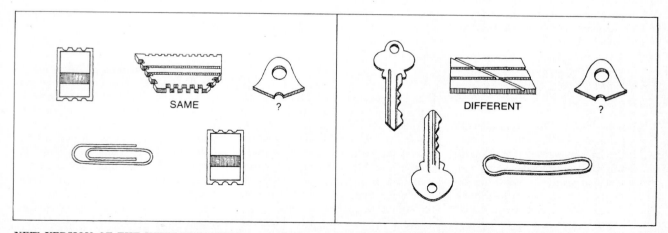

NEW VERSION OF THE INTERROGATIVE was taught by arranging an object and plastic symbols to form questions: "What is [Object A] the same as?" or "What is [Object A] different from?" Sarah had to replace question marker with the appropriate object.

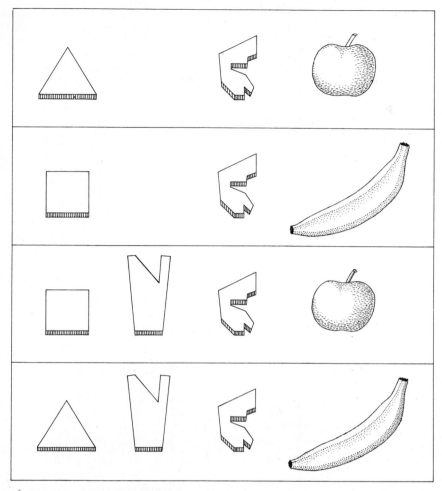

TEACHING LANGUAGE WITH LANGUAGE was the next step. Sarah was taught to put the symbol for "name of" between the word for "apple" and an apple and also between the word for "banana" and a banana. She learned the concept "not name of" in the same way. Thereafter Sarah could be taught new nouns by introducing them with "name of."

name of" between them. After she was able to perform both operations correctly new nouns could be taught quickly and explicitly. The plastic words for "raisin" and "name of" could be placed next to a real raisin and Sarah would learn the noun. Evidence of such learning came when Sarah subsequently requested "Mary give raisin Sarah" or set down "Raisin different apple."

An equally interesting linguistic leap occurred when Sarah learned the predicate adjective and could write such sentences as "Red color of apple," "Round shape of apple" and "Large size of apple." When asked for the relation between "Apple is red ? Red color of apple" and given "same" and "different" as choices, she judged the sentences to be the same. When given "Apple is red ? Apple is round," she judged the sentences to be different. The distinctions between similar and different, first learned with actual objects, was later

applied by Sarah in linguistic constructions.

In English the conditional consists of the discontinuous elements "if-then," which are inconvenient and conceptually unnecessary. In symbolic logic the conditional consists of the single sign ⊃, and we taught Sarah the conditional relation with the use of a single plastic word. Before being given language training in the conditional, she was given contingency training in which she was rewarded for doing one thing but not another. For example, she was given a choice between an apple and a banana, and only when she chose the apple was she given chocolate (which she dearly loved). "If apple, then chocolate, if banana, then no chocolate" were the relations she learned; the same relations were subsequently used in sentences to teach her the name for the conditional relation.

The subject was introduced with the

written construction: "Sarah take apple ? Mary give chocolate Sarah." Sarah was provided with only one plastic word: the conditional particle. She had to remove the question mark and substitute the conditional in its place to earn the apple and the chocolate. Now she was presented with: "Sarah take banana ? Mary no give chocolate Sarah." Again only the conditional symbol was provided. When Sarah replaced the question mark with the conditional symbol, she received a banana but no chocolate. After several such tests she was given a series of trials on each of the following pairs of sentences: "Sarah take apple if-then Mary give chocolate Sarah" coupled with "Sarah take banana if-then Mary no give chocolate Sarah," or "Sarah take apple if-then Mary no give chocolate Sarah" coupled with "Sarah take banana if-then Mary give chocolate Sarah."

At first Sarah made many errors, taking the wrong fruit and failing to get her beloved chocolate. After several of her strategies had failed she paid closer attention to the sentences and began choosing the fruit that gave her the chocolate. Once the conditional relation had been learned she was able to apply it to other types of sentence, for example "Mary take red if-then Sarah take apple" and "Mary take green if-then Sarah take banana." Here Sarah had to watch Mary's choice closely in order to take the correct action. With the paired sentences "Red is on green if-then Sarah take apple" and "Green is on red if-then Sarah take banana," which involved a change in the position of two colored cards, Sarah was not confused and performed well.

As a preliminary to learning the class concepts of color, shape and size Sarah was taught to identify members of the classes red and yellow, round and square and large and small. Objects that varied in most dimensions but had a particular property in common were used. Thus for teaching the word "red" a set of dissimilar, unnamed objects (a ball, a toy car, a Life Saver and so on) that had no property in common except redness were put before the chimpanzee. The only plastic word available to her was "red." After several trials on identifying red with a set of red objects and yellow with a set of yellow objects, Sarah was shifted to trials where she had to choose between "red" and "yellow" when she was shown a colored object. Finally completely new red and yellow objects were presented to her, including small cards that were identical except for their color.

Again she performed at her usual level of accuracy.

Sarah was subsequently taught the names of shapes, "round" and "square," as well as the size names "large" and "small." These words formed the basis for teaching her the names of the class concepts "color of," "shape of" and "size of." Given the interrogative "Red ? apple" or "Yellow ? banana," Sarah was required to substitute the plastic word for "color of" for the question mark. In teaching class names a good many sentences were not written on the board but were presented as hybrids. The hybrid sentences consisted of a combination of plastic words and real objects arranged in the proper sentence sequence on Sarah's worktable. Typical sentences were "Yellow ?" beside a real yellow balloon or "Red ?" beside a red wood block.

The hybrid sentences did not deter Sarah in the least. Her good performance showed that she was able to move with facility from symbols for objects to actual objects. Her behavior with hybrid constructions recalls the activity of young children, who sometimes combine spoken words with real objects they are unable to name by pointing at the objects.

Was Sarah able to think in the plastic-word language? Could she store information using the plastic words or use them to solve certain kinds of problem that she could not solve otherwise? Additional research is needed before we shall have definitive answers, but Sarah's performance suggests that the answers to both questions may be a qualified yes. To think with language requires being able to generate the meaning of words in the absence of their external representation. For Sarah to be able to match "apple" to an actual apple or "Mary" to a picture of Mary indicates that she knows the meaning of these words. It does not prove, however, that when she is given the word "apple" and no apple is present, she can think "apple," that is, mentally represent the meaning of the word to herself. The ability to achieve such mental representation is of major importance because it frees language from simple dependence on the outside world. It involves displacement: the ability to talk about things that are not actually there. That is a critical feature of language.

The hint that Sarah was able to understand words in the absence of their external referents came early in her language training. When she was given

a piece of fruit and two plastic words, she was required to put the correct word for the fruit on the board before she was allowed to eat it. Surprisingly often, however, she chose the wrong word. It then dawned on us that her poor performance might be due not to errors but to her trying to express her preferences in fruit. We conducted a series of tests to determine her fruit preferences, using actual fruits in one test and only fruit names in the other. Sarah's choices between the words were much the same as her choices between the actual fruits. This result strongly suggests that she could generate the meaning of the fruit names from the plastic symbols alone.

We obtained clearer evidence at a later stage of Sarah's language training. In the same way that she could use

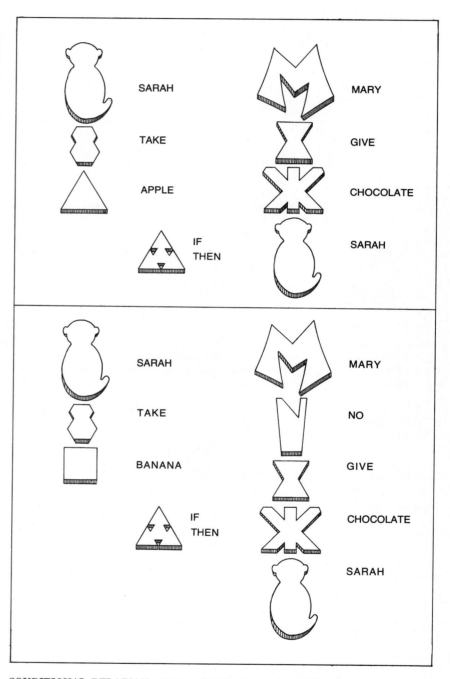

CONDITIONAL RELATION, which in English is expressed "if...then," was taught to Sarah as a single word. The plastic symbol for the conditional relation was placed between two sentences. Sarah had to pay attention to the meaning of both sentences very closely in order to make the choice that would give her a reward. Once the conditional relation was learned by means of this procedure, the chimpanzee was able to apply it to other situations.

"name of" to learn new nouns, she was able to use "color of" to learn the names of new colors. For instance, the names "brown" and "green" were introduced in the sentences "Brown color of chocolate" and "Green color of grape." The only new words at this point were "brown" and "green." Later Sarah was confronted with four disks, only one of which was brown, and when she was instructed with the plastic symbols "Take brown," she took the brown disk. Since chocolate was not present at any time during the introduction of the color name "brown," the word "chocolate" in the definition must have been sufficient to have Sarah generate or picture the property brown.

What form does Sarah's supposed internal representation take? Some indication is provided by the results of a test of ability to analyze the features of an object. First Sarah was shown an actual apple and was given a series of paired comparisons that described the features of the apple, such as red v. green, round v. square and so on. She had to pick the descriptive feature that belonged to the apple. Her feature analysis of a real apple agreed nicely with our own, which is evidence of the interesting fact that a chimpanzee is capable of decomposing a complex object into features. Next the apple was removed and the blue plastic triangle that was the word for "apple" was placed before her and again she was given a paired-comparison test. She assigned the same features to the word that she had earlier assigned to the object. Her feature analysis revealed that it was not the physical properties of the word (blue and triangle) that she was describing but rather the object that was represented by the word [see bottom illustration at right].

To test Sarah's sentence comprehension she was taught to correctly follow these written instructions: "Sarah insert apple pail," "Sarah insert banana pail," "Sarah insert apple dish" and "Sarah insert banana dish." Next instructions were combined in a one-line vertical sequence ("Sarah insert apple pail Sarah insert banana dish"). The chimpanzee responded appropriately. Then the second "Sarah" and the second verb "insert" were deleted to yield the compound sentence: "Sarah insert apple pail banana dish." Sarah followed the complicated instructions at her usual level of accuracy.

The test with the compound sentence is of considerable importance, because it provides the answer to whether or not

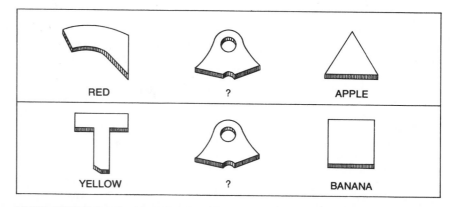

CLASS CONCEPT OF COLOR was taught with the aid of sentences such as "Red ? apple" and "Yellow ? banana." Sarah had to replace the interrogative symbol with "color of."

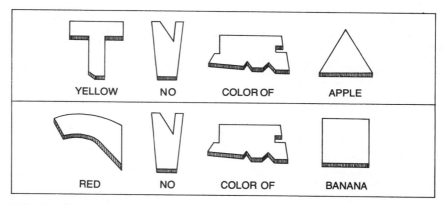

NEGATIVE CONCEPT was introduced with "no-not." When asked "Yellow ? apple" or "Red ? banana," Sarah had to replace interrogative symbol with "color of" or "not color of."

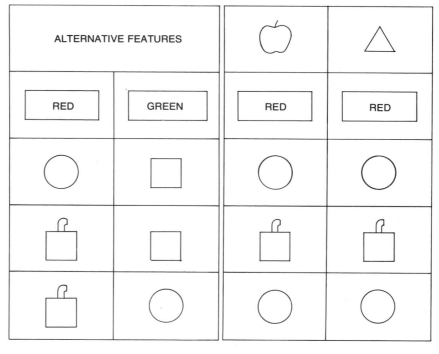

FEATURE ANALYSIS of an actual apple and the plastic word for "apple" was conducted. Sarah was shown an apple or the word and made to choose from alternative features: red or green, round or square, square with stem or plain square and square with stem or round. Sarah gave plastic word for "apple" same attributes she had earlier assigned to apple.

Sarah could understand the notion of constituent structure: the hierarchical organization of a sentence. The correct interpretation of the compound sentence was "Sarah put the apple in the pail and the banana in the dish." To take the correct actions Sarah must understand that "apple" and "pail" go together but not "pail" and "banana," even though the terms appear side by side. Moreover, she must understand that the verb "insert" is at a higher level of organization and refers to both "apple" and "banana." Finally, Sarah must understand that she, as the head noun, must carry out all the actions. If Sarah were capable only of linking words in a simple chain, she would never be able to interpret the compound sentence with its deletions. The fact is that she interprets them correctly. If a child were to carry out the instructions in the same way, we would not hesitate to say that he recognizes the various levels of sentence organization: that the subject dominates the predicate and the verb in the predicate dominates the objects.

Sarah had managed to learn a code, a simple language that nevertheless included some of the characteristic features of natural language. Each step of the training program was made as simple as possible. The objective was to reduce complex notions to a series of simple and highly learnable steps. The same program that was used to teach Sarah to communicate has been successfully applied with people who have language difficulties caused by brain damage. It may also be of benefit to the autistic child.

In assessing the results of the experiment with Sarah one must be careful not to require of Sarah what one would require of a human adult. Compared with a two-year-old child, however, Sarah holds her own in language ability. In fact, language demands were made of Sarah that would never be made of a child. Man is understandably prejudiced in favor of his own species, and members of other species must perform Herculean feats before they are recognized as having similar abilities, particularly language abilities. Linguists and others who study the development of language tend to exaggerate the child's understanding of language and to be extremely skeptical of the experimentally demonstrated language abilities of the chimpanzee. It is our hope that our findings will dispel such prejudices and lead to new attempts to teach suitable languages to animals other than man.

Slips of the Tongue

by Victoria A. Fromkin
December 1973

They are a good deal more than amusing (or embarrassing) errors of speech. The collection and analysis of such errors provides important clues to how speech is organized in the nervous system

The Reverend William A. Spooner, dean and warden of New College, Oxford, is famous in the English-speaking world as the man who had a special talent for slips of the tongue in which two sounds of an intended utterance are transposed. Although it is not certain that he actually made slips of this type, many "spoonerisms" are legendary. "Work is the curse of the drinking classes," he is alleged to have said when he meant "Drink is the curse of the working classes." Among other well-known spoonerisms are (in an address to a rural audience) "Noble tons of soil" and (in chiding a student) "You have hissed all my mystery lectures. I saw you fight a liar in the back quad; in fact, you have tasted the whole worm." Perhaps the most endearing of these slips is "the queer old dean" for "the dear old queen."

Speech errors have been used in literature by such writers as Rabelais, Shakespeare, Schiller and George Meredith. Nearly 300 years before the transposition speech error became known as a spoonerism, Henry Peacham quotes in *The Compleat Gentleman* a man who said "Sir, I must goe dye a beggar" instead of "I must goe buy a dagger." In recent years humorous bloopers made by radio and television announcers have been published in books and even preserved on records. The general awareness of the regularity of the occurrence of speech errors is shown in a column by Herb Caen in the *San Francisco Chronicle* of March 7, 1972: "The Tuck-Fortner Report [newscasts] is off Channel 2, much to the relief of those who worry about spoonerisms. Oddly enough, it was Mike Tuck who committed the only near miss in the history of the program, introducing Banker Fortney Stark as 'Fartney Stark.'"

In *The Psychopathology of Everyday Life* Sigmund Freud attempted to show that "[such] disturbances of speech may be the result of complicated psychical influences, of elements outside the same word, sentence or sequence of spoken words." In discussing the unconscious forces that he postulated as the cause of speech errors, Freud speculated "whether the mechanisms of this [speech] disturbance cannot also suggest the probable laws of the formation of speech."

Karl Spencer Lashley, a pioneer in neurophysiology, regarded speech as the "window through which the physiologist can view the cerebral life." He regarded speech errors as evidence that behavior can only be accounted for by positing "a series of hierarchies of organization: the order of vocal movements in pronouncing the word, the order of words in the sentence, the order of sentences in the paragraph." Disordering of these hierarchical units, he said, may occur at any stage, which would account for the diversity of observed speech errors.

In spite of the universality of various types of speech error, it was not until the 19th century that scholars began to pay serious attention to such utterances as evidence for psychological and linguistic theories. Hermann Paul, a German philologist, was probably the first linguist to suggest that an examination of speech errors might provide important clues to one cause of language change. Other linguists have been interested in slips of the tongue as a means of finding out what it is we learn and store in our minds when we learn a language.

A person's knowledge of a language cannot be equated solely with the words and sentences he utters and understands. If all the utterances of a person, or a number of persons, were recorded for an hour, a day, a week, a month, a year or even a lifetime, the corpus of these utterances would not in itself constitute the language he speaks. No one book can contain a complete human language. It is highly unlikely that this English sentence will have been printed before: "The Watergate scandal was caused by green-skinned, three-headed, cloven-footed Martians dressed in pink tights who penetrated the top-secret files of the Pentagon." Whether or not it is true, the preceding sentence is a grammatical English sentence that can be understood by any person with a knowledge of the language, yet it could not have been included in an English-language book before I had written it.

What makes it possible for a person to produce and understand novel sentences? If we are to understand the nature of language, we must be able to explain this ability. It cannot be accounted for simply by listing all possible sentences; in principle the number of sentences is infinite. For any sentence of length n one can produce a sentence of length $n + 1$. For example: "This is the house that Jack built. This is the malt that lay in the house that Jack built. It is questionable that this is the malt that lay in the house that Jack built. I know that it is questionable that this is the malt that lay in the house that Jack built."

Given the finite storage capacity of the brain, one cannot store all possible sentences of a language. We can of course store the words of a language because they are finite in number. In no language, however, are sentences formed by putting words together at random. "Built Jack that house the is this" is not an English sentence. Furthermore, although the number of words in a language is finite, the speakers of a language have the ability to create and adopt new words, for example Brillo and Kleenex. But just as there are rules for well-formed sentences, so there are rules for well-formed words; "Glooper" could be an acceptable word for a new product, but "nga" would never be used in English even though it is a perfectly good word in the Twi language of the Ashanti in western Africa.

Knowledge of a language must therefore include rules for the formation of words and sentences. In order to account for a speaker's ability to form a potentially infinite set of sentences and for his linguistic judgments concerning the well-formedness of words and sentences, linguistic theorists posit that what is learned in language acquisition is a grammar that includes a finite set of basic elements and a finite set of rules for their combination, including a recursive element to allow the formation of sentences of unlimited length [*see illustration on next page*]. Furthermore, there must be a hierarchy of such elements: discrete elements of sound (phonemes) combine in restricted ways to form syllables, which combine to form meaningful units (morphemes or words), which are combined to form phrases, which are combined into sentences [*see top illustration on page 184*].

All attempts to describe language and to account for our linguistic abilities assume the discreteness of each of these linguistic units. Yet the sounds we produce and the sounds we hear when we are talking are continuous signals, and examination of the physical properties of these acoustic signals does not reveal individual discrete sounds, words or phrases [*see bottom illustration on page 5*]. It has been impossible, however, to account for our linguistic abilities without positing a grammar consisting of discrete units and rules. This has always been intuitively accepted, as is indicated by the ancient Hindu myth in which the god Indra is said to have broken speech down into its distinct elements, thereby creating language. The classical Greeks also recognized the difference between the continuous nature of speech and the discrete nature of language. The messenger of the gods, Hermes, is also the god of speech because he was always on the move. In Plato's *Cratylus* dialogue (the oldest extant philosophical essay dealing exclusively with language) one of Hermes' namesakes, Hermogenes, asks Socrates if language can be analyzed by taking it apart. Socrates answers that doing so is the only way one can proceed.

The reality of the discrete elements of language and their rules of combination cannot be found by looking into the brains of speakers. It is here that systematic errors of speech can yield useful evidence.

Looked at from the viewpoint of linguistic behavior or performance, speech can be considered a communication system in which the concept to be conveyed must undergo a number of transformations. The message is generated in the brain of the speaker, encoded into the linguistic form of the language being spoken and transformed into neural signals that are sent to the muscles of the vocal tract, which transform the message into articulatory configurations. The acoustic signal must then be decoded by the listener to recover the original message. Thus the input signal that presumably starts as a string of individual discrete sounds organized into phrases and words ends up as a semicontinuous signal that the receiver must change back into the original string of discrete units. The grammar that represents our knowl-

edge of the language allows us to encode and decode an utterance.

Difficulties are encountered in attempts to model the actual behavior of a speaker because the only phenomena in this communication system that can be examined are the semicontinuous muscular movements of the vocal tract, the dynamic articulatory configurations and the acoustic signals. As in other communication systems, however, noise in any of the stages or connecting channels involved in speech can distort the original message. Most errors of speech would seem to be the result of noise or interference at the stage of linguistic encoding. Such errors can tell us something about a process that is not otherwise observable, and about the abstract grammar that underlies linguistic behavior.

Over the past five years I have re-

WILLIAM A. SPOONER was famous for his reputed lapses of speech, in which he would transpose two or more sounds, for example "blushing crow" for "crushing blow." Such speech errors are now called spoonerisms. This caricature of Spooner is by Sir Leslie Ward, whose work appeared in *Vanity Fair* under the pseudonym of Spy. Spooner was born in 1844 and died in 1930. A clergyman, he served as dean and warden of New College, Oxford.

corded more than 6,000 spontaneous errors of speech. In order to prevent the inclusion of errors of perception each item has been attested to by at least one other person. The deviant utterances that I give as examples hereafter are taken from this corpus.

According to all linguists who have analyzed spontaneous speech errors, the errors are nonrandom and predictable. Although one cannot predict when an error will occur or what the particular error will be, one can predict the kinds of error that will occur. Such predictions are based on our knowledge of the mental grammar utilized by speakers when they produce utterances. For example, many errors involve the abstract, discrete elements of sound we call phonemes. Although we cannot find these elements either in the moving articulators or in the acoustic signal, the fact that we learn to read and write with alphabetic symbols shows that they exist. In addition, if these discrete units were not real units used in speaking, we could not explain speech errors in which such segments must be involved. Substitution of one segment for another occurs: a later phoneme may be anticipated ("taddle tennis" instead of "paddle tennis"); a phoneme may persevere ("I can't cook worth a cam" instead of "I can't cook worth a damn"), or two segments may be transposed ("Yew Nork" instead of "New York"). Such segmental errors can involve vowels as well as consonants ("budbegs" instead of "bedbugs"). Moreover, two consonants that form a cluster can be either split or moved as a unit ("tendahl" instead of "Stendahl" and "foon speeding" instead of "spoon feeding") [*see top illustration on page 185*]. Such errors demonstrate that even though we do not produce discrete elements of sound at the stage of muscular movement in speech, discrete segments do exist at some earlier stage.

It is not the phonetic properties of sounds alone that determine the more abstract representation of phonemes. Sounds such as those represented by the "ch" in "church" and the "j" and "dge" in "judge" are clusters of two consonants on the phonetic level. This is shown by the fact that in the regular tempo of conversation the following two sentences will be pronounced identically by most people: " 'Why choose,' she said" and " 'White shoes,' she said." Yet linguists have posited that in words such as "choose," "church," "chain" and "judge" these phonetic clusters are single phonemes. The fact that the "ch" and "j" sounds in such words are never split in

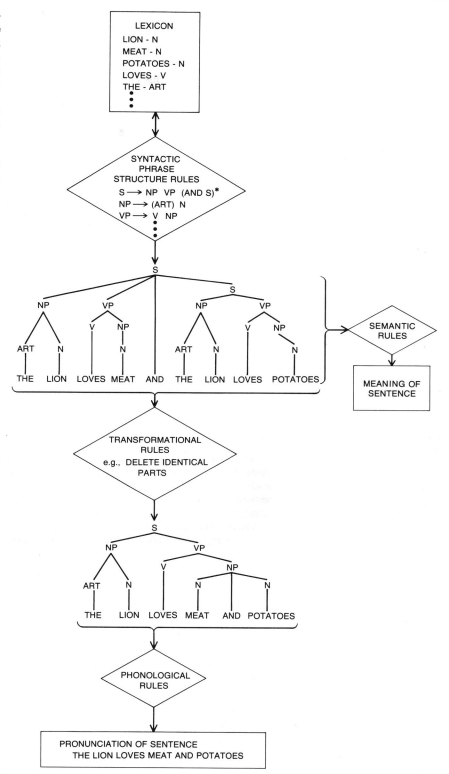

GRAMMAR OF A LANGUAGE consists of a finite set of basic elements (lexicon) and a finite set of rules for combining the basic elements such as nouns (*N*), verbs (*V*), articles (*ART*) and so forth. In order to generate a sentence (*S*), noun phrases (*NP*) and verb phrases (*VP*) are combined according to syntactic rules. The semantic rules determine whether or not the sentence generated is meaningful. Transformational rules enable a speaker to permute the sentence without altering its meaning. Phonological rules determine how the sentence is articulated. Errors at various stages can result in production of a deviant sentence, for example "The meat loves lion and potatoes" or "The lion loves peat and motatoes."

SENTENCE	[THE WILLOWY LIONESS LOVES THE WIRY LION]
PHRASES	[[THE WILLOWY LIONESS] [LOVES [THE WIRY LION]]]
	NOUN PHRASE VERB PHRASE
	NOUN PHRASE
WORDS	[[[THE] [WILLOWY] [LIONESS]] [[LOVES] [[THE] [WIRY] [LION]]]]
	ARTICLE ADJECTIVE NOUN VERB ARTICLE ADJECTIVE NOUN
MORPHEMES	[[[THE] [WILLOW + Y] [LION + NESS]] [LOVE + S] [[THE] [WIR + Y] [LION]]]]
PHONEMES	TH + E + W + I + LL + OW + Y + L + I + O + NN + E + SS + L + O + VE + S + TH + E + W + I + R + Y + L + I + O + N

HIERARCHY OF LINGUISTIC ELEMENTS is depicted. A sentence is composed of noun phrases and verb phrases. Phrases are made up of phrases or individual words and words in turn consist of morphemes, the basic units of meaning. Morphemes are made up of discrete elements of sound called phonemes. Spelling of the phonemes does not represent their sounds in a one-to-one fashion.

speech errors, although other consonant clusters such as "sp" and "gl" are, bears out this analysis. When these sounds are involved in speech errors, they always move as a single unit, as in "chee cane" instead of "key chain" and "sack's jute" instead of "Jack's suit." In cases where they represent two discrete phonemes, however, they can be independently disordered as in "Put the white boos in the shocks" for "Put the white shoes in the box." Speech errors therefore support the abstract analysis of linguists.

Segmental errors are constrained by rules of grammar that dictate the allowable sequence of sounds. Although "slips of the tongue" can be incorrectly uttered as "stips of the lung," it cannot be uttered as "tlip of the sung" because the sound "tl" is not allowed as the beginning of an English word. It is not the inability to say "tl" that inhibits such errors; we can say it easily enough. Rather it is a grammatical constraint in the English language. It is in this sense that speech errors are predictable and nonrandom.

Phonemic segments have been classified into intersecting sets dependent on shared properties. Thus the sounds that are produced by a closure of the lips, such as /p/, /b/ and /m/ (the diagonals are used to distinguish the sounds from the alphabetic letters), are classified as labials. The sounds produced by raising the tip of the tongue to the top of the teeth, such as /t/, /d/ and /n/, are alveolars. The sounds produced by raising the back of the tongue to the soft palate, such as /k/, /g/ and the /ng/ in "sing," are velars.

Such classes have been used to describe the sounds of all languages, but they had no basis in linguistic theory until recently. Roman Jakobson suggested a set of universal features that could be used to describe the sound system of all languages. These features, somewhat revised, were then incorporated into the theory of generative phonology by Morris Halle, who developed them further in collaboration with Noam Chomsky. It was shown that if segments are not viewed as being composites of features in the grammar of a language, certain regularities would be obscured, and the grammar written by the linguist would fail to correctly model a speaker's linguistic knowledge.

There has been some debate in linguistic circles over whether or not these universal phonetic features have any psychological reality. Some argue that they merely provide an elegant description of the sound system and do not exist as elements in the mental grammar of speakers. Just as speech errors show that discrete segments are real units, so also do they attest to the reality of phonetic features. Among the features posited in the universal set are the binary-valued features: voiced/voiceless and nasal/oral. Sounds produced with vocal-cord vibrations are voiced; sounds produced with an open glottis are voiceless. Nasal sounds are produced by lowering the soft palate to allow some air to escape through the nose while making a sound; oral sounds are produced by raising the soft palate to block off the nasal passage. In speech errors a single feature can be

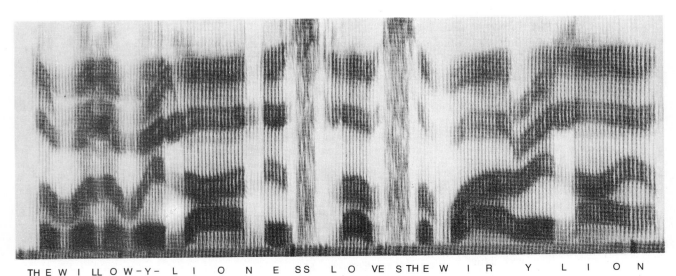

THE WILLOW-Y-LI O N E SS LO VE STHEWI R Y LI O N

SOUND SPECTROGRAM of the utterance "The willowy lioness loves the wiry lion" shows the speech sounds as a series of bands with the lowest sound frequencies at bottom and the highest frequencies at top. Note that the acoustical signal is semicontinuous.

disordered while all other features remain as intended; for example, "clear blue sky" was transposed to "glear plue sky." There was a voicing switch: the voiceless velar /k/ became a voiced /g/ and the voiced labial /b/ became a voiceless /p/ [*see bottom illustration at left*].

Unless the individual features have an independent existence in the mental grammar such errors cannot be accounted for. Prior to or simultaneous with the stage in the production process when neural signals are sent to the appropriate muscles, the specifications for voicing or not voicing must have been disordered. Similar transpositions can occur with nasal/oral features.

Speech errors involve more than sound units. In all languages different meanings are expressed by different strings of phonemes. That is, knowing a language enables one to associate certain sounds with certain meanings. One learns the vocabulary of the meaningful units of a language by learning not only the sounds but also what the sounds mean. Since the words of a language can consist of more than one meaningful element, words themselves cannot be the most elemental units of meaning. "Tolerant," "sane," "active" and "direct" are all English words; so are "intolerant," "insane," "inactive" and "indirect." The latter set includes the meanings of the former plus the meaningful unit "in-," which in these instances means "not."

In learning a language we learn these basic meaningful elements called morphemes and how to combine them into words. Speech errors show that there can be a breakdown in the application of the rules of word formation. The result is an uttered word that is possible but nonexistent. For example, "groupment" was said instead of "grouping," "intervenient" for "intervening," "motionly" for "motionless," "ambigual" for "ambiguous" and "bloodent" for "bloody." It is clear from such examples that rules for word formation must exist; otherwise there is no way to explain the deviant word forms. Obviously we do not have such words stored in our mental dictionary. Speech errors suggest that we learn morphemes as separate items and the rules for their combination. This ability enables us to create new words.

Many morphemes have alternative pronunciations depending on their context. The indefinite-article morpheme in English is either "a" or "an" depending on the initial sound of the word that follows: a coat, a man, an orange coat, an old man. This rule of language depends

ERRORS	EXAMPLES	
CONSONANT ERRORS		
ANTICIPATION	A READING LIST	A LEADING LIST
	IT'S A REAL MYSTERY	IT'S A MEAL MYSTERY
PERSEVERATION	PULLED A TANTRUM	PULLED A PANTRUM
	AT THE BEGINNING OF THE TURN	AT THE BEGINNING OF THE BURN
REVERSALS (SPOONERISMS)	LEFT HEMISPHERE	HEFT LEMISPHERE
	A TWO-PEN SET	A TWO-SEN PET
VOWEL ERRORS		
REVERSALS	FEET MOVING	FUTE MEEVING
	FILL THE POOL	FOOL THE PILL
OTHER ERRORS		
ADDITION	THE OPTIMAL NUMBER	THE MOPTIMAL NUMBER
MOVEMENT	ICE CREAM	KISE REAM
DELETION	CHRYSANTHEMUM PLANTS	CHRYSANTHEMUM P ANTS
CONSONANT CLUSTERS SPLIT OR MOVED	SPEECH PRODUCTION	PEACH SEDUCTION
	DAMAGE CLAIM	CLAMMAGE DAME

SEGMENTAL ERRORS IN SPEECH can involve vowels as well as consonants. Some typical types of substitution of sounds are shown. Such errors provide evidence that the discrete phonetic segments posited by linguistic theory exist in the mental grammar of the speaker.

	VOICED ORAL	VOICED NASAL	VOICELESS ORAL
LABIALS	BAT	MAT	PAT
	TAB	TAM	TAP
	BEAT	MEAT	PEET
	BEST	MESSED	PEST
	LIB	LIMB	LIP
	CAB	CAM	CAP
	AMBLE	AMBLE	AMPLE
ALVEOLARS	DIP	NIP	TIP
	CAD	CAN	CAT
	CANDOR	CANNER	CANTOR
	DOLE	KNOLL	TOLL
	DOOR	NOR	TORE
	RAID	RAIN	RATE
	RIDE	RHINE	RIGHT
VELARS	GIRL	*	CURL
	GREASE	*	CREASE
	GUARD	*	CARD
	LUG	LUNG	LUCK
	SAG	SANG	SACK
	ANGLE	ANGLE	ANKLE
	FINGER	SINGER	SINKER

LANGUAGE SOUNDS are categorized by certain universal features such as voiced/voiceless and nasal/oral. Some examples of voiced, oral, nasal and voiceless sounds are shown here. In speech errors a single feature may be disordered while the other features remain as intended. For example, when a person says "cedars of Lemadon" instead of "cedars of Lebanon," the nasality features of the /b/ and the /n/ are reversed. The intended oral labial /b/ becomes a nasal labial /m/ and the intended nasal alveolar /n/ becomes an oral alveolar /d/. Such reversal suggests that these features must also exist in mental grammars.

on the morpheme and not on the sound. We do make the "a" sound before a vowel ("America is") and the "an" sound before a consonant ("Roman court"). But errors such as "an istem" for "a system" or "a burly bird" for "an early bird" show that when segmental disordering occurs that changes a noun beginning with a consonant to a noun beginning with a vowel, or vice versa, the indefinite article is also changed so that it conforms to the grammatical rule. The rule also operates when entire words are disordered, as when "an example of courage" was produced as "a courage of example."

This operation is accomplished automatically, and such errors tell us something about the ordering of events in the brain. The disordering of the words or the phonemic segments must occur before the indefinite article is specified, or alternatively the rule that determines the indefinite article must reapply or feed back after the disordering has occurred. Furthermore, the monitoring function of the grammatical rule must specify the sounds of the indefinite article prior to the stage where neural signals are sent to the vocal muscles, since the rule does not change a structure such as "Rosa is" to "Rosan is." The existence of similar rules, called morphophonemic rules, and the ordering of their application are shown over and over again in speech errors.

The errors I have cited show that when we speak, words are structured into larger syntactic phrases that are stored in a kind of buffer memory before segments or features or words are disordered. This storage must occur prior to the articulatory stage. We do not select one word from our mental dictionary and say it, then select another word and say it. We organize an entire phrase and in many cases an entire sentence. This process can be demonstrated by the examination of errors in disordered phrases and sentences: "Nerve of a vergeous breakdown" instead of "Verge of a nervous breakdown"; "Seymour sliced the knife with a salami" instead of "Seymour sliced the salami with a knife"; "He threw the window through the clock" instead of "He threw the clock through the window"; "I broke the whistle on my crotch" instead of "I broke the crystal on my watch."

If these phrases had not been formed in some buffer storage, the transpositions could not have occurred. Furthermore, the intonation contour (stressed syllables and variations in pitch) of the utterance often remains the same as it is in the intended phrase even when the

words are disordered. In the intended utterance "Seymour sliced the salami with a knife" the highest pitch would be on "knife." In the disordered sentence the highest pitch occurred on the second syllable of "salami." The pitch rise is determined by the grammatical structure of the utterance. It must be constructed prior to articulation and is dependent on the syntactic structure rather than on the individual words. Thus syntactic structures also are shown to be units in linguistic behavior.

When words are exchanged, they are usually exchanged with words of the

same grammatical category; nouns are exchanged with nouns, adjectives with adjectives and so on. This phenomenon shows that words are represented in memory along with their grammatical characteristics. Indeed, when different grammatical classes are involved in a speech error, there is often a restructuring of the words to correct what otherwise would be syntactically incorrect. "I think it is reasonable to measure with care" was not transformed into "I think it is care to measure with reasonable" but rather into "I think it is careful to measure with reason." Such corrections

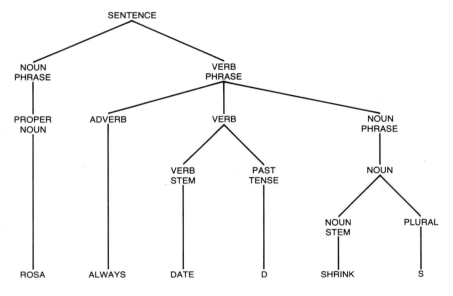

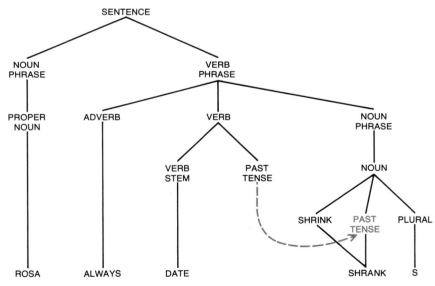

DISORDERING OF SYNTACTIC ELEMENTS can result in transformation of a sentence such as "Rosa always dated shrinks" into "Rosa always date shranks." The syntactical hierarchical structure of the intended sentence is shown in the top diagram. The error seems to have been caused by a disordering of the past-tense element, which mistakenly became attached to the noun node, as the bottom diagram illustrates. The shift probably occurred because "shrink" is a verb as well as a noun. After the disordering the phonological rules produced "shrank" and since the plural element was not disordered, "shranks" resulted.

reveal that there is constant monitoring at different stages of the speech-production chain. Although some errors emerged, a compounding of errors does not usually occur. In speech errors we never find a total disruption of the permissible syntactic structure, such as "Breakdown nervous a of verge."

But syntactic rules can be broken or misapplied, and syntactic elements can be disordered. Misstatements such as "If he swimmed in the pool nude" and "The last I knowed about it" indicate that words are stored in a basic form. To produce a past tense we do not select a stored past-tense form of a word but apply the rule of past-tense formation to the elemental morpheme. The regular rule for past-tense formation must have been wrongly applied to produce "swimmed" and "knowed." In these two instances the mistakes recorded were made by university professors who do not regularly say "swimmed" or "knowed." The reality of such rules is also shown by the forms produced by children before they have learned that there are exceptions to the rules they have generalized. Children regularly say "swimmed," "knowed," "bringed" and "singed" even though they have never heard these words spoken. Language acquisition involves constructing rules rather than merely imitating what one hears. It is these rules that may be wrongly applied in speech errors [see illustration on preceding page].

The negation element in sentences is another example of mistaken rule application: "I regard this as imprecise" came out "I disregard this as precise." The error shows that in producing a negative sentence a speaker must generate an abstract negative element that is or-dered in the string according to the rules of the language. The negative element in this sentence is independent of the particular words and can be disordered just as other units can be disordered. The sentence also shows that phonologically the negative element must be determined after the structure of the sentence is imposed. Only then can the negative plus "regard" be realized as either "do not regard" or as "disregard." A model of linguistic performance cannot posit a chain process of word selection; a hierarchical order exists.

Speech errors can involve entire words. A common type of error is a blend of two words: "shrig soufflé" for "shrimp and egg soufflé," "prodeption of speech" for "production and perception of speech." A more interesting blend, called a portmanteau word by Lewis Carroll, combines two words with similar meanings into one: "instantaneous" and "momentary" into "momentaneous," "splinters" and "blisters" into "splisters," "shifting" and "switching" into "swifting" and "edited" and "annotated" into "editated." This type of error reveals that the idea of the message is generated independently of the particular words selected from the mental dictionary to represent these concepts. A speaker seems to match the semantic features of words with the semantic notion to be conveyed. When there are alternatives, synonyms or near-synonyms, the speaker may be unsure of what word will best express his thoughts and in the moment of indecision may select two words and blend them.

The involuntary substitution of one word for the intended word shows that the meaning of a word is not an indissoluble whole. The semantic representation of a word is a composite of hierarchically ordered semantic features. In word selection one finds that the substituted and the original word often fall into the same semantic class: "blond eyes" for "blond hair," "bridge of the neck" for "bridge of the nose," "When my tongues bled" for "When my gums bled," "my boss's husband" for "my boss's wife" and "There's a small Chinese—I mean Japanese—restaurant."

Some errors show that antonyms are substituted: "like" for "hate," "big" for "small," "open" for "shut" and "hot" for "cold." Whatever the psychological causes of such slips, they show the ways we represent language in our stored mental grammar. The person who substituted "dachshund" for "Volkswagen" apparently selected a word with the semantic features "small, German." In the selection he underspecified the features to be matched.

There are many other varieties of speech error. All of them must be accounted for in a model of speech production. By positing the same units and rules required in a linguistic grammar, many of the errors can be categorized and explained. Speech therefore does provide a window into the cerebral life. By carefully studying speech errors we can get a view of the discrete elements of language and can see the grammatical rules at work. We also can look into the mental dictionary and get some notion of the complexity of the specifications of words and how the dictionary is organized. Throughout history men have speculated, theorized and conjectured about the nature of human language. Speech errors provide good data for testing some of these theories.

22 Bilingualism and Information Processing

by Paul A. Kolers
March 1968

A person who can speak two languages has clearly mastered two sets of symbols. Experiments that cause the two sets to interact provide important clues to how the mind works

Is the human mind too complex to be a profitable object of study? Many investigators have felt that it is, and yet one approach to it has always seemed promising. One of the principal activities of the human mind is the manipulation of symbols; might not an investigation of the way people use symbols yield some insights into the workings of the mind?

If so, a person who can speak two languages with reasonable fluency is of particular interest, because he works with two distinct sets of symbols. By presenting a bilingual subject with information in one language and then testing him in the other, the investigator should be able to learn much about the mental operations involved in the acquisition, storage and retrieval of the information. This has been the objective of experiments my colleagues and I have conducted with bilingual subjects in the Research Laboratory of Electronics at the Massachusetts Institute of Technology and in the Center for Cognitive Studies at H rvard University.

At the outset a qualification is in order. The experiments were concerned only with words, whereas the mind also receives and manipulates information in many other forms. One can remember the appearance of an object, the tonal quality of a musical instrument, the texture of a surface or the smell of a flower without being able to describe them precisely in words. The reader can remind himself of this fact by trying to find words for the smell of a rose. Nonetheless, much of a human being's thinking is expressed in words; they are clearly his principal means of receiving, storing, manipulating and transmitting information. The question of how words are involved in these processes is now the subject of intensive inquiry.

Let me proceed to our own work with an anecdote. Once when I was visiting Belgrade I set out with a colleague to buy a certain kind of decorated shoe—a part of the national costume of Yugoslavia—that had caught his eye. We tried several shops, where, with a combination of German, French, guidebook Serbian and gestures, he tried to get what he wanted. Finally we found a shop that had the shoes, but not in the right size.

As we started to leave, two other men came into the store speaking Italian. My friend listened and then said in Spanish, "They don't have that size; I just asked." One of the newcomers said, "Why do you speak Spanish to us? We're speaking Italian." "I know," said my friend in Spanish, "but I don't speak Italian. Can't you understand me? I understand you." "Well then," said the other man in French, "it is not so good. How is your French?" My friend answered in French, "I don't understand why you don't understand Spanish when you know Italian. My French is poor. Do you speak German?" "But yes, all right, let us speak German. Where do you come from?" My friend replied in German, "The United States. And where are you from?" The reply—in English—was "We're from New York," and everyone laughed. The entire exchange, involving the use of five languages, lasted for less than a minute.

I tell this story not only because it illustrates a number of aspects of the skilled use of languages but also because it was in thinking about the implications of the episode that I became interested in bilingualism. One point the story makes about the skilled user of two or more languages is that he can switch readily from one language to another. A second point is that the changeover is usually total: the people in the episode did not speak a mixture of Italian, Spanish, French, German and English; they spoke one or another exclusively.

Let us consider what such switching entails. In some languages, such as English and French, the meaning of a sentence is strongly dependent on the sequence of the words. The point is well made by the contrast between "The dog bit the man" and "The man bit the dog." The individual words are identical; the meanings are not. In other languages, such as German and Latin, meaning is less dependent on word order because the subjects and objects of sentences are indicated by case endings and the declension of articles. The difference in German between "Der Hund biss den Mann" and "Den Mann biss der Hund" is more one of emphasis than of meaning. Even though the order of words is different, both sentences translate as "The dog bit the man," although the second sentence might be taken to indicate a particular man.

There are of course many rules that characterize the use of a language. The body of rules is the grammar of the language; the individual words are its lexicon. The two men speaking in the Belgrade store did at least three things when they switched languages. They selected words from five different lexicons. They used words in different order, that is, they used different grammatical rules to generate meaningful sequences of words. They also made sounds in different ways, that is, they used a German accent for German, a French accent for French and so on. Moreover, although they were performing a complicated psychological task in switching among linguistic codes, they did not really have to think about the process.

One of our experiments was aimed at assessing the psychological cost of such code-switching. We were interested not only in the mental processes of a bilingual person when he hears or reads either of his languages but also in what is involved when he speaks or writes either of them. Our approach made use of passages of connected discourse, some of which violated normal grammatical rules. In one session bilingual subjects read such passages silently and then were tested for comprehension of what they had read. In a second session they read the passages aloud.

Four abbreviated passages are shown in the illustration on the next page. Two of them are wholly unilingual—one in English and one in French. The other two are mixed; both are made up of some English words and some French ones, but in the first the word order is English and in the second it is French. All four passages convey the same message.

Before testing our subjects we had established how much time other subjects needed to read unilingual passages of the same length as the experimental passages and get a score of 75 percent correct on a comprehension test. Our experimental subjects were then asked to read the various unilingual and mixed passages in exactly that length of time. One might think that in order to under-stand a mixed passage a subject would have to translate all the words into one language or to switch between linguistic codes in some other way. If so, one might expect that the subjects would be so busy translating and switching that they would have less time to consider the meaning of the passage. Hence they would get a lower score on a comprehension test of a mixed passage than on one of a unilingual passage.

Our findings, however, were that the subjects had almost identical scores on comprehension tests following the silent reading of unilingual and mixed passages. I concluded that a skilled reader of two languages can—in reading silently—comprehend a passage readily no matter to what extent words from either language are mixed in the passage. He apparently does not have to do any switching between linguistic codes when the passages are read. (We have not yet done the experiment to test if the same ease of comprehension is evident when a bilingual person listens to a message in which words from his two languages are mixed.)

The results were markedly different when we had our subjects read various passages aloud instead of silently. They needed more time to read the mixed passages than to read the unilingual ones. Evidently reading aloud entailed some kind of code-switching between lan-guages; the reader could not move as smoothly through "his horse, followed de deux bassets" as he could through "his horse, followed by two hounds."

We had constructed the passages in such a way that the unilingual ones contained an average of 110 words of English or French. The mixed passages contained 55 words from each language. We therefore were in a position to measure the amount of time required for code-switching by seeing how long it took a subject to read one passage in English and one in French and then subtracting the average of those times from the amount of time it took to read a mixed passage. Dividing the difference by the number of linguistic transitions in a mixed passage—the number of times a switch occurred between English and French—we determined that the average amount of time required for each switch in code was a third of a second. That is, it took a subject a third of a second longer, on the average, to read something like "his horse, followed de deux bassets" than to read "his horse, followed by two hounds."

Doubtless some of the difference is attributable to mechanical effects: the subject must physically adjust his vocal apparatus in switching from the sounds of one language to the sounds of another. We are not sure how much of the difference is due to such adjustments, but

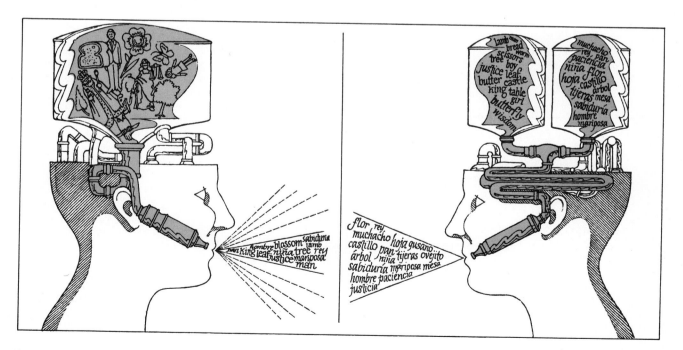

TWO HYPOTHESES about the way a bilingual person handles information are represented by two arrangements of tanks. One hypothesis (*left*) is that all his information is stored centrally, or in one tank, and that he has access to it equally with both languages, which are represented by the various taps. The other (*right*) is that his information is stored in linguistically associated ways, or in separate tanks. Experiments by the author indicated that the actual situation of a bilingual person combines parts of both hypotheses.

His horse, followed by two hounds, made the earth resound under its even tread. Drops of ice stuck to his cloak. A strong wind was blowing. One side of the horizon lighted up, and in the whiteness of the early morning light, he saw rabbits hopping at the edge of their burrows.

Son cheval, suivi de deux bassets, en marchant d'un pas égal faisait résonner la terre. Des gouttes de verglas se collaient à son manteau. Une brise violente soufflait. Un côté de l'horizon s'éclaircit; et, dans la blancheur du crépuscule, il aperçut des lapins sautillant au bord de leurs terriers.

His horse, followed de deux bassets, faisait la terre résonner under its even tread. Des gouttes de verglas stuck to his manteau. Une violente brise was blowing. One side de l'horizon lighted up, and dans la blancheur of the early morning light, il aperçut rabbits hopping at the bord de leurs terriers.

Son cheval, suivi by two hounds, en marchant d'un pas égal, made resound the earth. Drops of ice se collaient à son cloak. A wind strong soufflait. Un côté of the horizon s'éclaircit; et, in the whiteness du crépuscule, he saw des lapins sautillant au edge of their burrows.

SIMILAR PASSAGES of connected discourse were used in experiments with bilingual persons. The passages present the same message in four ways: unilingually in English and French and bilingually in mixed form, one favoring English word order and the other French. Subjects reading mixed passages silently lost no time switching between languages, whereas in reading aloud they took longer with mixed passages than with unilingual ones.

from control experiments involving code-switching in English alone we have concluded that a significant portion of the code-switching interval is occupied by a mental operation. The operation can be described as a "call time," meaning the amount of time the mind needs to organize a set of procedures for handling a piece of information. The length of call time probably varies from person to person. It may vary also with the procedure being called. In reading a science textbook, for example, one sees words, pictures, formulas and other kinds of symbol and uses different procedures for each of them. The length of time required to call the appropriate procedures may also differ.

The experiments with mixed passages involved the important matter of context. Clearly the fact that each of the passages had a context—a thematic continuity—made it easier for the subjects to comprehend the passages. In some instances context is created by the system of symbols itself, as when a writer uses words to tell the reader what topic he is discussing. Other systems of symbols are different. Computer programmers and engineers, for example, cannot usually understand each other's programs or circuit drawings until they are told separately what the program or the drawing is designed to do—what its context is. (How subtle one's dependence on context can be is illustrated by a recent newspaper story that described the bewilderment of a foreign visitor to New York when he saw a sign saying, "BUS STOP. NO STANDING." Lacking the context that would be familiar to any New Yorker driving a car, he at first took the sign to mean that he was supposed to sit down while waiting for the bus.)

Words and other symbols, however, are not always embedded in a context. I wanted to investigate how the mind dealt with words that were isolated from context. To that end I undertook two other experiments. Before I describe them I need to supply some context.

Many bilingual people say that they think differently and respond with different emotions to the same experience in their two languages. For example, reading a poem or a play in French and reading its translation in English are said to create markedly different feelings and impressions. It is difficult to assess these introspective statements, if only because emotive texts are notoriously difficult to translate well. As Robert Frost once remarked, when a poem is translated, the poetry is often lost.

Nonetheless, if one accepts the premise that such statements reflect a genuine mental experience, one wonders about its nature. In particular we wondered whether the difference in impression arises from the difficulty of translating words accurately or from some overall property of languages and the contexts in which they are used. To put the question another way, we wondered how verbal symbols are stored in the mind.

Perhaps a metaphor will help to clarify the issue. Regard the mind as a storage tank and languages as taps. Is all the information that words represent stored in some central tank in the mind, so that if a person is bilingual he has access to the same information even though he is using two different taps? If so, one could expect a variety of taps: some could be large and some small; some could release the contents of the tank as a spray and some as a stream. That is, the taps might be regarded as the rules of grammar that affect the translation of information in the mind into sentences. The information being tapped would always be the same, but its appearance and form would differ (according to the grammar being used) in such characteristics as word order, tense agreement and the like.

Another possibility is that the information in the mind of a bilingual person depends fundamentally on the language that was used to put it there. To continue the metaphor, such a person would have two tanks in his mind, each with its own tap. The tanks would reflect a situation in which the rules for using a language are indelibly stamped on the information stored, so that the bilingual person has access to different information when he uses the different taps.

The first of the two alternatives can be described as common storage of information. The second entails separate storage [see illustration on page 189]. The alternatives define two extreme ways of characterizing the issue. If common storage were the case, the differences in reading a poem in two languages would be due entirely to the difficulty of translation. If separate storage were the case, the difference would be due to other kinds of experience. The fact is, as I shall show with a description of the experiments, that neither extreme alternative correctly describes the mental storage of information. A third arrangement that combines features of the other two seems to be required.

The method I chose for examining the extreme alternatives was a word-association test in which the subject is required to say the first word that comes to mind in response to a stimulus word. For example, a large percentage of English-speaking adults respond to "table" with "chair" and to "black" with "white." My subjects were students whose native languages were German, Spanish or Thai but who were also fluent in English. In my tests the subjects responded in their native language to a list of words in that language; they responded in English to the same list in

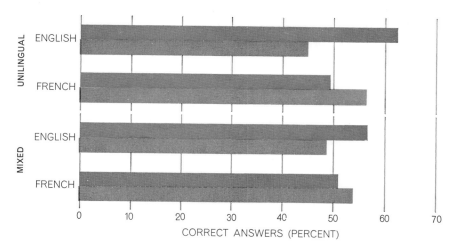

WRITTEN TESTS of comprehension of unilingual and mixed passages produced these results for Americans (*black*) and Europeans (*color*). The scores are roughly equivalent for all conditions, although the subjects did somewhat better with texts favoring their native syntax.

BILINGUAL SIGNS, a common sight in Quebec, are indicative of a situation in which use of two languages is an ordinary matter. Quebec often uses pictorial signs as an alternative.

	ENGLISH	GERMAN	SPANISH	THAI
EVOCATIVE	man	Mann	hombre	poo chai
	table	Tisch	mesa	dto
	bread	Brot	pan	ka-nom bpung
	boy	Junge	muchacho	dek poo chai
	blossom	Blüte	flor	dauk mai barn
	girl	Mädchen	niña	dek poo ying
	butter	Butter	mantequilla	nur-ie
	scissors	Schere	tijeras	gkan gkrai
ABSTRACTIONS	freedom	Freiheit	libertad	say-ree parp
	justice	Gerechtigkeit	justicia	yoo-dti tum
	law	Gesetz	ley	gkot mai
	honor	Ehre	honor	gkee-at-dti
	patience	Geduld	paciencia	kwam ot-ton
	wisdom	Weisheit	sabiduría	kwam raub roo
	duty	Pflicht	el deber	nah tee
	civilization	Zivilisation	civilización	ah-ra-ya tum
THINGS	lamb	Lamm	ovejita	look gkaa
	thorn	Dorn	espina	nam
	butterfly	Schmetterling	mariposa	pee sur-ah
	worm	Wurm	gusano	naun
	smoke	Rauch	humo	kwan
	castle	Schloss	castillo	bprah-sart
	tree	Baum	árbol	dton mai
	Norway	Norwegen	Noruega	nor-way
FEELINGS	pain	Schmerz	dolor	chjep bpoo-at
	hate	Hass	odio	kwam gklee-at
	jealousy	Eifersucht	celos	heung
	fear	Furcht	miedo	kwam gklau
	love	Liebe	amor	kwam ruk
	guilt	Schuld	culpa	kwam pit
	sadness	Traurigkeit	tristeza	kwam sow
	pity	Mitleid	piedad	song sarn

LEXICON OF WORDS used in word-association tests of the kind shown in the upper illustration on the opposite page was in four categories. The first contains words that evoke similar responses when used as stimulus words; for example, most people hearing "man" will respond "woman." Other categories are self-explanatory. Thai words are presented here in transliteration, whereas subjects familiar with the language saw them in Thai alphabet.

English, and they responded in one language to stimulus words presented in the other. A typical selection of words is shown in all four languages in the illustration above.

Consider the German words *Haus* (house) and *Tisch* (table). Suppose a person fluent in German and English who was taking the German-German association test responded to *Tisch* with *Haus*. Would he respond to *table* with *house* or with some other word, such as *chair*? And how would he respond when the stimulus was in one language and he was asked to react in the other?

If the hypothesis of a common store of information were correct, one would expect a large percentage of responses to be similar in all the tests, since the concepts with which the subject was dealing would be essentially the same regardless of the language he was speaking. On the other hand, if information were stored according to language, one would expect the percentage of such direct translations to be low; for example, the subject might respond to *Tisch* with *Haus* in the German-German test and to *table* with *chair* in the English-English test.

Our finding was that about a fifth of the responses were the same in a bilingual subject's two languages. That is too large a percentage to warrant the belief that the meanings of words were stored completely in linguistically separate tanks. On the other hand, the large number of responses (about a quarter of the total) confined to one language or another enabled us to reject the idea that the meanings existed in a single tank for which the languages were merely taps. The bilingual person does not have a single store of meanings in his mind that he taps with his two languages. What it comes down to is that access to the information one has in one's mind is in some cases restricted to the language by which—or, more broadly, the context in which—it was encoded.

What are these cases? An indication is provided by the different responses we received to different categories of words. Some of the words we used referred to concrete objects; examples are *lamb, thorn, tree.* Other words were more abstract: *freedom, justice, wisdom, materialism.* Still other words—*hate, jealousy, love, guilt*—referred to feelings.

Our results revealed that words referring to concrete, manipulable objects were more likely to elicit similar responses in the bilingual person's two languages than abstract words. The abstract words in turn elicited a larger number of similar responses than the words referring to feelings. To put the matter another way, *love* and *Liebe* or *democracy* and *Demokratie* do not mean the same thing to someone familiar with English and German, even though they are dictionary translations of one another. He has different contexts and different expectations for each of the two words in the pairs. In contrast, words that refer to objects that people in various countries manipulate in similar ways—objects such as pencils, books and desks—have very similar meanings in the two languages. The idea that there are operational definitions of terms, as many philosophers of science put it, seems to have some psychological reality as one basis of meaning.

Our work showed that some information can be stored in such a way that it is readily accessible in either of two languages. Other information is, in terms of its accessibility, closely bound to the language by which it was stored in the mind. In another set of experiments we explored the way in which words are stored and retrieved. The question was: Are words perceived and then stored in the memory as individual items or does the process take place in terms of their meanings?

Our experiment was based on a phenomenon first studied in detail by Nancy C. Waugh, a former colleague of mine who is now at the Harvard Medical School. She found that if a subject was presented with a unilingual list of words, some of which were repeated, his ability to recall a given word was directly proportional to the number of times it had been repeated. If a subject is shown, say, 120 words one at a time for about a second each, and if a few of the words are repeated on the list, he is twice as likely to recall a word presented four times as one presented twice.

My colleagues and I wondered what the result would be if a list were presented with some words appearing in two languages. Taking as an example the English word *fold* and its French translation *pli*, would a bilingual subject seeing each of them two or three times in a long list of words presented singly recall *fold* and *pli* according to the frequency with which each appeared or would his recall reflect the frequency of occurrence of the common meaning of the two words? An English-French list typical of the ones we used appears in the top illustration on the next page; the reader must remember that the subject saw the words one at a time and not in a complete array as in the illustration. Among the words that translate each other are *fold* and *pli* and *ten* and *dix;* among the words that are not translated are *herd* and *fonds* (funds).

The results showed that the percentage of recall increased linearly with the frequency of occurrence of meaning [*see bottom illustration on next page*]. Presenting *fold* twice and *pli* twice produces the same effect on the recall of either word as presenting either one four times. Since *fold* and *pli* neither look alike nor sound alike, it cannot be the words themselves that interact in perception and memory. Our subjects did not see and store the words individually as visual or phonetic objects; they stored them in terms of their meaning.

The implication is clear that the subjects were able to code and store verbal items in some form other than the language in which the items appeared. A further implication is that information repeated in different languages (different symbol systems) is as well retained as information repeated in a single language. The amount of information that can be retained, however, is not increased by using different symbol systems for storing it, but access to the information is increased.

To put the point more concretely, suppose one wanted to give a student two lessons in geography. If the student knew two languages, he would retain as much geography from one lesson in each language as from two lessons in one of them. Moreover, he would be able to talk about geography readily in both languages. On the other hand, teaching him geography in one language and also teaching him a second language would not necessarily enable him to express his knowledge of geography in the second language without some kind of additional instruction. The information one has and the mechanisms or rules used to acquire it are clearly separate aspects of memory.

I have so far described two aspects of the use of verbal symbol systems: the mental switching that characterizes the successful use of different languages and one of the ways language limits access to information stored in the memory. A third aspect involves the set of rules a

INTRALINGUAL

ENGLISH	ENGLISH
table	dish
boy	girl
king	queen
house	window

SPANISH	SPANISH
mesa	silla
muchacho	hombre
rey	reina
casa	madre

INTERLINGUAL

ENGLISH	SPANISH
table	silla
boy	niña
king	reina
house	blanco

SPANISH	ENGLISH
mesa	chair
muchacho	trousers
rey	queen
casa	mother

TYPICAL RESPONSES in a word-association test were given by a subject whose native language was Spanish. He was asked to respond in Spanish to Spanish stimulus words, in English to the same words in English and in each language to stimulus words in the other.

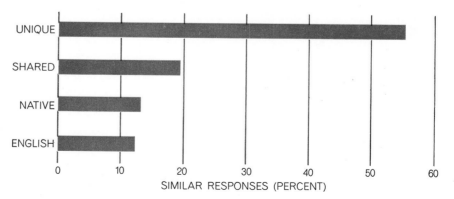

SIMILAR RESPONSES (PERCENT)

SUMMARY OF RESPONSES to interlingual word-association tests shows that more than half of the responses were unique, that is, not shared between languages. For example, in the upper illustration on this page the response *blanco* to *house* in the English-Spanish test differed from the response *window* to *house* in the English-English test. In contrast, *silla* was the response to both *table* and *mesa* and would be scored as a "native" response; answers of *reina* and *queen* to *king* are translations and are scored as "shared" responses.

ten	nerve	riz	tique
herd	truffe	isthme	preux
fold	paste	dix	fouet
soul	ice	glace	game
spout	gust	riz	clash
fonds	soul	âme	deux
jeu	truffe	fonds	game
tain	dix	crook	leaf
deux	preux	pli	bulk
pli	seing	bonne	golf
stub	ten	pli	bonne
bonne	nerf	spout	rampe
herd	rampe	golf	seing
âme	maid	two	gust
fold	maid	whip	clash
tain	jig	pâte	two
fold	truffe	psaume	whip
pli	gust	maid	âme
gust	preux	leaf	maid
bulk	cook	bonne	rampe
fouet	preux	clash	soul
fold	bulk	leaf	tain
riz	ice	glace	deux
riz	jeu	leaf	golf
two	juge	whip	fouet

STORAGE OF WORDS was tested with lists in which a subject saw, one at a time, words in both his languages. Some were repeated in the same language, others in both languages by means of translations; for example, *ten* and *dix* translate each other. Recall is improved by repetition. The question was whether recall of translated words would reflect the frequency with which their common meaning appeared or only the frequency with which the words themselves appeared. The results showed that words are stored in terms of their meanings.

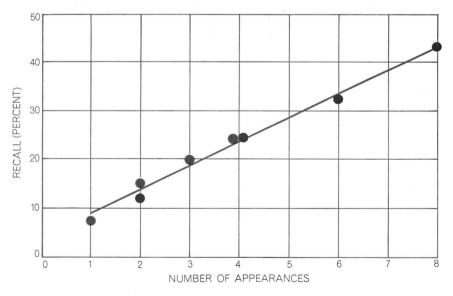

PERCENT OF RECALL was essentially the same for words repeated in one language (*colored circles*) and for words repeated as translations (*black circles*). Since most of the translations, such as *snow* and *neige*, do not resemble one another, the results show that the concept is the decisive factor in recall and that two languages increase access to concepts.

person learns for employing a language. In some of our experiments we found that such rules affect his linguistic performance in subtle ways.

Earlier I described how our bilingual subjects switched between their languages. Such switching is not always perfect, particularly in the daily use of language. Linguists use the word calque, which is the French word for "imitation," to describe the interference of one linguistic system with another. Examples of calques appear in the semi-Germanic sentences "Throw the baby out the window a bottle" and "Throw mama from the train a kiss." I have heard Hebrew-speaking people (Israeli students in the U.S.) inadvertently say "spoontea" for "teaspoon" and "cuptea" for "teacup." (In Hebrew the adjective always follows the noun.) Once I heard such a student say "washdisher" for "dishwasher." The last example is of particular linguistic interest because the Hebrew for "dishwasher" translates literally as "washerdish"; the speaker, however, combined the Hebrew word order with the English sequence of syllables.

In sum, speakers of a language develop linguistic habits, or characteristic ways of ordering words. One effect of these habits was revealed when our bilingual subjects were asked to read aloud linguistically mixed passages of the kind described at the beginning of this article *see illustration, page 190*]. The rules we had used for constructing the passages gave rise to many cases in which the normal word order of English or French was violated. Two examples in the illustration are "made resound the earth" and "une violente brise."

Subjects reading the passages aloud sometimes said "made the earth resound" and "une brise violente." Thus they showed that their experience with the normal syntactic forms affected their way of speaking words presented visually. In effect, the students were producing calques, but in a direction opposite to the normal one. Usually a calque distorts a verbal expression by applying a syntactic form of one language to words in another. In our experiment the subjects' ingrained skills in using the rules of English and French induced them to rectify word sequences that had been distorted deliberately.

The various experiments I have described embody some significant implications for both education and the study of the mind. Education entails the acquisition of information and the use of mental skills. Languages, as I have shown, can train one's mind in the way it orders and uses information. The phenomenon of bilingualism enables us to give people information or teach people a skill in one language and find out if the information or the skill can be expressed in another language. In this way we can separate for study the mental processes used in acquiring or manipulating information from the information itself.

One example of the difference between mental skills and information is found in mathematics. Nearly all our bilingual subjects remarked during interviews that they did mathematical operations in the language in which they were taught the operations. They could always tell us the results of their operations in either language, and they could even describe what operations they had performed and how they had performed them, but the operations could be performed in only one way. Indeed, a bilingual colleague once told me that, having moved from France to the U.S. at the age of 12, he does his arithmetic in French and his calculus in English.

The point to be made is that mental activities and information learned in one context are not necessarily available for use in another. They often have to be learned anew in the second context, although perhaps with less time and effort. The fact is, however, that relatively little is known about how the activities of the mind affect one another. The study of bilingualism, being a study of the interaction of symbol systems and the way they affect one's acquisition and use of information, promises to provide valuable information on these questions.

IMPORTANCE OF CONTEXT in understanding a language is indicated by a foreign visitor's reaction to a sign such as this one in New York. Not being an American motorist, he thought the sign meant that he should sit on the curb while he waited for a bus.

23

Problem-Solving

by Martin Scheerer
April 1963

The intelligent solution of a problem seems to involve more than trial and error. Experiments show that it often requires a fresh insight based on a sudden shift in the way the problem is viewed

A cat is penned in a wooden cage, the door of which can be released by a tug on a latchstring. The cat has never seen a latchstring. In an effort to get out it tries to squeeze between the bars and claws and bites at them in a random fashion until, by pure chance, it happens to claw at a loop in the string and pull. After gaining its freedom the cat is put back in the cage. Again it squeezes and claws and bites and finally happens to pull the string. On repeated trials the cat gets to the string a little sooner each time, and eventually it pulls the loop as soon as it is placed in the cage.

A hungry chimpanzee confined in a cage sees a banana outside the bars just beyond its reach. After some futile attempts to get the banana by reaching through the bars the chimpanzee discovers a stick lying on the floor of the cage. In one swift action the ape picks up the stick and with it retrieves the banana.

The cat and the chimpanzee each faced a problem and solved it in a very different way. The manner in which a cat or a chimpanzee—or a human being—solves a problem is a fundamental characteristic of the animal or person. The behavior manifested in solving a problem, moreover, provides a convenient window through which to observe mental processes. Since the turn of the century the experimental investigation of problem-solving has been a fruitful source of information on how animals and men think and learn.

The course of this experimentation has been heavily influenced by a canon laid down by the British zoologist and comparative psychologist C. Lloyd Morgan: Never attribute behavior in an animal to a high level of thinking or knowing if the behavior can be explained in terms of lower processes; in other words, always explain behavior in terms of the simplest possible mechanism.

In 1898 the U.S. psychologist Edward Lee Thorndike undertook to apply this principle of psychological parsimony in a comprehensive study of problem-solving in the cat and other animals. Thorndike's definition of "problem" is still widely accepted: A problem exists when the goal that is sought is not directly attainable by the performance of a simple act available in the animal's repertory; the solution calls for either a novel action or a new integration of available actions. It was Thorndike who performed the cat-in-the-cage experiment described at the beginning of this article. He posed these questions: Is it necessary to assume that the cat has intelligence in the human meaning of the term? Does the solution—pulling the string—require any understanding or insight or can it be achieved quite mechanically?

Thorndike noted that the cat pulled the string by chance and that the time it required to trip the latch declined gradually in successive trials. He concluded that the solution behavior could be explained quite simply: The string was a stimulus and the tugging was a response. The tugging was rewarded by escape. From this and similar experiments Thorndike derived his principle of learning: Whatever behavior is rewarded is "stamped in" and whatever behavior is not rewarded or is punished is "stamped out." This principle is at the heart of contemporary stimulus-response psychology, which was shaped not only by Thorndike but also by I. P. Pavlov, John B. Watson, Clark Hull and many others. In this view the tugging behavior is a learned habit, acquired through repeated "reinforcement," or reward. There is no need to assume that the cat has any understanding of why the tugging leads to escape; there is no need to assume any kind of intelligence other than a plasticity that allows the learning of new habits.

Then the Gestalt psychologists came on the scene. They emphasized the tendency of the mind to organize and integrate and to perceive situations, including problems, as total structures. They argued that more is involved in problem-solving than a sequence of stimuli and responses. One of the founders of Gestalt psychology, Wolfgang Köhler, objected specifically to Thorndike's test situations. The cat, he maintained, cannot possibly behave intelligently in the cage because the release mechanism is hidden and therefore not part of the perceived situation, and because its functioning is too complicated for an animal to unravel. Isolated on Tenerife in the Canary Islands during World War I, Köhler carried out a classic series of experiments with chimpanzees. One of his problem situations was the one involving the banana and the stick. In this case the chimpanzee's solution did not come gradually and was not the result of trial and error. It was intelligent behavior, Köhler said, based on a perception of what was required to solve the problem: some way of overcoming the distance barrier.

The insight that leads to a solution, in the Gestalt view, stems from this perception of the requirements of a problem. Max Wertheimer, another founder of Gestalt psychology, provided a good example to support this point of view. Suppose a child who already knows how to get the area of a rectangle is asked to find the formula for the area of a parallelogram. If the child thinks about it, Wertheimer said, he will be struck by the fact that a parallelogram would look like a rectangle were it not for the fact that

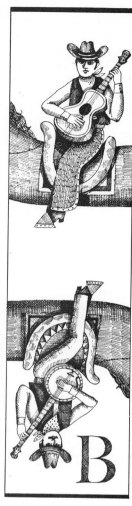

HORSE-AND-RIDER PUZZLE illustrates the power of fixation. The problem is to place drawing *B* on drawing *A* in such a way that the riders are properly astride the horses. This drawing is adapted from the original version. The correct solution is on page 202.

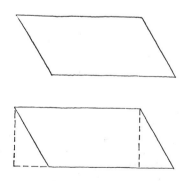

PARALLELOGRAM (*top*) is equal in area to a rectangle of the same base and altitude because the "protuberance" at one end is equal to the "gap" at the other (*bottom*).

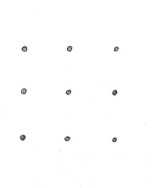

NINE DOTS are arranged in a square. The problem is to connect them by drawing four continuous straight lines without lifting pencil from paper. Solution is on page 201.

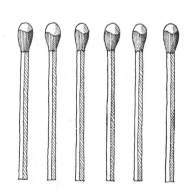

SIX MATCHES must be assembled to form four congruent equilateral triangles each side of which is equal to the length of the matches. The solution appears on page 201.

one side has a "protuberance" and the other side has a "gap" [*see illustration above*]. He formulates the hypothesis: "Get rid of the protuberance and fill in the gap." Then he realizes that the protuberance is equivalent to the gap; if he moves the protruding corner to the indented side, the figure is converted into a rectangle of the same base and altitude. Hence the formula is the same as it is for a rectangle.

With Morgan's warning in mind one can ask at this point if it is necessary to assume that the child has done more than go through a process of trial and error and call on previously learned hab-

its. The Gestalt answer is that although there may be trial and error it is not a blind, or random, sequence as Thorndike believed. Productive thinking is not accidental success or the mere application of bits of past experience. The problem has a structure of its own that points the way to its solution. Only within this total framework, or context, does the problem-solver draw selectively on relevant knowledge.

This view of problem-solving has direct implications for theories of learning and teaching. It is interesting, in passing, to consider how the thought process outlined above differs from the way the formula for the area of a parallelogram is usually taught. A geometry teacher would probably give the formula $b \times a$ (base times altitude) and offer the following proof. He would extend the base line and drop perpendiculars to construct two triangles and then demonstrate that the triangles are congruent. But he would probably not have pointed out in advance the simple reason why one should want to prove the congruence of the triangles. A bright student might grasp the reason but others would never attain that insight. Fortunately, insight achieved in the solving of a problem can be explained to others, who should then have precisely the same understanding attained by the original problem-solver. This true understanding has two major advantages beyond the intrinsic pleasure of grasping something: it can be retained easily and it can be transferred to other, similar problems. Once a student understands the reason the area of a parallelogram is given by $b \times a$, he can figure out how to get the area of a triangle or a trapezoid.

Wertheimer and Karl Duncker, who was then at the University of Berlin, explored the nature of the process by which people gain or fail to gain insight into problems. They found that although men have the capacity for genuine insight and often attain it, not everyone gains insight into a problem in the same way or at the same stage—or ever. Insight is often delayed or thwarted by "fixation" on an inappropriate solution. If the chimpanzee fails to realize that it simply cannot get the banana without a tool and keeps reaching through the bars, it will not notice the stick; the fixation stands in the way of a correct solution.

The author's own work in problem-solving has been centered on this phenomenon of fixation. He found that it operates in many ways. Sometimes a person clings misguidedly to a false premise or assumption concerning the task before him. Consider two simple problems that are made difficult by this fixation [see lower illustrations on preceding page]. The first requires that nine dots be connected by four straight lines drawn without lifting the pencil from the paper. This cannot be done unless one extends the lines beyond the dots [see illustration at bottom right, page 201]. But almost everyone assumes—although it is not stated as a condition of the problem—that he must stay within the group of dots. The second problem, assembling six matches of equal length to form four equilateral triangles with sides equal to the length of the matches, cannot be solved as long as one assumes that the matches must lie in one plane, and virtually everyone who tries it assumes just that. The assumption is implicit; most people do not even know they have made it. The way to the correct solution —an equilateral tetrahedron, or pyramid

RING-AND-PEG PROBLEM could be solved with a piece of string with which to tie the two sticks together. The only string in the room hung on a nail on the wall. When it hung there alone, every subject solved the problem. When it was used to suspend a cardboard, an old calendar or a cloudy mirror, some people failed. When the string was a hanger for functional things such as a sign, a clear mirror or a current calendar, more than half failed.

—is opened as soon as one realizes that the matches need not lie flat. This shift from one premise to a new one is what Gestalt psychologists call a "reformulation," or "recentering," of one's thoughts.

The power of fixation and recentering is illustrated by a problem the author developed in collaboration with the neuropsychiatrist Kurt Goldstein and Edwin G. Boring of Harvard University. The puzzle, which the author first came upon in an advertisement, involves a drawing of two misshapen horses and a drawing of two riders [see upper illustration, page 197]. The problem is to place the drawing of the riders (B) on the other drawing (A) in such a way that the riders are properly astride the horses. (The reader can try this himself by tracing the two drawings on two strips of paper.) The overwhelming tendency is to try to place each rider on one of the horses drawn in A. It is quite clear that this will not work (the horses are back-to-back in A and belly-to-belly in B, and the space between the horses is much less than the distance between the two riders) but most people keep trying. The correct solution requires a complete recentering of one's perception of the elements of the puzzle. The two horses in A must be broken into parts, so to speak, after which the head and the hindquarters of one combine respectively with the hindquarters and the head of the other to form two new horses. Then, when one of the strips is turned 90 degrees with respect to the other, the riders fit nicely on the newly created horses [see illustration, page 202]. In this case a solution is inhibited by a fixation that arises from the perceptual make-up of the puzzle. Another puzzle presents a similar problem with more abstract shapes [see top illustration, page 201].

Duncker discovered that fixation often interferes when the solution of a test problem requires the use of a familiar object in a novel way. Suppose someone needs a screw driver and one is not available. He could make do with any thin and sufficiently hard object—a coin, for example. But to see this possibility he must shift from his usual idea of "coin as money" to the new functional concept of "coin as screw driver," and this is a difficult kind of shift for many people to make. (Substitution of a coin, to be sure, seems rather obvious because it is a familiar expedient, but a person who thinks of it independently should be credited with a truly creative insight.) Duncker found that it was particularly hard for a person to think of an object as adaptable for a novel

WAGON AND WEIGHTS were used in the author's analogue of the river-crossing problem. The wagon was constructed on a double-seesaw principle. Flanges at the ends locked the front wheels if no weight was placed in the container (*top*) and the rear wheels if too much weight was loaded (*second from top*). The wheels turned and the wagon rolled only when either one large weight or one or two small ones were loaded (*two lower pictures*).

function if he had just put it to its conventional use. In one experiment the task was to suspend a piece of string from a wooden ledge. The subject had no hooks but he did have a gimlet; the solution was to screw the gimlet into the wood, leave it there and hang the string on it. Subjects given a preliminary task in which they employed the gimlet to make holes were less likely than others to think of using it as a peg.

The author sought to extend Duncker's investigation of "functional fixedness" in a series of experiments con-

ducted with Maurice Huling of the University of Kansas. The problem, originally developed with Zelda S. Klapper and Herman Witkin of the State University of New York College of Medicine in Brooklyn, required the subject to put two rings on a peg from a position six feet from the rings and the peg. He could not do it without a tool to extend his reach. Except when he was picking up the rings and putting them on the peg, he was allowed to move about the room, and he could use anything he saw. There were two sticks in the room, but neither

was long enough to bridge the gap alone; they had to be joined together. The only piece of string in the room was one by which an object hung from a nail on the wall [*see illustration on page 198*]. The string was in clear view but it was embedded in a meaningful context. It was predicted that it might not be seen as an available piece of string; although not hidden perceptually, it would prove to be psychologically inaccessible for anything but its present function.

At first 16 volunteers were given the problem with a piece of string hanging alone on the nail. All of them took down the string, tied the sticks together and with them placed the rings on the peg. The experimental series was then begun with the string holding things that had no real function: a piece of blank cardboard, an old calendar and a cloudy mirror. It was predicted that the string would still be psychologically available, and virtually everyone tested in these situations did indeed solve the problem. In the next phase the objects hung on the wall had definite functions: a current calendar, a clear mirror and a "No Smoking" sign. These could be expected to have a "stay put" quality. Fifty-six per cent of the subjects failed with the current calendar, 69 per cent with the intact mirror and 53 per cent with the "No Smoking" sign.

In each case the string had been tied with a square knot, which was placed in plain sight above the nail and looked eminently untieable. The subjects who failed to take down the string did not think they were forbidden to make use of it; they simply did not think to do so, as could be ascertained from their comments (they had been encouraged to think aloud) and follow-up interviews. Moreover, almost everyone decided quickly that he needed a string. This means that in this phase of the experiment more than half of the individuals sought a string for nearly the entire 20-minute test period but did not think of using for their purpose a string that was one of the most prominent things in their field of view.

In one situation the subject himself was asked to hang the object on the wall. While he was occupied with some unrelated written problems the departmental secretary came into the room, apologized for intruding and left a mirror on the table, explaining that mirrors were being put in all the laboratory cubicles "for an experiment next week." The experimenter said casually: "I suppose this should be hung up. Would you do

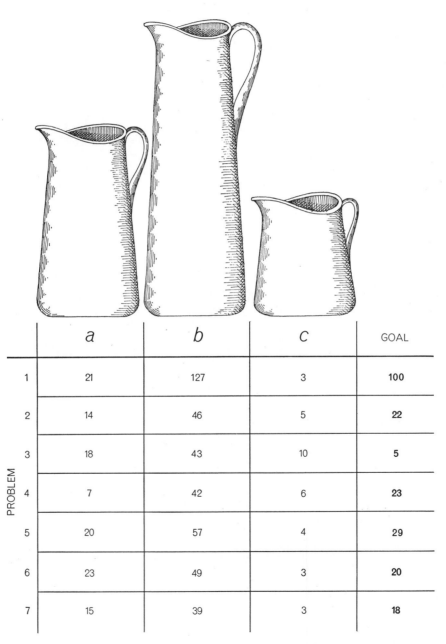

PROBLEM	a	b	c	GOAL
1	21	127	3	100
2	14	46	5	22
3	18	43	10	5
4	7	42	6	23
5	20	57	4	29
6	23	49	3	20
7	15	39	3	18

FIXATION because of habit is illustrated by this series of problems. In each a quantity of water (*right*) must be measured out; there is an unlimited supply of water but the only tools available are three pitchers, *a*, *b* and *c*, the volumes of which are specified for each problem. Once the subject hits on a successful pattern of filling and pouring ($b - a - 2c$) he tends to follow that pattern even when, in Problems 6 and 7, there is an easier solution.

it for me?" The subject hung the mirror on the nail (the only one in the room) and went back to his paper work. Fifteen minutes later he was given the ring-and-peg problem. In spite of the direct experience with the piece of string, the failure rate in this situation was 50 per cent.

The results were quite different when the string was handled ahead of time but was handled as "string." In what was called a "test of manual dexterity" we had a group of volunteers hang up the old calendar, the cardboard or the clear mirror using tweezers to tie the string. The object was left on the wall. When these subjects undertook the ring-and-peg problem after a 15-minute interval, only one out of 36 failed. Apparently even a functional mirror, if hung on the wall in the course of a "dexterity test," did not later take on the coloration of something that belonged on the wall. Instead the mirror and the string were perceived as two things left on the wall after fulfilling a specific but transient purpose. The string remained a string, not just a means of hanging things.

The follow-up interviews with people who had failed showed how persistent a fixation can be. The experimenter began by pointing in the general direction of the object on the wall and asking: "What about that?" The hint was enough for only five out of 47 people. When the experimenter then asked, "What about that mirror [or calendar and so on]?" only four more saw the solution. Many of the others responded: "What about it?" Still others suggested making the sign or mirror into a shovel-like tool with one of the sticks, wrapping the sticks in the sign or somehow employing the screw eyes in the back of the mirror. When the experimenter finally asked directly, "What about the string?" all 38 of the remaining subjects expressed surprise, chagrin and self-reproach as they admitted this was indeed a solution.

Fixation had been reported to be a function of involvement in a situation. To see if an increase in "psychological distance" would help to overcome it, some observers were allowed to watch as a "subject" ran through the motions of trying to solve the problem. The subject was excused when he reached the point of verbalizing the need for something with which to fasten the two sticks together. The observers were then asked to work out the problem in their minds. Only one out of seven of these observers failed, compared with the more than half of the deeply involved subjects

who had tried to solve the same problem in action.

One of the difficulties in the study of problem-solving is that the experimenter can never be sure just what is going on in the subject's mind. He can ask after the experiment is over, but the subject may forget details or may reconstruct his thought processes incorrectly. Even when the person being tested thinks aloud in the course of the solution, he may not mention everything that occurs to him. It is desirable, therefore, to construct a problem that invites and encourages a running translation of thought into visible action. James M. Elliott and the author worked out such a situation in another experiment at the

University of Kansas.

The problem chosen was essentially the familiar one of the river crossing. Eight soldiers have to cross a river. The only means of transportation is a small boat in which two little boys are playing; the boat can carry at most two boys or one soldier. How do the soldiers get across? If the reader will try to solve this problem before reading on, he will understand the difficulties our subjects faced.

The river puzzle was converted into one involving physical objects and requiring a sequence of discrete moves on the part of the person attempting it. A crude wagon was substituted for the boat, and eight large weights and two small ones for the soldiers and the boys

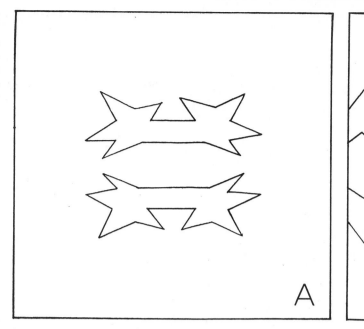

PERCEPTUAL FIXATION demonstrated by the horse-and-rider puzzle operates also with these abstract shapes. The problem here is to place element B on element A in such a way that two closed figures are formed. The solution to this problem appears on page 203.

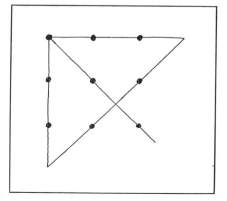

DOT PROBLEM is solved by extending the lines beyond the dots. But most people assume incorrectly that they may not do this.

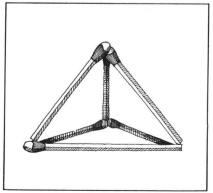

MATCH PROBLEM is solved by building a three-dimensional pyramid. Most people wrongly assume that matches must lie flat.

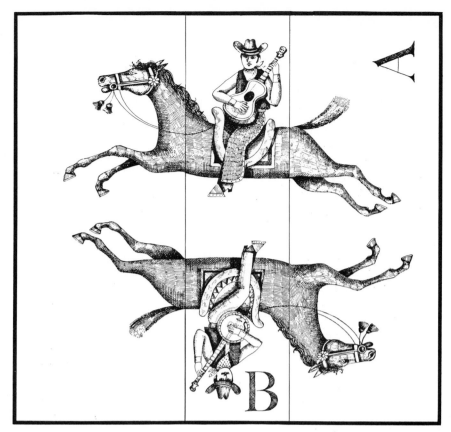

SOLUTION of the horse-and-rider puzzle requires a "recentering." The horses cannot be used as they are drawn in A but must be abstracted into their component parts and recombined into two new horses. Then, if drawing A is rotated 90 degrees, the riders fit properly.

see illustration, page 199]. The wagon wheels locked if no weights were placed placed in it and also if more than one large weight or two small ones were loaded. Each subject was told that his task was to transport all the weights in the wagon from one side of a table ("Lawrence") to the other side ("Topeka"), that the wheels must roll freely, that he could make as many trips as he wished and that there were no hidden tricks or gadgets on the wagon—that its rolling was a function of the amount of weight in it.

The solution consists in realizing that a precondition for getting the large weights across is to have one small weight on each side. The way to achieve this is to begin by taking both small weights across to Topeka. After one of them has returned the wagon to Lawrence the first large one can make the trip to Topeka. Then the small weight originally left in Topeka serves its purpose, getting the wagon back to Lawrence. Now the entire cycle must be repeated, and so on until all the weights are across.

Two experiments were performed. In the first the problem was simply given

to 49 individuals. In the second the subjects were divided into groups and interrupted at certain points in order to know what they were thinking or planning. In both cases the participants were asked to think aloud and were observed as their thoughts took the form of concrete behavior, recording each loading of a weight and each abortive or successful movement of the wagon.

No two individuals proceeded in exactly the same way but there were some striking similarities in the behavior of the volunteers. They began by exploring the various weight loadings that would allow the wagon to roll. They soon discovered that it would carry either one large weight or one or two small ones. After this discovery most of them formulated a hypothesis: "Take one weight over at a time, thus transporting them all in repeated trips." This hypothesis led 40 of the 49 into the error of promptly loading one large weight and taking it to Topeka—only to realize when they got there that it was impossible to get the wagon back without taking the weight back again.

Once they realized it did no good to start by transporting a large weight

alone, most of the subjects decided: "Take at least two weights over in order to return the wagon with one." This "rider" hypothesis, combined with the knowledge that the wagon would not roll with too much weight, usually led to the idea of transporting one large and one small weight—a combination that accounted for 52 per cent of the trial loadings at this stage. Virtually all the subjects who made that attempt said they intended to get the wagon back from Topeka with the small weight—that it seemed the best "rider" for the purpose. And although the wagon would clearly not roll with a large and small weight aboard, they returned again and again to that combination. For 30 of the subjects who persevered at it, the mean number of repetitions was 6.1. Many of them tried to rationalize the fixation as an attempt to find some special way of placing the weights so that the wagon would roll.

The reason for the fixation is fairly clear. These subjects had decided that they needed to carry a rider, and that the small weight was a logical one because it was less of an extra load than a second large weight. Even the few subjects who considered taking the two small weights across together saw one as a rider for the other only on a preliminary trip; thereafter, they thought, it would be a rider for a large one—so they might as well face the small-plus-large problem at the outset. Some went so far as to load the two small weights and still failed to see that it was the essence of the solution. All of these subjects were fixating on what appeared to them to be the goal: transporting the large weights to Topeka. For them the small weights had lost the quality of weights to be transported and were seen as riders only. It was therefore a detour from the major goal to transport two small weights first to Topeka merely in order to leave one there. The solution required them to shift to the perception of both small weights as tools to be taken across on a preliminary trip.

When individuals loading a large and a small weight were interrupted and asked, as the experimenter pointed to the other small weight, "What about this one? Have you ever thought of using them together?" a few were able to solve the problem. But most of them said something like: "It looks the same... I could take these two [small ones] over, but after one trip I couldn't do any more... I'd still be faced with the problem of getting the large ones over."

Even as they finally hit on the correct

first step of transporting the two small weights, many subjects failed to see the point. Some got back to Lawrence with a small weight and then tried once again to load a large and a small weight together. Even more of them got safely through the next steps of sending over one large weight and returning the waiting small one but failed to see that they had to start all over again at that point with the two small weights. In other words, they had not yet attained the second major insight: the cyclical nature of the solution.

Eventually all the subjects did solve the problem and all but two of them understood the solution. On questioning later, 36 per cent of them expressed the underlying principle in spatial terms: "You need a small one on each side at all times." Another 41 per cent expressed it in temporal terms, reciting the required sequence of events in the cycle. The remaining 23 per cent were unable to verbalize the principle clearly.

The various problems discussed here illustrate several causes of fixation in problem-solving. A person may start with an implicit but incorrect premise. He may fail to perceive an object's suitability for a solution because it must be used in a novel way or because it is embedded in a conventional context. Or he may be unwilling to accept a detour that delays the achievement of his goal. Any type of fixation can be strengthened by too much motivation. Herbert D. Birch, now at the Albert Einstein College of Medicine, found that if a chimpanzee is too hungry it will not do as well at a problem requiring a detour—the Köhler banana problem, for example—as an animal that is only moderately hungry. The overly hungry chimpanzee fixates rigidly on the goal, striving to no avail to reach the banana. On the human level there is some evidence that strong ego-involvement in a problem makes for overmotivation and is detrimental to a solution.

One final factor affecting fixation is habituation. There is truth to William James's statement that habit is the "flywheel of society," but one might add that habit can also be the flypaper of society. The direct availability of a habitual mode of response may make it much harder to break with habit and approach a problem afresh. This effect was beautifully illustrated some years ago by Abraham S. Luchins, who was then associated with Wertheimer at the New School for Social Research. The subject is asked to measure out mentally a given quantity of water; the tools available to him are three pitchers of specified sizes [see illustration on page 200]. Take the first problem: With three pitchers that hold three, 21 and 127 quarts, and with an unlimited supply of water, measure out 100 quarts. The solution is to fill the 127-quart vessel (b), pour off enough to fill the 21-quart pitcher (a) and then enough to fill the three-quart pitcher (c) twice. This leaves the desired 100 quarts in the big pitcher (b). The reader is invited to do the whole series.

Most people solve Problem 6 by pouring water from the filled 49-quart vessel into the 23-quart vessel and then twice into the three-quart pitcher, and they follow the same routine in Problem 7. But both problems have much simpler solutions. Problem 6 can be solved by filling a and pouring from it into c once; Problem 7 can be solved by filling a and c and pouring them into an empty b.

But because Problems 1 through 5 all call for the $b - a - 2c$ solution the subject becomes habituated to it, consciously or not, and holds to the same pattern even when it is inappropriate. This fixation is exploited in the traditional childhood game in which one child is called on to pronounce as the other spells out: "MAC DONALD...MAC HENRY...MAC MAHON...MACHINERY." The victim is trapped into pronouncing the last "name" as "Mac Hinery" instead of "machinery."

If insight is the essential element in intelligent problem-solving, fixation is its archenemy. Fixation is overcome and insight attained by a sudden shift in the way the problem or the objects involved in it are viewed. The work described in this article has pointed to some of the factors that necessitate this sudden shift, but precisely what brings it about is still unknown. It remains the central problem of problem-solving.

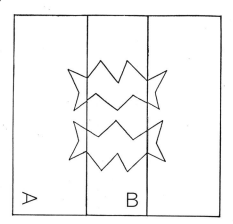

RECENTERING also solves this problem. The abstract shapes of A are broken up and rotated 90 degrees. B then fits properly.

IV

PERSONALITY AND
BEHAVIOR DISORDERS

PERSONALITY AND BEHAVIOR DISORDERS

IV

INTRODUCTION

Although the articles in this section are less closely related than those in the other sections, they are all concerned with individual differences in reacting to the environment. When we speak of personality, we usually refer to the characteristics and modes of behavior that make one individual different from others and determine his unique adjustment to environment. Some of these characteristics—such as physical attributes, intelligence, and special talents—depend upon innate potentials. Others are largely a product of the particular culture in which one is raised, as well as individual experiences with parents and peers. The potentialities present at birth are molded by life experiences to form the adult personality.

In the introduction to Section I we noted the importance of early experiences for the development of personality. Although early experiences are indeed crucial in forming personality, the role of innate attributes should not be overlooked. In "The Origin of Personality" Alexander Thomas, Stella Chess, and Herbert Birch explore the nature of inborn differences in temperament—the individual's "style" of responding to the environment. In a careful study of the behavior of infants two or three months after birth, marked individual differences in style were evident even at this very early age—differences that could hardly be attributed to differences in parental treatment. For example, of two infants from the same family, one might be characteristically active, easily distracted, and willing to accept new objects and people. The other might be predominantly quiet, persistent, and unwilling to accept anything new. A follow-up study of the same children over a 14-year period indicates that, for most of the children, characteristics of temperament tended to persist. The authors propose that the important factor in shaping personality is the interaction between innate characteristics and environment. If the two influences harmonize, then healthy development will follow; if not, psychological difficulties can be expected.

Your opinion of yourself affects many aspects of your behavior. In "Studies in Self-Esteem" Stanley Coopersmith describes an investigation of the kinds of experiences that lead to a feeling of competency and personal worth, and how such feelings (or the lack of them) can influence personal conduct. The study, which followed preadolescent boys into adulthood, gathered data on such variables as homelife, attitudes, abilities, reactions to stress, and personality traits; these variables were then correlated with ratings of self-esteem. Some of the results are surprising, or at least contrary to popular opinion. For example, neither physical attractiveness, height, family size, income, nor social status showed any consistent relation to feelings of self-esteem. Those interested in raising the self-esteem of their children will find some useful guidelines in Coopersmith's data concerning the different backgrounds of children with high and low self-esteem. Perhaps the most important finding is the relation between self-esteem and parental discipline.

A child's experiences with his parents and peers is of critical importance for later behavior. Harry and Margaret Harlow have conducted extensive studies concerning the effects of early social experience on adult behavior in monkeys. Some of their findings are summarized in their article "Social Deprivation in Monkeys." Because monkeys undergo a relatively long period of development before reaching maturity—a period of close attachment to the mother and social interaction with other young monkeys—their development is similar to that of the human child. The most significant finding of the Harlow studies is that physical contact with an attentive mother and play activity with other young monkeys are both essential for normal development. Infant monkeys raised in isolation for the first six months of life with an artificial mother (a wire figure covered with terry cloth and equipped with a nursing bottle) show severe abnormalities in later life. They engage in such bizarre behavior as biting or tearing at parts of their body, or clasping their head between their arms while sitting and rocking for long periods of time; they rarely engage in social interaction with other monkeys; they are difficult to mate and, if successfully mated, make very poor mothers, tending to abuse or neglect their infants. Infant monkeys raised with their own mothers, but without contact with other young monkeys during the early months, show similar abnormalities in social behavior as adults. Regardless of the degree of exposure to other monkeys after the initial period of isolation, these animals never develop normal patterns of social interaction. After investigating a number of different methods of early rearing, the Harlows conclude that although contact with a mother and with other young monkeys during the first six months of life are both crucial for normal social development, play with peers is probably the more important. Contact with other infant monkeys may compensate to some extent for the lack of mothering.

Emotional stress, however defined, can produce physical illness. Asthma, high blood pressure, skin disorders, and gastrointestinal disturbances are examples of ailments that may often be psychosomatic, that is, attributable to emotional rather than physical causes. In "Psychological Factors in Stress and Disease" Jay Weiss investigates the types of stress that lead to ulcers. One interesting finding is that "executive" rats—rats trained to press a lever in order to avoid electric shock—develop ulcers; rats who receive the same number of shocks but are powerless to avoid them do not develop ulcers. Apparently, under certain conditions the constant alertness required to prevent the shock produces a state of tension that eventually results in ulcers. The precise conditions under which ulceration will occur are shown to depend on two variables: the variety of coping responses that an animal can make in a stress-producing situation and the type of feedback these coping attempts produce. Based on this and other research the author has developed a theory that predicts when ulceration will occur. The theory has obvious practical implications and it appears that the principles discovered in these animal experiments may apply to humans as well.

In "Hyperactive Children" Mark Stewart describes a behavior syndrome that occurs in about four percent of all school children. He presents evidence that this syndrome—characterized by restlessness, irritability, inability to concentrate, destructiveness, and overactivity—may result from a congenital defect of the reticular formation of the brain stem (an area important in controlling consciousness and attention). Although early experiences have a powerful influence on emotion and social development (as noted in the articles by Levine, p. 13, and Harlow and Harlow, p. 225, the contribution of inborn, constitutional, factors cannot be overlooked.

In "Schizophrenia" Don Jackson describes the symptoms, possible causes, and treatment of the most prevalent type of mental disorder. More than fifty percent of all neuropsychiatric hospital beds are occupied by patients diagnosed as schizophrenic. There is much debate as to the cause of the disorder. Jackson believes that the primary causes are psychological—stemming from a faulty parent-child relationship—although there is also strong evidence for a genetic predisposition to the illness. Most experts now believe that the schizophrenic diagnosis includes a group of disorders, with some symptoms in common, rather than a single disorder. In some cases, inherited biological weaknesses may be primarily responsible for the schizophrenic symptoms; in others, environmental factors may play the major role.

The treatment of mental illness in the United States has changed profoundly over the past 20 years. One outstanding change has been the shift in the scene of care for severely disturbed patients from large state hospitals to small community mental health centers; at the same time there has been a pronounced decline in the number of psychiatric inpatients. One factor in this shift has been the discovery of drugs capable of altering acute psychotic behavior and severe depression. Another has been the development of a treatment method called the therapeutic community. In "The Therapeutic Community" Richard Almond describes the use of this method at the Yale-New Haven Hospital. A key element of the method is a close relationship between staff and patients; the attempt to maintain a sense of patient-staff community is unique to the approach. When combined with various forms of psychotherapy, the therapeutic community has proved to be effective, and offers an interesting prototype against which to judge various proposals for social change.

In the last article in this section, "Behavioral Psychotherapy," Albert Bandura describes one of the most recent psychotherapeutic methods for treating behavior disorders. This method departs from the more traditional approaches to psychotherapy, which are concerned primarily with helping the patient attain insight into the origins of his problems. Behavioral therapy attempts to apply the psychological principles of learning to the treatment of behavior disorders. In treating autistic children, for example, behavioral therapists reinforce desired behavior with either attention or food rewards, and ignore (or even punish) undesirable behavior. Operant conditioning techniques (see the introduction to Section III) have proved effective in substituting desirable for undesirable behavior. The main thesis of those who practice behavioral therapy is that behavior that departs from accepted social norms should not be viewed as a disease but as the way a person has learned to cope with environment demands. Treatment is thus a problem of teaching new "social learning," rather than delving into the psychological traumas of childhood.

The Origin of Personality

by Alexander Thomas, Stella Chess, and Herbert G. Birch
August 1970

*Children differ in temperament from birth. What is the
nature of these temperamental differences, and how do
they interact with environmental influences in the
formation of personality?*

Mothers, nurses and pediatricians are well aware that infants begin to express themselves as individuals from the time of birth. The fact that each child appears to have a characteristic temperament from his earliest days has also been suggested by Sigmund Freud and Arnold Gesell. In recent years, however, many psychiatrists and psychologists appear to have lost sight of this fact. Instead they have tended to emphasize the influence of the child's early environment when discussing the origin of the human personality.

As physicians who have had frequent occasion to examine the family background of disturbed children, we began many years ago to encounter reasons to question the prevailing one-sided emphasis on environment. We found that some children with severe psychological problems had a family upbringing that did not differ essentially from the environment of other children who developed no severe problems. On the other hand, some children were found to be free of serious personality disturbances although they had experienced severe family disorganization and poor parental care. Even in cases where parental mishandling was obviously responsible for a child's personality difficulties there was no consistent or predictable relation between the parents' treatment and the child's specific symptoms. Domineering, authoritarian handling by the parents might make one youngster anxious and submissive and another defiant and antagonistic. Such unpredictability seemed to be the direct consequence of omitting an important factor from the evaluation: the child's own temperament, that is, his own individual style of responding to the environment.

It might be inferred from these opinions that we reject the environmentalist tendency to emphasize the role of the child's surroundings and the influence of his parents (particularly the mother) as major factors in the formation of personality, and that instead we favor the constitutionalist concept of personality's being largely inborn. Actually we reject both the "nurture" and the "nature" concepts. Either by itself is too simplistic to account for the intricate play of forces that form the human character. It is our hypothesis that the personality is shaped by the constant interplay of temperament and environment.

We decided to test this concept by conducting a systematic long-term investigation of the differences in the behavioral reactions of infants. The study would be designed to determine whether or not these differences persist through childhood, and it would focus on how a child's behavioral traits interact with specific elements of his environment. Apart from satisfying scientific curiosity, answers to these questions would help parents and teachers—and psychiatrists —to promote healthy personality development.

After much preliminary exploration we developed techniques for gathering and analyzing information about individual differences in behavioral characteristics in the first few months of life, for categorizing such differences and for identifying individuality at each stage of a child's life. This technique consisted in obtaining detailed descriptions of children's behavior through structured interviews with their parents at regular intervals beginning when the child had reached an age of two to three months. Independent checks by trained observers established that the descriptions of the children's behavior supplied by the parents in these interviews could be accepted as reliable and significant.

Analyzing the data, we identified nine characteristics that could be reliably scored on a three-point scale (medium, high and low): (1) the level and extent of motor activity; (2) the rhythmicity, or degree of regularity, of functions such as eating, elimination and the cycle of sleeping and wakefulness; (3) the response to a new object or person, in terms of whether the child accepts the new experience or withdraws from it; (4) the adaptability of behavior to changes in the environment; (5) the threshold, or sensitivity, to stimuli; (6) the intensity, or energy level, of responses; (7) the child's general mood or "disposition," whether cheerful or given to crying, pleasant or cranky, friendly or unfriendly; (8) the degree of the child's distractibility from what he is doing; (9) the span of the child's attention and his persistence in an activity.

The set of ratings in these nine characteristics defines the temperament, or behavioral profile, of a child, and the profile is discernible even as early as the age of two or three months. We found that the nine qualities could be identified and rated in a wide diversity of population samples we studied: middle-class children, children of working-class Puerto Ricans, mentally retarded children, children born prematurely and children with congenital rubella ("German measles"). Other investigators in the U.S. and abroad have identified the same set of characteristics in children.

Equipped with this means of collecting and analyzing the required data on individual children through standard interviews with their parents, we proceeded to our long-term study of the development of a large group of children. We obtained the willing collaboration of 85 families, with a total of 141 children, who agreed to allow us to follow their children's development from birth over a period of years that by now extends to

HALLIE, a six-month-old experimental subject, is shown in motion picture taken during an observation session. In frames beginning at top left and running downward she pulls at rings hanging above her crib and repeatedly pushes away stuffed animal. She demonstrates a high level of concentration and persistence by rejecting animal each time it is given and continuing to play with the rings.

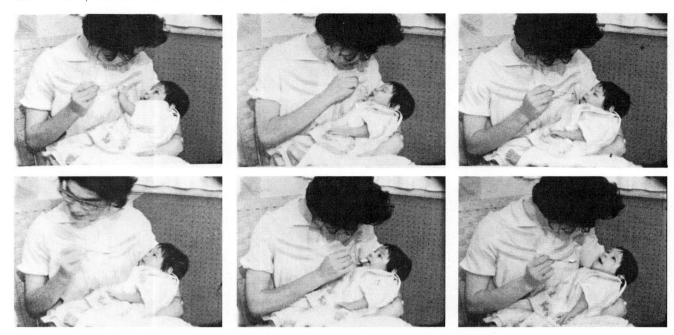

POSITIVE RESPONSE is displayed by Hallie when she was three months old as she is fed a new food, Cream of Wheat, for the first time. When her mother presents her with a spoonful of the food, she accepts it eagerly, swallows it and unhesitatingly accepts more.

more than a decade. Our parents have cooperated magnificently in all the interviews and tests, and in the 14 years since the study was started only four families (with five children) have dropped out. In order to avoid complicating the study by having to consider a diversity of socioeconomic influences we confined the study to a homogeneous group, consisting mainly of highly educated families in the professions and business occupations.

We have observed the children's development throughout their preschool period and their years in nursery and elementary school. Their parents have been interviewed at frequent intervals, so that descriptions of the children's behavior have been obtained while the parents' memory of it was still fresh. The interviews have focused on factual details of how the children behaved in specific situations, avoiding subjective interpretations as much as possible. We have supplemented the parental interviews with direct observation and with information obtained from the children's teachers. The children have also been examined with various psychological tests. Youngsters who have shown evidence of behavioral disturbances have received a complete psychiatric examination. The detailed behavioral data collected on all the children have been analyzed both in statistical and in descriptive terms.

Our preliminary exploration had already answered our first question: Children do show distinct individuality in temperament in the first weeks of life, independently of their parents' handling or personality style. Our long-term study has now established that the original characteristics of temperament tend to persist in most children over the years. This is clearly illustrated by two striking examples. Donald exhibited an extremely high activity level almost from birth. At three months, his parents reported, he wriggled and moved about a great deal while asleep in his crib. At six months he "swam like a fish" while being bathed. At 12 months he still squirmed constantly while he was being dressed or washed. At 15 months he was "very fast and busy"; his parents found themselves "always chasing after him." At two years he was "constantly in motion, jumping and climbing." At three he would "climb like a monkey and run like an unleashed puppy." In kindergarten his teacher reported humorously that he would "hang from the walls and climb on the ceiling." By the time he was seven Donald was encountering difficulty in school because he was unable to sit still long enough to learn anything and disturbed the other children by moving rapidly about the classroom.

Clem exemplifies a child who scored high in intensity of reaction. At four and a half months he screamed every time he was bathed, according to his parents' report. His reactions were "not discriminating—all or none." At six months during feeding he screamed "at the sight of the spoon approaching his mouth." At nine and a half months he was generally "either in a very good mood, laughing or chuckling," or else screaming. "He laughed so hard playing peekaboo he got hiccups." At two years his parents reported: "He screams bloody murder when he's being dressed." At seven they related: "When he's frustrated, as for example when he doesn't hit a ball very far, he stomps around, his voice goes up to its highest level, his eyes get red and occasionally fill with tears. Once he went up to his room when this occurred and screamed for half an hour."

Of course a child's temperament is not immutable. In the course of his development the environmental circumstances may heighten, diminish or otherwise modify his reactions and behavior. For example, behavior may become routinized in various areas so that the basic temperamental characteristics are no longer evident in these situations. Most children come to accept and even take pleasure in the bath, whatever their initial reactions may have been. The characteristics usually remain present, however, and may assert themselves in new situations even in the form of an unexpected and mystifying reaction. An illustration is the case of a 10-year-old girl who had been well adjusted to school. Entering the fifth grade, Grace was transferred from a small school to a large new one that was strongly departmentalized and much more formal. The change threw her into a state of acute fear and worry. Her parents were

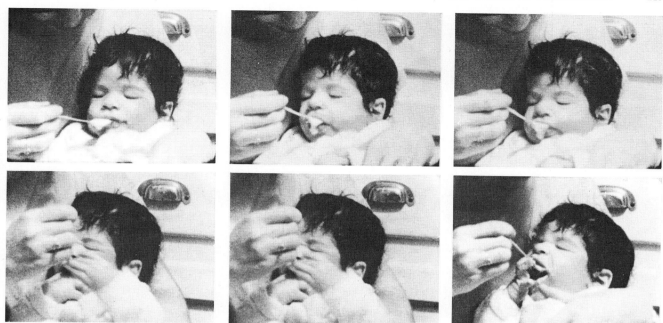

NEGATIVE RESPONSE is demonstrated by Hallie's younger brother, Russ, during his first exposure to a cereal at three months of age. He refuses to swallow the new food, spits it out, pushes the spoon away, grimaces and tilts his head away from the spoon.

puzzled, because Grace had many friends and had been doing very well in her studies. On reviewing her history, however, we found that she had shown withdrawal reactions to new situations during infancy and also on entrance into kindergarten and the first and second grades. Her parents and Grace had forgotten about these early reactions, because from the third grade on she was entirely happy in school. In the light of the early history it now became apparent that Grace's fear at the transfer to the new school, confronting her with a new scholastic setup, new fellow-students and a new level of academic demand, arose from her fundamental tendency to withdraw from new situations and to be slow to adapt to them.

Not all the children in our study have shown a basic constancy of temperament. In some there have apparently been changes in certain characteristics as time has passed. We are analyzing the data in these cases to try to determine if changes in the children's life situations or in specific stresses are responsible for the apparent fluctuations in temperament. We may find that inconsistency in temperament is itself a basic characteristic in some children.

When we analyzed the behavioral profiles of the children in an endeavor to find correlations among the nine individual attributes, we found that certain characteristics did cluster together. The clusters defined three general types of temperament (although some of the children did not fit into any of the three).

One type is characterized by positiveness in mood, regularity in bodily functions, a low or moderate intensity of reaction, adaptability and a positive approach to, rather than withdrawal from, new situations. In infancy these children quickly establish regular sleeping and feeding schedules, are generally cheerful and adapt quickly to new routines, new foods and new people. As they grow older they learn the rules of new games quickly, participate readily in new activities and adapt easily to school. We named this group the "easy children," because they present so few problems in care and training. Approximately 40 percent of the children in our total sample could be placed in this category.

In contrast, we found another constellation of characteristics that described "difficult children." These children are irregular in bodily functions, are usually intense in their reactions, tend to withdraw in the face of new stimuli, are slow to adapt to changes in the environment and are generally negative in mood. As infants they are often irregular in feeding and sleeping, are slow to accept new foods, take a long time to adjust to new routines or activities and tend to cry a great deal. Their crying and their laughter are characteristically loud. Frustration usually sends them into a violent tantrum. These children are, of course, a trial to their parents and require a high degree of consistency and tolerance in their up-

bringing. They comprised about 10 percent of the children in our sample.

The third type of temperament is displayed by those children we call "slow to warm up." They typically have a low activity level, tend to withdraw on their first exposure to new stimuli, are slow to adapt, are somewhat negative in mood and respond to situations with a low intensity of reaction. They made up 15 percent of the population sample we studied. Hence 65 percent of the children could be described as belonging to one or another of the three categories we were able to define; the rest had mixtures of traits that did not add up to a general characterization.

Among the 141 children comprising our total sample, 42 presented behavioral problems that called for psychiatric attention. Not surprisingly, the group of "difficult children" accounted for the largest proportion of these cases, the "slow to warm up children" for the next-largest proportion and the "easy children" for the smallest proportion. About 70 percent of the "difficult children" developed behavioral problems, whereas only 18 percent of the "easy children" did so.

In general easy children respond favorably to various child-rearing styles. Under certain conditions, however, their ready adaptability to parental handling may itself lead to the development of a behavioral problem. Having adapted readily to the parents' standards and expectations early in life, the child on moving into the world of his peers and

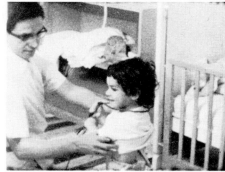

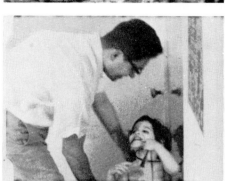

TWO YEARS OLD, Hallie plays with her father as he tries to change her clothes. He gets shirt off after struggling to lift it over her head, but she holds on with cord. She runs away, provoking chase, and tries to escape as he buttons her shirt. Hallie displays

school may find that the demands of these environments conflict sharply with the behavior patterns he has learned at home. If the conflict between the two sets of demands is severe, the child may be unable to make an adaptation that reconciles the double standard.

The possible results of such a dissonance are illustrated in the case of an "easy child" we shall call Isobel. Reared by parents who placed great value on individuality, imagination and self-expression, she developed these qualities to a high degree. When she entered school, however, her work fell far below her intellectual capabilities. She had difficulties not only in learning but also in making friends. It was found that the problems arose from her resistance to taking instruction from her teacher and to accepting her schoolmates' preferences in play. Once the nature of the conflict was recognized it was easily remedied in this case. We advised the parents to combine their encouragement of Isobel's assertions of individuality with efforts to teach her how to join constructively in activities with her teacher and schoolmates. The parents adopted this strategy, and within six months Isobel began to function well in school life.

In the case of difficult children the handling problem is present from the outset. The parents must cope with the child's irregularity and the slowness with which he adapts in order to establish conformity to the family's rules of living. If the parents are inconsistent, impatient or punitive in their handling of the child, he is much more likely to react negatively than other children are. Only by exceptionally objective, consistent treatment, taking full account of the child's temperament, can he be brought to get along easily with others and to learn appropriate behavior. This may take a long time, but with skillful handling such children do learn the rules and function well. The essential requirement is that the parents recognize the need for unusually painstaking handling; tactics that

work well with other children may fail for the difficult child.

For children in the "slow to warm up" category the key to successful development is allowing the child to adapt to the environment at his own pace. If the teacher or parents of such a child pressure him to move quickly into new situations, the insistence is likely to intensify his natural tendency to withdraw. On the other hand, he does need encouragement and opportunity to try new experiences. Bobby was a case in point. His parents never encouraged him to participate in anything new; they simply withdrew things he did not like. When, as an infant, he rejected a new food by letting it

TYPE OF CHILD	ACTIVITY LEVEL	RHYTHMICITY	DISTRACTIBILIT
	The proportion of active periods to inactive ones.	Regularity of hunger, excretion, sleep and wakefulness.	The degree to which extraneous stimuli a behavior.
"EASY"	VARIES	VERY REGULAR	VARIES
"SLOW TO WARM UP"	LOW TO MODERATE	VARIES	VARIES
"DIFFICULT"	VARIES	IRREGULAR	VARIES

TEMPERAMENT of a child allows him to be classified as "easy," "slow to warm up" or "difficult" according to how he rates in certain key categories in the authors' nine-point

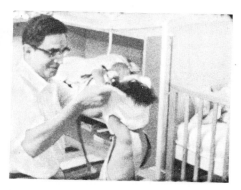

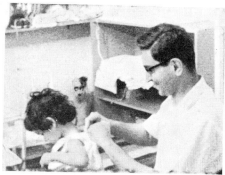

many temperamental characteristics such as intensity, positive mood and high activity.

dribble out of his mouth, they eliminated it from his diet. When he backed away from other children in the playground, they kept him at home. By the age of 10 Bobby was living on a diet consisting mainly of hamburgers, applesauce and medium-boiled eggs, and in play he was a "loner." Any activity that required exposure to new people or new demands was distasteful or even impossible for him. Yet he was adept and took pleasure in activities he could pursue by himself and at his own speed.

In general our studies indicate that a demand that conflicts excessively with any temperamental characteristics and

capacities is likely to place a child under heavy and even unbearable stress. This means that parents and teachers need to recognize what a specific child can and cannot do. A child with a high activity level, for example, should not be required to sit still through an eight-hour automobile trip; frequent stops should be made to allow him to run around and give vent to his energy. A persistent child who does not like to be distracted from a project should not be expected to come running when he is called unless he has been told in advance how much time he will have before he is called.

Obviously a detailed knowledge of a child's temperamental characteristics can be of great help to parents in handling the child and avoiding the development of behavioral problems. A highly adaptable child can be expected to accept new foods without resistance and even welcome them. On the other hand, a nonadaptable, intense child may need to have the same food offered at each meal for several days until he comes to accept it; if the mother takes away a rejected food, tries it again some weeks later and again retreats in the face of protests, the child simply learns that by fussing enough he will have his way. An adaptable child who is caught sticking things into electric sockets may need only one lecture on the danger to give up this practice; an easily distractible child may merely need to have his attention diverted to some other activity; a persistent child may have to be removed bodily from the hazard.

Understanding a child's temperament is equally crucial in the school situation. His temperamental traits affect both his approach to a learning task and the way he interacts with his teacher and classmates. If the school's demands on him go against the grain of these traits, learning may be difficult indeed. Hence the teacher has a need to know not only the

child's capacities for learning but also his temperamental style.

A pupil who wriggles about a great deal, plays continually with his pencils and other objects and involves himself in activities with the student next to him—in short, a child with a high activity level—obviously requires special handling. If the teacher decides the child does not want to learn and treats him accordingly, the youngster is apt to conclude that he is stupid or unlikable and react with even worse behavior. The teacher is best advised to avoid expressions of annoyance and to provide the child with constructive channels for his energy, such as running necessary errands, cleaning the blackboard and so on. Similarly, a "slow to warm up" child requires patience, encouragement and repeated exposure to a learning task until he becomes familiar with it and comfortable in attacking it. Children with the "difficult" constellation of traits of course present the most taxing problem. They respond poorly to a permissive, *laissez faire* attitude in the teacher and angrily to learning tasks they cannot master immediately. The teacher needs to be firm and patient; once the child has been tided over the period (which may be long) of learning rules or becoming familiar with a new task, he will function well and confidently. *Laissez faire* treatment is also detrimental for youngsters who are low in persistence and easily distracted from their work. Such a child will do poorly if few demands are made and little achievement is expected of him. He must be required to function up to his abilities.

The paramount conclusion from our studies is that the debate over the relative importance of nature and nurture only confuses the issue. What is important is the interaction between the two—between the child's own character-

APPROACH `HDRAWAL	ADAPTABILITY	ATTENTION SPAN AND PERSISTENCE	INTENSITY OF REACTION	THRESHOLD OF RESPONSIVENESS	QUALITY OF MOOD
esponse to a new t or person.	The ease with which a child adapts to changes in his environment.	The amount of time devoted to an activity, and the effect of distraction on the activity.	The energy of response, regardless of its quality or direction.	The intensity of stimulation required to evoke a discernible response.	The amount of friendly, pleasant, joyful behavior as contrasted with unpleasant, unfriendly behavior.
VE APPROACH	VERY ADAPTABLE	HIGH OR LOW	LOW OR MILD	HIGH OR LOW	POSITIVE
WITHDRAWAL	SLOWLY ADAPTABLE	HIGH OR LOW	MILD	HIGH OR LOW	SLIGHTLY NEGATIVE
HDRAWAL	SLOWLY ADAPTABLE	HIGH OR LOW	INTENSE	HIGH OR LOW	NEGATIVE

personality index (*color*). The categories are only a general guide to temperament. Of the 141 subjects 65 percent could be categorized, but 35 percent displayed a mixture of traits. Such a child might, for example, be rated "easy" in some ways and "difficult" in others.

TEMPERAMENTAL QUALITY	RATING	2 MONTHS	6 MONTHS
ACTIVITY LEVEL	HIGH	Moves often in sleep. Wriggles when diaper is changed.	Tries to stand in tub and splashes. Bounces in crib. Crawls after dog.
	LOW	Does not move when being dressed or during sleep.	Passive in bath. Plays quietly in crib and falls asleep.
RHYTHMICITY	REGULAR	Has been on four-hour feeding schedule since birth. Regular bowel movement.	Is asleep at 6:30 every night. Awakes 7:00 A.M. Food intake is constant.
	IRREGULAR	Awakes at a different time each morning. Size of feedings varies.	Length of nap varies; so does food intake.
DISTRACTIBILITY	DISTRACTIBLE	Will stop crying for food if rocked. Stops fussing if given pacifier when diaper is being changed.	Stops crying when mother sings. W remain still while clothing is change given a toy.
	NOT DISTRACTIBLE	Will not stop crying when diaper is changed. Fusses after eating, even if rocked.	Stops crying only after dressing is finished. Cries until given bottle.
APPROACH/WITHDRAWAL	POSITIVE	Smiles and licks washcloth. Has always liked bottle.	Likes new foods. Enjoyed first bath i a large tub. Smiles and gurgles.
	NEGATIVE	Rejected cereal the first time. Cries when strangers appear.	Smiles and babbles at strangers. Pl with new toys immediately.
ADAPTABILITY	ADAPTIVE	Was passive during first bath; now enjoys bathing. Smiles at nurse.	Used to dislike new foods; now acc them well.
	NOT ADAPTIVE	Still startled by sudden, sharp noise. Resists diapering.	Does not cooperate with dressing. Fusses and cries when left with sitte
ATTENTION SPAN AND PERSISTENCE	LONG	If soiled, continues to cry until changed. Repeatedly rejects water if he wants milk.	Watches toy mobile over crib intent "Coos" frequently.
	SHORT	Cries when awakened but stops almost immediately. Objects only mildly if cereal precedes bottle.	Sucks pacifier for only a few minute and spits it out.
INTENSITY OF REACTION	INTENSE	Cries when diapers are wet. Rejects food vigorously when satisfied.	Cries loudly at the sound of thunder Makes sucking movements when vitamins are administered.
	MILD	Does not cry when diapers are wet. Whimpers instead of crying when hungry.	Does not kick often in tub. Does not smile. Screams and kicks when tem perature is taken.
THRESHOLD OF RESPONSIVENESS	LOW	Stops sucking on bottle when approached.	Refuses fruit he likes when vitamins are added. Hides head from bright l
	HIGH	Is not startled by loud noises. Takes bottle and breast equally well.	Eats everything. Does not object to diapers being wet or soiled.
QUALITY OF MOOD	POSITIVE	Smacks lips when first tasting new food. Smiles at parents.	Plays and splashes in bath. Smiles a everyone.
	NEGATIVE	Fusses after nursing. Cries when carriage is rocked.	Cries when taken from tub. Cries wh given food she does not like.

BEHAVIOR of a child reveals that he has a distinct temperament early in life. These reports taken from interviews with the parents of the children studied by the authors show that temperamental differences are apparent when a child is only two months old. As a child grows his temperament tends to remain constant in quality: if he wriggles while his diaper is being changed at two months,

istics and his environment. If the two influences are harmonized, one can expect healthy development of the child; if they are dissonant, behavioral problems are almost sure to ensue.

It follows that the pediatrician who undertakes to supervise the care of a newborn child should familiarize himself with his young patient's temperamental as well as physical characteristics. He will then be able to provide the parents with appropriate advice on weaning, toilet training and the handling of other needs as the child develops. Similarly, if a behavioral disorder arises, the psychiatrist will need to understand both the child's temperament and the environmental demands in conflict with it in order to find a helpful course of action. His function then will often be to guide rather than "treat" the parents.

1 YEAR	2 YEARS	5 YEARS	10 YEARS
...alks rapidly. Eats eagerly. Climbs into ...erything.	Climbs furniture. Explores. Gets in and out of bed while being put to sleep.	Leaves table often during meals. Always runs.	Plays ball and engages in other sports. Cannot sit still long enough to do homework.
...nishes bottle slowly. Goes to sleep ...sily. Allows nail-cutting without ...ssing.	Enjoys quiet play with puzzles. Can listen to records for hours.	Takes a long time to dress. Sits quietly on long automobile rides.	Likes chess and reading. Eats very slowly.
...aps after lunch each day. Always ...inks bottle before bed.	Eats a big lunch each day. Always has a snack before bedtime.	Falls asleep when put to bed. Bowel movement regular.	Eats only at mealtimes. Sleeps the same amount of time each night.
...ll not fall asleep for an hour or more. ...oves bowels at a different time each ...y.	Nap time changes from day to day. Toilet training is difficult because bowel movement is unpredictable.	Food intake varies; so does time of bowel movement.	Food intake varies. Falls asleep at a different time each night.
...ies when face is washed unless it is ...ade into a game.	Will stop tantrum if another activity is suggested.	Can be coaxed out of forbidden activity by being led into something else.	Needs absolute silence for homework. Has a hard time choosing a shirt in a store because they all appeal to him.
...es when toy is taken away and ...ects substitute.	Screams if refused some desired object. Ignores mother's calling.	Seems not to hear if involved in favorite activity. Cries for a long time when hurt.	Can read a book while television set is at high volume. Does chores on schedule.
...pproaches strangers readily. Sleeps ...ell in new surroundings.	Slept well the first time he stayed overnight at grandparents' house.	Entered school building unhesitatingly. Tries new foods.	Went to camp happily. Loved to ski the first time.
...ffened when placed on sled. Will not ...ep in strange beds.	Avoids strange children in the playground. Whimpers first time at beach. Will not go into water.	Hid behind mother when entering school.	Severely homesick at camp during first days. Does not like new activities.
...as afraid of toy animals at first; now ...ays with them happily.	Obeys quickly. Stayed contentedly with grandparents for a week.	Hesitated to go to nursery school at first; now goes eagerly. Slept well on camping trip.	Likes camp, although homesick during first days. Learns enthusiastically.
...ntinues to reject new foods each ...e they are offered.	Cries and screams each time hair is cut. Disobeys persistently.	Has to be hand led into classroom each day. Bounces on bed in spite of spankings.	Does not adjust well to new school or new teacher; comes home late for dinner even when punished.
...ays by self in playpen for more than ...hour. Listens to singing for long ...riods.	Works on a puzzle until it is completed. Watches when shown how to do something.	Practiced riding a two-wheeled bicycle for hours until he mastered it. Spent over an hour reading a book.	Reads for two hours before sleeping. Does homework carefully.
...es interest in a toy after a few ...utes. Gives up easily if she falls ...ile attempting to walk.	Gives up easily if a toy is hard to use. Asks for help immediately if undressing becomes difficult.	Still cannot tie his shoes because he gives up when he is not successful. Fidgets when parents read to him.	Gets up frequently from homework for a snack. Never finishes a book.
...ghs hard when father plays roughly. ...eamed and kicked when temperature ...taken.	Yells if he feels excitement or delight. Cries loudly if a toy is taken away.	Rushes to greet father. Gets hiccups from laughing hard.	Tears up an entire page of homework if one mistake is made. Slams door of room when teased by younger brother.
...es not fuss much when clothing is ...led on over head.	When another child hit her, she looked surprised, did not hit back.	Drops eyes and remains silent when given a firm parental "No." Does not laugh much.	When a mistake is made in a model airplane, corrects it quietly. Does not comment when reprimanded.
...ts out food he does not like. Giggles ...en tickled.	Runs to door when father comes home. Must always be tucked tightly into bed.	Always notices when mother puts new dress on for first time. Refuses milk if it is not ice-cold.	Rejects fatty foods. Adjusts shower until water is at exactly the right temperature.
...s food he likes even if mixed with ...liked food. Can be left easily with ...angers.	Can be left with anyone. Falls to sleep easily on either back or stomach.	Does not hear loud, sudden noises when reading. Does not object to injections.	Never complains when sick. Eats all foods.
...s bottle; reaches for it and smiles. ...ghs loudly when playing peekaboo.	Plays with sister; laughs and giggles. Smiles when he succeeds in putting shoes on.	Laughs loudly while watching television cartoons. Smiles at everyone.	Enjoys new accomplishments. Laughs when reading a funny passage aloud.
...s when given injections. Cries when ...alone.	Cries and squirms when given haircut. Cries when mother leaves.	Objects to putting boots on. Cries when frustrated.	Cries when he cannot solve a homework problem. Very "weepy" if he does not get enough sleep.

his high activity level is likely to be expressed at one year through eager eating and a tendency "to climb into everything." A five-year-old child who behaved quietly in infancy may dress slowly and be able to sit quietly and happily during long automobile rides. Color indicates those temperamental characteristics that are crucial to classifying a child as "easy," "slow to warm up" and "difficult."

Most parents, once they are informed of the facts, can change their handling to achieve a healthier interaction with the child.

Theory and practice in psychiatry must take into full account the individual and his uniqueness: how children differ and how these differences act to influence their psychological growth. A given environment will not have the identical functional meaning for all children. Much will depend on the temperamental makeup of the child. As we learn more about how specific parental attitudes and practices and other specific factors in the environment of the child interact with specific temperamental, mental and physical attributes of individual children, it should become considerably easier to foster the child's healthy development.

25 Studies in Self-Esteem

by Stanley Coopersmith
February 1968

The opinion an individual has of himself is clearly an important component of his behavior. How this component is shaped and how it influences personal conduct is investigated in a group of boys

One of the more significant concerns of modern society is how to produce competent and self-respecting citizens. Faced with conditions of poverty, increasing expectations and changing values, the public has turned to psychologists and other behavioral scientists for guidance. The question is no longer how to avoid maladjustment and insecurity but rather how to generate those capacities that enable an individual to function effectively in his private, personal and public activities. This emphasis on the constructive aspects of personality marks a change from the traditional ways of thinking about mental and behavioral disorders. Whereas earlier theories focused on difficulties that were already present and sought to determine how they arose, current efforts are concerned with the processes by which healthy and effective individuals develop. This "approach to health" orientation rather than the "avoidance of illness" one is consistent with views in the modern medical sciences. According to such views procedures that develop the resistance of the organism are far preferable to attempts to treat symptoms after they have arisen. It is much more sensible, for example, to immunize the population against poliomyelitis or smallpox than to try to treat the ravages produced by these infections.

Applying the same reasoning to the problem of psychological health, we should devote more attention to finding specific ways to build up the constructive capacities of human personality so that it can deal effectively with the stresses to which it will inevitably be subjected and can eliminate those conditions that have destructive consequences. The strategy of strengthening the organism is the same for psychology as it is for medicine, with the major difference that psychology focuses on the acquisition of socially learned capacities and skills rather than taking physiological measures.

This requires first of all that we identify more specifically than has been done in the past just what those constructive resources and potentialities are. We also need more detailed and accurate knowledge of what kinds of experience are necessary for the development of competent and effective behavior and feelings of inner comfort and acceptance. The main requirements for such development are rather obvious. They include expectations of success (hope), motivation to achieve, initiative and the ability to deal with anxiety. Probably the most important requirement for effective behavior, central to the whole problem, is self-esteem.

Philosophers from time immemorial have recognized that the feeling of personal worth plays a crucial role in human happiness and effectiveness. Only recently, however, have self-esteem and its effects received systematic study. Among the first modern thinkers to write on this subject, early in this century, were the psychologist William James, the philosopher George H. Mead and the psychologist Alfred Adler. The last, of course, founded his system of diagnosis and treatment on the negative aspect of this theme: that feelings of inferiority and inadequacy underlie many neurotic disturbances.

James shrewdly observed: "A man... with powers that have uniformly brought him success with place and wealth and friends and fame, is not likely to be visited by the morbid diffidences and doubts about himself which he had when he was a boy, whereas he who has made one blunder after another and still lies in middle life among the failures at the foot of the hill is liable to grow all sick-lied o'er with self-distrust, and to shrink from trials with which his powers can really cope."

Although the importance of self-esteem in influencing behavior is widely appreciated, most of the ideas and evidence on the subject remain rather vague and intuitive. Clinicians are well aware in a general way that many of the disturbed patients who come to them for treatment feel themselves to be incompetent and socially rejected. It is universally recognized that self-confidence and an optimistic assessment of one's abilities contribute markedly to business success and the formation of friendships. There is also a popular belief, less firmly based, that the development of self-esteem depends on physical attractiveness, ability, social status and material welfare.

Objective and scientifically organized research is now beginning to produce a body of tested information on the subject. Over the past eight years a group of us, working with the support of the National Institute of Mental Health first at Wesleyan University and then at the University of California at Davis, have conducted a series of studies of self-esteem, applying the techniques of modern clinical, laboratory and field investigation. The social scientists involved in these studies were Betty James Beardslee, David G. Lowy, Alice L. Coopersmith and myself. Our subjects were a representative sample of normal boys whom we followed from preadolescence to early adulthood. Starting with thorough examinations of their self-esteem (as indicated by various criteria) and their abilities, personality traits, attitudes, behavior and family background, we later observed how they fared in dealing with school, job and social demands as they grew up.

BEANBAG EXPERIMENT was designed to explore the relation between a subject's level of self-esteem (as determined from other tests) and the level of the goals he sets for himself. A higher score could be won by tossing the beanbag into a more distant target.

THE CHOICE of which target he would shoot for had to be made by the boy before he proceeded to aim and toss. He could try for a safe shot but one that would win him a low score or he could aspire to achieving a high goal, although one with more risk attached to it.

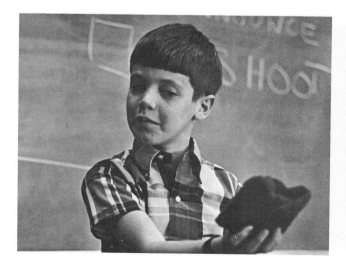

THE SHOT followed the boy's announcement of the target he had selected. All the boys who participated in the experiment agreed as to what the ideal score would be but those with high self-esteem displayed greater assurance that they could actually achieve the ideal.

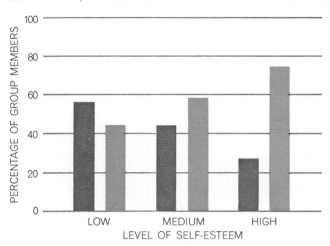

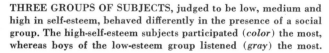

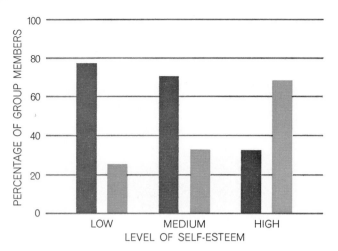

THREE GROUPS OF SUBJECTS, judged to be low, medium and high in self-esteem, behaved differently in the presence of a social group. The high-self-esteem subjects participated (*color*) the most, whereas boys of the low-esteem group listened (*gray*) the most.

AVOIDANCE OF DISAGREEMENT during a discussion was displayed oftener by boys of the medium- and low-esteem groups. In contrast to the high-level group, they tended to withdraw from argument (*gray*) rather than express an independent opinion (*color*).

The subjects—middle-class, urban boys aged 10 to 12—were normal in the sense that they had no pathological personality disturbances and came from intact families. Our first problem was to obtain reliable measures of their levels of self-esteem. Since one's own evaluation of his self-esteem may be far from accurate, we resorted to two additional indexes. One was the teachers' report on those aspects of each boy's behavior—such as relative self-assurance or timidity and reactions to failures and criticism—that presumably reflected the boy's level of self-esteem. For the other index we employed psychological tests (the Rorschach and the thematic apperception test) that indicate a person's unconscious self-evaluation. We found that in more than 80 percent of the cases the ratings by these indexes were substantially in accord with the boy's own estimate of his self-esteem.

After determining the individual boys' levels of self-esteem and rating them according to three categories—high, medium or low in self-esteem—our investigations proceeded along three lines. These were (1) laboratory tests of the subjects' memory, perception, level of aspiration, conformity and responses to stress; (2) clinical tests and interviews designed to show their levels of ability, personality traits, attitudes, insights and styles of response; (3) studies, including interviews with their parents, that looked into factors of upbringing or experience that might be related to each boy's self-esteem.

From these items of information we were able to draw a fairly detailed picture of the formative influences and personal characteristics associated with

each level of self-esteem. I shall describe them at the three levels, but since we were primarily concerned with identifying the constructive aspects of psychological health our main interest was in the high-self-esteem group, and the following descriptions are largely in terms of comparison with that group.

We found, not very surprisingly, that youngsters with a high degree of self-esteem are active, expressive individuals who tend to be successful both academically and socially. They lead rather than merely listen in discussions, are eager to express opinions, do not sidestep disagreement, are not particularly sensitive to criticism, are highly interested in public affairs, showed little destructiveness in early childhood and are little troubled by feelings of anxiety [*see illustrations above and on page 223*]. They appear to trust their own perceptions and reactions and have confidence that their efforts will meet with success. They approach other persons with the expectation that they will be well received. Their general optimism stems not from fantasies but rather from a well-founded assessment of their abilities, social skills and personal qualities. They are not self-conscious or preoccupied with personal difficulties. They are much less frequently afflicted with psychosomatic troubles—such as insomnia, fatigue, headaches, intestinal upset—than are persons of low self-esteem. (This immunity of people with high self-esteem has also been observed in adults by Morris Rosenberg of the National Institute of Mental Health, who reported on a hospital study of normal patients.)

The boys in our group who were char-

acterized by a medium level of self-esteem were similar to high-esteem subjects in most qualities of behavior and attitudes. They tended, for example, to be optimistic, expressive and able to take criticism. In certain respects, however, they were distinctly different from both the high-esteem and the low-esteem subjects. They showed the strongest tendency to support of the middle-class value system and compliance with its norms and demands. They were also the most uncertain in their self-ratings of their personal worth and tended to be particularly dependent on social acceptance. The dependent attitude of the medium-self-esteem subjects and their behavior gave evidence that uncertainty about one's worth should not be confused with low self-esteem; the consequences are markedly different. Whereas persons with low self-esteem, convinced of their inferiority, are fearful of social encounters, persons who are unsure of their worth tend to be active in seeking social approval and experiences that will lead to enhancement of their self-evaluation.

In contrast, the boys with low self-esteem presented a picture of discouragement and depression. They felt isolated, unlovable, incapable of expressing or defending themselves and too weak to confront or overcome their deficiencies. They were fearful of angering others and shrank from exposing themselves to notice in any way. In the presence of a social group, at school or elsewhere, they remained in the shadows, listening rather than participating, sensitive to criticism, self-conscious, preoccupied with inner problems. This dwelling on their own difficulties not only intensified their feelings of malaise but also isolated them from opportunities for the friendly relationships such persons need for support.

By examining our subjects' styles of expression, in drawings and other creative products, we obtained further insight into the effects of the various levels of self-esteem. The boys with high self-esteem were consistently freer and more original in creativity than those with lower levels of self-confidence [see illustration on next page]. Their drawings were characterized by activity, humor and sensitivity to details of costume, attitude and behavior. The drawings by boys of medium self-esteem were more restrained and static; for example, their pictures of the bearded figure (apparently a popular contemporary subject for youngsters) were less vigorous and less complex than those of the high-self-esteem group. The boys with low self-esteem clearly showed their lack of confidence by drawing small, constrained and distorted figures. In general the figures drawn by the three categories of subjects revealed distinct differences in their perceptions of themselves and other people.

Our exploration of the factors that lead to the development of high self-esteem produced a number of surprises, or at least contradictions of popular clichés. Let me first list the factors we found to have little or nothing to do with self-esteem in our sample of subjects. We found no consistent relation between self-esteem and physical attractiveness, height, the size of the boy's family, early trauma, breast- or bottle-feeding in infancy or the mother's principal occupation (that is, whether she spent her time at home as a housewife or went out to work). Even more surprising, our subjects' self-esteem depended only weakly, if at all, on family social position or income level. Studies by other investigators confirm that what we observed in our boys is also true of adults: the proportion of individuals with high self-esteem is almost as high in low social classes as it is in the higher classes. Our subjects tended to gauge their individual worth primarily by their achievements and treatment in their own interpersonal environment rather than by more general and abstract norms of success. It appears that we should reexamine the common definition of success: probably most persons define success for themselves not in terms of some external, abstract standard but in the more direct terms of their day-to-day personal relationships.

Looking into the backgrounds of the boys who possess high self-esteem, we were struck first and foremost by the

close relationships that existed between these boys and their parents. The parents' love was not necessarily expressed in overt shows of affection or the amount of time they spent with their children; it was manifested by interest in the boys' welfare, concern about their companions, availability for discussion of the boys' problems and participation in congenial joint activities. The mother knew all or most of her son's friends, and the mother and father gave many other signs that they regarded the boy as a significant person who was inherently worthy of their deep interest. Basking in this appraisal, the boy came to regard himself in a similar, favorable light.

A second and more surprising finding was that the parents of the high-self-esteem children proved to be less permissive than those of children with lower self-esteem [see lower illustration on page 224]. They demanded high standards of behavior and were strict and consistent in enforcement of the rules. Yet their discipline was by no means harsh; indeed, these parents were less punitive than the parents of the boys whom we found to be lacking in self-esteem. They used rewards rather than corporal punishment or withdrawal of love as disciplinary techniques, and their sons praised their fairness. We found that the parents of the low-self-esteem

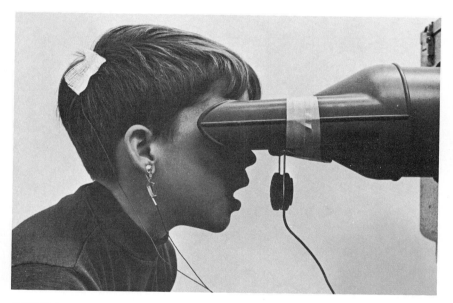

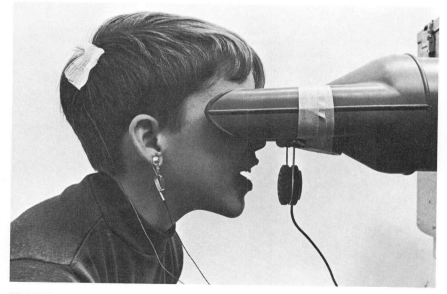

PROJECTOR was employed in tests timing a boy's recognition of words shown one by one. The words used were either neutral; threatening, such as "monster" (top), or pleasant, such as "ice cream" (bottom). To signify recognition the boy spoke into the microphone; his reaction was also recorded by the two electrodes. Boys whose self-appraisal was positive recognized threatening words quicker than boys whose self-appraisal was negative.

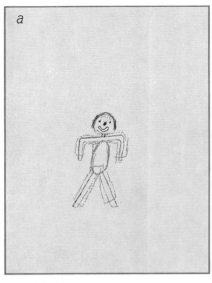

BOYS' DRAWINGS were made following instructions to "Draw a person and complete the drawing in 10 minutes." The first two figures are from the collection of drawings by boys judged to be low in self-esteem (*a, b*). The figures made by this group were constrained and distorted. Next are shown two drawings executed by subjects in the medium-self-esteem group (*c, d*). More originality, complexity and humor were displayed in the drawings made by boys with high self-esteem (*e, f*). Many of the men drawn had beards.

boys, on the other hand, tended to be extremely permissive but inflicted harsh punishment when the children gave them trouble. These boys considered their parents unfair, and they took the absence of definitely stated rules and limits for their behavior as a sign of lack of parental interest in them.

The family life of the high-self-esteem boys was marked not only by the existence of a well-defined constitution for behavior but also by a democratic spirit. The parents established the principles and defined the powers, privileges and responsibilities of the members, but they presided as benevolent despots: they were respectful toward dissent, open to persuasion and generally willing to allow the children a voice in the making of family plans. It seems safe to conclude that all these factors—deep interest in the children, the guidance provided by well-defined rules of expected behavior, non-punitive treatment and respect for the children's views—contributed greatly to the development of the boys' high self-esteem.

Does the level of one's aspirations, or goals, play a part in one's achievement of self-esteem? This is a complex question. It might be supposed from abstract theory that anyone can attain success and consequent high self-esteem simply by setting his goals at a low enough level. Our findings, however, tend to refute that idea. We found that low aspirations do not promote self-esteem; on the contrary, they proved to be characteristic of boys who failed to develop high self-esteem. The boys with high self-esteem had significantly higher goals than those with only medium or low self-esteem did. In tests designed to indicate the level of goals they set for themselves the high-esteem boys had a mean score of 86.3; the medium-esteem group, 76.7; the low-esteem group, only 70.1. These tests measured the boys' actual hopes or expectations rather than a theoretical ideal. For example, one test involved skills at various levels of difficulty in tossing a beanbag. Boys at all levels of self-esteem agreed on the ideal skill they would have liked to strive for, but when they were asked which skill they expected to succeed in, the boys of high self-esteem chose higher levels of skill than the others. Similarly, the subjects generally agreed on a list of desirable occupations they would like to enter, but the boys of high self-esteem expressed higher ambitions than the others as to the occupations they actually expected to enter.

Not only did the subjects with high self-esteem have higher goals; they were also more successful in achieving their goals. Those lacking in self-esteem ran behind in performance as well as in ambition; they tended to fall shorter of attaining their lower goals.

The high expectations of the boys with high self-esteem clearly reflected the influence of their parents. The parents of these boys specifically indicated that they placed greater value on the achieve-

ment of standards of excellence by their children than on adjustment or accommodation to other persons. They set up definite standards of performance that enabled the child to know whether or not he had succeeded in a task, how far he had fallen short when he failed, and what efforts would be required in order to achieve success. That is to say, they presented the child with challenges to his capacities and thus led him to learn and appreciate the reach of his strengths.

Is high self-esteem likely to result from outstanding competence or virtue in a particular field, such as athletic prowess or uncompromising honesty? Here again a careful examination of the facts raises questions about the common belief. Theoretically it can be supposed

that the especially talented individual, placing a high value on the behavior at which he excels and deprecating those behaviors in which he is inferior, might develop a high degree of general self-confidence. In practice, however, one is subject to many social influences that affect self-evaluation. The home, the school, friends and other associations generally lead one to accept group norms and values. It is well known, for example, that children who do poorly in school nevertheless place as high a value on intelligence and good grades as able students do. Consequently, although an athlete or other person with special capacities obtains considerable gratification from his achievements, he is unlikely to accept this special competence alone as the principal basis for evaluating his

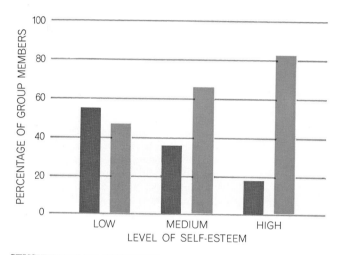

SENSITIVITY TO CRITICISM was high (*gray*) when self-evaluation was low. Except in the low-self-esteem group, most subjects were moderately or slightly sensitive to criticism (*color*). The findings are based on interviews during which the boys explained why they had or had not participated in the earlier group discussions.

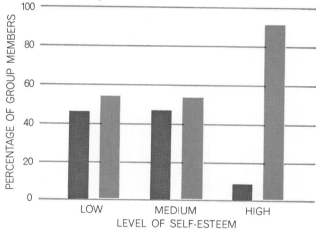

CONCERN WITH PUBLIC AFFAIRS (*color*) was evinced by boys with a higher level of self-esteem, in contrast to the other subjects, about half of whom expressed indifference (*gray*). During interviews a number of the boys who had been found lacking in self-regard expressed a wish to avoid involvement with other people.

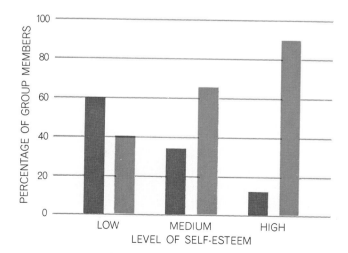

CHILDHOOD DESTRUCTIVENESS was considerable (*gray*) when self-esteem was low and little (*color*) when it was high. The ratings are based on mothers' reports of the boys' early behavior.

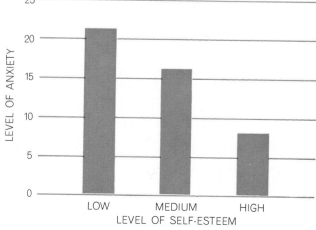

LEVEL OF ANXIETY in the three groups of subjects was rated on the basis of the frequency of feelings of distress reported by the subjects and of psychosomatic symptoms reported by their mothers.

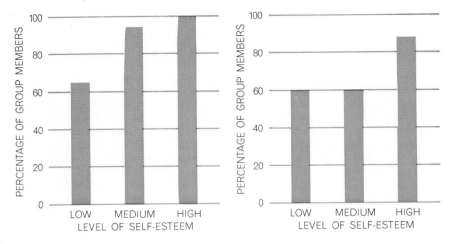

CHILD REARING ATTITUDES of the subjects' mothers were revealed through interview and questionnaire. Mothers of the high-self-esteem boys displayed the most interest in and concern for the child. For example, they knew all or most of his friends (*left*). They also appeared to be more careful and consistent in enforcing limits on his behavior (*right*).

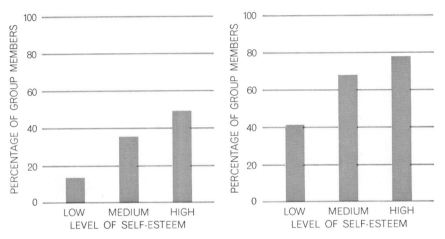

LESS PERMISSIVENESS but more respect for the child's rights were shown by mothers of boys with high self-esteem. Strict in enforcing rules, they used rewards rather than corporal punishment or withdrawal of love as disciplinary measures (*left*). Most mothers of boys in this group agreed that children should have a say in the making of family plans (*right*).

worth as a person. He may, indeed, tend to dwell on his deficiencies and be low in overall self-esteem.

The findings from these studies concerning the factors that contribute to the formation of high self-esteem suggest important implications for parents, educators and therapists. They indicate that children develop self-trust, venturesomeness and the ability to deal with adversity if they are treated with respect and are provided with well-defined standards of values, demands for competence and guidance toward solutions of problems. It appears that the development of independence and self-reliance is fostered by a well-structured, demanding environment rather than by largely unlimited permissiveness and freedom to explore in an unfocused way. From our studies of a sample of preadolescent boys in a typical American environment we have become convinced that learning at an early age to respond constructively to challenges and troublesome conditions is essential to becoming a self-respecting individual.

We are now studying other selected groups for further light on this process. Among the questions inviting further exploration are the nature of the rules and limits on behavior that can contribute most effectively to building youngsters' self-esteem and the appropriate ages for presenting particular demands and challenges to them. We are also exploring the therapeutic problem of finding ways to raise the self-esteem of persons who have already developed a low self-evaluation.

Social Deprivation
in Monkeys

by Harry F. and Margaret Kuenne Harlow
November 1962

*Maternal care has long been known to influence
the emotional development of infants. New studies
with rhesus monkeys suggest that peer relations
may play an even more decisive role*

In *An Outline of Psychoanalysis*, published posthumously in 1940, Sigmund Freud was able to refer to "the common assertion that the child is psychologically the father of the man and that the events of his first years are of paramount importance for his whole subsequent life." It was, of course, Freud's own historic investigations, begun a half-century before, that first elucidated the role of infantile experiences in the development of the personality and its disorders. The "central experience of this period of childhood," he found, is the infant's relation to his mother. Freud's ideas have now shaped the thinking of two generations of psychologists, psychiatrists and psychoanalysts. Much evidence in support of his deep insights has been accumulated, particularly from clinical studies of the mentally ill. Contemporary writers stress inadequate or inconsistent mothering as a basic cause of later disorders such as withdrawal, hostility, anxiety, sexual maladjustment, alcoholism and, significantly, inadequate maternal behavior!

The evidence from clinical studies for this or any other view of human personality development is qualified, however, by an inherent defect. These studies are necessarily retrospective: they start with the disorder and work backward in time, retracing the experiences of the individual as he and his relatives and associates recall them. Inevitably details are lost or distorted, and the story is often so confounded as to require a generous exercise of intuition on the part of the investigator. Nor does evidence obtained in this manner exclude other possible causes of personality disorder. Against arguments in favor of a biochemical or neurological causation of mental illness, for example, there is no way to show that the patient began life with full potentiality for normal development. Given

the decisive influence ascribed to the mother-infant relation, there may be a tendency in the reconstruction of the past to overlook or suppress evidence for the influence of other significant early relations, such as the bonds of interaction with other children. Little attention has been given, in fact, to child-to-child relations in the study of personality development. Yet it can be supposed that these play a significant part in determining the peer relations and the sexual role of the adult. Plainly there is a need to study the development of per-

ABNORMAL MOTHER, raised with a cloth surrogate instead of her mother, rejects her infant, refusing to let it nurse. Infants of four such mothers, raised under same conditions as infants of good mothers, developed relatively normally in spite of poor maternal care.

INFANTS PLAY in one of the playpens used in experiments described in two preceding illustrations. Both infants, photographed when they were six months old, had normal mothers.

sonality forward in time from infancy. Ideally the study should be conducted under controlled laboratory conditions so that the effects of single variables or combinations of variables can be traced.

Acceding to the moral and physical impossibility of conducting such an investigation with human subjects, we have been observing the development of social behavior in large numbers of rhesus monkeys at the Primate Laboratory of the University of Wisconsin. Apart from this primate's kinship to man, it offers a reasonable experimental substitute because it undergoes a relatively long period of development analogous to that of the human child and involving intimate attachment to its mother and social interaction with its age-mates. With these animals we have been able to observe the consequences of the deprivation of all social contact for various lengths of time. We have also raised them without mothers but in the company of age-mates and with mothers but without age-mates.

We have thereby been able to make some estimate of the contribution of each of these primary affectional systems to the integrated adult personality. Our observations sustain the significance of the maternal relation, particularly in facilitating the interaction of the infant with other infants. But at the same time we have found compelling evidence that opportunity for infant-infant interaction under optimal conditions may fully compensate for lack of mothering, at least in so far as infant-infant social and heterosexual relations are concerned. It seems possible—even likely—that the infant-

mother affectional system is dispensable, whereas the infant-infant system is the *sine qua non* for later adjustment in all spheres of monkey life. In line with the "paramount importance" that Freud assigned to experience in the first years of life, our experiments indicate that there is a critical period somewhere between the third and sixth months of life during which social deprivation, particularly deprivation of the company of its peers, irreversibly blights the animal's capacity for social adjustment.

Our investigations of the emotional development of our subjects grew out of the effort to produce and maintain a colony of sturdy, disease-free young animals for use in various research programs. By separating them from their mothers a few hours after birth and placing them in a more fully controlled regimen of nurture and physical care we were able both to achieve a higher rate of survival and to remove the animals for testing without maternal protest. Only later did we realize that our monkeys were emotionally disturbed as well as sturdy and disease-free. Some of our researches are therefore retrospective. Others are in part exploratory, representing attempts to set up new experimental situations or to find new techniques for measurement. Most are incomplete because investigations of social and behavioral development are long-term. In a sense, they can never end, because the problems of one generation must be traced into the next.

Having separated the infant from its mother, our procedure was to keep it alone in a bare wire cage in a large room with other infants so housed. Thus each

little monkey could see and hear others of its kind, although it could not make direct physical contact with them. The 56 animals raised in this manner now range in age from five to eight years. As a group they exhibit abnormalities of behavior rarely seen in animals born in the wild and brought to the laboratory as preadolescents or adolescents, even after the latter have been housed in individual cages for many years. The laboratory-born monkeys sit in their cages and stare fixedly into space, circle their cages in a repetitive stereotyped manner and clasp their heads in their hands or arms and rock for long periods of time. They often develop compulsive habits, such as pinching precisely the same patch of skin on the chest between the same fingers hundreds of times a day; occasionally such behavior may become punitive and the animal may chew and tear at its body until it bleeds. Often the approach of a human being becomes the stimulus to self-aggression. This behavior constitutes a complete breakdown and reversal of the normal defensive response; a monkey born in the wild will direct such threats and aggression at the approaching person, not at itself. Similar symptoms of emotional pathology are observed in deprived children in orphanages and in withdrawn adolescents and adults in mental hospitals.

William A. Mason, now at the Yerkes Laboratories of Primate Biology, compared the behavior of six of these animals, which were then two years old and had been housed all their lives in individual cages, with a matched group of rhesus monkeys that had been captured in the wild during their first year of life and housed together in captivity for a while before being individually housed in the laboratory. The most striking difference was that all the animals that had been born in the wild—and not one of the laboratory-born animals—displayed normal sex behavior. That the laboratory-born animals were not lacking in sex drive was indicated by the fact that the males frequently approached the females and the females displayed part of the pattern of sexual presentation. But they did not orient themselves correctly and they did not succeed in mating. Moreover, the monkeys born in the wild had apparently learned to live with others in a stable hierarchy of dominance, or "pecking order"; consequently in the pairing test they fought one another less and engaged more often in social grooming. They would also release a companion from a locked cage more frequently than did the laboratory-

NORMAL MOTHER-INFANT RELATION among monkeys involves close bodily contact between the two. This pair and three similar pairs were used in a study of the relative importance of maternal and peer relations in the social development of the young. Each pair was housed alone, but the infants had access to a common playpen. In this situation the young developed normally.

born animals, which usually ignored their caged partner's plight.

The severity of the affliction that grips these monkeys raised in the partial isolation of individual wire cages has become more apparent as they have grown older. They pay little or no attention to animals in neighboring cages; those caged with companions sit in opposite corners with only rare interaction. No heterosexual behavior has ever been observed between male and female cagemates, even between those that have lived together for as long as seven years.

When efforts have been made to bring about matings, by pairing animals during the female's estrus, they have sometimes fought so viciously that they have had to be parted. Attempts to mate the socially deprived animals with sexually adequate and experienced monkeys from

MOTHERLESS INFANTS, raised from birth by cloth surrogates, play in a specially constructed playroom supplied with equipment for climbing and swinging. These animals, plus one other not seen in this photograph, were kept in individual cages and brought together in the playroom for 20 minutes a day. Although they had no maternal care whatever, they developed normally in every respect.

the breeding colony have been similarly frustrated.

In the summer of 1960 we undertook to devise a group-psychotherapy situation for 19 of these animals—nine males and 10 females—by using them to stock the monkey island in the municipal zoo in Madison, Wis. This was their first experience outside the laboratory, and they had much to learn in order to survive. They had to learn to drink water from an open trough instead of from a tube in the wall of a cage, to compete for food in a communal feeding situation, to huddle together or find shelter from inclement weather, to climb rocks and avoid the water surrounding the island. Most difficult of all, they had to learn to live together. Within the first few days they made all the necessary physical adjustments. The three casualties—a male that

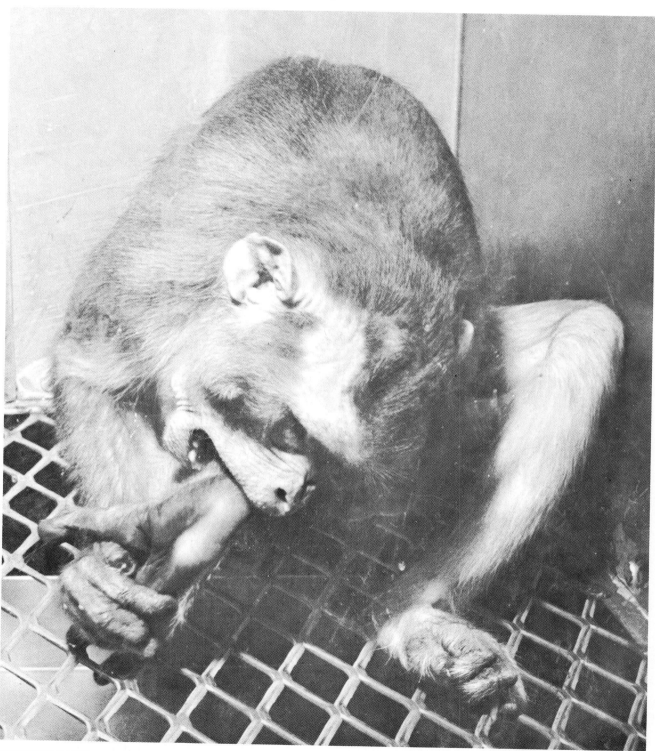

MONKEYS RAISED IN PARTIAL ISOLATION from birth to six months develop severe abnormalities of behavior. This animal, now full-grown, bites itself at the approach of the photographer. Animals raised in isolation often display such self-punishing behavior when a human being appears. They defend themselves adequately, however, against other monkeys and are often extremely aggressive.

EXPERIMENTAL CONDITION	PRESENT AGE	BEHAVIOR				
		NONE	LOW	ALMOST NORMAL	PROBABLY NORMAL	NORMAL
RAISED IN ISOLATION (TOTAL)						
CAGE-RAISED FOR 2 YEARS	4 YEARS	■ □ ▨				
CAGE-RAISED FOR 6 MONTHS	14 MONTHS	□ ▨ ■				
CAGE-RAISED FOR 80 DAYS	10½ MONTHS			■ □ ▨		
(PARTIAL) CAGE-RAISED FOR 6 MONTHS	5 TO 8 YEARS	■	▨		□	
SURROGATE-RAISED FOR 6 MONTHS	3 TO 5 YEARS	■	▨			
RAISED WITH MOTHER						
NORMAL MOTHER; NO PLAY WITH PEERS	1 YEAR		▨ ■			□
MOTHERLESS MOTHER; PLAY IN PLAYPEN	14 MONTHS			□	▨ ■	□
NORMAL MOTHER; PLAY IN PLAYPEN	2 YEARS				■ □	▨
RAISED WITH PEERS						
FOUR RAISED IN ONE CAGE; PLAY IN PLAYROOM	1 YEAR				■	▨ □ ▨
SURROGATE-RAISED; PLAY IN PLAYPEN	2 YEARS					▨ ■ □
SURROGATE-RAISED; PLAY IN PLAYROOM	21 MONTHS					■ □ ▨

■ PLAY
□ DEFENSE
▨ SEX

RESULTS OF EXPERIMENTS are summarized. The monkey's capacity to develop normally appears to be determined by the seventh month of life. Animals isolated for six months are aberrant in every respect. Play with peers seems even more necessary than mothering to the development of effective social relations.

drowned and two females that were injured and had to be returned to the laboratory—resulted from the stress of social adjustment. Fighting was severe at first; it decreased as effective dominance relations were established and friendship pairs formed. Grooming appeared in normal style and with almost normal frequency. A limited amount of sex behavior was observed, but it was infantile in form, with inadequate posturing by both females and males. In the hope of promoting therapy along this line we introduced our largest, strongest and most effective breeding-colony male to the island around the middle of summer. He immediately established himself at the head of the dominance order. But in spite of his considerable persistence and patience he did not succeed in starting a single pregnancy.

Back in the laboratory these animals ceased to groom and fought more frequently. In pairings with breeding-colony monkeys, not one male has achieved a normal mount or intromission and only one female has become pregnant. After two years we have had to conclude that the island experience was of no lasting value.

As the effects of the separation of these monkeys from their mothers in infancy were first becoming apparent in 1957 we were prompted to undertake a study of the mother-infant affectional bond. To each of one group of four animals separated from their mothers at birth we furnished a surrogate mother: a welded wire cylindrical form with the nipple of the feeding bottle protruding from its "breast" and with a wooden head surmounting it. The majority of the animals, 60 in all, were raised with cozier surrogate mothers covered by terry cloth. In connection with certain experiments some of these individuals have had both a bare-wire and a cloth-covered mother. The infants developed a strong attachment to the cloth mothers and little or none to the wire mothers, regardless of which one provided milk. In fright-inducing situations the infants showed that they derived a strong sense of security from the presence of their cloth mothers [see the article "Love in Infant Monkeys," by Harry F. Harlow, beginning on page 94]. Even after two years of separation they exhibit a persistent attachment to the effigies.

In almost all other respects, however, the behavior of these monkeys at ages ranging from three to five years is indistinguishable from that of monkeys raised in bare wire cages with no source of contact comfort other than a gauze diaper pad. They are without question socially and sexually aberrant. No normal sex behavior has been observed in the living cages of any of the animals that have been housed with a companion of the opposite sex. In exposure to monkeys from the breeding colony not one male and only one female has shown normal mating behavior and only four females have been successfully impregnated. Compared with the cage-raised monkeys, the surrogate-raised animals seem to be less aggressive, whether toward themselves or other monkeys. But they are also younger on the average, and their better dispositions can be attributed to their lesser age.

Thus the nourishment and contact comfort provided by the nursing cloth-covered mother in infancy does not produce a normal adolescent or adult. The surrogate cannot cradle the baby or communicate monkey sounds and gestures. It cannot punish for misbehavior or attempt to break the infant's bodily attachment before it becomes a fixation. The entire group of animals separated from their mothers at birth and raised in individual wire cages, with or without surrogate, must be written off as potential breeding stock. Apparently their early social deprivation permanently impairs their ability to form effective relations with other monkeys, whether the opportunity was offered to them in the second six months of life or in the second to the fifth year of life.

One may correctly assume that total social isolation, compared with the partial isolation in which these subjects were reared, would produce even more devastating effects on later personality development. Such disastrous effects have been reported in the rare cases of children who have been liberated after months or years of lonely confinement in a darkened room. We have submitted a few monkeys to total isolation. Our purpose was to establish the maximum of social deprivation that would allow survival and also to determine whether or not there is a critical period in which social deprivation may have irreversible effects.

In our first study a male and a female were housed alone from birth for a period of two years, each one in its own cubicle with solid walls. Their behavior could be observed through one-way vision screens and tested by remote control. The animals adapted to solid food slowly, but they had normal weight and good coats when they were removed from the isolation boxes at the end of two years. Throughout this period nei-

ther animal had seen any living being other than itself.

They responded to their liberation by the crouching posture with which monkeys typically react to extreme threat. When placed together, each one crouched and made no further response to the other. Paired with younger monkeys from the group raised in partial isolation, they froze or fled when approached and made no effort to defend themselves from aggressive assaults. After another two years, in which they were kept together in a single large cage in the colony room, they showed the same abnormal fear of the sight or sound of other monkeys.

We are now engaged in studying the effects of six months of total social isolation. The first pair of monkeys, both males, has been out of isolation for eight months. They are housed, each monkey in its own cage, in racks with other monkeys of their age that were raised in the partial isolation of individual wire cages. For 20 minutes a day, five days a week, they are tested with a pair of these monkeys in the "playroom" of the laboratory. This room we designed to stimulate the young monkeys to a maximum of activity. It was not until the 12th and 27th week respectively that the two totally deprived monkeys began to move and climb about. They now circulate freely but not as actively as the control animals. Although frequently attacked by the

controls, neither one has attempted to defend itself or fight back; they either accept abuse or flee. One must be characterized as extremely disturbed and almost devoid of social behavior. The other resembles a normal two-month-old rhesus infant in its play and social behavior, and the indications are that it will never be able to make mature contacts with its peers.

A considerably more hopeful prognosis is indicated for two groups of four monkeys raised in total isolation for the much shorter period of 80 days. In their cubicles these animals had the contact comfort of a cloth-covered surrogate. They were deficient in social behavior during the first test periods in the playroom. But they made rapid gains; now, eight months later, we rate them as "almost normal" in play, defense and sex behavior. At least seven of the eight seem to bear no permanent scars as the result of early isolation.

Our first few experiments in the total isolation of these animals would thus appear to have bracketed what may be the critical period of development during which social experience is necessary for normal behavior in later life. We have additional experiments in progress, involving a second pair that will have been isolated for six months and a first pair that will have been isolated for a full year. The indications are that six months of isolation will render the animals per-

"TOGETHER-TOGETHER" EXPERIMENT involved raising four motherless infants in one cage and giving them 20 minutes a day in the playroom. At one year of age they are normal, but during their early months they spent most of the time huddled in this position.

manently inadequate. Since the rhesus monkey is more mature than the human infant at birth and grows four times more rapidly, this is equivalent to two or three years for the human child. On the other hand, there is reason to believe that the effects of shorter periods of early isolation, perhaps 60 to 90 days or even more, are clearly reversible. This would be equivalent to about six months in the development of the human infant. The time probably varies with the individual and with the experiences to which it is exposed once it is removed from isolation. Beyond a brief period of neonatal grace, however, the evidence suggests that every additional week or month of social deprivation increasingly imperils social development in the rhesus monkey. Case studies of children reared in impersonal institutions or in homes with indifferent mothers or nurses show a frightening comparability. The child may remain relatively unharmed through the first six months of life. But from this time on the damage is progressive and cumulative. By one year of age he may sustain enduring emotional scars and by two years many children have reached the point of no return.

In all of these experiments in partial and total isolation, whether unwitting or deliberate, our animals were deprived of the company of their peers as well as of their mothers. We accordingly undertook a series of experiments designed to distinguish and compare the roles of mother-infant and infant-infant relations in the maturation of rhesus monkey behavior. Our most privileged subjects are two groups of four monkeys each, now two years old, that were raised with their mothers during the first 18 and 21 months respectively and with peers from the first weeks. Each mother-infant pair occupied a large cage that gave the infant access to one cell of a four-unit playpen. By removing the screens between the playpens we enabled the infants to play together in pairs or as foursomes during scheduled observation periods each day. In parallel with these two groups we raised another group of four in a playpen setup without their mothers but with a terrycloth surrogate in each home cage.

From the time the mothers let them leave their home cages, after 20 or 30 days, the mothered infants entered into more lively and consistent relations with one another than did the four motherless ones. Their behavior evolved more rapidly through the sequence of increasingly complex play patterns that reflects the maturation and learning of the infant

GROUP PSYCHOTHERAPY for monkeys raised in isolation in the laboratory was attempted by removing them to the semiwild conditions of the zoo after they reached maturity. Here their behavior improved; they began to play together and groom one another. But when they were returned to the laboratory, they reverted to their earlier abnormal behavior.

monkey and is observed in a community of normal infants. The older they grew and the more complex the play patterns became, the greater became the observable difference between the mothered and the motherless monkeys. Now, at the end of the second year, the 12 animals are living together in one playpen setup, with each original group occupying one living cage and its adjoining playpen. All are observed in daily interaction without the dividing panels. The early differences between them have all but disappeared. Seven of the eight mothered animals engage in normal sexual activity and assume correct posture. The deviant is a male, and this animal was the social reject in its all-male group of four. Of the two motherless males, one has recently achieved full adult sexual posture and the other is approaching it. The two motherless females appear normal, but it remains to be seen whether or not their maternal behavior will reflect their lack of mothering.

Observation of infants with their mothers suggests reasons for the differences in the early social and sexual behavior of these playpen groups. From early in life on the infant monkey shows a strong tendency to imitate its mother; this responding to another monkey's behavior carries over to interaction with its peers. It is apparent also that sexual activity is stimulated by the mother's grooming of the infant. Finally, as the mother begins occasionally to reject its offspring in the third or fourth month,

the infant is propelled into closer relations with its peers. These observations underlie the self-evident fact that the mother-infant relation plays a positive role in the normal development of the infant-infant and heterosexual relations of the young monkey.

That the mother-infant relation can also play a disruptive role was demonstrated in another experiment. Four females that had been raised in the partial isolation of individual wire cages—and successfully impregnated in spite of the inadequacy of their sexual behavior—delivered infants within three weeks of one another. This made it possible to set up a playpen group composed of these "motherless" mothers and their infants. The maternal behavior of all four mothers was completely abnormal, ranging from indifference to outright abuse. Whereas it usually requires more than one person to separate an infant from its mother, these mothers paid no attention when their infants were removed from the cages for the hand-feeding necessitated by the mothers' refusal to nurse. Two of the mothers did eventually permit fairly frequent nursing, but their apparently closer maternal relations were accompanied by more violent abuse. The infants were persistent in seeking contact with their mothers and climbed on their backs when they were repulsed at the breast. In play with one another during the first six months, the infants were close to the normally mothered animals in maturity of play, but they played less.

In sexual activity, however, they were far more precocious. During the eight months since they have been separated from their mothers, they have exhibited more aggression and day-to-day variability in their behavior than have the members of other playpen groups. The two male offspring of the most abusive mothers have become disinterested in the female and occupy the subordinate position in all activities.

More study of more babies from motherless mothers is needed to determine whether or not the interrelations that characterize this pilot group will characterize others of the same composition. There is no question about the motherless mothers themselves. The aberration of their maternal behavior would have ensured the early demise of their infants outside the laboratory. As for the infants, the extremes of sexuality and aggressiveness observed in their behavior evoke all too vivid parallels in the behavior of disturbed human children and adolescents in psychiatric clinics and institutions for delinquents.

Another pilot experiment has shown that even normal mothering is not enough to produce socially adequate offspring. We isolated two infants in the exclusive company of their mothers to the age of seven months and then brought the mother-infant pairs together in a playpen unit. The female infant took full advantage of the play apparatus provided, but in three months the male was never seen to leave its home cage, and its mother would not permit the female to come within arm's reach. Social interaction of the infants was limited to an occasional exchange of tentative threats. For the past two months they have been separated from their mothers, housed in individual cages and brought together in the playroom for 15 minutes each day. In this normally stimulating environment they have so far shown no disposition to play together. Next to the infants that have been raised in total isolation, these are the most retarded of the infants tested in the playroom.

It is to the play-exciting stimulus of the playroom that we owe the unexpected outcome of our most suggestive experiment. The room is a relatively spacious one, with an eight-foot ceiling and 40 square feet of floor space. It is equipped with movable and stationary toys and a wealth of climbing devices, including an artificial tree, a ladder and a burlap-covered climbing ramp that leads to a platform. Our purpose in constructing the playroom was to provide the monkeys with opportunities to move about in the three-dimensional world to which, as arboreal animals, they are much more highly adapted than man. To assess the effects of different histories of early social experience we customarily turn the animals loose in the room in groups of four for regularly scheduled periods of observation each day.

The opportunities afforded by the playroom were most fully exploited by two groups of four infants that otherwise spent their days housed alone in their cages with a cloth surrogate. In terms of "mothering," therefore, these monkeys were most closely comparable to the four that were raised with surrogates in the playpen situation. These animals were released in the playroom for 20 minutes a day from the first month of life through the 11th, in the case of one group, and through the second year in the case of the other. In contrast with all the other groups observed in the playroom, therefore, they did their "growing up" in this environment. Even though their exposure to the room and to one another was limited to 20 minutes a day, they enacted with great spirit the entire growth pattern of rhesus-monkey play behavior.

They began by exploring the room and each other. Gradually over the next two or three months they developed a game of rough-and-tumble play, with jumping, scuffling, wrestling, hair-pulling and a little nipping, but with no real damage, and then an associated game of flight and pursuit in which the participants are alternately the threateners and the threatened. While these group activities evolved, so did the capacity for individual play exploits, with the animals running, leaping, swinging and climbing, heedless of one another and apparently caught up in the sheer joy of action. As their skill and strength grew, their social play involved shorter but brisker episodes of free-for-all action, with longer chases between bouts. Subsequently they developed an even more complex pattern of violent activity, performed with blinding speed and integrating all objects, animate and inanimate, in the room. Along with social play, and possibly as a result or by-product, they began to exhibit sexual posturing—immature and fleeting in the first six months and more frequent and adult in form by the end of the year. The differences in play activity that distinguish males and females became evident in the first two or three months, with the females threatening and initiating rough contact far less frequently than the males and withdrawing from threats and approaches far more frequently.

Thus in spite of the relatively limited opportunity for contact afforded by their daily schedule, all the individuals in these two groups developed effective infant-infant play relations. Those observed into the second year have shown the full repertory of adult sexual behavior. At the same chronological age these motherless monkeys have attained as full a maturity in these respects as the infants raised with their mothers in the playpen.

Another group of four motherless animals raised together in a single large cage from the age of two weeks is yielding similar evidence of the effectiveness of the infant-infant affectional bond. During their first two months these animals spent much of their time clinging together, each animal clutching the back of the one just ahead of it in "choo-choo" fashion. They moved about as a group of three or four; when one of them broke away, it was soon clutched by another to form the nucleus of a new line. In the playroom the choo-choo linkage gave way to individual exploratory expeditions. During periods of observation, whether in their home cage or in the playroom, these animals have consistently scored lower in play activity than the most playful groups. We think this is explained, however, by the fact that they are able to spread their play over a 24-hour period. At the age of one year they live amicably together. In sex behavior they are more mature than the mother-raised playpen babies. No member of the group shows any sign of damage by mother-deprivation.

Our observations of the three groups of motherless infants raised in close association with one another therefore indicate that opportunity for optimal infant-infant interaction may compensate for lack of mothering. This is true at least in so far as infant-infant and sexual relations are concerned. Whether or not maternal behavior or later social adjustment will be affected remains to be seen.

Of course research on nonhuman animals, even monkeys, will never resolve the baffling complex roles of various kinds of early experience in the development of human personality. It is clear, however, that important theoretical and practical questions in this realm of interest can be resolved by the use of monkeys. The close behavioral resemblance of our disturbed infants to disturbed human beings gives us the confidence that we are working with significant variables and the hope that we can point the way to reducing the toll of psychosocial trauma in human society.

27 Psychological Factors in Stress and Disease

by Jay M. Weiss
June 1972

A new technique separates the psychological and physical factors in stressful conditions. In studies with rats the psychological factors were the main cause of stomach ulcers and other disorders

One of the most intriguing ideas in medicine is that psychological processes affect disease. This concept is not new; it dates back to antiquity, and it has always been controversial. To counter those skeptics who believed that "no state of mind ever affected the humors of the blood," Daniel Hack Tuke, a noted 19th-century London physician, compiled an exhaustive volume, *Illustrations of the Influence of the Mind on the Body.* He concluded:

"We have seen that the influence of the mind upon the body is no transient power; that *in health* it may exalt the sensory functions, or suspend them altogether; excite the nervous system so as to cause the various forms of convulsive action of the voluntary muscles, or to depress it so as to render them powerless; may stimulate or paralyze the muscles of organic life, and the processes of Nutrition and Secretion—causing even death; that *in disease* it may restore the functions which it takes away in health, reinnervating the sensory and motor nerves, exciting healthy vascularity and nervous power, and assisting the *vis medicatrix Naturae* to throw off disease action or absorb morbid deposits." Through the years many other individuals have voiced their belief in the importance of psychological factors in disease, and they have carved out the field known as psychosomatic medicine. It is a field filled with questions, and we are still seeking better evidence on the role of the psychological factors.

Our ability to determine the influence of psychological factors on disease entered a new phase recently with the application of experimental techniques. Formerly the evidence that psychological factors influence disease came from the observations of astute clinicians who noted that certain psychological conditions seemed to be associated with particular organic disorders or with the increased severity of disorders. But such evidence, no matter how compelling, is correlational in nature. Although a psychological characteristic or event may coincide with the onset or advance of a disorder, one cannot be certain that it actually has any effect on the disease process; the psychological event may simply occur together with the disease or may even be caused by the disease. In addition it is always possible that the apparent correlation between the psychological variable and the disease is spurious; that among the myriad of other factors in the physical makeup of the patient and in his life situation lies a different critical element the observer has failed to detect. Such considerations can be ruled out only by accounting for every possible element in the disease process, which obviously is impractical.

The development of experimental techniques for inducing disease states in animals has made the task of determining whether or not psychological factors affect disease much easier. When an investigator can establish conditions that will cause a pathology to develop in experimental animals in the laboratory, he does not have to wait for the disease to arise and then attempt to determine if a particular factor had been important; instead he can introduce that factor directly into his conditions and see if it does indeed affect the development of the disease. Moreover, the use of experimental procedures enables the investigator to deal with the numerous other variables that might influence the disease. Even so, the investigator certainly cannot regulate or even be aware of all the variables that affect a disease. Such variables will, however, be distributed randomly throughout the entire population of experimental subjects. When the experimenter applies some treatment to one randomly selected group of subjects and not to another, he knows that any consistent difference between the treatment group and the control group will have been caused by the experimental treatment and not by the other variables, since those variables are distributed randomly throughout both groups.

Recently I have been studying the influence of psychological factors on certain experimentally induced disorders, particularly the development of gastric lesions or stomach ulcers. As the prob-

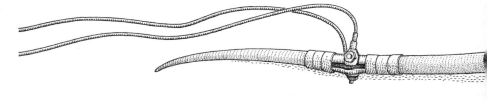

TRANSPARENT-PLASTIC CHAMBER is one type of apparatus used in stress ulcer experiments with rats. The rat is housed in the chamber for the entire 48-hour stress session.

lem of gastrointestinal ulcers has become more widespread (the disease currently causes more than 10,000 deaths each year in the U.S. and afflicts one out of every 20 persons at some point in their life) pathologists have continued to refine techniques of studying ulceration experimentally. Within the past 15 years, beginning with the pioneering work of Serge Bonfils and his associates at the Institut d'Hygiène in Paris, investigators have discovered that experimental animals can develop gastric lesions under stressful environmental conditions. The finding that lesions can be induced by manipulating an animal's external environment opened the way for experimental study of the psychological conditions that are brought about by stressful environmental events.

The experimental techniques had to be refined still further, however, for studying the influence of psychological variables. The reason is that when experimental animals are exposed to an environmental stressor (a stressor is a stress-inducing agent), the effects of psychological variables may be confounded with the effects of the physical stressors. For example, suppose rats are made to swim for an hour in a tank from which they cannot escape, and these animals then develop organic pathology whereas control animals (those not exposed to the swim stressor) show no pathology at all. Although it is evident that the pathology was induced by the swim stressor, how can we assess the role of any psychological factor in producing this pathology? Certainly the pathology might have been affected by the fear the animal experienced, by its inability to escape, by the constant threat of drowning. But what about the extraordinary muscular exertion the stressful situation required, with its attendant debilitation and exhaustion of tissue resources? Clearly in such an experiment it is not possible to determine if psychological variables influenced the development of pathology, since the pathology might have been due simply to the direct impact of the swim stressor itself. Thus in order to study the role of psychological factors one must devise a means of assessing the importance of psychological variables apart from the impact of the physical stressor on the organism.

The method I have used is to expose two or more animals simultaneously to exactly the same physical stressor, with each animal in a different psychological condition. I then look to see if a consistent difference results from these conditions; such a difference must be due to psychological variables since all the animals received the same physical stressor. To illustrate this technique, let us consider an experiment on the effects of the predictability of an electric shock on ulceration.

Two rats received electric shocks simultaneously through electrodes placed on their tail, while a third rat served as a control and received no shocks. Of the two rats receiving shocks, one heard a beeping tone that began 10 seconds before each shock. The other rat also heard the tone, but the tone sounded randomly with respect to the

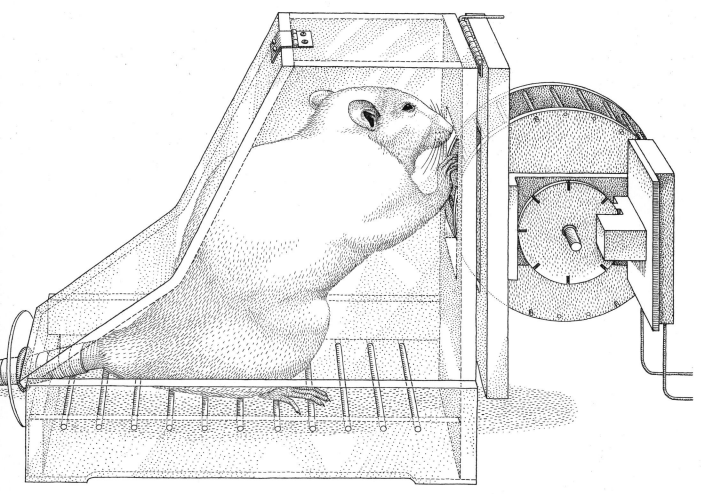

Shocks are delivered through electrodes attached to the tail. A disk secured to the tail by a piece of tubing prevents the rat from pulling its tail into the chamber and biting off the electrodes. The rat receives no food during the experiment, but water is available.

shock. Thus both these animals received the same shocks, but one could predict when the shocks would occur whereas the other could not. Since the physical stressor was the same for the two animals, any consistent difference between them in the amount of ulceration would be the result of the difference in the predictability of the stressor, the psychological variable being studied.

This raises a most important point: If such experiments are to be valid, one must be sure that the physical stressor, in this case the electric shock, is the same for all animals in the test. When these studies were begun, the standard way of administering electric shock to experimental rats was to place them on a grid floor whose bars were electrically

charged. That method of delivering an electric shock was clearly inadequate for the present experiments, since rats can lessen the shock on a grid floor by changing their posture or can even terminate the shock completely by jumping. The experimenter is faced with a serious problem if one group of rats is able to perform such maneuvers more effectively than another group. In the predictability experiment, for example, the rats that are able to predict shock would surely have been able to prepare for such postural changes more effectively than the rats that were unable to predict shock, so that the groups would have differed with respect not only to the predictability of the stressor but also to the amount of shock received. That would essentially invali-

date the experiment. The tail electrode, which is used in all the experiments discussed here, was developed specifically to avoid the possibility of unequal shock. Because the electrode is fixed to the tail, the rat cannot reduce or avoid the shock by moving about. In addition, with the fixed electrode it is possible to wire the electrodes of matched animals in series, so that both animals are part of the same circuit. Thus all the shocks received by the matched subjects are equal in duration and have an identical current intensity, which appears to be the critical element in determining the discomfort of shock.

As was to be expected, the control rats that received no shock developed very little gastric ulceration or none. A

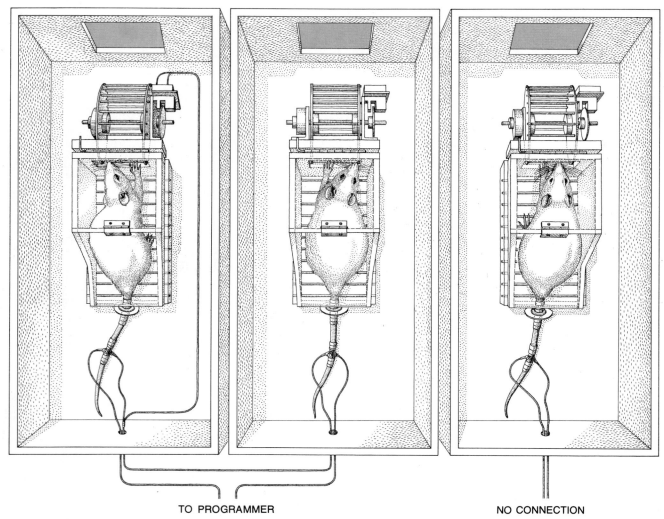

TO PROGRAMMER   NO CONNECTION

BASIC TRIPLET PARADIGM for the ulceration experiments consists in placing three rats, matched for weight and age, in individual soundproof compartments with one-way-mirror windows. Each rat is prepared in exactly the same way and then randomly assigned to one of the three experimental conditions: avoidance-escape, yoked and control. In this illustration the rat on the left is the avoidance-escape subject. It can terminate the programmed shock by turning the wheel. Moreover, turning the wheel between shocks will postpone the shock. The rat in the center is electrically wired in series to the first rat, so that when the first rat receives a shock, the yoked rat simultaneously receives a shock of the same intensity and duration. The actions of the yoked rat do not affect the shock sequence. The electrodes on the tail of the control rat on the right are not connected, and this rat does not receive shocks at any time. At the end of the experimental session the rats are sacrificed and the length of their gastric lesions is measured.

striking result of the experiment was that rats able to predict when the shocks would occur also showed relatively little ulceration, whereas those that received the same shocks unpredictably showed a considerable amount of ulceration [*see top illustration at right*]. In short, the results demonstrated clearly that the psychological variable of predictability, rather than the shock itself, was the main determinant of ulcer severity.

Even though some rats in the foregoing experiment could predict the shock, they were helpless in that they could not avoid the shock. How will stress reactions, such as gastric ulcers, be altered if an animal has control over a stressor instead of being helpless? A recent series of experiments conducted in our laboratory at Rockefeller University has yielded a considerable amount of new information on effects of coping behavior, and also has given us some insight into why these effects arise.

To study the effects of coping behavior, three rats underwent experimental treatment simultaneously, just as in the predictability experiment. Two of the rats again received exactly the same shocks through fixed tail electrodes wired in series, while the third rat served as a nonshock control. In the coping experiments, however, the difference between the two rats receiving shock was not based on predictability (all matched shocked rats in these experiments received the same signals) but rather was based on the fact that one rat could avoid or escape the shock whereas the other could not do anything to escape it.

Since albino rats tend to lose weight when stressed, at first I simply measured the effects of avoidance-escape versus helplessness in terms of changes in the rate of weight gain. In this experimental arrangement one rat of each shocked pair could avoid the shock by jumping onto a platform at the rear of its enclosure during a warning signal, thereby preventing the shock from being given to itself or its partner. If the avoidance-escape rat failed to jump in time, so that shock occurred, it could still jump onto the platform to terminate the shock for itself and its partner. Thus the avoidance-escape rat could affect the occurrence and duration of shock by its responses, whereas its partner, called the yoked subject, received exactly the same shocks but was helpless: its responses had no effect at all on shock. The control rat, which received no shock, was simply allowed to explore its apparatus during the experiment. It is important to note that in all these experiments the three rats were assigned to their respec-

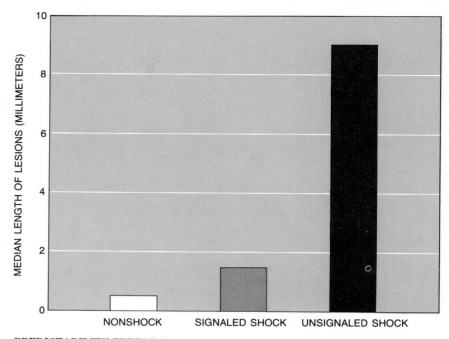

PREDICTABILITY EXPERIMENT showed that if a rat could predict when shocks would occur, it developed less gastric ulceration than a rat that received the same shocks unpredictably. One rat heard a "beep" before each shock, whereas for the other rat the "beep" occurred randomly with respect to the shock. A third rat, a control subject, heard the sound but received no shocks. Thus the only difference between the rats receiving shocks was psychological, and this psychological variable strongly affected the degree of ulceration.

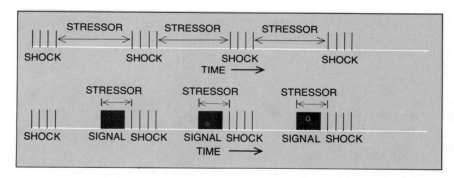

STRESSFUL SITUATION (called "stressor") is created by the electric shock and the stimuli associated with the shock. When there is no warning-signal stimulus, the stressor condition extends through the entire time between shocks. When a warning of the shock is given, however, the stressor condition tends to be restricted to the warning signal.

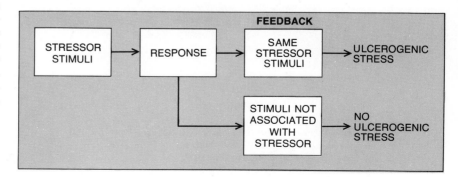

COPING ATTEMPTS OR RESPONSES made by the rat in trying to escape from the stressor are related to ulcerogenic stress only if the responses fail to produce stimuli that are not associated with the stressor. If coping responses produce stimuli not associated with the stressor, the rat receives relevant feedback and ulcerogenic stress does not occur.

tive condition randomly just before the first trial.

The results showed that the yoked, helpless rats lost considerably more weight than the avoidance-escape rats. Over the several days of test sessions the yoked, helpless rats suffered an 80 percent reduction from "normal" weight gain (as measured in the control rats), whereas the reduction of weight gain in the avoidance-escape rats was only 30 percent. Again a psychological factor, in this case a difference in coping behavior, exerted a more powerful influence on stress responses than the occurrence of the physical stressor did.

A second experiment was immediately undertaken to test the generality of these findings, employing a different apparatus and measuring a different pathological response: gastric ulceration. In this case the avoidance-escape rat could avoid shock not by jumping onto a platform but by reaching through a hole in a small restraint cage to touch a panel mounted just outside. The avoidance-escape animal again had a yoked partner, which received the same shocks but was helpless, and a nonshock control. The rats were subjected to one continuous stress session lasting 21 hours, with the shocks—each preceded by a signal—scheduled to occur at the rate of one per minute. After the conclusion of the session all animals were sacrificed and their stomachs were examined for gastric lesions.

The effects of coping behavior were again found to be beneficial. The rats that were able to avoid and escape shock were found to show considerably less gastric ulceration than their yoked, helpless partners. And again the results pointed up how remarkable the effects of coping behavior could be. Whereas the stomach of the average avoidance-escape rat was found to have 1.6 millimeters of lesioned tissue, the average yoked rat had 4.5 millimeters of lesions, or roughly three times as much ulceration as the average avoidance-escape rat.

In both avoidance-escape experiments the shock was always preceded by a warning, so that the rats could predict when a shock was going to occur. Hence the avoidance-escape rat always had a signal to inform it when to respond. What would happen if there was no signal before the shock? Would the avoidance-escape rat again show less ulceration than a yoked subject?

To find out a large experiment was conducted in which three different warning-signal conditions were set up: no warning signal, a single uniform signal preceding the shock as in the earlier experiments, and a series of different signals that acted like a clock and therefore gave more information about when a shock would occur than the single uniform signal did. For these studies each rat was placed in a chamber with a large wheel [*see illustration on pages 234 and 235*]. If the avoidance-escape rat turned the wheel at the front of the apparatus, the shock was postponed for 200 seconds, or if shock had begun, it was immediately terminated and the next shock did not occur for 200 seconds. Thus the avoidance-escape conditions were exactly the same except for the difference in the warning signals. Each avoidance-escape rat had a yoked, helpless partner and both received exactly the same signals and shocks. A rat that never received a shock also was included in every case as a control subject.

The results showed that regardless of the warning-signal condition avoidance-escape rats developed less gastric ulceration than yoked, helpless rats [*see illustration at left*]. Although the presence of a warning signal did reduce ulceration in both avoidance-escape and yoked groups, the avoidance-escape rats always developed less ulceration.

All the experimental findings on coping behavior that I have described up to this point have been opposite to the result found by Joseph V. Brady, Robert Porter and their colleagues in an experiment with monkeys [see "Ulcers in 'Executive' Monkeys," by Joseph V. Brady; SCIENTIFIC AMERICAN, October, 1958]. They reported that in four pairs of monkeys the animals that could avoid shock by pressing a lever developed severe gastrointestinal ulcers and died, whereas yoked animals that received the same shocks but could not perform the avoidance response survived with no apparent ill effects. Why were these results so markedly different?

With careful study of the data from the 180 rats that were used in the coping-behavior and warning-signal experiment, it was possible to develop a theory that may explain how coping behavior affects gastric ulceration. This theory can account for the results I have

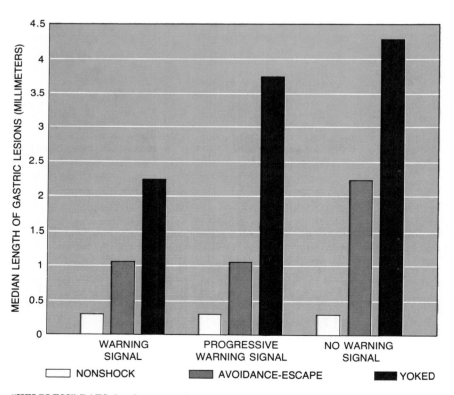

"HELPLESS" RATS develop more ulcers than their counterparts that can avoid or escape shock by performing a simple task, even though both rats have received exactly the same shocks. In all situations the avoidance-escape rat could terminate or postpone the shock by turning the wheel in front of it; its yoked partner received the same shocks but was unable to affect the shock sequence by its behavior. The control rat was never shocked. Regardless of the warning-signal conditions, rats that could do something to stop the shock developed less ulceration than their yoked, helpless mates. Ulceration was more extensive in both groups when there was no warning signal. The yoked, helpless rats unexpectedly developed almost as much ulceration with the progressive warning signal as with no warning signal.

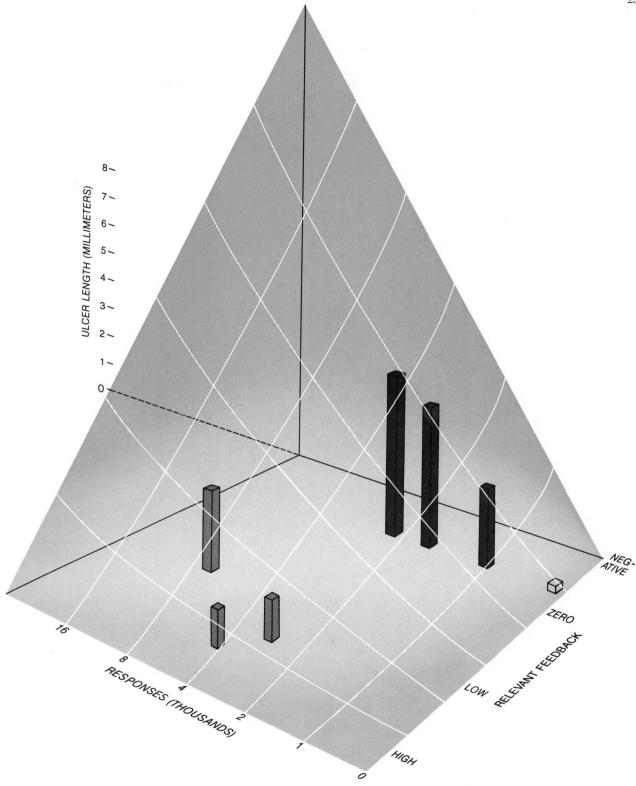

ULCER LENGTH (MILLIMETERS)

8
7
6
5
4
3
2
1
0

RESPONSES (THOUSANDS)

16
8
4
2
1
0

NEG-ATIVE

ZERO

LOW

RELEVANT FEEDBACK

HIGH

RESPONSE RATE was found to be related to the amount of ulcer-ation: the greater the number of responses, the more the ulcera-tion. Moreover, increasing the amount of relevant feedback de-creases ulceration. Combining these variables produces this three-dimensional graph. Here data from the illustration on the opposite page are replotted. The yoked, helpless rats given the progressive warning signal (*middle black bar*) made more responses than help-less rats given only a brief warning signal (*lowest black bar*). Help-less rats shocked without a warning signal made more responses than the other helpless rats and had the highest ulceration (*tallest black bar*). The single white bar represents the control rats that received no shocks in all three conditions, since their response rate and ulceration was nearly the same in all cases. (They devel-oped some ulceration because they too were in a mildly stressful condition.) The avoidance-escape rats that received no warning signal made the greatest number of coping responses and had a high amount of ulceration (*tallest gray bar*). The avoidance-escape rats given the progressive warning signal (high feedback) made more responses (*middle gray bar*) than avoidance-escape rats that heard the brief warning signal before the shock (*right gray bar*).

240

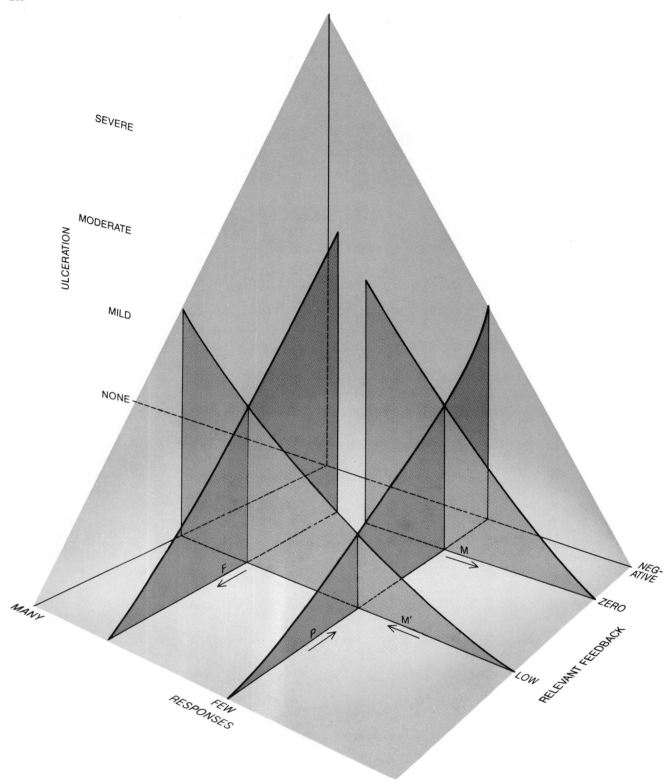

SEVERE

MODERATE

ULCERATION

MILD

NONE

MANY

F

M

NEG-
ATIVE

ZERO

P

M'

LOW

RELEVANT FEEDBACK

FEW

RESPONSES

PREDICTIVE MODEL of the relation between responses, feedback and ulceration is shown here. It predicts that the highest rate of ulceration will occur when the number of coping responses is very high and the feedback is very low or negative. The model can explain why the "executive" monkeys developed more ulcers than their "helpless" counterparts. The executive monkeys could postpone a shock by pressing a lever. Their response rate was quite high, but the amount of relevant feedback they received was low. Thus increased response rate along the low-feedback plane (*M'* in *illustration*) led to increased ulceration in the executive monkeys.

For the "helpless" monkeys, even though they received zero feedback (*Plane M*), their low response rate put them in the low-ulceration area. Similarly, if a high-relevant-feedback situation is changed into a negative-relevant-feedback situation (for example, a previously correct response suddenly begins to produce punishment), the model predicts a rapid increase in ulceration (*Plane P*) even at low levels of response. Finally, increasing feedback to a very high level should reduce ulceration to a very low amount (*Plane F*) even if the response rate is high. Results of experiments conducted to test these predictions are shown on page 242.

obtained and also can reconcile the seemingly contradictory results of the "executive monkey" experiment.

The theory states that stress ulceration is a function of two variables: the number of coping attempts or responses an animal makes, and the amount of appropriate, or "relevant," feedback these coping attempts produce. When an animal is presented with a stressor stimulus, the animal will make coping attempts or responses. The first proposition is simply that the more responses one observes, the greater is the ulcerogenic (ulcer-producing) stress. (Note that this does not say that the behavioral responses themselves cause ulceration, only that the amount of coping behavior and the amount of ulcerogenic stress tend to rise together.) If the responses, however, immediately produce appropriate feedback —that is, if the responses bring about stimuli that have no connection with the stressor—ulcerogenic stress will not occur. On the other hand, if the responses fail to produce such stimuli, then ulcerogenic stress will occur [see bottom illustration on page 237].

Perhaps the most important concept in this theory is that of feedback. The appropriate feedback is called relevant feedback. It consists of stimuli that are not associated with the stressful situation. Relevant feedback occurs when a response produces stimuli that differ from the stressor. The amount of relevant feedback produced depends on how different the stimulus situation becomes and how far removed these new stimuli are from any association with the stressor.

We can now specify how the two variables, responding and relevant feedback, are related to ulceration. Ulceration increases as the number of responses increases, and ulceration decreases as the amount of relevant feedback increases. Combining these two produces a function that forms a three-dimensional plane [see illustration on page 239]. From this model one can predict the amount of ulceration that is expected to occur in any stressful situation by specifying the number of coping attempts or responses the animal makes and the amount of relevant feedback these responses produce.

The model explains why animals able to perform effective coping responses usually develop fewer ulcers than helpless animals. Whenever a helpless animal makes a coping attempt, the response necessarily produces no relevant feedback because it has no effect on the stimuli of the animal's environment. Thus if helpless animals make an appreciable number of coping attempts, which many of them do, they will develop ulcers because of the lack of relevant feedback. Animals that have control in a stressful situation, however, do receive relevant feedback when they respond. In my experiments, for example, the avoidance-escape rats could terminate warning signals and shocks (thereby producing silence and the absence of shocks), so that their responses produced stimuli that were dissociated from the stressor. Hence animals in control of a stressor can usually make many responses and not develop ulcers because they normally receive a substantial amount of relevant feedback for responding.

It is evident that, according to the theory, the effectiveness of coping behavior in preventing ulceration depends on the relevant feedback that coping responses produce; simply to have control over the stressor is in and of itself not beneficial. This means that conditions certainly can exist wherein an animal that has control will ulcerate severely. Specifically, in cases of low relevant feedback ulceration will be severe if the number of responses made is high [see illustration on opposite page].

I believe the foregoing statement tells us precisely why the executive monkeys died of severe gastrointestinal ulceration while performing an avoidance response. First of all, the responding of the monkeys was maintained at a very high rate in that experiment because they had to respond once every 20 seconds to avoid shock. In addition, the executives were actually selected for their high rate of responding. On the basis of a test before the experiment began, the monkey in each pair that responded at the higher rate was made the avoidance animal while its slower partner was assigned to the yoked position. Thus on the basis of their response rate the executive monkeys were more ulcer-prone from the beginning than their yoked partners. With regard to the relevant feedback for responding, the feedback for avoidance responding was quite low. There were no warning signals, and so the executives' rapid-fire responses could not turn off any external signals and therefore did not change the external-stimulus environment at all. As a result the relevant feedback came entirely from internal cues. Evidently this feedback was not sufficient to counteract the extremely high response condition, so that the executive animals developed ulcers and died. At the same time the yoked animals probably made very few responses or coping attempts because the shocks were few and far between, thanks to the high responding of the executives. It is no wonder, then, that the yoked animals in this case survived with no apparent ill effects.

Further evidence in support of this model has emerged, both in an analysis of earlier experiments and in new direct tests with rats. Reviewing those experiments in which hyperactive avoidance-escape rats happened to be paired with low-responding yoked rats under conditions similar to those of the executive-monkey experiment, I found that high-responding avoidance-escape animals developed more ulceration than their helpless partners, which replicated the results of the monkey pairs [see top illustration on next page]. I then went on to test the model directly by examining the effects of very poor relevant feedback and excellent relevant feedback.

The first experiment examined the effects of very poor relevant feedback, which should, of course, produce severe ulceration. In this case avoidance-escape rats, having spent 24 hours in a normal avoidance situation with a warning signal, were given a brief pulse of shock every time they performed the correct response. Although the avoidance-escape rats had control over the stressor, their responses now produced the wrong kind of feedback: the stressor stimulus itself. The feedback in this condition is even worse than it is in the zero-relevant-feedback, or helplessness, condition. The results showed that even though these rats had control over the stressor, they developed severe gastric ulceration, in fact more ulceration than helpless animals receiving the same shocks [see middle illustration on next page].

Having found that very poor feedback would cause severe ulceration, I conducted an experiment to determine if excellent feedback could reduce and possibly eliminate ulceration in a stressful situation. Initially the shock was administered without a warning signal, and under this condition the avoidance-escape rats will normally develop a considerable amount of gastric ulceration. Presumably ulceration occurs because the relevant feedback for responding is low, as in the case of the executive monkeys. Then a brief tone was added to the experiment. When the rat now performed its coping response, it not only postponed shock but also sounded the tone. Because the tone immediately followed the response, and the response postponed the shock, the tone was not associated with the shock. Thus the tone produced a change in the stimulus situa-

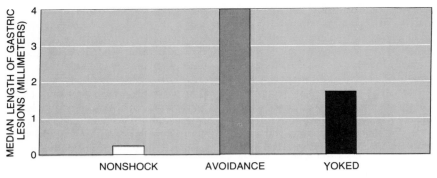

REPLICATION of the executive-monkey situation with data from experiments in which rats received unsignaled shocks offers support for the theoretical model of ulcerogenic stress. Matched pairs of high-responding avoidance rats and low-responding yoked rats were statistically selected and their ulcers measured. As the model predicts, the avoidance rats showed higher ulceration and the low-responding yoked rats had less ulceration.

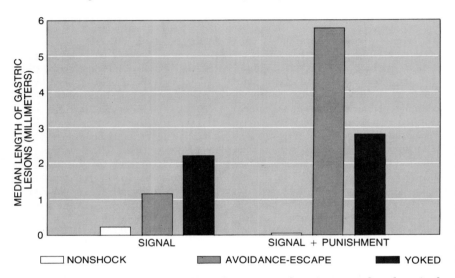

NEGATIVE RELEVANT FEEDBACK produces severe ulceration even when the animal has control over the shock. In the warning-signal condition avoidance-escape rats learned to perform a response to avoid a shock whenever a tone sounded. In the punishment situation during the last half of the experiment the rats received a shock every time they performed the previously learned correct response. With this negative relevant feedback the avoidance-escape rats developed more ulcers than their yoked, helpless mates did.

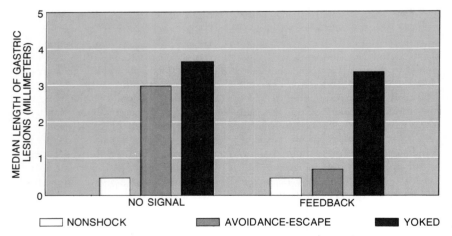

EXCELLENT RELEVANT FEEDBACK following a correct response drastically reduces the amount of ulceration in rats. In the no-signal condition the avoidance-escape rat could postpone the shock by turning a wheel but there was no feedback other than the absence of shock. In the feedback condition a signal followed immediately after every correct response. The number of responses by avoidance-escape rats in both conditions was the same.

tion that constituted excellent relevant feedback. The result was striking. Although the rats in this situation received about as many shocks as the counterparts that were not given the tone feedback, they developed a small amount of ulceration; in fact, they developed only slightly more ulceration than controls receiving no shocks at all did [*see bottom illustration at left*].

Hence by manipulating the feedback consequences of responding, rats could be made to develop extensive gastric ulceration in an otherwise nonulcerogenic condition or could be protected almost completely from developing ulcers in a condition that was normally quite ulcerogenic. The fact that these results are consistent with the proposed model means that we are beginning to develop some idea of why the remarkable effects of psychological variables in stress situations occur.

It appears that the principles discovered in these animal experiments may operate in human situations as well. For example, Ronald Champion of the University of Sydney and James Geer and his associates at the State University of New York at Stony Brook have shown that if people are given inescapable shocks, the individuals who think they can terminate these shocks by clenching a fist or pressing a button show less emotional arousal as measured by electrical skin resistance than individuals who receive the same shocks and are also asked to clench a fist or press the button but are told that the shocks are inescapable. These findings can be explained using the model derived from the animal experiments, again emphasizing the role of relevant feedback. The people who thought they had control over the shock perceived their responses as producing the shock-free condition, that is, they saw their responses as producing relevant feedback. In contrast, the people who thought they were helpless necessarily perceived their responses as producing no relevant feedback. Thus for humans, as for rats, the same variables seem important in describing the effects of behavior in stress situations. On the other hand, the experiments with humans alert us to how important higher cognitive processes are in people, showing that verbal instructions and self-evaluation can determine feedback from behavior, which will subsequently affect bodily stress reactions.

Other stress responses have been measured in addition to gastric ulceration, for example the level of plasma corticosterone in the blood and the amount of body weight the animals lost during the stress session. In many instances the results reflect those found with gastric ulcers, showing that ulceration may be only one manifestation of a more general systemic stress response. The correlation between measures is by no means perfect, so that it is evident that all physiological systems participating in stress reactions are not affected in the same way by a given stress condition. Certain systems in the body may be severely taxed by one set of conditions whereas other systems may be hardly affected at all, or actually may be benefited. For example, I have observed that heart weight tends to decrease in certain conditions, and this effect is seen more often in animals that are able to avoid and escape shock. We do not yet even know what this change indicates, but it suggests that certain conditions protecting one organ system, such as the gastrointestinal tract, might adversely affect another, such as the cardiovascular system.

Perhaps the most exciting biochemical system we have begun to study involves the catecholamines of the central nervous system. Eric A. Stone, Nell Harrell and I have studied changes in the level of norepinephrine in the brain. This substance is a suspected neurotransmitter that is thought to play a major role in mediating active, assertive responses, and several investigators have suggested that depletion of norepinephrine is instrumental in bringing about depression in humans. We found that animals able to avoid and escape shock showed an increase in the level of brain norepinephrine, whereas helpless animals, which received the same shocks, showed a decrease in norepinephrine. At the same time Martin Seligman, Steven Maier and Richard L. Solomon of the University of Pennsylvania have found that dogs given inescapable shocks will subsequently show signs of behavioral depression, but that dogs that are able to avoid and escape shocks do not show such depression. It may well be that the causal sequence leading from "helplessness" to behavioral depression depends on biochemical changes in the central nervous system, such as changes in brain norepinephrine. This would indicate that depressed behavior often can be perpetuated in a vicious circle: the inability to cope alters neural biochemistry, which further accentuates depression, increasing the inability to cope, which further alters neural biochemistry, and so on. We need to know more about this cycle and how to break it.

Hyperactive Children

by Mark A. Stewart
April 1970

Certain children are more than usually restless, noisy, destructive and distractible. Their behavior appears to be a distinct disease syndrome that may well be innate

Parents and teachers have long been aware of a youthful syndrome that is succinctly described in a short story in verse for children written a century ago (and here translated) by a German physician, Heinrich Hoffmann:

> *Fidgety Phil,*
> *He won't sit still;*
> *He wriggles,*
> *And giggles...*

at the dinner table, and when his father admonishes him, it only results in

> *The naughty restless child*
> *Growing still more rude and wild.*

Fidgeting in itself is hardly an unusual or alarming behavior in children, but it is a matter for concern when it is accompanied by a cluster of other symptoms that characterize what is known as the "hyperactive-child syndrome." Typically a child with this syndrome is continually in motion, cannot concentrate for more than a moment, acts and speaks on impulse, is impatient and easily upset. At home he is constantly in trouble because of his restlessness, noisiness and disobedience. In school he is readily distracted, rarely finishes his work, tends to clown and talk out of turn in class and becomes labeled a discipline problem.

Clinicians developed an active interest in the syndrome during the 1918 epidemic of encephalitis in the U.S. Among the children who were stricken and recovered from the acute phase of the attack, many later showed a catastrophic change in personality: they became hyperactive, distractible, irritable, unruly, destructive and antisocial. It then began to be noted that the same cluster of behavior problems commonly occurred in children who had suffered brain damage from other causes, particularly from head injury or oxygen lack during or shortly after delivery. Hyperactivity therefore came to be called the "brain damage" syndrome. It has been found, however, that most children diagnosed as hyperactive do not have a history suggesting brain injury. An early history, for instance, of prenatal or birth complications that might have caused brain damage is no more common among hyperactive children than among normal children. Some clinicians still hold to the brain-damage theory, noting that many hyperactive children show suggestive signs such as clumsiness, squinting and speech difficulties, but these symptoms might well arise from functional disorders of the brain rather than from structural damage.

The hyperactivity syndrome is not confined to children. Many adults exhibit the same cluster of symptoms. In adult life, however, certain of the basic characteristics—high energy, aggressiveness, lack of inhibitions—may be helpful in one's work, whereas in childhood, when one is required to sit still at a desk and concentrate on studies for long periods, the restlessness associated with the syndrome may be a great handicap and give rise to severe problems.

Many years ago Charles Bradley of the Emma Pendleton Bradley Home made the paradoxical discovery that stimulating drugs, such as amphetamine (benzedrine), tend to calm hyperactive children and improve their behavior. The drug enables such children to sit still, concentrate and get their work done. On the other hand, barbiturate sedatives, it has been found, tend to *increase* the restlessness of a hyperactive child.

My own interest in the syndrome developed from a more general interest in the chemical basis of psychiatric disorders. In the psychiatry clinic of the St. Louis Children's Hospital we had seen many hyperactive patients, and we estimated that about 4 percent of suburban grade school children were afflicted with this disorder. The syndrome suggested intriguing questions in basic biology. Is the hyperactive temperament hereditary? Does it have a basis in disordered metabolism? How early does it show itself in a child? Do children outgrow the troublesome behavior or do the problems persist through adolescence and into adulthood? As an approach to clarification of these questions I decided to study the natural history of the syndrome in children. With the help of associates at the Washington University School of Medicine and with support from the National Institute of Mental Health we undertook a program of investigations.

Our first project was to establish a systematic description of the nature and incidence of the symptoms as a base for follow-up studies of patients. For this purpose we selected a sample of hyperactive children and compared them with a control group of normal children. The patients were 37 schoolchildren (32 boys and five girls) aged five through 11 who were being treated in the psychiatry clinic of Children's Hospital; all showed pronounced symptoms of overactivity and inability to maintain concentration but had no chronic disease or special sensory defect. The controls were first-grade children who generally matched the patient group except for their younger average age. This age difference could be disregarded in comparing the two groups for symptoms of hyperactivity, because the hyperactive children had developed most of their symptoms before they entered the first grade.

Using a questionnaire that covered the child's present and past symptoms, his medical and developmental history, his school record and the family history, we interviewed the mother of each child in the patient group and the control group. The interview took between one hour and two hours, and as far as possible the replies to the questions were recorded verbatim. The answer for each symptom was later scored positive or negative according to predetermined criteria. For example, the answer to the question "Has he worn out furniture and toys?" was scored positive if the child had worn out a new bicycle in less than a year or if he had used his baby crib so badly that it could not be handed on to the next child. On questions that did not provide such objective criteria we looked for other forms of confirmatory evidence. For instance, to the question "Does he rock, jiggle, fidget?" the answer was scored positive only if the mother thought the child's behavior in these respects was very different from that of her other children and if other observers had remarked on the behavior. In most cases a symptom was scored positive only if the behavior had persisted over a period of years.

The results showed that the hyperactive patients were strikingly different from the controls. The differences were most marked on symptoms that have been accepted as particularly characteristic of the syndrome [*see illustration on next page*]. For example, 81 percent of the patients were described as unable to sit still at meals, as against only 8 percent of the controls; 84 percent of the patients were said by their mothers to be unable to finish projects, whereas among the controls none was found to be lacking in this ability. Substantial per-

Die Geschichte vom Zappel-Philipp.

"THE STORY OF FIDGETY PHILIPP" is one of the cautionary tales in *Struwwelpeter* (*Shock-headed Peter*), a children's book in verse written a century ago by Heinrich Hoffmann. The tale of a "hyperactive" child named Philipp is told in three drawings and 36 lines of doggerel. In the first picture (*top at right*) Philipp begins rocking back and forth on his chair after his father asks "I wonder if Philipp is able to sit still today at the table?" In the second picture Philipp loses his balance and grabs frantically at the tablecloth. In the third picture Philipp has crashed to the floor, where he lies covered by the tablecloth, food and broken dishes.

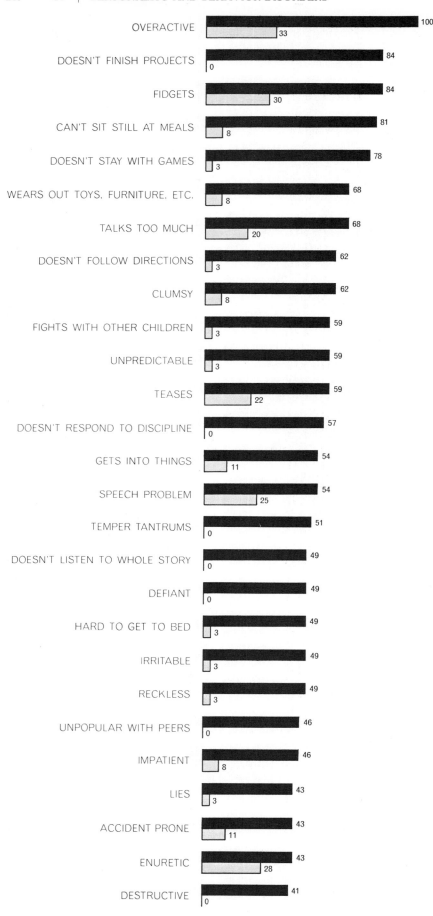

centages of the children in the control group were reported to be overactive, fidgety, overtalkative or given to teasing, but even in these necessarily subjective answers the control children had a much lower positive score as a group than the patients did. All in all the catalogue of symptoms indicated clearly that the patients were distinctly different in temperament from normal children.

Along with their fidgetiness and inability to concentrate the hyperactive children showed many forms of antisocial behavior. They were given to fighting with other children, irritability, defiance, lying and destructiveness, and nearly half were said to be unpopular with other children. About one in four of the patients had been caught stealing (usually money from members of their family), and about one in 10 had been guilty of vandalism, setting fires, cruelty to animals and truancy. Consulting their teachers, we found that half of the patients had had to be disciplined in school, more than a third had had to repeat grades and the same proportion had histories of repeated fighting in school.

The hyperactive children's troubles had generally started at a very early age. About half of the mothers had begun to notice that their child was unusual before he was two years old. We found no indication that the behavioral disorder was significantly related to complications in the mother's pregnancy or delivery, to a family history of mental disease or to absence of the child's parents from home; there was no statistical difference between the patients' family backgrounds and the control children's in these respects. The patients did tend, however, to have a history of feeding problems, disturbed sleep and generally poor health in the first year of life, and many had been handicapped by delayed development of speech and poor coor-

COMMON SYMPTOMS of hyperactivity were scored (*at left*) in a study that compared 37 young patients (32 boys and five girls) from the psychiatric clinic of the St. Louis Children's Hospital with a control group of children attending first grade in two suburban schools. The symptoms were scored by interviewing the mothers of the two groups. The black bars indicate the percentage of young patients with each symptom; the gray bars show percentages for the control group. There are obviously many more "fidgety Philipps" among the 37 patients than among the nonpatients.

dination. All of this suggested the possibility of inborn difficulties.

We followed up this study of young children with a similar survey of teen-agers who had previously been seen in our clinic for the same disorder. This sample consisted of 45 youngsters (41 boys and four girls) between the ages of 12 and 16. On the average they had first come to the clinic about five years previously, and all had definitely been diagnosed at that time as hyperactive on the basis of several symptoms. For the follow-up study we used a questionnaire for interviewing the mothers that was much like the one we had employed in the survey of the sample of younger children. In this case we added interviews with the teen-agers themselves, asking them about their symptoms, their general behavior at home and in school, their attitudes toward school and their self-evaluation.

Our interviews with the mothers indicated that these children had not changed much since we first saw them. Of the 45 teen-agers 14 had deteriorated or at least not improved in behavior, 26 had improved somewhat and only five were said to be more or less free of their original symptoms. Most of the youngsters were still notably restless, unable to concentrate or finish jobs, overtalkative and poor in school performance. A large majority were described by their mothers as being low in self-esteem and tending to feel picked on (questions that we had unfortunately neglected to include in the earlier study of young children). It turned out that the teen-agers showed a distinct increase (over the younger sample) in impatience, resistance to discipline, irritability and lying. Substantial proportions of them engaged in fighting and stealing, and deviant behavior such as running away from home, going with a "bad crowd" and playing hooky; drinking was not uncommon. In our interviews with the teen-agers themselves, many said they found it hard to study and were not interested in school. A third of the mothers said their child was so hard to handle that they had seriously considered sending him away to a boarding school or an institution. Four out of 10 of the mothers could think of no career for which their child would be suited.

These youngsters were clearly abnormal, but not seriously so in the usual psychiatric terms. Three of the 45 have a record of antisocial behavior so extensive that they might be called "sociopaths." The others are best described as individuals with personality problems.

We have not yet compared these teen-agers with a control group. That their problems are not typical of teen-agers' problems in general has already been indicated, however, by the results of a study by Jean W. Macfarlane and her associates at the University of California at Berkeley. They found that in a large sample of normal teen-age boys from roughly the same socioeconomic background as our group the frequency of overactivity was only 17 percent; of irritability, 12 percent; of quarrelsomeness, 4 percent; of lying, 8 percent; of stealing, zero.

We have found evidence of another kind that hyperactive children start life with a temperament that is distinctly abnormal. In clinical practice I have been impressed by the frequency with which hyperactive children turn out to have had a history of an accidental poisoning early in life—usually before the age of three. This might be expected, because the medicine cabinet is a prime target for children's curiosity, and a hyperactive child is more likely than a normal one to get into such things as soon as he can toddle and climb. The question has considerable practical importance; if active children do indeed run a higher than normal danger of accidental poisoning, extra precautions to prevent access to drugs and toxins should be taken in such households. We decided to look into the facts concerning the extent of this hazard for hyperactive children.

Two medical students at Washington University followed up 90 young children who had been treated at Children's Hospital for accidental poisoning six years earlier. They interviewed the mothers and teachers of the children with our standard questionnaire for eliciting symptoms of the hyperactivity syndrome. At the time of the interviews these children were eight or nine years old. It turned out that a third of the 58 boys could be diagnosed as hyperactive, using fairly rigorous criteria, an incidence considerably higher than the 7 percent figure we have found in a control population of boys. We also sent questionnaires to the mothers of 80 hyperactive children visiting our clinic and to the mothers of an equal number of normal second-grade children. Again the returns showed that 22 percent of the hyperactive children, as against only 8 percent of the controls, had had an accidental poisoning.

This finding, it seems to me, strongly supports the thesis that the syndrome manifests itself at an early age and that hyperactive children may be innately different from other children. It is consistent with the fact that 80 percent of the responding parents in our first study of young children in the early grades and 60 percent of those in our study of teen-agers reported they knew their children were unusual before they reached school age. Alexander Thomas, Stella Chess and Herbert G. Birch of the New York University School of Medicine, who have made an extensive study of the behavioral development of children from birth, have found that certain patterns observable at a very early age foreshadow later disorders of behavior. The investigators conclude that many disorders may be traceable to inborn temperament.

In our own experience with hyperactive children in the clinic we have commonly found that the child's father had been troublesome as a youngster, that he may have dropped out of school and that as an adult he is characteristically restless and short-tempered. Our interviews with the mothers in our first study did not disclose any significant difference between the patient group and the control group in this aspect of the family history, but the interviews did not actually yield much information on the subject. We plan to explore the question directly and in detail in further studies. An investigation at the genetic level is already in progress: a medical geneticist at Washington University is analyzing the chromosomes of a group of children from our clinic. This inquiry was prompted by the recent discovery of an association of aggressive antisocial behavior with a peculiarity of the XYY karyotype. This is a chromosomal abnormality in which a male is born with two Y chromosomes instead of one.

It seems highly significant that the hyperactivity syndrome is much more common in boys than in girls (the ratio in the various groups studied is six to one or more) and that boys are also afflicted more frequently with other behavioral problems such as infantile autism, reading disability and delayed speech development. There is every reason to believe these are inborn differences and not the result of biased treatment of boys by parents and teachers. Moreover, difficulties in reading and speech are often familial. It appears that some inherited eccentricities of behavior or learning may be sex-linked or that the male nervous system may be peculiarly prone to certain failures in early development; conceivably both of these hypotheses are true.

The idea that hyperactivity has a biological basis is further strengthened by the dramatic change in behavior produced in many of these children by a stimulating drug (such as amphetamine or methylphenidate). Under the influence of the drug the hyperactive child (in at least half of all cases) becomes quieter, exhibits a longer attention span and greater perseverance with assigned work, performs better in school and is generally easier to get along with. It has been found that amphetamine has a somewhat similar effect on the performance of normal adults who are assigned a boring or complex task. Russell Davis of the University of Cambridge reported, for example, that in an experiment along these lines men who were given the drug became absorbed in the task, apparently as a result of the focusing of all their attention on it. The stimulating drug, in short, seems to bring about a more acute and better-organized responsiveness to the environment.

It is known that the amphetamines act on the reticular formation in the brain stem, a key area controlling consciousness and attention. When amphetamine is administered to a subject, one can usually tell he is aroused simply by observing his behavior: he becomes more attentive, alert and frequently more talkative. Objective evidence of "arousal" can also be seen in changes that occur in his brain waves as shown by an electroencephalogram. It is also known that amphetamine produces specific effects on the metabolism of norepinephrine, or noradrenalin, in the brain cells. Norepinephrine probably controls the transmission of nerve impulses by some key nerve cells; it is highly concentrated in areas such as the hypothalamus and brain stem, which have much to do with mood and awareness. In recent experiments Sebastian P. Grossman of the University of Chicago found that the injection of a minute amount of norepinephrine in the reticular formation of a rat lowers the animal's activity level and responsiveness; injection of acetylcholine has the opposite effect. Since amphetamine is known to stimulate the release of norepinephrine from nerve endings, it seems entirely possible that the drug's effect on the behavior of hyperactive children may be due to its action at this critical juncture. It may repair a deficit in the activity of norepinephrine or in some other way restore the normal balance of activity between norepinephrine and acetylcholine.

This idea gains credence from the fact that hyperactive children often behave very differently from their usual selves when they are under tension. A child who has been described by his mother as a demon may be an angel when he comes to the psychiatrist's office. Most hyperactive children tend to be subdued in a strange situation and to display their bad behavior only when they feel at home. The explanation may lie in a stress-induced release of norepinephrine in the brain cells. Thus a state of anxiety may produce the same effect as a dose of amphetamine—through exactly the same mechanism.

It has been known for many years that removal of the frontal lobes of the brain produces hyperactivity in monkeys. Harry F. Harlow and his associates at the University of Wisconsin narrowed down the critical area: hyperactivity and apparent distractibility could be produced in monkeys by removing a section of granular cortex toward the rear of the frontal lobe. In a related series of experiments George D. Davis of the Louisiana State University School of Medicine has found that the effects of lobectomy in monkeys can be reversed with a stimulating drug; it reduces the animals' overactivity and improves their concentration.

As a practicing child psychiatrist I am of course concerned primarily with treatment of the hyperactivity syndrome. Amphetamine and other stimulants produce such good results that it is tempting to base treatment on use of a drug. Its effect is only temporary, however; when the drug wears off, the child reverts to his usual behavior. Furthermore, continuance of the drug into the teens runs the danger that the child may overuse it or become a habitual drug user. We therefore employ the drugs only to enable a hyperactive child to make a good start in school and prevent him from becoming resentful and insecure. My colleagues and I devote ourselves principally to adjusting the environment to the needs of the handicapped child.

This approach entails giving practical advice to the parents and helping them to apply techniques of behavioral therapy. We also assist the child's teachers in planning ways to work around his difficulties in learning. Educating the parents and teachers in what the problems of hyperactive children are and how to handle them appears to offer the best hope for enabling the patients to grow up to be confident and happy in spite of the limitations of their temperament.

Schizophrenia

by Don D. Jackson
August 1962

This grave mental illness now hospitalizes at least 250,000 Americans. Its investigators have sought to explain it on either a physiological or a psychological basis. The latter explanation is currently favored

Schizophrenia is a major public health problem compounded of the private and individually unique catastrophes of its victims. The diagnosis of schizophrenia accounts for more than half of the mentally ill patients who fill more than half of the hospital beds in this country. Typically the disorder overtakes younger people—"between the ages of 18 and 28." Often it maims them for life: the schizophrenic entering a state hospital has little better than an even chance of ever returning to society as a functioning member. The symptoms of the disease are behavioral, and they are as diverse as the personalities of the patients themselves. Of schizophrenics in general it can be said only that they show little or no response or inappropriate response to other people and to their environment. Frequently they exhibit secondary symptoms, including hallucinations and delusions, confusion, fluctuation of mood from manic to depressed, stupor and catatonic rigidity. In a sense the symptoms are the disease. There is no agreement among therapists and investigators as to the underlying nature of schizophrenia and its cause.

It is not for lack of study that schizophrenia remains a mysterious and intractable disease. Since the turn of the century it has occupied the forefront of psychiatry in the U.S. and Europe. From a survey of the huge literature that I have recently completed I can testify that the difficulties arise not only from the nature of the disease and the unsatisfactory character of its victims as research subjects but also from the human frailty of its investigators. The symptoms of schizophrenia are ambiguous and so various from culture to culture that the consistency of diagnosis and recorded data must be correspondingly low. The chronic patients in state hospitals, who are readily available and therefore the subjects most often stud-

ied, are members of a subculture: the mental hospital. The social effect of being imprisoned and of feeling abandoned and the physical effect of poor diet and lack of exercise bring on behavioral problems and even physiological and constitutional changes that are peculiar to this culture.

But the study of schizophrenia must include also study of its investigators. They have tended to gravitate toward one of two extremes: to investigation of some easily isolated and controllable aspect of the patient—his urine, for example—or to generalized sociological observations that may be interesting but that are difficult to prove or to replicate. On the whole the largest effort has gone into the search for some neat biological explanation for schizophrenia, and hence a cure, at the expense of broader research. Certainly it would be agreeable if some abnormal biochemical process or some pathological change in the brain could be made to explain the malfunctioning of the schizophrenic, because a drug or an operation could then undoubtedly be devised to cure him. If the accumulating literature proves anything, however, it shows with increasing clarity that there will be no such simple answer to schizophrenia.

Fortunately this bleak conclusion does not constitute the sole finding of my survey of the literature. I also note encouraging signs in recent years of willingness to encompass broader questions. Instead of chopping the patient into bits in order to study the variables in isolation, the trend is now toward study of the many variables involved—physiological, psychological and social—in their interaction.

The Taxonomy of Mental Illness

Schizophrenia is one of the many categories of mental illness worked out by

19th-century European psychiatrists in confident expectation that the laboratory would soon match diagnosis with specific cure. In the psychiatric classification of Emil Kraepelin it was first called dementia praecox, meaning early, as contrasted with senile, deterioration of the brain. In 1911 Eugen Bleuler renamed the disorder "schizophrenia," from the Greek for "split" (*schizein*) and "mind" (*phren*). The term was intended to express the common observation that patients exhibit a splitting of psychic function in which one set of ideas, or "complexes," dominates the personality for a time while others are suppressed. Bleuler also pointed out that there is no anatomical deterioration of the brain and that the affliction does not occur exclusively or primarily in the young, as Kraepelin's label implied. Bleuler urged that the disorder be called "the group of schizophrenias," because he felt that psychiatrists were dealing with a variety of disorders linked by certain common symptoms.

Unfortunately Bleuler's cautioning too often goes unheeded nowadays, and many research reports prove meaningless because the author tells nothing about his cases except that they are "schizophrenic." Kraepelin originally distinguished four subclasses of the disorder: hebephrenic, characterized by undue concern with the body image, hypochondriac symptoms and silliness; catatonic, characterized by mute, rigid withdrawal; paranoid, characterized by suspicious, embittered attitudes and feelings of persecution; and simple schizophrenia, characterized by an insidious onset leading to withdrawal, confusion and secret grandiosity. The usefulness of Kraepelin's classification is attested by the fact that it continues in use to this day in hospital psychiatry. In the standard nomenclature of U.S. psychiatry schizophrenia is broken down into nine forms, to which most psychiatrists add two paranoid syndromes. Many authorities now feel that the picture of schizophrenia is too mixed to permit such fine-grained classification. They point out that it is much easier to classify chronic, hospitalized patients than to classify more acute cases at onset.

Next to schizophrenia the most common diagnoses on admission to state hospitals in the U.S. are senile psychosis and alcoholism, which respectively account for roughly 20 per cent and 10 per cent of all patients. In both cases the behavioral disorder is usually accompanied by some observable constitutional defect. Involutional melancholia, which principally afflicts women at the crisis of menopause, is the diagnosis in 10 to 15 per cent of the patients. In a dwindling number of cases the patients are initially diagnosed as suffering from manic-depressive psychosis. This condition is characterized by the cyclic emotionality implied by its name and is distinguished from schizophrenia because the patient does not show the flattening or disengagement of emotional response to others. In the medical records of the U.S. today the manic-depressive shows up increasingly in the depressive phase of his illness. Whatever the diagnosis on admission, as Lionel S. Penrose of University College London observed in 1941, the longer a patient remains in a mental hospital, the more the diagnosis tends to become that of schizophrenia.

Agreement as to diagnosis may conceal the most diametrically opposed opinions as to the nature of the disease. In the view of classical psychiatry schizophrenia was a "thinking disorder." The patient could say, for example, "Mother is dead," while smiling because he lacked all feeling or because his feelings were inappropriate. This lack of apparent feeling led Sigmund Freud to the conclusion, early in the century, that the schizophrenic was too narcissistic— that is, too self-preoccupied—to be reached by the psychotherapist. It was not until the 1920's that the U.S. psychiatrist Harry Stack Sullivan and his associates came forward with the view that the schizophrenic's apparent lack of emotion hid an extreme sensitivity; they found that their patients were able to form intense relationships in psychotherapy. On the other hand, the more organically minded investigators understand the lack of emotional response as a defect, and they postulate an anatomical or physiological cause. One can say in general that the closer an investigator is to the medical sciences and to European traditions in medicine, the more likely he is to ascribe organic causation to the symptoms of schizophrenia. Correspondingly, the closer he is to the behavioral sciences and to U.S. traditions, the more likely he is to view schizophrenia as a psychologically determined condition.

For their part schizophrenics seem to be obligingly responsive to the attitude of the investigator. A patient may seem hopelessly ill to the organically oriented psychiatrist, and with the same patient a psychologically oriented psychiatrist may strike immediate promise and future hope. Who is to say how much such factors may influence the eventual outcome, not only in particular cases but also in the ultimate understanding and management of this cruel disorder?

The Genetic Hypothesis

One of the most fruitful hypotheses, measured in terms of the volume of work it has inspired, holds that schizophrenia is a hereditary disease. Most human geneticists have long since set aside such primitive notions as "poor protoplasm," advanced by 19th-century German physicians in explanation of many afflictions, from leprosy to insomnia. They recognize also that the entity of personality embraces many variables to which the Mendelian laws of single-factor inheritance are inapplicable. The principal difficulty in the way of this line of research, however, remains the fact that the same individuals who provide the genetic inheritance of the schizophrenic also furnish the early environment in the overwhelming majority of cases. It has therefore been an impossible task to sort out the relative influences of nature and nurture.

The idea of studying identical twins in order to accomplish this sorting out was suggested as early as 1885 by the English mathematician and geneticist Francis Galton. Today the most widely quoted evidence for a hereditary cause of schizophrenia comes from the study of the disease in identical twins conducted by Franz J. Kallmann of the Columbia University College of Physicians and Surgeons. He showed that if one identical twin is located in a state hospital suffering from schizophrenia, there is an 85 per cent chance that the other twin will be found to suffer from the same disorder. This is an impressive figure, even discounting the fact that concordant pairs are much more likely to attract attention than discordant ones. Identical twins, however, have been the subject of intensive psychological study, and it is clear that the relation involves something more than just two individuals who have a similar genetic inheritance. In twins, as in other pairs of individuals who are emotionally close to each other, the condition known as *folie à deux* has been commonly observed. The two partners tend to develop shared delusions and symptoms and to become mentally ill at about the same time. A study of the case histories of sibling pairs reveals a strong homosexual element that shows up in the content of their delusions and seems related to difficulty in

FIVE PIONEERS in the study and treatment of schizophrenia are, reading from left to right, the psychiatrists Sigmund Freud of Austria, Frieda Fromm-Reichmann of the U.S.,

distinguishing "me" from "you." The condition is four times more common in women than in men and typically results in two spinster sisters living in semi-seclusion in their 30's or 40's. This is undoubtedly related to the fact that in our culture "closeness" between brothers is likely to receive opprobrious notice because of suspicion of homosexuality, whereas intimacy between women is acceptable. Published reports on fraternal as well as identical-twin pairs show a much higher concordance for schizophrenia among female pairs. One report, in fact, shows that female fraternal twins were nearly 50 per cent concordant, a figure that compares with Kallmann's finding for identical twins.

What about identical twins who are reared apart? There is a fiction rampant to the effect that schizophrenia tends to afflict both twins simultaneously. In a careful search of the literature I have been able to turn up only two instances that partially satisfy the terms of this story. In each case the twins were adopted by relatives on opposite sides of their natural families and were well aware of each other's existence; in fact, they were caught in the middle of family feuding. The effects of heredity and environment could not be said to have been separated in these cases. In an intensive effort to assess the incidence of schizophrenia, without regard to simultaneity, in pairs of identical twins reared apart, a group of investigators led by H. H. Newman and Frank N. Freeman collected 19 cases after scouring the entire U.S. This labor came to no conclusion be-

cause the investigating team disagreed on the relative weight to be accorded to nature and nurture in these cases.

Apart from identical twins the statistics show that schizophrenia does tend to "run in families." To some investigators the figures suggest the classical Mendelian dominant mode of inheritance; to others the genetic factor appears recessive. But all of these statistical series betray evidence that cultural influences are at work. The shadow of *folie à deux* is apparent, for example, in a Swiss study that shows that sister pairs and mothers and daughters are more likely to be found in mental hospitals than brother pairs and fathers and sons. Two recent Scandinavian studies reveal an almost complete absence of the disease in the fathers of schizophrenics and a significantly higher incidence in mothers. But geneticists do not claim that schizophrenia is a sex-linked disorder!

Some geneticists have attempted to tie schizophrenia to other aspects of inheritance: to type of physique or to a predisposing "schizoid personality," characterized by tendencies to introversion. These studies have foundered on the observation that schizophrenics and their relatives come in all shapes and sizes and on the discovery that the schizophrenic patient has been found to be extroverted as often as introverted prior to his illness.

The more modern idea is that schizophrenia is a hereditarily determined disease that requires psychogenic stress for its precipitation. Such a proposition is difficult to prove one way or the other. Until the ill-defined abstraction of "per-

sonality" can be broken down into enduring traits that are shown to have a genetic basis it is surely fruitless to look for a genetic mechanism behind the symptomatic disorder of schizophrenia. If the apparently unitary and measurable "trait" of intelligence comes under suspicion, as it has in recent years, then personality must seem even less subject to hereditary determination. All are agreed that sick patients come from sick families, but the question of whether this commonplace observation rests on psychological or physiological grounds or both has scarcely been broached.

Biochemical Investigation

It would appear that a genetic cause of schizophrenia would have to manifest itself in some metabolic or other biochemical defect. No such defect has been uncovered in 60 years of persistent investigation. Biochemical investigation of schizophrenia usually pursues one of two major courses: (1) the body chemistry of "normals" is compared with that of schizophrenics or (2) the same drug is administered to the two classes of subjects and the difference in effect, if any, is compared. A review of published reports indicates that work along both lines has been largely inspired by chance discoveries or by purely empirical leads. In the early 1900's, for example, Sir David Bruce observed that the administration of thyroid-gland extract had an apparently beneficial effect on schizophrenics. There followed a large number of papers on the activity of the thy-

Emil Kraepelin of Germany, Eugen Bleuler of Switzerland and Harry Stack Sullivan of the U.S. Their researches in this field span a period of approximately 75 years, extending from the last quarter of the 19th century through the first half of the 20th century.

roid gland in schizophrenia. Manfred Sakel of Germany made a similar finding with respect to insulin; hundreds of papers have since explored the carbohydrate metabolism of schizophrenics.

The most recent notable surge of effort along these lines has surrounded the role of serotonin in the biochemistry of the human organism. This substance, originally discovered in the lining of the intestine, was found to play an important role in the function of smooth (involuntary) muscle. Eventually it was isolated from various sites in the central nervous system, in particularly high concentration from certain parts of the brain stem. Some investigators then measured serotonin in schizophrenics and reported it to be high, although a few others found it to be low.

What brought serotonin to the center of the stage in biochemical studies of schizophrenics was the finding that lysergic acid diethylamide (LSD) is antagonistic to serotonin in its action on smooth muscle. LSD had already attracted attention because it induced hallucinations and other symptoms in volunteer subjects; investigators were encouraged to believe that they had come on a means to induce "experimental psychoses" [see "Experimental Psychoses," by Six Staff Members of the

LARGEST MENTAL HOSPITAL in the U.S. is the Pilgrim State Hospital near New York City. Of the 13,991 patients there on March 31, 1958, 60 per cent were schizophrenic. Of the 535,000 patients in all public mental hospitals in the U.S. in 1959, approximately 50

Boston Psychopathic Hospital; SCIENTIFIC AMERICAN, June, 1955]. It was postulated that LSD might produce its peculiar behavioral effects by competition with serotonin in the central nervous system. This idea acquired even more stirring implications from the finding that reserpine, a tranquilizer already in wide use in mental hospitals, apparently produced its effects by a parallel sort of action. It was only one more step to the

per cent were schizophrenic. Fifty-three per cent of these were women; 47 per cent, men.

conclusion that schizophrenia was a disorder of serotonin metabolism and another step to the use of serotonin in the treatment of schizophrenics. Some investigators went so far as to inject the substance into the ventricles of patients' brains, a rather difficult neurosurgical procedure.

The enthusiasm over serotonin was heightened by the discovery of a breakdown product of adrenalin called adrenochrome. This substance bears a structural resemblance to LSD and to mescaline, the active ingredient in the hallucinatory mushrooms and peyote cactus employed in religious rituals by the Indians of the U.S. Southwest and the Mexican highlands. The discoverers of adrenochrome found that it induced hallucinations when they administered it to themselves. They proposed, therefore, that an excess of adrenochrome in the biochemistry of schizophrenics brings on their psychotic symptoms.

Further research has failed to sustain these ideas and the hopes they excited. The function of serotonin in the central nervous system remains unknown. A serotonin antagonist called 2-bromolysergic acid produces none of the mental symptoms characteristic of LSD. Chlorpromazine, a tranquilizer more effective than reserpine in quieting schizophrenics, shows no sign of biochemical competition with serotonin. Adrenochrome has yet to be found in the body and has been labeled a laboratory artifact. A painstaking study of the turnover of adrenal substances in the bodies of normal and schizophrenic women by direct measurement from the adrenal arteries and veins has shown no detectable differences. Finally, the much heralded experimental psychoses have turned out to be nothing other than "toxic psychoses," familiar to clinicians for many years and clearly differentiated from schizophrenic states. In toxic psychosis, whether it is induced by drugs or by bodily poisons as in uremia, the patient suffers from depression of higher cerebral function and deficiency in interpersonal transactions. The schizophrenic does not necessarily show such depression and is often capable of complex interpersonal relations.

Toxic psychosis is familiar to anyone who has weathered a cocktail party. As is well known, alcohol affects different people differently and the same person differently at different times. By the same token mescaline might enhance the religious ecstasy of a member of the peyote cult and might have quite another effect on an Irishman on a Saturday night in a bawdyhouse. Studies that

set out to compare the reactions of schizophrenics and volunteers to drugs must therefore be designed with adequate respect for psychological variables.

Customarily investigators rely on placebos (inert substances) as controls for the drugs being administered. Yet a recent study has shown that the placebo and the tranquilizer function with equal effect in improving the schizophrenic's ability to stop soiling himself. Withdrawal of either substance was accompanied by regression in behavior, and restoration was accompanied by improvement again. This study casts doubt on hundreds of previous investigations that have served to demonstrate the efficacy of tranquilizers as such in the management of schizophrenic patients. It should serve as a caution against hastily conceived programs for testing drugs without proper regard for the context in which they are given.

Failure to observe this practical rule explains most of the false enthusiasms and disappointments that the biochemical approach to schizophrenia has engendered in the past. Although much of importance is being learned about the mechanisms of the living cell and of the body, these advances have shed no light on schizophrenia. It has not been shown that any biochemical substance is involved in the cause of the disorder. It is not even known if schizophrenia is accompanied by an increase in the production of any chemical substance in the body. These questions are not unworthy of investigation, but they cannot be usefully pursued in isolation.

Psychological Causation

Some of the hopes vested in drug-induced psychoses have recently been transferred to purely psychological methods for producing the so-called experimental psychoses. One of the most effective of these techniques is to cut down environmental stimulation to a minimum. Apparently the human organism requires a certain rate of sensory input in order to maintain the functioning of its perceptual apparatus. When the input is naturally lowered, as it is in sleep, those projections of already registered percepts called dreams occur. That the dreaming process has physiological significance as well has been shown by Nathaniel Kleitman of the University of Chicago, who has established that dreaming is essential to physical well-being. Sensory deprivation is accomplished in a number of ways in the laboratory—by submerging the sub-

THREE LARGEST MENTAL HOSPITALS in New York are located in this one section of Long Island. On March 31, 1958, they contained 32,277 patients, of whom 18,993 were schizophrenic. Of the 51,458 schizophrenics in all New York state hospitals at that time, about 60 per cent had been hospitalized 10 years or more and only 13 per cent one year or less.

ject in water at body temperature, for example, or by confining him in a room with his hands isolated in special cuffs, a translucent mask over his eyes and no sound but the hum of an air conditioner. After relatively brief periods, in a majority of cases, the subject begins to have hallucinations and to experience the most unpleasant psychosis-like reactions [see "The Pathology of Boredom," by Woodburn Heron; SCIENTIFIC AMERICAN Offprint 430].

These studies have led some investigators to postulate a psychological mechanism for the induction of schizophrenia. It is thought that the victim is driven by severe anxiety to repress and reject the input of sensory experience from the environment that has become so disturbing to him. Such withdrawal, combined with attempts at restructuring his experience, leads to hallucination and the formation of a delusional system. The psychoses of old age suggest an interesting parallel; in these cases defects in the sensory system lead to disorientation and misperception of environmental cues and therefore to disturbed behavior. One of the most familiar examples of this process is the paranoid feeling on the part of a deaf elderly individual that "people are talking about me."

It is difficult to test hypotheses of this kind, for instance to determine objectively whether a schizophrenic's difficulty in assimilating perceptions is constitutional or learned. Schizophrenics are notoriously uncoöperative, and one cannot be sure how to motivate them properly to do their best on, say, an intelligence test. The evaluation of such a test presents further problems, because the patient may have been daydreaming in school and not taking in material that he "should" have learned and was otherwise capable of learning at a given chronological age in school. Psychological studies of schizophrenics show a ruling tendency toward scatter—that is, toward a chaotic mixture of good and bad performance.

Family Study and Therapy

Some useful insights have come from recent studies of the families of schizophrenics. The so-called Benjamin proverbs have long been used in making the diagnosis of schizophrenia. To the question "What is the meaning of the old proverb 'A rolling stone gathers no moss'?" the sick person characteristically gives a literal rather than an interpretive answer. Now there are indications that the parents of schizophrenics also answer in a literal fashion. Such answers on the patient's part may therefore be regarded as the result of a learning process rather than a thinking disorder.

Ordinarily a physician treats just one person: his patient. In psychiatry the intimacy of the therapist-patient relation has reinforced tradition. Psychiatrists have been slow to think of the disturbed family that may have produced the disturbed patient. This is not to say that the importance of family relations in the genesis of schizophrenia has gone without recognition. But the early psychoanalytic papers, in accordance with the plot of the Oedipus complex, focused on the patient's relation to his mother and neglected the family system. Many therapists today continue to rely on the "patient's-eye view" of the family and conduct only the most superficial interviews with parents, siblings and, in the case of mature patients, spouses.

It was not until the 1950's that therapists began to see the patient's family as a group and to undertake conjoint family therapy. At the National Institute of Mental Health, Murray Bowen arranged for families and patients to live together at the hospital; at other institutions the families visit the hospital once or twice a week for sessions of therapy. As might be expected, such experience has encouraged the formulation of new hypotheses. Among these is the "double bind" theory advanced by Gregory Bateson, Jay Haley, John H. Weakland and me, which sees the traumatic situation of the schizophrenic as arising fundamentally from aberration in communication. The "binder," who may be parent or spouse, demands two quite different and mutually contradictory responses from the patient at the same time but on two levels of communication, as by voice and by action. The patient is so dependent on the binder that he is strongly inhibited against acknowledging or pointing out the contradiction; yet he can neither ignore nor fail to respond to this paralyzing injunction. In a model situation, a mother says to her child: "Don't be so obedient!" She thereby places the child in an impossible paradox. If he obeys the injunction, he is disobedient; if he disobeys, he is obedient. In a real situation the contradiction is, of course, covert and arises perhaps from parental hostility that is camouflaged by the external cultural trappings of the parent-child relation. Such disturbed patterns of communication may obtain in other relations; the motion picture *Gaslight*, in which a husband willfully subjects his wife to such treatment, has added the verb "to gaslight" to the language. In

a study of a mental-hospital ward Alfred H. Stanton and Morris S. Schwartz, then working at the Chestnut Lodge Sanitarium, found in every case where a patient became assaultive or had a psychotic episode there was a covert disagreement between the psychotherapist and the physician who ran the ward.

Another observation from family studies relates the patient's condition and progress to "family homeostasis." In some cases it has been found that the family system is able to function "normally" only at the expense of the patient's mental health. Ulcers, heart attacks, gall bladder disfunction and other

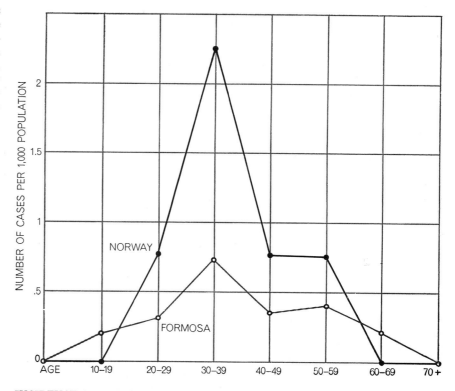

INCIDENCE OF SCHIZOPHRENIA in the total population of a community was studied both for the island of Formosa and for a small fishing village in Norway. The studies, by different investigators, were made in the 1940's. As the graph shows, the incidence of schizophrenia was highest in both communities among members of the 30-to-39-year-old age group.

INVESTIGATOR	YEAR	NUMBER OF PAIRS		INCIDENCE OF SCHIZOPHRENIA	
		FRATERNAL	IDENTICAL	FRATERNAL	IDENTICAL
LUXENBERGER	1930	60	21	3.3	66.6
ROSANOFF	1934	101	41	10.0	67.0
ESSEN-MOLLER	1941	24	7	16.7	71.0
SLATER	1951	115	41	14.0	76.0
KALLMANN	1946	517	174	14.5	85.6
KALLMANN	1952	685	268	14.5	85.6

IDENTICAL AND FRATERNAL TWINS have been studied by several investigators to discover if schizophrenia has a genetic basis. All agree in finding that both identical twins are more likely to have the disease than are both fraternal twins. But the figures vary widely from one study to another, suggesting that factors other than the genetic may be at work.

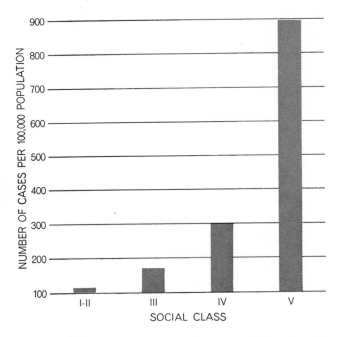

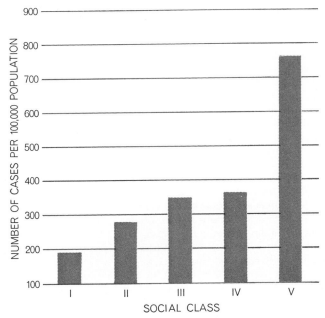

RELATION OF CLASS MEMBERSHIP to mental illness in a U.S. community was studied among patients undergoing psychiatric treatment, in and out of hospitals, in New Haven, Conn. Class membership was determined by residence, education and occupation. As the chart shows, the rate of schizophrenia was nearly nine times higher in the lowest class than in the two upper classes together.

FIRST ADMISSIONS of male schizophrenics to mental hospitals in Great Britain over a five-year period suggests the relation of class membership to mental illness in that country. Class status, as determined by the British census, is based solely on occupation. Unskilled workers make up the lowest class; professionals and administrators of various sorts constitute the two upper classes.

disorders appear to afflict other members of the family with suspicious frequency just at that time in conjoint family therapy when the patient makes a significant change for the better.

These insights from the first tentative steps in family therapy suggest the promise of deeper investigation of the family. There is need especially for longitudinal study of representative families over long periods of time. In cases where schizophrenia develops such study would show not only the character of the family at the time of crisis but also the earlier environment and the patterns of interpersonal relations and personality structure it promoted.

The Sociocultural Milieu

In undertakings of this kind psychiatry must enlist the collaboration of sociology and anthropology. Without the broader perspective of these other disciplines psychiatrists tend to generalize their observations of a few atypical patients into resounding pronouncements about mankind everywhere. A remarkable example of collaborative enterprise is the Nova Scotia study, led by Alexander H. Leighton of the Cornell University Medical College, which established the incidence and characteristic symptomatic patterns of mental illness

in three sociocultural groups in that community. Another is the Midtown Manhattan study, initiated by the late Thomas A. C. Rennie of Cornell, which has shown that psychiatrists may have underestimated the incidence of schizophrenia by some 300 per cent.

Considering the dimensions of schizophrenia as a public health problem, there is a dearth of straightforward statistics about it. State hospital admissions apparently offer a poor indication of the true incidence of the disease in the population. A recent survey of a portion of Salt Lake City indicates an incidence of 3 per cent, far in excess of the .85 per cent that figures in so many genetic studies. The work of August B. Hollingshead and Fredrick C. Redlich of the Yale University School of Medicine has demonstrated that the lowest socioeconomic group has 12 times the incidence of hospitalized schizophrenia compared with the highest. People living singly and in an economically deprived condition in the heart of a large city develop the illness far more often than their rural counterparts do.

Such findings barely suggest the insights into the true nature of the disease that can come from a full picture of its epidemiology. Sociologists have shown, moreover, that something more than mere head-counting is involved in gath-

ering statistics on mental illness. To evaluate the incidence of mental illness in a given social group, it is necessary to consider the character and degree of behavioral deviation from the group norms that will be tolerated by its members. It is obvious that a widely scattered rural population may accommodate many individuals who in a more closely knit community would interfere with their neighbors' lives to such an extent that they would be labeled insane. The culture of a group also has much to do with the nature of the disease as it occurs among the members. The patterns of schizophrenic psychosis that show up in Irish-American families contrast sharply, for example, with those of Italian-American families [see "Schizophrenia and Culture," by Marvin K. Opler; SCIENTIFIC AMERICAN Offprint 444].

Sociological studies have also illuminated the process of therapy in surprising ways. It has been shown that therapy is much more likely to be successful when therapist and patient come from similar social backgrounds and share similar value systems and goals. A review of the records of a New York hospital revealed that the social background, income and age of the patients were plainly correlated with the kind of treatment administered, ranging from electroshock to psychotherapy. This study also showed that while the foreign-born older patients tended to receive organic therapies, they also tended to get out of the hospital sooner than the middle-class, youthful schizophrenic. The longer stay in the hospital was evidently a function of the therapist-patient relation and not of the severity of the illness.

Theory and Therapy

Such observations lend support to the view, held by many, that there is in practice little or no relation between theory and therapy in schizophrenia. One can readily agree that this applies to the more radical approaches to therapy that have been advanced from time to time. Egas Moniz, the Portuguese psychiatrist and surgeon, designed and promoted the now discredited prefrontal lobotomy for schizophrenia on the strength of the purely empirical observation that lobotomized cats exhibited more placid and less excitable dispositions. The surgical interruption of the tract linking the thalamus and the frontal lobes in the human brain also produced more manageable patients but no cure for their affliction [see "Prefrontal Lobotomy: Analysis and Warning," by Kurt Goldstein; SCIENTIFIC AMERICAN Offprint 445]. An equally narrow and empirical observation suggested the first shock therapy. On the strength of the mistaken observation that epileptics do not develop schizophrenia it was thought that schizophrenics might be cured by subjecting them to convulsive seizures. The rationale for this kind of therapy now takes somewhat different forms, depending on the agent employed.

The few groups that relate theory to therapy on a one-to-one basis today stand at the extremes of the continuum from organic to psychological cause. For example, certain groups in Italy attribute schizophrenia to parasitic infestation, and so they purge the patients. On the other hand, there are American and a few European workers who attribute schizophrenia to family interaction and treat their patients by conjoint family psychotherapy. More frequently one finds investigators used the same techniques but espoused different theories of the disease. In two different centers, for example, large doses of reserpine and electroshock were employed to produce profound regression in schizophrenic patients. Both groups theorized that by such techniques they interrupted self-exciting circuits in the brain and facilitated reintegration of the patient. One group, however, viewed schizophrenia as an organic disorder and the other viewed it as a psychological disorder.

No matter what the theoretical viewpoint of the therapist, the tool most commonly used in the treatment of schizophrenia is the social milieu. In Europe, Canada and the U.S. mental hospitals universally stress the importance of work therapy, group therapy, the therapeutic community, open-door policies, television, dances and afternoon tea. There are few hospitals where the physicians do not attribute a large part of the efficacy of other kinds of treatment, including insulin-coma therapy as well as tranquilizers, to the interpersonal relations of patients and staff. The basic reorientation in the structure and function of the mental hospital throughout the nations of the West has had marked effect in eliminating what were regarded as usual symptoms of schizophrenia in former times—incontinence, smearing of feces and marked catatonic disorder of motility. Indeed, it seems to be fairly well recognized that medication of any sort supports the hospital staff in its traditional medical role and therefore has an important effect on therapy, whatever the direct action on the patient may be.

Progress in therapy, it is clear, has derived from the accumulation of empirical lore and not from theoretical foresight. If present attempts at therapy are to contribute to the improvement of therapy in the future, the therapist-investigator must emphasize the design and method of collecting data. Whatever his private persuasion, if he carefully reports his results, his colleagues and his successors in the work will learn something. As has been suggested in this discussion, the behavior of the investigator himself requires study in the investigation of so complex a subject as disturbed human behavior. The impulse of the organically oriented investigator to reduce the subject to a single cause, on the one hand, and the soul-saving tendencies of the psychotherapist, on the other, have on occasion muddied the waters. The chasm between them remains unbridged. But while it is my impression that the evidence for the psychosocial nature of schizophrenia has been mounting for the past 10 years, I see little reason to claim victory for either side, nor much sense in taking an either-or position. Such continuing conflict between polar positions is not strange in science. It is good evidence that serious effort is being made to study schizophrenia.

The Therapeutic Community

by Richard Almond
March 1971

*In this new approach to treating mental disturbance
the ward is a self-governing community. Shared values
and social role-playing reinforce therapy based on
open discussion of patients' problems*

The treatment of mental illness in the U.S. has changed profoundly over the past 20 years. An outstanding change has been the shift in the scene of care for severely disturbed patients from large state hospitals to the psychiatric wards of general hospitals and, more recently, to Federally supported community mental health centers. There has also been a pronounced decline in the number of psychiatric inpatients. One factor in this shift has been the discovery of drugs capable of altering acute psychotic behavior and severe depression. Another has been the trend toward reducing the prison-like atmosphere in large state hospitals. The third, which is not widely known outside the mental health profession, has been the development of a method of treatment that is called the therapeutic community.

The term describes a way of operating a small psychiatric unit in a hospital. Ideally a unit will have between 20 and 40 patients; a large hospital may have more than one therapeutic community. A key constituent of the method is a close relationship between the staff and the patients, who share the work and activities of the unit and participate in the making of decisions affecting it. Methods of treatment include psychotherapy, drug therapy when indicated, various group activities and therapies and family treatment. It is the attempt at maintaining a sense of patient-staff community, however, that is unique to this approach.

The system is exemplified by the psychiatric in-patient ward of the Yale–New Haven Hospital. It is a 24-bed unit within a general hospital that is part of the Yale University School of Medicine. The unit's constitution, which was written by patients, describes the ward as "a community whose goal is that each can learn how to be responsible for himself and is able to help himself through helping others." The same document confronts the arriving patient with a list of meetings of nine different types in addition to individual therapy. The meetings include several small group-therapy sessions, family group meetings, leaderless group meetings and a large number of community meetings.

Much of the work of the community meetings involves deciding questions of the privileges the individual patient is to have; his privilege status is first worked out periodically in negotiations between himself and an advisory board made up of patients. Values and behavioral norms within the patient-staff community are explicit and consistent. Patients are expected to behave normally, to socialize, to discuss real problems openly in the many group meetings and to participate in the decisions and activities of the unit.

For many patients the exposure to a therapeutic community for a period of weeks or months has proved helpful. The

COMMUNITY MEETING brings together the patients and staff members of a ward at the Yale–New Haven Hospital that is organized as a therapeutic community (*left*). The partici-

method does not work for everybody. Its implications are nonetheless important not only for psychiatry but also for other social experiments that seek to deal with the problems of living in a complex society.

The therapeutic community was foreshadowed by a widespread 19th-century technique known as "moral treatment" and by the approach termed "milieu therapy," which was developed early in this century by the German psychiatrist Hermann Simon and introduced in the U.S. some 40 years ago by William C. Menninger. In milieu therapy the psychiatrist, on the basis of understanding derived from psychotherapy with the patient, prescribed a particular approach to be taken by the members of the staff engaged in nursing and occupational therapy. The approach entailed the first recognition that the patient was responsive to his environment, but conceptually it did not advance far beyond the traditional doctor-patient relationship. An individual physician treated an individual patient; the milieu was regarded as an extension of the doctor.

Milieu therapy attracted the interest of social scientists, who undertook a number of studies of hospital units practicing it. Two major observations emerged. First, in the mental hospital, even a hospital where intensive psychotherapy is practiced, there is a "patient culture": a set of behavioral norms maintained within the patient group. The patient culture may be at variance with the therapeutic efforts of the staff; indeed, it may be largely unknown to the staff. Second, hospitals emphasizing psychotherapy are plagued by problems of communication among staff members and between patients and staff. Often these problems lead to a deterioration in the behavior of patients.

Much of the trouble in such hospitals appears to relate to issues of authority. A hospital, like any organization, needs some system of authority for maintaining its function. Asylums, prisons and state hospitals maintain order largely through physical and psychological coercion. Psychoanalysis, emphasizing maximum freedom for the patient, is at the opposite pole. Initial experiments with psychotherapy in hospitals emphasized freedom and minimum use of authority. Disruptive behavior by patients was tolerated as far as possible while the psychiatrist sought to bring about a lasting change through psychotherapy.

The therapeutic community as a hospital technique developed somewhat later than the approach oriented to psychotherapy. It grew in part from the same therapeutic impetus that had given rise to psychotherapy hospitals and in part from the difficulties encountered by those hospitals. The first therapeutic community was established shortly after World War II by the British psychiatrist Maxwell Jones. He organized a treatment unit at Belmont Hospital as a community where staff and patients were closely associated and the usual boundary between them was blurred by giving patients a share in decision-making and by holding a variety of group meetings where patients were encouraged to take part as equals and as therapists for one another. The atmosphere was permissive, but at times the staff asserted authority in order to protect the functioning of the unit. At other times the patients demonstrated surprising abilities for self-government and therapeutic collaboration.

My interest in the therapeutic community as an object of investigation developed in the course of work in several mental hospitals (including large state hospitals), institutions practicing intensive psychotherapy and finally a

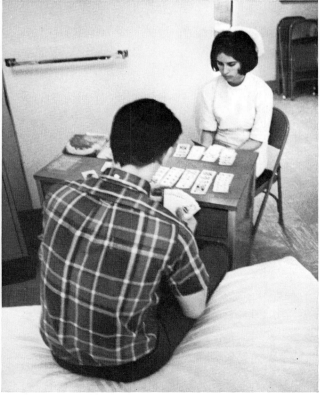

pants are voting on privileges to be awarded to a patient. Informal discussion of patients' problems is encouraged. A patient, a nurse and a social worker talk things over in hospital corridor (*middle*) and a patient and a nurse play cards in the patient's room (*right*).

number of therapeutic communities. Informal observation led me to conclude that the therapeutic community could create a ward atmosphere in which patients behave for the most part quite "normally" and can return rapidly to their families and jobs. It also seemed to me that in a well-run therapeutic community the difficult problem of authority could be resolved somewhere between coercion and permissiveness. An important ingredient of the solution

seemed to be the culture of the community. Staff and patients in effective therapeutic communities share a set of norms that emphasize an atmosphere of comradeship along with earnest, open confrontation of patients' problems.

These preliminary observations suggested the usefulness of a more careful examination of the culture of the therapeutic community. A group then in the department of psychiatry at the Yale School of Medicine decided to under-

take such a study, with the psychiatric ward of the Yale–New Haven Hospital as our subject. The therapeutic community established there by Thomas Detre about 10 years ago is regarded as a good example of the type. Our study group included Sandra Boltax, a psychiatrist working in the ward; Kenneth Keniston, a social psychologist, and myself.

We formulated a number of questions for the study. What in fact are the cultural values (concepts of the desirable)

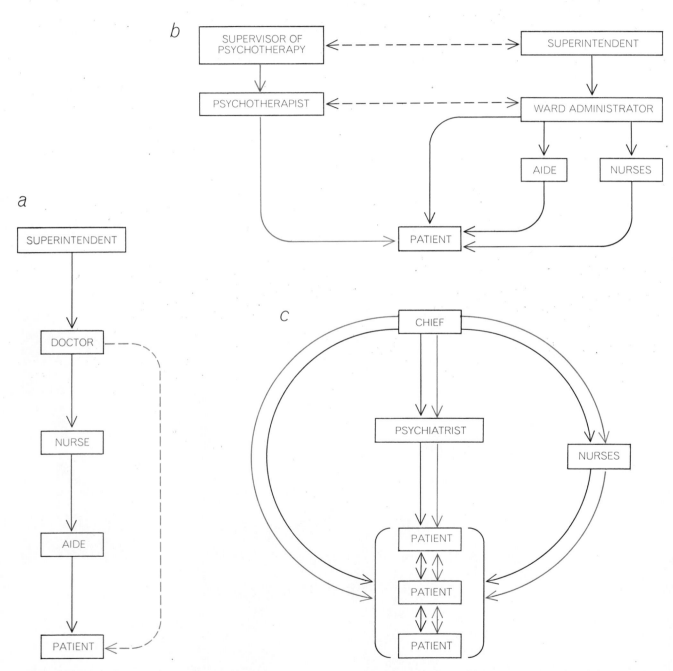

THERAPEUTIC COMMUNITY differs from two other kinds of psychiatric unit as indicated by these diagrams. In the "asylum" situation (*a*) patient care is given largely by aides. Authority relations (*black arrows*) dominate; only occasionally is there a therapeutic relation (*color*) between a doctor and a patient. In a psychotherapy

hospital (*b*) the population is smaller and more people can relate to a patient. Consensus tends to be poor between the therapeutic and the authority system, however, because they are oriented toward different goals. In the therapeutic community (*c*) every relation is assumed to have both a therapeutic and an authority aspect.

and norms (specific desired behavior) of the community? How is the culture of the community related to issues of authority and dependency? Is the culture transmitted effectively to new patients? How does the culture influence patient behavior? How do patients differ from one another in their experience of the ward culture? How does the exposure to psychiatric treatment, together with such a ward culture, affect the lives of patients after they leave the hospital?

To investigate these questions we used techniques from both psychiatry and the social sciences. For preliminary hypotheses we approached the ward in much the same way that an anthropologist approaches a primitive society. We observed the activities of the unit, interviewed patients and staff members and examined material written by and about the unit.

Eventually we concentrated on two major procedures. One we called the hospital-career study. It was an investigation of a patient's total experience in the ward. We interviewed patients at length to determine their views of their hospitalization, kept notes on the formal and informal therapy experiences, examined patients' charts and reviewed records of the changes of drugs and privileges affecting the patients. From all these data we assembled an account of each patient's experience in the hospital.

The second procedure made use of an attitude inventory that we developed to explore the value system of the unit. On the basis of our early observations we constructed questionnaire items that reflected the major norms of the unit as we perceived them. We organized the items into six scales: (1) be open—share problems and feelings with others here; (2) be a member—join in, feel an involvement and a loyalty to the community and its members; (3) take responsibility—your improvement and that of others is up to you, the patient; (4) have faith in the ward—trust in the effectiveness of this place and of the staff and the patients; (5) view family realistically—do not blame them for your problems, learn to adapt to family troubles; (6) face problems—difficulties will be diminished only if they are confronted directly in discussion and thinking. Although we separated these scales, it was clear from the outset that there might be a close relation between two or more of them.

In our questionnaire we also included scales from other studies of psychiatric hospitals to bring out two important and previously observed dimensions of patient experience. One was authority. The other was dependency—the patient's

SCALE	SAMPLE ITEM
MEMBERSHIP	Other patients can help me get well just as much as the staff can.
OPENNESS	The more a patient can open up about his problems the better.
RESPONSIBILITY	It is most important to take an active part in helping other patients get better.
FAITH IN WARD	Everyone here — patients and staff alike — is trying to help me get better.
FAMILY REALISM	I should not expect too much of my family because they have problems too.
FACE PROBLEMS	There is no psychological problem that can't be helped by facing it and trying to understand it.

VALUE SYSTEM of the therapeutic community at the Yale–New Haven Hospital was explored with a questionnaire that included 10 items for each of six scales (*left*) reflecting ward's major norms. Responses ranged from "strong agreement" to "strong disagreement."

SAMPLE ITEM	MEAN SCORE	LOADING ON FACTOR I
Each patient's major problems should be known to the staff and other patients.	5.42	.60
The more a patient can open up about his problems the better.	5.98	.60
I shouldn't mind when my personal problems are brought up in the group.	5.00	.54
I like to go to lots of hospital activities, such as O.T. and dances and patient government.	4.19	.50
For a patient who has to be hospitalized, groups are the most important treatment.	4.41	.49
Everyone here — patients and staff alike — is trying to help me get better.	5.82	.48
A patient should prefer talking with any other patient over reading a book.	4.30	.46
The staff here is trying to make a permanent improvement in my life.	5.79	.43
A patient should not worry about whether the things he tells his doctor will remain confidential.	4.79	.41
If I do not get better, it will be my own fault.	5.15	.39
It is most important to take an active part in helping other patients get better.	5.91	.38
Patients shouldn't have to tell each other about how they came to be on the ward.	2.75	—.69
A new patient should be allowed to be alone and not have to talk all the time, although being in groups may help too.	3.52	—.65
I wish people would leave me alone.	2.55	—.63
A disturbed patient should not have to talk about how he is doing or feeling in the large meetings.	2.98	—.62
There should not be so much pressure here for patients to conform to the system of the ward.	3.41	—.58
A patient should not get too involved with other patients while here.	3.00	—.53
I wish my doctor would keep many of the problems I discuss with him confidential between him and the staff.	4.38	—.49
A patient in the hospital shouldn't be forced to be friendly with other patients with completely different kinds of backgrounds.	3.01	—.48
It's asking too much for a patient to discuss his problems quickly after admission.	3.79	—.46
Things such as O.T. and recreation may be pleasant ways to spend time, but they probably do little to help patients get well again.	3.01	—.45
If another patient tells me about some trouble he is having, I should discuss it with him but leave it up to him whether to tell anyone else.	3.86	—.44
Families who live far away should not be expected to attend the meetings.	3.99	—.44
When a patient is sick, it is extra hard for him to live in a ward with patients of so many races and religions.	2.23	—.43
Most of the work the patients do around here helps the hospital more than it helps the patients.	2.06	—.41

FACTOR ANALYSIS of questionnaire scores (on a scale running from 1 for disagreement to 7 for agreement) brought together items responded to similarly by many patients and thus defined the major dimensions of the entire set of answers. The ward's value system, "social openness and ward involvement," emerged as Factor I. Items with highest and lowest "loadings" on (in effect, correlations with) Factor I are listed together with average scores.

sense of nurture or deprivation by the institution. A patient was asked to fill out the questionnaire, which presented questions randomly, four times: on the day of admission, after one week, after one month and at discharge. (The average stay was 10 weeks.) We also had a representative sample of the staff fill out the questionnaire.

To investigate the value structure of the unit we applied to the data from the questionnaire the statistical procedure known as factor analysis, which reduces a large number of variables (120 questionnaire items in our study) to a much smaller number of entities that are termed factors. Each factor can then be characterized by examining the loading, or contribution, of each of the original variables to it.

The results of factor analysis of our data were quite clear-cut. The values of the unit emerged as a single factor. Most of the items from our six scales were heavily loaded for that factor. This was notably true of the scale and items reflecting openness, membership and, to a lesser extent, faith in the ward and taking responsibility. We designated the factor as a whole "social openness and ward involvement." It was now possible to measure this dimension by making a scale out of the items that were loaded highest and lowest.

The social-openness factor has interesting relations to the dimensions of authority and nurture, which emerged as the other two major factors in the analysis. Our measure of authority consisted of items reflecting an observation made in earlier studies: in a hospital situation attitudes toward authority are indicated by the patients' degree of preference for control by the staff, for strict rules and for suppression of abnormal behavior. Patients agreeing with such items can be said to desire the hospital to be a benign autocracy.

The workers who developed this authority dimension had predicted that it would be the opposite of the prevailing attitude in a therapeutic community. Our finding only partly supported that prediction. A preference for a benign autocracy was not equivalent to a rejection of the therapeutic community. This finding reflects the fact that the culture of the Yale–New Haven ward does not include permissiveness but rather the firm and open use of authority by patients as well as staff in appropriate situations.

The dimension of dependency (nurture or deprivation) was also distinct from the dimension of social openness.

Again the pattern is complex and reveals something about the dimension and about the setting in the Yale–New Haven ward. The patients who experienced the ward as a depriving place tended to reject its norms. On the other hand, acceptance of the social-openness view was independent of experiencing the ward as a nurturing place. This result supported our observation of the ward as a serious, businesslike place where the staff opposed the idea that an easy, comfortable life was good for the patients.

We next examined changes during hospitalization in patients' scores for social openness. Here we found strong support for our impression that the ward's efforts to bring patients into the unit's culture were successful. The average scores for a sample of 65 consecutively admitted patients shifted consistently to greater agreement with staff views. This average shift was highly significant by statistical criteria. Scores for the dimensions of authority and nurture did not shift in such a consistent fashion. This result confirmed our observation that much of the time spent in group meetings and other social situations was directed to bringing newer patients into agreement with the unit's values.

By examining ratings of patients' be-

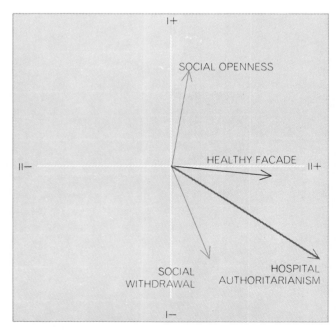 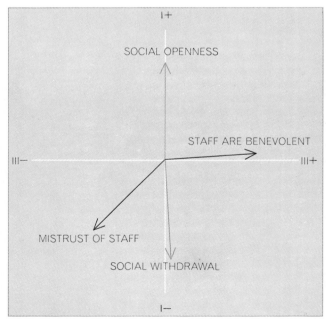

"FACTOR SPACE" MAPS indicate the relations of the Factor I items defined in the preceding illustration with other items representing authoritarianism (*left*) and dependency (*right*), which emerged as Factors II and III respectively. Each group of items is plotted by using its total loadings on two factors as coordinates. Social openness and withdrawal by definition plot close to the Factor I axis. The map at the left shows that authoritarianism, a de-

sire for firm authority, is not (as might have been expected) the exact inverse of social openness, although it does correlate somewhat with withdrawal. The map at the right shows that mistrust of the staff (deprivation) is somewhat related to rejection of the ward culture but a view of the staff as benevolent (nurture) is almost totally unrelated to either pole of the therapeutic-community factor, which thus appears to be independent of nurture and deprivation.

havior made by staff members we were also able to ascertain that patients not only improved during their stay but also behaved increasingly in accord with the norms of social openness. Looking into the relation between change of value and change of behavior, we made an unexpected finding: Desired behavior tended to precede desired attitudes. Patients were acting in accord with the unit's values before registering such changes in a questionnaire on attitudes.

Studies of change in attitude and behavior increasingly indicate that modifying behavior is one of the most powerful ways of modifying attitudes. The more common expectation that a change in attitude leads to a change in behavior is undoubtedly based on extensive exposure to advertising and other forms of propaganda. It appears, however, that even these techniques are in part effective because they confirm what people have already done and reinforce their inclination to do it again.

In understanding this phenomenon among patients in a therapeutic community our career-study material proved helpful. In it we had several descriptions by perceptive patients of the initial phase of hospitalization. What these patients emphasized was the unexpected quality of their first experiences in the unit. Most of them had expected the atmosphere of either a sanitarium rest cure or a "snake pit." Instead they encountered staff members and other patients who wanted to know about their troubles.

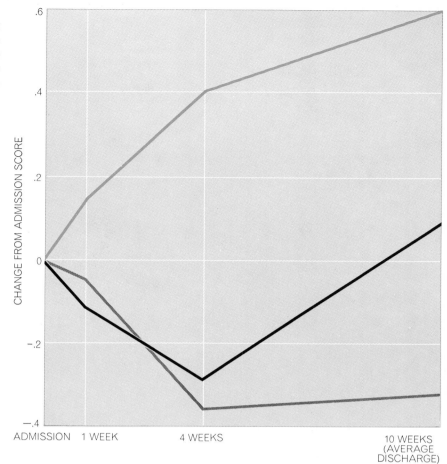

CHANGES IN AVERAGE SCORES of patients are shown for social openness (*color*), staff benevolence (**black**) and authoritarianism (*gray*). Changes are statistically significant for openness throughout, for staff benevolence at four weeks and for authoritarianism at four weeks and at discharge. The staff score on openness was 1.2 units higher than the patients' admission score; half of that discrepancy was made up by the time of discharge.

One patient, describing her first day in the ward, said: "I was quite taken aback when people would come up and say to me, 'Why were you brought here?' " Recounting her reaction over the next few days, she said: "I began talking with very many people, staff and patients alike. I began seeing the problems I had.... I was becoming more objective.... I had never been quite so clear about what got me into this illness." Describing how she became part of the ward and learned its customs, she said: "It was through talking, actually. The intensity of this ward is impressive.... [It] keeps things so intense that you do adjust quickly and begin to see your own problems more objectively because you're constantly thrown into situations where you must talk about it.... People here all have many things in common and seem genuinely to be interested in one another's welfare."

Another patient commented: "When I came in, I just wanted to be by myself,

but patients began questioning me.... They tell you to talk with patients, ask them about their problems."

Such descriptions were universal among the patients studied. It became clear that from the moment a patient reaches the ward he encounters expectations that derive from the value system of social openness. The behavior of experienced patients and of staff members puts the newcomer under strong pressure to act according to the unit's norms, that is, to trust others, talk openly with them about problems and thus become an involved member of the community. The initial efforts of the social system are directed toward inducing the patient to *act* differently. Only later does he accept the system of belief reflected by his actions.

A change of attitude is still a critical part of the therapeutic-community process, although its place in the social fabric is not what we originally supposed. Our

view was that patients are transformed by having their attitudes on how to behave or feel changed. In actuality the function of attitude change is to sustain the social process and culture of the unit.

The social-openness style of therapeutic-community life is not self-sustaining. It is a culture in chronic disequilibrium. It asks patients to act open, involved, responsible and "noncrazy" just when they are feeling most closed, passive and sick. It asks patients and staff alike to expose themselves to the sick behavior of other patients at close quarters and to relate to it in ways that will induce change. These difficult tasks are motivated and guided by the culture.

The norms of social openness define the role of the patient in the therapeutic community. This definition of role operates against the multiple pressures at the time of admission that tend to fix the patient's view of himself and society's view of him as permanently deviant. Indeed,

PRIVILEGE STATUS   PATIENT EVALUATION   THERAPEUTIC APPROACH

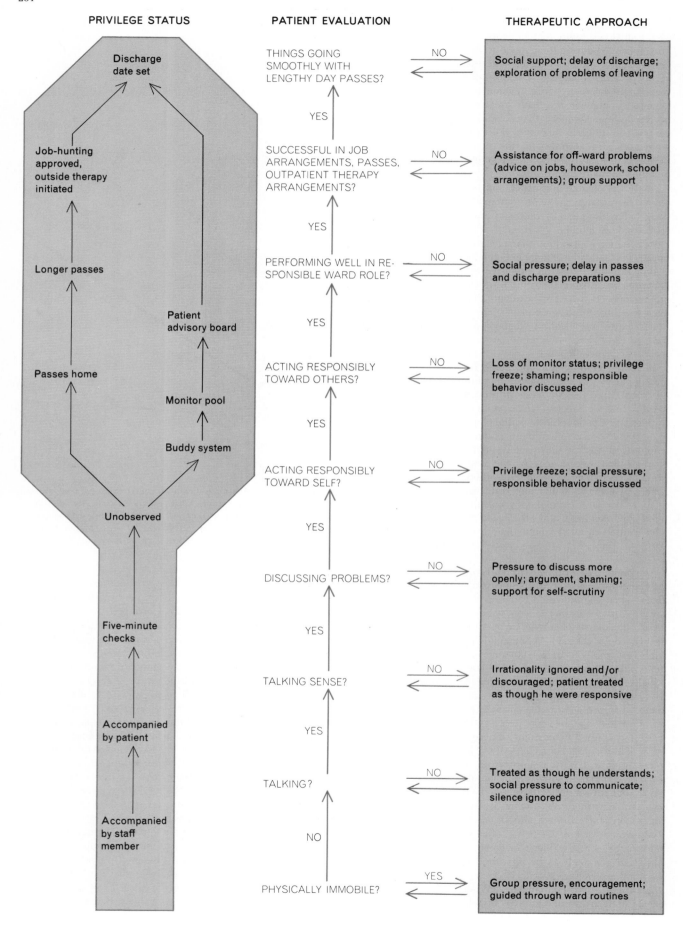

PRIVILEGE STATUS

- Discharge date set
- Job-hunting approved, outside therapy initiated
- Longer passes
- Passes home
- Patient advisory board
- Monitor pool
- Buddy system
- Unobserved
- Five-minute checks
- Accompanied by patient
- Accompanied by staff member

PATIENT EVALUATION

- THINGS GOING SMOOTHLY WITH LENGTHY DAY PASSES? — NO
  - YES
- SUCCESSFUL IN JOB ARRANGEMENTS, PASSES, OUTPATIENT THERAPY ARRANGEMENTS? — NO
  - YES
- PERFORMING WELL IN RESPONSIBLE WARD ROLE? — NO
  - YES
- ACTING RESPONSIBLY TOWARD OTHERS? — NO
  - YES
- ACTING RESPONSIBLY TOWARD SELF? — NO
  - YES
- DISCUSSING PROBLEMS? — NO
  - YES
- TALKING SENSE? — NO
  - YES
- TALKING? — NO
  - NO
- PHYSICALLY IMMOBILE? — YES

THERAPEUTIC APPROACH

- Social support; delay of discharge; exploration of problems of leaving
- Assistance for off-ward problems (advice on jobs, housework, school arrangements); group support
- Social pressure; delay in passes and discharge preparations
- Loss of monitor status; privilege freeze; shaming; responsible behavior discussed
- Privilege freeze; social pressure; responsible behavior discussed
- Pressure to discuss more openly; argument, shaming; support for self-scrutiny
- Irrationality ignored and/or discouraged; patient treated as though he were responsive
- Treated as though he understands; social pressure to communicate; silence ignored
- Group pressure, encouragement; guided through ward routines

the entire culture of the therapeutic community can be seen, at the simplest level of analysis, as seeking to neutralize the effects of hospital admission. Since the decision to admit a patient inevitably follows a complex process involving the failure of other efforts to cope with problems, the neutralization of its effects can be a major task.

Not all therapeutic communities are necessarily dedicated to this goal of rehabilitation toward functioning outside the institution. With certain chronic disorders such as alcoholism, drug addiction and schizophrenia it may be more important to help patients adapt to functioning within the institution. In any case it appears that the core of a therapeutic community is the process of role-channeling of individuals from one behavioral status to another that is more adaptive.

It is to be expected that individual patients will react differently to the therapeutic-community approach. One of the most meaningful ways to distinguish different but recurring types of hospital experience was found to be the examination of a profile of attitude change over the course of hospitalization. Three major patterns could be discerned; we called the groups of patients characterized by the respective patterns preconverts, unit converts, and rejectors or renegers. Preconverts, whose social-openness scores were consistently high in the first week of hospitalization, were less disturbed people who tended to be from higher social classes. Unit converts, whose scores rose after a delay of at least a week, were almost all adolescents, more severely disturbed and slower at improving in behavior. Rejectors and renegers, whose scores were low or had dropped after an initial increase, were older patients who improved the least and were from lower-social-class backgrounds.

The preconvert pattern is exemplified by the case of Mary, a housewife in her early thirties who came to the ward because of an attempt at suicide following a period of marital conflict and personal crises. Her upper-middle-class background had provided her with a number of experiences related to life in a typical therapeutic community—experi-

ences such as college, summer camp and work with the League of Women Voters. Hospitalization provided an immediate sense of relief simply by removing her from the situation generating her depression. She was immediately exposed to patients and staff who pressed her to discuss with them the events leading to her hospitalization. Moreover, since she wanted to "do well" in the hospital— move quickly through the hierarchy of privilege—she rapidly assessed the unit's norms of good behavior and sought to comply with them.

Such a patient is likely to follow one of two paths during hospitalization. She might tend to a steady pattern of self-revelation, acceptance of comments from others (including her husband) and continued therapeutic progress. Mary, however, attempted to "play at" the patient's role by doing what appeared to be a good job but avoiding involvement in the critical issue of marital tension. Gradually a crisis developed as Mary began to respond to her ward physician and other staff members as she had to her husband. Only through a series of angry outbursts, which were pointed out to her by the staff, did she begin to realize the self-defeating aspects of her behavior. Thereafter she was able to interact more with her husband in joint therapy and to plan for discharge and follow-up therapy as an out-patient.

The typical unit convert has quite a different experience of hospitalization. Many of these patients come into the hospital with serious disturbances in their perceptions of reality, that is, with a psychosis. An adolescent whom we studied closely is an example. Bill had not had the kind of prior social experience that would make the culture of a therapeutic community familiar. The deterioration of his functioning before he entered the hospital was preceded by a long history of social withdrawal. In addition he, like many other such patients, came from a family in which oddness or irrationality was unintentionally encouraged or reinforced.

In the hospital Bill was at first mistrustful of the staff and of the strong pressure on him to expose his feelings and thoughts. He was able to become involved in the social and governmental

activities of the ward only after developing a secure relationship with his ward physician and other members of the staff. They sensed this need and gave him more of their time than they would give to an average patient. The involvement of his parents in treatment activities of the ward and evidence on their part of a willingness to change were also critical. As is the case with many adolescent patients, when Bill developed trust in the ward, he became a strong proponent of therapeutic-community values.

Patients of the third group usually have few experiences similar to those in the therapeutic community and are often seriously ill. Hence they have great difficulty accepting the values of the therapeutic community. Even if such a patient wants to respond, his passivity and unfamiliarity with the concept of open discussion of feelings and problems can retard his progress.

Charles, a man in his fifties who was hospitalized for alcoholism and depression, refused to relate to other patients or to take part in the ward's program of patient responsibility. He insisted that he had only medical ailments and threatened to sign out of the hospital. He was given treatment for his drinking, but attempts to involve him in discussion of his psychological difficulties were unsuccessful. He was discharged after a month with a staff appraisal that further hospital therapy would not then be helpful.

The experiences of the three types of patient after discharge are usually different. With preconverts a history of prior good functioning, plus continued therapeutic attention to the issues that precipitated the crisis, combine to give a generally successful record on follow-up. Unit converts tend on follow-up to be doing fairly well but with occasional periods of upset. Depending on the ability of the patient and his family to anticipate such crises and to get help on them, such patients are capable of improvement in their life course following hospitalization. Patients in the third group do least well on follow-up, probably not only because they got less from hospitalization but also because their prior experience and psychological impairment limited both their response in the hospital and their functioning later.

PROCESS OF HOSPITALIZATION in a therapeutic community involves a progression (*upward on the diagram*) through a series of evaluations, with the degree of observation or privilege status (*left*) and the applicable therapy (*right*) depending on the patient's condition. For example, a patient entering the hospital mute and psychotic might progress as indicated. The community takes part in helping the patient to move from one level to the next. The privileges are rewards for improvement but are not tied directly to the specific evaluating questions listed here. Discharge to home would generally occur at the top level.

Role-channeling is not limited to the psychiatric setting. It is a major ingredient in such self-help groups as Alcoholics Anonymous; Synanon, which deals with narcotics addicts, and Recovery Inc., which is concerned with former mental patients. It also appears in

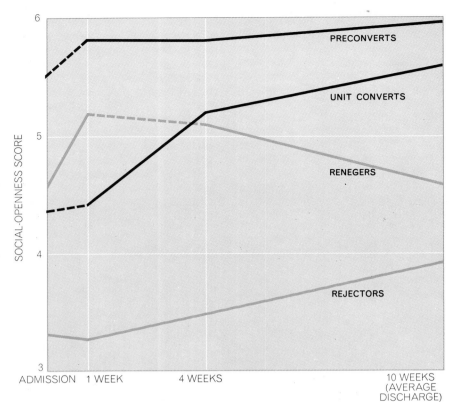

FOUR TYPES OF PATIENT are defined by scores on social openness. In each case portions of the profile that defines the type are shown by the solid lines. Preconverts enter the group disposed to adopt its values. Unit converts tend to be more severely disturbed but improve behaviorally with help from the group. Renegers and rejectors improve least.

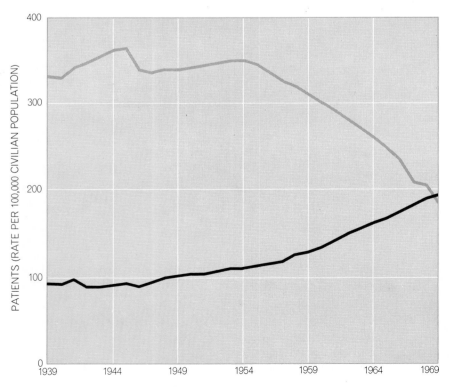

TREND toward more, briefer hospitalization is shown by data for U.S. state and county mental hospitals. Resident population (color) is down but annual admissions (black) are up.

the healing cults of primitive societies, where social involvement in the cult and learning role behavior through others in the cult are important ingredients. The therapeutic-community approach therefore seems to be a fundamental human social pattern and to represent a rediscovery rather than a discovery.

Role-channeling may have relevance for many social problems that involve institutions and individuals. Prisons, for example, are notorious as training grounds for criminal careers and are rarely noted for achieving rehabilitation of inmates. Society's emphasis on punishment and deterrence and the usually powerful inmate culture constitute major obstacles to the introduction of a role-channeling approach directed toward noncriminal roles for released prisoners. Nonetheless, experimental projects involving the use of other inmates as role models have been tried with considerable success.

Similarly, job training of "hard core" unemployed men from urban ghettos has been most successful when trainees have been encouraged to develop a strong peer-group loyalty. This attitude then provides a bridge to the work setting, where a trainee's adjustment is aided by an experienced "buddy" from his own neighborhood and ethnic background.

Therapeutic-community patterns also have relevance for current social change. Young people alienated from established social institutions are experimenting with such ventures as communal living, organizations for political activism and encounter groups. These "alternate institutions" frequently emphasize values similar to those of a therapeutic community: group cohesion and commitment; open communication, particularly about personal problems; helping and being helped by peers, and "participant democracy," meaning involvement of the entire group in decision-making. The motivation for these new social patterns is similar to the motivation behind role-channeling in a therapeutic community: a wish to influence the end state of the individual that results from his contact with an organization. Many young people wish to avoid what they feel are the dehumanizing effects of living, studying or working in large organizations. The cultures of their experimental groups seek to facilitate new social roles that will enable participants to find new personal solutions to living in a complex society. For existing organizations that may wish to shift their internal function toward such goals, the therapeutic community may offer valuable guidelines.

Behavioral Psychotherapy

by Albert Bandura
March 1967

Abnormal behavior can be thought of not as a symptom of a hidden illness but as a problem of "social learning," and can be treated directly by methods that are derived from principles of learning

In recent years there has been a fundamental departure from conventional views regarding the nature, causes and treatment of psychological disorders. Most theories of maladaptive behavior are based on the disease concept, according to which abnormalities in behavior are considered to be symptoms of an underlying neurosis or psychic illness. Today many psychotherapists are advancing the view that behavior that is harmful to the individual or departs widely from accepted social and ethical norms should be viewed not as some kind of disease but as a way—which the person has learned—of coping with environmental demands. Treatment then becomes a problem in "social learning." The abnormal behavior can be dealt with directly, and in seeking to modify it the therapist can call on principles of learning that are based on experimentation and are subject to testing and verification.

The concepts of symptom and disease are quite appropriate in physical disorders. Changes in tissues or in their functioning do in fact occur, and they can be verified whether or not there are external manifestations. Where psychological problems are concerned, however, analogy with physical disease can be misleading. The psychic conditions that are assumed to underlie behavioral malfunctioning are merely abstractions from the behavior that are given substance and often endowed with powerful motivating properties. Each of the many conventional theories of psychopathology has its own favored set of hypothetical internal agents. Psychotherapists of differing theoretical background and affiliation tend to find evidence for their own preferred psychodynamic agents but not for those cited by other schools. Freudians unearth Oedipus complexes Ad-

lerians discover inferiority feelings with compensatory power-strivings, Rogerians find inappropriate self-concepts and existentialists are likely to diagnose existential crises and anxieties.

A correlate of the disease approach is the assumption that in order to gain lasting benefits from psychotherapy the client must achieve awareness of the concealed forces causing his actions, and the development of this insight is usually one of the primary goals of conventional therapy. A study of the results of psychotherapy made by Ralph W. Heine at the University of Chicago School of Medicine suggested, however, that a client's insights and emergent "unconscious" could be predicted more accurately from knowledge of his therapist's theoretical system than from the client's actual developmental history. It would seem from this finding and others that insight may primarily represent a conversion to the therapist's point of view rather than a process of self-discovery. It is therefore not surprising that insight can be achieved without any real effect on the difficulties for which the patient originally sought help. A chronic stutterer converted to Freudianism or Jungianism—or to any other theoretical system—will not necessarily begin to speak fluently. His stuttering behavior is more likely to be eliminated by the necessary relearning experiences than by the gradual discovery of predetermined insights.

Stuttering is a well-defined motor behavior, but I should make it clear that what are called behavioral therapies apply to the full range of psychological events: attitudinal and emotional as well as motor. Some forms of behavioral therapy bring about major changes in people's actions by modifying their emotional responses; on the other hand,

enduring changes in attitude can be most successfully effected through modifications in overt behavior. In the final analysis all modes of psychotherapy are behavioral, since the client's behavior—broadly defined to include conceptual, emotional and motor expression—is the only reality the psychotherapist can deal with and modify. Indeed, while conventional therapists are promoting insights, they may simultaneously (if inadvertently) reward desirable patterns of behavior and show disapproval of abnormal behavior; they may reduce anxieties through their supportive reactions to a client's statements; they exhibit attitudes, values and patterns of behavior that a client is inclined to emulate. Many of the therapeutic changes that occur in conventional psychotherapy may therefore arise primarily from the unwitting application of social-learning principles. The point is that these beneficial results can be obtained more readily when the principles are applied in a more considered and systematic way. I shall describe a number of different approaches to treatment based on learning principles and review some studies, many of them controlled investigations, in which such procedures have been tested.

In our research at Stanford University we have found that almost any learning outcome that results from direct experience can also come about on a vicarious basis through observation of other people's behavior and its consequences for them. Indeed, providing an appropriate "model" may accelerate the learning process, and one method of social-learning therapy is therefore based on modeling the desired behavior. This is particularly suitable in the treatment of gross deficits in behavior, as in the case of a child (usually diagnosed as

268

PRINCIPLES OF LEARNING are utilized in the simple course of therapy suggested by these drawings. An extremely withdrawn pre-kindergarten boy whose solitary play is usually "reinforced" by the teacher's solicitude (a) is instead rewarded for joining a group by the teacher's devoting her full attention to him and the group (b). When the original reinforcement is resumed as a check on the treatment, he reverts to his former behavior (c). Then the therapeutic reinforcement is reinstituted and the desired behavior is well established (d). In time the child's enjoyment of his new behavior maintains his sociable interaction without special attention (e).

schizophrenic or autistic) who does not speak, interact with other people or even respond to their presence.

O. Ivar Lovaas of the University of California at Los Angeles has recently devised modeling procedures that hold promise of developing the intellectual and interpersonal capabilities of schizophrenic children. In teaching a mute child to talk, for example, the therapist first rewards any visual attentiveness and even random sounds made by the child. When vocalization has been increased, the rewards are limited to occasions on which sounds are made in response to a sound uttered by the therapist, and then to precise verbal reproduction of specific sounds, words and phrases modeled by the therapist. When the child has acquired a vocabulary and can imitate new words easily, the therapist goes on to teach the meaning of words, grammatical structure and even abstract verbal concepts by the modeling procedures. Lovaas has also taught schizophrenic children a variety of skills and social patterns of behavior by modeling the desired behavior and rewarding the child when he emulates it. The most impressive thing about this form of treatment is that it can be conducted under the supervision of nurses, students and parents, to whom the methods are easily taught.

In a very different application of modeling principles, George A. Kelly of Brandeis University conceived a role-enactment form of therapy for adults who want to develop new personality characteristics. The client is provided with a personality sketch and given demonstrations of the desired behavior; he then has opportunities to practice the new patterns in a protected therapeutic situation before being encouraged to apply them as he goes about his everyday life.

Often therapists, instead of having to fill a behavioral vacuum, have the problem of eliminating strongly established abnormal behavior. In an early study at the University of Iowa, Gertrude E. Chittenden tested the efficacy of a symbolic modeling procedure for dealing with children's hyperaggressive reactions to frustration. It has been widely assumed that either witnessing or participating in aggressive behavior serves to reduce, at least temporarily, the incidence of such behavior. The overall evidence from studies conducted in our laboratory and elsewhere strongly indicates that psychotherapies employing these conventional "cathartic" procedures may actually be increasing aggres-

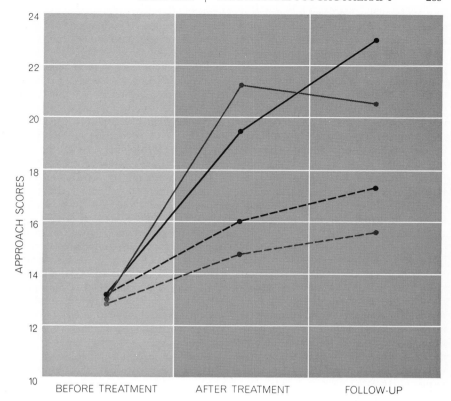

FEAR OF DOGS, as measured by an "approach score," abated most for children who watched displays in which "models" played with dogs in a party atmosphere (*solid black curve*) or in a neutral context (*solid gray*). The change was less for children who were merely in the party atmosphere (*broken black*) or who saw no child models (*broken gray*).

sive tendencies rather than reducing them. In contrast, therapy based on social-learning principles concentrates at the outset on developing constructive alternative modes of behavior. Chittenden had domineering and hyperaggressive children watch a series of scenes in which dolls representing preschool children exhibited first aggressive reactions to common frustrating situations and then cooperative reactions; the consequences of the aggressive reactions were shown as being unpleasant and those of the cooperative ones as being rewarding. Children for whom the different reactions and consequences were modeled showed a lasting decrease in aggressive, domineering behavior compared with a group of similarly hyperaggressive children who received no treatment.

We have found that phobias and inhibitions can be eliminated by having the fearful person observe a graduated sequence of modeled activities beginning with presentations that are easily tolerated. In a controlled test of this therapy, nursery school children who were afraid of dogs (according to their parents' statements and tests of "dog avoidance" behavior) were assigned to one of four groups. Children in the first group par-

ticipated in eight brief sessions in which they watched a child without fear interact more and more closely with a dog—approaching it, playing with it, petting it and so on—with the entire procedure taking place in a "positive" party setting designed to counteract anxiety reactions. The second group saw the same sequence but in a neutral context. In order for us to assess the effects of exposure to the dog alone the third group saw the dog in a party setting but without the child model; the fourth joined the party activities but was not exposed to either the model or the dog.

The tests for avoidance behavior were readministered after the completion of treatment and again a month later. The tests were quite severe, requiring the child not only to touch, pet and walk a dog but also to remain alone in a room with it, to hand-feed it and finally to climb into a playpen with the animal. The test scores showed that most of the children who had received the modeling treatment had essentially lost their fear of dogs [*see illustration on this page*]. The favorable results were largely confirmed by a second experiment in which the same modeled behavior was presented to some children in filmed performances while children in a control group watched a different motion picture. Finally the control children, whose fear of dogs had remained unchanged, were shown the therapeutic movies, after which their fear was in turn substantially diminished. One of the obvious advantages of the modeling technique in psychotherapy is that it lends itself to the treatment of groups of people. Moreover, the success of the filmed version of the modeling suggests that it may be possible to develop therapeutic films to be used in preventive programs directed against certain common fears and anxieties before they became strongly established.

There is increasing evidence that behavior commonly attributed to internal psychic conditions is in fact largely regulated by its own external, environmental consequences. Positive reinforcement—the modification of behavior through alteration of its rewarding outcomes—is therefore an important procedure in behavioral therapy. The techniques are those of operant conditioning, which was developed largely by B. F. Skinner and his colleagues at Harvard University.

Three elements are necessary to the proper implementation of operant conditioning in psychotherapy. The first is that the reinforcement, or incentive, system must be capable of maintaining the client's motivation and responsiveness; the system can involve tangible rewards, opportunities to engage in enjoyable activities, praise and attention or the satisfaction of a job well done. The second is that the reinforcement must be made conditional on the occurrence of the desired behavior, correctly timed and applied on a regular basis. The third is that there must be a dependable way to elicit the desired behavior either by demonstrating it or by rewarding small improvements in the direction of more complex forms of behavior.

The application of these elements is illustrated by a case reported by Arthur W. Staats, then at Arizona State University, and William H. Butterfield. They treated a 14-year-old delinquent boy who, in addition to having a long history of aggressive, destructive behavior, had never received a passing grade in eight and a half years of school and who read at the second-grade level. He was considered to be uneducable, incorrigible and mentally retarded.

The therapists undertook to teach him to read—first single words, then sentences and finally brief stories. For each

word the boy learned he received points that he saved and "exchanged" for phonograph records and other things he wanted or for sums of money. In four and a half months he made notable advances in reading-test scores [see illustration below]. Moreover, the brief treatment program produced generalized educational and psychological effects: he received passing grades in all his subjects for the first time and his aggressively defiant behavior ceased. The entire program, which was administered by a probation officer, involved a total expenditure of $20.31 for the exchange items!

The effectiveness of operant conditioning was demonstrated most convincingly by Florence R. Harris, Montrose M. Wolf and Donald M. Baer at the University of Washington. In their method grossly abnormal behavior in children is successively eliminated, reinstated and eliminated again by varying its social consequences.

First the psychologists observe the child in question to note the frequency of the behavior disorder, the context in which it occurs and the reaction of the teacher. In one case an extremely withdrawn little boy in nursery school spent about 80 percent of the time in solitary activities. Observation revealed that the teacher unwittingly "reinforced" his solitary behavior by paying a great deal of attention to him, consoling him and encouraging him to play with the other children. When he did happen to join the others, the teacher took no particular notice.

In the second phase of the program a new set of reinforcement practices is substituted. In the case of the solitary little boy, for example, the teacher stopped rewarding solitary play with attention and support. Instead, whenever the child sought out other children, the teacher immediately joined the group and gave it her full attention. Soon the boy was spending about 60 percent of his time playing with the other children.

After the desired change in behavior has been produced, the original reinforcement practices are reinstated to determine if the original behavior was in fact maintained by its social consequences. In this third stage, for example, the teacher again paid no attention to the child's sociability but instead responded with comforting ministrations and concern whenever he was alone. The effect of this traditional "mental hygiene" treatment was to increase the child's withdrawal to the original high level.

Finally the therapeutic activity is reintroduced, the abnormal behavior is eliminated and the desired behavior pattern is generously reinforced until it is well enough established to be maintained by its own implicit satisfactions. Once the little boy was again playing with other children the teacher was able to reduce her direct involvement with the group; the child derived increasing enjoyment from his new behavior pattern and eventually maintained it without any special attention.

Children with a wide variety of be-

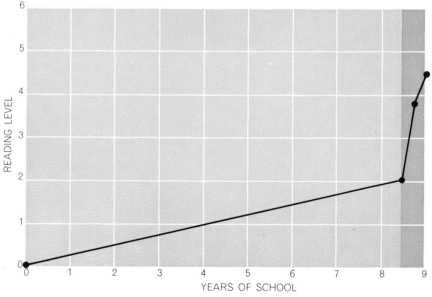

DELINQUENT ADOLESCENT BOY was reading at the second-grade level after more than eight years in school. In half a year of therapy his reading level had more than doubled.

havior disorders have participated in this form of treatment, and in each case their maladaptive behavior was eliminated, reinstated and removed a second time by alterations in the teacher's "social responsiveness." Clearly child-rearing and therapeutic practices should be evaluated carefully in terms of the effects they have on their recipients rather than in terms of the humanitarian intent of teachers or psychotherapists.

Certain widespread psychological problems must be treated primarily at the social rather than the individual level. By altering the reinforcement contingencies of a social group it may be possible to affect the behavior of each member in beneficial ways, whereas working with individuals would yield trifling results. Recently incentive programs have been applied on a group basis in psychiatric hospitals and in institutions for retarded children and for delinquent adolescents. Operant conditioning therapies have, for example, restored some social competence and self-reliance in severely impaired psychiatric patients. The traditional hospital routine tends to reinforce docile behavior and

dependence; the therapy rewards self-sufficiency, social relations and progress in vocational training. At the Anna State Hospital in Illinois, Teodoro Ayllon and Nathan H. Azrin found that psychotic patients would work productively in the rehabilitation program if activities and material comforts they wanted were made dependent on the completion of their assignments; the patients quickly lapsed into their customary lethargy when the incentives were discontinued and the privileges were made available routinely as before [see illustration on page 272].

There is an obverse side to the positive-reinforcement method. Abnormal behavior that persists because it leads to rewarding outcomes can often be eliminated simply by withholding the usual positive reinforcement. Tantrums, hyperaggressive behavior, chronic eating problems, psychosomatic and hypochondriacal complaints, psychotic talk and even the bizarre behavior of autistic children have been found to abate gradually when the solicitous concern they usually evoke is not forthcoming. This process is greatly facilitated if alterna-

tive behavior patterns are rewarded at the same time.

A third major category of therapeutic methods derived from learning theory is based on the principle of "counter-conditioning." These methods are appropriate for treating the conditions most frequently seen in a conventional interview-therapy practice: anxiety reactions, chronic tensions, inhibitions, phobias and psychosomatic reactions. The objective in counterconditioning is to induce strong positive responses in the presence of stimuli that ordinarily arouse fear or other unfavorable reactions in the client. As positive responses are repeatedly associated with the threatening events, the anxiety is gradually eliminated. Although psychotherapeutic applications of this principle were reported by Mary Cover Jones as long ago as 1924, the approach received little attention until some 30 years later, when Joseph Wolpe, now at the Temple University School of Medicine, worked out procedures that increased the range of disorders subject to treatment by counterconditioning.

In Wolpe's "desensitization" method

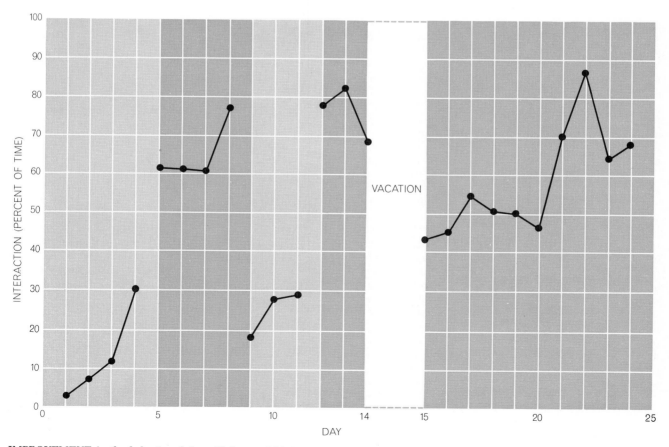

IMPROVEMENT in the behavior of the withdrawn child (see illustration on page 268) is indicated by the increasing time spent in social interaction. Before treatment began and during the time when his solitary play was rewarded with attention he was usually alone (light colored areas), but he played with others when such behavior was reinforced by the teacher's responses (dark areas).

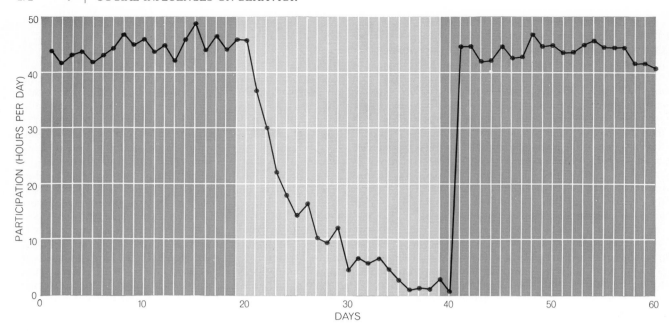

PARTICIPATION in rehabilitation activities increased for a group of 44 schizophrenic patients when privileges were made conditional on their successful completion of assignments (*dark colored areas*), and decreased when the same rewards were provided whether or not they took part in the activities (*light area*). The colored spots indicate the total number of hours of participation each day.

the therapist—working with information obtained from interviews and psychological tests—first constructs a "hierarchy," or ranked list, of situations to which the client reacts with increasing degrees of anxiety (or avoidance or inhibition, as the case may be). Then the therapist induces in the client a state of deep muscular relaxation—a state incompatible with anxiety—and asks the client to visualize the weakest item in the hierarchy of anxiety-arousing stimuli. If any tension results, the client is told to stop imagining the threatening situation and the relaxation process is resumed; if the relaxation remains unimpaired in the imagined presence of the stimulus, the patient is presented with the next item in the hierarchy. So it goes throughout the graduated series, with the intensity of the disturbing situations being increased from session to session until the most threatening situations have been completely neutralized.

Favorable clinical reports on counterconditioning have recently been borne out by a number of experimental studies in which changes in behavior were assessed objectively. Arnold A. Lazarus, now at Temple University, evaluated clients afflicted with acrophobia (fear of heights), claustrophobia or impotence after they had been treated either by conventional group psychotherapy or by group desensitization. Of the 18 clients treated by desensitization, 13 completely recovered from their phobias. The con-

ventional treatment was successful in only two out of 17 cases, and of the 15 people whose phobias were essentially unmodified 10 were thereupon treated successfully by group desensitization. A follow-up study indicated that 80 percent of the clients for whom desensitization had been successful maintained their recovery as measured by a stringent criterion: the recurrence of even weak phobic responses was rated as a failure.

At the University of Illinois, Gordon L. Paul studied the relative efficacy of counterconditioning and conventional methods in treating college students who suffered from extreme anxiety about public speaking. One group received interview therapy intended to produce insight. A second group underwent desensitization treatments in which relaxation was associated with imagined public-speaking situations of a progressively more threatening nature. A third group was given a form of placebo treatment, and a control group had no treatment at all.

After six weeks the students' response to a stressful public-speaking test was evaluated according to three sets of criteria: their own reports as to just how disturbed they felt, physiological indicators of anxiety and an objective judgment of the extent to which their speaking behavior was disrupted. Students in all three of the treatment conditions showed less behavior indicative of anxiety, and reported less distress, than the

untreated control group. Only the students in the counterconditioned group achieved a significant reduction in physiological arousal compared with the controls, however. In each case the counterconditioned group showed greater improvement than the insight group and the placebo group, which did not differ significantly from each other [*see illustration on page 273*]. In a follow-up period the counterconditioned students reported experiencing less anxiety about speaking than the other three groups. An interesting aspect of this study was that the therapists, who in their regular practice favored insight-directed methods, rated the students treated by desensitization as most improved and also indicated a better prognosis for them. A subsequent study by Paul and Donald Shannon indicated that desensitization administered on a group basis can be similarly effective in eliminating disabling anxieties.

A number of current investigations are directed at identifying the specific components of counterconditioning therapy that account for its success. In these experiments Gerald C. Davison and Earl D. Schubot of Stanford and Peter J. Lang of the University of Wisconsin devise treatment procedures with well-defined differences and then make objective measurements of behavioral changes. The preliminary results of their studies suggest that the critical factor is the close association of relaxation with the stimuli that arouse anxiety, particularly in the treatment of severe anxiety disorders.

I have been discussing specific kinds of procedures for rather specific psychological problems. Many people seeking psychotherapy present multiple problems, and these call for combinations of procedures. (The developments in behavioral therapy in some respects parallel those in medicine, where all-purpose therapies of limited efficacy were eventually replaced by powerful specific procedures designed to treat particular physical disorders.) The treatment process is not piecemeal, since favorable changes in one area of behavior tend to produce beneficial modifications in other areas. In many instances a circumscribed problem has wide social consequences, and a change in such an area can have pervasive psychological effects.

Psychotherapists who think in terms of diseases often assume that the direct modification of abnormal behavior may result in what they call "symptom substitution." The available evidence reveals, however, that induced behavioral changes at least persist in themselves and often have favorable effects on other areas of psychological functioning. To be sure, a poorly designed course of therapy aimed only at eliminating maladaptive behavior patterns does not in itself guarantee that desired modes of response will take their place. The client may revert to alternative and equally unsatisfactory courses of action, and the therapist may be faced with the task of eliminating a succession of ineffective patterns of behavior. This problem can be forestalled by including procedures

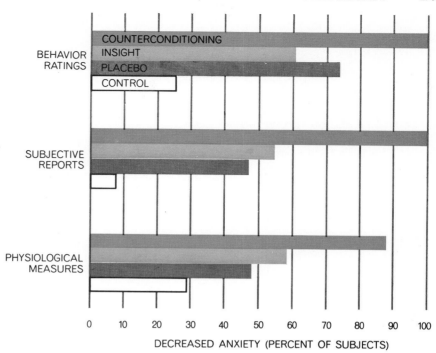

PUBLIC-SPEAKING phobia was treated by counterconditioning, by an "insight" method and by a placebo treatment. There was also an untreated control group. The chart gives the percent of subjects who showed decreased anxiety (according to three different criteria).

in the original treatment that are designed to foster desirable alternative modes of behavior.

Preliminary applications of social-learning approaches to psychotherapy indicate that these methods hold considerable promise; they need to be developed further, extended to the treatment of multiple problems and evaluated after a sufficient period has elapsed. Many new methods of psychotherapy have been introduced enthusiastically and then have been retired by controlled studies. The fact that social-learning

therapies are based on established principles of behavior and are subjected to experimental study at each stage of development gives us reason to expect them to weather the test of time. The day may not be far off when psychological disorders will be treated not in hospitals or mental hygiene clinics but in comprehensive "learning centers," when clients will be considered not patients suffering from hidden psychic pathologies but responsible people who participate actively in developing their own potentialities.

V

SOCIAL INFLUENCES ON BEHAVIOR

SOCIAL INFLUENCES ON BEHAVIOR

V

INTRODUCTION

Individual behavior is influenced by the social context in which it occurs. Most of our life is spent in interaction with other people. Their responses to us are a major factor determining our attitudes and actions. Social influences were acknowledged in earlier articles in this volume when considering such topics as the importance of early experiences with parents and peers for the development of appropriate adult social behavior, or the effect of interaction with others on feelings of self-esteem. In this section, however, we are concerned more with attitudes and attitude change, the effect of social groups on the behavior and attitudes of the individual, and the ways in which people interact within groups and against other groups.

In "Attitude and Pupil Size" Eckhard Hess describes a unique method for measuring a person's private attitude toward some person, object, or group. Because people do not always fully or truthfully express their true attitudes, an involuntary response (such as pupil dilation) can provide a clue to the individual's true feelings.

How attitudes change after a decision has been made is discussed by Leon Festinger in "Cognitive Dissonance." After we make a choice between equally attractive alternatives, we tend to change our appraisal of the alternatives in favor of the decision. For example, if you are selecting a house for purchase, you may find two with nearly equal advantages and disadvantages. Once you decide between the two, however, you will find many more advantages in favor of the house you purchased and new reasons why the other would have been a poor choice. By altering your appraisal so as to reduce any anxiety that you may have made a wrong decision, you are reducing *cognitive dissonance*. The theory of cognitive dissonance is based on the assumption that we want our behavior and attitudes to be consistent. If we find that they are inconsistent (dissonant), we try to reduce the dissonance by changing either our behavior or attitudes, or both. Festinger's theory has important implications for the way in which social pressures may produce changes in attitude or behavior. He presents some interesting studies of lying and yielding to temptation.

As social beings, we function as members of several groups. Family, socioeconomic, national, and racial groups, social clubs, and religious and political organizations are but a few of the groups by which we are linked with other people in varying degrees of organization and closeness. The group to which a person belongs is sometimes called an "ingroup"; those who do not belong are the "outgroup." In "Experiments in Intergroup Discrimination" Henri Tajfel examines the social and psychological factors that contribute to prejudice toward, and discrimination against, outgroups. He describes the depressing cycle whereby the determinants of intergroup attitudes and behavior reinforce each other. A conflict of economic or social interests between two groups may lead to discriminatory behavior; such behavior creates attitudes of prejudice; these attitudes in turn lead to new forms of discriminatory behavior that may create new economic or social disparities, and thus perpetuate the vicious circle. An experiment by Tajfel shows how easy it is to elicit outgroup discrimination in the laboratory. The results suggest that there are clear social norms that specify how one should behave in relation to an outgroup, and that these norms exert a powerful influence on behavior, even when such motivating conditions as conflict of interest or prior hostility are lacking.

Whether or not observing violence and aggression on television or in films predisposes the viewer to aggressive acts has been the subject of much debate in recent years. Some authorities believe that exposure to filmed violence and brutality prompts disturbed individuals to express their aggressions by similar destructive acts. Other equally eminent authorities argue that watching other people behave aggressively serves as a cathartic experience, providing a safe release for the viewer's hostile impulses. Unfortunately, research data on this topic is sparse. The studies reported by Leonard Berkowitz in "The Effects of Observing Violence" tend to support the first view. They suggest that there is little, if any, cathartic effect from watching aggression. Quite the contrary, observing violent behavior does arouse aggressive impulses, particularly if the viewer is already angry and if the observed aggression is portrayed as justifiable—that is, if the victim deserves his beating. Fortunately, aroused aggressive impulses are usually inhibited by social restraints and quickly dissipate—but the potential danger of filmed violence still exists.

If a teacher expects a child to perform poorly in school, the child probably will. In "Teacher Expectations for the Disadvantaged" Robert Rosenthal and Lenore Jacobson demonstrate that a teacher's expectations, however erroneous, of a pupil's potential achievement provide a fairly good prediction of how the child will actually perform. The teachers in this classroom study were told that special test information indicated that certain of their students were "potential academic spurters"; in actuality, the children so identified were simply chosen at random from the class. The authors investigated several variables that might account for the significant gains of the children in the experimental group. They concluded that the teachers unwittingly communicated their expectations to the children, changing both the students' conception of themselves and their motivational level. The effect of teacher expectations was particularly pronounced in the lower grades.

An extremely controversial aspect of discrimination against outgroups has revolved around the question of whether there are genetic differences between blacks and whites, particularly in intelligence. One of the arguments put forward by ardent segregationists as a justification for separate educational systems is that black children have innately lower intelligence than white children. Most studies using standard intelligence tests do show a somewhat lower average IQ for black children than for white children. But this difference can be explained by a number of factors related to environmental differences and the nature of the intelligence tests, rather than on genetic grounds. Discussions of this issue, many of which have appeared in prestigious journals, have too often involved a great deal of nonsense with no basis in scientific fact. "Intelligence and Race" by Walter Bodmer and Luigi Cavalli-Sforza, provides a balanced treatment of the issue.

"Pictorial Perception and Culture" by Jan Deregowski, raises the question of whether people of one culture perceive a picture differently than people of another culture. He reports on a series of experiments done in Africa that indicate that differences do exist, and argues that picture perception does depend on some form of learning. To the question "Do pictures offer us a universal language?" Deregowski answers a clear no.

The last article in this section, "The Origins of Alienation" by Urie Bronfenbrenner, examines the profound changes taking place in the lives of young Americans. It seems clear that the degree of estrangement between young people and adults is greater today than it has been in the past. The article explores the origins of alienation and attempts to identify some of the circumstances that give rise to it. Several proposals for dealing with alienation are made on the basis of research reviewed in the article. The problem and the cure lie not in the alienated individuals themselves, but in the social institutions that produce alienation by their failure to be more responsive to psychological needs in a democratic society.

Attitude and Pupil Size

by Eckhard H. Hess
April 1965

Dilation and constriction of the pupils reflect not only changes in light intensity but also ongoing mental activity. The response is a measure of interest, emotion, thought processes and attitudes

One night about five years ago I was lying in bed leafing through a book of strikingly beautiful animal photographs. My wife happened to glance over at me and remarked that the light must be bad—my pupils were unusually large. It seemed to me that there was plenty of light coming from the bedside lamp and I said so, but she insisted that my pupils were dilated. As a psychologist who is interested in visual perception, I was puzzled by this little episode. Later, as I was trying to go to sleep, I recalled that someone had once reported a correlation between a person's pupil size and his emotional response to certain aspects of his environment. In this case it was difficult to see an emotional component. It seemed more a matter of intellectual interest, and no increase in pupil size had been reported for that.

The next morning I went to my laboratory at the University of Chicago. As soon as I got there I collected a number of pictures—all landscapes except for one seminude "pinup." When my assistant, James M. Polt, came in, I made him the subject of a quick experiment. I shuffled the pictures and, holding them above my eyes where I could not see them, showed them to Polt one at a time and watched his eyes as he looked at them. When I displayed the seventh picture, I noted a distinct increase in the size of his pupils; I checked the picture, and of course it was the pinup he had been looking at. Polt and I then embarked on an investigation of the relation between pupil size and mental activity.

The idea that the eyes are clues to emotions—"windows of the soul," as the French poet Guillaume de Salluste wrote—is almost commonplace in literature and everyday language. We say

"His eyes were like saucers" or "His eyes were pinpoints of hate"; we use such terms as "beady-eyed" or "bug-eyed" or "hard-eyed." In his *Expressions of Emotion in Man and Animals* Charles Darwin referred to the widening and narrowing of the eyes, accomplished by movements of the eyelids and eyebrows, as signs of human emotion; he apparently assumed that the pupil dilated and contracted only as a physiological mechanism responsive to changes in light intensity.

This light reflex is controlled by one of the two divisions of the autonomic nervous system: the parasympathetic system. Later investigators noted that pupil size is also governed by the other division of the autonomic system—the sympathetic system—in response to strong emotional states and that it can vary with the progress of mental activity. On a less sophisticated level some people to whom it is important to know what someone else is thinking appear to have been aware of the pupil-size phenomenon for a long time. It is said that magicians doing card tricks can identify the card a person is thinking about by watching his pupils enlarge when the card is turned up, and that Chinese jade dealers watch a buyer's pupils to know when he is impressed by a specimen and is likely to pay a high price. Polt and I have been able to study the pupil response in detail and to show what a remarkably sensitive indicator of certain mental activities it can be. We believe it can provide quantitative data on the effects of visual and other sensory stimulation, on cerebral processes and even on changes in fairly complex attitudes.

Most of our early experiments related pupil size to the interest value and "emotionality" of visual stimuli. Our

techniques for these studies are quite simple. The subject peers into a box, looking at a screen on which we project the stimulus picture. A mirror reflects the image of his eye into a motion-picture camera. First we show a control slide that is carefully matched in overall brightness to the stimulus slide that will follow it; this adapts the subject's eyes to the light intensity of the stimulus slide. At various points on the control slide are numbers that direct the subject's gaze to the center of the field. Meanwhile the camera, operating at the rate of two frames per second, records the size of his pupil. After 10 seconds the control slide is switched off and the stimulus slide is projected for 10 seconds; as the subject looks at it the camera continues to make two pictures of his eye per second. The sequence of control and stimulus is repeated about 10 or 12 times a sitting. To score the response to a stimulus we compare the average size of the pupil as photographed during the showing of the control slide with its average size during the stimulus period. Usually we simply project the negative image of the pupil, a bright spot of light, on a screen and measure the diameter with a ruler; alternatively we record the changes in size electronically by measuring the area of the pupil spot with a photocell.

In our first experiment, before we were able to control accurately for brightness, we tested four men and two women, reasoning that a significant difference in the reactions of subjects of different sex to the same picture would be evidence of a pupil response to something other than light intensity. The results confirmed our expectations: the men's pupils dilated more at the sight of a female pinup than the women's

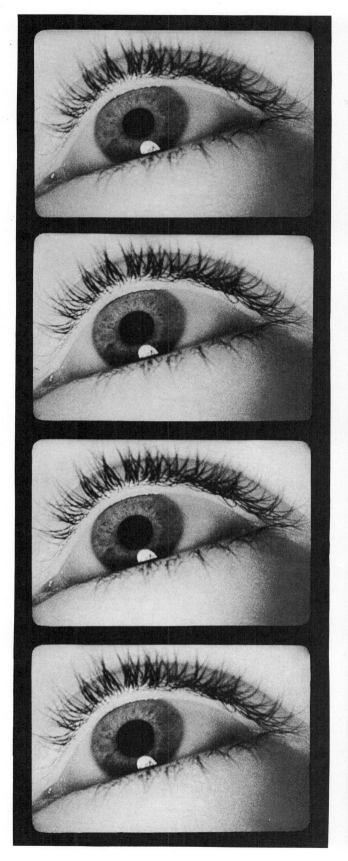

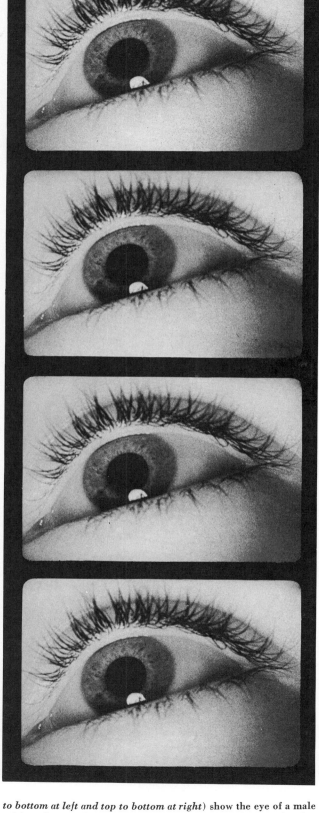

PUPIL SIZE varies with the interest value of a visual stimulus. In the author's laboratory a subject's eye is filmed as he looks at slides flashed on a screen. These consecutive frames (*top to bottom at left and top to bottom at right*) show the eye of a male subject during the first four seconds after a photograph of a woman's face appeared. His pupil increased in diameter 30 percent.

SUBJECT in pupil-response studies peers into a box, looking at a rear-projection screen on which slides are flashed from the pro-jector at right. A motor-driven camera mounted on the box makes a continuous record of pupil size at the rate of two frames a second.

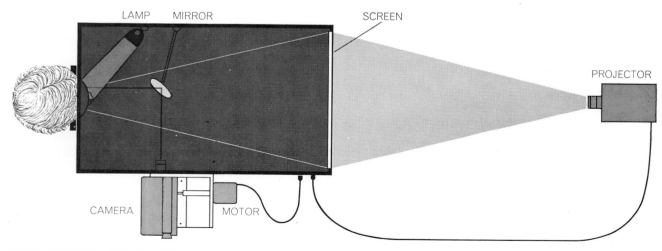

PUPIL-RESPONSE APPARATUS is simple. The lamp and the camera film work in the infrared. A timer advances the projector every 10 seconds, flashing a control slide and a stimulus slide alternately. The mirror is below eye level so that view of screen is clear.

did; the women showed a greater response than the men did to a picture of a baby or of a mother and baby and to a male pinup [*see illustration at right*]. We interpreted dilation in these cases as an indication of interest.

We then undertook another demonstration designed to eliminate the role of brightness. In this experiment we did not show a control slide; only the general room lighting illuminated the rear-projection screen of the apparatus during the control period. When the stimulus slide came on, every part of the screen was therefore at least somewhat brighter than it had been during the control period. If the eye responded only to changes in light intensity, then the response by all subjects to any stimulus ought to be negative; that is, the pupil should constrict slightly every time. This was not the case; we got positive responses in those subjects and for just those stimuli that would have been expected, on the basis of the results of the first study, to produce positive responses. We also got constriction, but only for stimuli that the person involved might be expected to find distasteful or unappealing.

These negative responses, exemplified by the reaction of most of our female subjects to pictures of sharks, were not isolated phenomena; constriction is as characteristic in the case of certain aversive stimuli as dilation is in the case of interesting or pleasant pictures. We observed a strong negative response, for example, when subjects were shown a picture of a cross-eyed or crippled child; as those being tested said, they simply did not like to look at such pictures. One woman went so far as to close her eyes when one of the pictures was on the screen, giving what might be considered the ultimate in negative responses. The negative response also turned up in a number of subjects presented with examples of modern paintings, particularly abstract ones. (We were interested to note that some people who insisted that they liked modern art showed strong negative responses to almost all the modern paintings we showed them.) The results are consistent with a finding by the Soviet psychologist A. R. Shachnowich that a person's pupils may constrict when he looks at unfamiliar geometric patterns.

We have come on one special category of stimuli, examples of which are pictures of dead soldiers on a battlefield, piles of corpses in a concentration camp and the body of a murdered gang-

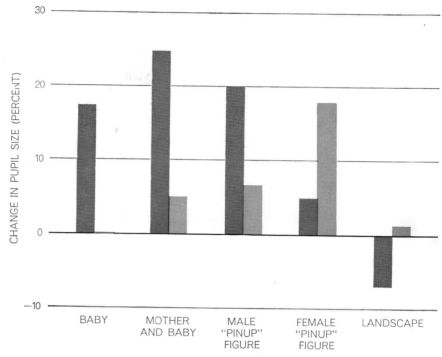

DIFFERENT RESPONSES to the same picture by female subjects (*gray bars*) and male (*colored bars*) established that the pupil response was independent of light intensity. The bars show changes in average area of pupils from the control period to the stimulus period.

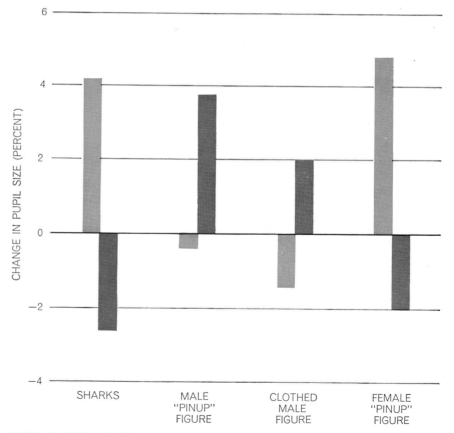

ROLE OF BRIGHTNESS was also eliminated in an experiment in which the screen was unlighted before the stimulus appeared. Whereas responses to light alone would therefore have resulted in constriction, some pictures caused dilation in men (*colored bars*) and women (*gray*). In this experiment pupil diameter was tabulated rather than area.

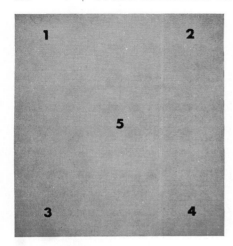

CONTROL SLIDE provides calibration for experiments involving direction of gaze (*opposite page*). The subject looks at the five numbers in sequence and the camera records the resulting movements of his pupil.

ster. One might expect these to be "negative," and indeed they do produce extreme pupil constriction in some subjects, but they elicit a very different pattern of responses in others. On initial exposure the subject often responds with a large increase, rather than a decrease, in pupil size. Then, with repeated presentations, there is a shift to a negative response; the shift is usually accomplished after three to five exposures, and the time interval between those exposures seems to make little difference. Our impression was that these were negative stimuli with an additional "shock" content that prompted a strong emotional reaction. To check this hypothesis we attached electrodes to the hands of some of our volunteers and recorded their galvanic skin response, a measure of the electrical resistance of the skin that has been correlated with emotional level and is a component of most so-called lie-detector tests. As we had anticipated, stimuli we had classified as "shocking" got a high galvanic skin response along with the initial high pupil response in most subjects. After repeated presentations the skin response decreased rapidly as the pupil response shifted from dilation to constriction.

Although we have dealt primarily with positive stimuli, the evidence suggests that at least with respect to visual material there is a continuum of responses that ranges from extreme dilation for interesting or pleasing stimuli to extreme constriction for material that is unpleasant or distasteful to the viewer. In the presence of uninteresting

or boring pictures we find only slight random variations in pupil size.

One of the most interesting things about the changes in pupil size is that they are extremely sensitive, sometimes revealing different responses to stimuli that at the verbal level seem to the person being tested quite similar. We once demonstrated this effect with a pair of stimulus photographs that in themselves provided an interesting illustration of the relation between pupil size and personality. In a series of pictures shown to a group of 20 men we included two photographs of an attractive young woman. These two slides were identical except for the fact that one had been retouched to make the woman's pupils extra large and the other to make them very small. The average response to the picture with the large pupils was more than twice as strong as the response to the one with small pupils; nevertheless, when the men were questioned after the experimental session, most of them reported that the two pictures were identical. Some did say that one was "more feminine" or "prettier" or "softer." None noticed that one had larger pupils than the other. In fact, they had to be shown the difference. As long ago as the Middle Ages women dilated their pupils with the drug belladonna (which means "beautiful woman" in Italian). Clearly large pupils are attractive to men, but the response to them—at least in our subjects—is apparently at a nonverbal level. One might hazard a guess that what is appealing about large pupils in a woman is that they imply extraordinary interest in the man she is with!

Pupillary activity can serve as a measure of motivation. We have investigated the effect of hunger, which is a standard approach in psychological studies of motivation. It occurred to us that a person's physiological state might be a factor in the pupil response when we analyzed the results of a study in which several of the stimulus slides were pictures of food—rather attractive pictures to which we had expected the subjects to respond positively. The general response was positive, but about half of the people tested had much stronger responses than the others. After puzzling over this for a while we checked our logbook and found that about 90 percent of the subjects who had evinced strong responses had been tested in the late morning or late afternoon—when, it seemed obvious, they should have been hungrier than the people tested soon after breakfast or lunch.

To be sure, not everyone is equally hungry a given number of hours after eating, but when we tested two groups controlled for length of time without food, our results were unequivocal: the pupil responses of 10 subjects who were "deprived" for four or five hours were more than two and a half times larger than those of 10 subjects who had eaten a meal within an hour before being tested. The mean responses of the two groups were 11.3 percent and 4.4 percent respectively.

Interestingly enough the pupils respond not only to visual stimuli but also to stimuli affecting other senses. So far our most systematic research on nonvisual stimuli has dealt with the sense of taste. The subject places his head in a modified apparatus that leaves his mouth free; he holds a flexible straw to which the experimenter can raise a cup of the liquid to be tasted. During the test the taster keeps his eyes on an X projected on the screen, and the camera records any changes in pupil size.

Our first study involved a variety of presumably pleasant-tasting liquids—carbonated drinks, chocolate drinks and milk—and some unpleasant-tasting ones, including concentrated lemon juice and a solution of quinine. We were surprised to find that both the pleasant and the unpleasant liquids brought an increase in pupil size compared with a "control" of water. Then we decided to test a series of similar liquids, all presumably on the positive side of the "pleasant-unpleasant" continuum, to see if, as in the case of visual material, some of the stimuli would elicit greater responses than others. We selected five "orange" beverages and had each subject alternate sips of water with sips of a beverage. One of the five orange beverages caused a significantly larger average increase in pupil size than the others did; the same drink also won on the basis of verbal preferences expressed by the subjects after they had been through the pupil-size test. Although we still have a good deal of work to do on taste, particularly with regard to the response to unpleasant stimuli, we are encouraged by the results so far. The essential sensitivity of the pupil response suggests that it can reveal preferences in some cases in which the actual taste differences are so slight that the subject cannot even articulate them—a possibility with interesting implications for market research.

We have also had our volunteers listen to taped excerpts of music while

DIRECTIONAL ANALYSIS reveals where a subject was looking when each frame of film was made as well as how large his pupil was. Superposed on the upper reproduction of Leon Kroll's "Morning on the Cape" are symbols showing the sequence of fixations by a female subject looking at the painting; a man's responses are shown below. The light-color symbols indicate a pupil size about the same as during the preceding control period; open symbols denote smaller responses and dark-color symbols larger responses. The experimenters determine the direction of gaze by shining light through the film negative; the beam that passes through the image of the pupil is projected on a photograph of the stimulus (in this case the painting) and its position is recorded.

the camera monitors their pupil size. We find different responses to different compositions, apparently depending on individual preference. As in the case of the taste stimuli, however, the response to music seems always to be in a positive direction: the pupil becomes larger when music of any kind is being played. We have begun to test for the effect of taped verbal statements and individual words, which also seem to elicit different pupil responses. Research in these areas, together with some preliminary

work concerning the sense of smell, supports the hypothesis that the pupil is closely associated not only with visual centers in the brain but also with other brain centers. In general it strongly suggests that pupillary changes reflect ongoing activity in the brain.

It is not surprising that the response of the pupil should be intimately associated with mental activity. Embryologically and anatomically the eye is an extension of the brain; it is almost

as though a portion of the brain were in plain sight for the psychologist to peer at. Once it is, so to speak, "calibrated" the pupil response should make it possible to observe ongoing mental behavior directly and without requiring the investigator to attach to his subject electrodes or other equipment that may affect the very behavior he seeks to observe.

More than 50 years ago German psychologists noted that mental activity (solving arithmetical problems, for ex-

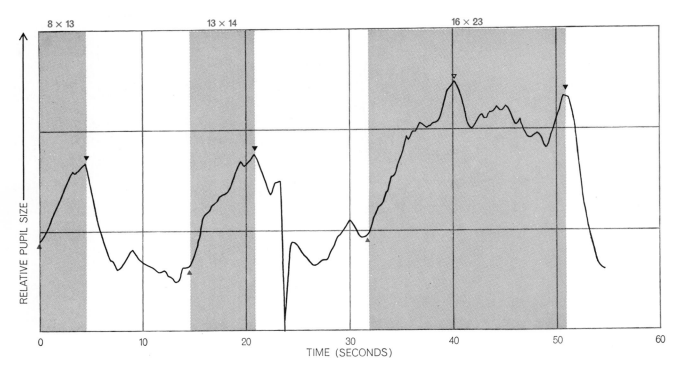

CHANGES IN PUPIL SIZE are traced in a subject doing the three mental-arithmetic problems shown at the top. Beginning when the problem is posed (*colored triangles*), the pupil dilates until the answer is given (*solid black triangles*). This subject appears to have reached a solution of the third problem (*open triangle*) and then to have reconsidered, checking his answer before giving it.

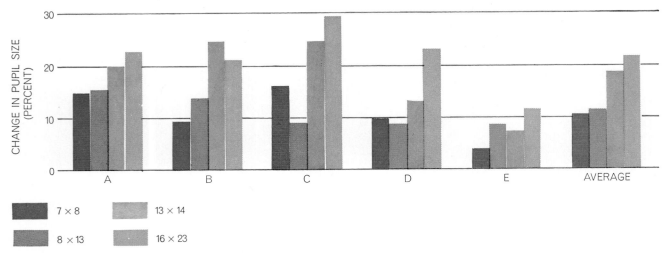

INDIVIDUAL DIFFERENCES in pupil response while solving multiplication problems reflect the fact that two of the five subjects, *D* and *E*, could do mental arithmetic with less effort than the others. The change in pupil size was computed by comparing the average size in the five frames before the problem was posed with the average in the five frames just before the answer was given.

ample) caused a gross increase in pupil size. We decided this would be a good area for detailed study in an effort to see how precise and differentiated an indicator the response could be. We present mental-arithmetic problems of varying difficulty to volunteers and then obtain a continuous trace of their pupil response by measuring the filmed images of the pupil with a photocell [*see upper illustration on opposite page*]. As soon as the problem is presented the size of the pupil begins to increase. It reaches a maximum as the subject arrives at his solution and then immediately starts to decrease, returning to its base level as soon as the answer is verbalized. If the subject is told to solve the problem but not give the answer, there is some decrease at the instant of solution but the pupil remains abnormally large; then, when the experimenter asks for the solution, the pupil returns to its base level as the subject verbalizes the answer.

In one study we tested five people, two who seemed to be able to do mental arithmetic easily and three for whom even simple multiplication required a lot of effort. The pupil-response results reflect these individual differences [*see lower illustration on opposite page*] and also show a fairly consistent increase in dilation as the problems increase in difficulty. Individual differences of another kind are revealed by the trace of a subject's pupil size. Most subjects do have a response that drops to normal as soon as they give the answer. In some people, however, the size of the pupil decreases momentarily after the answer is given and then goes up again, sometimes as high as the original peak, suggesting that the worried subject is working the problem over again to be sure he was correct. Other people, judging by the response record, tend to recheck their answers before announcing them.

We have found a similar response in spelling, with the maximum pupil size correlated to the difficulty of the word. The response also appears when a subject is working an anagram, a situation that is not very different from the kind of mental activity associated with decision-making. We believe the pupil-response technique should be valuable for studying the course of decision-making and perhaps for assessing decision-making abilities in an individual.

It is always difficult to elicit from someone information that involves his private attitudes toward some person or concept or thing. The pupil-

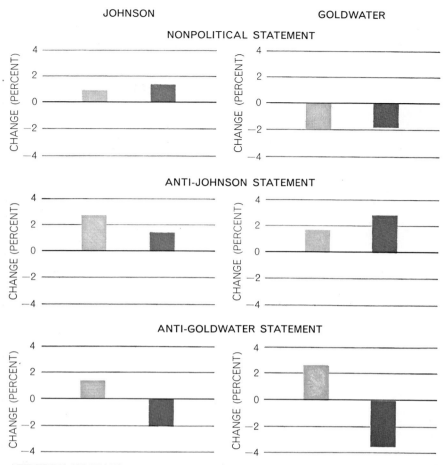

ATTITUDE CHANGES are revealed by responses to Johnson (*left*) and Goldwater (*right*) before (*light bars*) and after (*dark bars*) subjects read a statement supplied by the experimenter. Nonpolitical material had no appreciable effect. The anti-Johnson material had the expected effect. Bitter anti-Goldwater material made response to both candidates negative.

response technique can measure just such attitudes. We have established that the correlation between a person's expressed attitude and his "measured pupil" attitude can vary widely, depending on the topic. For example, we tested 64 people with five pictures of foods and also asked them to rank the foods from favorite to least preferred. When we matched each person's verbal report with his pupil response, we obtained 61 positive correlations—a result one could expect to get by chance only once in a million times.

The correlation is poor in an area that involves social values or pressures, however. For example, we do not get such good agreement between pupillary and verbal responses when we show women pictures of seminude men and women. Nor did we get good correlation when we did a political study last fall. We showed photographs of President Johnson and Barry Goldwater to 34 University of Chicago students, faculty members and employees. Everyone professed to be in favor of Johnson and

against Goldwater. The pupil-response test, however, had indicated that about a third of these people actually had a slightly more positive attitude toward Goldwater than toward Johnson.

To be sure, the pupil test may overemphasize the effect of physical appearance; certainly our data do not prove that a third of the subjects went on to vote for Goldwater. But the results do raise the interesting possibility that at least some of them did, and that in the liberal atmosphere of the university these people found it difficult to utter any pro-Goldwater sentiment. The results suggest that our technique, by which we measure a response that is not under the control of the person being tested, may yield more accurate representations of an attitude than can be obtained with even a well-drawn questionnaire or with some devious "projective" technique in which a person's verbal or motor responses are recorded in an effort to uncover his real feelings.

For me the most interesting aspect

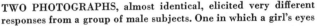

TWO PHOTOGRAPHS, almost identical, elicited very different responses from a group of male subjects. One in which a girl's eyes were retouched, as at left, to make the pupils large got a greater response than one in which the pupils were made small (*right*).

of our work has been the measurement of changes in attitude. We begin by determining the pupil response of one of our volunteers to someone's picture. Then we have the subject read some kind of informative material, we retest for the response and compare the "before" and "after" scores. In one case the reading material consisted of a passage indicating that the man whose picture had been displayed was the former commandant of the concentration camp at Auschwitz. When we then remeasured the subject's pupil response to the man in question, we found that a more negative attitude had clearly developed as a result of the intervening reading.

Take another and more hypothetical example: Suppose a patient seeking psychotherapy has a fear of people with beards. We ought to be able to get a pupillary measure of his attitude by showing him photographs of bearded men, among others, and then be able to check on the course of treatment by repeating the test later. Regardless of whether what intervenes is straightforward information, psychotherapy, political propaganda, advertising or any other material intended to change attitudes, it should be possible to monitor the effectiveness of that material by measuring changes in pupil size, and to

do this with a number of people at any desired interval.

One recent study along these lines will illustrate the possibilities. We showed five different photographs of President Johnson and five of Goldwater, along with a single photograph of former presidents Kennedy and Eisenhower, to three groups of people. One group thereupon read anti-Johnson material, another read anti-Goldwater material and the third read some excerpts from a psychology journal that had no political content. Then each group was retested.

Now the people who had read the anti-Johnson material showed a slightly smaller response than before to Johnson and a slightly larger response than before to Goldwater. Some extremely negative anti-Goldwater material, which one of my assistants apparently found very easy to write, had a different kind of effect. It did cause the expected decrease in the response to Goldwater, but it also caused a large drop in the response to Johnson and even to Eisenhower! The only person who was unaffected was Kennedy. This may indicate that bitter campaign propaganda can lower a person's attitude toward politicians in general, Kennedy alone being spared for obvious reasons.

The pupil response promises to be

a new tool with which to probe the mind. We are applying it now in a variety of studies. One deals with the development in young people of sexual interest and of identification with parents from preschool age to high school age. In an attempt to establish personality differences, we are tabulating the responses of a number of subjects to pictures of people under stress and pictures of the same people after they have been released from the stressful situation. Our other current study deals with volunteers who are experiencing changes in perception as the result of hypnotic suggestion. In the perception laboratory of Marplan, a communications-research organization that has supported much of our work, Paula Drillman is studying responses to packages, products and advertising on television and in other media. Several laboratories at Chicago and elsewhere are employing our techniques to study such diverse problems as the process of decision-making, the effect of certain kinds of experience on the attitudes of white people toward Negroes and the efficacy of different methods of problem-solving. Those of us engaged in this work have the feeling that we have only begun to understand and exploit the information implicit in the dilations and constrictions of the pupil.

Cognitive Dissonance

by Leon Festinger
October 1962

*It is the subject of a new theory based on experiments
showing that the grass is usually not greener on the
other side of the fence and that grapes are sourest
when they are in easy reach*

There is an experiment in psychology that you can perform easily in your own home if you have a child three or four years old. Buy two toys that you are fairly sure will be equally attractive to the child. Show them both to him and say: "Here are two nice toys. This one is for you to keep. The other I must give back to the store." You then hand the child the toy that is his to keep and ask: "Which of the two toys do you like better?" Studies have shown that in such a situation most children will tell you they prefer the toy they are to keep.

This response of children seems to conflict with the old saying that the grass is always greener on the other side of the fence. Do adults respond in the same way under similar circumstances or does the adage indeed become true as we grow older? The question is of considerable interest because the adult world is filled with choices and alternative courses of action that are often about equally attractive. When they make a choice of a college or a car or a spouse or a home or a political candidate, do most people remain satisfied with their choice or do they tend to wish they had made a different one? Naturally any choice may turn out to be a bad one on the basis of some objective measurement, but the question is: Does some psychological process come into play immediately after the making of a choice that colors one's attitude, either favorably or unfavorably, toward the decision?

To illuminate this question there is another experiment one can do at home, this time using an adult as a subject rather than a child. Buy two presents for your wife, again choosing things you are reasonably sure she will find about equally attractive. Find some plausible excuse for having both of them in your possession, show them to your wife and ask her to tell you how attractive each one is to her. After you have obtained a good measurement of attractiveness, tell her that she can have one of them, whichever she chooses. The other you will return to the store. After she has made her choice, ask her once more to evaluate the attractiveness of each of them. If you compare the evaluations of attractiveness before and after the choice, you will probably find that the chosen present has increased in attractiveness and the rejected one decreased.

Such behavior can be explained by a new theory concerning "cognitive dissonance." This theory centers around the idea that if a person knows various things that are not psychologically consistent with one another, he will, in a variety of ways, try to make them more consistent. Two items of information that psychologically do not fit together are said to be in a dissonant relation to each other. The items of information may be about behavior, feelings, opinions, things in the environment and so on. The word "cognitive" simply emphasizes that the theory deals with relations among items of information.

Such items can of course be changed. A person can change his opinion; he can change his behavior, thereby changing the information he has about it; he can even distort his perception and his information about the world around him. Changes in items of information that produce or restore consistency are referred to as dissonance-reducing changes.

Cognitive dissonance is a motivating state of affairs. Just as hunger impels a person to eat, so does dissonance impel a person to change his opinions or his behavior. The world, however, is much

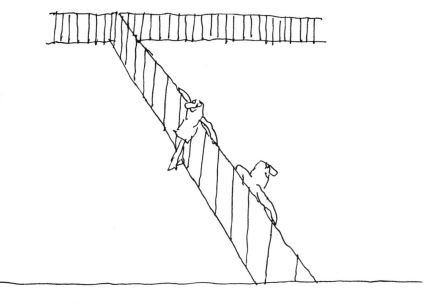

The grass is not always greener on the other side of the fence

Blechman

Consequences of making a decision between two reasonably attractive alternatives

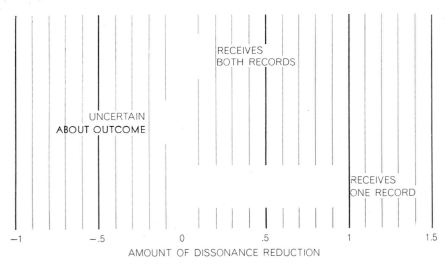

RECEIVES
BOTH RECORDS

UNCERTAIN
ABOUT OUTCOME

RECEIVES
ONE RECORD

−1   −.5   0   .5   1   1.5

AMOUNT OF DISSONANCE REDUCTION

**DISSONANCE REDUCTION is a psychological phenomenon found to occur after a person
has made a choice between two approximately equal alternatives. The effect of the phenomenon is to enhance the attractiveness of the chosen object or chosen course of action.
The chart summarizes the results of an experiment in which high school girls rated the
attractiveness of 12 "hit" records before and after choosing one of them as a gift. Substantial dissonance reduction occurred under only one of three experimental conditions described in the text. Under two other conditions no systematic reduction was observed.**

more effectively arranged for hunger
reduction than it is for dissonance reduction. It is almost always possible to find
something to eat. It is not always easy to
reduce dissonance. Sometimes it may be
very difficult or even impossible to
change behavior or opinions that are
involved in dissonant relations. Consequently there are circumstances in which
appreciable dissonance may persist for
long periods.

To understand cognitive dissonance
as a motivating state, it is necessary
to have a clearer conception of the conditions that produce it. The simplest
definition of dissonance can, perhaps,
be given in terms of a person's expectations. In the course of our lives we have
all accumulated a large number of expectations about what things go together
and what things do not. When such an
expectation is not fulfilled, dissonance
occurs.

For example, a person standing un-
protected in the rain would expect to get
wet. If he found himself in the rain and
he was not getting wet, there would exist
dissonance between these two pieces
of information. This unlikely example is
one where the expectations of different
people would all be uniform. There are
obviously many instances where different people would not share the same
expectations. Someone who is very self-
confident might expect to succeed at
whatever he tried, whereas someone
who had a low opinion of himself might
normally expect to fail. Under these circumstances what would produce dissonance for one person might produce
consonance for another. In experimental
investigations, of course, an effort is
made to provide situations in which expectations are rather uniform.

Perhaps the best way to explain the
theory of cognitive dissonance is to show
its application to specific situations. The
rest of this article, therefore, will be devoted to a discussion of three examples
of cognitive dissonance. I shall discuss
the effects of making a decision, of lying
and of temptation. These three examples by no means cover all the situations
in which dissonance can be created. Indeed, it seldom happens that everything
a person knows about an action he has
taken is perfectly consistent with his
having taken it. The three examples,
however, may serve to illustrate the
range of situations in which dissonance
can be expected to occur. They will also
serve to show the kinds of dissonance-
reduction effects that are obtained under a special circumstance: when dissonance involves the person's behavior

and the action in question is difficult to change.

Let us consider first the consequences of making a decision. Imagine the situation of a person who has carefully weighed two reasonably attractive alternatives and then chosen one of them—a decision that, for our purposes, can be regarded as irrevocable. All the information this person has concerning the attractive features of the rejected alternative (and the possible unattractive features of the chosen alternative) are now inconsistent, or dissonant, with the knowledge that he has made the given choice. It is true that the person also knows many things that are consistent or consonant with the choice he has made, which is to say all the attractive features of the chosen alternative and unattractive features of the rejected one. Nevertheless, some dissonance exists and after the decision the individual will try to reduce the dissonance.

There are two major ways in which the individual can reduce dissonance in this situation. He can persuade himself that the attractive features of the rejected alternative are not really so attractive as he had originally thought, and that the unattractive features of the chosen alternative are not really unattractive. He can also provide additional justification for his choice by exaggerating the attractive features of the chosen alternative and the unattractive features of the rejected alternative. In other words, according to the theory the process of dissonance reduction should lead, after the decision, to an increase in the desirability of the chosen alternative and a decrease in the desirability of the rejected alternative.

This phenomenon has been demonstrated in a variety of experiments. A brief description of one of these will suffice to illustrate the precise nature of the effect. In an experiment performed by Jon Jecker of Stanford University, high school girls were asked to rate the attractiveness of each of 12 "hit" records. For each girl two records that she had rated as being only moderately attractive were selected and she was asked which of the two she would like as a gift. After having made her choice, the girl again rated the attractiveness of all the records. The dissonance created by the decision could be reduced by increasing the attractiveness of the chosen record and decreasing the attractiveness of the rejected record. Consequently a measurement of dissonance reduction could be obtained by summing both of these kinds of changes in ratings made before and after the decision.

Different experimental variations were employed in this experiment in order to examine the dynamics of the process of dissonance reduction. Let us look at three of these experimental variations. In all three conditions the girls, when they were making their choice, were given to understand there was a slight possibility that they might actually be given both records. In one condition they were asked to rerate the

records after they had made their choice but before they knew definitely whether they would receive both records or only the one they chose. The results for this condition should indicate whether dissonance reduction begins with having made the choice or whether it is suspended until the uncertainty is resolved. In a second condition the girls were actually given both records after their choice and were then asked to rerate

Further consequences of making a difficult decision

all the records. Since they had received both records and therefore no dissonance existed following the decision, there should be no evidence of dissonance reduction in this condition. In a third condition the girls were given only the record they chose and were then asked to do the rerating. This, of course, resembles the normal outcome of a decision and the usual dissonance reduction should occur.

The chart on page 290 shows the results for these three conditions. When the girls are uncertain as to the outcome, or when they receive both records, there is no dissonance reduction—that is, no systematic change in attractiveness of the chosen and rejected records. The results in both conditions are very close to zero—one slightly positive, the other slightly negative. When they receive only the record they chose, however, there is a large systematic change in rating to reduce dissonance. Since dissonance reduction is only observed in this last experimental condition, it is evident that dissonance reduction does not occur during the process of making

a decision but only after the decision is made and the outcome is clear.

Let us turn now to the consequences of lying. There are many circumstances in which, for one reason or another, an individual publicly states something that is at variance with his private belief. Here again one can expect dissonance to arise. There is an inconsistency between knowing that one really believes one thing and knowing that one has publicly stated something quite different. Again, to be sure, the individual knows things that are consonant with his overt, public behavior. All the reasons that induced him to make the public statement are consonant with his having made it and provide him with some justification for his behavior. Nevertheless, some dissonance exists and, according to the theory, there will be attempts to reduce it. The degree to which the dissonance is bothersome for the individual will depend on two things. The more deviant his public statement is from his private belief, the greater will be the dissonance. The greater the amount of justification the person has for having made the public statement, the less bothersome the dissonance will be.

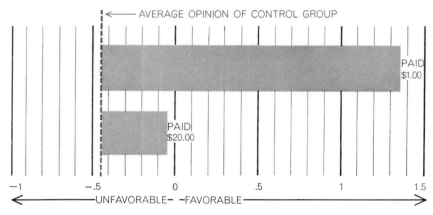

CONSEQUENCES OF LYING are found to vary, depending on whether the justification for the lie is large or small. In this experiment students were persuaded to tell others that a boring experience was really fun. Those in one group were paid only $1 for their co-operation; in a second group, $20. The low-paid students, having least justification for lying, experienced most dissonance and reduced it by coming to regard the experience favorably.

How can the dissonance be reduced? One method is obvious. The individual can remove the dissonance by retracting his public statement. But let us consider only those instances in which the public statement, once made, cannot be changed or withdrawn; in other words, in which the behavior is irrevocable. Under such circumstances the major avenue for reduction of the dissonance is change of private opinion. That is, if the private opinion were changed so that it agreed with what was publicly stated, obviously the dissonance would be gone. The theory thus leads us to expect that after having made an irrevocable public statement at variance with his private belief, a person will tend to change his private belief to bring it into line with his public statement. Furthermore, the degree to which he changes his private belief will depend on the amount of justification or the amount of pressure for making the public statement initially. The less the original justification or pressure, the greater the dissonance and the more the person's private belief can be expected to change.

An experiment recently conducted at Stanford University by James M. Carlsmith and me illustrates the nature of this effect. In the experiment, college students were induced to make a statement at variance with their own belief. It was done by using students who had

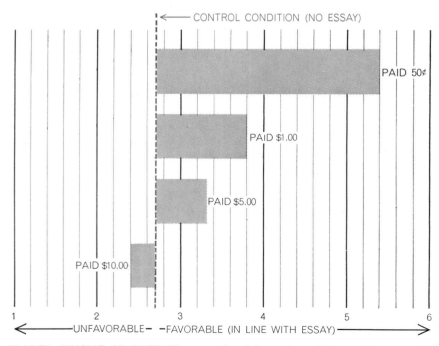

GRADED CHANGE OF OPINION was produced by paying subjects various sums for writing essays advocating opinions contrary to their beliefs. When examined later, students paid the least had changed their opinion the most to agree with what they had written. Only the highest paid group held to their original opinion more strongly than did a control group.

volunteered to participate in an experiment to measure "motor performance." The purported experiment lasted an hour and was a boring and fatiguing session. At the end of the hour the experimenter thanked the subject for his participation, indicating that the experiment was over. The real purpose of the hour-long session, however, was to provide each subject with an identical experience about which he would have an unfavorable opinion.

At the end of the fatiguing hour the experimenter enlisted the subject's aid in preparing the next person for the experiment. The subject was led to believe that, for experimental purposes, the next person was supposed to be given the impression that the hour's session was going to be very interesting and lots of fun. The subject was persuaded to help in this deception by telling the next subject, who was waiting in an adjoining room, that he himself had just finished the hour and that it had indeed been very interesting and lots of fun. The first subject was then interviewed by someone else to determine his actual private opinion of the experiment.

Two experimental conditions were run that differed only in the amount of pressure, or justification given the subject for stating a public opinion at variance with his private belief. All subjects, of course, had the justification of helping to conduct a scientific experiment. In addition to this, half of the subjects were paid $1 for their help—a relatively small amount of money; the other subjects were paid $20—a rather large sum for the work involved. From the theory we would expect that the subjects who were paid only $1, having less justification for their action, would have more dissonance and would change their private beliefs more in order to reduce the dissonance. In other words, we would expect the greatest change in private opinion among the subjects given the least tangible incentive for changing.

The upper illustration on the opposite page shows the results of the experiment. The broken line in the chart shows the results for a control group of subjects. These subjects participated in the hour-long session and then were asked to give their private opinion of it. Their generally unfavorable views are to be expected when no dissonance is induced between private belief and public statement. It is clear from the chart that introducing such dissonance produced a change of opinion so that the subjects who were asked to take part in a deception finally came to think better of the session than did the control subjects. It

The effect of rewards on lying

is also clear that only in the condition where they were paid a dollar is this opinion change appreciable. When they were paid a lot of money, the justification for misrepresenting private belief is high and there is correspondingly less change of opinion to reduce dissonance.

Another way to summarize the result is to say that those who are highly rewarded for doing something that involves dissonance change their opinion less in the direction of agreeing with what they did than those who are given very little reward. This result may seem surprising, since we are used to thinking that reward is effective in creating change. It must be remembered, however, that the critical factor here is that the reward is being used to induce a behavior that is dissonant with private opinion.

To show that this result is valid and not just a function of the particular situation or the particular sums of money used for reward, Arthur R. Cohen of New York University conducted a similar experiment in a different context. Cohen paid subjects to write essays advocating an opinion contrary to what

they really believed. Subjects were paid either $10, $5, $1 or 50 cents to do this. To measure the extent to which dissonance was reduced by their changing their opinion, each subject was then given a questionnaire, which he left unsigned, to determine his private opinion on the issue. The extent to which the subjects reduced dissonance by changing their opinion to agree with what they wrote in the essay is shown in the lower illustration on the opposite page. Once again it is clear that the smaller the original justification for engaging in the dissonance-producing action, the greater the subsequent change in private opinion to bring it into line with the action.

The final set of experiments I shall discuss deals with the consequences of resisting temptation. What happens when a person wants something and discovers that he cannot have it? Does he now want it even more or does he persuade himself that it is really not worth having? Sometimes our common general understanding of human behavior can provide at least crude answers to such questions. In this case,

293

however, our common understanding is ambiguous, because it supplies two contradictory answers. Everyone knows the meaning of the term "sour grapes"; it is the attitude taken by a person who persuades himself that he really does not want what he cannot have. But we are also familiar with the opposite reaction. The child who is not allowed to eat candy and hence loves candy passionately; the woman who adores expensive clothes even though she cannot afford to own them; the man who has a hopeless obsession for a woman who spurns his attentions. Everyone "understands" the behavior of the person who longs for what he cannot have.

Obviously one cannot say one of these reactions is wrong and the other is right; they both occur. One might at least, however, try to answer the question: Under what circumstances does one reaction take place and not the other? If we examine the question from the point of view of the theory of dissonance, a partial answer begins to emerge.

Imagine the psychological situation that exists for an individual who is tempted to engage in a certain action but for one reason or another refrains. An analysis of the situation here reveals its similarity to the other dissonance-producing situations. An individual's knowledge concerning the attractive aspects of the activity toward which he was tempted is dissonant with the knowledge that he has refrained from engaging in the activity. Once more, of course, the individual has some knowledge that is consonant with his behavior in the situation. All the pressures, reasons and justifications for refraining are consonant with his actual behavior. Nevertheless, the dissonance does exist, and there will be psychological activity oriented toward reducing this dissonance.

As we have already seen in connection with other illustrations, one major way to reduce dissonance is to change one's opinions and evaluations in order to bring them closer in line with one's actual behavior. Therefore when there is

dissonance produced by resisting temptation, it can be reduced by derogating or devaluing the activity toward which one was tempted. This derivation from the theory clearly implies the sour-grapes attitude, but both theory and experiment tell us that such dissonance-reducing effects will occur only when there was insufficient original justification for the behavior. Where the original justification for refraining from the action was great, little dissonance would have occurred and there would have been correspondingly little change of opinion in order to reduce dissonance. Therefore one might expect that if a person had resisted temptation in a situation of strong prohibition or strong threatened punishment, little dissonance would have been created and one would not observe the sour-grapes effect. One would expect this effect only if the person resisted temptation under conditions of weak deterrent.

This line of reasoning leaves open the question of when the reverse effect occurs—that is, the situation in which desire for the "unattainable" object is increased. Experimentally it is possible to look at both effects. This was done by Elliot Aronson and Carlsmith, at Stanford University, in an experiment that sheds considerable light on the problem. The experiment was performed with children who were about four years old. Each child was individually brought into a large playroom in which there were five toys on a table. After the child had had an opportunity to play briefly with each toy, he was asked to rank the five in order of attractiveness. The toy that the child liked second best was then left on the table and the other four toys were spread around on the floor. The experimenter told the child that he had to leave for a few minutes to do an errand but would be back soon. The experimenter then left the room for 10 minutes. Various techniques were employed to "prohibit" the child from playing with the particular toy that he liked second best while the experimenter was out of the room.

For different children this prohibition was instituted in three different ways. In one condition there was no temptation at all; the experimenter told the child he could play with any of the toys in the room and then took the second-best toy with him when he left. In the other two conditions temptation was present: the second-best toy was left on the table in the experimenter's absence. The children were told they could play with any of the toys in the room except

Temptation accompanied by a severe threat

Temptation accompanied by a mild threat

the one on the table. The children in one group were threatened with mild punishment if they violated the prohibition, whereas those in the other group were threatened with more severe punishment. (The actual nature of the punishment was left unspecified.)

During his absence from the room the experimenter observed each child through a one-way mirror. None of the children in the temptation conditions played with the prohibited toy. After 10 minutes were up the experimenter returned to the playroom and each child was again allowed to play briefly with each of the five toys. The attractiveness of each toy for the child was again measured. By comparing the before and after measurements of the attractiveness of the toy the child originally liked second best, one can assess the effects of the prohibition. The results are shown in the chart on this page.

When there was no temptation—that is, when the prohibited toy was not physically present—there was of course no dissonance, and the preponderant result is an increase in the attractiveness of the prohibited toy. When the temptation is present but the prohibition is enforced by means of a severe threat of punishment, there is likewise little dissonance created by refraining, and again the preponderant result is an increase in the attractiveness of the prohibited toy. In other words, it seems clear that a prohibition that is enforced in such a way as not to introduce dissonance results in a greater desire for the prohibited activity.

The results are quite different, however, when the prohibition is enforced by only a mild threat of punishment. Here we see the result to be expected from the theory of dissonance. Because the justification for refraining from playing with the toy is relatively weak, there is appreciable dissonance between the child's knowledge that the toy is attractive and his actual behavior. The tendency to reduce this dissonance is strong enough to more than overcome the effect apparent in the other two conditions. Here, as a result of dissonance reduction, we see an appreciable sour-grapes phenomenon.

The theory of cognitive dissonance obviously has many implications for everyday life. In addition to throwing light on one's own behavior, it would seem to carry useful lessons for everyone concerned with understanding human behavior in a world where everything is not black and white.

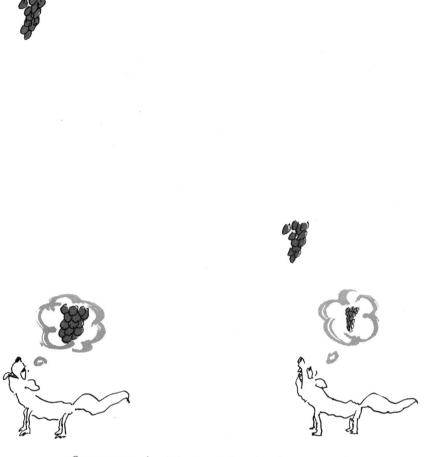

Consequences of resisting temptation when deterrence varies

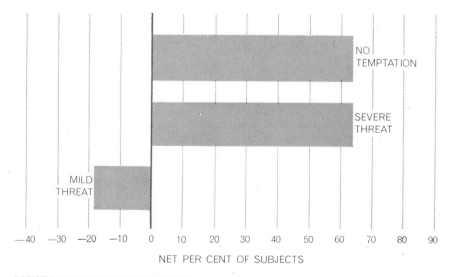

NET PER CENT OF SUBJECTS

CONSEQUENCES OF TEMPTATION were explored by prohibiting children from playing with a desirable toy. Later the children were asked to re-evaluate the attractiveness of the forbidden toy. In one case the prohibition was enforced by removing the toy from the child's presence. In the second case the prohibition took the form of a threat of severe punishment; in the third case, a threat of mild punishment. The chart shows the net per cent of children who thought the forbidden toy more attractive after the experiment than before. ("Net per cent" means the per cent who found the toy more attractive minus the per cent who found it less so.) Evidently only those threatened mildly experienced much dissonance, and they reduced it by downgrading toy's desirability. Others thought the toy more desirable.

34

Experiments in Intergroup Discrimination

by Henri Tajfel
November 1970

Can discrimination be traced to some such origin as social conflict or a history of hostility? Not necessarily. Apparently the mere fact of division into groups is enough to trigger discriminatory behavior

Intergroup discrimination is a feature of most modern societies. The phenomenon is depressingly similar regardless of the constitution of the "ingroup" and of the "outgroup" that is perceived as being somehow different. A Slovene friend of mine once described to me the stereotypes—the common traits attributed to a large human group—that are applied in his country, the richest constituent republic of Yugoslavia, to immigrant Bosnians, who come from a poorer region. Some time later I presented this description to a group of students at the University of Oxford and asked them to guess by whom it was used and to whom it referred. The almost unanimous reply was that this was the characterization applied by native Englishmen to "colored" immigrants: people coming primarily from the West Indies, India and Pakistan.

The intensity of discrimination varies more than the nature of the phenomenon. In countries with long-standing intergroup problems—be they racial as in the U.S., religious as in Northern Ireland or linguistic-national as in Belgium—tensions reach the boiling point more easily than they do elsewhere. In spite of differing economic, cultural, historical, political and psychological backgrounds, however, the *attitudes* of prejudice toward outgroups and the *behavior* of discrimination against outgroups clearly display a set of common characteristics. Social scientists have naturally been concerned to try to identify these characteristics in an effort to understand the origins of prejudice and discrimination.

The investigative approaches to this task can be roughly classified into two categories. Some workers stress the social determinants of prejudice and discrimination. Others emphasize psycho-

logical causation. In *The Functions of Social Conflict,* published in 1956, Lewis A. Coser of Brandeis University established a related dichotomy when he distinguished between two types of intergroup conflict: the "rational" and the "irrational." The former is a means to an end: the conflict and the attitudes that go with it reflect a genuine competition between groups with divergent interests. The latter is an end in itself: it serves to release accumulated emotional tensions of various kinds. As both popular lore and the psychological literature testify, nothing is better suited for this purpose than a well-selected scapegoat.

These dichotomies have some value as analytical tools but they need not be taken too seriously. Most cases of conflict between human groups, large or small, reflect an intricate interdependence of social and psychological causation. Often it is difficult, and probably fruitless, to speculate about what were the first causes of real present-day social situations. Moreover, there is a dialectical relation between the objective and the subjective determinants of intergroup attitudes and behavior. Once the process is set in motion they reinforce each other in a relentless spiral in which the weight of predominant causes tends to shift continuously. For example, economic or social competition can lead to discriminatory behavior; that behavior can then in a number of ways create attitudes of prejudice; those attitudes can in turn lead to new forms of discriminatory behavior that create new economic or social disparities, and so the vicious circle is continued.

The interdependence of the two types of causation does not manifest itself only in their mutual reinforcement. They actually converge because of the psychological effects on an individual of his so-

ciocultural milieu. This convergence is often considered in terms of social learning and conformity. For instance, there is much evidence that children learn quite early the pecking order of evaluations of various groups that prevails in their society, and that the order remains fairly stable. This applies not only to the evaluation of groups that are in daily contact, such as racial groups in mixed environments, but also to ideas about foreign nations with which there is little if any personal contact.

In studies conducted at Oxford a few years ago my colleagues and I found a high consensus among children of six and seven in their preference for four foreign countries. The order was America, France, Germany and Russia, and there was a correlation of .98 between the preferences of subjects from two different schools. As for adults, studies conducted by Thomas F. Pettigrew in the late 1950's in South Africa and in the American South have shown that conformity is an important determinant of hostile attitudes toward blacks in both places (above and beyond individual tendencies toward authoritarianism, which is known to be closely related to prejudice toward outgroups).

These studies, like many others, were concerned with attitudes rather than behavior, with prejudice rather than discrimination. Discrimination, it is often said, is more directly a function of the objective social situation, which sometimes does and sometimes does not facilitate the expression of attitudes; the attitudes of prejudice may be socially learned or due to tendencies to conform, but they are not a very efficient predictor of discriminatory behavior. According to this view, psychological considerations are best suited to explaining and predict-

297

A

MATRIX 1

−19	−16	−13	−10	−7	−4	−1	0	1	2	3	4	5	6
6	5	4	3	2	1	0	−1	−4	−7	−10	−13	−16	−19

MATRIX 2

12	10	8	6	4	2	0	−1	−5	−9	−13	−17	−21	−25
−25	−21	−17	−13	−9	−5	−1	0	2	4	6	8	10	12

B

MATRIX 3

1	2	3	4	5	6	7	8	9	10	11	12	13	14
14	13	12	11	10	9	8	7	6	5	4	3	2	1

MATRIX 4

18	17	16	15	14	13	12	11	10	9	8	7	6	5
5	6	7	8	9	10	11	12	13	14	15	16	17	18

C

MATRIX 5

−14	−12	−10	−8	−6	−4	−2	−1	3	7	11	15	19	23
23	19	15	11	7	3	−1	−2	−4	−6	−8	−10	−12	−14

MATRIX 6

17	14	11	8	5	2	−1	−2	−3	−4	−5	−6	−7	−8
−8	−7	−6	−5	−4	−3	−2	−1	2	5	8	11	14	17

FIRST EXPERIMENT conducted by the author and his colleagues utilized these six matrices. The numbers represented points (later translated into awards or penalties in money) to be assigned by a subject to other individuals; by checking a box the subject assigned the number of points in the top of the box to one person and the number in the bottom of the box to another person; he did not know the identity of these people but only whether each was a member of his own group or "the other group." (The groups had been established by the experimenters on grounds that were artificial and insignificant.) Each matrix appeared three times in a test booklet with each row of numbers labeled to indicate whether the subject was choosing between two members of his own group (ingroup) other than himself, two members of the outgroup or one member of the ingroup and one member of the outgroup. Choices were scored to see if subjects chose for fairness, maximum gain to their own group or maximum difference in favor of the ingroup.

ing the genesis and functioning of attitudes; the facts of intergroup discrimination are best related to, and predicted from, objective indexes of a social, economic and demographic nature.

Although I have no quarrel with this view, I am left with a nagging feeling that it omits an important part of the story. The fact is that behavior toward outgroups shows the same monotonous similarity as attitudes do, across a diversity of socioeconomic conditions. This apparent diversity may, of course, obscure an underlying common factor of "rational" conflict, of struggle to preserve a *status quo* favorable to oneself or to obtain an equitable share of social opportunities and benefits. Another kind of underlying regularity is nonetheless common to a variety of social situations and is an important psychological effect of our sociocultural milieu. It is the assimilation by the individual of the various norms of conduct that prevail in his society.

For the purposes of this article I shall define social norms as being an individual's expectation of how others expect him to behave and his expectation of how others will behave in any given social situation. Whether he does or does not behave according to these expecta-

tions depends primarily on his understanding of whether or not and how a situation relates to a specific set of expectations. If a link is made between the one and the other—if an individual's understanding of a situation in which he finds himself is such that in his view certain familiar social norms are pertinent to it—he behaves accordingly.

There is nothing new to this formulation; it is inherent in most studies and discussions of intergroup prejudice and discrimination that stress the importance of conformity. The point I wish to make is broader. Conformity contributes to hostile attitudes and behavior toward specified groups of people in situations that are usually characterized by a history of intergroup tensions, conflicts of interest and early acquisition by individuals of hostile views about selected outgroups. We are dealing, however, with a process that is more general and goes deeper than the learning of value judgments about a specific group and the subsequent acting out of accepted patterns of behavior toward that group. The child learns not only whom he should like or dislike in the complex social environment to which he is exposed but also something more basic. An individual constructs his own "web of social affiliations" by applying principles of order

and simplification that reduce the complexity of crisscrossing human categorizations. Perhaps the most important principle of the subjective social order we construct for ourselves is the classification of groups as "we" and "they"—as ingroups (any number of them to which we happen to belong) and outgroups. The criteria for these assignments may vary according to the situation, and their emotional impact may be high or low, but in our societies this division into groups most often implies a competitive relation between the groups. In other words, intergroup categorizations of all kinds may bring into play what seems to the individual to be the appropriate form of intergroup behavior.

What this essentially means is that the need to bring some kind of order into our "social construction of reality" (a term recently used by Peter L. Berger of the New School for Social Research and Thomas Luckmann of the University of Frankfurt) combines with the hostility inherent in many of the intergroup categorizations to which we are continually exposed to develop a "generic norm" of behavior toward outgroups. Whenever we are confronted with a situation to which some form of intergroup categorization appears directly relevant, we are likely to act in a manner that discrimi-

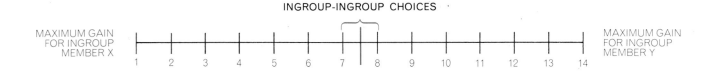

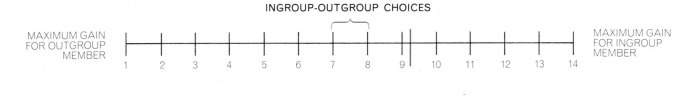

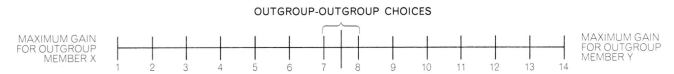

RESULTS WERE SCORED by ranking the choices from 1 to 14 depending on which box was checked. The end of the matrix at which the ingroup member got the minimum number of points (and the outgroup member the maximum) was designated 1; the other end, giving the ingroup member the maximum, was 14. The mean choices (*colored vertical lines*) are shown here. In the intergroup situation the subjects gave significantly more points to members of their own group than to members of the other group. In the intragroup situations, however, the means of the choices fell at Rank 7.5, between the choices of maximum fairness (*brackets*).

nates against the outgroup and favors the ingroup.

If this is true, if there exists such a generic norm of behavior toward outgroups, several important consequences should follow. The first is that there may be discrimination against an outgroup even if there is no reason for it in terms of the individual's own interests—in terms of what he can gain as a result of discriminating against the outgroup. The second consequence is that there may be such discrimination in the absence of any previously existing attitudes of hostility or dislike toward the outgroup. And the third consequence, following directly from the second, is that this generic norm may manifest itself directly in behavior toward the outgroup before any attitudes of prejudice or hostility have been formed. If this reasoning is correct, then discriminatory intergroup behavior can sometimes be expected even if the individual is not involved in actual (or even imagined) conflicts of interest and has no past history of attitudes of intergroup hostility.

At the University of Bristol, in collaboration with Claude Flament of the University of Aix-Marseille, R. P. Bundy and M. J. Billig, I have conducted experiments designed to test this prediction and others that follow from it. The main problem was to create experimental conditions that would enable us to assess the effects of intergroup categorization per se, uncontaminated by other variables, such as interactions among individuals or preexisting attitudes. We aimed, moreover, to look at the behavior rather than the attitudes of the subjects toward their own group and the other group, to ensure that this behavior was of some importance to them and to present them with a clear alternative to discriminating against the outgroup that would be a more "sensible" mode of behavior.

Perhaps the best means of conveying the way these criteria were met is to describe the procedure we followed in the first experiments and its variants in subsequent ones. Our subjects were 64 boys 14 and 15 years old from a state, or "comprehensive," school in a suburb of Bristol. They came to the laboratory in separate groups of eight. All the boys in each of the groups were from the same house in the same form at the school, so that they knew each other well before the experiment. The first part of the experiment served to establish an intergroup categorization and in the second part we assessed the effects of that categorization on intergroup behavior.

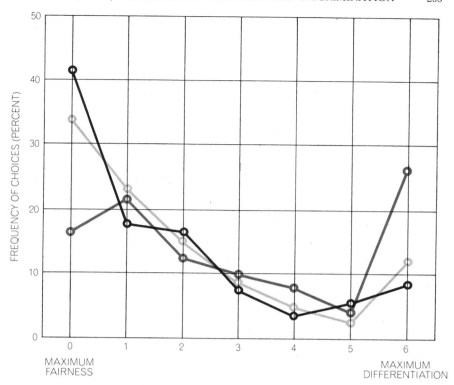

INTERGROUP DISCRIMINATION was a deliberate strategy in the ingroup-outgroup choices (*colored curve*) and fairness a deliberate strategy in the ingroup-ingroup (*gray*) and outgroup-outgroup (*black*) choices. This is indicated by the fact that the frequencies of intergroup choices differed significantly from those of the intragroup choices only at the extreme points of the distribution, the points of maximum fairness and of maximum discrimination. (For this analysis the two fairest choices in each matrix, the two middle ones, were ranked together as 0 and departures in either direction were scored from 1 to 6.)

In the first part the boys were brought together in a lecture room and were told that we were interested in the study of visual judgments. Forty clusters of varying numbers of dots were flashed on a screen. The boys were asked to estimate the number of dots in each cluster and to record each estimate in succession on prepared score sheets. There were two conditions in this first part of the experiment. In one condition, after the boys had completed their estimates they were told that in judgments of this kind some people consistently overestimate the number of dots and some consistently underestimate the number, but that these tendencies are in no way related to accuracy. In the other condition the boys were told that some people are consistently more accurate than others. Four groups of eight served in each of the two conditions.

After the judgments had been made and had been ostentatiously "scored" by one of the experimenters, we told the subjects that, since we were also interested in other kinds of decision, we were going to take advantage of their presence to investigate these as well, and that for

ease of coding we were going to group them on the basis of the visual judgments they had just made. In actuality the subjects were assigned to groups quite at random, half to "underestimators" and half to "overestimators" in the first condition, half to "better" and half to "worse" accuracy in the second one.

Instructions followed about the nature of the forthcoming task. The boys were told that it would consist of giving to others rewards and penalties in real money. They would not know the identity of the individuals to whom they would be assigning these rewards and penalties since everyone would have a code number. They would be taken to another room one by one and given information as to which group they were in. Once in the other room they were to work on their own in separate cubicles. In each cubicle they would find a pencil and a booklet containing 18 sets of ordered numbers, one to each page. It was stressed that on no occasion would the boys be rewarding or penalizing themselves; they would always be allotting money to others. At the end of the task each boy would be brought back into

A

MATRIX 1

19	18	17	16	15	14	13	12	11	10	9	8	7
1	3	5	7	9	11	13	15	17	19	21	23	25

MIP

MD

MJP
MJP
MIP
MD

MATRIX 2

23	22	21	20	19	18	17	16	15	14	13	12	11
5	7	9	11	13	15	17	19	21	23	25	27	29

B

MATRIX 3

7	8	9	10	11	12	13	14	15	16	17	18	19
1	3	5	7	9	11	13	15	17	19	21	23	25

MD

MIP
MJP
MIP
MJP
MD

MATRIX 4

11	12	13	14	15	16	17	18	19	20	21	22	23
5	7	9	11	13	15	17	19	21	23	25	27	29

SECOND EXPERIMENT involved new matrices. Each was presented in four versions labeled (as in the illustration at the bottom of this page) to indicate whether the choice was between members of different groups or between two members of the same group; the intergroup choices sometimes had the ingroup member's points in the top row and sometimes had them in the bottom row. The objective now was to analyze the influence of three variables on the subjects' choices: maximum ingroup profit (*MIP*), maximum joint profit (*MJP*) and maximum difference in favor of the ingroup member (*MD*). These varied according to different patterns in the Type *A* and Type *B* matrices and in the different versions; in some cases the maxima were together at one end of the matrix and in other cases they were at opposite ends. For example, in the ingroup-over-outgroup version of Type *A* matrices the maximum ingroup profit and maximum difference were at one end and the maximum joint profit at the other end (*colored type*); in the outgroup-over-ingroup version of the same matrices the three maxima were together at the right-hand end of the matrices (*black type*). Type *B* ingroup-over-outgroup versions, on the other hand, distinguish the difference in favor of ingroup from the other two gains (*color*).

Booklet for group preferring Klee

These numbers are rewards for:

✓

member no. 74 of Klee group

25	23	21	19	17	15	13	11	9	7	5	3	1

member no. 44 of Kandinsky group

19	18	17	16	15	14	13	12	11	10	9	8	7

Please fill in below details of the box you have just chosen:

Amount

Reward for member no. 74 of Klee group   21

Reward for member no. 44 of Kandinsky group   17

PAGE OF BOOKLET, presenting a single matrix, is reproduced as a subject might have marked it. In addition to checking a box, the subject filled in the blanks below it to confirm his choice. The page heading reminded him which group he was in. The awards were made to persons identified only by number and group; the subject did not know who they were but only their group identification.

the first room and would receive the amount of money the other boys had awarded him. The value of each point they were awarding was a tenth of a penny (about a tenth of a U.S. cent). After these instructions were given, the boys were led individually to their cubicles to fill out their booklets.

On each page in the booklet there was one matrix consisting of 14 boxes containing two numbers each. The numbers in the top row were the rewards and penalties to be awarded to one person and those in the bottom row were those to be awarded to another. Each row was labeled "These are rewards and penalties for member No. ___ of your group" or "...of the other group." The subjects had to indicate their choices by checking one box in each matrix. On the cover of each booklet and at the top of each page was written: "Booklet for member of the ___ group."

There were six matrices [see illustration, page 297] and each of them appeared three times in the booklet—once for each of three types of choice. There were ingroup choices, with the top and the bottom row signifying the rewards and penalties to be awarded to two members of the subject's own group (other than himself). Then there were outgroup choices, with both rows signifying the rewards and penalties for a member of the other group. Finally there were intergroup, or "differential," choices, one row indicating the rewards and penalties to be awarded to an ingroup member (other than himself) and the other the points for an outgroup member. (The top and bottom positions of ingroup and outgroup members were varied at random.)

The results for the intergroup choices were first scored in terms of ranks of choices. In each matrix Rank 1 stood for the choice of the term that gave to the member of the ingroup the minimum possible number of points in that matrix; Rank 14, at the opposite extreme of the matrix, stood for the maximum possible number of points. Comparable (but more complex) methods of scoring were adopted for the other two kinds of choice, the ingroup choices and the outgroup ones, and for comparison of these choices with those made in the differential situation.

The results were striking. In making their intergroup choices a large majority of the subjects, in all groups in both conditions, gave more money to members of their own group than to members of the other group. All the results were—at a very high level of statistical significance

—above both Rank 7.5, which represents the point of maximum fairness, and the mean ranks of the ingroup and outgroup choices. In contrast the ingroup and outgroup choices were closely distributed about the point of fairness. Further analysis made it clear that intergroup discrimination was the deliberate strategy adopted in making intergroup choices.

Before continuing, let us review the situation. The boys, who knew each other well, were divided into groups defined by flimsy and unimportant criteria. Their own individual interests were not affected by their choices, since they always assigned points to two other people and no one could know what any other boy's choices were. The amounts of money were not trivial for them: each boy left the experiment with the equivalent of about a dollar. Inasmuch as they could not know who was in their group and who was in the other group, they could have adopted either of two reasonable strategies. They could have chosen the maximum-joint-profit point of the matrices, which would mean that the boys as a total group would get the most money out of the experimenters, or they could choose the point of maximum fairness. Indeed, they did tend to choose the second alternative when their choices did not involve a distinction between ingroup and outgroup. As soon as this differentiation was involved, however, they discriminated in favor of the ingroup. The only thing we needed to do to achieve this result was to associate their judgments of numbers of dots with the use of the terms "your group" and "the other group" in the instructions and on the booklets of matrices.

The results were at a very high level of statistical significance in all eight separately tested groups of eight boys. In view of the consistency of the phenomenon we decided to analyze it further and also to validate it with a different criterion for intergroup categorization. We tested three new groups of 16 boys each, this time with aesthetic preference as the basis of the division into two groups. The boys were shown 12 slides, six of which were reproductions of paintings by Paul Klee and six by Wassily Kandinsky, and they were asked to express their preference for one or the other of these two "foreign painters." The reproductions were presented without the painter's signature, so that half of the subjects could be assigned at random to the "Klee group" and half to the "Kandinsky group."

The matrices that confronted the boys

subsequently in their individual cubicles were different from those in the first experiment. We were now interested in assessing the relative weights of some of the variables that may have pulled their decisions in one direction or the other. In this experiment we looked at three variables: maximum joint profit, or the largest possible joint award to both people; maximum ingroup profit, or the largest possible award to a member of the ingroup, and maximum difference, or the largest possible difference in gain between a member of the ingroup and a member of the outgroup in favor of the former.

There were four different matrices [see top illustration on opposite page]. As in the first experiment, there were three types of choice: between a member of the ingroup and a member of the outgroup, between two members of the ingroup and between two members of the outgroup. In the outgroup-over-ingroup version of Type A matrices (that is, where the numbers in the top row represented amounts given to a member of the outgroup and in the bottom row to a member of the ingroup) the three gains—joint profit, ingroup profit and difference in favor of the ingroup—varied together; their maxima (maximum joint profit, maximum ingroup profit and maximum difference) were all at the same end of the matrix. In the ingroup-over-outgroup version, ingroup profit and difference in favor of ingroup went together in one direction and were in direct conflict with choices approaching maximum joint profit. In the Type B matrices outgroup-over-ingroup versions again represented a covariation of the three gains; in the ingroup-over-outgroup versions, difference in favor of ingroup varied in the direction opposite to joint profit and ingroup profit combined.

A comparison of the boys' choices in the various matrices showed that maximum joint profit exerted hardly any effect at all; the effect of maximum ingroup profit and maximum difference combined against maximum joint profit was strong and highly significant; the effect of maximum difference against maximum joint profit and maximum ingroup profit was also strong and highly significant. In other words, when the subjects had a choice between maximizing the profit for all and maximizing the profit for members of their own group, they acted on behalf of their own group. When they had a choice between profit for all and for their own group combined, as against their own group's winning *more* than the outgroup at the sacrifice of both of these utilitarian advantages, it was the maximization of *difference* that seemed more important to them.

Evidence leading in the same direction emerged from the other two types of choice, between two members of the ingroup and between two members of the outgroup: the ingroup choices were consistently and significantly nearer to the maximum joint profit than were the outgroup ones—and this was so in spite of the fact that giving as much as possible to two members of the outgroup in the choices applying solely to them presented no conflict with the ingroup's interest. It simply would have meant giving more to "the others" without giving any less to "your own." This represented, therefore, a clear case of gratuitous discrimination. We also included in the second experiment some of the original matrices used in the first one, with results much the same as before. Again all the results in this experiment were at a high level of statistical significance.

In subsequent experiments we tested the importance of fairness in making the choices, the effect on the choices of familiarity with the situation and the subjects' ideas about the choices that others were making. Fairness, we found, was an important determinant; most of the choices must be understood as being a compromise between fairness and favoring one's own group. We found that discrimination not only persisted but also increased when the entire situation became more familiar to the subjects. With familiarity there was also an increase (when the boys were asked to predict the other subjects' behavior) in their expectation that other boys were

discriminating.

Much remains to be done to analyze the entire phenomenon in greater detail and to gain a fuller understanding of its determining conditions, but some clear inferences can already be made. Outgroup discrimination is extraordinarily easy to trigger off. In some previous studies of group conflict, such as one conducted by Muzafer Sherif at the University of Oklahoma, groups had to be placed in intense competition for several days for such results to occur [see "Experiments in Group Conflict," by Muzafer Sherif; SCIENTIFIC AMERICAN, Offprint 454]; in other situations behavior of this kind can occur without direct conflict if it is based on previously existing hostility. Yet neither an objective conflict of interests nor hostility had any relevance whatever to what our subjects were asked to do. It was enough for them to see themselves as clearly categorized into an ingroup and an outgroup, flimsy as the criteria for this division were— even though the boys knew one another well before the experiments, their own individual gains were not involved in their decisions and their actions could have been aimed to achieve the greatest common good.

It would seem, then, that the generic norm of outgroup behavior to which I have referred does exist and that it helps to distort what might have been more reasonable conduct. This norm determines behavior—as other social norms do—when an individual finds himself in a situation to which, in his view, the norm applies. Behavior is never motiveless, but it is a crude oversimplification to think that motives in social situations include no more than calculations of

self-interest or that they can be derived from a few supposedly universal human drives such as aggression toward the outsider, the need to affiliate and so on. To behave socially is a complex business. It involves a long learning process; it is based on the manipulation of symbols and abstractions; it implies the capacity for modification of conduct when the situation changes—and social situations never remain static. To behave *appropriately* is therefore a powerful social motive, and attempting to do so means to behave according to one's best understanding of the situation. Judgments of what is appropriate are determined by social norms, or sets of expectations.

It seems clear that two such norms were understood by our subjects to apply to the situation we imposed on them: "groupness" and "fairness." They managed to achieve a neat balance between the two, and one might assume that in real-life situations the same kind of balance would apply. Unfortunately it is only too easy to think of examples in real life where fairness would go out the window, since groupness is often based on criteria more weighty than either preferring a painter one has never heard of before or resembling someone else in one's way of counting dots. Socialization into "groupness" is powerful and unavoidable; it has innumerable valuable functions. It also has some odd side effects that may—and do—reinforce acute intergroup tensions whose roots lie elsewhere. Perhaps those educators in our competitive societies who from the earliest schooling are so keen on "teams" and "team spirit" could give some thought to the operation of these side effects.

The Effects of Observing Violence

by Leonard Berkowitz
February 1964

Experiments suggest that aggression depicted in television and motion picture dramas, or observed in actuality, can arouse certain members of the audience to violent action

An ancient view of drama is that the action on the stage provides the spectators with an opportunity to release their own strong emotions harmlessly through identification with the people and events depicted in the play. This idea dates back at least as far as Aristotle, who wrote in *The Art of Poetry* that drama is "a representation . . . in the form of actions directly presented, not narrated; with incidents arousing pity and fear in such a way as to accomplish a purgation of such emotions."

Aristotle's concept of catharsis, a term derived from the Greek word for purgation, has survived in modern times. It can be heard on one side of the running debate over whether or not scenes of violence in motion pictures and television programs can instigate violent deeds, sooner or later, by people who observe such scenes. Eminent authorities contend that filmed violence, far from leading to real violence, can actually have beneficial results in that the viewer may purge himself of hostile impulses by watching other people behave aggressively, even if these people are merely actors appearing on a screen. On the other hand, authorities of equal stature contend that, as one psychiatrist told a Senate subcommittee, filmed violence is a "preparatory school for delinquency." In this view emotionally immature individuals can be seriously affected by fighting or brutality in films, and disturbed young people in particular can be led into the habit of expressing their aggressive energies by socially destructive actions.

Until recently neither of these arguments had the support of data obtained by controlled experimentation; they had to be regarded, therefore, as hypotheses, supported at best by unsystematic observation. Lately, however, several psychologists have undertaken laboratory tests of the effects of filmed aggression. The greater control obtained in these tests, some of which were done in my laboratory at the University of Wisconsin with the support of the National Science Foundation, provides a basis for some statements that have a fair probability of standing up under continued testing.

First, it is possible to suggest that the observation of aggression is more likely to induce hostile behavior than to drain off aggressive inclinations; that, in fact, motion picture or television violence can stimulate aggressive actions by normal people as well as by those who are emotionally disturbed. I would add an important qualification: such actions by normal people will occur only under appropriate conditions. The experiments point to some of the conditions that might result in aggressive actions by people in an audience who had observed filmed violence.

Second, these findings have obvious social significance. Third, the laboratory tests provide some important information about aggressive behavior in general. I shall discuss these three statements in turn.

Catharsis appeared to have occurred in one of the first experiments, conducted by Seymour Feshbach of the University of Colorado. Feshbach deliberately angered a group of college men; then he showed part of the group a filmed prizefight and the other students a more neutral film. He found that the students who saw the prizefight exhibited less hostility than the other students on two tests of aggressiveness administered after the film showings. The findings may indicate that the students who had watched the prizefight had vented their anger vicariously.

That, of course, is not the only possible explanation of the results. The men who saw the filmed violence could have become uneasy about their own aggressive tendencies. Watching someone being hurt may have made them think that aggressive behavior was wrong; as a result they may have inhibited their hostile responses. Clearly there was scope for further experimentation, particularly studies varying the attitude of the subjects toward the filmed aggression.

Suppose the audience were put in a frame of mind to regard the film violence as justified—for instance because a villain got a beating he deserved. The concept of symbolic catharsis would predict in such a case that an angered person might enter vicariously into the scene and work off his anger by thinking of himself as the winning fighter, who was inflicting injury on the man who had provoked him. Instead of accepting

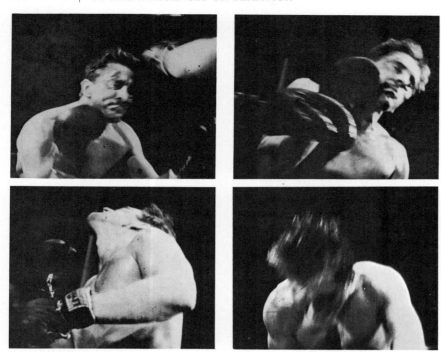

FILMED AGGRESSION shown in author's experiments was from the motion picture *Champion* and included these scenes in which Kirk Douglas receives a bad beating. Watchers had been variously prepared; after showing they were tested for aggressive tendencies.

this thesis, my associates and I predicted that justified film aggression would lead to stronger rather than weaker manifestations of hostility. We believed that the rather low volume of open hostility in the Feshbach experiment was attributable to film-induced inhibitions. If this were so, an angered person who saw what appeared to be warranted aggression might well think he was justified in expressing his own hostile desires.

To test this hypothesis we conducted three experiments. Since they resulted in essentially similar findings and employed comparable procedures, I shall describe only the latest. In this experiment we brought together two male college students at a time. One of them was the subject; the other was a confederate of the experimenter and had been coached on how to act, although of course none of this was known to the subject. Sometimes we introduced the confederate to the subject as a college boxer and at other times we identified him as a speech major. After the introduction the experimenter announced that the purpose of the experiment was to study physiological reactions to various tasks. In keeping with that motif he took blood-pressure readings from each man. Then he set the pair to work on the first task: a simple intelligence test. During this task the confederate either deliberately insulted the subject—

for example, by remarks to the effect that "You're certainly taking a long time with that" and references to "cow-college students" at Wisconsin—or, in the conditions where we were not trying to anger the subject, behaved in a neutral manner toward him. On the completion of the task the experimenter took more blood-pressure readings (again only to keep up the pretense that the experiment had a physiological purpose) and then informed the men that their next assignment was to watch a brief motion picture scene. He added that he would give them a synopsis of the plot so that they would have a better understanding of the scene. Actually he was equipped with two different synopses.

To half of the subjects he portrayed the protagonist of the film, who was to receive a serious beating, as an unprincipled scoundrel. Our idea was that the subjects told this story would regard the beating as retribution for the protagonist's misdeeds; some tests we administered in connection with the experiment showed that the subjects indeed had little sympathy for the protagonist. We called the situation we had created with this synopsis of the seven-minute fight scene the "justified fantasy aggression."

The other subjects were given a more favorable description of the protagonist. He had behaved badly, they were told, but this was because he had been vic-

timized when he was young; at any rate, he was now about to turn over a new leaf. Our idea was that the men in this group would feel sympathetic toward the protagonist; again tests indicated that they did. We called this situation the "less justified fantasy aggression."

Then we presented the film, which was from the movie *Champion;* the seven-minute section we used showed Kirk Douglas, as the champion, apparently losing his title. Thereafter, in order to measure the effects of the film, we provided the subjects with an opportunity to show aggression in circumstances where that would be a socially acceptable response. We separated each subject and accomplice and told the subject that his co-worker (the confederate) was to devise a "creative" floor plan for a dwelling, which the subject would judge. If the subject thought the floor plan was highly creative, he was to give the co-worker one electric shock by depressing a telegraph key. If he thought the floor plan was poor, he was to administer more than one shock; the worse the floor plan, the greater the number of shocks. Actually each subject received the same floor plan.

The results consistently showed a greater volume of aggression directed against the anger-arousing confederate by the men who had seen the "bad guy" take a beating than by the men who had been led to feel sympathy for the protagonist in the film [*see illustration on opposite page*]. It was clear that the people who saw the justified movie violence had not discharged their anger through vicarious participation in the aggression but instead had felt freer to attack their tormentor in the next room. The motion picture scene had apparently influenced their judgment of the propriety of aggression. If it was all right for the movie villain to be injured aggressively, they seemed to think, then perhaps it was all right for them to attack the villain in their own lives—the person who had insulted them.

Another of our experiments similarly demonstrated that observed aggression has little if any effectiveness in reducing aggressive tendencies on the part of an observer. In this experiment some angered men were told by another student how many shocks they should give the person, supposedly in the next room, who had provoked them. Another group of angered men, instead of delivering the shocks themselves, watched the other student do it. Later the members of both groups had an opportunity to deliver the shocks personally. Consist-

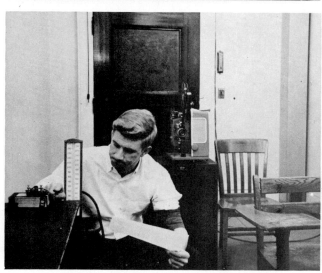

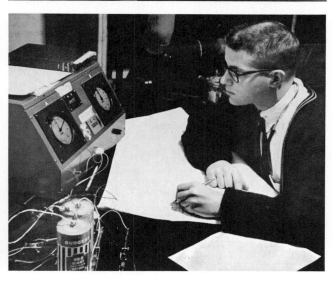

TYPICAL EXPERIMENT tests reaction of angered man to filmed violence. Experiment begins with introduction of subject (*white shirt*) to a man he believes is a co-worker but who actually is a confederate of the author's. In keeping with pretense that experiment is to test physiological reactions, student conducting the experiment takes blood-pressure readings. He assigns the men a task and leaves; during the task the confederate insults the subject. Experimenter returns and shows filmed prizefight. Confederate leaves; experimenter tells subject to judge a floor plan drawn by confederate and to record opinion by giving confederate electric shocks. Shocks actually go to recording apparatus. The fight film appeared to stimulate the aggressiveness of angered men.

ently the men who had watched in the first part of the experiment now displayed stronger aggression than did the people who had been able to administer shocks earlier. Witnessed aggression appeared to have been less satisfying than self-performed aggression.

Our experiments thus cast considerable doubt on the possibility of a cathartic purge of anger through the observation of filmed violence. At the very least, the findings indicated that such a catharsis does not occur as readily as many authorities have thought.

Yet what about the undoubted fact that aggressive motion pictures and violent athletic contests provide relaxation and enjoyment for some people? A person who was tense with anger sometimes comes away from them feeling calmer. It seems to me that what happens here is quite simple: He calms down not because he has discharged his anger vicariously but because he was carried away by the events he witnessed. Not thinking of his troubles, he ceased to stir himself up and his anger dissipated. In addition, the enjoyable motion

picture or game could have cast a pleasant glow over his whole outlook, at least temporarily.

The social implications of our experiments have to do primarily with the moral usually taught by films. Supervising agencies in the motion picture and television industries generally insist that films convey the idea that "crime does not pay." If there is any consistent principle used by these agencies to regulate how punishment should be administered to the screen villain, it would seem to be the talion law: an eye for an eye, a tooth for a tooth.

Presumably the audience finds this concept of retaliation emotionally satisfying. Indeed, we based our "justified fantasy aggression" situation on the concept that people seem to approve of hurting a scoundrel who has hurt others. But however satisfying the talion principle may be, screenplays based on it can lead to socially harmful consequences. If the criminal or "bad guy" is punished aggressively, so that others do to him what he has done to them,

the violence appears justified. Inherent in the likelihood that the audience will regard it as justified is the danger that some angered person in the audience will attack someone who has frustrated *him,* or perhaps even some innocent person he happens to associate with the source of his anger.

Several experiments have lent support to this hypothesis. O. Ivar Lövaas of the University of Washington found in an experiment with nursery school children that the youngsters who had been exposed to an aggressive cartoon film displayed more aggressive responses with a toy immediately afterward than a control group shown a less aggressive film did. In another study Albert Bandura and his colleagues at Stanford University noted that preschool children who witnessed the actions of an aggressive adult in a motion picture tended later, after they had been subjected to mild frustrations, to imitate the kind of hostile behavior they had seen.

This tendency of filmed violence to stimulate aggression is not limited to children. Richard H. Walters of the Uni-

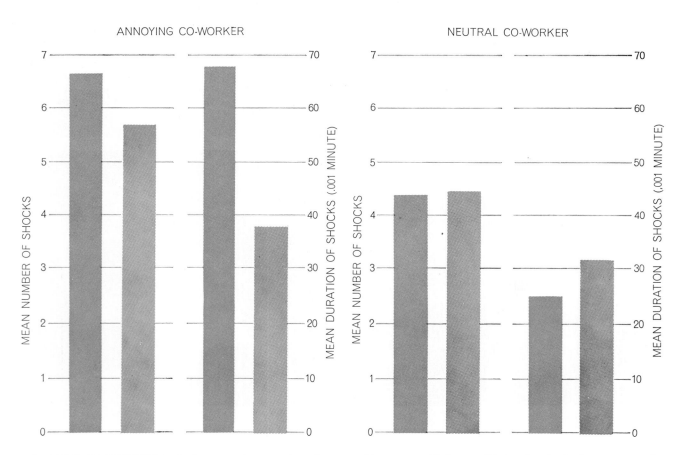

RESPONSES OF SUBJECTS invited to commit aggression after seeing prizefight film varied according to synopsis they heard beforehand. One (*colored bars*) called Douglas' beating deserved; the other (*gray bars*) said it was undeserved. After the film the subjects were told they could give electric shocks to an annoying or neutral co-worker based on his "creativeness" in doing a task. Seeing a man receive what had been described as a well-deserved beating apparently lowered restraints against aggressive behavior.

versity of Waterloo in Ontario found experimentally that male hospital attendants who had been shown a movie of a knife fight generally administered more severe punishment to another person soon afterward than did other attendants who had seen a more innocuous movie. The men in this experiment were shown one of the two movie scenes and then served for what was supposedly a study of the effects of punishment. They were to give an electric shock to someone else in the room with them each time the person made a mistake on a learning task. The intensity of the electric shocks could be varied. This other person, who was actually the experimenter's confederate, made a constant number of mistakes, but the people who had seen the knife fight gave him more intense punishment than the men who had witnessed the nonaggressive film. The filmed violence had apparently aroused aggressive tendencies in the men and, since the situation allowed the expression of aggression, their tendencies were readily translated into severe aggressive actions.

These experiments, taken together with our findings, suggest a change in approach to the manner in which screenplays make their moral point. Although it may be socially desirable for a villain to receive his just deserts at the end of a motion picture, it would seem equally desirable that this retribution should not take the form of physical aggression.

The key point to be made about aggressiveness on the basis of experimentation in this area is that a person's hostile tendencies will persist, in spite of any satisfaction he may derive from filmed violence, to the extent that his frustrations and aggressive habits persist. There is no free-floating aggressive energy that can be released through a wide range of different activities. A drive to hurt cannot be reduced through attempts to master other drives, as Freud proposed, or by observing others as they act aggressively.

In fact, there have been studies suggesting that even if the angered person performs the aggression himself, his hostile inclinations are not satisfied unless he believes he has attacked his tormentor and not someone else. J. E. Hokanson of Florida State University has shown that angered subjects permitted to commit aggression against the person who had annoyed them often display a drop in systolic blood pressure. They seem to have experienced a physiological relaxation, as if they had satisfied their aggressive urges. Systolic pressure

declines less, however, when the angered people carry out the identical motor activity involved in the aggression but without believing they have attacked the source of their frustration.

I must now qualify some of the observations I have made. Many aggressive motion pictures and television programs have been presented to the public, but the number of aggressive incidents demonstrably attributable to such shows is quite low. One explanation for this is that most social situations, unlike the conditions in the experiments I have described, impose constraints on aggression. People are usually aware of the social norms prohibiting attacks on others, consequently they inhibit whatever hostile inclinations might have been aroused by the violent films they have just seen.

Another important factor is the attributes of the people encountered by a person after he has viewed filmed violence. A man who is emotionally aroused does not necessarily attack just anyone. Rather, his aggression is directed toward specific objectives. In other words, only certain people are capable of drawing aggressive responses from him. In my theoretical analyses of the sources of aggressive behavior I have suggested that the arousal of anger only creates a readiness for aggression. The theory holds that whether or not this predisposition is translated into actual aggression depends on the presence of appropriate cues: stimuli associated with the present or previous instigators of anger. Thus if someone has been insulted, the sight or the thought of others who have provoked him, whether then or earlier, may evoke hostile responses from him.

An experiment I conducted in conjunction with a graduate student provides some support for this train of thought. People who had been deliberately provoked by the experimenter were put to work with two other people, one a person who had angered them earlier and the other a neutral person. The subjects showed the greatest hostility, following their frustration by the experimenter, to the co-worker they disliked. He, by having thwarted them previously, had acquired the stimulus quality that caused him to draw aggression from them after they had been aroused by the experimenter.

My general line of reasoning leads me to some predictions about aggressive behavior. In the absence of any strong inhibitions against aggression, people who have recently been angered and have then seen filmed aggression will be more likely to act aggressively than people who have not had those experiences. Moreover, their strongest attacks will be directed at those who are most directly connected with the provocation or at others who either have close associations with the aggressive motion picture or are disliked for any reason.

One of our experiments showed results consistent with this analysis. In this study male college students, taken separately, were first either angered or not angered by A, one of the two graduate

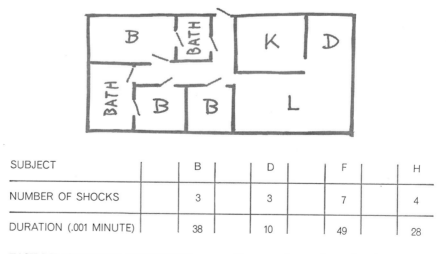

SUBJECT		B		D		F		H
NUMBER OF SHOCKS		3		3		7		4
DURATION (.001 MINUTE)		38		10		49		28

TASK BY ANNOYING CO-WORKER supposedly was to draw a floor plan. Actually each subject saw the floor plan shown here. The subject was asked to judge the creativeness of the plan and to record his opinion by pressing a telegraph key that he thought would give electric shocks to the co-worker: one shock for a good job and more for poor work. Responses of eight subjects who saw prizefight film are shown; those in color represent men told that Douglas deserved his beating; those in black, men informed it was undeserved.

ANGERED SUBJECTS

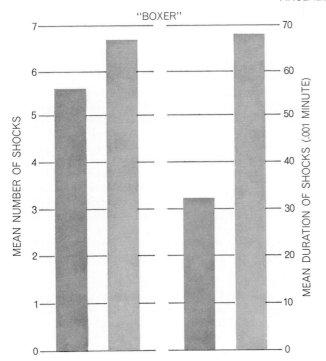

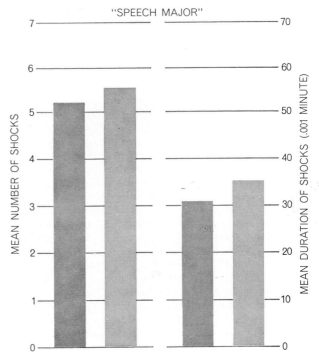

CO-WORKER'S INTRODUCTION also produced variations in aggressiveness of subjects. Co-worker was introduced as boxer or as speech major; reactions shown here are of men who were angered by co-worker and then saw either a fight film (*colored bars*) or a neutral film (*gray bars*). Co-worker received strongest attacks when subjects presumably associated him with fight film.

UNANGERED SUBJECTS

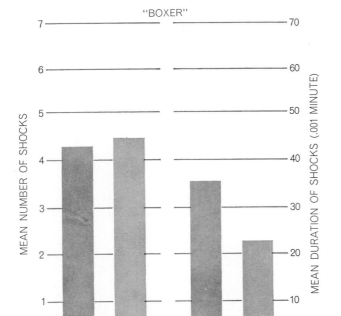

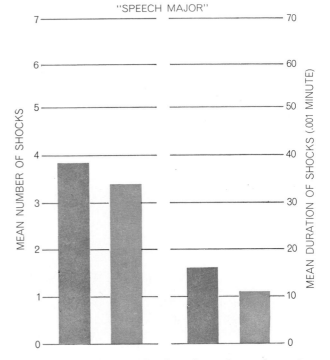

SIMILAR TEST, varied by the fact that the co-worker behaved neutrally toward the subjects and therefore presumably did not anger them, produced these reactions. The greater number of shocks given to the co-worker introduced as a boxer than to the one introduced as a speech major apparently reflected a tendency to take a generally negative attitude toward persons identified as boxers.

students acting as experimenters. A had been introduced earlier either as a college boxer or as a speech major. After A had had his session with the subject, B, the second experimenter, showed the subject a motion picture: either the prizefight scene mentioned earlier or a neutral film. (One that we used was about canal boats in England; the other, about the travels of Marco Polo.)

We hypothesized that the label "college boxer" applied to A in some of the cases would produce a strong association in the subject's mind between A and the boxing film. In other words, any aggressive tendencies aroused in the subject would be more likely to be directed at A the college boxer than at A the speech major. The experiment bore out this hypothesis. Using questionnaires at the end of the session as the measures of hostility, we found that the deliberately angered subjects directed more hostility at A, the source of their anger, when they had seen the fight film and he had been identified as a boxer. Angered men who had seen the neutral film showed no particular hostility to A the boxer. In short, the insulting experimenter received the strongest verbal attacks when he was also associated with the aggressive film. It is also noteworthy that in this study the boxing film did not influence the amount of hostility shown toward A when he had not provoked the subjects.

A somewhat inconsistent note was introduced by our experiments, described previously, in "physiological reactions." Here the nonangered groups, regardless of which film they saw, gave the confederate more and longer shocks when they thought he was a boxer than when they understood him to be a speech major [see bottom illustration on opposite page]. To explain this finding I assume that our subjects had a negative attitude toward boxers in general. This attitude may have given the confederate playing the role of boxer the stimulus quality that caused him to draw aggression from the angered subjects. But it could only have been partially responsible, since the insulted subjects who saw the neutral film gave fewer shocks to the boxer than did the insulted subjects who saw the prizefight film.

Associations between the screen and the real world are important. People seem to be emotionally affected by a screenplay to the extent that they associate the events of the drama with their own life experiences. Probably adults are less strongly influenced than children because they are aware that the film is make-believe and so can dissociate it from their own lives. Still, it seems clear from the experiments I have described that an aggressive film can induce aggressive actions by anyone in the audience. In most instances I would expect that effect to be short-lived. The emotional reaction produced by filmed violence probably dies away rather rapidly as the viewer enters new situations and encounters new stimuli. Subjected to different influences, he becomes less and less ready to attack other people.

Television and motion pictures, however, may also have some persistent effects. If a young child sees repeatedly that screen heroes gain their ends through aggressive actions, he may conclude that aggression is desirable behavior. Fortunately screenplays do not consistently convey that message, and in any event the child is exposed to many other cultural norms that discourage aggression.

As I see it, the major social danger inherent in filmed violence has to do with the temporary effects produced in a fairly short period immediately following the film. For that period, at least, a person—whether an adult or a child—who had just seen filmed violence might conclude that he was warranted in attacking those people in his own life who had recently frustrated him. Further, the film might activate his aggressive habits so that for the period of which I speak he would be primed to act aggressively. Should he then encounter people with appropriate stimulus qualities, people he dislikes or connects psychologically with the film, this predisposition could lead to open aggression.

What, then, of catharsis? I would not deny that it exists. Nor would I reject the argument that a frustrated person can enjoy fantasy aggression because he sees characters doing things he wishes he could do, although in most cases his inhibitions restrain him. I believe, however, that effective catharsis occurs only when an angered person perceives that his frustrater has been aggressively injured. From this I argue that filmed violence is potentially dangerous. The motion picture aggression has increased the chance that an angry person, and possibly other people as well, will attack someone else.

Teacher Expectations for the Disadvantaged

by Robert Rosenthal and Lenore F. Jacobson
April 1968

*It is widely believed that poor children lag in school
because they are members of a disadvantaged group.
Experiments in a school suggest that they may also
do so because that is what their teachers expect*

One of the central problems of American society lies in the fact that certain children suffer a handicap in their education which then persists throughout life. The "disadvantaged" child is a Negro American, a Mexican American, a Puerto Rican or any other child who lives in conditions of poverty. He is a lower-class child who performs poorly in an educational system that is staffed almost entirely by middle-class teachers.

The reason usually given for the poor performance of the disadvantaged child is simply that the child is a member of a disadvantaged group. There may well be another reason. It is that the child does poorly in school because that is what is expected of him. In other words, his shortcomings may originate not in his different ethnic, cultural and economic background but in his teachers' response to that background.

If there is any substance to this hypothesis, educators are confronted with some major questions. Have these children, who account for most of the academic failures in the U.S., shaped the expectations that their teachers have for them? Have the schools failed the children by anticipating their poor performance and thus in effect teaching them to fail? Are the massive public programs of educational assistance to such children reinforcing the assumption that they are likely to fail? Would the children do appreciably better if their teachers could be induced to expect more of them?

We have explored the effect of teacher expectations with experiments in which teachers were led to believe at the beginning of a school year that certain of their pupils could be expected to show considerable academic improvement during the year. The teachers thought the predictions were based on tests that had been administered to the student body toward the end of the preceding school year. In actuality the children designated as potential "spurters" had been chosen at random and not on the basis of testing. Nonetheless, intelligence tests given after the experiment had been in progress for several months indicated that on the whole the randomly chosen children had improved more than the rest.

The central concept behind our investigation was that of the "self-fulfilling prophecy." The essence of this concept is that one person's prediction of another person's behavior somehow comes to be realized. The prediction may, of course, be realized only in the perception of the predictor. It is also possible, however, that the predictor's expectation is communicated to the other person, perhaps in quite subtle and unintended ways, and so has an influence on his actual behavior.

An experimenter cannot be sure that he is dealing with a self-fulfilling prophecy until he has taken steps to make certain that a prediction is not based on behavior that has already been observed.

If schoolchildren who perform poorly are those expected by their teachers to perform poorly, one cannot say in the normal school situation whether the teacher's expectation was the cause of the performance or whether she simply made an accurate prognosis based on her knowledge of past performance by the particular children involved. To test for the existence of self-fulfilling prophecy the experimenter must establish conditions in which an expectation is uncontaminated by the past behavior of the subject whose performance is being predicted.

It is easy to establish such conditions in the psychological laboratory by presenting an experimenter with a group of laboratory animals and telling him what kind of behavior he can expect from them. One of us (Rosenthal) has carried out a number of experiments along this line using rats that were said to be either bright or dull. In one experiment 12 students in psychology were each given five laboratory rats of the same strain. Six of the students were told that their rats had been bred for brightness in running a maze; the other six students were told that their rats could be expected for genetic reasons to be poor at running a maze. The assignment given the students was to teach the rats to run the maze.

From the outset the rats believed to have the higher potential proved to be the better performers. The rats thought to be dull made poor progress and sometimes would not even budge from the starting position in the maze. A questionnaire given after the experiment showed that the students with the allegedly brighter rats ranked their subjects as brighter, more pleasant and more likable than did the students who had the allegedly duller rats. Asked about their methods of dealing with the rats, the students with the "bright" group turned out to have been friendlier, more enthusiastic and less talkative with the animals than the students with the "dull" group had been. The students with the "bright" rats also said they handled their animals more, as well as more gently,

than the students expecting poor performances did.

Our task was to establish similar conditions in a classroom situation. We wanted to create expectations that were based only on what teachers had been told, so that we could preclude the possibility of judgments based on previous observations of the children involved. It was with this objective that we set up our experiment in what we shall call Oak School, an elementary school in the South San Francisco Unified School District. To avoid the dangers of letting it be thought that some children could be expected to perform poorly we estab-

lished only the expectation that certain pupils might show superior performance. Our experiments had the financial support of the National Science Foundation and the cooperation of Paul Nielsen, the superintendent of the school district.

Oak School is in an established and somewhat run-down section of a middle-sized city. The school draws some students from middle-class families but more from lower-class families. Included in the latter category are children from families receiving welfare payments, from low-income families and from Mexican-American families. The

VERBAL ABILITY of children in kindergarten and first grade was tested with questions of this type in the Flanagan Tests of General Ability. In the drawings at top the children were asked to cross out the thing that can be eaten; in the bottom drawings the task was to mark "the thing that is used to hit a ball." The tests are published by Science Research Associates, Inc., of Chicago.

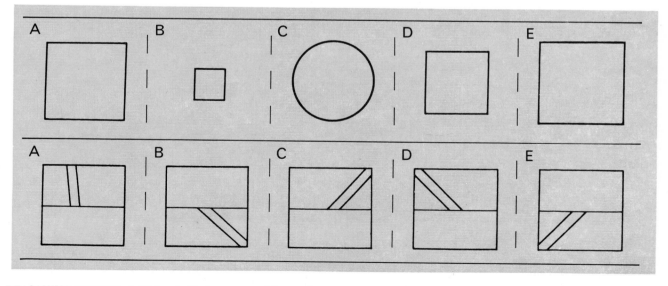

REASONING ABILITY of children in kindergarten and first grade was tested with abstract drawings. The children were told that four of the drawings in each example followed the same rule and one did not. The task was to mark the exception. In the drawings at top the exception is the circle; at bottom all the drawings except the first one have parallel lines that terminate at a corner.

school has six grades, each organized into three classes—one for children performing at above-average levels of scholastic achievement, one for average children and one for those who are below average. There is also a kindergarten.

At the beginning of the experiment in 1964 we told the teachers that further validation was needed for a new kind of test designed to predict academic blooming or intellectual gain in children. In actuality we used the Flanagan Tests of General Ability, a standard intelligence test that was fairly new and therefore unfamiliar to the teachers. It consists of two relatively independent subtests, one

focusing more on verbal ability and the other more on reasoning ability. An example of a verbal item in the version of the test designed for children in kindergarten and first grade presents drawings of an article of clothing, a flower, an envelope, an apple and a glass of water; the children are asked to mark with a crayon "the thing that you can eat." In the reasoning subtest a typical item consists of drawings of five abstractions, such as four squares and a circle; the pupils are asked to cross out the one that differs from the others.

We had special covers printed for the test; they bore the high-sounding ti-

tle "Test of Inflected Acquisition." The teachers were told that the testing was part of an undertaking being carried out by investigators from Harvard University and that the test would be given several times in the future. The tests were to be sent to Harvard for scoring and for addition to the data being compiled for validation. In May, 1964, the teachers administered the test to all the children then in kindergarten and grades one through five. The children in sixth grade were not tested because they would be in junior high school the next year.

Before Oak School opened the follow-

ADVANCED TESTS were given to children in second and third grades and grades four through six. Two examples from the test of verbal reasoning for grades four through six appear here. In the example at top the children were asked to "find the beverage." In the bottom example the instruction that the pupils received from the teacher was "Find the one you are most likely to see in the city."

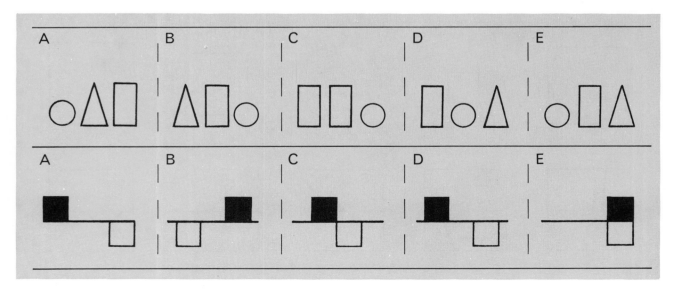

REASONING TEST for children in grades four through six was based on the same principles as the test for younger children but used more sophisticated examples. At top the exception is *C*, which has no triangle. In the example at bottom the exception is *E*, because in all the other drawings the black and white squares are not aligned vertically. The tests were used to measure pupils' progress.

ing September about 20 percent of the children were designated as potential academic spurters. There were about five such children in each classroom. The manner of conveying their names to the teachers was deliberately made rather casual: the subject was brought up at the end of the first staff meeting with the remark, "By the way, in case you're interested in who did what in those tests we're doing for Harvard...."

The names of the "spurters" had been chosen by means of a table of random numbers. The experimental treatment of the children involved nothing more than giving their names to their new teachers as children who could be expected to show unusual intellectual gains in the year ahead. The difference, then, between these children and the undesignated children who constituted a control group was entirely in the minds of the teachers.

All the children were given the same test again four months after school had started, at the end of that school year and finally in May of the following year. As the children progressed through the grades they were given tests of the appropriate level. The tests were designed for three grade levels: kindergarten and first grade, second and third grades and fourth through sixth grades.

The results indicated strongly that children from whom teachers expected greater intellectual gains showed such gains [see illustration below]. The gains, however, were not uniform across the grades. The tests given at the end of the first year showed the largest gains among children in the first and second grades. In the second year the greatest gains were among the children who had been in the fifth grade when the "spurters" were designated and who by the time of the final test were completing sixth grade.

At the end of the academic year 1964–1965 the teachers were asked to describe the classroom behavior of their pupils. The children from whom intellectual growth was expected were described as having a better chance of being successful in later life and as being happier, more curious and more interesting than the other children. There was also a tendency for the designated children to be seen as more appealing, better adjusted and more affectionate, and as less in need of social approval. In short, the children for whom intellectual growth was expected became more alive and autonomous intellectually, or at least were so perceived by their teachers. These findings were particularly striking among the children in the first grade.

An interesting contrast became apparent when teachers were asked to rate the undesignated children. Many of these children had also gained in I.Q. during the year. The more they gained, the less favorably they were rated.

From these results it seems evident that when children who are expected to gain intellectually do gain, they may be benefited in other ways. As "personalities" they go up in the estimation of their teachers. The opposite is true of children who gain intellectually when improvement is not expected of them. They are looked on as showing undesirable behavior. It would seem that there are hazards in unpredicted intellectual growth.

A closer examination revealed that the most unfavorable ratings were given to the children in low-ability classrooms who gained the most intellectually. When these "slow track" children were in the control group, where little intellectual gain was expected of them, they were rated more unfavorably by their teachers if they did show gains in I.Q. The more they gained, the more unfavorably they were rated. Even when the slow-track children were in the experimental group, where greater intellectual gains were expected of them, they were not rated as favorably with respect to their control-group peers as were the children of the high track and the medium track. Evidently it is likely to be difficult for a slow-track child, even if his I.Q. is rising, to be seen by his teacher as well adjusted and as a potentially successful student.

How is one to account for the fact that the children who were expected to gain did gain? The first answer that comes to mind is that the teachers must have spent more time with them than with the children of whom nothing was said. This hypothesis seems to be wrong, judging not only from some questions we asked the teachers about the time they spent with their pupils but also from the fact that in a given classroom the more the "spurters" gained in I.Q., the more the other children gained.

Another bit of evidence that the hypothesis is wrong appears in the pattern of the test results. If teachers had talked to the designated children more, which would be the most likely way of invest-

GAINS IN INTELLIGENCE were shown by children by the end of the academic year in which the experiment was conducted in an elementary school in the San Francisco area. Children in the experimental group (dark bars) are the ones the teachers had been told could be expected to show intellectual gains. In fact their names were chosen randomly. Control-group children (light bars), of whom nothing special was said, also showed gains.

ing more time in work with them, one might expect to see the largest gains in verbal intelligence. In actuality the largest gains were in reasoning intelligence.

It would seem that the explanation we are seeking lies in a subtler feature of the interaction of the teacher and her pupils. Her tone of voice, facial expression, touch and posture may be the means by which—probably quite unwittingly—she communicates her expectations to the pupils. Such communication might help the child by changing his conception of himself, his anticipation of his own behavior, his motivation or his cognitive skills. This is an area in which further research is clearly needed.

Why was the effect of teacher expectations most pronounced in the lower grades? It is difficult to be sure, but several hypotheses can be advanced. Younger children may be easier to change than older ones are. They are likely to have less well-established reputations in the school. It may be that they are more sensitive to the processes by which teachers communicate their expectations to pupils.

It is also difficult to be certain why the older children showed the best performance in the follow-up year. Perhaps the younger children, who by then had different teachers, needed continued contact with the teachers who had influenced them in order to maintain their improved performance. The older children, who were harder to influence at first, may have been better able to maintain an improved performance autonomously once they had achieved it.

In considering our results, particularly the substantial gains shown by the children in the control group, one must take into account the possibility that what is called the Hawthorne effect might have been involved. The name comes from the Western Electric Company's Hawthorne Works in Chicago. In the 1920's the plant was the scene of an intensive series of experiments designed to determine what effect various changes in working conditions would have on the performance of female workers. Some of the experiments, for example, involved changes in lighting. It soon became evident that the significant thing was not whether the worker had more or less light but merely that she was the subject of attention. Any changes that involved her, and even actions that she only thought were changes, were likely to improve her performance.

In the Oak School experiment the fact that university researchers, supported by

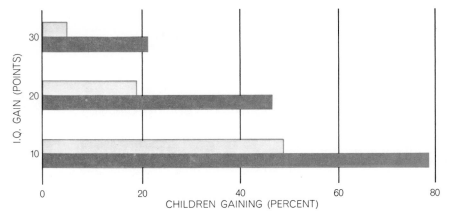

CHILDREN IN LOWER GRADES showed the most dramatic gains. The chart shows the percent of children in the first and second grades by amount of their gains in I.Q. points. Again dark bars represent experimental-group children, light bars control-group children. Two lower sets of bars include children from higher groups, so that lowest set sums results.

Federal funds, were interested in the school may have led to a general improvement of morale and effort on the part of the teachers. In any case, the possibility of a Hawthorne effect cannot be ruled out either in this experiment or in other studies of educational practices. Whenever a new educational practice is undertaken in a school, it cannot be demonstrated to have an intrinsic effect unless it shows some excess of gain over what Hawthorne effects alone would yield. In our case a Hawthorne effect might account for the gains shown by the children in the control group, but it would not account for the greater gains made by the children in the experimental group.

Our results suggest that yet another base line must be introduced when the intrinsic value of an educational innovation is being assessed. The question will be whether the venture is more effective (and cheaper) than the simple expedient of trying to change the expectations of the teacher. Most educational innovations will be found to cost more in both time and money than inducing teachers to expect more of "disadvantaged" children.

For almost three years the nation's schools have had access to substantial Federal funds under the Elementary and Secondary Education Act, which President Johnson signed in April, 1965. Title I of the act is particularly directed at disadvantaged children. Most of the programs devised for using Title I funds focus on overcoming educational handicaps by acting on the child—through remedial instruction, cultural enrichment and the like. The premise seems to be that the deficiencies are all in the child

and in the environment from which he comes.

Our experiment rested on the premise that at least some of the deficiencies—and therefore at least some of the remedies—might be in the schools, and particularly in the attitudes of teachers toward disadvantaged children. In our experiment nothing was done directly for the child. There was no crash program to improve his reading ability, no extra time for tutoring, no program of trips to museums and art galleries. The only people affected directly were the teachers; the effect on the children was indirect.

It is interesting to note that one "total push" program of the kind devised under Title I led in three years to a 10-point gain in I.Q. by 38 percent of the children and a 20-point gain by 12 percent. The gains were dramatic, but they did not even match the ones achieved by the control-group children in the first and second grades of Oak School. They were far smaller than the gains made by the children in our experimental group.

Perhaps, then, more attention in educational research should be focused on the teacher. If it could be learned how she is able to bring about dramatic improvement in the performance of her pupils without formal changes in her methods of teaching, other teachers could be taught to do the same. If further research showed that it is possible to find teachers whose untrained educational style does for their pupils what our teachers did for the special children, the prospect would arise that a combination of sophisticated selection of teachers and suitable training of teachers would give all children a boost toward getting as much as they possibly can out of their schooling.

Intelligence and Race

by Walter Bodmer and Luigi Luca Cavalli-Sforza
October 1970

Do the differences in I.Q. scores between blacks and whites have a genetic basis? Two geneticists, reviewing the evidence, suggest that the question cannot be answered in present circumstances

To what extent might behavioral differences between social classes and between races be genetically determined? This question is often discussed, although generally not at a scientific level. Recently attention has been focused on the average differences in intelligence, as measured by I.Q., between black and white Americans by the educational psychologist Arthur R. Jensen and the physicist William Shockley. We are geneticists who are interested in the study of the interaction between heredity and environment. Our aim in this article is to review, mainly for the nongeneticist, the meaning of race and I.Q. and the approaches to determining the extent to which I.Q. is inherited. Such a review can act as a basis for the objective assessment of the evidence for a genetic component in race and class I.Q. differences.

We should first define what we mean by terms such as "heredity," "intelligence" and "race." Heredity refers to those characteristics of an individual that are inherited from past generations. The primary functional unit of heredity is the gene. The human genome—the complete set of genes in an individual—consists of perhaps as many as 10 million genes. Some of these genes and their expression can now be analyzed at the biochemical level. Complex behavioral traits such as intelligence, however, are most probably influenced by the combined action of many genes. The inheritance of differences known to be deter-

mined by one gene or a few genes can be reliably predicted, but the tools for dealing with the inheritance of more complex characteristics are still relatively ineffective.

What is intelligence? A rigorous, objective definition of such a complicated characteristic is not easy to give, but for the purposes of this discussion one can focus on qualities that can actually be observed and measured. One instrument of measurement for intelligence is a test such as the Stanford-Binet procedure. Such a test is devised to measure a capacity to learn or, more generally, the capacity to benefit from experience.

Intelligence tests are based on the solution of brief problems of various kinds and on the response to simple questions. The total score is standardized for a given age by comparing it with the values of a large sample of a given reference population (such as native-born American whites). The final standardized score, which is called the intelligence quotient, is usually computed so that it is given on a scale for which the average of the reference population is 100, and for which the spread is such that about 70 percent of the individuals have I.Q.'s in the range of 85 to 115 and 5 percent have I.Q.'s either below 70 or above 130 (corresponding to a standard deviation of about 15 points).

The Stanford-Binet test and other procedures yield results that correspond

reasonably well to one another. More ambitious attempts have been made to measure the "general intelligence factor." There is a tendency among the more optimistic psychologists to consider such tests as measuring an "innate" or potential ability. Any given test, however, depends on the ability acquired at a given age, which is inevitably the result of the combination of innate ability and the experience of the subject. Intelligence tests are therefore at most tests of achieved ability.

This limitation is confirmed by the dependence of all intelligence tests on the particular culture of the people they are designed to test. The transfer of tests to cultures different from the one for which they were designed is usually difficult, and sometimes it is impossible. Attempts to design tests that are genuinely "culture-free" have so far failed.

A check on the usefulness of I.Q. measurements is provided by examining their reliability (equivalent to short-term consistency), their stability (equivalent to long-term consistency) and their validity. For the Stanford-Binet test the average difference between repeat tests after a short time interval ranges from 5.9 points at an I.Q. of 130 to 2.5 for I.Q.'s below 70, indicating a fairly high reproducibility. The long-term consistency of the test is less impressive, particularly if the age at the first test is lower than five or six. Repetitions of testing after a period of years may show large discrepancies (up to 20 to 30 I.Q. points), and these differences increase with the number of years between tests.

There is at present no definition of intelligence that is precise enough to answer questions of validity in general terms. The validity of a particular test must therefore be related to its predictive aims. If the aim is to predict future school performance, then the validity is measured by how well I.Q. predicts that performance. The prediction will be on a probability basis, meaning that a higher I.Q. will usually but not always be associated with better school performance. There is, in fact, fairly general agreement that there is a high correlation between intelligence tests and success in school. The same is true for success in jobs and, in general, in society. I.Q. tests do have some predictive value on a probability basis, although this is limited to performance in contemporary American and European society. In this sense I.Q. tests do have some validity.

Races are subgroups that emerge within the same species. Like other species, the human species is made up of individuals whose genetic composition is so similar that in principle any male can mate with any female and give rise to fertile progeny. In the course of evolution this highly mobile species has spread over the entire surface of the earth. Even today, however, most individuals live out their lives within a small area. This pattern, together with geographic and other barriers, leads to considerable reproductive isolation of groups living in different regions.

Ecological factors, such as geology, climate and flora and fauna, may differ widely in the different habitats of a species. Natural selection, that is, the preferential survival and reproduction of individuals better fitted to their local environment, inevitably creates differences among these somewhat localized groups. In addition the isolation of one group from another allows differences to arise by the random sampling to which genes are subject from generation to generation; this process results in what is called random genetic drift.

Isolated subgroups of the same species therefore tend to differentiate. The process is a slow one: hundreds—more probably thousands—of generations may be necessary for biological differences to become easily noticeable. When sufficient time has elapsed for the differences to become obvious, we call the subgroups races.

In man biological differentiation is usually accompanied or preceded by cultural differentiation, which is a much faster process than biological evolution. The two kinds of differentiation inevitably interact. Cultural differences may contribute to perpetuation of the geographic barriers that lead to reproductive isolation. For example, religious differences may promote reproductive isolation. In the U.S. differences in skin color, which reflect biological differentiation, usually reduce the chances of marriage between groups. This effect, however, is probably a direct psychological consequence not of the difference in skin color but of the parallel cultural divergence.

The relative contributions of biological and cultural factors to complex characteristics such as behavioral differences, including those that distinguish one race from another, are exceedingly difficult to identify. In this connection it is instructive to consider characteristics in which differences can easily be attributed to biological factors. It is clear, for example, that differences in skin color are mostly biological. There is a predominantly nongenetic factor—tanning—that operates during the life of an individual; it is a short-term physiological adaptation and is generally reversible. Apart from this adaptation, most of the differences in skin color both within and among races are genetic.

There are many differences among individuals that are totally under genetic control, that is, they are not subject to even the small physiological adaptation mentioned for skin color. These genetic differences are called genetic polymorphisms when the alternative versions of the genes determining them each occur within a population with a substantial frequency. Such genetic traits are generally detected by chemical or immunological tests, as in the case of the "blood groups." (There are three genes, A, B and O, that determine the ABO blood type.)

The frequencies of polymorphic genes vary widely among races. For example, in Oriental populations the frequencies of the A, B and O genes are respectively 49 percent, 18 percent and 65 percent; in Caucasian populations they are 29 percent, 4 percent and 68 percent. Such polymorphisms are a valuable aid in understanding the nature and magnitude of the biological similarities and differences among races, since they show what kinds of factor can be due solely to heredity. The inheritance of the more conspicuous face and body traits, however, is complex and not well understood, which decreases their value for the biological study of races.

The analysis of genetic polymorphisms demonstrates three very important features of the nature and extent of genetic variation within and among races. First, the extent of variation with-

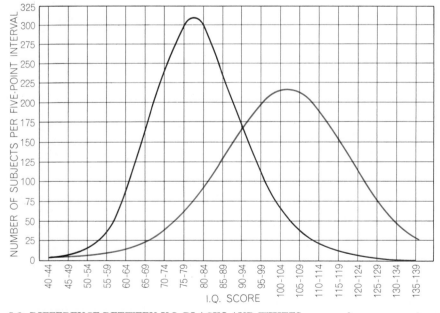

I.Q. DIFFERENCE BETWEEN U.S. BLACKS AND WHITES emerges from a comparison of the I.Q. distribution in a representative sample of whites (*colored curve*) with the I.Q. distribution among 1,800 black children in the schools of Alabama, Florida, Georgia, Tennessee and South Carolina (*black curve*). Wallace A. Kennedy of Florida State University, who surveyed the students' I.Q., found that the mean I.Q. of this group was 80.7. The mean I.Q. of the white sample is 101.8, a difference of 21.1 points. The two samples overlap distinctly, but there is also a sizable difference between the two means. Other studies show a difference of 10 to 20 points, making Kennedy's result one of the most extreme reported.

in any population generally far exceeds the average differences between populations. Second, the differences between populations and races are mostly measured by differences in the relative frequencies of a given set of genes rather than by qualitative differences as to which gene is present in any particular population. Thus any given genetic combination may be found in almost any race, but the frequency with which it is found will vary from one race to another. Third, the variation from race to race is mostly not sharp but may be almost continuous at the boundaries between races. This is the consequence of hybridization's occurring continuously at these boundaries in spite of isolation, or of the formation of hybrid groups by recent migration followed by the more complete mixing of formerly isolated groups.

As we have noted, intelligence must be a complex characteristic under the control of many genes. Extreme deviations from normal levels, as in cases of severe mental retardation, can, however, be attributed to single gene differences. Such deviations can serve to illustrate important ways in which genetic factors can affect behavior. Consider the disease phenylketonuria. Individuals with this disease receive from both of their parents a mutated version of the gene controlling the enzyme that converts one amino acid, phenylalanine, into another, tyrosine. That gene allows phenylalanine to accumulate in the blood and in the brain, causing mental retardation. The accumulation can be checked early in life by a diet deficient in phenylalanine.

The difference between the amounts of phenylalanine in the blood of people with phenylketonuria and that in the blood of normal people, which is closely related to the primary activity of the gene causing phenylketonuria, clearly creates two genetic classes of individuals [*see bottom illustration on next page*]. When such differences are compared with differences in I.Q., there is a slight overlap, but individuals afflicted with phenylketonuria can be distinguished clearly from normal individuals. This simply reflects the fact that the phenylketonuric genotype, that is, the genetic constitution that leads to phenylketonuria, is associated with extreme mental retardation. If differences in head size and hair color in phenylketonuric individuals and normal individuals are compared, however, they show a considerable overlap. Although it can be said that the phenylketonuric genotype has

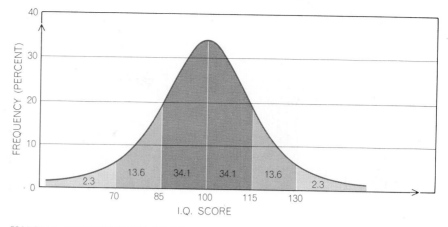

NORMAL DISTRIBUTION OF I.Q. for a population whose mean is 100 is shown by curve. The standard deviation, that is, the usual measure of variation, is about 15 points and the distance in either direction from this mean is measured in multiples of the standard deviation. Thus about 34 percent have an I.Q. with a value that lies between 85 and 100, another 34 percent of the population have an I.Q. score of 100 to 115 points (*dark color*). Those with very high or low scores are a smaller part of population: about 2 percent have an I.Q. below 70, whereas another 2 percent have an I.Q. above 130 (*light color*).

on the average a significant effect on both head size and hair color, measurements of these characteristics cannot be used to distinguish the phenylketonuric genotype from the normal one. The reason is that the variation of head size and hair color is large compared with the average difference. Thus the genetic difference between phenylketonuric and normal individuals contributes in a major way to the variation in blood phenylalanine levels but has only a minor, although significant, effect on head size and hair color.

The phenylketonuric genotype is very rare, occurring with a frequency of only about one individual in 10,000. It therefore has little effect on the overall distribution of I.Q. in the population. It is now known, however, that a large fraction of all genes are polymorphic. Among the polymorphic genes must be included many whose effect on I.Q. is comparable to the effect of the phenylketonuric genotype on head size or hair color. These genotype differences cannot be individually identified, but their total effect on the variation of I.Q. may be considerable.

The nature of phenylketonuria demonstrates another important point: The expression of a gene is profoundly influenced by environment. Phenylketonuric individuals show appreciable variation. This indicates that the genetic difference involved in phenylketonuria is by no means the only factor, or even the major factor, affecting the level of phenylalanine in the blood. It is obvious that dietary differences have a large effect, since a phenylalanine-deficient diet

brings the level of this amino acid in the blood of a phenylketonuric individual almost down to normal. If an individual receives the phenylketonuric gene from only one parent, his mental development is not likely to be clinically affected. Nevertheless, he will tend to have higher than normal levels of phenylalanine in his blood. The overall variation in phenylalanine level is therefore the result of a combination of genetic factors and environmental factors. Measuring the relative contribution of genetic factors to the overall variation is thus equivalent to measuring the relative importance of genetic differences in determining this type of quantitative variation.

When we turn to the analysis of a complex characteristic such as I.Q., which is influenced by many genes each contributing on the average a small effect, we can expect the characteristic to be even more strongly affected by the previous history of the individual and by a host of other external, nongenetic or in any case unrelated factors, which can together be called the "environment." It is necessary to resort to statistical analysis in order to separate the effects of these various factors. Consider an experiment of nature that allows the separation, at least roughly, of environmental factors from genetic factors. This is the occurrence of two types of twins: twins that are "identical," or monozygous (derived from only a single zygote, or fertilized egg, and therefore genetically identical), and twins that are "fraternal," or dizygous (derived from two separate zygotes and therefore genetically different).

Clearly the difference between the

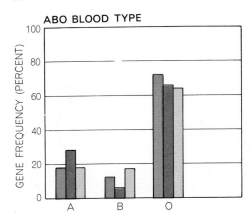

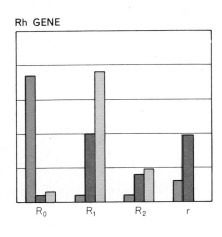

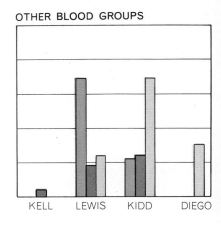

ABO BLOOD TYPE

Rh GENE

OTHER BLOOD GROUPS

GENE FREQUENCY (PERCENT)

A B O

R_0 R_1 R_2 r

KELL LEWIS KIDD DIEGO

FREQUENCIES OF POLYMORPHIC GENES among Africans, Caucasians and Orientals provide a means of differentiating these three races. (A polymorphic gene is one of a group that accounts for variability in a particular characteristic.) About half of the

two members of a monozygous pair is determined only by environmental factors. It would seem that the distribution of such differences among a number of pairs might tell us how much two individuals can differ because of environmental factors alone. The members of monozygous pairs do not generally have identical I.Q.'s. The members of a given twin pair can differ by as much as 20 I.Q. points, although in the majority of cases they differ by less than 10. Hence environmental differences can have an effect on I.Q. whose average magnitude is comparable to, or slightly larger than, the difference between the I.Q. scores of the same individual who has been tested more than once over a period of time.

To see whether or not, and if so to what extent, genetic differences are found, we turn to dizygous twins. Here we know that in addition to the environment genetic factors also play a role in differentiating the members of a pair. The differences in I.Q. among dizygous pairs show a greater spread than those among monozygous pairs, indicating

that the addition of genetic diversity to the purely environmental factors increases, on the average, the overall difference between members of a pair. Hence genetic factors that can contribute to the differentiation of I.Q.'s also exist among normal individuals.

It might seem that the twin data could easily provide a measure of the relative importance of genetic variation and environmental variation. A comparison of the average difference between the members of a monozygous pair and the average difference between the members of a dizygous pair should be a good index of the comparative importance of genetic factors and environmental ones. (A minor technical point should be mentioned here. As is customary in all modern statistical analysis, it is better to consider not the mean of the differences but the mean of their squares. This is comparable to, and can easily be transformed into, a "variance," which is a well-known measure of variation.)

There are two major contrasting reasons why such a simple measure is not entirely satisfactory. First, the difference

between members of a dizygous pair represents only a fraction of the genetic differences that can exist between two individuals. Dizygous twins are related to each other as two siblings are; therefore they are more closely related than two individuals taken at random from a population. This implies a substantial reduction (roughly by a factor of two) in the average genetic difference between dizygous twins compared with that between two randomly chosen individuals. Second, the environmental difference between members of a pair of twins encompasses only a fraction of the total environmental difference that can exist between two individuals, namely the difference between individuals belonging to the same family. This does not take into account differences among families, which are likely to be large. Within the family the environmental differences between twins are limited. For instance, the effect of birth order is not taken into account. Differences between ordinary siblings might therefore tend to be slightly greater than those between dizygous twins. It also seems possible

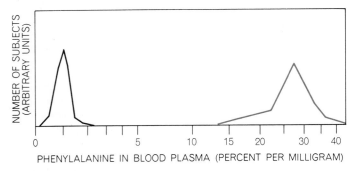

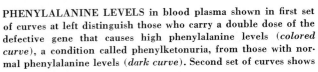

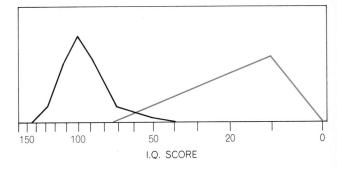

NUMBER OF SUBJECTS (ARBITRARY UNITS)

0   5   10   15   20   30   40

PHENYLALANINE IN BLOOD PLASMA (PERCENT PER MILLIGRAM)

150   100   50   20   0

I.Q. SCORE

PHENYLALANINE LEVELS in blood plasma shown in first set of curves at left distinguish those who carry a double dose of the defective gene that causes high phenylalanine levels (*colored curve*), a condition called phenylketonuria, from those with normal phenylalanine levels (*dark curve*). Second set of curves shows that this genotype has a direct effect on intelligence: phenylketonurics (*colored curve*) have low I.Q.'s because accumulation of phenylalanine and its by-products in blood and nerve tissue damages the brain. Individuals with functioning gene (*dark curve*) have normal I.Q.'s. In the third set phenylalanine levels are related

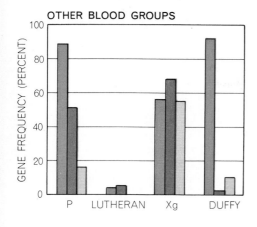

OTHER BLOOD GROUPS

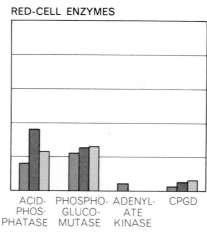

RED-CELL ENZYMES

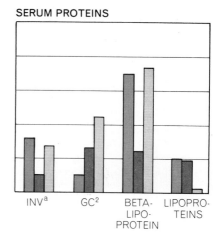

SERUM PROTEINS

polymorphic systems in man are shown. Average differences in frequencies between Africans (*color*) and Caucasians (*dark color*) are 22 percent, those between Africans and Orientals (*light color*) are 30 percent, those between Caucasians and Orientals are 22 percent.

that the environmental differences between monozygotic twins, who tend to establish special relations with each other, are not exactly comparable to those between dizygotic twins. In short, whereas the contrast between monozygotic and dizygotic twin pairs minimizes genetic differences, it also tends to maximize environmental differences.

In order to take account of such difficulties one must try to use all available comparisons between relatives of various types and degrees, of which twin data are only a selected case. For technical reasons one often measures similarities rather than differences between two sets of values such as parent I.Q.'s and offspring I.Q.'s. Such a measure of similarity is called the correlation coefficient. It is equal to 1 when the pairs of values in the two sets are identical or, more generally, when one value is expressible as a linear function of the other. The correlation coefficient is 0 when the pairs of measurements are completely independent, and it is intermediate if there is a relation between the two sets such

that one tends to increase when the other does.

The mean observed values of the correlation coefficient between parent and child I.Q.'s, and between the I.Q.'s of pairs of siblings, are very nearly .5. This is the value one would expect on the basis of the simplest genetic model, in which the effects of any number of genes determine I.Q. and there are no environmental influences or complications of any kind. It seems probable, however, that the observed correlation of .5 is coincidental. Complicating factors such as different modes of gene action, tendencies for like to mate with like and environmental correlations among members of the same family must just happen to balance one another almost exactly to give a result that agrees with the simplest theoretical expectation. If we ignored these complications, we might conclude naïvely (and in contradiction to other evidence, such as the observation of twins) that biological inheritance of the simplest kind entirely determines I.Q.

Instead it is necessary to seek a means

of determining the relative importance of environmental factors and genetic factors even taking account of several of the complications. In theory this measurement can be made by computing the quotients known as heritability estimates. To understand what such quotients are intended to measure, consider a simplified situation. Imagine that the genotype of each individual with respect to genes affecting I.Q. can be identified. Individuals with the same genotype can then be grouped together. The differences among them would be the result of environmental factors, and the spread of the distribution of such differences could then be measured. Assume for the sake of simplicity that the spread of I.Q. due to environmental differences is the same for each genotype. If we take the I.Q.'s of all the individuals in the population, we obtain a distribution that yields the total variation of I.Q. The variation within each genotype is the environmental component. The difference between the total variation and the environmental component of variation leaves a component of the total variation

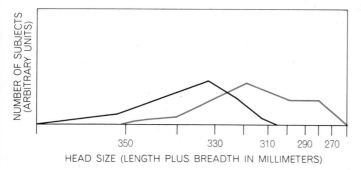

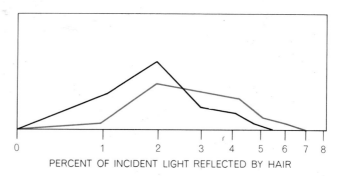

to head size (displayed as the sum of head length and breadth), and in the fourth set phenylalanine levels are related to hair color (displayed as the percentage of light with a wavelength of 700 millimicrons reflected by the hair). In both cases it is obvious that the phenylketonuric genotype has a significant effect on each of these

characteristics: the reflectance is greater and the head size is smaller (*colored curves*) among phenylketonurics than they are among normal individuals (*dark curves*). Yet the distribution of these characteristics is such that they cannot be used to distinguish those afflicted with phenylketonuria from those who are not.

that may be accounted for by genetic differences. This component, when expressed as a fraction of the total variance, is one possible measure of heritability.

In practice, however, the estimation of the component of the total variation that can be accounted for by genetic differences (from data on correlations between relatives) always depends on the construction of specific genetic models, and is therefore subject to the limitations of the models. One problem lies in the fact that there are a number of alternative definitions of heritability depending on the genetic model chosen, because the genetic variation may have many components that can have quite different meanings. A definition that includes only those parts of the genetic variation generally considered to be most relevant in animal and plant breeding is often used. This is called heritability in the narrow sense. If all genetic sources of variation are included, then the heritability estimate increases and is referred to as heritability in the broad sense.

The differences between these esti-

mates of heritability can be defined quite precisely in terms of specific genetic models. The resulting estimates of heritability, however, can vary considerably. Typical heritability estimates for I.Q. (derived from the London population in the early 1950's, with data obtained by Sir Cyril Burt) give values of 45 to 60 percent for heritability in the narrow sense and 80 to 85 percent for heritability in the broad sense.

A further major complication for such heritability estimates has the technical name "genotype-environment interaction." The difficulty is that the realized I.Q. of given genotypes in different environments cannot be predicted in a simple way. A given genotype may develop better in one environment than in another, but this is not necessarily true for any other genotype. Even if it is true, the extent of the difference may not be the same. Ideally one would like to know the reaction of every genotype in every environment. Given the practically infinite variety of both environments and genotypes, this is clearly impossible. Moreover, in man there is no way of con-

trolling the environment. Even if all environmental influences relevant to behavioral development were known, their statistical control by appropriate measurements and subsequent statistical analysis of the data would still be extremely difficult. It should therefore be emphasized that because estimates of heritability depend on the extent of environmental and genetic variation that prevails in the population examined at the time of analysis, they are not valid for other populations or for the same population at a different time.

In animals and plants the experimental control of the environment is easier, and it is possible to explore "genotype-environment" interactions. An interesting experiment was conducted by R. Cooper and John P. Zubek of the University of Manitoba with two lines of rats in which genetic differences in the rats' capacity to find their way through a maze had been accumulated by artificial selection. The two lines of rats had been selected to be either "bright" or "dull" at finding their way through the maze. When rats from these lines were raised for one generation in a "restricted" environment that differed from the "normal" laboratory conditions, no difference between the lines could be found. Both bright and dull animals performed at the same low level. When they were raised in a stimulating environment, both did almost equally well [see illustration, page 325]. Since the difference between the lines is genetic, the effect of environmental conditions should be reversible in future generations. This experiment is particularly relevant to differences in I.Q. because of the structure of human societies. If "ghetto" children tend to have I.Q. scores lower, and the children of parents of high social and economic status to have scores higher, than the level one would expect if both groups of children were reared in the same environment, then heritability estimates may be biased upward.

The only potential safeguard against such bias is provided by the investigation of the same genotype or similar genotypes in different environments. In man this can be done only through the study of adopted children. A particularly interesting type of "adoption" is that in which monozygous twins are separated and reared in different families from birth or soon afterward. The outcome is in general a relatively minor average decrease in similarity. Following the same line of reasoning, the similarity between foster parents and adopted children can be measured and contrasted with that between biological parents and their

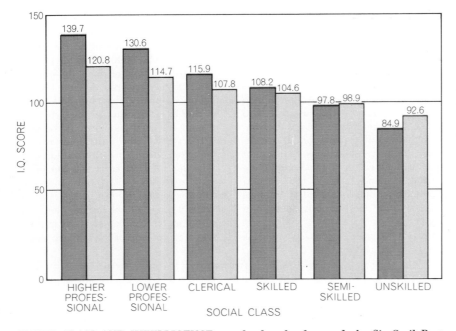

SOCIAL CLASS AND INTELLIGENCE are closely related, a study by Sir Cyril Burt of the University of London indicates. Set of bars at left shows the mean I.Q. for higher professionals (*dark bar*) is 139.7, children of higher professionals have a mean I.Q. of 120.8 (*light bar*). Second set of bars shows that lower professionals have a mean I.Q. of 130.6, children of lower professionals have a mean I.Q. of 114.7. Third set shows that clerical workers have a mean I.Q. of 115.9, their children have a mean I.Q. of 107.8. Fourth set shows that skilled workers have a mean I.Q. of 108.2, their children have a mean I.Q. of 104.6. Fifth set shows that semiskilled workers have a mean I.Q. of 97.8, their children have a mean I.Q. of 98.9. Sixth set shows that unskilled workers have a mean I.Q. of 84.9, their children have a mean I.Q. of 92.6. Mean I.Q.'s of wives (*not shown*) correlate well with husbands'. Above the mean children's I.Q. tends to be lower than that of parents. Below it children's I.Q. tends to be higher. Social mobility maintains distribution because those individuals with high I.Q.'s tend to rise whereas those with low I.Q.'s tend to fall.

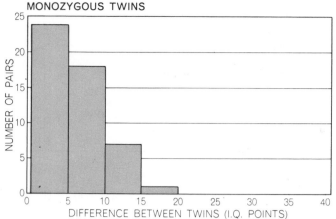

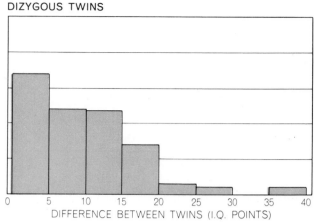

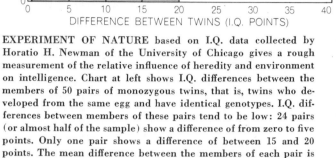

EXPERIMENT OF NATURE based on I.Q. data collected by Horatio H. Newman of the University of Chicago gives a rough measurement of the relative influence of heredity and environment on intelligence. Chart at left shows I.Q. differences between the members of 50 pairs of monozygous twins, that is, twins who developed from the same egg and have identical genotypes. I.Q. differences between members of these pairs tend to be low: 24 pairs (or almost half of the sample) show a difference of from zero to five points. Only one pair shows a difference of between 15 and 20 points. The mean difference between the members of each pair is 5.9 points. Since the genotypes in each pair are identical it appears that the environmental effect tends to be small. Second chart shows I.Q. differences between 45 pairs of dizygous twins, that is, twins with different genotypes who developed from separate eggs. In this case the mean difference in I.Q. between the members of these pairs is about 10 points. Thus a fairly large difference appears to be attributable to heredity. Such a comparison does not separate the effects of heredity and environment precisely. Members of monozygous pairs have very similar environments, whereas genotypes of dizygous twins are less different on the average by a factor of two than those of unrelated individuals. Comparison thus underestimates effect of heredity but also minimizes environmental influence.

children. A few such studies have been conducted. They show that the change of family environment does indeed have an effect, although it is not as great as that of biological inheritance. The correlation between foster parents and their adopted children is greater than 0, but it is undoubtedly less than that between biological parents and their offspring.

A complete analysis of such data is almost impossible because environmental variation among families and genotype-environment interactions of various kinds must be responsible for the observed effects in ways that make it difficult to disentangle their relative importance. Adoption and rearing apart take place in conditions far from those of ideal experiments, and so any conclusions are bound to be only semiquantitative. On the basis of all the available data, with allowance for these limitations, the heritability of intelligence, as measured by I.Q., is still fairly high. It must be kept in mind, however, that the environmental effects in such studies are generally limited to the differences among and within families of a fairly homogeneous section of the British or American population. They cannot be extrapolated to prediction of the effects of greater differences in environment, or of other types of difference.

There are significant differences in mean I.Q. among the various social classes. One of the most comprehensive and widely quoted studies of such dif-

ferences and the reasons for their apparent stability over the years was published by Burt in 1961 [see illustration on opposite page]. His data come from schoolchildren and their parents in a typical London borough. Socioeconomic level was classified, on the basis of type of occupation, into six classes. These range from Class 1, including "university teachers, those of similar standing in law, medicine, education or the church and the top people in commerce, industry or civil service," to Class 6, including "unskilled laborers, casual laborers and those employed in coarse manual work." There are four main features of these data:

1. Parental mean I.Q. and occupational class are closely related. The mean difference between the highest and the lowest class is over 50. Although occupational class is determined mostly by the father, the relatively high correlation between the I.Q.'s of husband and wife (about .4) contributes to the differentiation among the classes with respect to I.Q.

2. In spite of the significant variation between the parental mean I.Q.'s, the residual variation in I.Q. among parents within each class is still remarkably large. The mean standard deviation of the parental I.Q.'s for the different classes is 8.6, almost three-fifths of the standard deviation for the entire group. That standard deviation is about 15, and it is usual for the spread of I.Q.'s in any group.

3. The mean I.Q. of the offspring for each class lies almost exactly between the parental mean I.Q.'s and the overall population mean I.Q. of 100. This is expected because it is only another way of looking at the correlation for I.Q. between parent and child, which as we have already seen tends to be about .5 in any given population.

4. The last important feature of the data is that the standard deviations of the I.Q. of the offspring, which average 13.2, are almost the same as the standard deviation of the general population, namely 15. This is another indication of the existence of considerable variability of I.Q. within social classes. Such variability is almost as much as that in the entire population.

The most straightforward interpretation of these data is that I.Q. is itself a major determinant of occupational class and that it is to an appreciable extent inherited (although the data cannot be used to distinguish cultural inheritance from biological). Burt pointed out that, because of the wide distribution of I.Q. within each class among the offspring and the regression of the offspring to the population mean, appreciable mobility among classes is needed in each generation to maintain the class differences with respect to I.Q. He estimated that to maintain a stable distribution of I.Q. differences among classes, at least 22 percent of the offspring would have to change class, mainly as a function of I.Q., in each generation. This figure is

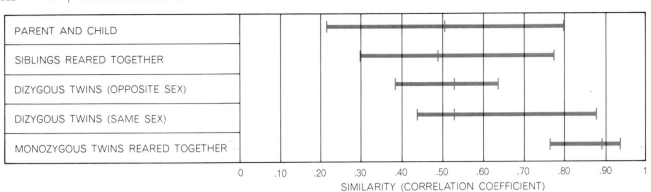

PARENT AND CHILD		
SIBLINGS REARED TOGETHER		
DIZYGOUS TWINS (OPPOSITE SEX)		
DIZYGOUS TWINS (SAME SEX)		
MONOZYGOUS TWINS REARED TOGETHER		

0   .10   .20   .30   .40   .50   .60   .70   .80   .90   1

SIMILARITY (CORRELATION COEFFICIENT)

CORRELATION COEFFICIENTS are calculations of similarity, for example, between the I.Q.'s of two sets of relatives such as parents and children. A coefficient of 1 indicates identity, 0 indicates independence of one value from the other. These data were collected from published literature by L. Erlenmeyer-Kimling and Lissy F. Jarvik of the New York State Psychiatric Institute to derive measurements of comparative effects of heredity and environment, taking into account all possible effects of relatedness between individuals. The horizontal line at top indicates that the coefficients of samples of parents and children from different studies range from about .20 to .80. Second horizontal line indicates that coefficients for siblings reared together range from .30 to about .78. Range for dizygous (fraternal) twins of opposite sex is .38 to .65; for dizygous twins of same sex it is .43 to .88. The mean (*vertical line intersecting each horizontal line*) for each of these four sets of relatives is about .50. Monozygous (identical) twins, however, have a range of .77 to .92 with a mean of .89. Mean coefficient of .50 is that which would be expected if there were no environmental effects in I.Q. Since other evidence indicates that environment exerts a significant effect, these calculations must be further refined.

well below the observed intergenerational social mobility in Britain, which is about 30 percent.

Fears that there may be a gradual decline in I.Q. because of an apparent negative correlation between I.Q. and fertility have been expressed ever since Francis Galton pointed out this correlation for the British ruling class in the second half of the 19th century. If there were such a persistent association, if I.Q. were at least in part genetically determined and if there were no counteracting environmental effects, such a decline in I.Q. could be expected. The fact is that no significant decline has been detected so far. The existing data, although they are admittedly limited, do not support the idea of a persistent negative correlation between I.Q. and overall reproductivity.

The existence of culturally, and often racially, reproductively isolated subgroups within a human population almost inevitably leads to social tensions, which are the seeds of racism. This has been true throughout the history of mankind, and is by no means unique to the present tensions among different racial groups such as those between blacks and whites in the U.S. Conflicts between religious groups, such as Protestants and Catholics in Northern Ireland, are examples of the same type of social tension. Cultural divergence is often accompanied by relative economic deprivation in one group or the other, which aggravates the tensions between them.

The striking outward differences between blacks and whites, mainly of

course the color of their skin, must be a major extra factor contributing to the racial tensions between them. If the cultural differences between the Protestants and Catholics of Ireland disappeared, there would be no way of telling the two groups apart. The same is not true for black and white Americans. Many generations of completely random mating would be needed to even out their difference in skin color.

Such mating has not taken place in the U.S. The average frequency of marriages between blacks and whites throughout the U.S. is still only about 2 percent of the frequency that would be expected if marriages occurred at random with respect to race. This reflects the persistent high level of reproductive isolation between the races, in spite of the movement in recent years toward a strong legal stand in favor of desegregation. Hawaii is a notable exception to this separation of the races, although even there the observed frequency of mixed marriages is still only 45 to 50 percent of what would be expected if matings occurred at random.

The socioeconomic deprivation of one racial group with respect to another inevitably raises the question of whether or not the difference has a significant genetic component. In the case of U.S. blacks and whites the question has recently been focused on the average difference in I.Q. Many studies have shown the existence of substantial differences in the distribution of I.Q. in U.S. blacks and whites. Such data were obtained in an extensive study published by Wallace A. Kennedy of Florida State University and

his co-workers in 1963, based on I.Q. tests given to 1,800 black children in elementary school in five Southeastern states (Florida, Georgia, Alabama, Tennessee and South Carolina). When the distribution these workers found is compared with a 1960 sample of the U.S. white population, striking differences emerge. The mean difference in I.Q. between blacks and whites is 21.1, whereas the standard deviation of the distribution among blacks is some 25 percent less than that of the distribution among whites (12.4 v. 16.4). As one would expect, there is considerable overlap between the two distributions, because the variability for I.Q., like the variability for most characteristics, within any population is substantially greater than the variability between any two populations. Nevertheless, 95.5 percent of the blacks have an I.Q. below the white mean of 101.8 and 18.4 percent have an I.Q. of less than 70. Only 2 percent of the whites have I.Q.'s in the latter range.

Reported differences between the mean I.Q.'s of blacks and whites generally lie between 10 and 20, so that the value found by Kennedy and his colleagues is one of the most extreme reported. The difference is usually less for blacks from the Northern states than it is for those from the Southern states, and clearly it depends heavily on the particular populations tested. One well-known study of Army "Alpha" intelligence-test results, for example, showed that blacks from some Northern states achieved higher average scores than whites from some Southern states, although whites always scored higher than blacks from the same state. There are many uncertainties and variables that influence the outcome of I.Q. tests, but the observed mean differences between U.S. blacks and whites are undoubtedly more or less reproducible and are quite striking.

There are two main features that clearly distinguish I.Q. differences among social classes described above from those between blacks and whites. First, the I.Q. differences among social classes relate to the environmental variation within the relatively homogeneous British population. It cannot be assumed that this range of environmental variation is comparable with the average environmental difference between black and white Americans. Second, and more important, these differences are maintained by the mobility among occupational classes that is based to a significant extent on selection for higher I.Q. in the higher occupational classes. There is clearly no counterpart of this mobility with respect to the differences between U.S. blacks and whites; skin color effectively bars mobility between the races.

The arguments for a substantial genetic component in the I.Q. difference between the races assume that existing heritability estimates for I.Q. can reasonably be applied to the racial difference. These estimates, however, are based on observations within the white population. We have emphasized that heritability estimates apply only to the population studied and to its particular environment. Thus the extrapolation of existing heritability estimates to the racial differences assumes that the environmental differences between the races are comparable to the environmental variation within them. Since there is no basis for making this assumption, it follows that there is no logical connection between heritabilities determined within either race and the genetic difference between them. Whether or not the variation in I.Q. within either race is entirely genetic or entirely environmental has no bearing on the question of the relative contribution of genetic factors and environmental factors to the differences between the races.

A major argument given by Jensen in favor of a substantial genetic component in the I.Q. difference is that it persists even when comparisons are made between U.S. blacks and whites of the same socioeconomic status. This status is defined in terms of schooling, occupation and income, and so it is necessarily a measure of at least a part of the environmental variation, comparable to the class differences we have discussed here.

Taken at face value—that is, on the assumption that status is truly a measure of the total environment—these data would indicate that the I.Q. difference is genetically determined. It is difficult to see, however, how the status of blacks and whites can be compared. The very existence of a racial stratification correlated with a relative socioeconomic deprivation makes this comparison suspect. Black schools are well known to be generally less adequate than white schools, so that equal numbers of years of schooling certainly do not mean equal educational attainment. Wide variation in the level of occupation must exist within each occupational class. Thus one would certainly expect, even for equivalent occupational classes, that the black level is on the average lower than the white. No amount of money can buy a black person's way into a privileged upper-class white community, or buy off more than 200 years of accumulated racial prejudice on the part of the whites, or reconstitute the disrupted black family, in part culturally inherited from the days of slavery. It is impossible to accept the idea that matching for status provides an adequate, or even a substantial, control over the most important environmental differences between blacks and whites.

Jensen has suggested other arguments in defense of his thesis that the average I.Q. difference between blacks and whites is entirely genetic or mostly so, and he has challenged readers of his paper in the *Harvard Educational Review* to consider them. One is a set of data on blacks that is quite similar to those we have cited for whites; it shows the filial regression of I.Q. or related measurements as a function of the social class of the parents. The only conclusion one can draw is that among blacks the inheritance of I.Q. must also be fairly high. No conclusion can be drawn from these data concerning environmental differences between blacks and whites that affect I.Q., and it is this that is the real issue.

Jensen also discusses differences between the races in rates of early motor development, and in other developmental rates, which are believed to be correlated with I.Q. The argument must, by implication, be that developmental rates are determined mostly by genetic factors. Environmental influences on such rates are widely recognized, so that this information does not help to clarify the situation concerning I.Q. Moreover, Jensen makes the statement, based on the well-known "Coleman report," that American Indians, in spite of poor schooling, do not show the same I.Q. gap as blacks. According to the Coleman report, however, American Indians typically go to schools where whites are in the majority, which is not the case for most of the schools attended by black children. (The actual difference between whites and Indians may be greater, be-

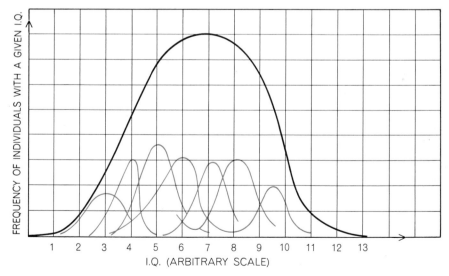

HERITABILITY is a measure of the relative effects of heredity and environment on characteristics such as I.Q. The heritability estimate is based on the assumption that a population consists of several groups each distinguished by a different genotype and I.Q. distribution (*colored curves*). The total of these I.Q. distributions equals the I.Q. spread for the population (*black curve*). By definition those in each group have the same genotype, thus any variation in a group is environmental. Heredity's effect on the total I.Q. distribution can be calculated by averaging together the I.Q. spread of each group and subtracting the result from the total I.Q. spread. The remainder is the total variation due to genetic factors.

cause the sample may not have adequately represented the 70 to 80 percent of American Indians who live on reservations.) The differences between Indians and blacks or whites are clearly no easier to assess than those between blacks and whites.

Jensen states that because the gene pools of whites and blacks are known to differ and "these genetic differences are manifested in virtually every anatomical, physiological and biochemical comparison one can make between representative samples of identifiable racial groups ...there is no reason to suppose that the brain should be exempt from this generalization." As geneticists we can state with certainty that there is no a priori reason why genes affecting I.Q., which differ in the gene pools of blacks and whites, should be such that on the average whites have significantly more genes increasing I.Q. than blacks do. On the contrary, one should expect, assuming no tendency for high-I.Q. genes to accumulate by selection in one race or the other, that the more polymorphic genes there are that affect I.Q. and that differ in frequency in blacks and whites, the less likely it is that there is an average genetic difference in I.Q. between the races. The same argument applies to the differences between any two racial groups.

Since natural selection is the principal agent of genetic change, is it possible that this force has produced a significant I.Q. difference between American blacks and whites? Using the simple theory with which plant and animal breeders predict responses to artificial selection, one can make a rough guess at the amount of selection that would have been needed to result in a difference of about 15 I.Q. points, such as exists between blacks and whites. The calculation is based on three assumptions: that there was no initial difference in I.Q. between Africans and Caucasians, that the heritability of I.Q. in the narrow sense is about 50 percent and that the divergence of black Americans from Africans started with slavery about 200 years, or seven generations, ago. This implies a mean change in I.Q. of about two points per generation. The predictions of the theory are that this rate of change could be achieved by the complete elimination from reproduction of about 15 percent of the most intelligent individuals in each generation. There is certainly no good basis for assuming such a level of selection against I.Q. during the period of slavery.

It seems to us that none of the above arguments gives any support to Jensen's conclusion. The only observation that could prove his thesis would be to compare an adequate sample of black and white children brought up in strictly comparable environments. This seems practically impossible to achieve today.

What can be said concerning environmental differences that are known or suspected to affect I.Q.? First it should be mentioned that, in spite of high I.Q. heritability estimates, the mean intrapair I.Q. difference found by Horatio H. Newman and his co-workers at the University of Chicago between monozygotic twins reared apart was 8 and the range was from 1 to 24. Therefore even within the white population there is substantial environmental variation in I.Q.

The following known environmental effects are also worth mentioning:

1. There is a systematic difference of as much as five I.Q. points between twins and nontwins, irrespective of socioeconomic and other variables. This reduction in the I.Q. of twins could be due either to the effects of the maternal environment *in utero* or to the reduced attention parents are able to give each of two very young children born at the same time.

2. It has been reported that the I.Q. of blacks tested by blacks was two to three points higher than when they were tested by whites.

3. Studies of the effects of protein-deficient diets administered to female rats before and during pregnancy (conducted by Stephen Zamenhof and his co-workers at the University of California School of Medicine in Los Angeles) have shown a substantial reduction in total brain DNA content of the offspring and hence presumably a reduction in the number of brain cells. The reductions were correlated with behavioral deficiencies and in man could be the basis for substantial I.Q. differences. There can be no doubt that in many areas the poor socioeconomic conditions of blacks are correlated with dietary deficiency. Dietary deficiencies in early childhood are likely to have similar consequences.

4. The very early home environment has long been thought to be of substantial importance for intellectual development. There are clear-cut data that demonstrate the detrimental effects of severe early sensory deprivation. There can be little doubt that both the lower socio-

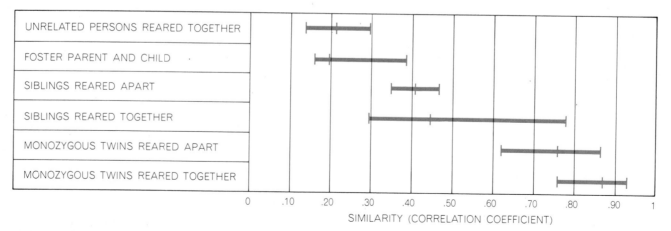

EFFECTS OF ENVIRONMENT can be measured by comparing correlation coefficients of individuals with similar genetic backgrounds reared in different environments and those with different backgrounds reared in the same environment. Published data collected by Erlenmeyer-Kimling and Jarvik show that unrelated persons reared together have coefficients that range from about .15 to slightly over .30. Coefficients for foster-parents and children range from .16 to almost .40. Siblings reared apart have coefficients that range from more than .30 to more than .40. Siblings reared together have coefficients that range from .30 to almost .80. Monozygous twins reared apart have coefficients that range from more than .60 to above .80, and monozygous twins reared together have coefficients of more than .70 to more than .90. It appears that environment affects intelligence but not as strongly as heredity does.

economic status of U.S. blacks and a cultural inheritance dating back to slavery must on the average result in a less satisfactory home environment; this may be particularly important during the preschool years. Here again animal experiments support the importance of early experience on brain development.

5. Expectancy of failure usually leads to failure.

In his *Harvard Educational Review* article Jensen chooses to minimize environmental effects such as these. We believe, however, that there is no evidence against the notion that such influences, among other environmental factors, many of which doubtless remain to be discovered, could explain essentially all the differences in I.Q. between blacks and whites.

We do not by any means exclude the possibility that there could be a genetic component in the mean difference in I.Q. between races. We simply maintain that currently available data are inadequate to resolve this question in either direction. The only approach applicable to the study of the I.Q. difference between the races is that of working with black children adopted into white homes and vice versa. The adoptions would, of course, have to be at an early age to be sure of taking into account any possible effects of the early home environment. The I.Q.'s of black children adopted into white homes would also have to be compared with those of white children adopted into comparable white homes. To our knowledge no scientifically adequate studies of this nature have ever been undertaken. It is questionable whether or not such studies could be done in a reasonably controlled way at the present time. Even if they could, they would not remove the effects of prejudice directed against black people in most white communities. We therefore suggest that the question of a possible genetic basis for the race I.Q. difference will be almost impossible to answer satisfactorily before the environmental differences between U.S. blacks and whites have been substantially reduced.

Apart from the intrinsic difficulties in answering this question, it seems to us that there is no good case for encouraging the support of studies of this kind on either theoretical or practical grounds. From a theoretical point of view it seems unlikely that such studies would throw much light on the general problem of the genetic control of I.Q., because any racial difference would be a small fraction of the total variation in I.Q. The mere fact that even the rela-

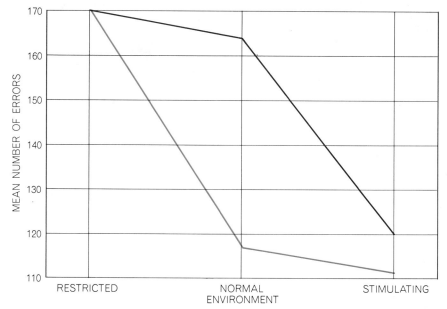

GENOTYPE-ENVIRONMENT INTERACTION is measured in these results from an experiment carried out by R. Cooper and John P. Zubek of the University of Manitoba. The experiment involved two strains of rats: those that were bred to be "bright," that is, clever at finding their way through a maze, and those that were "dull." In a normal environment bright rats (*colored curve*) made only 120 errors, whereas dull rats made about 168 errors. When both strains were raised in a restricted environment, however, both made about 170 errors. When raised in a stimulating environment, both kinds of rats did equally well.

tively crude studies on the inheritance of I.Q. conducted so far have not taken advantage of racial differences suggests that these are not the most convenient differences to investigate. Much basic work on the biology and biochemistry of mental development under controlled conditions, making use of known genetic differences, is needed before a fuller understanding of the inheritance of I.Q. can be achieved.

Perhaps the only practical argument in favor of research on the race I.Q. difference is that, since the question that the difference is genetic has been raised, an attempt should be made to answer it. Otherwise those who now believe—we think on quite inadequate evidence—that the difference is genetic will be left to continue their campaigns for an adjustment of our educational and economic systems to take account of "innate" racial differences.

A demonstration that the difference is not primarily genetic could counter such campaigns. On the other hand, an answer in the opposite direction should not, in a genuinely democratic society free of race prejudice, make any difference. Our society professes to believe there should be no discrimination against an individual on the basis of race, religion or other a priori categorizations, including sex. Our accepted ethic holds that each individual should be given equal and maximum opportunity, ac-

cording to his or her needs, to develop to his or her fullest potential. Surely innate differences in ability and other individual variations should be taken into account by our educational system. These differences must, however, be judged on the basis of the individual and not on the basis of race. To maintain otherwise indicates an inability to distinguish differences among individuals from differences among populations.

We are not unaware of the dangers of either overt or implicit control of scientific inquiry. The suppression of Galileo and the success of T. D. Lysenko are two notorious examples of the evils of such control. Most investigators, however, do accept certain limitations on research on human beings, for example in the right of an individual not to be experimented on and in the confidentiality of the information collected by organizations such as the Bureau of the Cen[sus]. In the present racial climate of the [...] studies on racial differences in I.Q[...] ever well intentioned, could [...] misinterpreted as a form of [...] lead to an unnecessary a[...] racial tensions. Since w[...] for the present at lea[...] can be made for su[...] scientific or practic[...] see any point in [...] the use of pub[...] There are m[...] problems f[...]

38

Pictorial Perception and Culture

by Jan B. Deregowski
November 1972

Do people of one culture perceive a picture differently from people of another? Experiments in Africa show that such differences exist, and that the perception of pictures calls for some form of learning

A picture is a pattern of lines and shaded areas on a flat surface that depicts some aspect of the real world. The ability to recognize objects in pictures is so common in most cultures that it is often taken for granted that such recognition is universal in man. Although children do not learn to read until they are about six years old, they are able to recognize objects in pictures long before that; indeed, it has been shown that a 19-month-old child is capable of such recognition. If pictorial recognition is universal, do pictures offer us a lingua franca for intercultural communication? There is evidence that they do not: cross-cultural studies have shown that there are persistent differences in the way pictorial information is interpreted by people of various cultures. These differences merit investigation not only because improvement in communication may be achieved by a fuller understanding of them but also because they may provide us with a better insight into the nature of human percep-

tail!' And the boy will say: 'Oh! yes and there is the dog's nose and eyes and ears!' Then the old people will look again and clap their hands and say, 'Oh! yes, it is a dog.' When a man has seen a picture for the first time, his book education has begun."

Mrs. Donald Fraser, who taught health care to Africans in the 1920's, had similar experiences. This is her description of an African woman slowly discovering that a picture she was looking at portrayed a human head in profile: "She discovered in turn the nose, the mouth, the eye, but where was the other eye? I tried by turning my profile to explain why she could only see one eye but she hopped round to my other side to point out that I possessed a second eye which the other lacked."

There were also, however, reports of vivid and instant responses to pictures: "When all the people were quickly seated, the first picture flashed on the sheet was that of an elephant. The wildest excitement immediately prevailed, many of the people jumping up and shouting, fearing the beast must be alive, while those nearest to the sheet sprang up and fled. The chief himself ─ealthily forward and peeped be─ to see if the animal had ─hen he discovered that the y was only the thickness of great roar broke the stillness

Thus the evidence gleaned from the insightful but unsystematic observations quoted is ambiguous. The laborious way some of these Africans pieced together a picture suggests that some form of learning is required to recognize pictures. Inability to perceive that a pattern of lines and shaded areas on a flat surface represents a real object would render all pictorial material incomprehensible. All drawings would be perceived as being meaningless, abstract patterns until the viewer had learned to interpret and organize the symbolic elements. On the other hand, one could also argue that pictorial recognition is largely independent of learning, and that even people from cultures where pictorial materials are uncommon will recognize items in pictures, provided that the pictures show familiar objects. It has been shown that an unsophisticated adult African from a remote village is unlikely to choose the wrong toy animal when asked to match the toy to a picture of, say, a lion. Given a photograph of a kangaroo, however, he is likely to choose at random from the array of toys. Yet one can argue that this sample was not as culturally remote as those described above. It is therefore probably safer to assume that utter incomprehension of pictorial material may be observed only in extremely isolated human populations.

Conventions for depicting the spatial arrangement of three-dimensional ob-

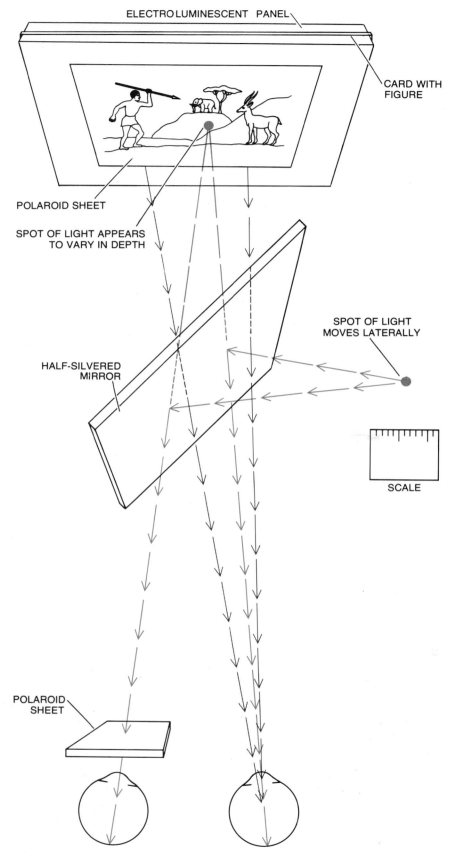

ELECTROLUMINESCENT PANEL

CARD WITH FIGURE

POLAROID SHEET

SPOT OF LIGHT APPEARS TO VARY IN DEPTH

SPOT OF LIGHT MOVES LATERALLY

HALF-SILVERED MIRROR

SCALE

POLAROID SHEET

APPARATUS FOR STUDYING PERCEIVED DEPTH enables the subject to adjust a spot of light so that it appears to lie at the same depth as an object in the picture. The light is seen stereoscopically with both eyes but the picture is seen with only one eye. Africans unfamiliar with pictorial depth cues set the light at the same depth on all parts of the picture.

jects in a flat picture can also give rise to difficulties in perception. These conventions give the observer depth cues that tell him the objects are not all the same distance from him. Inability to interpret such cues is bound to lead to misunderstanding of the meaning of the picture as a whole. William Hudson, who was then working at the National Institute for Personnel Research in Johannesburg, stumbled on such a difficulty in testing South African Bantu workers. His discovery led him to construct a pictorial perception test and to carry out much of the pioneering work in cross-cultural studies of perception.

Hudson's test consists of a series of pictures in which there are various combinations of three pictorial depth cues. The first cue is familiar size, which calls for the larger of two known objects to be drawn considerably smaller to indicate that it is farther away. The second cue is overlap, in which portions of nearer objects overlap and obscure portions of objects that are farther away; a hill is partly obscured by another hill that is closer to the viewer. The third cue is perspective, the convergence of lines known to be parallel to suggest distance; lines representing the edges of a road converge in the distance. In all but one of his tests Hudson omitted an entire group of powerful depth cues: density gradients. Density gradients are provided by any elements of uniform size: bricks in a wall or pebbles on a beach. The elements are drawn larger or smaller depending on whether they are nearer to the viewer or farther away from him.

Hudson's test has been applied in many parts of Africa with subjects drawn from a variety of tribal and linguistic groups. The subjects were shown one picture at a time and asked to name all the objects in the picture in order to determine whether or not the elements were correctly recognized. Then they were asked about the relation between the objects. (What is the man doing? What is closer to the man?) If the subject takes note of the depth cues and makes the "correct" interpretations, he is classified as having three-dimensional perception. If the depth cues are not taken into account by the subject, he is said to have two-dimensional perception [see illustration on preceding page]. The results from African tribal subjects were unequivocal: both children and adults found it difficult to perceive depth in the pictorial material. The difficulty varied in extent but appeared to persist through most educational and social levels.

Further experimentation revealed that the phenomenon was not simply the result of the pictorial material used in the test. Subjects were shown a drawing of two squares, one behind the other and connected by a single rod [see top illustration at right]. They were also given sticks and modeling clay and asked to build a model of what they saw. If Hudson's test is valid, people designated as two-dimensional perceivers should build flat models when they are shown the drawing, whereas those designated as three-dimensional perceivers should build a cubelike object. When primary-school boys and unskilled workers in Zambia were given Hudson's test and then asked to build models, a few of the subjects who had been classified as three-dimensional responders by the test made flat models. A substantial number of the subjects classified as two-dimensional perceivers built three-dimensional models. Thus Hudson's test, although it is more severe than the construction task, appears to measure the same variable.

The finding was checked in another experiment. A group of Zambian primary-school children were classified into three-dimensional and two-dimensional perceivers on the basis of the model-building test. They were then asked to copy a "two-pronged trident," a tantalizing drawing that confuses many people. The confusion is a direct result of attempting to interpret the drawing as a three-dimensional object [see top illustration on next page]. One would expect that those who are confused by the trident would find it difficult to recall and draw. The students actually made copies of two tridents: the ambiguous one and a control figure that had three simple prongs. To view the figure the student had to lift a flap, which actuated a timer that measured how long the flap was held up. The student could view the figure for as long as he wanted to, but he could not copy it while the flap was open. After the flap was closed the student had to wait 10 seconds before he began to draw. The delay was introduced to increase the difficulty of copying the figure. The results confirmed that the students who were three-dimensional perceivers spent more time looking at the ambiguous trident than at the control trident, whereas the two-dimensional perceivers did not differ significantly in the time spent viewing each of the two tridents.

Do people who perceive pictorial

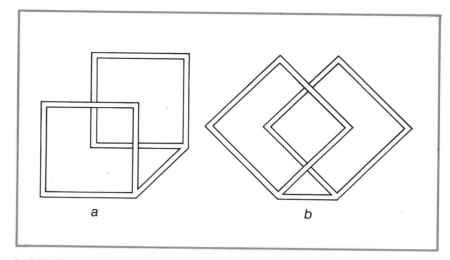

CONSTRUCTION-TASK FIGURES consist of two squares connected by a single rod. Most subjects from Western cultures see the figure a as a three-dimensional object, but when the figure is rotated 45 degrees (right), they see it as being flat. Subjects from African cultures are more likely to see both figures as being flat, with the two squares in the same plane.

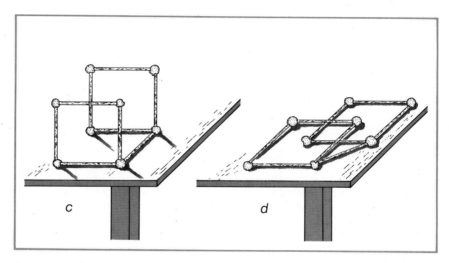

STICK-AND-CLAY MODELS of the figure a in the top illustration were made by test subjects. Almost all the three-dimensional perceivers built a three-dimensional object (left). Subjects who did not readily perceive depth in pictures tended to build a flat model (right).

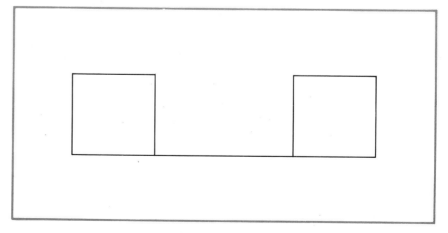

"SPLIT" DRAWING was preferred by two-dimensional perceivers when shown a model like figure c and given a choice between the split drawing and figure a in top illustration.

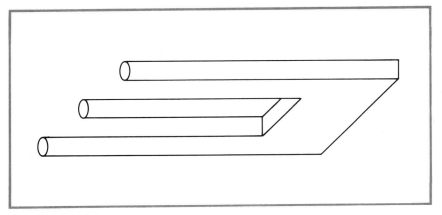

AMBIGUOUS TRIDENT is confusing to observers who attempt to see it as a three-dimensional object. Two-dimensional perceivers see the pattern as being flat and are not confused.

depth really see depth in the picture or are they merely interpreting symbolic depth cues in the same way that we learn to interpret the set of symbols in "horse" to mean a certain quadruped? An ingenious apparatus for studying perceived depth helped us to obtain an answer. This is how the apparatus is described by its designer, Richard L. Gregory of the University of Bristol:

"The figure is presented back-illuminated, to avoid texture, and it is viewed through a sheet of Polaroid. A second sheet of Polaroid is placed over one eye crossed with the first so that no light from the figure reaches this eye. Between the eyes and the figure is a half-silvered mirror through which the figure is seen but which also reflects one or more small light sources mounted on an optical bench. These appear to lie in the figure; indeed, optically they *do* lie in the figure provided the path length of the lights to the eyes is the same as that of the figure to the eyes. But the small light sources are seen with both eyes while the figure is seen with only *one* eye because of the crossed Polaroids. By moving the lights along their optical bench, they may be placed so as to lie at the same distance as any selected part of the figure."

A Hudson-test picture that embodied both familiar-size and overlap depth cues was presented in the apparatus to a group of unskilled African workers, who for the most part do not show perception of pictorial depth in the Hudson test and in the construction test [*see illustration on page 328*]. The test picture showed a hunter and an antelope in the foreground and an elephant in the distance. The subjects set the movable light at the same apparent depth regardless of whether they were asked to place it above the hunter, the antelope or the elephant. In contrast, when three-dimensional perceivers were tested, they set the light farther away from themselves when placing it on the elephant than when setting it on the figures in the foreground. The result shows that they were not simply interpreting symbolic depth cues but were actually seeing depth in the picture.

When only familiar size was used as the depth cue, neither group of subjects placed the movable light farther back for the elephant. The result should not be surprising, since other studies have shown that familiar-size cues alone do not enable people even in Western cultures to see actual depth in a picture, even though they may interpret the picture three-dimensionally.

The fact that depth was seen in the picture only in the presence of overlap cues is of theoretical interest because it had been postulated that a perceptual mechanism for seeing depth cues where none are intended is responsible for certain geometric illusions, for example overestimating the length of the vertical limb of the letter *L*. If the mechanism is the same as the one for the perception of pictorial depth in Hudson's tests, then one would expect a decrease in the perception of geometric illusions in people who have low three-dimensional scores.

Do people who find pictures of the

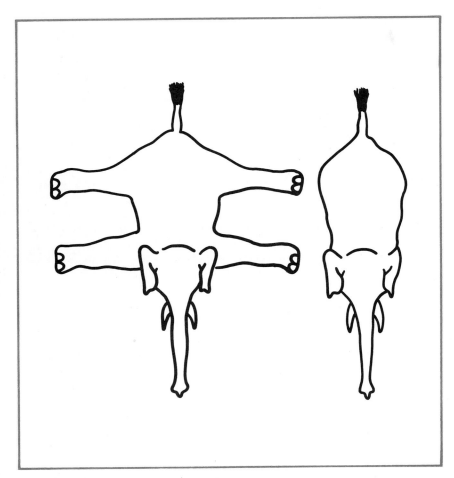

SPLIT-ELEPHANT DRAWING (*left*) was generally preferred by African children and adults to the top-view perspective drawing (*right*). One person, however, did not like the split drawing because he thought the elephant was jumping around in a dangerous manner.

perspective type difficult to interpret tend to prefer pictures that depict the essential characteristics of an object even if all those characteristics cannot be seen from a single viewpoint? Here again the first systematic cross-cultural observations were carried out by Hudson. He showed African children and adults pictures of an elephant. One view was like a photograph of an elephant seen from above; the other was a top view of an elephant with its legs unnaturally split to the sides. With only one exception all the subjects preferred the drawing of the split elephant [see bottom illustration on opposite page]. The one person who did not prefer the drawing said that it was because the elephant was jumping about dangerously.

Other studies have shown that preference for drawings of the split type is not confined to meaningful pictures but also applies to geometric representations. Unskilled Zambian workers were shown a wire model and were asked to make a drawing of it. Only an insignificant proportion of them drew a figure that had pictorial depth; most drew a flat figure of the split type [see bottom illustration on page 329]. They also preferred the split drawing when they were shown the model and were asked to choose between it and a perspective drawing. Then the process was reversed, and the subjects were asked to choose the appropriate wire model after looking at a drawing. Only a few chose the three-dimensional model after looking at the split drawing; instead they chose a flat wire model that resembled the drawing. Paradoxically the split drawing had proved to be less efficient than the less preferred perspective drawing when an actual object had to be identified.

Although preference for drawings of the split type has only recently been studied systematically, indications of such a preference have long been apparent in the artistic styles of certain cultures, for example the Indians of the northwestern coast of North America. Other instances of the split style in art are rock paintings in the caves of the Sahara and primitive art found in Siberia and New Zealand. What art historians often fail to note is that the style is universal. It can be found in the drawings of children in all cultures, even in those cultures where the style is considered manifestly wrong by adults.

Perspective drawings and drawings of the split type are not equally easy to interpret. Even industrial draftsmen with a great deal of experience in interpreting engineering drawings, which are essentially of the split type, find it more difficult to assemble simple models from engineering drawings than from perspective drawings.

One theory of the origin of the split style was put forward by the anthropologist Franz Boas. His hypothesis postulated the following sequence of events. Solid sculpture was gradually adapted to the ornamentation of objects such as boxes or bracelets. In order to make a box or a bracelet the artist had to reduce the sculpture to a surface pattern and include an opening in the solid form, so that when the sculptured object was flattened out, it became a picture of the split type. It is possible that this development led to the beginnings of split drawings and that the natural preference of the style ensured its acceptance. There is no historical evidence that this evolution actually took place, however, and it does seem that the hypothesis is unnecessarily complicated.

The anthropologist Claude Lévi-Strauss has proposed a theory in which the split style has social origins. According to him, split representation can be explored as a function of a sociological theory of split personality. This trait is common in "mask cultures," where privileges, emblems and degrees of prestige are displayed by means of elaborate masks. The use of these mask symbols apparently generates a great deal of per-

STYLIZED BEAR rendered by the Tsimshian Indians on the Pacific coast of British Columbia is an example of split drawing developed to a high artistic level. According to anthropologist Franz Boas, the drawings are ornamental and not intended to convey what an object looks like. The symbolic elements represent specific characteristics of the object.

sonality stress. Personalities are torn asunder, and this finds its reflection in split-style art.

Both Boas' and Lévi-Strauss's hypotheses ignore the universality of the phenomenon. If one accepts the existence of a fundamental identity of perceptual processes in all human beings and extrapolates from the data I have described, one is led to postulate the following. In all societies children have an aesthetic preference for drawings of the split type. In most societies this preference is suppressed because the drawings do not convey information about the depicted objects as accurately as perspective drawings do. Therefore aesthetic preference is sacrificed on the altar of efficiency in communication.

Some societies, however, have developed the split drawing to a high artistic level. This development occurs if the drawings are not regarded as a means of communication about objects or if the drawings incorporate cues that compensate for the loss of communication value due to the adoption of the split style. Both of these provisions are found in the art of the Indians of the Pacific Northwest. These pictures were intended to serve primarily as ornaments. They also incorporate symbolic elements that enable the viewer to interpret the artist's intention. Every such code, however, carries the penalty that communication is confined to people familiar with the code. Highly stylized art is not likely to be easily understood outside of its specific culture. Thus whereas the same psychological processes under the influence of different cultural forces may lead to widely different artistic styles, the styles arrived at are not equally efficient in conveying the correct description of objects and evoking the perception of pictorial depth.

What are the forces responsible for the lack of perception of pictorial depth in pictures drawn in accordance with the efficacious conventions of the West? At present we can only speculate. Perhaps the basic difficulty lies in the observers' inability to integrate the pictorial elements. They see individual symbols and cues but are incapable of linking all the elements into a consolidated whole. To the purely pragmatic question "Do drawings offer us a universal lingua franca?" a more precise answer is available. The answer is no. There are significant differences in the way pictures can be interpreted. The task of mapping out these differences in various cultures is only beginning.

The Origins of Alienation

by Urie Bronfenbrenner
August 1974

*It seems clear that the degree of estrangement
between young people and adults in the U.S.
is currently higher than it has been in other
times. The causes lie in evolutionary changes
in the American family*

Profound changes are taking place in the lives of America's children and young people. The institution that is at the center of these changes and that itself shows the most rapid and radical transformation is the American family, the major context in which a person grows up. The primary causes and consequences of change, however, lie outside the home. The causes are to be found in such unlikely quarters as business, urban planning and transportation systems; the ultimate effects of change are seen most frequently in American schools and—not as often but more disturbingly—in the courts, clinics and mental and penal institutions. The direction of change is one of disorganization rather than constructive development.

The disorganization is experienced at two levels. In the first instance it affects the structure and function of society and its primary institutions; then it is rapidly reflected in the structure and function of individual human beings, particularly those who are still in the process of development: children and young people. The crux of the problem lies in the failure of the young person to be integrated into his society. He feels uninterested, disconnected and perhaps even hostile to the people and activities in his environment. He wants "to do his own thing" but often is not sure what it is or with whom to do it. Even when he thinks he has found it—and them—the experience often proves unsuccessful and interest wanes.

This feeling, and fact, of disconnectedness from people and activities has a name that has become familiar: alienation. My purpose here is to explore the origins of alienation, to identify the circumstances that give rise to it and to consider how these circumstances might be altered in order to reverse the process. As I have suggested, although alienation ul-timately affects the individual, it has its roots in the institutions of the society, and among these institutions the family plays a particularly critical role. I can therefore begin my inquiry by examining the changes that have taken place in the American family over recent decades.

Family Structure

The family of 1974 is significantly different from the family of only 25 years ago. Today almost 45 percent of the nation's mothers work outside the home. The greatest increase has occurred for mothers of preschool children: one in every three mothers with children under six is working today. As more mothers go to work, the number of other adults in the family who could care for the child has shown a marked decrease. For example, 50 years ago half of the households in Massachusetts included at least one adult besides the parents; today the figure is only 4 percent.

The divorce rate among families with children has risen substantially during the past 20 years. The percent of children from divorced families is almost twice what it was a decade ago. If present trends continue, one child in six will lose a parent through divorce by the time he is 18.

In 1970, 10 percent of all children under six—2.2 million of them—were living in single-parent families with no father in the home, almost double the rate for a decade ago. The average income for a single-parent family with children under six was $3,100 in 1970—well below the "poverty" line ($4,000 per year for a family of four). Even when the mother worked, her average income of $4,200 barely exceeded the poverty level. Among families in poverty 45 percent of all children under six were living in single-parent households; in nonpov-erty families the corresponding figure was only 3.5 percent.

Of the 5.6 million preschool children whose mothers are in the labor force, one million live in families below the poverty line. Another million children of working mothers live in near-poverty (income between $4,000 and $7,000 for a family of four). All these children would have to be on welfare if the mother did not work. Finally, there are about 2.5 million children under six whose mothers do not work but whose family income is below the poverty level. Without counting the many thousands of children in families above the poverty line who are in need of child-care services, this makes a total of about 4.5 million children under six whose families need some help if normal family life is to be sustained.

The situation is particularly critical for the families of black Americans. Of all black children 53 percent live in families below the poverty line; the corresponding figure for whites is 11 percent. Of all black children 44 percent have mothers who are in the labor force; the corresponding figure for whites is 26 percent. Of all black children more than 30 percent live in single-parent families; the corresponding figure for whites is 7 percent. The census does not provide comparable information for other groups living under duress, such as American Indians, Mexican Americans and whites living in Appalachia. If and when such data become available, they are likely to show similar trends.

During the past decade many of us have become familiar with the plight of poor families in general terms, but we may not yet have recognized the impact of poverty at the concrete level and our own direct responsibility for its destructive effects. A case in point is the scandal of infant mortality. At the latest count, in 1972, the U.S. ranked 14th in the world in combating mortality during the first year of life—behind East Germany—and our ranking had been dropping steadily. The overall figures for the U.S., dismaying as they are, mask even greater inequities. Infant mortality is almost twice as high for nonwhites as for whites; within New York City it is three times as high in central Harlem as it is in Forest Hills. Several different studies have related infant mortality to inadequate prenatal care. What happens if that care is delivered to poor people? The answer to that question is available in data from the maternal- and infant-care projects the Department of Health, Education, and Welfare financed in the mid-1960's in slum sections of 14 cities. In the target areas of such programs there was a dramatic drop in infant mortality: from 34.2 per 1,000 live births in 1964 to 21.5 in 1969 in Denver, from 33.4 to 13.4 in Omaha, from 25.4 in 1965 to 14.3 in 1969 in Birmingham. Among the populations served by these programs there were also significant reductions in premature births, in repeated teen-age pregnancy, in conceptions by women over 35 and in the number of families with more than four children. It is a reflection of

our distorted priorities that these programs are currently in jeopardy even though their proposed replacement through revenue-sharing is not yet on the horizon. The phasing out of these programs will result in a return of mortality to the earlier levels: more infants will die.

The record in infant and maternal care is only one example of this country's failure to support its children and families living in poverty. It is not only disadvantaged families, however, that experience frustration and failure; for families that can get along the rats may be gone but the rat race remains. The demands of a job that claims mealtimes, evenings and weekends as well as days; the trips and moves necessary to get ahead or simply to hold one's own; the increasing time spent commuting, entertaining, going out, meeting social and community obligations—all of these produce a situation in which a child often spends more time with a passive baby-sitter than with a participating parent.

The forces undermining the parental role are particularly strong in the case of fathers. Compare, for example, the results of a study of middle-class fathers

who told interviewers they were spending an average of 15 to 20 minutes a day playing with their one-year-old infants with another study in which the father's voice was actually recorded by means of a microphone attached to the infant's shirt. "The data indicate that fathers spend relatively little time interacting with their infants. The mean number of interactions per day was 2.7, and the average number of seconds per day was 37.7."

Another factor reducing interaction between parents and children is the changing physical environment in the home, in which proliferating television-viewing areas and playrooms and "family rooms" and master bedrooms increasingly separate the generations. Perhaps the ultimate in isolation is reached in a "cognition crib" described in a brochure I received recently in the mail. It is equipped with a tape recorder that can be actuated by the sound of the infant's voice. Frames built into the sides of the crib make possible the insertion of "programmed play modules for sensory and physical practice." The modules come in sets of six, which the parent is "encouraged to change" every three months in order to keep pace with the child's development. Since "faces are what an infant sees first, six soft plastic faces... adhere to the window." Other modules include mobiles, a crib aquarium, a piggy bank and "ego-building mirrors." Parents are hardly mentioned except as potential purchasers.

Isolation

It is not only parents of whom children are deprived but also people in general. Developments of recent decades—many in themselves beneficent—conspire to isolate children from the rest of society. The fragmentation of the extended family, the separation of residential and business areas, the breakdown of neighborhoods, zoning ordinances, occupational mobility, child-labor laws, the abolition of the apprentice system, consolidated schools, supermarkets, television, separate patterns of social life for different age groups, the working mother, the delegation of child care to specialists—all these manifestations of progress operate to decrease opportunity and incentive for meaningful contact between children and people older or younger than themselves.

This erosion of the social fabric isolates not only the child but also his family. In particular, with the breakdown of the community, the neighborhood and the extended family and the rise in the

INFANT MORTALITY (deaths before one year of age) is one of the indexes of maternal and child care by which the U.S. no longer ranks well among advanced industrial nations. Recent studies have correlated infant mortality specifically with poor prenatal health care.

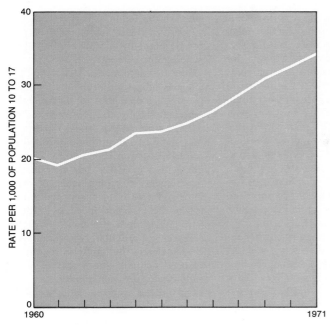

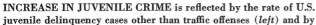

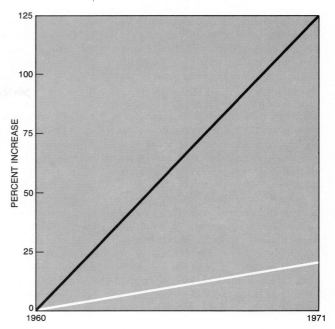

INCREASE IN JUVENILE CRIME is reflected by the rate of U.S. juvenile delinquency cases other than traffic offenses (*left*) and by the large increase in arrests of people under 18 (*black*) compared with the smaller increase (*white*) for those 18 and over (*right*).

number of homes from which the father is absent, increasingly great responsibility has fallen on young mothers. For some of them the resulting pressures appear to be mounting beyond the point of endurance. The growing number of divorces is now accompanied by a new phenomenon: the unwillingness of either parent to take custody of the child. In more and more families the woman is fleeing without waiting for a formal separation. Increasing numbers of married women are being reported to police departments as missing, and news reports indicate a quantum leap in the number of runaway wives whom private detectives, hired by fathers who are left with the children, are trying to find.

There is a more gruesome trend: The killing of infants under one year of age has been increasing sporadically since 1957. The infanticide rate rose from 3.1 per 100,000 of the infant population in that year to 4.7 in 1970. A similar pattern appears for less violent forms of child abuse that involve bodily injury. A 1970 survey of more than 1,300 families projected a nationwide total of from two to four million battered-child cases a year, with the highest rates occurring among adolescents. Significantly, more than 90 percent of the incidents took place in the child's home. The most severe injuries occurred in single-parent homes and were inflicted by the mother herself, a fact that reflects the desperation of the situation faced by some young mothers today.

The centrifugal forces generated with-

in the family by its increasing isolation propel its members in different directions. As parents spend more time in work and community activities, children are placed in or gravitate toward organized or informal group settings. Between 1965 and 1970 the number of children enrolled in day-care centers doubled, and the demand today far exceeds the supply. More and more children come home from school to an empty house or apartment. When he is not in preschool or school, the child spends increasing amounts of time in the company of only his age-mates; the vacuum created by the withdrawal of parents and other adults has been filled by the informal peer group. A recent study has found that at every age and grade level children today show greater dependence on their peers than they did a decade ago. A parallel investigation indicates that such susceptibility to group influence is higher among children from homes in which at least one parent is frequently absent. Moreover, peer-oriented youngsters describe their parents as being less affectionate and less firm in discipline. Attachment to age-mates appears to be influenced more by a lack of attention and concern at home than by any positive attraction of the peer group itself; in fact, these children have a rather negative view of their friends and of themselves as well. They are pessimistic about the future, they rate lower in responsibility and leadership and they are more likely to engage in such antisocial behavior as lying, teasing other children,

playing hooky or "doing something illegal."

These, of course, are among the milder consequences of alienation. The more serious manifestations are reflected in the rising rates of youthful runaways, school dropouts, drug abuse, suicide, delinquency, vandalism and violence documented for the White House Conference on Children in 1970 and in more recent government publications. The proportion of youngsters between the ages of 10 and 18 arrested for drug abuse doubled between 1964 and 1968. Since 1963 juvenile delinquency has been increasing at a higher rate than the juvenile population; more than half of the crimes involve vandalism, theft or breaking and entry; if the present trends continue, one in every nine youngsters will appear in juvenile court before the age of 18. These figures index only offenses that are detected and prosecuted. One wonders how high the numbers must climb before we acknowledge that they reflect deep and pervasive problems in the treatment of children and youth in our society.

The Neglected Family

What is the ultimate source of these problems? Where do the roots of alienation lie? Studies of human behavior have yielded few generalizations that are firmly grounded in research and broadly accepted by specialists, but there are two answers to the foregoing questions that do meet these exacting criteria.

1. Over the past three decades liter-

ally thousands of investigations have been conducted to identify the developmental antecedents of behavior disorders and social pathology. The results point to an almost omnipresent overriding factor: family disorganization.

2. Much of the same research also shows that the forces of disorganization arise primarily not from within the family but from the circumstances in which the family finds itself and from the way of life that is imposed on it by those circumstances.

Specifically, when those circumstances and the way of life they generate undermine relationships of trust and emotional security between family members, when they make it difficult for parents to care for, educate and enjoy their children, when there is no support or recognition from the outside world for one's role as a parent and when time spent with one's family means frustration of career, personal fulfillment and peace of mind, then the development of the child is adversely affected. The first symptoms are emotional and motivational: disaffection, indifference, irresponsibility and inability to follow through in activities requiring applica-

tion and persistence. In less favorable family circumstances the reaction takes the form of antisocial acts injurious to the child and to society. Finally, for children who come from environments in which the capacity of the family to function has been most severely traumatized by such destructive forces as poverty, ill health and discrimination, the consequences for the child are seen not only in the spheres of emotional and social maladjustment but also in the impairment of the most distinctive of human capacities: the ability to think, to deal with concepts and numbers at even the most elementary level.

The extent of this impairment in contemporary American society, and its roots in social disorganization, are reflected in recent studies. A New York State commission on education studied more than 300 schools and reported that 58 percent of the variation in student achievement could be predicted by three socioeconomic factors: broken homes, overcrowded housing and the educational level of the head of the household; when racial and ethnic variables were introduced into the analysis, they accounted for less than an additional 2 per-

cent of the variation. And there is a secular trend: each year "more and more children throughout the state are falling below minimum competence."

How are we to reverse this trend? The evidence indicates that the most promising solutions do not lie within the child's immediate setting, the classroom and the school. An impressive series of investigations, notably the studies published by James Coleman in 1966 and by Christopher Jencks in 1972, demonstrate that the characteristics of schools, of classrooms and even of teachers predict very little of the variation in school achievement. What does predict it is family background, particularly the characteristics that define the family in relation to its social context: the world of work, neighborhood and community.

The critical question thus becomes: Can our social institutions be changed—old ones modified and new ones introduced—so as to rebuild and revitalize the social context that families and children require for their effective function and growth? Let me consider some institutions on the contemporary American scene that are likely to have the greatest impact, for better or for worse, on the welfare of America's children and young people.

Day Care

Day care is coming to America. The question is what kind. Shall we, in response to external pressures to "put people to work" or for considerations of personal convenience, allow a pattern to develop in which the care of young children is delegated to specialists, further separating the child from his family and reducing the family's and the community's feeling of responsibility for their children? Or will day care be designed, as it can be, to reinvolve and strengthen the family as the primary and proper agent for making human beings human?

As Project Head Start demonstrated, preschool programs can have no lasting constructive impact on the child's development unless they affect not only the child himself but also the people who constitute his enduring day-to-day environment. This means that parents and other people from the child's immediate environment must play a prominent part in the planning and administration of day-care programs and also participate actively as volunteers and aides. It means that the program cannot be confined to the center but must reach out into the home and the community so that the entire neighborhood is caught up in activities in behalf of its children. We

INCREASE IN VIOLENT CRIME is reflected in Federal Bureau of Investigation statistics covering murders and nonnegligent manslaughters (*black curve and scale at left*) and robberies (*white curve and scale at right*) known to and reported by police departments.

need to experiment with putting day-care centers within reach of the significant people in the child's life. For some families this will mean neighborhood centers, for others centers at the place of work. A great deal of variation and innovation will be required to find the appropriate solutions for different groups in different settings.

Such solutions confront a critical obstacle in contemporary American society. The keystone of an effective day-care program is parent participation, but how can parents participate if they work full time—which is one of the main reasons the family needs day care in the first place? I see only one possible solution: increased opportunities and rewards for part-time employment. It was in the light of this consideration that the report of the White House Conference urged business and industry, and governments as employers, to increase the number and the status of part-time positions. In addition the report recommended that state legislatures enact a "Fair Part-Time Employment Practices Act" to prohibit discrimination in job opportunity, rate of pay, fringe benefits and status for parents who sought or engaged in part-time employment.

I should like to report the instructive experience of one state legislator who attempted to put through such a bill, Assemblywoman Constance Cook of New York. Mrs. Cook sent me a copy of her bill as it had been introduced in committee. It began, "No employer shall set as a condition of employment, salary, promotion, fringe benefits, seniority" and so on that an employee who is the parent or guardian of a child under 18 years of age shall be required to work more than 40 hours a week. Forty hours a week, of course, is full time; Mrs. Cook informed me that there was no hope of getting a bill through with a lower limit. It turned out that even 40 hours was too low. The bill was not passed even in committee. The pressure from business and industry was too great, and they insisted on the right to require their employees to work overtime.

(There is a ray of hope, however. In the settlement of the United Automobile Workers' 1973 strike against the Chrysler Corporation a limit was placed for the first time on the company policy of mandatory overtime.)

These concerns bring me to what I regard as the most important single factor affecting the welfare of the nation's children. I refer to the place and status of women in American society. Whatever the future trend may be, the fact remains that in our society today the care of chil-

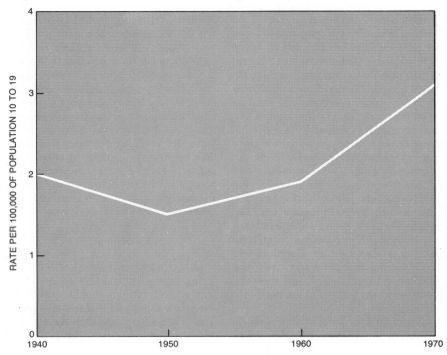

JUVENILE SUICIDE RATE (for adolescents from 10 to 19 years old) has risen recently. The rate for the population as a whole, in contrast, has stayed around 11 since World War II.

dren depends overwhelmingly on women, and specifically on mothers. Moreover, with the withdrawal of the social supports for the family to which I alluded above, the position of women and mothers has become more and more isolated. With the breakdown of the community, the neighborhood and the extended family an increasing responsibility for the care and upbringing of children has fallen on the young mother. Under these circumstances it is not surprising that many young women in America are in revolt. I understand and share their sense of rage, but I fear the consequences of some of the solutions they advocate, which will have the effect of isolating children still further from the kind of care and attention they need. There is, of course, a constructive implication to this line of thought, in that a major route to the rehabilitation of children and youth in American society lies in the enhancement of the status and power of women in all walks of life—in the home as well as on the job.

Work and Responsibility

One of the most significant effects of age segregation in our society has been the isolation of children from the world of work. Once children not only saw what their parents did for a living but also shared substantially in the task; now many children have only a vague notion of the parent's job and have had little or

no opportunity to observe the parent (or for that matter any other adult) fully engaged in his or her work. Although there is no systematic research evidence on this subject, it appears likely that the absence of such exposure contributes significantly to the growing alienation among children and young people. Experience in other modern urban societies indicates that the isolation of children from adults in the world of work is not inevitable; it can be countered by creative social innovations. Perhaps the most imaginative and pervasive of these is the common practice in the U.S.S.R., in which a department in a factory, an office, an institute or a business enterprise adopts a group of children as its "wards." The children's group is typically a school classroom, but it may also include a nursery, a hospital ward or any other setting in which children are dealt with collectively. The workers visit the children's group wherever it may be and also invite the youngsters to their place of work in order to familiarize the children with the nature of their activities and with themselves as people. The aim is not vocational education but rather acquaintance with adults as participants in the world of work.

There seems to be nothing in such an approach that would be incompatible with the values and aims of our own society, and this writer has urged its adaptation to the American scene. Acting on this suggestion, David A. Goslin of the

Russell Sage Foundation persuaded the Detroit *Free Press* to participate in an unusual experiment as a prelude to the White House Conference on Children. By the time it was over two groups of 12-year-old children, one from a slum area and the other predominantly middle class, had spent six to seven hours a day for three days in virtually every department of the newspaper, not just observing but participating actively in the department's work. There were boys and girls in the pressroom, the city room, the composing room, the advertising department and the delivery department. The employees of the *Free Press* entered into the experiment with serious misgivings, but, as a documentary film that was made of the project makes clear, the children were not bored, nor were the adults—and the paper did get out every day.

If a child is to become a responsible person, he not only must be exposed to adults engaged in demanding tasks but also must himself participate in such tasks. In the perspective of cross-cultural research one of the most salient characteristics of the U.S. is what Nicholas Hobbs, a former president of the American Psychological Association, has called "the inutility of childhood." Our children are not entrusted with any real responsibilities. Little that they do really matters. They are given duties rather than responsibilities; the ends and means have been determined by someone else and their job is to fulfill an assignment involving little judgment, decision making or risk. This practice is intended to protect children from burdens beyond their years, but there is reason to believe it has been carried too far in contemporary American society and has contributed to the alienation of young people and their alleged incapacity to deal constructively with personal and social problems. The evidence indicates that children acquire the capacity to cope with difficult situations when they have an opportunity to take on consequential responsibilities in relation to others and are held accountable for them.

School

Although training for responsibility by giving responsibility clearly begins in the family, the institution that has probably done the most to keep children insulated from challenging social tasks is the American school system. For historical reasons rooted in the separation of church and state this system has been isolated from responsible social concern in both content and actual location. In terms of content, education in America, when viewed from a cross-cultural perspective, seems peculiarly one-sided, emphasizing subject matter to the exclusion of another fundamental aspect of the child's development for which there is no generally accepted term in our educational vocabulary: what the Germans call *Erziehung*, the Russians *vospitanie* and the French *éducation*. Perhaps the best equivalents are "upbringing" or "character education," expressions that sound outmoded and irrelevant to us. In many countries of western and eastern Europe, however, the corresponding terms are the names of what constitutes the core of the educational process: the development of the child's qualities as a person—his values, motives and patterns of social response.

Our schools, and consequently our children, are also physically insulated from the life of the community, neighborhood and families the schools purport to serve and from the life for which they are supposedly preparing the children. And the insularity is repeated within the school system itself, where children are segregated into classrooms that have little social connection with one another or with the school as a common community for which members can take active responsibility.

During the past decade the trend toward segregation of the school from the rest of the society has been accelerated by the forces of social disorganization to which I have referred. As a result the schools have become one of the most potent breeding grounds of alienation in American society. For this reason it is of crucial importance for the welfare and development of school-age children that schools be reintegrated into the life of the community.

It is commonplace among educators to affirm that the task of the school is to prepare the child "for life." There is one role

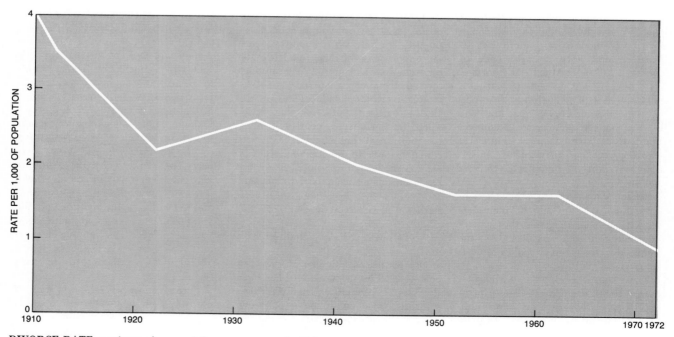

DIVORCE RATE, a mirror of some of the pressures on the U.S. family, has doubled in each of the past two 30-year periods. Divorce now comes somewhat later in marriage, so that the number of children involved in each divorce has risen disproportionately.

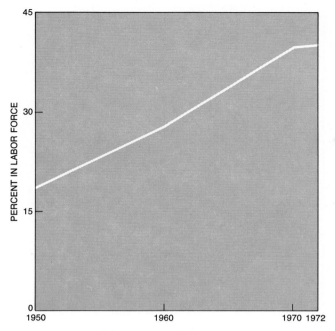
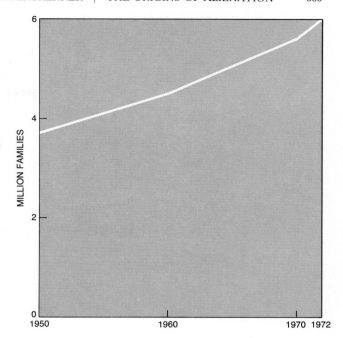

STRESS ON MOTHERS is suggested by data for working mothers (*left*) and for families headed by women (*right*). The curve at left shows specifically the labor-force participation rate for married women whose husbands are present and who have children up to 17 years old at home. The female heads of families include women who are single, divorced or widowed or whose husbands are absent.

in life the overwhelming majority of all children will ultimately play but for which they are given virtually no concrete preparation. It is parenthood. In cross-cultural observations I have been struck by the American child's relative lack of ease in relating to infants and young children, engaging their interest and enjoying their company. With the important exception of certain minority groups, including blacks, many young people never have experience in extended care of a baby or a young child until they have their own.

A solution to this problem, which speaks as well to the need to give young people in our society genuine and consequential responsibility, is to introduce truly functional courses in human development into the regular school curriculum. These would be distinguished in a number of important ways from units on "family life" as they are now usually taught in junior high school (chiefly to girls who do not plan to go on to college). Now the material is typically presented in vicarious form, that is, through reading or discussion or possibly through role-playing rather than actual role-taking. In contrast, the approach being proposed here would have as its core a responsible and active concern for the lives of young children and their families. Such an experience could be facilitated by locating day-care centers and preschool programs in or near schools so that they could be made an integral part

of the curriculum. The older children would work with the younger ones on a regular basis, both at school and in the young children's homes, where they would have an opportunity to become acquainted with the youngsters' families and their circumstances.

Neighborhood

Much of what happens to children and families is determined by the ecology of the neighborhood in which the family lives. The implication of this principle for our own times is illustrated in a research report on the effect of some "new towns" on the lives of children. The study compared the reactions of children living in 18 new model communities in West Germany with those of youngsters living in older German cities. The research was conducted by the Urban and Planning Institute in Nuremberg. According to a report in *The New York Times*, in the new towns, "amid soaring rectangular shapes of apartment houses with shaded walks, big lawns and fenced-in play areas, the children for whom much of this has been designed apparently feel isolated, regimented and bored." The study found that the children gauged their freedom not by the extent of open areas around them but by the liberty they had to be among people and things that excited them and fired their imagination.

The implications of such research are

self-evident. In the planning and design of new communities, housing projects and urban renewal, both public and private planners need to give explicit consideration to the kind of world being created for the children who will grow up in these settings. Particular attention should be given to the opportunities the environment presents (or precludes) for the involvement of children with people who are both older and younger than themselves.

Among the specific factors to be considered are the location of shops and businesses where children can have contact with adults at work, recreational and day-care facilities readily accessible to parents as well as children, provision for a family neighborhood center and family-oriented facilities and services, the availability of public transportation and —perhaps most important of all—places to walk, sit and talk in common company.

It may be fitting to end this discussion with a proposal for nothing more radical than providing a setting in which young and old can simply sit and talk. The fact that such settings are disappearing and have to be recreated deliberately points both to the roots of the problem and to its remedy. The evil and the cure lie not in the victims of alienation but in the social institutions that produce alienation, and in their failure to be responsive to the most human needs and values of a democratic society.

BIBLIOGRAPHIES

I. BIOLOGICAL AND DEVELOPMENTAL DETERMINERS OF BEHAVIOR

1. Brain Changes in Response to Experience

CHEMICAL AND ANATOMICAL PLASTICITY OF BRAIN. Edward L. Bennett, Marian C. Diamond, David Krech and Mark R. Rosenzweig in *Science*, Vol. 146, No. 3644, pages 610–619; October 30, 1964.

EFFECTS OF ENVIRONMENT ON DEVELOPMENT OF BRAIN AND BEHAVIOR. Mark R. Rosenzweig in *Biopsychology of Development*, edited by Ethel Tobach. Academic Press, 1971.

ENVIRONMENTAL INFLUENCES ON BRAIN AND BEHAVIOR OF YEAR-OLD RATS. Walter H. Riege in *Developmental Psychobiology*, Vol. 4, No. 2, pages 157–167; 1971.

QUANTITATIVE SYNAPTIC CHANGES WITH DIFFERENTIAL EXPERIENCE IN RAT BRAIN. Kjeld Møllgaard, Marian C. Diamond, Edward L. Bennett, Mark R. Rosenzweig and Bernice Lindner in *International Journal of Neuroscience*, Vol. 2, No. 2, pages 113–128; August, 1971.

2. Stress and Behavior

ADRENOCORTICAL ACTIVITY AND AVOIDANCE LEARNING AS A FUNCTION OF TIME AFTER AVOIDANCE TRAINING. Seymour Levine and F. Robert Brush in *Physiology & Behavior*, Vol. 2, No. 4, pages 385–388; October, 1967.

HORMONES AND CONDITIONING. Seymour Levine in *Nebraska Symposium on Motivation: 1968*, edited by William J. Arnold. University of Nebraska Press, 1968.

EFFECTS OF PEPTIDE HORMONES ON BEHAVIOR. David de Wied in *Frontiers in Neuroendocrinology*, edited by William F. Ganong and Luciano Martini. Oxford University Press, 1969.

THE NEUROENDOCRINE CONTROL OF PERCEPTION. R. I. Henkin in *Perception and Its Disorders: Proceedings of the Association for Research in Nervous Mental Disease*, 32, edited by D. Hamburg. Williams & Wilkins, 1970.

3. The Visual Cortex of the Brain

DISCHARGE PATTERNS AND FUNCTIONAL ORGANIZATION OF MAMMALIAN RETINA. Stephen W. Kuffler in *Journal of Neurophysiology*, Vol. 16, No. 1, pages 37–68; January, 1953.

INTEGRATIVE PROCESSES IN CENTRAL VISUAL PATHWAYS OF THE CAT. David M. Hubel in *Journal of the Optical Society of America*, Vol. 53, No. 1, pages 58–66; January, 1963.

RECEPTIVE FIELDS, BINOCULAR INTERACTION AND FUNCTIONAL ARCHITECTURE IN THE CAT'S VISUAL CORTEX. D. H. Hubel and T. N. Wiesel in *Journal of Physiology*, Vol. 160, No. 1, pages 106–154; January, 1962.

THE VISUAL PATHWAY. Ragnar Granit in *The Eye, Volume II: The Visual Process*, edited by Hugh Davson. Academic Press, 1962.

4. Pleasure Centers in the Brain

THE BEHAVIOR OF ORGANISMS: AN EXPERIMENTAL ANALYSIS. B. F. Skinner. Appleton-Century-Crofts, 1938.

DIENCEPHALON. Walter Rudolf Hess. Grune & Stratton, 1954.

PSYCHOSOMATIC DISEASE AND THE "VISCERAL BRAIN": RECENT DEVELOPMENTS BEARING ON THE PAPEZ THEORY OF EMOTION. Paul D. MacLean in *Psychosomatic Medicine*, Vol. 11, pages 338–353; 1949.

5. "Imprinting" in a Natural Laboratory

"IMPRINTING" IN ANIMALS. Eckhard H. Hess in *Scientific American*, Vol. 198, No. 3, pages 81–90; March, 1958.

IMPRINTING IN BIRDS. Eckhard H. Hess in *Science*, Vol. 146, No. 3648, pages 1128–1139; November 27, 1964.

INNATE FACTORS IN IMPRINTING. Eckhard H. Hess and Dorle B. Hess in *Psychonomic Science*, Vol. 14, No. 3, pages 129–130; February 10, 1969.

DEVELOPMENT OF SPECIES IDENTIFICATION IN BIRDS: AN INQUIRY INTO THE PRENATAL DETERMINANTS OF PERCEPTION. Gilbert Gottlieb. University of Chicago Press, 1971.

NATURAL HISTORY OF IMPRINTING. Eckhard H. Hess in *Integrative Events in Life Processes: Annals of The New York Academy of Sciences*, Vol. 193, 1972.

6. The Object in the World of the Infant

THE CONSTRUCTION OF REALITY IN THE CHILD. Jean Piaget. Basic Books, 1954.

THE CHILD AND MODERN PHYSICS. Jean Piaget in *Scientific American*, Vol. 196, No. 3, pages 46–51; March, 1957.

CAUSALITÉ, PERMANENCE ET RÉALITÉ PHÉNOMÉNALES: ETUDES DE PSYCHOLOGIE EXPÉRIMENTALE. A. Michotte. Louvain, Belgium: Publications Universitaires, 1962.

THE NATURE OF PERCEPTUAL ADAPTATION. Irvin Rock. Basic Books, 1966.

THE VISUAL WORLD OF INFANTS. T. G. R. Bower in *Scientific American*, Vol. 215, No. 6, pages 80–92; December, 1966.

SPACE PERCEPTION IN EARLY INFANCY: PERCEPTION WITHIN A COMMON AUDITORY-VISUAL SPACE. Eric Aronson and Shelley Rosenbloom in *Science*, Vol. 172, No. 3988, pages 1161–1163; June 11, 1971.

7. The "Visual Cliff"

BEHAVIOR OF LIGHT- AND DARK-REARED RATS ON A VISUAL CLIFF. E. J. Gibson, T. J. Tighe and R. D. Walk in *Science*, Vol. 126, No. 3,262, pages 80–81; July 5, 1957.

THE MECHANISM OF VISION. XI. A PRELIMINARY TEST OF INNATE ORGANIZATION. K. S. Lashley and J. T. Russell in *Journal of Genetic Psychology*, Vol. 45, No. 1, pages 136–144; September, 1934.

SPACE PERCEPTION OF TORTOISES. R. M. Yerkes in *The Journal of Comparative Neurology*, Vol. 14, No. 1, pages 17–26; March, 1904.

VISUALLY CONTROLLED LOCOMOTION AND VISUAL ORIENTATION IN ANIMALS. James J. Gibson in *The British Journal of Psychology*, Vol. 49, Part 3, pages 182–194; August, 1958.

II. PERCEPTION AND AWARENESS

8. Stabilized Images on the Retina

THE ORGANIZATION OF BEHAVIOR. D. O. Hebb. Wiley, 1949.

VISUAL EFFECTS OF VARYING THE EXTENT OF COMPENSATION FOR EYE MOVEMENTS. Lorrin A. Riggs and S. Ülker Tulunay in *Journal of the Optical Society of America*, Vol. 9, No. 8, pages 741–745; August, 1959.

VISUAL PERCEPTION APPROACHED BY THE METHOD OF STABILIZED IMAGES. R. M. Pritchard, W. Heron and D. O. Hebb in *Canadian Journal of Psychology*, Vol. 14, No. 2, pages 67–77; 1960.

9. The Processes of Vision

THE KINETIC DEPTH EFFECT. H. Wallach and D. N. O'Connell in *Journal of Experimental Psychology*, Vol. 45, No. 4, pages 205–218; April, 1953.

THE RELATION OF EYE MOVEMENTS, BODY MOTILITY AND EXTERNAL STIMULI TO DREAM CONTENT. William Dement and Edward A. Wolpert in *Journal of Experimental Psychology*, Vol. 55, No. 6, pages 543–553; June, 1958.

THE SENSES CONSIDERED AS PERCEPTUAL SYSTEMS. James J. Gibson. Houghton Mifflin, 1966.

COGNITIVE PSYCHOLOGY. Ulric Neisser. Appleton-Century-Crofts, 1967.

10. Eidetic Images

THE EIDETIC CHILD. Heinrich Klüver in *A Handbook of Child Psychology*, edited by Carl Murchison. Clark University Press, 1931.

EIDETIC IMAGERY, I: FREQUENCY. Ralph Norman Haber and Ruth B. Haber in *Perceptual and Motor Skills*, Vol. 19, pages 131–138; 1964.

EIDETIC IMAGERY: A CROSS-CULTURAL WILL-O -THE-WISP? Leonard W. Doob in *The Journal of Psychology*, Vol. 63, pages 13–34; 1966.

11. Visual Illusions

SENSATION AND PERCEPTION IN THE HISTORY OF EXPERIMENTAL PSYCHOLOGY. Edwin Garrigues Boring. Appleton-Century, 1942.

OPTICAL ILLUSIONS. S. Tolansky. Pergamon, 1964.

EYE AND BRAIN. R. L. Gregory. McGraw-Hill, 1966.

WILL SEEING MACHINES HAVE ILLUSIONS? R. L. Gregory in *Machine Intelligence I*, edited by N. L. Collins and Donald Michie. American Elsevier, 1967.

12. Multistability in Perception

THE ANALYSIS OF SENSATIONS AND THE RELATION OF THE PHYSICAL TO THE PSYCHICAL. Ernst Mach. Dover, 1959.

AMBIGUITY OF FORM: OLD AND NEW. Gerald H. Fisher in *Perception and Psychophysics*, Vol. 4, No. 3, pages 189–192; September, 1968.

TRIANGLES AS AMBIGUOUS FIGURES. Fred Attneave in *The American Journal of Psychology*, Vol. 81, No. 3, pages 447–453; September, 1968.

13. Perception of Disoriented Figures

RECOGNITION UNDER OBJECTIVE REVERSAL. George V. N. Dearborn in *The Psychological Review*, Vol. 6, No. 4, pages 395–406; July, 1899.

THE ANALYSIS OF SENSATIONS AND THE RELATION OF THE PHYSICAL TO THE PSYCHICAL. Ernst Mach, translated from the German by C. M. Williams. Dover, 1959.

ORIENTATION AND SHAPE I AND II in *Human Spatial Orientation*. I. P. Howard and W. B. Templeton. Wiley, 1966.

SIMILARITY IN VISUALLY PERCEIVED FORMS. Erich Goldmeier in *Psychological Issues*, Vol. 8, No. 1, Monograph 29; 1972.

ORIENTATION AND FORM. Irvin Rock. Academic Press, 1974.

14. Vision and Touch

ADAPTATION OF DISARRANGED HAND-EYE COORDINATION CONTINGENT UPON RE-AFFERENT STIMULATION. Richard Held and Alan Hein in *Perceptual and Motor Skills*, Vol. 8, No. 2, pages 87–90; June, 1958.

AN ESSAY TOWARDS A NEW THEORY OF VISION. George Berkeley. Dutton, 1910.

THE NATURE OF PERCEPTUAL ADAPTATION. Irvin Rock. Basic Books, 1966.

PERCEPTION. Julian Hochberg. Prentice-Hall, 1964.

PERCEPTUAL ADAPTATION TO INVERTED, REVERSED, AND DISPLACED VISION. Charles S. Harris in *Psychological Review*, Vol. 72, No. 6, pages 419–444; November, 1965.

15. Sources of Ambiguity in the Prints of Maurits C. Escher

SOME FACTORS DETERMINING FIGURE-GROUND ARTICULATION. M. R. Harrower in *British Journal of Psychology*, Vol. 26, No. 4, pages 407–424; 1936.

PERCEPTION. Hans-Lukas Teuber in *Handbook of Physiology: Section 1—Neurophysiology, Vol. 3*. Edited by H. W. Magoun. Williams & Wilkins, 1961.

THE GRAPHIC WORK OF M. C. ESCHER. M. C. Escher. Balantine, 1971.

THE WORLD OF M. C. ESCHER, edited by J. L. Locher. Abrams, 1971.

NEW ASPECTS OF PAUL KLEE'S BAUHAUS STYLE. M. L. Teuber in *Paul Klee, Paintings and Watercolors from the Bauhaus Years, 1921–1931*. Des Moines Art Center, 1973.

III.   MEMORY, LEARNING AND THINKING

16. The Control of Short-term Memory

HUMAN MEMORY: A PROPOSED SYSTEM AND ITS CONTROL PROCESSES. R. C. Atkinson and R. M. Shiffrin in *Advances in the Psychology of Learning and Motivation Research and Theory: Vol. II*, edited by K. W. Spence and J. T. Spence. Academic Press, 1968.

MEMORY SEARCH. Richard M. Shiffrin in *Models of Human Memory*, edited by Donald A. Norman. Academic Press, 1970.

FORGETTING: TRACE EROSION OR RETRIEVAL FAILURE. Richard M. Shiffrin in *Science*, Vol. 168, No. 3939, pages 1601–1603; June 26, 1970.

HUMAN MEMORY AND THE CONCEPT OF REINFORCE-
MENT. R. C. Atkinson and T. D. Wickens in *The
Nature of Reinforcement,* edited by R. Glaser.
Academic Press, 1971.

AN ANALYSIS OF REHEARSAL PROCESSES IN FREE RECALL.
D. Rundus in *Journal of Experimental Psychology,*
Vol. 89, pages 63–77; July, 1971.

17. How We Remember What We See

EMERGENCE AND RECOVERY OF INITIALLY UNAVAILABLE
PERCEPTUAL MATERIAL. Ralph Norman Haber and
Mathew Hugh Erdelyi in *Journal of Verbal Learning and Verbal Behavior,* Vol. 6, No. 4, pages
618–628; August, 1967.

DIRECT MEASURES OF SHORT-TERM VISUAL STORAGE.
Ralph Norman Haber and L. G. Standing in *The
Quarterly Journal of Experimental Psychology,*
Vol. 21, Part 1, pages 43–54; February, 1969.

PROCESSING OF SEQUENTIALLY PRESENTED LETTERS.
Ralph Norman Haber and Linda Sue Nathanson
in *Perception and Psychophysics,* Vol. 5, No. 6,
pages 359–361; June, 1969.

18. How to Teach Animals

THE BEHAVIOR OF ORGANISMS. B. F. Skinner. Appleton-
Century-Crofts, 1938.

19. The Split Brain in Man

CEREBRAL COMMISSUROTOMY. J. E. Bogen, E. D. Fisher
and P. J. Vogel in *Journal of the American Medical
Association,* Vol. 194, No. 12, pages 1328–1329;
December 20, 1965.

CEREBRAL ORGANIZATION AND BEHAVIOR. R. W. Sperry
in *Science,* Vol. 133, No. 3466, pages 1749–1757;
June 2, 1961.

LANGUAGE AFTER SECTION OF THE CEREBRAL COM-
MISSURES. M. S. Gazzaniga and R. W. Sperry in
Brain, Vol. 90, Part 1, pages 131–148; 1967.

OBSERVATIONS ON VISUAL PERCEPTION AFTER DIS-
CONNEXION OF THE CEREBRAL HEMISPHERES IN
MAN. M. S. Gazzaniga, J. E. Bogen and R. W.
Sperry in *Brain,* Vol. 88, Part 2, pages 221–
236; 1965.

20. Teaching Language to an Ape

SYNTACTIC STRUCTURES. Noam Chomsky. Mouton, 1957.

THE GENESIS OF LANGUAGE. Edited by F. Smith and
G. A. Miller. M.I.T. Press, 1966.

BEHAVIOR OF NONHUMAN PRIMATES: VOLS. III–IV.
Edited by Fred Stollnitz and Allan M. Schrier.
Academic Press, 1971.

LANGUAGE IN CHIMPANZEE? David Premack in *Science,*
Vol. 172, No. 3985, pages 808–822; May 21, 1971.

A FIRST LANGUAGE: THE EARLY STAGES. Roger Brown.
Harvard University Press, 1973.

21. Slips of the Tongue

THE NON-ANOMALOUS NATIVE OF ANOMALOUS UTTER-
ANCES. Victoria A. Fromkin in *Language,* Vol. 47,
No. 1, pages 27–52; March, 1971.

LANGUAGE AND MIND. Noam Chomsky. Harcourt Brace
Jovanovich, 1972.

SPEECH ERRORS AS LINGUISTIC EVIDENCE. Edited by
Victoria A. Fromkin. Mouton, 1973.

22. Bilingualism and Information-Processing

LANGUAGES IN CONTACT: FINDINGS AND PROBLEMS. Uriel
Weinrich. Linguistic Circle of New York, 1953.

PROBLEMS OF BILINGUALISM. Edited by John Mac-
namara. *The Journal of Social Issues,* Vol. 23, No.
2; April, 1967.

READING AND TALKING BILINGUALLY. Paul A. Kolers
in *The American Journal of Psychology,* Vol. 79,
No. 3, pages 357–376; September, 1966.

WORDS AND THINGS. Roger Brown. Free Press, 1958.

23. Problem-Solving

A DEMONSTRATION OF INSIGHT: THE HORSE-AND-RIDER
PUZZLE. Martin Scheerer, Kurt Goldstein and
Edwin G. Boring in *The American Journal of Psy-
chology,* Vol. 54, No. 3, pages 437–438; July, 1941.

MECHANIZATION IN PROBLEM-SOLVING: THE EFFECT
OF EINSTELLUNG. Abraham S. Luchins in *Psy-
chological Monographs,* Vol. 54, No. 6, Whole
No. 248, pages 1–95; 1942.

PRODUCTIVE THINKING. Max Wertheimer. Harper, 1945.

IV. PERSONALITY AND BEHAVIOR DISORDERS

24. The Origin of Personality

BIRTH TO MATURITY: A STUDY IN PSYCHOLOGICAL
DEVELOPMENT. Jerome Kagan and H. A. Moss.
Wiley, 1962.

THE WIDENING WORLD OF CHILDHOOD: PATHS TOWARD
MASTERY. Lois Barclay Murphy. Basic Books, 1962.

YOUR CHILD IS A PERSON: A PSYCHOLOGICAL APPROACH

TO PARENTHOOD WITHOUT GUILT. Stella Chess,
Alexander Thomas and Herbert G. Birch. Viking
Press, 1965.

TEMPERAMENT AND BEHAVIOR DISORDERS IN CHILDREN.
Alexander Thomas, Stella Chess and Herbert G.
Birch. New York University Press, 1968.

25. Studies in Self-Esteem

ANTECEDENTS OF SELF-ESTEEM. Stanley Coopersmith. W. H. Freeman, 1967.

THE PRACTICE AND THEORY OF INDIVIDUAL PSYCHOLOGY. Alfred Adler. Translated by P. Radin. Harcourt, Brace, 1924.

SOCIETY AND THE ADOLESCENT SELF-IMAGE. Morris Rosenberg. Princeton University Press, 1965.

26. Social Deprivation in Monkeys

AFFECTIONAL RESPONSES IN THE INFANT MONKEY. Harry F. Harlow and Robert R. Zimmermann in Science, Vol. 130, No. 3373, pages 421–432; August 21, 1959.

DETERMINANTS OF INFANT BEHAVIOR. Edited by B. M. Foss. Methuen, 1961.

THE DEVELOPMENT OF LEARNING IN THE RHESUS MONKEY. Harry F. Harlow in Science in Progress: Twelfth Series, edited by Wallace R. Brode, pages 239–269. Yale University Press, 1962.

THE HETEROSEXUAL AFFECTIONAL SYSTEM IN MONKEYS. Harry F. Harlow in American Psychologist, Vol. 17, No. 1, pages 1–9; January, 1962.

LOVE IN INFANT MONKEYS. Harry F. Harlow in Scientific American, Vol. 200, No. 6, pages 68–74; June, 1959.

27. Psychological Factors in Stress and Disease

SOMATIC EFFECTS OF PREDICTABLE AND UNPREDICTABLE SHOCK. Jay M. Weiss in Psychosomatic Medicine, Vol. 32, pages 397–408; 1970.

EXPERIMENTALLY INDUCED GASTRIC LESIONS: RESULTS AND IMPLICATIONS OF STUDIES IN ANIMALS. Robert Ader in Advances in Psychosomatic Medicine, Vol. 6, pages 1–39; 1971.

EFFECTS OF COPING BEHAVIOR IN DIFFERENT WARNING SIGNAL CONDITIONS ON STRESS PATHOLOGY IN RATS. Jay M. Weiss in Journal of Comparative and Physiological Psychology, Vol. 77, No. 1, pages 1–30; October, 1971.

28. Hyperactive Children

A DEVELOPMENTAL STUDY OF THE BEHAVIOR PROBLEMS OF NORMAL CHILDREN BETWEEN 21 MONTHS AND 14 YEARS. J. W. Macfarlane, L. Allen and M. P. Honzik. University of California Press, 1954.

THE HYPERACTIVE CHILD SYNDROME. Mark A. Stewart, Ferris N. Pitts, Jr., Alan G. Craig and William Dieruf in American Journal of Orthopsychiatry, Vol. 36, No. 5, pages 861–867; October, 1966.

29. Schizophrenia

CULTURAL ASPECTS OF DELUSION: A PSYCHIATRIC STUDY OF THE VIRGIN ISLANDS. E. A. Weinstein. Free Press, 1962.

THE ETIOLOGY OF SCHIZOPHRENIA. Edited by Don D. Jackson, Basic Books, 1960.

HUMAN BEHAVIOR. Claire Russell and W. M. S. Russell. Little, Brown, 1961.

SCHIZOPHRENIA: SOMATIC ASPECTS. Edited by Derek Richter. Macmillan, 1957.

30. The Therapeutic Community

THE THERAPEUTIC COMMUNITY: A NEW TREATMENT METHOD IN PSYCHIATRY. Maxwell Jones. Basic Books, 1953.

THE PSYCHIATRIC HOSPITAL AS A SMALL SOCIETY. William Caudill. Harvard University Press, 1958.

COMMUNITY AS DOCTOR: NEW PERSPECTIVES ON A THERAPEUTIC COMMUNITY. Robert N. Rapoport. Charles C Thomas, 1960.

MILIEU THERAPEUTIC PROCESS. Richard Almond, Kenneth Keniston and Sandra Boltax in Archives of General Psychiatry, Vol. 21, No. 4, pages 431–442; October, 1969.

31. Behavioral Psychotherapy

BEHAVIORAL MODIFICATIONS THROUGH MODELING PROCEDURES. Albert Bandura in Research in Behavior Modification, edited by Leonard Krasner and Leonard P. Ullmann. Holt, Rinehart & Winston, 1965.

EXPERIMENTS IN BEHAVIOR THERAPY. H. J. Eysenck. Pergamon Press, 1964.

PRINCIPLES OF BEHAVIOR MODIFICATION. Albert Bandura. Holt, Rinehart & Winston, 1969.

PSYCHOTHERAPY BY RECIPROCAL INHIBITION. Joseph Wolpe. Stanford University Press, 1958.

SOCIAL LEARNING AND PERSONALITY DEVELOPMENT. Albert Bandura and Richard H. Walters. Holt, Rinehart & Winston, 1963.

V. SOCIAL INFLUENCES ON BEHAVIOR

32. Attitude and Pupil Size

PUPIL SIZE AS RELATED TO INTEREST VALUE OF VISUAL STIMULI. Eckhard H. Hess and James M. Polt in Science, Vol. 132, No. 3423, pages 349–350; August 5, 1960.

PUPIL SIZE IN RELATION TO MENTAL ACTIVITY DURING SIMPLE PROBLEM-SOLVING. Eckhard H. Hess and James M. Polt in Science, Vol. 143, No. 3611, pages 1190–1192; March 13, 1964.

33. Cognitive Dissonance

COGNITIVE CONSEQUENCES OF FORCED COMPLIANCE. Leon Festinger and James M. Carlsmith in *The Journal of Abnormal and Social Psychology*, Vol. 58, No. 2, pages 203–210; March, 1959.

PREPARATORY ACTION AND BELIEF IN THE PROBABLE OCCURRENCE OF FUTURE EVENTS. Ruby B. Yaryan and Leon Festinger in *The Journal of Abnormal and Social Psychology*, Vol. 63, No. 3, pages 603–606; November, 1961.

A THEORY OF COGNITIVE DISSONANCE. Leon Festinger. Bow, Peterson, 1957.

WHEN PROPHECY FAILS. Leon Festinger, Henry W. Riecken and Stanley Schachter. University of Minnesota Press, 1956.

34. Experiments in Intergroup Discrimination

THE NATURE OF PREJUDICE. Gordon W. Allport. Addison-Wesley, 1954.

RACIAL AND CULTURAL MINORITIES. G. E. Simpson and J. M. Yinger. Harper & Row, 1965.

TOWARD A THEORY OF MINORITY-GROUP RELATIONS. Hubert M. Blalock, Jr. Wiley, 1967.

PREJUDICE AND ETHNIC RELATIONS. John Harding, Harold Proshansky, Bernard Kutner and Isidor Chein in *The Handbook of Social Psychology, Vol. V: Applied Social Psychology*, edited by Gardner Lindzey and Elliot Aronson. Addison-Wesley, 1969.

COGNITIVE ASPECTS OF PREJUDICE. Henri Tajfel in *The Journal of Social Issues*, Vol. 25, No. 4, pages 79–97; Autumn, 1969.

35. The Effects of Observing Violence

AGGRESSION: A SOCIAL PSYCHOLOGICAL ANALYSIS. Leonard Berkowitz. McGraw-Hill, 1962.

EFFECTS OF FILM VIOLENCE ON INHIBITIONS AGAINST SUBSEQUENT AGGRESSION. Leonard Berkowitz and Edna Rawlings in *Journal of Abnormal and Social Psychology*, Vol. 66, No. 5, pages 405–412; May, 1963.

ENHANCEMENT OF PUNITIVE BEHAVIOR BY AUDIOVISUAL DISPLAYS. Richard H. Walters, Edward Llewellyn Thomas and C. William Acker in *Science*, Vol. 136, No. 3519, pages 872–873; June 8, 1962.

IMITATION OF FILM-MEDIATED AGGRESSIVE MODELS. Albert Bandura, Dorothea Ross and Sheila A. Ross in *Journal of Abnormal and Social Psychology*, Vol. 66, No. 1, pages 3–11; January, 1963.

TELEVISION IN THE LIVES OF OUR CHILDREN. Wilbur Schramm, Jack Lyle and Edwin B. Parker. Stanford University Press, 1961.

36. Teacher Expectations for the Disadvantaged

COVERT COMMUNICATION IN THE PSYCHOLOGICAL EXPERIMENT. Robert Rosenthal in *Psychological Bulletin*, Vol. 67, No. 5, pages 356–367; May, 1967.

THE EFFECT OF EXPERIMENTER BIAS ON THE PERFORMANCE OF THE ALBINO RAT. Robert Rosenthal and Kermit L. Fode in *Behavioral Science*, Vol. 8, No. 3, pages 183–189; July, 1963.

EXPERIMENTER EFFECTS IN BEHAVIORAL RESEARCH. Robert Rosenthal. Appleton-Century-Crofts, 1966.

PYGMALION IN THE CLASSROOM: TEACHER EXPECTATION AND PUPILS' INTELLECTUAL DEVELOPMENT. Robert Rosenthal and Lenore Jacobson. Holt, Rinehart, Winston, 1968.

SOCIAL STRATIFICATION AND ACADEMIC ACHIEVEMENT. Alan B. Wilson in *Education in Depressed Areas*, edited by A. Harry Passow. Teachers College Press, Columbia University, 1966.

37. Intelligence and Race

INTRODUCTION TO QUANTITATIVE GENETICS. D. S. Falconer. Oliver and Boyd, 1960.

INTELLIGENCE AND SOCIAL MOBILITY. Cyril Burt in *The British Journal of Statistical Psychology*, Vol. 14, Part 1, pages 3–24; May, 1961.

MONOZYGOTIC TWINS BROUGHT UP APART AND BROUGHT UP TOGETHER: AN INVESTIGATION INTO THE GENETIC AND ENVIRONMENTAL CAUSES OF VARIATION IN PERSONALITY. James Shields. Oxford University Press, 1962.

GENETICS AND INTELLIGENCE: A REVIEW. L. Erlenmeyer-Kimling and Lissy F. Jarvik in *Science*, Vol. 142, No. 3598, pages 1477–1479; December 13, 1963.

HOW MUCH CAN WE BOOST IQ AND SCHOLASTIC ACHIEVEMENT? Arthur R. Jensen in *Harvard Educational Review*, Vol. 39, No. 1, pages 1–123; Winter, 1969.

DISCUSSION; HOW MUCH CAN WE BOOST IQ AND SCHOLASTIC ACHIEVEMENT? *Harvard Educational Review*, Vol. 39, No. 2, pages 273–356; Spring, 1969.

38. Pictorial Perception and Culture

GEOGRAPHY AND ATLAS OF PROTESTANT MISSIONS. Harlan P. Beach. New York Volunteer Movement for Foreign Missions, 1901.

THE STUDY OF THE PROBLEM OF PICTORIAL PERCEPTION

AMONG UNACCULTURATED GROUPS. William Hudson in *International Journal of Psychology*, Vol. 2, No. 2, pages 89–107; 1967.

DIFFICULTIES IN PICTORIAL DEPTH PERCEPTION IN AFRICA. Jan B. Deregowski in *The British Journal of Psychology*, Vol. 59, Part 3, pages 195–204; August, 1968.

PERCEPTION OF THE TWO-PRONGED TRIDENT BY TWO-AND THREE-DIMENSIONAL PERCEIVERS. J. B. Deregowski in *Journal of Experimental Psychology*, Vol. 82, No. 1, Part 1, pages 9–13; October, 1969.

RESPONSES MEDIATING PICTORIAL RECOGNITION. Jan B. Deregowski in *The Journal of Social Psychology*, Vol. 84, First Half, pages 27–33; June, 1971.

39. Origins of Alienation

PROFILES OF CHILDREN: WHITE HOUSE CONFERENCE ON CHILDREN. U.S. Government Printing Office, 1970.

REPORT TO THE PRESIDENT: WHITE HOUSE CONFERENCE ON CHILDREN. U.S. Government Printing Office, 1970.

TWO WORLDS OF CHILDHOOD: U.S. AND U.S.S.R. Urie Bronfenbrenner. Russell Sage Foundation, 1970.

YOUTH TRANSITION TO ADULTHOOD: REPORT OF THE PANEL ON YOUTH OF THE PRESIDENT'S SCIENTIFIC ADVISORY COMMITTEE. University of Chicago Press, 1974.

BRAIN CHANGES IN RESPONSE TO EXPERIENCE

Mark R. Rosenzweig, Edward L. Bennett, and Marian Cleeves Diamond   FEBRUARY 1972

Chapter 1

I. SUMMARY

Does experience produce any observable change in the brain? This question was studied in a series of experiments which for the most part followed the same general format. At weaning, sets of three males were taken from each rat litter and each was assigned randomly to a different group. One animal remained in a standard laboratory group cage, one rat was placed in an enriched environment, and the third was put in an impoversihed environment. In the enriched environment, several rats lived together in a large cage fitted out with a variety of toys, whereas impoverished animals lived alone in a small bare cage. At the end of the experimental period, the rats were sacrificed and their brains removed. Individual portions of the dissected brains were weighed and frozen until chemical analysis could be performed.

In their initial studies the authors found that the different experiences altered the weight of the brain samples and the amount of acetylcholinesterase in them. Rats with enriched experience had a greater weight of cerebral cortex, a greater thickness of cortex, and a greater total activity of acetycholinesterase, but less activity of this enzyme per unit of tissue weight. Such rats also had considerably increased amounts of the glial enzyme, cholinesterase, probably because of the increase in the number of glial cells. Although the enriched environment did not produce more nerve cells per unit of tissue, it did produce larger cell bodies and nuclei; and further chemical analysis revealed an increased ratio of RNA to DNA. In most of the experiments, the greatest differences were observed in the occipital cortex. In this area the enriched environment has also been shown to produce an increase in the number of spines on pyramidal cell dendrites, and a careful examination of the synoptic junctions in the third layer revealed that rats from enriched environments had synapses that were much larger than similar junctions in their impoverished littermates.

The differences between the three conditions could have been attributable to differences in the amount of handling. Animals in the enriched group were handled each day when new playthings were put in the cage, whereas animals in the impoverished environment were handled only once a week for weighing. However, when animals in both groups were handled once a day, the usual differences in brain chemistry and structure developed. Another possibility was that the differences in the stressful aspects of the environments were responsible for the results; but stress induced by daily electric shock was unable to effect cerebral changes. Does the enriched environment simply accelerate neural maturation? This does not seem likely; changes in the thickness of cerebral cortex and some of the other changes resulting from an enriched environment go in the opposite direction to what is found in normal growth. Moreover, an enriched environment can produce as great an increase in brain weight in fully mature rats as it does in young rats.

One of the major problems in measuring the effects of experience on the brain is finding an appropriate baseline. The authors have used as their baseline the normal laboratory environment, but in studies with wild deer mice it was shown that even the enriched laboratory environment is impoverished in comparison with the animals' natural habitat.

II. GLOSSARY

acetylcholine — one of the neurotransmitters.
acetylcholinesterase — an enzyme which rapidly breaks down the neurotransmitter acetycholine.
apical dendrite — the relatively long dentrite on pyramidal cells running in line with the cell axon.
axon — the part of the neuron which conducts impulses away from the dendrites and cell body to the post-synaptic cell.
basal dendrites — relatively short dendrites on pyramidal cells running tangential to the apical dentrite and axon.
bouton — synaptic bulb containing the synaptic vesicles which release the transmitter substance into the synaptic cleft.
dendritic spines — tiny projections from the dendrites of a nerve cell.

glial cells — cells found in the nervous system which transport materials between capillaries and nerve cells as well as forming the fatty sheath found around the axons of some neurons.
occipital cortex — the cortex of the posterior lobe of the cerebrum which has primarily a visual function.
perfuse — injecting first saline and then a fixative through the circulatory system of a sacrificed animal to rinse the system of blood and to preserve it.
pyramidal cell — cells in the cortex with pyramid-shaped cell bodies.
synapses — gaps between neurons across which neural activity must be conducted by neurotransmitters.
synaptic vesicles — vesicles containing the transmitter substance which is released into the synaptic cleft when an electrical signal reaches the bouton.

III. ESSAY STUDY QUESTIONS

1. Discuss the characteristics of rodents which make them ideal subjects for certain kinds of investigation.
2. Describe the general procedure which was used in most of the experiments.
3. "Enriched" and "impoverished" are only relative terms. Discuss.
4. List the changes in the brain produced by the differences in environment.
5. What was the reason for the experiments on wild deer mice? What were the results?
6. It is possible that the brain changes resulted not from learning and memory, but from other aspects of the experimental situation. On what basis do the authors dismiss this possibility?
7. The human brain is more likely than animal brains to provide answers concerning the relations between experience and brain structure. Discuss.

STRESS AND BEHAVIOR
Chapter 2

Seymour Levine   JANUARY 1971

I. SUMMARY

Information about stress, whether from inside or from outside the body, is received by the central nervous system and eventually transmitted to the hypothalamus. The hypothalamus secretes a substance called corticotropin-releasing factor (CRF), which stimulates the release of adrenocorticotrophic hormone (ACTH) from the anterior pituitary. This in turn stimulates the cortex of the adrenal gland to increase its synthesis and secretion of hormones, particularly those known as glucocorticoids. In man the predominant glucocorticoid is hydrocortisone; in many lower animals, such as the rat, it is corticosterone. This entire mechanism is controlled by a feedback system. When the glucocorticoid level in the blood is elevated, the process leading to the secretion of ACTH is inhibited, and ACTH secretion is stimulated by reduced glucocorticoid levels.

There is direct evidence that the activities of the pituitary-adrenal system play an important role in controlling overt behavior. When the pituitary gland was removed from rats, their learning of a shuttle-box avoidance response was severely retarded, but if they were also given replacement injections of ACTH, their original learning ability was restored. Moreover, when intact animals were injected with ACTH during the learning period, extinction of the avoidance responses was greatly prolonged. Similarly, extinction was prolonged in rats from which the adrenals had been removed, presumably because adrenal hormones were no longer present to restrict the output of ACTH. Conversely, restricting ACTH output with injections of glucocorticoids, such as corticosterone or the synthetic dexamethasone, accelerated the rate of extinction. Curiously, these glucocorticoids promoted extinction even in the absence of the pituitary gland, indicating that glucocorticoids can produce this effect by acting directly on the central nervous system, as well as by their effects on ACTH secretion. However, a truncated 10-amino-acid version of the ACTH molecule which has no influence on adrenal secretions can also retard extinction. Injection of this molecular fragment improved passive avoidance in normal animals as well as in animals from which the pituitary had been removed, but in these latter animals hydrocortisone had no effect.

Hormones of the adrenal cortex also seem to play a role in sensory functions. Patients whose adrenal gland has been surgically removed or is functioning poorly show a marked increase in the ability to detect sensory signals, particularly those of taste, smell, hearing, and proprioception. On the other hand, the increased adrenal secretions associated with Cushing's syndrome lead to a dulling of the senses. Although a deficiency of adrenal cortex hormones leads to increased sensitivity, it also disrupts the patient's ability to integrate sensory signals, thus producing a variety of perceptual deficits. Rats have shown an improvement in time perception in response to treatment with glucocorticoids. In a situation in which an electric shock was applied every 20 seconds unless a lever was pressed to postpone the shock for another 20 seconds, the experimental rats treated with glucocorticoids learned to perform more efficiently than controls. They lengthened the interval between bar presses and took fewer shocks.

II. GLOSSARY

adrenals — endocrine glands situated over the kidneys which secrete hormones that help the body "adapt" to stressful stimulation.

adrenocorticotrophic hormone (ACTH) — pituitary hormone which causes the adrenal cortex to increase the production and release of hormones.

corticosterone — the main glucocorticoid in many lower animals, including the rat.

corticotropin-releasing factor (CRF) — substance secreted by the hypothalamus which controls the release of ACTH from the pituitary.

Cushing's syndrome — a disease marked by excessive secretion from the adrenal cortex.

dexamethasone — a synthetic glucocorticoid known to be a potent inhibitor of ACTH.

estrogen — female sex hormone secreted by the ovaries.

extinction — reducing the frequency of a conditioned response by withholding the reinforcement or punishment that usually follows it.

general stress syndrome — a system of defensive reactions mobilized by the pituitary-adrenal system in response to stress.

glucocorticoids — a class of steroid hormones secreted by the adrenal glands.

hippocampus — a structure just below the cortex suspected of housing receptor sites for hormones of the adrenal cortex.

hormones — organic substances secreted by endocrine glands and transported through the circulatory system to other parts of the body, where they have their effects.

hydrocortisone — the main glucocorticoid in man.

hypothalamus — structure in the basal area of the brain which controls the release of hormones from the pituitary.

pituitary — the endocrine gland whose secretions are controlled by the hypothalamus and which in turn control the activities of many of the other glands in the body.

progesterone — hormone secreted by the corpus luteum of the ovary to prepare the reproductive organs for pregnancy.

proprioception — perception of signals arising from within the body.

prostate — gland of the male reproductive system whose size and secretions are controlled by testosterone.

reticular formation — a structure in the core of the brain stem known to influence arousal, attention, and sleep.

seminal vesicles — organ which stores sperm.

shuttle box — a two-compartment avoidance apparatus where an animal must learn to move to the other compartment in response to a conditioned stimulus in order to avoid a shock.

testosterone — male sex hormone secreted primarily by the testes.

III. ESSAY STUDY QUESTIONS

1. There seem to be two ways in which glucocorticoids can influence behavior, by acting directly on the nervous system, or by influencing the levels of ACTH. Give the evidence confirming the operation of each of these two modes of action.
2. Describe Selye's concept of the general stress syndrome.
3. Describe the pituitary-adrenal feedback system.
4. What effects do changes in the pituitary-adrenal system have on the acquisition and extinction of a conditioned avoidance response?
5. What evidence is there that the pituitary-adrenal system can influence the extinction of appetitive responses?
6. What is habituation, and how is it affected by hormones of the pituitary-adrenal system?
7. What effects do the adrenal's hormones have on sensory function?
8. Levine concludes that in many situations effective behavior in adult life may depend on exposure to some optimum level of stress. On what observations does he base this conclusion? Discuss.

THE VISUAL CORTEX OF THE BRAIN
David H. Hubel   NOVEMBER 1963

Chapter 3

I. SUMMARY

When visual stimuli impinge on the retina of the eye, this information is encoded and transmitted in the form of nerve impulses to the visual cortex. Hubel and his colleague, Wiesel, have tried to determine the function of different steps in the nervous pathway between retina and cortex by recording the electrical activity of individual neurons in the visual system of the cat in response to a variety of visual stimuli presented to the retina.

Kuffler reported that the receptive fields of retinal ganglion cells were of two types, both having a circular center with an opposing periphery. One type has an "on" center with an "off" periphery while the other had the opposite arrangement. Hubel and Wiesel found similar receptive fields for lateral geniculate cells except that at this stage of the visual system there was an enhanced capacity for the periphery of the re-

ceptive fields to cancel the effects of the center. In the visual cortex, Hubel and Wiesel found two types of cells, which they termed simple and complex. Simple cells could be divided into static "on" and "off" areas but instead of the circular arrangement seen at more peripheral levels of the nervous system, simple cortical cells were most sensitive to stimuli with straight-line boundaries presented in a specific position and at a specific orientation. Complex cells were sensitive to the same type of stimuli, that is straight-line stimuli at a specific orientation, but they responded to stimulation anywhere in the receptive field. Complex and simple cortical cells sensitive to stimuli of the same orientation were found to be organized anatomically into vertical columns in the cortex. An anatomical model of the visual system was suggested by Hubel to account for these observations.

II. GLOSSARY

axon — the principal fiber of the neuron, which is responsible for transmitting nervous impulses from one part of the nervous system to another.

bipolar cells — retinal neurons that receive direct input from receptor cells and synapse on retinal ganglion cells.

cerebrum — upper part of the mammalian brain consisting of two hemispheres [cerebral hemispheres] separated by a deep fissure.

chiasm — point at which some of the axons forming the optic nerve cross over to the opposite side.

complex cortical cells — cells of the visual cortex that respond to straight-line stimuli with the appropriate orientation presented to any part of the receptive field.

converge — when a number of neurons synapse on a single neuron, they are said to converge.

cornea — transparent outer surface of the eyeball.

cortex — a layer of grey nervous tissue that covers most of the external surface of the brain.

fovea — the central part of the retina, which is used for "fine" vision.

lateral geniculate bodies — a pair of clusters of cell bodies of neurons receiving input from retinal ganglion cells and projecting to layer IV of the cortex.

microelectrode — an electrical conductor with a tip so small that it can be used to record the electrical activity of individual neurons in the brain.

off-center cell — a cell with a receptive field consisting of a small circular area that gives "off" responses when stimulated and a periphery that gives "on" responses.

off response — when the firing rate of a neuron increases with the offset of the sensory stimulus.

on response — when the firing rate of a neuron increases with the onset of a sensory stimulus.

on-center cell — a cell with a receptive field consisting of a small circular "on" area and a periphery that produces "off" responses.

optic nerve — the bundle of axons of retinal ganglion cells that leaves the retina and projects to the lateral geniculate bodies.

receptive field of a cell — is the area of the retina that, when stimulated, will produce a change in the activity of that cell.

receptor cells — cells in the retina of the eye that, when stimulated by incoming patterns of light, transmit this information in the form of an electrical potential to the bipolar cells.

retina — the innermost layer of cells on the back of the eyeball, on which incoming visual images are projected.

retinal ganglion cells — the cells that receive input from the bipolar cells and pass it via the optic nerve to the lateral geniculate bodies.

simple cortical cells — cortical cells that respond to a straight line of specific orientation and location.

synapse — a cleft between the termination of an axon and the next neuron in the neural path.

III. ESSAY STUDY QUESTIONS

1. How can microelectrode recording as opposed to neuroanatomical investigation be used to determine the function of a neural structure?
2. Describe Kuffler's work on the retinal ganglion cells.
3. Explain why cells specialized for precise visual discrimination are likely to have smaller field centers.
4. Compare the visual fields of lateral geniculate cells, simple cortical cells, and complex cortical cells.
5. Describe Hubel's idea of how lateral geniculate, simple cortical, and complex cortical cells are interconnected.
6. Describe the columnar organization of the visual cortex.

PLEASURE CENTERS IN THE BRAIN

Chapter 4

James Olds   OCTOBER 1956

I. SUMMARY

Recent research has indicated that there seem to be specific centers in the brain which are responsible for feelings of pleasure. These areas have been particularly difficult to study because they are enclosed beneath the cortex of the brain and because complex behaviors associated with feelings of pleasure have been difficult to assess. The first difficulty was overcome by stimulating the brain with a fine needle electrode that could be inserted into the subcortical areas and fixed in position without producing extensive damage along the electrode path. The second was overcome by using the technique devised by B. F. Skinner for assessing the rewarding effects of a stimulus. Animals were stimulated each time they pressed a lever and the frequency of responding was used as a measure of the rewarding effects of the stimulation.

In their initial series of tests Olds and his colleagues attempted to implant electrodes in the mid-brain reticular system, but their aim was poor and the tip of the electrode in one animal ended up in a nerve pathway projecting from the rhinencephalon. In their first experiment this animal was placed in a large square box; whenever he went to a certain corner of the box he received a small electrical stimulation through the electrode. As a result he continually returned to that corner, and on subsequent tests the rat was directed to other parts of the box by making the stimulation contingent upon his presence in a particular location. After confirming that stimulation to certain brain structures could have rewarding effects in other subjects, Olds compared the re-warding effects of stimulation applied to various brain areas. Here Skinner's technique provided the means. Each rat was placed in a Skinner box in which each bar press delivered a stimulation to the rat's own brain. When electrodes were implanted in the classical sensory and motor systems, response rates stayed at the chance level of 10 to 25 an hour, but when the animals were rewarded by stimulation of areas of the hypothalamus and certain other mid-brain regions, which Hess and others had found to be related to consumatory behaviors, response rates were much higher. Animals with electrodes in these areas would stimulate themselves at rates between 500 and 5,000 times per hour. Rewarding effects were also observed in the rhinencephalon but the effects were milder, producing self-stimulation at rates of about 200 times per hour. Stimulation of some regions appeared to be even more reinforcing than natural reinforcers; hungry animals would often ignore food in favor of pressing a lever that would deliver brain stimulation.

Why is electrical stimulation so rewarding? Olds's working hypothesis was that rewarding brain stimulation activates some of the nerve cells that are excited during the satisfaction of biological drives. Supporting this view was the finding that an animal's appetite for electric stimulation to some brain regions seemed to increase as hunger increased, whereas the rewarding effect of stimulation of other areas could be abolished by castration and then restored by injections of testosterone.

II. GLOSSARY

cortex — layer of neural tissue covering the cerebral hemispheres.

fissures — furrows on the surface of the brains of some animals, including man.

fornix — tract connecting the hippocampus and the hypothalamus.

hypothalamus — structure of the diencephalic region of the brain stem that supports high rates of self-stimulation.

photomicrograph — an enlarged photograph of a microscopic object.

phrenology — the doctrine that the shape of the skull and its protuberances reflect the development of various parts of the brain and the mental faculties that they control.

reticular system — system of undifferentiated short-axon neurons in the core of the mid-brain that seems to control sleep and wakefulness.

rhinencephalon — area of the brain comprised of the hippocampus, fornix, and associated structures.

Skinner box — a box in which rewards are delivered contingent on a lever press.

testosterone — male testicular hormone.

thalamus — structure of the diencephalic region of the brainstem situated just above the hypothalamus.

III. ESSAY STUDY QUESTIONS

1. Summarize the knowledge of brain function that existed when Olds and his colleagues began their work.
2. The rewarding functions of subcortical structures were difficult to assess for two reasons. Explain. What methods were used to overcome these problems?
3. What evidence does Olds provide to support his view that the rewarding effects of electrical brain stimulation are attributable to the excitation of neurons that are active during the satisfaction of natural drives?
4. The animals pressed the lever at extremely high rates for stimulation to some brain areas, but when the current was turned off they ceased pressing almost immediately. Discuss this apparent paradox in view of Olds's interpretation of the rewarding effects of brain stimulation.
5. Briefly describe the procedures involved in implanting permanent subcortical electrodes.
6. What is a Skinner box? Explain how it was used to study rewarding brain stimulation.
7. Does Olds's work have implications for the study of the functions of the human brain? Discuss.

"IMPRINTING" IN A NATURAL LABORATORY

Eckhard H. Hess   AUGUST 1972

Chapter 5

I. SUMMARY

The phenomenon of imprinting has become widely known largely through the work of Konrad Lorenz. In the 1930's Lorenz observed that newly hatched goslings would develop a strong attachment for any moving object—the mother, under normal circumstances—that was present in the period after hatching. Lorenz regarded this phenomenon as being different from the usual kind of learning because of its rapidity and apparent permanence, but the majority of researchers have regarded imprinting as a standard form of learning. They have studied it using methods much the same as those used in the study of other learning processes. In every case efforts were made to manipulate or stringently control the imprinting process. Usually the subjects are incubator-hatched birds kept in isolation until the imprinting experience, to prevent the interaction of early social experience. Various objects, including duck decoys, dolls, flashing lights, and rotating disks, have been used as the artificial parent, and often the young bird's movements relative to the imprinting object have been monitored automatically.

Since in such studies the birds have been incubated, hatched, and reared in artificial conditions, it is possible that the behavior observed under such conditions is not directly relevant to what actually happens in nature. For example, in opposition to the results of Lorenz's early field studies, imprinting as studied in the laboratory appears to be only a temporary phenomemon. In many of the author's studies he has applied many of the procedures commonly used in laboratory experiments for recording behavior to the study of imprinting in natural conditions. The first step in these so called field-laboratory studies of imprinting was to obtain a detailed inventory of the events that occur during natural imprinting, to provide the essential reference point for the assessment of experimental manipulations of the imprinting process.

In the natural environment all the eggs in a clutch hatch at approximately the same time, even though they were laid at different times, while in controlled laboratory conditions the mallard eggs in a given clutch hatch over a two- or three-day period. Periodic cooling of the eggs while the mother is absent seems to be one variable which increases the synchronization of hatching. A clutch of mallard eggs periodically removed from an incubator and placed in a room at seven degrees hatches over a period of a day and a half instead of the usual two and a half days. Cooling, however, cannot play a major role in the natural environment. In June the temperature of the clutch is not significantly reduced when the mother is absent from the nest yet hatching in June is still sychronized. Synchronization appears to result from the vocal interaction between the mother and the unhatched ducklings. When the sounds of a duckling who had pipped its shell were recorded and played to females at various stages of incubation, there were no responses during the first two weeks of incubation, a few responses in the third week, and consistent responses in the fourth. Conversely, when a recording of a female mallard's vocalizations was played intermittently to eggs in the 24 hours prior to hatching, the total number of duckling vocalizations increased steadily while the proportion occurring during silent periods on the tape diminished. The author has found that a combination of cooling the eggs daily, placing them in contact with each other, and transmitting parental calls through a microphone in the nest causes artificially-incubated eggs to hatch as synchronously as eggs do in nature. Moreover, this auditory interaction before hatching may play a major role in the imprinting process. The results of preliminary studies indicate that the prehatching vocalization by the mother may in fact facilitate the eventual imprinting of the offspring to her.

Such studies, although only in their beginning stages, have clearly demonstrated the importance of studying imprinting under natural conditions; they have also demonstrated the value of objective laboratory techniques and instrumentation.

II. GLOSSARY

Celsius – Centigrade.
clutch – all of the eggs incubated at one time by a given bird.
field-laboratory method – the application of laboratory procedures to the study of animals in their natural habitat.
filial – pertaining to offspring.

imprinting – the strong attachment formed by many young birds and animals for their parents or other moving objects present shortly after birth.
kilohertz – thousands of cycles per second.
pip – to break through the shell of an egg.
sound spectrogram – a chart presenting the analysis of sounds into component frequency bands as a function of time.

III. ESSAY STUDY QUESTIONS

1. Discuss the suitability of laboratory as opposed to field studies in the understanding of imprinting.
2. In opposition to Lorenz's original conclusions many experiments have shown imprinting to be only a temporary phenomenon. Discuss.
3. What is the field-laboratory method?
4. In laboratory conditions imprinting in ducklings has been found to be most effective in the 27th day after incubation but this cannot be true of natural imprinting. Explain.
5. What factors account for the relative synchrony of hatching in naturally incubated ducklings?
6. Why is it biologically important that all the eggs in a clutch hatch at approximately the same time?
7. Describe the vocal interaction between parent and offspring in the period before and after hatching.
8. What is the relation between temperature and the length of incubation?
9. It is clear that periodic temperature reductions are not an important factor in the synchronized hatching of a clutch of eggs. Explain.
10. What is the effect of effort and punishment on imprinting?

THE OBJECT IN THE WORLD OF THE INFANT

T. G. R. Bower   OCTOBER 1971

Chapter 6

I. SUMMARY

According to traditional theories only the sense of touch has the intrinsic ability to distinguish solids from nonsolids; the ability to distinguish solid objects visually is the result of learning to associate visual cues with tactile impressions. And it seems that a similar situation must exist when babies observe an object move behind another. An adult knows that the object is still there and that it has not ceased to exist but it is hard to understand how an infant could know that the object is still there by using vision alone. How can vision provide information about the location of an invisible object? Touch must play a critical role in the development of the ability to deal with hidden objects. The hand can go around obstacles to reach such objects, and only as a result of such explorations can an infant come to know that the object is still there.

In order to study the development of the visual perception of solidity and permanence, the infants "surprise" was assessed. In one series of studies an illusion was produced with a binocular shadow-caster, a device consisting of two light projectors with polarizing filters and a rear projection screen. An object made of translucent plastic is suspended between the lights and the screen so that it casts a double shadow on the rear of the screen. The subject views the screen with polarizing goggles that allow only one shadow to be visible to each eye. When these two images are combined by the normal processes of binocular vision, the object appears in front of the subject looking very real and tangible although, of course, lacking any real substance. In the first experiment with infants between 16 and 24 weeks, the results were unambiguous. None of the infants showed any surprise when he touched the real object suspended in front of him, but every infant showed marked surprise when his hand failed to make contact with the illusion. Moreover, subjects younger than two weeks responded emotionally to quickly approaching objects or quickly approaching illusions generated by the binocular shadow-caster.

These findings are fatal to traditional theories of the development of the visual perception of solidity. It is very unlikely that such young subjects had been exposed to situations where they could have learned to fear approaching objects and expect them to have tactile properties. Thus, there seems to be an innate unity of the senses, with visual properties specifying tactual qualities. The conclusive support for this view was supplied by a study on newborn infants. All newborn infants touched and grasped real objects without any sign of disturbance, but the illusory object produced a howl as soon as the infant's hand went to the intangible object's location.

Is there also an innate ability to know that an object is still there when it disappears behind another? Attempts to answer this question were inconclusive, but they led to a startling observation: young infants seem to be unable to identify a stationary object with the same object when it is moving. For example, when a target object was moved on a circular trajectory and stopped, every infant continued to look along the trajectory after fixating for a moment on the stationary object. It was as if the infants had been tracking a moving object, had noticed a different stationary object, and then looked farther on to find the moving object again. Another experiment showed that infants will look in the place where a stationary object had been seen after watching it move off to a new location. A toy train situated directly in front of the infants moved slowly to the left and stopped at a new position before returning to the original position, and the infants watched this cycle being repeated 10 times. Then, as the train with lights flashing moved to the right the infants looked to the left where the stationary train had "appeared" on previous cycles. Thus, movements and objects seem to have different meanings for young infants. Supporting this view was the observation that infants less than 16 weeks old tracked a moving object until it went behind a screen and anticipated its reappearance on the other side but when a different object emerged, they continued to track with no sign of surprise. Older infants also tracked the object in motion but when a different object appeared, they often glanced back to the starting point looking for the original. This indicates that the younger infants do not respond to moving objects but to movements. Older infants have learned to recognize an object by its features rather than by its place or movements.

II. GLOSSARY

binocular — involving two eyes.
binocular shadow-caster — a device consisting of two light projectors with polarizing filters and a rear-projection screen for producing stereoscopic images.

stereoscopic — a three-dimensional percept produced by viewing two images of an object taken from slightly different points of view, one with each eye.

III. ESSAY STUDY QUESTIONS

1. What is the traditional view of how infants acquire the ability to visually perceive solidity and permanence?
2. The study of the development of the perception of solidity and permanence in human infants is technically difficult. Explain.
3. Describe the operation of the binocular shadow-caster.
4. The author believes that infants under two weeks of age are not completely awake when they are lying on their backs. On what evidence does he base this conclusion and what implications does it have for developmental research?
5. What evidence supports the view that the ability of human infants to perceive tactual qualities in visual stimuli is innate?
6. Do infants know that an object still exists when it passes behind another?
7. Describe the evidence which suggests that young infants do not recognize the identity of a moving object with the same object when it is still.
8. What evidence indicates that young infants do not respond to moving objects but to movements, and not to stationary objects but to places?
9. Describe the results of the multiple-mother experiment.
10. In adults most eye movements are not under conscious control. In view of this fact evaluate the use of direction of gaze as a measure of what an infant sees or expects to see.
11. The object concept does not seem to be present in newborn infants. Does this necessarily mean that it is a concept which must be learned?

THE "VISUAL CLIFF"

Eleanor J. Gibson and Richard D. Walk   APRIL 1960

Chapter 7

I. SUMMARY

As an infant progresses past the toddling stage, he becomes less and less likely to fall from high places. One commonsense view of this improved performance is that the infant is learning to perceive depth by a gradual trial-and-error process. Is experience really the teacher or is the ability to perceive and avoid a brink part of the child's original endowment? A major problem in answering such a question is to devise a suitable experimental apparatus. Gibson and Walk report experiments employing a device called the visual cliff which has been widely used for this purpose. The visual cliff consists of a board laid across a heavy piece of glass; on one side of the board there is no apparent support for the glass thus giving the impression of a cliff.

Infants ranging from 6 to 14 months were tested on the visual cliff, and all the children who moved off the central board had a strong tendency to avoid the deep side. The results of this experiment do not show that depth perception is innate in humans, but the results of other visual cliff studies do show that depth perception in some animals is well-developed at birth. The chick, for example, can be tested shortly after birth because it is born with the well-developed locomotor system that it needs to forage for its own food. The chick never makes a mistake on the visual cliff. In fact, all animals appear to have well-developed depth perception by the time their locomotor abilities are developed enough for them to be tested. This finding is consistent with evolutionary doctrine, since it is important for the survival of the species that individuals have well-developed depth perception before they are capable of independent locomotion. Furthermore, it is not likely that such a vital capacity would depend on the possibly fatal accidents which would occur during learning.

Gibson and Walk have tried to study the development of motion parallax and texture density as depth cues using the visual cliff. Since neither newborn chicks nor dark-reared rats seemed to respond to differences in textural density, it appears that of the two cues only motion parallax is an innate cue for depth perception.

II. GLOSSARY

motion parallax — as the observer moves his head from side to side, distant objects are displaced less than near objects.

nocturnal — pertaining to the night.

texture density — differences in pattern density seen clearly when the same pattern is viewed at different distances.

vibrissae — long, bristly hairs growing from the mouth region of certain animals.

visual cliff — a device used for testing depth perception which consists of a board laid across a heavy piece of glass. On one side of the glass there is no apparent support for the glass, thus giving the impression of a cliff.

III. ESSAY STUDY QUESTIONS

1. The presence of those very abilities that allow some newborn organisms to be tested on the visual field preclude the possibility of generalizing these findings to human babies. Discuss.
2. Summarize the major conclusions that can be drawn from the results of visual-cliff experiments.
3. Why would the young chick be expected to perform better than a human infant on the visual cliff? Why should the chick be better than the turtle? Why should the chick be better than the rat?
4. Poor performance on the visual cliff does not necessarily mean poor perception. Explain.
5. What evidence is there that motion parallax and not texture density is an innate cue for depth perception?
6. What are the effects of dark-rearing?

STABILIZED IMAGES ON THE RETINA

Chapter 8

Roy M. Pritchard JUNE 1961

I. SUMMARY

During normal vision the eye is constantly moving, even during apparent fixation on a stationary object. As a result the image of the object is kept in constant movement on the retina. One way to study the function of these movements is to eliminate them, but this is difficult to do without endangering the eye. A safer but equally effective technique is to allow the eye to remain in motion but to attach the visual stimulus to the eyeball itself. As the eye moves the stimulus moves, but the image on the retina remains stationary. Under these viewing conditions the visual image begins to fade after a few seconds, eventually disappearing completely but returning to view a few seconds later. Pritchard and his colleagues have studied this stabilized image phenomenon to draw valuable inferences about the organization of the visual system. Presumably the fading is some type of neural adaptation process, and by examining patterns of fading one can determine something about what neural elements are organized to function as a unit.

In general, simple figures were found to vanish rapidly and reappear as a complete image, whereas more complex targets often disappeared and reappeared in parts. Complex figures thus remained at least partially in view for a larger proportion of time. These patterns of disappearing and reappearing in complex figures confirmed the predictions of two different theories of perception. The "cell-assembly" theory stresses the importance of experience in the development of perception. The recognizable parts of an object are presumed to correspond to neural perceptual elements established by experience. Supporting this view is that things that we have learned to be meaningful units fade as units. For example, if the word "BEER" is the target figure, meaningful groups of letters such as 'BEE" are much more likely to behave in unison than meaningless combinations such as "EEP." On the other hand, there is also support for the Gestalt theory, which stresses the importance of innate tendencies to see various patterns as "wholes." If an irregular shape is presented, there is a strong tendency for the more distorted features to fade, leaving a more regular figure which then acts as a unit.

II. GLOSSARY

closure — the tendency of the visual system to "fill in" a partially completed figure.

cornea — transparent outer covering of the front of the eye.

fovea — the part of the retina which is the center of focus and which mediates "fine" vision.

iris — contractile structure controlling the size of the pupil.

lens — structure which focuses the visual image on the retina.

Necker cube — a line drawing of a cube.

pupil — aperture through which light enters the eye.

retina — layer of cells including visual receptors lining the back of the eyeball.

III. ESSAY STUDY QUESTIONS

1. Describe the three kinds of involuntary eye movement.
2. Describe the technique for producing a stabilized image.
3. What evidence supplied by stabilized-image research suggests that learning plays an important part in the development of our visual systems?
4. What basic concepts of Gestalt psychology are consistent with the effects of stabilized images?
5. What is the function of involuntary eye movements in form and color perception?

THE PROCESS OF VISION

Ulric Neisser   SEPTEMBER 1968

I. SUMMARY

The analogy between eye and camera is an obvious one, but inherent in it are some misleading implications. It implies that the individual's perceptual experience is determined by an optical pattern or image projected from the retina into the nervous system. The fact is that the internal representations of visual experience are not mere reflections of the retinal image. The retinal image of any object undergoes continuous changes of shape, size, location, and color; nevertheless, the perceived characteristics of the object appear relatively fixed and stable.

What properties of the incoming optic array determine the way things look? One approach to this problem is ecological optics, the study of the patterns of reflected light that are formed when real objects and surfaces are naturally illuminated. Such study, however, does not take into account the characteristic saccadic movements of the human eye, which serve to focus various parts of the retinal image on the fovea for detailed inspection. Visual perceptions of the world are somehow constructed on the basis of information taken in during many different fixations.

In addition to specifying the properties of the visual stimulus that are important for perception, one must consider how this information is processed. Neisser believes that the mechanisms of visual processing are similar to those of visual memory. Visual memory differs from perception because it is based primarily on stored rather than on current information, but it involves the same kind of synthesis.

II. GLOSSARY

afterimage — image of a visual object which outlasts the visual stimulus.

binocular — involving two eyes.

binocular parallax — the differences in a single visual display as viewed by each eye. Such differences are greatest for close objects.

congenitally — from birth.

ecological optics — the study of patterns of light reflected from "everyday" objects and surfaces.

eidetic image — a visual image which seems to be external to the observer.

fovea — central part of the retina mediating "fine" vision.

homunculus — some image theories of perception are unsatisfactory because in order to explain perception they must postulate the existence of a homunculus (small man) in the brain which perceives the retinal image.

introspective — examining one's own consciousness.

kinetic depth effect — certain moving two-dimensional patterns are seen as three-dimensional objects.

monocular — involving one eye.

retina — inner layer of cells lining the rear of the eyeball onto which the visual image is projected.

saccade — a flick of the eye taking less than a twentieth of a second and occurring several times a second during the visual inspection of a scene.

size constancy — the size of an object is perceived quite accurately at various distances despite differences in the size of the retinal image.

III. ESSAY STUDY QUESTIONS

1. In what two ways is the term visual image used?
2. What unfortunate implications does the eye-camera analogy have for the study of vision?
3. Neisser discusses two kinds of questions about visual perception. What are they?
4. Why was there the tendency to regard some visual cues as secondary?
5. What evidence is there that what one sees is a composite based on information accumulated over a period of time?
6. What are the three kinds of visual memory discussed by Neisser?
7. Describe Sperling's demonstration that memories can be momentarily stored in the form of afterimages.
8. What is the evidence that imagining is similar to visual perception?
9. What evidence is there that most people have visual images?

EIDETIC IMAGES

Ralph Norman Haber   APRIL 1969

Chapter 10

I. SUMMARY

Certain individuals report the presence of a sharp visual image that persists for many seconds or even minutes after they have finished looking at a scene. There have been numerous investigations of these eidetic images, most conducted before 1935, but loose methods and the failure to develop convincing explanations of the findings led most psychologists to ignore the phenomenon. This early work indicated eidetic imagery was relatively rare after puberty but common among young school-age children.

When Haber and his colleagues attempted to study this phenomenon they initially screened elementary-school children—more than 500 in all. Children were shown pictures presented against a gray background; when the pictures were removed, they were asked to continue looking at the background and to report what they were seeing. Both during the initial viewing and the subsequent test, subjects were instructed to scan the field with their eyes rather than to fixate on a single point. If a subject reported seeing something, the experimenter asked if he was actually seeing something or remembering it from when the picture was in view. About half of the children screened said they saw something after the stimulus was removed, but nearly all these reports were of images which were fleeting and indistinct. However, between 5 and 10 percent of the children reported images which lasted longer and presented some sharp detail. These subjects were termed eidetic and subjected to further tests, demonstrations, and examinations.

The main criticisms directed at reports of eidetic imagery have generally centered around the lack of evidence that the children were in fact reporting the experience of a visual image rather than just describing their memory of the stimulus. The argument for the existence of eidetic imagery has usually been based on the fact that some of the reports of supposed images are incredibly detailed, but there is no reason to doubt that some children may have good enough memories to be capable of the same feats from memory alone. Haber believes that resting the case for eidetic imagery on the fidelity of the reports is a mistake, since the amount of detail that an eidetic child can report is in general not phenomenally good, although there are some phenomenal exceptions. There is no reason to assert that an eidetic image has to be complete or that it must last long enough before it fades for the child to describe all the content. Then what does differentiate eidetic images from other kinds of images or from memory? The only clear distinction between eidetic images and afterimages is in terms of location. Afterimages seem to result from the differential adaptation of retinal receptors and thus fixation is required to produce an afterimage. Moreover, once produced it cannot be moved in relation to the retina; when the eye moves, the image moves with it. In all of the present studies scanning was required during the initial inspection of the stimulus, and was invariably reported with the subsequent description of the image even though the image itself apparently remained stationary.

What evidence is there that the children were actually viewing an image? The differences between images and memories are subtle, and the possibility that the experimental situation and the questions themselves caused the children to think that they are actually viewing eidetic images is a possibility that cannot be ignored. But there were a number of observations which support the visual character of eidetic imagery: (1) Some eidetic children said that they could remember parts of the picture which were not in the image. (2) A conscious attempt to label parts of the stimulus interfered with the fidelity of the report. (3) Nearly all the eidetic children reported the same pattern of fading. (4) When asked to move their images to another surface, eidetic children reported that it fell off the edge of the background. (5) When the children formed an image of letters exposed individually in a window, they all reported that the image moved to the left as each new letter appeared in the window. (6) Children were most capable of reporting details that they had scanned most recently. (7) Some eidetic children reported that the image of a Necker cube spontaneously reversed in depth. (8) Some children could combine an eidetic image with the new visual display to produce an entirely new picture.

II. GLOSSARY

afterimage — a faint and fleeting image which remains after fixating a visual stimulus.

Emmert's law — the tendency of an afterimage to increase in size proportionally to the distance of the surface on which it is projected.

fixate — to focus one's eyes on a point.

fovea — small area near the center of the retina that is the only part of the retina capable of mediating detailed vision.

III. ESSAY STUDY QUESTIONS

1. How did Haber's findings differ from those of early investigators?
2. Describe the methods employed by Haber and his colleagues. Discuss the possibility that these procedures may have elicited reports of visual images from young children who were not actually experiencing them.
3. What are the differences between visual afterimages and eidetic images? What evidence is there that Haber's subjects were experiencing eidetic images rather than afterimages?
4. What evidence suggests that eidetic images exist? Evaluate each piece of evidence and come to a general conclusion.
5. Discuss the view that eidetic imagery is the basis of the so-called photographic memory.
6. In the author's view, the fact that children are most capable of reporting details of stimuli scanned most recently supports an imagery as opposed to a memory interpretation. Evaluate critically.
7. It appears that eidetic children can store visual information in the form of images or in the form of verbal memories, but not in both forms at once. Discuss.
8. Describe and evaluate the author's direct test for eidetic imagery.

VISUAL ILLUSIONS

Richard L. Gregory   NOVEMBER 1968

Chapter 11

I. SUMMARY

The visual system processes retinal images in a way that usually provides the organism with a fairly accurate representation of the external world, but there are a number of striking exceptions: the visual illusions. The study of visual illusions can provide valuable information concerning the visual processing mechanisms which under normal conditions accurately reflect the nature of the external environment. On the basis of such studies, Gregory has argued that only a small part of our total perception is included in the retinal image. Perception is largely a process of selecting the hypothesis about the stimulus object which is most consistent with current sensory input and past experience. Apparently, visual illusions occur when inappropriate cues cause an individual's internal model of the external stimulus to be distorted. In some cases [e.g. Necker cube] visual cues are ambiguous and the viewer fluctuates between two different models of the visual world even though the sensory input is unchanged.

Convincing support for Gregory's theory comes from studies showing that the well known Müller-Lyer illusion is the result of perspective cues being misinterpreted by the visual system. When the figures are viewed in the absence of a visible background, the illusion is still present, but both figures appear as corners in three dimensions. Moreover, there is a clear correlation between the magnitude of the illusion viewed on a surface and the depth that is perceived when the background is removed. Under normal viewing conditions, when two objects produce a retinal image of the same size, the object which is perceived as being more distant is perceived as being larger. Both lines of the Müller-Lyer illusion produce retinal images of the same size, but because differential depth cues are produced by the "arrowheads" the lines appear to differ in length. Paradoxically, the illusions occur even when it is obvious that the figures are flat. Apparently, perspective cues presented on a flat surface trigger the brain to compensate for differences in distance even when no such differences are perceived.

II. GLOSSARY

afterimage—visual image remaining for a short period of time after termination of the visual stimulus.

depth-cue scaling — size scaling established directly and automatically by depth cues.

depth-hypothesis scaling—size scaling which depends on the observer's hypothesis about the nature of the stimulus object.

distortion illusions — systematic distortions of perceived size or shape.

Emmert's law — the apparent size of an afterimage is directly related to the distance of the surface on which it is viewed.

Hering illusion — parallel lines appear bowed when they pass on either side of a point from which numerous straight lines radiate.

horizontal-vertical illusion — a vertical line looks longer than a horizontal line of the same length.

Müller-Lyer illusion — a line with out-directed arrowheads at each end looks shorter than the same line with in-directed arrowheads.

Necker cube — the line drawing of a transparent cube which spontaneously reverses in depth.

Penrose triangle — a three dimensional, closed triangular shape which is logically consistent over restricted portions, but impossible when viewed as a whole.

Poggendorff illusion — [line-displacement illusion] two segments of a diagonal line appear offset if the line passes behind a solid bar.

Ponso illusion — [the railway-line illusion] two identical rectangles between converging lines appear to differ in size, the line closer to the point of convergence appearing larger.

size constancy — the tendency of the same object presented at different distances to appear the same size even though the size of the retinal image is changed markedly.

size-weight illusion — the smaller of two objects of the same weight is judged as being the heavier.

stereoscopic information — visual information derived from disparities between the two retinal images.

III. ESSAY STUDY QUESTIONS

1. What is the main proposition examined by Gregory?
2. What evidence is there that the horizontal-vertical illusion is not the result of learned patterns of eye movement?
3. What was the common feature of early attempts to explain illusions?
4. Why are pictures paradoxical?
5. How can pictures be viewed without stereoscopic and background information? How does the Müller-Lyer illusion look under these conditions?
6. What evidence is there to support the conclusion that the magnitude of the Müller-Lyer illusion as it is viewed on a flat surface is related to the amount of depth perceived when the background is removed?
7. What evidence is there that at least part of size constancy is due to a central size-scaling mechanism?
8. What is the difference between depth-cue scaling and depth-hypothesis scaling?
9. The size constancy effect is not complete. Explain.
10. Summarize Gregory's view of perception.

MULTISTABILITY IN PERCEPTION

Chapter 12

Fred Attneave   DECEMBER 1971

I. SUMMARY

Some pictures and geometric figures change in appearance with continued viewing. The classic example is the Necker cube. At first, one of its faces seems to be at the front, but then the figure reverses in depth. Under continued viewing the two orientations will alternate spontaneously; sometimes one orientation is seen and sometimes the other, but never both simultaneously. The problem is to understand why the perceptions change even though the physical stimulus does not.

Figure-ground reversals are a commonly studied form of alternating figure. An example of such a reversal is the drawing which can be seen as either a goblet or a pair of faces; the various surface properties are attributed alternately to different parts of the drawing. Under natural conditions, many factors cooperate to determine the figure-ground relationship and ambiguity are, but in reversible figures such cues are absent and the nervous system alternates between "equiprobable" interpretations.

Some of the most striking and amusing ambigious figures are pictures that can be seen as either of two objects, for example, a duck or a rabbit, a young lady or an old woman, or a man's face or a woman's figure. Why should one aspect of an ambiguous figure, once it is "locked in," ever give way to the other? Indeed, some people can look for quite a while and see only one aspect of an ambiguous figure, especially if they are first exposed to a version of the figure biased in favor of one of the interpretations. Not until both aspects have been pointed out will the figure spontaneously alternate.

Ambiguities of depth characterize a large class of multistable figures, the Necker cube being the most familiar example. Necker concluded that the aspect seen depends entirely on the point of fixation. Although the fixation point is indeed important, it has been shown that depth reversal will readily occur without eye movement. To understand how depth relationships can be multistable, one must first consider how a three-dimensional perception can be derived from a two-dimensional drawing. A particular straight line on the retina can be produced by any one of an infinite number of external lines in an infinite number of orientations in a given plane. We should not be surprised, therefore, that depth is sometimes ambiguous; it is far more remarkable that the perceptual systems can select a particular orientation, or at worst can vacillate between just two or three possibilities. On what basis does the visual system perform this feat? The answer is found in the principle of Prägnanz, the idea that one perceives the simplest picture consistent with a given image. With reversible figures, there are two or more equally probable perceptions.

The multistable behavior of the perceptual system displays two notable characteristics. The first is that at any one moment only one aspect of the ambiguous figure can be seen; mixtures occur only fleetingly if at all. The second is that the different percepts alternate spontaneously. The most likely interpretation of such effects is that the alternative aspects of the figure are represented by activity in different neural structures, and when one structure becomes "fatigued," it gives way to the other, which is more excitable. If the activity in the two structures were mutually inhibitory, this would explain why only one aspect of the ambiguous figure can be perceived at a time.

II. GLOSSARY

equilateral — a triangle with three equal sides.
frontal lobes — the anterior portions of the cerebral hemisphere.
isosceles — a triangle with two equal sides.
Necker cube — a line drawing of a transparent cube which reverses in depth under continuous viewing.

Prägnanz — principle that one perceives the "best" picture consistent with a given retinal image.
retina — the layer of cells lining the rear of the eyeball which contains the visual receptors.
scalene — a triangle with three unequal sides.
Schröder stairs — a line drawing of transparent stairs which reverses in depth under steady viewing.

III. ESSAY STUDY QUESTIONS

1. Why does Attneave use the concept of multistability in his discussion of ambiguous figures?
2. When elements are grouped perceptually, they are partitioned; they are not simultaneously cross-classified. Explain.
3. Describe a case of multistability involving apparent movement.
4. It is difficult to separate the roles of simplicity and familiarity in perception. Explain.
5. Describe a case of perspective reversal where the color as well as the shape of the object can change.
6. Describe a case of perspective reversal where head movement induces apparent motion.
7. Describe and discuss the multistable states of triangles.
8. Describe physical and electronic systems which approximate the multistability characteristics of the perception of ambiguous figures.
9. Describe the physiological explanation of the perception of ambiguous figures which is suggested by Attneave.

THE PERCEPTION OF DISORIENTED FIGURES

Irvin Rock   JANUARY 1974

Chapter 13

I. SUMMARY

Since changing the orientation of a figure does not alter its internal geometric relations, it is difficult to understand why figures are difficult to identify when they are upside down or tilted. In order to understand this phenomenon, one must consider what changes are produced by changing the orientation of a figure. One obvious change is that rotating a figure produces a change in the orientation of the figure on the retina. The second change is that a rotated figure is in a different orientation to the vertical and horizontal axes of the environment. Which of these factors—the retinal or the environmental—is responsible for the perceptual difficulties produced by figure rotation? It is relatively easy to separate these two factors experimentally. If a square is taped to the wall with the bottom parallel to the floor, it looks like a square even when the head is tilted 45 degrees. Yet in this position, the retinal image is the same as that of a diamond viewed when the head is upright. Alternatively, if the square is rotated on the wall so that it becomes a diamond, it looks like a diamond whether the head is upright or tilted 45 degrees. Thus it is the figure's perceived orientation in the environment that determines its perceived shape, and not the orientation of the retinal image.

Why does the orientation of a figure with respect to the directional coordinates of the environment have such a profound effect on the perceived shape of a figure? Rock proposes that the nervous system encodes figures on the basis of these coordinates. For example, an isosceles triangle could be encoded as a closed symmetrical figure resting on a straight horizontal base with a point at the top and two straight sides of equal length. Obviously if such a figure were encoded in this manner, identification would be more difficult if the figure were rotated. But there is one kind of disorientation which has little effect on the recognition of figures: a mirror-image reversal. Thus, it seems that the "sides" of visual space are essentially interchangeable. The up-and-down directions, however, are not; they are distinctly different directions in our perceptual world. In the absence of visual or gravitational cues, a subject will assign top-bottom coordinates on the basis of this subjective reference system. For example, a figure drawn on a circular sheet of paper lying on the ground will be perceived as having a top and bottom in relation to the position of the subject's body. The vertical axis of the figure is seen as being aligned with the axis of the subject's head and body.

There are some cases, however, where the orientation of the retinal image and not the environmental assignment of direction seems to determine the perceived shape of the object. For example, if a viewer observes photographs with his head upside down between his legs, they will be just as difficult to recognize as when the picture is upside down and the head is upright. And conversely, if both the viewer's head and the pictures are inverted, the viewer has no difficulty in observing them.

Rock argues that when we view an object with our head tilted, we automatically compensate for this tilt in much the same way as we compensate for the size of distant objects. When a vertical luminous rod is viewed in a dark room by a tilted observer, the rod will appear vertical or almost so even though the retinal image is tilted. Thus body tilt must be taken into account and corrected for by the perceptual system. When we look at figures which are difficult to recognize when they are retinally disoriented, the difficulty increases as the degree of disorientation increases. This relationship may offer some insights into the mechanisms of this correction process. Rock suggests that to correct for retinal disorientation, the observer must visualize how the figure would look if it were rotated until it was upright with respect to the viewer himself. If this process of "mental" rotation requires visualizing the entire sequence of angular change, greater difficulty would be expected to be associated with greater angular change.

II. GLOSSARY

ambiguous figures —figures which can be perceived as either of two different objects.

orientation constancy — the orientation of objects can be perceived accurately with respect to the external environment regardless of the orientation of the viewer.

quadrilateral — four-sided figure.

retinal image — the pattern of energy striking the retina of the eye from a visual stimulus.

size constancy — objects of equal size viewed at varying distances appear to be the same size even though more distant objects produce a smaller retinal image.

transposition — changing a figure without altering its internal geometric relations.

vestibular apparatus — the organs of balance located in the inner ear.

III. ESSAY STUDY QUESTIONS

1. Describe the research which indicates that it is a figure's orientation in the environment rather than the orientation of its retinal image that determines its perceived shape.
2. According to Rock, why does the orientation of a figure with respect to the directional coordinates of the environment have such a profound effect on perceived shape?
3. What evidence is there that perceived shape can also depend on retinal orientation?
4. Explain the concept of orientational constancy. Compare it with size constancy.
5. Rock suggests that perception in general is based to a great extent on cognitive processes. What does this mean and what evidence does he offer to support his contention?
6. What evidence is there that orientational correction is difficult to achieve if the visual display has multiple components?
7. What factors make it difficult to read inverted material?
8. About 80 per cent of subjects reported seeing only the aspect of the ambiguous figure that was environmentally upright, even though the alternative was upright on their retina. Explain.
9. How does the author account for the fact that children often look at things upside down?
10. Briefly summarize Rock's conclusions.

VISION AND TOUCH   # Chapter 14

Irvin Rock and Charles S. Harris   MAY 1967

I. SUMMARY

Visual perception is much more than a simple copy of the retinal image. As a result, many investigators have assumed that one must learn how to see. Touch presumably educates vision, adding meaning to the initially meaningless jumble of retinal images. Rock and Harris report the results of a variety of experiments which test this view.

What happens when touch and vision provide conflicting information? If touch does in fact educate vision, the tactual information should be dominant, but the opposite seems to be the case. When subjects felt an object as they were viewing it through a lens which distorted its shape, they were not aware of the conflicting information and judged the shape to correspond to the visually perceived distortion even when the judgments were made tactually. This striking dominance of touch by vision has been termed visual capture.

After long periods of such exposure to conflicting tactual and visual information, there was considerable adaptation. When subjects first put on prisms which laterally displaced the perceived position of objects, performance was disrupted. When the observer first tried to point rapidly at an object, he missed, but after a few minutes of viewing his moving hand through the displacing prisms, the accuracy of his performance improved markedly. There are two interpretations of this adaptation. Perhaps subjects pointed more accurately because visual perception had changed to conform to the felt position of the hand even though the retinal image remained displaced. Conversely, the felt position of the hand may have changed to conform to the displaced retinal image. This latter interpretation has been convincingly supported by the observation that the accuracy of pointing improved only with the hand which had been viewed through the lens. If the change were in visual perception, adaptation should have occurred with both hands. Moreover, after such adaptation, there was a shift in pointing of the "practiced" hand at sounds even when the eyes were closed.

These and other related observations have provided strong support for the view that vision dominates touch, the felt position of our limbs being modified to conform to visual information. Furthermore, there is no convincing evidence for the widely accepted notion that touch educates vision.

II. GLOSSARY

adaptation — the improvement in performance observed during continued experience with distorted or displaced retinal images.

remembered-standard test — a subject perceives a standard stimulus object and at some later point selects a test stimulus which best matches the standard.

right-angle prism — prism which reverses the visual field from right to left.

visual capture — the tendency for vision to completely dominate touch when the two are in conflict.

III. ESSAY STUDY QUESTIONS

1. Visual perception is not a direct copy of the retinal image. Explain.
2. What do the authors mean when they refer to the sense of touch?
3. What observations have been generally assumed to support the view that touch educates vision?
4. What four pieces of information contradict the assumption that touch educates vision?
5. Describe the phenomenon of visual capture and the experiments used to demonstrate it.
6. What two explanations are there for adaptation to distorted vision?
7. Describe experiments that show that adaptation to displaced retinal images really reflects a change in position sense rather than a change in visual perception.
8. What evidence is there that adaptation to prisms reflects a sensory rather than a motor change?
9. Describe how a remembered-standard test was used to determine whether touch or vision was changed after prolonged exposure to conflicting data.
10. On what point do Rock and Harris disagree?

SOURCES OF AMBIGUITY IN THE PRINTS OF MAURITS C. ESCHER

Marianne L. Teuber   JULY 1974

Chapter 15

I. SUMMARY

Ambiguity is the most striking characteristic of the graphic art of Maurits C. Escher. There is the ambiguity of figure and ground; the ambiguity of two or three dimensions; the ambiguity of the reversible cube; and the ambiguous limits of the infinitely small. Moreover, in many cases this visual ambiguity goes hand in hand with ambiguity of meaning. Those works of Escher characterized by regular subdivisions of figure and ground have frequently been compared to the packed periodic structures of crystals and to the mathematical transformations of topology and non-Euclidean geometry; however, it is now clear that the original inspiration for these ambiguous patterns came from the psychological literature on visual perception. From Escher's own commentary on his prints, it is clear that he was familiar with the psychological literature relevant to his work. In particular, his style seems to have been influenced by early experiments on figure and ground by Edgar Rubin, by Kurt Koffka's 1935 book *Principles of Gestalt Psychology*, and by the experiments of Koffka's student, Molly R. Harrower. Only after he had mastered the construction of repeated ambiguous figure-ground relations did he recognize their similarity to certain aspects of crystallography.

Ambiguous figure-ground designs first appear in Escher's work in 1921, the same year that the reversible figure-ground patterns of Danish psychologist Edgar Rubin were published in German translation, and Escher's own commentary on these early prints leaves little doubt of Rubin's influence on them. After his early exposure to Rubin's ambiguous figure-ground patterns, Escher left his native Netherlands to live in Italy; it was only after departure from Italy in 1934 that he again returned to the figure-ground problem. It is apparent that some time between 1935 and 1938 Escher became acquainted with Koffka's *Principles of Gestalt Psychology*. In this book there is an entire chapter on the topic of figure and ground based to a large extent on Rubin's original research. Thus, through Koffka, Escher's dormant fascination and preoccupation with figure-ground relationships were revived.

Prior to 1936 Escher had concentrated on presentations of two-dimensional contiguous human and animal forms. In *Principles of Gestalt Psychology* Koffka demonstrates how two-dimensional lines and planes are viewed in three dimensions under certain conditions. As a result of this influence, in the years after 1936 three-dimensionality and ambiguity of depth became a prominent feature of Escher's work. The influence of experiments by Harrower was also evident in Escher's post-1936 work. By gradually changing the shape and the brightness contrast of repeated figure-ground relationships Escher produced an interesting effect: the figure gradually became the ground and the ground, the figure. Both shape and brightness contrast had been identified by Harrower in her 1936 article as important factors in the perception of figure-ground relationships.

Psychological studies were not Escher's only source of inspiration. Escher himself recognized the similarities of his regular subdivisions of a plane to the principles of crystallography; because of these similarities, most art historians have assumed that mathematical prototypes provided the original stimulus for his work. This conclusion is understandable because the influence of crystallographic theory was clearly present in Escher's later work. Yet the origins of his characteristic style from manipulations of the figure-ground reversal in the framework of early psychological literature is now quite clear.

II. GLOSSARY

Alhambra — a palace of the Moorish kings built in Spain in the 14th and 15th centuries.

crater illusion — changes from concave to convex in depth perception of a crater drawn on a flat surface when the apparent direction of illumination is changed from top to bottom.

crystallography — the study of the form and structure of crystals.

Gestalt psychology — a school of psychology that concentrated on the study of perception and had as its defining premise the idea that psychological processes can not be studied by analyzing them into their constituent elements.

lithograph — a print taken from a picture originally produced on a flat, specially prepared stone.

majolica — a kind of pottery coated with enamel and decorated with rich colours.

Necker cube — a two-dimensional line drawing of a cube that reverses in depth on continued inspection.

Schröder stairs — a line drawing of stairs that reverses in depth.

tesselated — formed of small squares or blocks in a mosaic pattern.

woodcut — a print from an engraved block of wood.

III. ESSAY STUDY QUESTIONS

1. Escher's work is characterized by ambiguity. Discuss the ambiguities incorporated in three of his works.
2. The impetus for Escher's work has been assumed to come from mathematical theories of structure. Why?
3. Select three of Escher's works from various stages of his career and discuss how these works were influenced by psychological studies of perception.
4. Describe the influence that each of the following individuals had on Escher's work: Edgar Rubin, Kurt Koffka, Molly R. Harrower, B. G. Escher, Kai von Fieandt, and Giovanni Battista Piranesi.
5. Describe the developments in Escher's style that occurred in the late 1930's. What factors seem to have influenced them?
6. Discuss the principle of equivalence as used by Escher.
7. Discuss Escher's use of perceptual impossibility.

THE CONTROL OF SHORT-TERM MEMORY

Richard C. Atkinson and Richard M. Shiffrin   AUGUST 1971

Chapter 16

I. SUMMARY

The authors propose a theory based on the idea that there are two modes of information storage, short-term and long-term, and that the storage and retrieval of information is best described in terms of the flow of information through the short-term store and the subject's control of the flow. According to the authors' view, information from the environment is processed by the sensory systems and entered into the short-term store, where it remains for a period of time under the control of the subject. By rehearsing, subjects can extend the length of time that an item will remain in this form, but the number of items which can be stored simultaneously in short-term memory is strictly limited. While information is held in short-term storage, it may be copied into the long-term store, which is assumed to be a storage system from which memories are not usually lost. While an item is being held in short-term storage, closely related information is activated and also brought into the short-term store. Thus, to retrieve information from long-term storage, the appropriate "probe information" is placed in the short-term store; this calls up subsets of related information that the subject "scans" for the desired information.

The research on this retrieval process involves a paradigm known as the free-recall task, in which subjects are presented with a long list of random words one at a time and are asked to recall them after an interval of time. An interesting result of such studies is that the probability of recalling each item is a function of its place in the list. There is an increased probability of recall for words near the beginning and end of the list termed the primacy and recency effects respectively. There is considerable evidence that the recency effect is due to retrieval from short-term storage and that the earlier portions of the serial-position curve reflect retrieval from long-term storage only. For example, if subjects are asked to do some difficult arithmetic calculations after the list has been presented so that all of the words will be lost from the short-term store, the recency effect is eliminated but the earlier portions of the curve are unaffected. Moreover, if variables that influence only the long-term store are manipulated, only the earlier portions of the curve show changes. The authors have attempted to explain the serial-position ef-

fect in terms of a rehearsal process. According to this view, as the words are presented the subjects actively rehearse those items held in short-term memory but only a small, fixed number of items can be maintained in short-term storage by rehearsal. Thus as each new word is presented one of the preceding items is dropped from short-term memory. The items that are still being rehearsed when the last item is presented are the ones which are immediately recalled, thus giving rise to the recency effect. Since the transfer of information from the short-term to the long-term is a function of the length of time an item has been rehearsed in the short-term store, those items at the start of the list, which are under rehearsal the longest before being displaced by subsequent items, are remembered better than items in the middle, thus giving rise to the primacy effect.

When rehearsal is blocked by having subjects perform arithmetic tasks in the interval between initial learning and the test, recall is a decreasing function of the learning-test interval. The amount of material introduced between learning and the test seems to be much more important in determining recall than the amount of time that has elapsed. Is the intervening activity a direct cause of items being dropped from short-term storage or does the intervening activity merely reduce recall by interfering with the number of times an item can be rehearsed? The fact that a signal-detection task interferes with rehearsal but not recall favors the first interpretation and shows that the loss of material from the short-term store is not only a function of the amount of intervening material but the type. It appears that forgetting is caused by entry into the short-term store of other similar information. Although the signal-detection task does not disrupt short-term memory, it does stop material in the short-term store from being transferred to the long-term mode. Thus it appears that rehearsal plays an important part in the transfer of information to long-term storage.

Forgetting has been commonly viewed as an erosion of the long-term memory trace by subsequent material but the authors view long-term memory as being permanent. In this view subsequent material produces forgetting by interfering with retrieval.

II. GLOSSARY

coding — putting information to be remembered in a context of additional, easily retrievable information.

imaging — a process in which verbal material is remembered through visual images.

interference theories — theories of memory which attribute forgetting to the erosion of a memory trace by subsequent learning.

mnemonic — any artificial technique of coding information to improve memory.

phenomenology — investigation of conscious experience.

primacy effect — the first few items in a list have a higher probability of being recalled than items in the middle of the list.

probe information — information put into short-term memory in order to call up a particular memory.

recency effect — the last few items in a list have a higher probability of being recalled than items in the middle of the list.

rehearsal — an overt or covert repetition of material to improve retention.

search set — a subset of information in the long-term store which is activated by the probe information.

serial-position effect — the U-shaped relation between serial position and the probability of recall.

III. ESSAY STUDY QUESTIONS

1. Describe some of the control processes which can be used to influence the flow of information through short-term memory.
2. Describe the authors' model of memory storage and retrieval.
3. What is the serial-position curve and what evidence is there that the primacy and recency effects are phenomena of long- and short-term storage respectively?
4. Describe the authors' interpretation of the serial-position effect and the data that support it.
5. What evidence is there that rehearsal is an important factor in the maintenance of information in the short-term store and the transfer of information to the long-term system?
6. What are the forgetting and transfer characteristics of the short-term store in the absence of rehearsal?
7. There are two interpretations for the effects of intervening activity on recall. What are they and which interpretation is supported by the experimental findings?
8. Forgetting is caused by entry into the short-term store of other, similar information. Explain.
9. What evidence shows that the mere presence of a trace in the short-term store is not enough to result in the transfer to long-term storage?
10. How do coding procedures improve memory?
11. In opposition to the interference theories of forgetting, the authors argue that information is held permanently in long-term storage. Explain. Describe the evidence supporting the authors' view.

HOW WE REMEMBER WHAT WE SEE

Ralph Norman Haber   MAY 1970

Chapter 17

I. SUMMARY

Subjects were shown 2,560 photographic slides at the rate of one every 10 seconds. Then, one hour later, they were shown 280 pairs of slides, each pair consisting of one slide from the original series and a new slide. They were able to identify the familiar slide in 85 to 95 percent of the cases. Thus it is clear that the human capacity for remembering pictures is appreciable. However, although a person may recognize a large proportion of the pictures that he has previously seen, he is frequently unable to recall the details of a specific picture when asked to do so. What happens to these omitted details? Are they never seen in the first place? Are they seen but then forgotten, or are they seen and remembered but in such a way that they are not retrievable under normal circumstances? To study these questions each subject was shown a detailed picture and asked to recall both verbally and by drawing everything about the picture that he could remember seeing. When the recall of further details seemed exhausted, the subjects engaged in dart throwing or work association for 30 minutes before being asked again to recall details of the picture. The dart-throwers' ability to recall the details of the picture neither improved nor deteriorated, but each word-associator recovered a number of details omitted from the earlier recall.

These results indicate that some information about fine pictorial details is maintained in memory but is not normally available for verbal report. Moreover, the relatively poor verbal recall of pictorial stimuli suggests that pictorial information is not normally stored in the form of a verbal code. When the pictorial memory process is compared with the process by which words, numbers, and other symbols are remembered, it becomes clear that the two systems are probably very different. In the case of pictures, the image is received and stored in pictorial form; whereas, where words or other symbols are concerned, the first step of memory is to extract the meaning from the visual form. Words are remembered as ideas, not as collections of letters.

The first step in the process of extracting linguistic information from its representational form and storing it conceptually is a brief moment of iconic or visual storage during which the image is scanned and coded. Several experiments by the author and other investigators have clarified what happens in this early stage of memory storage. One problem that was investigated was the source of the errors that are made when an individual is asked to recall several items in a detailed display. Do omissions indicate a limited memory capacity or are they due to a failure to perceive some of the items? In an experiment by Sperling, an array of tachistoscopically presented letters remained visible for 50 milliseconds. Once the display ended, the subject's task was to remember all the letters until a marker appeared that indicated which of the letters was to be reported. The important finding was that if the marker came on within 250 milliseconds of the array, there were virtually no errors. Thus, it is clear that all of the array was perceived and errors at longer intervals could not be the result of failure to perceive some of the details. These results also indicate that iconic storage persists for about 250 milliseconds. This conclusion was supported by the author's observation that if the intervals between light flashes are less than 250 milliseconds, subjects report that the light is continuously present. In another experiment a brief visual stimulus was presented to subjects who were asked to adjust the timing of a click so that it sounded at stimulus onset and again at offset. As expected, the second click followed the offset of a brief display by about 200 milliseconds, indicating that the iconic image was of that duration; however, with longer stimulus durations, the duration of the iconic image was shorter. Thus, it is clear that the initial phase of memory storage is visual, since subjects treat the memory as if it is a continuation of the visual stimulus. Iconic images seem to prolong a brief visual stimulus that does not last long enough to be recognized and entered into memory storage.

II. GLOSSARY

acronym — a word formed from the initial letters of other words.

iconic storage — memory storage that takes the form of a visual image.

tachistoscope — device for presenting precisely timed sequences of visual displays.

word association — a form of free association in which the subject responds to a presented word with the first word or idea that comes to mind.

III. ESSAY STUDY QUESTIONS

1. Recall, recognition, and relearning are three measures of memory. When comparing the facility with which verbal as opposed to pictorial information can be retained, it is important that the same measure of memory be used in both cases. Discuss with reference to the present article.

2. The author concludes that the capacity of memory for pictures may be unlimited. On what evidence is this conclusion based?

3. Although most people can recognize most pictures that they have seen before, they have difficulty recalling the details of the pictures when asked to do so. What explanations are there for this discrepancy between recall and recognition. What does the author's research indicate?

4. The author believes that scenes, faces, and pictures are remembered differently from linguistic material. What evidence does he offer in support of this position?

5. What evidence is there for the view that pictures are not normally stored in memory in the form of words?

6. The process of extracting linguistic material from its representational form and storing it conceptually appears to consist of several steps. Discuss.

7. Describe two methods for improving short-term memory.

8. What evidence is there that the inability to recall all of the items in a visual display is not entirely the result of a perceptual problem?

9. What is the duration of the iconic phase of memory storage? Describe the research which has a bearing on this issue.

10. What evidence is there that the iconic image is not totally a retinal phenomenon?

11. What experimental results show that the first stage of memory storage is visual?

12. Discuss the relation between iconic images and reading ability.

13. Once a letter is perceived, further viewing time is not required for processing the information, as long as the iconic image is not disrupted. Discuss.

HOW TO TEACH ANIMALS
Chapter 18

B. F. Skinner   December 1951

I. SUMMARY

Whenever a rewarding state of affairs follows a particular response, that response and responses similar to it are more likely to be repeated. There is nothing new about this principle, but what is new is a better understanding of how to use it effectively to control behavior. By controlling the contingencies between behavior and reinforcement, one can "shape" the behavior of others.

In order to train an organism to perform a desired response, one must find a stimulus which can serve as the reinforcement. Food, for example, is usually an effective reinforcement for animals who have been deprived of food prior to training. There are two important rules for effectively administering reinforcement. First, reinforcement must be administered in such a way that it remains effective. When food is used, for example, only small pieces should be used, so that the organism's hunger is not significantly reduced during the course of training. Second, reinforcement must be administered immediately following the desired response; even a slight delay greatly reduces the effectiveness of the reinforcement. Since most reinforcers are difficult to administer with the speed required, a conditioned reinforcer is often employed. This is a stimulus which acquires reinforcing properties of its own through being repeatedly paired with a reinforcer. A buzzer, for example, can be sounded at the same time meat is presented, until it acquires reinforcing properties. Then, when the dog makes the appropriate response, the buzzer can be sounded immediately, and regardless of where he is or what he is doing he will be reinforced immediately.

Often the desired response is one that is not in the animal's behavioral repertoire. In this case, the trainer or experimenter cannot wait for the appearance of the desired response to reinforce it, because this response may never occur spontaneously. He must shape the response by first reinforcing any activity which is part of the desired response, and then reinforcing closer and closer approximations until the desired response itself is produced. For example, to train a dog to turn on the radio, it may first be necessary to reinforce the dog for standing near the radio. Once this response is established, then the dog can be reinforced for touching the radio with his nose, then for touching areas closer and closer to the control knob, then for touching the knob, and finally for turning the radio on.

It is important to understand such simple learning situations, since they are common in everyday behavior. Although the reinforcements are more complex and subtle—attention, approval, or affection as opposed to food or water—the principles seem to be the same. We are almost always reinforcing or punishing the behavior of others whether we mean to or not.

II. GLOSSARY

conditioned reinforcer — a "neutral" stimulus which acquires reinforcing properties of its own by being repeatedly paired with a reinforcer.

extinguish — reduce the frequency of a response by withholding the reinforcer that usually follows it.

punishment — any stimulus which reduces the rate of a response that precedes it.

reinforcement — any stimulus which increases the rate of a response that precedes it.

III. ESSAY STUDY QUESTIONS

1. Describe the function of the conditioned reinforcer in training. How do you tell when it is working properly?
2. Describe how you would train a monkey to identify incompletely filled bottles in a bottling plant.
3. The limit of animal training is determined as much by the experimenter's skill as that of the animal. Discuss.
4. We are almost always reinforcing or punishing the behavior of others, whether we want to or not. Discuss.
5. Parents may actually train their children to be annoying. Explain.

THE SPLIT BRAIN IN MAN

Michael S. Gazzaniga   AUGUST 1969

Chapter 19

I. SUMMARY

The brain of man and other "higher" animals is a double organ consisting of left and right hemispheres connected by the corpus callosum and several other smaller commissures. Experimental examination of patients having some of the major commissures therapeutically sectioned has revealed much about the function of these structures and the general organization of the brain.

In general it has been found that following this split-brain operation each hemisphere functions independently as if it were a complete brain with its own capacities and capabilities; the major difference between the hemispheres being that in most individuals verbal abilities are controlled for the most part by the left hemisphere. Thus, when visual or tactual information is presented to the left hemisphere, the subject can respond to it verbally or manually with the right hand, but when the same information is presented to the right hemisphere the subject can not respond verbally but can identify it with the left hand.

The bisected-brain syndrome has also provided a valuable vehicle for determining the extent of ipsilateral motor control in human subjects. This can be examined by presenting information to one hemisphere and requiring a response from an ipsilateral limb based on this input. In general, it has been found that only gross movements are subject to such control. The split-brain patient has also provided a method for comparing the abilities of the two hemispheres. For example, it was found that the right hemisphere does in fact have some minor verbal abilities, the limits of which vary dramatically from subject to subject. Although the left hemisphere is commonly termed the dominant hemisphere, the right hemisphere has been found not to be inferior or subordinate in all respects.

II. GLOSSARY

cerebrum — the upper part of the brain, consisting of two hemispheres separated by a deep longitudinal fissure.

commissures — neural connections between the hemispheres.

contralateral — opposite side.

corpus callosum — the largest commissure.

cranium — skull.

cross-cuing — transferring information from one hemisphere to the other via non-neural routes.

hemisphere — either of the lateral halves of the cerebrum.

ipsilateral — same side.

optic chiasm — the point at which the optic nerve fibers from the nasal portion of the retina cross over to the contralateral hemisphere.

optic nerve — the nerve transmitting coded visual information from the eye to the brain.

unilateral — restricted to one side.

III. ESSAY STUDY QUESTIONS

1. Why are the effects of the split-brain operation most dramatic when sensory information can be limited to a single hemisphere?
2. How did Myers and Sperry limit visual input to a single hemisphere in cats? How was this accomplished in human patients?
3. Describe the effects on vision of sectioning the optic chiasm.
4. How can the extent of ipsilateral motor control be determined using a split-brain subject?
5. Describe the events which happen when the word "HEART" is presented to a split-brain subject so that the fixation point is between the "E" and the "A".
6. Describe the changes in the localization of verbal abilities which occur with increasing age.
7. Describe the phenomenon of unilateral emotions.
8. In what respects does the right hemisphere seem superior to the left?
9. Describe the experiment which showed that split-brain monkeys can process visual information more efficiently than normal monkeys.

TEACHING LANGUAGE TO AN APE

Ann James Premack and David Premack   OCTOBER 1972

Chapter 20

I. SUMMARY

The authors have taught a chimpanzee named Sarah to read and write with variously shaped and colored pieces of plastic, each representing a word. Why try to teach human language to an ape? The motive in this case was to better define the fundamental nature of language. Language is a general system of which human language is a particular, albeit remarkably refined, form. By teaching language to a chimpanzee it may be possible to identify those aspects of language that are uniquely human. Moreover, such experiments may reveal the nature of the chimpanzee's conceptual world and facilitate the comparative study of cognitive processes.

The first step was to exploit knowledge that Sarah already had; they mapped out the social transaction of giving, which is something that the chimpanzee does both in nature and in the laboratory. In order to map out the entire transaction of giving, the animal had to distinguish agents from objects, agents from one another, and objects from one another. Sarah initially had to put a pink plastic square on a "language board" mounted on the side of her cage in order to receive a slice of banana. Later several other fruits, the verb "give," and the plastic words that named each of them were introduced. To be certain that Sarah knew the meaning of "give" it was necessary to contrast "give" with other verbs. When she put "wash apple" on the board, she did not receive the apple; it was placed in a bowl and washed. At this stage Sarah had to place two words, "give apple," on the board to receive the apple. When recipients were named, three words were required; identification of the donor required yet another word. At every stage she had to observe the proper word sequence.

At first Sarah learned all her words in the context of social exchange, but later, when she had learned the concepts of "name of" and "not name of," it was possible to introduce new words in a more direct way. Subsequently, Sarah was trained in the uses of adjectives and conditional and interrogative statements. In order to teach her the concepts of color, shape, and size she was taught to identify members of the classes red and yellow, round and square, and large and small. Objects which varied in most dimensions but had one of the above properties in common were used for this purpose. In teaching class names many of the sentences were not "written" on the board but were presented as hybrids consisting of a combination of plastic words and real objects. For example, a typical hybrid sentence was "Yellow?" beside a banana. Her performance showed that she was able to move with facility from symbols for objects to the real objects.

Was Sarah able to think in her new language? Could she store information using the plastic words and use it to solve problems that she could not have otherwise solved? Additional research is required for unequivocal answers to these questions, but several aspects of Sarah's performance indicate that the answers may be a qualified yes. For Sarah to match the word "apple" with an actual apple indicates that she knows the meaning of the word, but it does not mean that she can think apple when she is presented with the word alone. The ability to achieve such mental representation is important because it frees language from direct dependence on the external world. The hint that Sarah could use words in the absence of their external referents came in a test where she was given a piece of fruit and two plastic words. While the task was to put the correct word for the fruit on the board, she frequently put up the wrong word. Subsequent tests indicated that she was trying to communicate her preference in fruit. This strongly suggests that Sarah could generate meanings of fruit from the symbols alone.

II. GLOSSARY

autistic — individuals who indulge in wishful thinking or phantasy to a pathological degree.

call system — a series of vocalizations used by some animals for intraspecific communication.

constituent structure — the hierarchical organization of a sentence.

displacement — the ability to talk about things that are not currently present.

language board — a sheet of steel on which Sarah placed her magnetized words.

III. ESSAY STUDY QUESTIONS

1. What was the objective of the authors' work and to what extent did they accomplish it?
2. Why did the authors teach Sarah to communicate with plastic chips rather than vocal patterns? Is this really language?
3. Until animals are taught language it will not be possible to study their cognitive processes for classifying stimuli, for storing and retrieving information, and for problem solving. Discuss.
4. In most psychological experiments many subjects are tested but the Premacks' conclusions are based on data from only a single organism. Discuss.
5. The test with the compound sentence was of considerable importance. Explain.
6. A chimpanzee is capable of decomposing a complex object into features. Explain.
7. What evidence is there that Sarah could think and solve problems in plastic word language?
8. How was Sarah trained to understand conditional statements?
9. What procedures were used to train Sarah to form concepts of color, shape, and size?
10. How was Sarah trained to understand questions?
11. Sarah could have learned more words if the symbols were similar to the objects they represented. Why did the authors not use this strategy?

SLIPS OF THE TONGUE

Victoria A. Fromkin DECEMBER 1973   # Chapter 21

I. SUMMARY

Given the finite storage capacity of the brain, it is not possible to store the infinite number of sentences that are possible in a given language. To account for a speaker's ability to form an infinite number of sentences, linguistic theorists have argued that what is learned in language acquisition is a grammar that includes a finite set of basic elements and a finite set of rules for their combination. Moreover, these discrete elements seem to be organized hierarchically, phonemes combining to form syllables that combine to form morphemes that combine to form sentences. The presence of such an organization of speech into discrete elements is not obvious since the sounds we produce and those we hear are continuous; however, a careful examination of the systematic errors of speech has provided strong support for the idea that the continuous flow of speech is based on a hierarchical organization of discrete elements.

The author studied more than 6,000 reports of errors in speech. The first thing that was obvious from this study was that errors in language were not random; they seemed to be based on the mental grammar utilized by speakers when they encode ideas into utterances. For example, errors such as the legendary spoonerisms are errors in the arrangement of the discrete elements of sounds called phonemes—spoonerisms result when two sounds in a given utterance are transposed (e.g., "thore some" instead of "sore thumb"). Such errors demonstrate that even though discrete elements of sound are not obvious in ordinary speech, organization in terms of discrete sounds does seem to exist at some earlier stage in the process. However, the organization of discrete sounds is not based entirely on our system of phonetic elements. The sound made by the last three letters in "judge" is represented by two consonants on the phonetic level, but these are never split in two by speech errors as are clusters like "cl," "sp," and "st"; when a sound such as "dge" or "ch" is involved in an error, it moves as a unit.

Some speech errors involve meaning as well as sound. These result from the fact that words of a language often consist of more than one meaningful element or morpheme. Some speech errors show that there can be a breakdown in the rules by which words are formed from the component morphemes. The result is words such as "irregardless," "ambigual," and "motionly," which are nonexistent but possible words. Such errors suggest that we learn morphemes and the rules for their combination separately, and that this gives us the ability to recognize and form new words. Many morphemes, such as the indefinite-article morpheme "a" or "an," have alternative pronunciations depending on their context. Errors such as "a burly bird" for "an early bird" show that when segmental disordering occurs that changes a word beginning with a vowel to one beginning with a consonant, or vice versa, the pronunciation of the indefinite article is changed to conform to grammatical rules despite the error. Moreover, when complete words are exchanged, they are usually exchanged with words of the same grammatical category, which indicates that words are represented in memory along with their grammatical characteristics.

Examples of speech errors indicate that when we speak, morphemes are structured into phrases in a kind of buffer memory before articulation. Most speech errors would not occur if each word in a sentence were processed chronologically. We do not select one word from our "mental dictionary" and say it before selecting and saying another. At some stage before articulation the entire phrase has been fabricated and it is apparently at this time that transpositions and substitutions arise. How could a word near the end of a sentence be transposed with one at the beginning unless the complete sentence were at some point stored as a unit before articulation?

II. GLOSSARY

alveolars — sounds produced by raising the tip of the tongue to the top of the teeth.
labials — sounds produced by closure of the lips.
morphemes — the meaningful units or words of a language.
nasal sounds — sounds produced by lowering the soft palate to allow some air to escape through the nose while making the sounds.
oral sounds — sounds produced by raising the soft palate to block the escape of air through the nose while making the sounds.

phonemes — discrete sounds that compose a language.
portmanteau — a blend of two words with similar meanings.
spoonerisms — slips of the tongue in which two sounds of an intended utterance are transposed; e.g., "The Sale of Two Tities is an intriguing novel."
velars — sounds produced by raising the back of the tongue to the soft palate.
voiced sounds — sounds produced with vocal cord vibrations.
voiceless sounds — sounds produced with an open glottis.

III. ESSAY STUDY QUESTIONS

1. A person's knowledge of a language cannot be equated solely with the words and sentences he utters and understands. How can a finite nervous system store the infinite number of sentences possible in a particular language?
2. Describe the classification of speech sounds. What evidence is there that the units of classification have an independent existence in the mental grammar?
3. What evidence is there that the internal schema for representing the elements of sounds does not always coincide with the phonetic representation of sounds?
4. What evidence is there that language acquisition involves constructing utterances from rules rather than merely imitating what is heard?
5. In cases where an incorrect word was used instead of the appropriate one, the substitute and original often fall into the same semantic class. What does this indicate?
6. What evidence is there that phrases are held in a kind of buffer memory before articulation?

BILINGUALISM AND INFORMATION PROCESSING

Chapter 22

Paul A. Kolers   MARCH 1968

I. SUMMARY

An investigation of the way people use symbols may provide valuable insights into the functioning of the mental processes, and people who can speak two languages are of particular interest in this regard because they work with two distinct sets of symbols. By presenting a bilingual subject with information in one language and requesting a response in the other, the investigator should be able to learn about the mental operations involved in the acquisition, storage, and retrieval of information.

In the first experiment reported by Kolers, the process of switching back and forth between languages was studied. In one test condition, bilingual subjects read passages silently and then were tested for comprehension; in a second condition, they read the passages aloud. Four kinds of passages were used. Two of them were unilingual—one in English and the other in French. The other two were mixed; both were made up of some English words and some French words, but in one the word order obeyed the rules of French grammar, whereas the other followed the rules of English. All subjects were required to read the passages at the same rate that had enabled control subjects to score 75 per cent on the comprehension test. One might expect that in order to understand a mixed passage a subject would have to translate all the words into one language or spend extra time switching from code to code. However, in the silent condition mixing languages produced no deficits in comprehension. On the other hand, subjects had difficulty reading mixed passages aloud. The amount of time required for each switch between languages was calculated to be about one third of a second.

To study the way languages are stored in the brain, word-association tests were given to bilingual subjects who were required to respond in their native language to words in that language, to respond in English to words in English, or to respond in one language to words in the other. If both languages were retained in a common store, one would expect the responses to be similar on all kinds of tests, since the concepts with which the subject was dealing would be similar regardless of the language involved. On the other hand, if information were stored in separate modes according to language, word associations in one language would only infrequently be subject to direct translation into the other language. The finding was that about one fifth of the responses were the same in a bilingual subject's two languages. On the basis of this intermediate degree of concordance, Kolers concluded that only in some cases is the access to stored information restricted to the language by which it was encoded. Words referring to concrete objects were more likely to elicit similar responses in the two languages than abstract words, and the abstract words, in turn, elicited a larger number of similar responses than did words referring to feelings.

If a unilingual list of words is presented one at a time to a subject, his ability to recall a given word is increased if the word is repeated in the list. Kolers and his colleagues found that in bilingual lists where subjects saw meanings repeated in each language, the percentage of recall increased linearly with the frequency of a particular meaning. Thus, it is clear that bilingual subjects do not store words as individual visual or phonetic objects, but in terms of their meanings. Information repeated in different languages was as well retained as information repeated in a single language.

II. GLOSSARY

bilingual — speaking two languages.
call time — the amount of time needed to organize a set of procedures for handling a piece of information.
calque — the interference which one linguistic system creates for another in bilingual subjects.
grammar — the many rules that characterize how the words of a language are used.

introspective — pertaining to an examination of one's own mental processes.
lexicon — the individual words of a language
transliteration — representing a word with the symbols of another language.
unilingual — speaking one language.
word-association test — a test where the subject responds to one word with the first word that comes to mind.

III. ESSAY STUDY QUESTIONS

1. Describe the experiment on code-switching. What were the results and what do they indicate?
2. The fact that reading mixed passages aloud produces deficits but reading them silently does not suggest that the deficits may be due to the motor aspects of speaking rather than to difficulties in information processing. Discuss.
3. Describe the two storage systems postulated by Kolers. Which kind of system did his data support?
4. In the bilingual word-association test, 20 per cent of the responses were the same in both languages. The interpretation of this finding is rather arbitrary, in the sense that it follows from all possible results except 0 per cent and 100 per cent. Discuss.
5. Discuss the interference that can occur when mixing speech in two different languages.
6. Information learned in one language is not necessarily available for use in the other. What evidence is there for this statement?
7. The author describes three aspects of the use of verbal symbol systems. What are they?

PROBLEM-SOLVING

Martin Scheerer   APRIL 1963

Chapter 23

I. SUMMARY

A problem exists when the goal that is sought is not directly attainable by the performance of a simple act available in the organism's repertory; thus the solution of a problem calls for either a novel action or a novel integration of standard responses. According to the trial-and-error view of problem-solving, solutions are attempted at random until the correct response is performed, resulting in the solution and, thus, the reward. This reward increases the probability that the correct response will be performed again in similar situations. This conception of problem-solving does not assume an understanding of the problem; the reward automatically "stamps in" the correct response. Others, however, have argued that there is more to problem-solving than a sequence of stimuli and responses. Gestalt psychologists have argued that solutions are often achieved not by blind, random behavior but by productive thinking and insight. Solutions involving true understanding or insight have two major advantages over trial-and-error solutions, besides the intrinsic pleasure of grasping something: they can be retained more easily, and they can be transferred more readily to other problems involving the same principles.

Although men as well as some other animals have the capacity for genuine insight, not every person gains insight into a given problem, and those that do frequently do not gain insight in the same way or at the same stage. Insight is often delayed or thwarted by fixation of an incorrect solution. Such fixation can have several different causes. First, a person may start with an implicit but incorrect premise. For example, subjects asked to form four equilateral triangles from six matches have a difficult time because they assume that all the matches must lie in a single plane. The solution is achieved easily once it is realized that this assumption has been made and that all the matches need not lie flat. A second source of fixation stems from the fact that subjects often fail to perceive an object's suitability for a solution, especially when it is embedded in a conventional context. In one experiment, for example, two sticks had to be tied together in order to solve the problem, and when a string was placed in the room all subjects solved the problem. However, when the string was used to hold up a sign, a mirror, or a calendar, over half the subjects failed to reach the correct solution. A third cause of fixation occurs when the most obvious way to the solution must be circumvented if the solution is to be eventually achieved. Finally, the availability of a habitual mode of response may make it harder to take a fresh approach required to solve a problem. This latter effect has been clearly demonstrated by the Luchins water problem.

Whatever the cause of fixation, its effects can be strengthened and insight delayed or completely eliminated by increasing the level of motivation. It has been shown that if a chimpanzee is too hungry, it will not do as well at a problem, such as the Kohler banana problem, which involves a detour in order to solve the problem. And for humans there is evidence that strong ego-involvement in a problem can interfere with the rapid discovery of the solution.

II. GLOSSARY

functional fixedness — not being able to see novel functions of objects in a situation in which they seem to be serving other functions.
Morgan's canon — always explain behavior in terms of the simplest possible mechanism.

recentering — shifting from a false premise or assumption to a new one which facilitates the solution of the problem.
reinforcement — any stimulus which increases the probability of a response which precedes it.

III. ESSAY STUDY QUESTIONS

1. What is Morgan's canon? Why is there the need for such a principle?
2. How does Thorndike's view of problem-solving differ from that of the Gestalt psychologists?
3. Discuss Harlow's view that trial-and-error problem-solving and insight are two stages in the process of learning how to solve problems: an organism is only capable of insight as the result of initial trial-and-error behavior.

4. Describe the four different factors which can lead to fixation.
5. Describe the horse-and-rider puzzle, the Luchins water problem, the match problem, the dot problem, the ring-and-peg problem, and the river-crossing problem. What important aspect of problem-solving does each of these problems illustrate?

THE ORIGIN OF PERSONALITY

Alexander Thomas, Stella Chess, Herbert C. Birch   AUGUST 1970

Chapter 24

I. SUMMARY

In recent years many psychiatrists and psychologists have tended to emphasize the influence of the child's early environment on the development of human personality, but there seem to be differences between children that cannot be attributed to environmental factors. Some children with severe psychological problems have a family upbringing similar to that of healthy children, and some children without major psychological problems have experienced severe family disorganization and poor parental care. The authors, however, do not reject the idea that the infant's environment is an important factor in the formation of personality; they argue instead that the personality is shaped by the constant interplay of temperament and environment. To test their hypothesis, the authors obtained detailed descriptions of the behavior of children by means of structured interviews with their parents, beginning when each child had reached the age of two or three months. The temperament, or behavioral profile, of a child was defined by ratings on nine different three-point scales. These behavioral profiles have been traced for over a decade in more than 100 children.

Initial observations confirmed that children do indeed show a distinct individuality in temperament in the first few weeks of life, which is apparently independent of their parents' handling or personality. Moreover, these initial characteristics seem to persist over the years in most children. When these behavioral profiles were examined more closely, it was found that some of the nine individual attributes seemed to cluster together. These clusters seemed to define three general classes of temperament. About 65 percent of the children could be described as belonging to one of the categories; the rest had a mixture of traits that did not add up to a general characterization. One group was named "easy children" because they presented few problems in care and training in contrast to the "difficult children." The third general type of temperament was termed "slow to warm up." These children were withdrawn, slow to adapt, and somewhat negative in mood.

The authors conclude that a demand that conflicts excessively with a child's personality characteristics and capacities is likely to place the child under heavy and perhaps even unbearable stress. Obviously, then, a detailed knowledge of a child's behavior profile can be of great help to parents in handling the child and avoiding the later development of behavioral problems. What is important in the development of the child is the interaction between the child's own characteristics and his environment. If the two influences are harmonized, one can expect healthy development of the child; if they are dissonant, behavioral problems are almost sure to ensue. Thus, there is no one correct way to raise children; a given environment will not affect all children in the same way, especially if they differ markedly in temperament.

II. GLOSSARY

congenital — present from birth.
constitutionalist — an individual who emphasizes the role of innate factors in human development.
environmentalist — an individual who emphasizes the role of experiential factors in human development.

nature — the side of the "nature-nurture" issue stressing heredity factors.
nurture — the side of the "nature-nurture" issue stressing the importance of environmental factors.
rubella — German measles.

III. ESSAY STUDY QUESTIONS

1. Why do the authors believe that the environment is not the only determining factor in the development of personality?
2. The authors argue that the personality is shaped by the constant interplay of temperament and environment. What experimental evidence do they offer in support of their contention?
3. According to the authors, what is the most important general principle to follow when rearing a child?
4. Describe the rearing practices recommended for children in the three general categories.

STUDIES IN SELF-ESTEEM

Stanley Coopersmith   FEBRUARY 1968   # Chapter 25

I. SUMMARY

There has been a change from the traditional ways of thinking about mental and behavioral disorders. The question is no longer how to avoid maladjustment, but rather how to generate those capacities that enable an individual to function effectively. Whereas earlier theories focused on difficulties that were already present and sought to determine how they arose, current efforts are frequently concerned with the process by which healthy and effective individuals develop. This approach is consistent with the view found in other areas of modern medical science that procedures developing the resistance of the organism are preferable to procedures for treating symptoms once they have arisen. Thus, there has been a recent shift of attention in psychology to finding specific ways to build up the constructive capacities of human personality, so that it can deal effectively with the stresses to which it will inevitably be subjected. This approach requires that we identify what these constructive capacities are, and then determine what experiences lead to their development.

It has long been recognized that a feeling of personal worth plays a crucial role in human happiness and effectiveness, but it has only been recently that a body of objective information has been collected on the topic of self-esteem. The author and his colleagues have contributed to this literature by applying the techniques of modern clinical, laboratory, and field investigation. The subjects were a representative sample of normal boys followed from preadolescence to early adulthood. Three measures were used to assess self-esteem—the child's own evaluation, a report from the child's teacher, and the results of Rorschach and thematic apperception tests. On the basis of these measures each boy was rated as possessing high, medium, or low self-esteem. The study of the boys in these three categories progressed along three separate lines: (1) laboratory tests of the subjects' memory, perception, level of aspiration, conformity, and response to stress; (2) clinical tests and interviews designed to show their levels of ability, personality traits, attitudes, insights, and styles of response; and (3) studies, including interviews with their parents, that looked into factors of upbringing that might be related to each boy's level of self-esteem.

Boys with a high degree of self-esteem were active, expressive individuals who tended to be successful both academically and socially. They were eager to express their own opinions, were not particularly sensitive to criticism, exhibited little destructive behavior, and were untroubled by feelings of anxiety. In general their optimism stemmed not from fantasies but from a well-founded assessment of their own qualities and skills. Boys with a medium level of self-esteem were similar to the high-esteem subjects, but they differed in several respects. They showed the strongest tendency to support the middle-class value system, and they were particularly dependent on social acceptance. In contrast, the boys with low self-esteem presented a picture of discouragement and depression. They felt isolated, unlovable, incapable of expressing or defending themselves, and too weak to overcome their deficiencies.

Study of the factors which appeared to lead to high self-esteem failed to confirm a number of widely held expectations. There was no consistent relation between self-esteem and physical attractiveness, height, family size, early trauma, breast- or bottle-feeding, or whether the mother worked or stayed home. Moreover, there was only a weak relation between family social position or income level and the child's self-esteem. However, two factors did prove to be related to the development of high self-esteem. First, the background of the high-self-esteem subject was typically characterized by close relationships with his parents. The mother knew all or most of her son's friends and the mother and father regarded their son as an individual worthy of their deep interest. The second and somewhat more surprising finding was that the parents of high-esteem children were less permissive than those of children of lower self-esteem. They demanded high standards of behavior and enforced these strictly but were by no means harsh; they tended to use rewards rather than corporal punishment or withdrawal of love to control their child's behavior.

II. GLOSSARY

insomnia — difficulty in sleeping.

representative sample — a sample whose characteristics mirror those of the population from which it was selected.

Rorschach test — a projective personality test commonly known as the inkblot test.

thematic apperception test — a projective personality test in which the subject makes up a story about a picture and his responses are interpreted by the psychologist.

III. ESSAY STUDY QUESTIONS

1. There has been a change of emphasis in the study of personality. Explain.
2. It is impossible to do an adequate job of studying the factors which lead to maladjustment without also identifying those which lead to normal personalities. Discuss.
3. Only boys were studied but the conclusions seem to have been generalized to children in general. What conclusions might have been different if girls rather than boys had been studied?
4. The author reports several relationships between the parent's behavior and the child's self-esteem and he assumes that these relationships indicate that the parent's behavior influenced the development of the self-esteem. But there is another possibility; perhaps the child's self-esteem develops very early and this influences the way in which the parents respond to their child. Discuss. Describe an experiment which would test these two possible interpretations of the data.
5. Correlation does not imply causation. Discuss with reference to the present article.
6. Uncertainty of one's worth should not be confused with low self-esteem. Explain.
7. Do feelings of self-esteem lead to certain patterns of behavior or do the patterns of behavior lead to feelings of self-esteem. Discuss.
8. Most persons define success for themselves not in terms of some absolute standard but in relation to people around them. Discuss and evaluate the evidence for this statement.
9. What two factors seemed to contribute to the development of high self-esteem?
10. How was self-esteem related to level of aspiration?

SOCIAL DEPRIVATION IN MONKEYS

Harry F. Harlow and Margaret Kuenne Harlow   NOVEMBER 1962

Chapter 26

I. SUMMARY

The events of early life are unquestionably of paramount importance in the development of personality disorders, and contemporary writers have especially emphasized the role of inadequate or inconsistent mothering. The Harlows have attempted to evaluate this hypothesis experimentally by using the rhesus monkey as a subject. Apart from this primate's obvious evolutionary kinship to man, it is a reasonable subject for such experiments because it undergoes a relatively long period of development like that of a human child, with intimate attachment to its mother and social interaction with its peers.

In the initial series of studies, the infant monkeys were separated from their mothers and housed individually in bare wire cages. The behavior of animals reared in such a manner was markedly different from that of animals reared with opportunity for normal social contacts. The isolated animals sat in their cages and stared fixedly into space, circled their cages in a stereotyped manner, and clutched their heads and rocked for long periods of time. Often self-destructive behaviors developed, and none of the isolated animals ever displayed normal sexual behavior, although they did not seem to lack sexual motivation. Moreover, the isolated animals had difficulty establishing a pecking order, and as a result they fought more. Six months of such total isolation rendered the infant monkeys permanently inadequate, but the effects of shorter periods of isolation were reversible.

In most experiments on early social isolation, infants are deprived of the company of their peers as well as their mothers, thus making it difficult, if not impossible, to determine the relative contribution of peer and maternal contact to normal development. The Harlows therefore raised rhesus monkeys without mothers but in the company of their peers, and with mothers but without their age-mates. Their observations confirmed the importance of the infant-mother relationship for normal development. However, they found that appropriate peer contact can compensate for the absence of the mother. Young monkeys reared in group pens without maternal care did not differ from mothered animals, at least in terms of play, defense, and sexual behavior. On the other hand, monkeys reared with mothers but no playmates showed severe behavioral disabilities. Apparently, peer relations are even more important than maternal care for normal social development.

II. GLOSSARY

critical period — a time during development when a response must be learned if it is to be learned at all.

estrus — the phase of the female's estrous cycle during which the female is receptive to the sexual advances of the male.

heterosexual behavior — sexual behavior between members of the opposite sex.

pecking order — the stable hierarchy of dominance established in many animal societies.

surrogate mother — substitute mother.

III. ESSAY STUDY QUESTIONS

1. What are some of the problems involved in the interpretation of clinical as opposed to experimental data?
2. Why did the Harlows use monkeys in their studies?
3. Explain how a pecking order can reduce combat in an animal society.
4. Describe the differences between those rhesus monkeys reared in isolation and those reared in the wild.
5. What were the differences between young monkeys raised in isolation and those raised in isolation with surrogate mothers?
6. What evidence is there that an abnormal mother-infant relationship can play a disruptive role in development?
7. Describe the experiments dealing with the relative importance of maternal and peer relationships.

PSYCHOLOGICAL FACTORS IN STRESS AND DISEASE

Jay M. Weiss   JUNE 1972

Chapter 27

I. SUMMARY

One of the most intriguing ideas in medicine is that psychological processes affect disease. Many individuals have emphasized the importance of psychological factors in physical disease, and the field of psychosomatic medicine has been based on this premise. Recently our ability to determine psychological factors involved in disease has advanced into a new phase with the development of the appropriate experimental protocols. Formerly the evidence of psychological influences on disease processes came from the observations of clinicians who noticed that certain psychological conditions seemed to be associated with particular organic disorders or with their increased severity. However, such correlational evidence, no matter how compelling, does not prove that psychological factors can produce or exacerbate disease. Although a certain psychological event may coincide with a specific disorder, there is no way to be sure it was the cause. The disease may have caused the psychological event; a third unidentified factor may have caused both the physical disorder and the psychological event, thus leading to the correlation; or the correlation may have been spurious. The development of experimental procedures for inducing disorders in experimental animals has made the task of identifying the psychological factors that affect disease much easier. The experimenter does not have to wait for a disease to occur, and then determine if a particular factor had an effect; instead he can introduce the suspected factor directly and see if in fact the disease does develop. Moreover, by assigning subjects to conditions at random, the experimenter knows that any consistent difference between the treatment and control groups has been caused by the experimental treatment and not by extraneous variables.

Weiss has used experimental procedures to study the effects of psychological variables on stomach ulcers. These investigations were based on the finding that environmental stress can induce stomach ulcers, but in order to show that the psychological effect rather than the stimulation per se was the critical factor, specific experimental procedures had to be employed. Two animals had to be exposed to exactly the same physical stress, with each animal in a different psychological condition. The usual procedure for stressing an experimental animal is to administer electric footshock through a grid floor, but some animals may be able to develop different strategies, such as jumping, so that animals in different groups may not receive exactly the same physical stress. To control for this possibility in all his experiments, Weiss administered the shock through electrodes attached to the tail. In the first experiment, two rats received electric shock through the tail electrodes, while a third, control rat received no shocks. Of the two rats receiving shock, one heard a beeping tone that began 10 seconds before each shock; the other heard the same tone but at random. Thus, both animals received exactly the same shock and tone, but only one could predict when the shock was coming. The result was that only those rats receiving unpredictable shock developed marked ulceration. But how would the animals react to stress in a situation in which they have control over it? To answer this question, three rats were tested simultaneously as in the predictability experiment; again, two rats received shock, while the third remained as an unshocked control. In this experiment, while both experimental animals heard the tone, only one could avoid or escape shock by jumping onto a platform. Both experimental animals received the same shock because when the one animal jumped on the platform, it turned the shock off for the other animal as well. The results showed that the helpless, yoked rats lost considerably more weight than the animals that could control the shock. A second experiment was performed to test the generality of this finding, employing a different apparatus and a different pathological response: gastric ulceration. The results were consistent with those of the previous experiment; the rats that were able to avoid or escape the shock showed considerably less ulceration than did the yoked controls. On the basis of these and other results, Weiss proposed a theory to explain how coping behavior is related to ulceration. According to this theory, ulceration is a function of two variables: the number of coping attempts that an animal makes; and the amount of appropriate feedback that these responses produce. Ulceration increases as the number of responses increases, and decreases as the amount of relevant feedback increases. Thus, coping behavior per se does not protect an animal from ulcers; only those coping responses do so that are followed by some indication that the response has effectively delayed or removed the stressful stimulation.

II. GLOSSARY

catecholamines — a class of substances, including norepinephrine and dopamine, which seem to play a role in neurotransmission.

corticosterone — the major steroid hormone secreted by the adrenal gland of rats.

correlational study — a study which reports the relationships between uncontrolled, naturally occurring events.

feedback — information received by an organism concerning the consequences of its behavior.

norepinephrine — a catecholamine suspected of being a central nervous system transmitter substance.

psychosomatic medicine — a field of medicine based on the premise that psychological factors play an important role in the development and treatment of physical illness.

random assignment — assigning subjects to conditions so that each subject has an equal probability of being assigned to each condition.

stomach ulcer — an open sore or lesion on the stomach wall.

ulcerogenic — ulcer-producing.

yoked subject — a subject who receives the same treatment as the experimental animal, the administration of the treatment to both animals being contingent on the behavior of the experimental subject.

III. ESSAY STUDY QUESTIONS

1. Explain the difference between a correlational study and a true experiment in which the experimenter manipulates and controls variables. What information can be obtained from each kind of investigation?
2. In experiments on the psychological factors involved in disease, it is important that treatment and control animals are subjected to the same physical stress. Explain. How did Weiss ensure that animals in various conditions of his experiment on coping behavior received the same electric shock?
3. Yoked controls are essential to study the effects of contingency. Explain.
4. What effect did signaled as opposed to unsignaled shock have on the development of stomach ulcers?
5. Describe the experiments which revealed the effect of coping behavior on the body's response to stress.
6. Describe Weiss's explanation of the relation between coping behavior and stress. What support is there for this view?
7. How does Weiss's theory reconcile his results with the seemingly contradictory results of Brady and Porter?
8. Random assignment does not guarantee equivalent groups. Discuss.
9. What effect did coping behavior have on ulcerogenesis in the various warning-signal conditions?
10. All physiological systems participating in stress reactions are not affected in the same way by a given stress condition. Explain and discuss.
11. Stress may initiate and perpetuate a vicious circle in some subjects. Explain.

HYPERACTIVE CHILDREN

Mark A. Stewart   APRIL 1970

Chapter 28

I. SUMMARY

Certain children are more than usually restless, noisy, destructive, and distractible, and this cluster of symptoms characterizes the hyperactive-child syndrome. The typical hyperactive child is continually in motion, cannot concentrate for more than a moment, acts impulsively, and is impatient and easily upset. At home he is constantly in trouble because of his restlessness, noisiness, and disobedience. In school he rarely finishes his work because of his restlessness and distractibility, and almost always turns out to be a discipline problem. Parents and teachers have long been aware of this problem, but clinicians did not develop an active interest in it before the encephalitis epidemic that occurred early in this century, the hyperactivity syndrome being common among those children who recovered from the acute phases of this illness. It was then noticed that the hyperactivity syndrome was common in children who had suffered brain damage from other causes. As a result of these early observations, it was assumed that the hyperactivity syndrome was the result of brain damage, but it has since been found that only a few children diagnosed as hyperactive have a history suggesting brain damage. For instance, an early history of prenatal or birth complications which may have caused brain damage is no more common among hyperactive children than among normal children.

In Stewart's study a sample of hyperactive children was compared with a control group of normal children. The control group was composed of first-grade children; the hyperactive group was composed of children aged 5 through 11 who were being treated for their malady. Information about the child's present and past symptoms, medical record, school record, and family history was gathered through extensive interviews with the parents. As expected, the hyperactive patients were markedly different from controls, especially in terms of the symptoms accepted as being characteristic of the syndrome, but along with these characteristics were many forms of antisocial behavior. Although about half the mothers of hyperactive children reported that they had noticed that their child was unusual before it had reached the age of two, there were no differences between the early medical and family backgrounds of control and hyperactive children. This suggested the possibility that the hyperactive syndrome may be inborn. In a follow-up experiment teenagers who had been hyperactive as young children were studied, information being collected by interviews with the subjects as well as the parents. The interviews indicated that these children had not changed much since they were originally treated as young children. Most were still notably restless, unable to concentrate or finish jobs, overtalkative, and poor in school performance. Moreover, substantial proportions of them engaged in fighting, stealing, and other forms of deviant behavior. In another study it was shown that hyperactive children were more likely than others to have a history of accidental poisoning. In view of the hyperactive child's tendency to get into things, extra precautions to prevent access to drugs and toxins should be taken in households with hyperactive children.

The fact that stimulating drugs such as amphetamines produce a dramatic improvement in the behavior of many hyperactive children suggests a biological basis for this syndrome. Amphetamines have effects on the activity of the reticular activating system, probably by affecting the activity of the neurotransmitter, norepinephrine. An injection of a small amount of norepinephrine into the reticular formation lowers the activity level and responsiveness of rats. Since amphetamine is known to stimulate the release of norepinephrine from nerve endings, its therapeutic action may occur on the reticular formation.

II. GLOSSARY

acetylcholine — a neurotransmitter which increases a rat's activity level when injected into the reticular formation.

amphetamines — a class of stimulating drugs which stimulate the release of norepinephrine.

autism — a psychotic state of childhood marked by almost complete unresponsiveness to social stimuli.

electroencephalogram — a record of the subject's brain waves.

encephalitis — inflammation of the brain.

frontal lobes — the two anterior portions of the cerebrum.

karyotype — appearance of somatic chromosomes.

lobectomy — excision or removal of parts of the frontal lobes for the treatment of certain severe cases of mental illness.

noradrenalin — norepinephrine.

norepinephrine — a neurotransmitter which decreases a rat's activity level when injected into the reticular formation.

reticular formation — structure in the brain stem known to influence consciousness, arousal, and attention.

sociopath — a person whose antisocial behavior reaches pathological levels.

III. ESSAY STUDY QUESTIONS

1. Describe the main features of the hyperactive-child syndrome.
2. What is the brain-damage syndrome? Why was the term coined?
3. What evidence is there that the hyperactive-child syndrome is produced by brain damage?
4. What evidence is there that the hyperactive-child syndrome is innate?
5. Explain how the failure to equate the control and hyperactive group in terms of age may have contributed significantly to some of the results.
6. Hyperactivity may be an inherited sex-linked trait. Discuss.
7. What happens to hyperactive children as they mature?
8. Discuss a possible biological basis for the hyperactive-child syndrome.
9. What recommendations does Stewart make for the care and treatment of hyperactive children?

SCHIZOPHRENIA

Don D. Jackson   AUGUST 1962 Chapter 29

I. SUMMARY

The defining characteristic shared by all schizophrenics is that they respond inappropriately or hardly at all to other people and to their environment, but the secondary symptoms, such as hallucinations, delusions, stupor, catatonic rigidity, confusion, and extreme fluctuations of mood, are so varied and ambiguous that consistency of diagnosis is low. Rather than being signs of an underlying disease, these symptoms are themselves the disease, since the underlying factors which produce them are unknown.

Because there has been almost no agreement about the nature of schizophrenia, its study and treatment have taken many different forms. For example, much study has been inspired by the idea that schizophrenia is a hereditary disease. The major difficulty with such study is that the same individuals who provide the genetic inheritance of the schizophrenic also furnish the early environment; thus, even though it is clear that schizophrenia does run in families, it is difficult to separate the influences of nature and nurture. In one study it was found that if one identical twin was hospitalized and diagnosed as schizophrenic, the probability that the other twin would be found suffering from the same disorder was .85. However, this figure is probably inflated because of the phenomenon of *folie à deux*, the tendency of emotionally involved individuals to develop the same psychiatric symptoms at the same time. A widely accepted view is that a susceptibility to schizophrenia can be inherited which requires the appropriate stress for its precipitation.

Many investigators have assumed schizophrenia to be the result of a biochemical imbalance, with much of the interest surrounding the role of the neurotransmitter, serotonin. The main support for a serotonin interpretation comes from the observation that LSD is antagonistic to serotonin in its action on smooth muscle, but there are other serotonin antagonists which produce none of the psychotomimetic effects of LSD. A difficulty encountered in trying to identify chemicals which can help schizophrenics is that even inert substances when substituted for treatments have a marked therapeutic effect. The effectiveness of these placebo treatments has tended to emphasize the psychological aspects of schizophrenia, as has the finding that hallucinations and other symptoms of schizophrenia can be produced by relatively short periods of sensory deprivation. It was not until the 1950's that therapists began to fully appreciate the role of the patient's family in his illness and began to undertake conjoint family therapy. In some cases it seemed that the family could only function smoothly at the expense of the patient's mental health; just when the patient improved significantly during conjoint family therapy, other members of the family began to suffer from a variety of afflictions.

It is surprising that there is often little agreement between a therapist's view of schizophrenia and the methods of treatment he employs. However, regardless of a therapist's theoretical point of view, he must emphasize the collecting of data if present attempts at therapy are to contribute to the improvement of therapy in the future. Whatever his persuasion, if he carefully collects and reports his data, they can be used to develop and improve therapeutic techniques.

II. GLOSSARY

adrenalin — a hormone which activates the sympathetic nervous system.

adrenochrome — a breakdown product of adrenalin.

catatonic — one of the classic subclasses of schizophrenia, characterized by mute, rigid withdrawal.

chlorpromazine — a commonly used tranquilizer.

delusion — a persistent, false belief.

dementia praecox — the original term for schizophrenia.

double bind — the theory that schizophrenia can be induced when a patient is placed in a situation where he must perform two different and mutually contradictory responses.

folie à deux — individuals who are emotionally close tend to develop the same symptoms of mental illness at about the same time.

fraternal twins — twins with different genetic material.

hallucination — a perception which has no physical reality.

hebephrenic — one of the classic subclasses of schizophrenia, characterized by hypochondria and silliness.

hypochondria — excessive concern with one's health in the absence of physical symptoms.

identical twins — twins with exactly the same genetic material.

insulin — a hormone secreted by the pancreas which helps regulate blood sugar levels.

involutional melancholia — a psychotic depressive reaction characterized by depression, agitation, and apprehension.

manic-depressive — a psychotic reaction characterized by long periods of excitement or depression or the fluctuation between them.

narcissism — self-love.

paranoid — one of the classic subclasses of schizophrenia, characterized by feelings of persecution.

placebos — inert substances which can have therapeutic effects if the patients believe that they will be effective.

prefrontal lobotomy — the connections between the frontal lobes and the rest of the brain are severed to treat severe psychotic reactions.

reserpine — a commonly used tranquilizer.

schizophrenia — a psychotic reaction characterized by the blunting of responsiveness to other people and the environment.

senile psychosis — psychotic reaction produced by neural changes accompanying extreme age.

serotonin — central nervous system neural-transmitter substance which is suspected of playing a role in schizophrenia.

shock therapy — inducing seizures and coma as a treatment for severe psychosis.

simple schizophrenia — one of the classic subclasses of schizophrenia, characterized by insidious onset leading to withdrawal, confusion, and grandiosity.

taxonomy — the branch of any science concerned with classification.

thyroid — an endocrine gland found in all mammals.

uremia — the presence of urinary constituents in the blood due to kidney malfunction.

III. ESSAY STUDY QUESTIONS

1. In schizophrenia, the symptoms of the disease are the disease. Explain.
2. The study of schizophrenia must include the study of its investigators. Discuss.
3. When studying schizophrenia, one finds it difficult to separate the effects of the disease from the effects of hospitalization. Explain.
4. Describe the subclasses of schizophrenia.
5. What implication does Bleuler's contention that schizophrenia should be called "the group of schizophrenias" have for its study and treatment?
6. What is the greatest problem involved in studying the genetic determinants of schizophrenia?
7. What evidence is there for a genetic factor in schizophrenia?
8. What two kinds of studies have been conducted to uncover the biochemical factors involved in schizophrenia?
9. What evidence is there to support the serotonin theory of schizophrenia? What findings have been at odds with this view?
10. It is important to administer placebo treatments when evaluating new therapies. Explain.
11. Describe the effects of sensory deprivation.
12. Discuss the double bind and family homeostasis concepts.
13. What kinds of individuals are most likely to be hospitalized for schizophrenia? Does this mean that schizophrenia is most common among these individuals?

THE THERAPEUTIC COMMUNITY

Richard Almond   MARCH 1971

Chapter 30

I. SUMMARY

Over the past 20 years there has been an appreciable decline in the number of psychiatric inpatients. One factor in this shift from inpatient care has been the development of a method of treatment termed the therapeutic community. This term describes a way of operating a small psychiatric unit in a hospital. The key constituent of this method is the close relationship between the staff and the patients, who share the work and participate in making decisions affecting the group. Methods of treatment include psychotherapy, drug therapy, and various group and family therapies but it is the attempt at maintaining a sense of patient-staff community that is unique to this approach. Values and behavioral norms within the community are explicit and consistent; patients are expected to behave normally, to socialize, to discuss their problems openly, and to participate in the decisions and activities of the unit. There are two problems which are frequently encountered in psychiatric wards which are at least partially solved by the community approach to therapy. The first is that there often is a patient culture that is largely unknown to the staff and that may be at variance with their therapeutic efforts. Second, psychiatric hospitals are often plagued by problems of communication among staff members and between patients and staff. In the therapeutic community the boundaries between staff and patients are blurred and patients take part as equals.

The author and his colleagues investigated a therapeutic community in the psychiatric ward of the Yale–New Haven Hospital. Two major investigatory procedures were used. One, the hospital-career study, was an investigation of the patients' total experience on the ward through interviews, questionnaires, and hospital records. The second procedure made use of an attitude inventory to explore the value system of the unit, to measure attitudes toward authority, and to measure dependency, the patients' sense of nurture or deprivation by the institution. The questionnaire responses were subjected to factor analysis and the results were quite clear. The items designed to measure the values of the unit loaded heavily for a single factor which the authors termed social openness and ward involvement and this factor had interesting relations to the dimensions of authority and deprivation.

The authority dimension, which was measured by the patients' degree of preference for control by staff, for strict rules, and for suppression of abnormal behavior, was surprisingly unrelated to the acceptance of the values and norms of the therapeutic community. A preference for authority was not related to a rejection of the therapeutic community. This lack of relation reflects the fact that the Yale–New Haven ward does not include permissiveness but rather the firm and open use of authority by patients as well as staff. The dimension of dependency was also relatively independent of the dimension of social openness and ward involvement. The patients who experienced the ward as a depriving place tended to reject its norms, but acceptance of the social-openness view was independent of experiencing the ward as a nurturing place. This result supported the observation of the ward as a serious businesslike place where the patients and staff opposed the idea that an easy comfortable life was good for the patients.

Changes over time in the patients' scores for social openness suggested that the ward's efforts to incorporate new patients into the ward culture were largely successful. The average scores for newly admitted patients shifted consistently to greater agreement with staff views. The behavior of the patients as well as their attitudes changed in accord with the norms of social openness. Surprisingly, however, these changes in behavior tended to precede changes in attitudes as measured by the questionnaire. Patients were acting in accord with the unit's values before registering such changes in a questionnaire on attitudes.

Not all patients responded in the same way to the therapeutic community. Three major patterns were discerned; individuals in these three groups were termed preconverts, unit converts, and rejectors. Preconverts, whose social-openness scores were consistently high even in the first week of hospitalization, were less disturbed and tended to be from higher social classes. Unit converts, whose scores did not rise until after at least a week of hospitalization, were almost all adolescents more severely disturbed and slower to respond to treatment than the preconverts. The rejectors were older patients who improved least and tended to be from lower-class backgrounds.

II. GLOSSARY

correlation — the degree to which changes in one variable are related to changes in another.
factor analysis — studying the intercorrelations between a number of observations to identify the factor or factors which produce them.
nurture — that which nourishes or fosters.
psychoanalysis — treatment for mental illness based on the teaching of Freud.

psychotherapy — any therapy using psychological techniques.
schizophrenia — a psychotic reaction characterized by a loss of contact with reality, intellectual deficits, and emotional blunting.
therapeutic community — a way of operating a small psychiatric unit so that the patients and staff share the work and activities of the unit and participate in the decisions that affect it.

III. ESSAY STUDY QUESTIONS

1. What is the therapeutic community? What evidence has Almond supplied to demonstrate the effectiveness of this procedure?
2. What were the goals of the author's research? To what extent were these goals accomplished?
3. What factors led to the development of the therapeutic community as a popular approach to the treatment of mental illness?
4. In the author's view how does the therapeutic community help patients return to their families and jobs?
5. What were the results of the factor analysis of the questionnaire responses?
6. How was the social-openness and ward-involvement factor related to the dimensions of authority and nurture? Explain.
7. Describe the changes in attitudes and behavior which occur in members of a therapeutic community.
8. It is usually assumed that changes in attitude precede changes in behavior. Why? Does this hold true for the development of social openness in a therapeutic community?
9. Describe the major patterns of attitude change observed by the author and his co-workers.
10. Role channeling is not limited to the psychiatric setting. Discuss.

BEHAVIORAL PSYCHOTHERAPY

Albert Bandura MARCH 1967

I. SUMMARY

Most theories of maladaptive behavior are based on the disease concept, according to which abnormal behavior is a symptom of an underlying illness. The concepts of symptom and disease are quite appropriate for physical disorders, but for most psychological problems the disease concept can be misleading. The pathological mental conditions that are assumed to underlie behavior malfunctions are merely abstractions which are then given substance from the abnormal behavior. Today many psychotherapists hold that abnormal behavior should not be viewed as a manifestation of an underlying disease, but as a way in which the person has learned to cope with environmental demands. Treatment then becomes a problem of learning, and the therapist can call on principles of learning that are based on experimentation to treat his patients. In fact, many of the gains achieved by traditional psychotherapy may result from the unwitting application of these social-learning principles.

One method of behavioral psychotherapy is based on modeling the desired behavior. Almost any human learning that results from direct experience can come about vicariously by observing other people's behavior and its consequences for them. For example, children who are afraid of dogs can have this fear reduced by watching other children play with dogs. Positive reinforcement, the modification of behavior by alteration of its rewarding consequences, is another important procedure in behavioral psychotherapy. Bandura reports the case of an extremely withdrawn boy

whose teacher was unwittingly reinforcing his "solitary" behavior by consoling him and encouraging him when he was alone and ignoring him when he did venture to interact with other children. When these contigencies were reversed, the child was soon spending 60 percent of his time playing with other children. When these contingencies were reversed, the evaluated carefully in terms of the effects they have on the children rather than in terms of the humanitarian intent of teachers, parents, and psychotherapists.

A third behavioral-psychotherapy technique is based on the principle of counterconditioning. The objective of counterconditioning is to induce positive responses in the presence of stimuli that ordinarily arouse feelings of fear or other unfavorable reactions. In Wolpe's desensitization method, the therapist constructs a ranked list of situations to which the patient generally reacts with increasing levels of anxiety. Then the subject is instructed to relax and to visualize the weakest item in the list. When this no longer disturbs muscular relaxation, he moves on to the next item, until eventually even the most threatening situations have been effectively neutralized.

Many new methods of psychotherapy based on little more than the convictions of their advocates have been introduced enthusiastically but have been "retired" by controlled experimentation. In contrast, learning therapies are based on established, experimentally derived principles; as such they appear to be much more effective, and as a result are likely to be much more durable.

II. GLOSSARY

acrophobia — irrational fear of heights.
autistic — pathologically absorbed in fantasy.
claustrophobia — irrational fear of closed places.
counterconditioning — eliminating the anxiety of threatening events by repeatedly pairing them with positive outcomes.
desensitization — a form of counterconditioning devised by Wolpe in which the patient attempts to remain relaxed while thinking through a ranked series of threatening events.

hypochondriac — a person who demonstrates frequent and unwarranted concern for his own health.
modeling — learning by observing the consequences of other people's behavior.
phobia — irrational fear.
placebo treatment — the subject believes he is being treated although in reality he is not.
positive reinforcement — any stimulus which produces an increase in the rate of a response that precedes it.

III. ESSAY STUDY QUESTIONS

1. Describe the disease concept and the alternative that Bandura is supporting.
2. The mental conditions that are assumed to underlie behavioral malfunctioning are merely abstractions that are then given substance from the abnormal behavior. Explain.
3. Describe Bandura's view of traditional psychotherapy as a form of behavioral psychotherapy.
4. What are the three kinds of behavioral psychotherapeutic techniques that Bandura discusses? Give an example of each.

5. What three things are necessary before positive reinforcement can be used to deal with human behavior problems?
6. After the effective application of positive reinforcement has successfully produced the desired behavior, the original reinforcement practices may, for a time, be reinstated. Why?
7. Describe how reinforcement therapy can be used to eliminate undesired behavior.
8. The idea that behavioral psychotherapy could lead to symptom substitution stems from belief in the disease concept of behavior malfunction. Explain.

ATTITUDE AND PUPIL SIZE

Eckhard H. Hess   APRIL 1965

Chapter 32

I. SUMMARY

It is generally assumed that pupil diameter is controlled only by fluctuations in light intensity. Hess and his colleagues explored the possibility that pupil size is related to the emotional tone and interest value of visual stimuli. The procedures involved in these studies were quite simple. The subjects looked into a box at a stimulus picture while the eye was being photographed at the rate of two frames per second. Before each stimulus picture was presented a control slide was viewed that carefully matched in overall brightness the stimulus slide that was to follow. The purpose of the control slide was to adapt the subject's eyes to the light intensity of the following stimulus slide.

In the first study four men and two women viewed a series of stimulus slides; the men's pupils were observed to dilate more at the sight of a female pinup than the women's did, but the women showed a greater response to a male pinup. In a second experiment, the control slide was not illuminated, so that in every case the presentation of the test stimulus involved an increase in illumination. In this case, the stimuli should have consistently produced constriction if pupil size is a function only of light intensity; yet dilation occurred in response to interesting pictures. Aversive stimuli were found to produce particularly marked constriction.

On the basis of these experiments Hess postulated the existence of a continuum of responses ranging from extreme dilation for material that is interesting or pleasing to the viewer to extreme constriction for material that is unpleasant or distasteful. One of the most interesting things about these changes in pupil size is that in some situations they were more sensitive to differences between stimuli than were responses at the verbal level. For example, two pictures of an attractive young woman were shown to a group of men. These pictures were identical except that they had been retouched, so that in one the girl had huge pupils, while in the other they were small. The average pupil dilation produced by the picture with large pupils was almost twice as great as that produced by the picture with small pupils; yet when questioned after the test, most of the men reported that they had not perceived any difference between the pictures.

Since the interest in a visual stimulus can fluctuate with the motivational state, one would expect that the degree of pupil dilation produced by a given picture would also be a function of the level of motivation. When two groups of subjects which had been deprived of food for different amounts of time were shown pictures of food, the results were unequivocal: dilation was much greater in the more deprived subjects. Another study showed that the iris can respond to nonvisual stimuli. During this study the subjects kept their eyes on a point projected on the screen so that the camera could record changes in pupil size. At the same time subjects sampled five orange drinks interspersed between sips of water. The orange drinks all produced pupil dilation but one of the five orange beverages caused a significantly larger average increase in pupil size than the others did; it was the drink that the subjects designated as their favorite. There were also changes in pupil size as the subjects solved mental arithmetic problems. As soon as the problem was presented the size of the pupil increased, reaching a maximum as the subject arrived at a solution and returning to baseline as soon as the answer was verbalized. Moreover, the difficulty of the problem was related fairly consistently to the degree of dilation.

The pupil response promises to be an important new tool with which to study mental activity and attitudes.

II. GLOSSARY

autonomic nervous system — the branch of the nervous system consisting of those ganglia and nerves connected to the spinal cord and brain stem that regulate the activities of the internal organs.
belladonna — a drug which increases pupil dilation.
galvanic skin response — a decrease in the electrical resistance of the surface of the skin in response to stressful stimulation.

parasympathetic nervous system — the division of the autonomic nervous system which generally acts in opposition to the sympathetic division to conserve bodily resources.
sympathetic nervous system — the division of the autonomic nervous system which generally acts in opposition to the parasympathetic division to mobilize body resources during emergencies.

III. ESSAY STUDY QUESTIONS

1. Describe the author's basic experimental paradigm.
2. Describe Hess' first experiment. What was its rationale?
3. Describe the experiment which showed that the size of a person's pupils can influence the way in which they are perceived by others. What other point does this experiment make?
4. What effect did hunger have on pupil size? What was the effect of taste? And of music?

5. Describe the changes in pupil size that accompany mental arithmetic.
6. What evidence is there that pupil size is related to preference? What exceptions are there to this view?
7. Discuss Hess' contention that pupil size may yield more accurate representations of attitude than the usual procedures. Evaluate the evidence that Hess uses to support his contention.
8. Describe Hess' experiments on political opinion.

COGNITIVE DISSONANCE

Leon Festinger   OCTOBER 1962

Chapter 33

I. SUMMARY

According to the theory of cognitive dissonance, if a person knows various things that are not psychologically consistent with one another, he will try to make them more consistent. Cognitive dissonance is thus a motivating state of affairs. Just as hunger impels a person to eat, dissonance impels him to change his opinions and his behavior. Perhaps the best way to explain the theory of cognitive dissonance is by example. Festinger reports examples of three common situations in which the effects of cognitive dissonance are clearly present. These three examples illustrate not only how dissonance develops, but how it can be reduced.

After a person irrevocably selects one of two attractive alternatives, all the information he has concerning the attractive features of the rejected alternative are in conflict with the knowledge that he has rejected it. Such dissonance can be reduced in two ways: he can persuade himself that the attractive features of the rejected alternative are really not so attractive; or he can provide additional justification for his choice by exaggerating the attractive features of the chosen article. High-school girls were allowed to select only one record from a pair they had previously rated as equal. After the choice, the girls again rated the records; this time the selected record was rated higher than the other.

Cognitive dissonance can be produced by lying; there is an inconsistency between knowing that one really believes one thing but has said another. When the statement is irrevocable, the main avenue for the reduction of this dissonance is a change of private opinion, but the degree to which the dissonance motivates the individual to change his opinion depends on two factors. First, the more deviant his public statement is from his private belief, the greater will be the dissonance. Second, the greater the amount of justification the person has for lying, the less bothersome will be the dissonance. In other words, those who are highly rewarded for lying are least likely to change their opinion to coincide with the lie.

The final example of dissonance deals with the consequences of resisting temptation. There are two common reactions when a person does not obtain something he wants. Everyone is familiar with the "sour grapes" reaction, but the opposite reaction may also occur: sometimes not achieving a goal seems to enhance its value. Under what circumstances does each reaction occur? The evaluation of such situations in terms of cognitive dissonance may provide a partial answer. When the goal is difficult or impossible to achieve, there is little dissonance created by not obtaining it, and as a result no devaluation of the goal is necessary to eliminate the dissonance. On the other hand, if there is insufficient justification for resisting temptation, considerable dissonance will be produced and the goal must be degraded to reduce it.

II. GLOSSARY

cognitive — pertaining to an item of knowledge.
cognitive dissonance— a motivating state of affairs produced by two pieces of knowledge that are psychologically inconsistent.

sour grapes — debasing a goal that one has failed to achieve.

III. ESSAY STUDY QUESTIONS

1. In what way is cognitive dissonance like hunger?
2. What evidence is there that cognitive dissonance does not occur during the process of making a decision, but only after the outcome is clear?
3. What are the ways of reducing dissonance after a decision?
4. The smaller the original justification for engaging in a dissonance-producing action, the greater is the subsequent change in private opinion. Explain.
5. When is the "sour grapes" phenomenon most likely to occur?
6. Give three experimental examples of cognitive dissonance.

EXPERIMENTS IN INTERGROUP DISCRIMINATION

Henri Tajfel   NOVEMBER 1970

Chapter 34

I. SUMMARY

Intergroup discrimination is a feature of most modern societies and the phenomenon is depressingly similar regardless of the constitution of the "ingroup" and the "outgroup." In spite of differing economic, cultural, historical, political, and psychological backgrounds, the attitudes of prejudice toward outgroups and the behavior of discrimination against outgroups display a set of common characteristics. The intensity of the discrimination varies more than its nature. Although much discriminatory behavior results from the fact that as young children we learn hostile attitudes and behavior toward specified groups of people or from the fact that we are in direct competition with certain groups of people, there is a more general factor which contributes to intergroup discrimination. There seems to be a strong tendency for individuals to simplify their view of social order by classifying groups as "we" or "they." Are they part of the ingroup or part of the outgroup? Unfortunately, in most societies this categorization carries with it an element of competition, so that whenever an individual is confronted with a situation which involves intergroup categorization, he is likely to act in a manner which discriminates against the outgroup and favors the ingroup. If this view of discrimination is accurate, several important consequences should follow. The first is that there may be discrimination against an outgroup even if there is no reason for it in terms of the individual's own interests; the second is that there may be discrimination in the absence of any previously existing attitudes of hostility; and finally discrimination may occur directly in the absence of prejudice.

Tajfel and his collaborators tested these hypotheses on groups of young boys 14 and 15 years of age. They came to the laboratory in groups of eight and they all knew each other before the start of the experiment. At first the boys were briefly shown clusters of dots and asked to estimate the number on each sheet. Then the eight subjects were divided randomly into two groups of four but they were told that the division was made in terms of their performance in estimating dots. In the next part of the task each boy had to decide on rewards and penalties to be allotted to the others. They did not know the individuals to whom these rewards and penalties were being allotted—only the group to which they belonged—and it was stressed that each individual's decisions would have no effect on the amount of money that he himself received. The subjects made the decisions by checking one box in each of a series of matrices. Each matrix consisted of 14 boxes, each with two numbers. The numbers in the top row were the rewards or penalties to be awarded to one person and those in the bottom row were to be awarded to another. There were ingroup choices, with the top and bottom rows signifying the rewards or penalties to be awarded to two unidentified members of his own group; there were outgroup choices; and finally there were intergroup choices with one row for an ingroup member and the other for an outgroup member. The results were striking. In making their intergroup choices a large majority of subjects gave more money to members of their own group than to members of the other. In contrast the ingroup and outgroup choices were closely distributed about the point of equality.

In a second experiment it was shown that when the subjects were given a choice between maximizing profit for all or maximizing profit for only those members of their own group, they did the latter. Moreover, it was found that subjects would be willing to decrease their own group's winnings in order to maximize the difference between the winnings of the two groups. When the choice was between two members of the same group, the ingroup choices were consistently and significantly nearer the maximum joint profit than were the outgroup ones. Thus, even when it did not affect their own group's winnings they gave less to the outgroup.

From these experiments it is clear that intergroup discrimination is extremely easy to trigger and it can occur in the absence of any objective conflict of interests or any hostility toward the individuals or groups involved. It does seem, therefore, that discrimination is the norm of intergroup behavior.

II. GLOSSARY

demographic — pertaining to an individual's vital and social statistics.
dialectical — pertaining to logical argumentation.
generic — characteristic of the individuals of a certain group or class.

social norm — an individual's expectation of how others expect him to behave and his expectation of how others will behave in any given social situation.
statistical significance — the degree to which a given experimental observation cannot be attributed to random or chance factors.

III. ESSAY STUDY QUESTIONS

1. What factors are usually viewed as being responsible for intergroup discrimination?
2. What factor does the author believe to be important in the production of intergroup discrimination? What predictions can be derived from this view?
3. Why is it important to make the distinction between prejudice and discrimination?
4. Do you think that the results would have been any different if girls instead of boys had been used in these studies? Discuss.
5. Describe the procedures and results of the first experiment. How did the second experiment differ from the first and what did this experiment show?
6. What was the major contribution of the research outlined in this article?
7. Tajfel has shown what is not necessary for discrimination to occur but he has not in fact offered a convincing interpretation of why it does occur. Discuss.
8. Describe Tajfel's view of why discrimination occurs in the absence of hostility or a conflict of interests. Evaluate this interpretation.
9. The main question raised by the author's work is why people develop a social norm which involves discriminatory behavior toward outgroups. How do you think such tendencies develop?

THE EFFECTS OF OBSERVING VIOLENCE

Leonard Berkowitz   FEBRUARY 1964

Chapter 35

I. SUMMARY

Eminent authorities have argued that violence in motion picture and television programs can have beneficial effects by allowing the viewer to purge himself of aggressive tendencies; authorities of equal stature have contended that filmed violence can instigate violent deeds. Both of these arguments were only hypotheses supported at best by unsystematic observations until the effects of filmed violence were assessed by controlled experimentation.

In one study, after hearing a synopsis of the entire film, subjects were shown a film segment of a man being badly beaten in a boxing match. Some subjects were given a synopsis indicating that the beating was deserved while others were given the impression that it was undeserved. All of the subjects went through the experiment with a partner whom they believed to be another subject but who was in fact a confederate of the experimenter. In one condition the confederate repeatedly insulted and provoked the subject while in the other condition he was neutral. After the film all of the subjects were shown a floor plan of a home which they were told had been prepared by the other subject (the confederate) and they were asked to administer painful shocks to the confederate in inverse relation to the quality of the floor plan. In actuality all subjects were shown the same floor plan so that the number of shocks they administered was a measure of their violent behavior. The subjects consistently administered more shocks to the anger-arousing confederate but, what is more important, they shocked this anger-arousing confederate most after seeing a film in which violence seemed to be justified. It was clear that the people who saw justified movie violence had not vicariously discharged their anger but were encouraged to attack their tormentor in the next room. In another version of this experiment the confederate was introduced to subjects as either a boxer or a speech major. Using questionnaires to measure hostility, it was found that the angered subjects directed more hostility at the confederate when he was viewed as a boxer, presumably because he was associated with the fight film. Thus, the strongest attacks were directed at those persons who had not only provoked the subjects but who had been associated with the aggressive film.

If violent films can induce violent behavior in experimental situations, why are there so few cases where aggressive incidents are demonstrably attributable to such films? One explanation for this is that most social situations, unlike the conditions in experimental studies of aggression, impose constraints on aggressive behavior. Consequently, people inhibit whatever hostile inclinations might have been aroused by a hostile film. Another important variable is the attributes of the people encountered by an individual after the film; a man whose violent tendencies have been aroused does not necessarily attack just anyone. Violent films can only create a predisposition for violence; for violence to actually occur the appropriate stimuli must trigger it. A final point is that only certain kinds of filmed violence seem to create a predisposition for aggression; it is not violence per se but justified violence which seems to be most effective in inducing a violent predisposition. Thus, one might question the film industry's tendency to ensure that the "bad guy" be violently punished for his own violent deeds. This "eye for an eye" philosophy is intended to demonstrate that crime does not pay, but it may be most effective in encouraging violent behavior.

II. GLOSSARY

catharsis — an opportunity for dissipating or purging a repressed emotion.
systolic blood pressure — pressure of the blood during the contraction of the ventricles of the heart.

talion law — an eye for an eye, a tooth for a tooth.

III. ESSAY STUDY QUESTIONS

1. What are the two opposing views of the effect of filmed violence on aggressive tendencies?
2. What experimental support does Berkowitz's research offer for his conclusion that filmed violence increases aggressive inclinations rather than dissipating them? What support is supplied by the research of other investigators?
3. What evidence does Berkowitz offer to support his notion that an individual is more likely to be subjected to film-induced violence by a viewer if he is associated in the viewer's mind with the film? There is evidence to the contrary if the data of the unangered subjects are carefully examined. Discuss.
4. The number of aggressive incidents which can be attributed to film violence is quite low. How does Berkowitz account for this fact in view of his belief that violent films encourage violence?
5. Describe and compare the various methods which have been used to measure violent or aggressive tendencies. How much do these measures reveal about the likelihood of an individual committing an overt violent act in a "natural" social situation?
6. Berkowitz tested only male college students but generalized his results to people in general. What effect might this have on the accuracy of his conclusions?
7. What is Berkowitz's view of the idea that aggressive films create a catharsis? What evidence does he offer for this view?
8. Berkowitz argues that the major social dangers inherent in a violent film are its temporary effects. What evidence is there for the existence of temporary effects?
9. To what extent has Berkowitz demonstrated that violent films are dangerous?

TEACHER EXPECTATIONS FOR THE DISADVANTAGED

Robert Rosenthal and Lenore F. Jacobson   APRIL 1968

Chapter 36

I. SUMMARY

One of the central problems in any modern society is that certain children perform poorly in school and thus remain handicapped to a certain extent throughout their lives. The reason usually given for the poor performance of some children is simply that they are members of the disadvantaged class. There may very well be another reason: the disadvantaged child may do poorly in school because that is what is expected of him. In other words, his shortcomings may not originate entirely in his ethnic, cultural, economic, and family background but in his teacher's response to that background. The idea behind this hypothesis is that a person's expectations of others can be communicated to them, influencing their behavior in subtle and unintended ways. In order to test this idea it was important to create a situation in which an individual's expectations were not based on assessment of past behavior. If school children who perform poorly are those expected by their teachers to perform poorly, one cannot say in the normal school situation whether the teacher's expectation was the cause of the poor performance or whether she simply made an accurate prognosis based on her knowledge of the student's past performance.

Such conditions were easy to establish in the laboratory by presenting subjects with groups of animals and telling them what kind of behavior to expect. Rosenthal carried out one experiment in which each subject was given a group of standard laboratory rats, but some were told that their rats had been bred for brightness in running a maze, while the others were told that their rats would probably perform poorly. From the outset the rats believed to have the higher potential proved to be better performers; those subjects who believed that they had superior rats rated their subjects as being more likable and spent more time handling them.

To establish the same conditions in a classroom situation the authors had to create expectations in the teachers which were not based on their previous observations. At the beginning of the experiment the teachers were told that further validation was needed for a new test designed to predict intellectual gain in children. Following administration of this test, which was in fact a standard test of intelligence, about 20 percent of the children were selected at random and designated as potential academic spurters. Thus, the difference between these children and the undesignated children who constituted the control group was entirely in the minds of the teachers. Over the next two years the children were given versions of the same intelligence test appropriate for their age group. The children who were "expected" to show greater intellectual gains performed better on these objective tests. The tests given at the end of the first year showed the largest gains among children in the first and second grades. In the second year the greatest gains were among the children who were then completing the sixth grade. Furthermore, the teachers viewed these supposed spurters as being happier, and more interesting and having a better chance of success than other children. An interesting contrast became apparent when the teachers were asked to rate the undesignated children. Many of these children had gained in I.Q. during the year, but the more they gained, the less favorably they were rated. Evidently it is likely to be difficult for a disadvantaged child, even if his I.Q. is rising, to be rated by the teacher as a well-adjusted and potentially successful student.

Thus, the experiment indicated that at least some of the educational problems faced by disadvantaged children rest not in the children themselves but in the attitudes of their teachers towards them. Perhaps more attention in educational research should be focused on the teacher. In the author's experiment, the I.Q.'s of children improved appreciably although nothing was done directly for them; the only people affected directly were the teachers.

II. GLOSSARY

Flanagan Tests of General Ability — a fairly new test of general intelligence.
Hawthorne effect — the performance of individuals is improved simply by subjecting their performance to experimental investigation.
I.Q. — intelligence quotient; mental age divided by chronological age times 100.

self-fulfilling prophecy — when an individual believes an event will happen, and behaves in such a way that subtle and unintended influences cause the event to occur.

III. ESSAY STUDY QUESTIONS

1. To test for the existence of a self-fulfilling prophecy, the experimenter must establish conditions in which an expectation is uncontaminated by the past behavior of the subject whose performance is being predicted. Discuss.
2. Describe Rosenthal's laboratory experiment on self-fulfilling prophecy.
3. Describe the procedures of the experiment at Oak School. What were the results of this experiment?
4. Even the control subjects showed appreciable gains in I.Q. What interpretation of this result is suggested by the authors?
5. Discuss the possibility that at least part of the improved performance of both experimental and control subjects was a result of prior experience with the various forms of the Flanagan Tests of General Ability. What groups should have been included in the experimental design to control for this possibility?
6. The more intellectual advances that "disadvantaged" children made, the less favorably they were rated by their teachers. Discuss.
7. More attention in educational research should be focused on the teacher rather than the student. Discuss.
8. Teachers seem to evaluate students at least partially in terms of the degree to which they live up to their expectations. What are the implications of this observation and how could one deal with the problem it creates?
9. How did the teachers influence the performance of their students?

INTELLIGENCE AND RACE

Walter F. Bodmer and
Luigi Luca Cavalli-Sforza   OCTOBER 1970

Chapter 37

I. SUMMARY

Jensen and Shockley have recently argued that the differences in I.Q. between black and white Americans have a genetic basis. Bodmer and Cavalli-Sforza offer a basis for the objective assessment of this claim, as they review the various methods of determining the extent to which I.Q. is inherited.

A complex characteristic such as the ability to perform on a so-called intelligence test is determined by many genes acting in concert and by a host of environmental factors. A comparison of monozygous and dizygous twins is one method that has been used to determine the relative contributions of environmental and genetic influences. The differences in I.Q. among dizygous twins show a greater spread than those among monozygous pairs, indicating that the additon of genetic diversity to the purely environmental factors increases the average difference between members of a pair. There are two major reasons, however, why the magnitude of the average I.Q. difference between monozygous and dizygous twins is not a good index of the relative contribution of heredity and environment. First, the difference between members of a dizygous pair is only a part of the genetic difference that can exist between two individuals. And second, the environmental difference between members of a pair of twins encompasses only a fraction of the environmental difference that can exist between two individuals. Another approach to this problem has been to compute a heritability quotient for I.Q. This is an estimate of the variability in I.Q. caused by genetic factors, expressed as a fraction of the total variability. One problem with this particular approach is that heritability estimates must always be computed within the framework of a particular model, and thus are always subject to the model's limitations. Another problem is the genotype-environment interaction; the expression of a particular genotype may require a suitable environment.

Arguments for a substantial genetic component in the I.Q. difference between whites and blacks in the U.S. assume that existing heritability estimates for I.Q. can be reasonably applied to racial differences, even though these estimates are based on the study of variability in I.Q. within white populations. It is clear that this assumption is not justified. Whether or not the variation in I.Q. within a given race is entirely genetic or entirely environmental has no bearing on the relative contribution of genetic factors and environmental factors to the differences between races. Another argument frequently advanced in favor of genetic interpretation of the I.Q. difference is that it persists even when comparisons are made between U.S. whites and blacks of the same socioeconomic status. However, in view of racial inequalities inherent in U.S. society, it is difficult to accept the idea that matching for status provides an adequate control for the environmental differences between blacks and whites. The only observation which could provide strong support for the view that there is a genetic basis for the racial discrepancy in I.Q. would be a comparison of large samples of black and white children brought up in identical environments. In view of the fact that racial prejudice is a prevalent feature of American society, such a comparison is not currently feasible.

The authors do not exclude the possibility of a genetic component in the mean difference in I.Q. between American whites and blacks. They do maintain, however, that currently available data are inadequate to resolve the issue, and that the results of investigations into this question are of no potential practical or theoretical value.

II. GLOSSARY

correlation coefficient – a number between –1 and +1 which describes the degree and direction of a linear relation between two variables.

dizygous twins – twins developing from two separate zygotes.

genetic polymorphisms – distinct genetic differences between individuals of a species that occur in fairly constant proportions within freely interbreeding populations.

genome – an individual's complete set of genes.

genotype – the genetic constitution of an organism.

heritability – the proportion of variation in a certain trait that can be attributed to genetic factors.

monozygous twins – twins developing from a single zygote.

phenylketonuria – an inherited inability to convert phenylalanine into tyrosine, which results in an accumulation of phenylalanine in the blood and brain, producing severe mental retardation.

races – subgroups of obviously different genetic composition that emerge within a species.

random genetic drift – genetic differences that arise between isolated populations of a species due to the random sampling to which genes are subject.

reliability – the ability of a test to give the same results when it, or different forms of it, are given to the same individuals on different occasions.

variance – a frequently used measure of variability.

zygote – fertilized egg.

III. ESSAY STUDY QUESTIONS

1. Describe the standardization of I.Q. scores.
2. Intelligence tests are tests of achieved ability, rather than tests of intelligence per se. Explain.
3. Since there are no "culture-free" tests of intelligence it is impossible to compare the intelligence of white and black Americans. Discuss. Discuss.
4. Discuss the reliability, stability, and validity of I.Q. tests.
5. Why do isolated subgroups of the same species tend to differentiate?
6. The analysis of genetic polymorphisms demonstrates important features of genetic variation within and between races. Discuss.
7. The nature of phenylketonuria demonstrates important points concerning the genetic control of I.Q. Discuss.
8. Some investigators have studied I.Q. in identical and fraternal twins in order to sort out the genetic and environmental influences. Explain.
9. What is a heritability estimate? What is the difference between heritability in the narrow sense and heritability in the broad sense? What problems are involved in interpreting heritability estimates?
10. What are the four main features of the data published by Burt in 1961?
11. What are the two main features that clearly distinguish I.Q. differences between social classes and those between blacks and whites?
12. Arguments for a substantial genetic component in the I.Q. difference between black and white Americans frequently are based on the assumption that existing heritability estimates for I.Q. can validly be applied to racial differences. Discuss.
13. The fact that the I.Q. difference persists even when comparisons are made between U.S. blacks and whites of the same socioeconomic status is not necessarily strong evidence for the existence of a substantial genetic component. Discuss.
14. Briefly describe and assess all of Jensen's arguments.
15. Describe examples of well-established environmental influences on I.Q.
16. The authors conclude that investigations into racial differences in I.Q. are not worthwhile. Explain.

PICTORIAL PERCEPTION AND CULTURE

Jan B. Deregowski NOVEMBER 1972

Chapter 38

I. SUMMARY

A picture is a pattern of lines and shaded areas on a flat surface that depicts some aspect of the real world. The ability to recognize objects in pictures is so common in most cultures that it is usually assumed to be universal; however, there is considerable evidence indicating that there are persistent differences in the way that individuals in different cultures perceive pictorial information. Cross-cultural studies of pictorial perception are important not only because they may improve communication between cultures but because they may provide insights into the basic nature of human perceptual mechanisms.

Inability to interpret the conventions for depicting the spatial arrangement of three-dimensional objects on two-dimensional surfaces leads to a misunderstanding of the meaning of the picture. William Hudson observed such difficulties in testing South African Bantu workers and developed a standard protocol for assessing these difficulties. Hudson presented a series of pictures that employed various combinations of three of the standard pictorial depth cues: familiar size, overlap, and perspective. The tests were presented to African subjects from a variety of tribal and linguistic groups. The results were unequivocal: many individuals, both children and adults, found it difficult to perceive depth in the pictorial material. The subsequent use of a "construction task" indicated that Hudson's results did not depend on the particular procedures he used. In this test subjects were shown a picture of two squares, one behind the other, joined by a single line. Their task was to construct a model of this picture from sticks and clay. Supporting Hudson's initial observation was that African subjects were more likely to construct two-dimensional models than were subjects from Western cultures. Although subjects were more likely to be rated as two-dimensional perceivers by Hudson's test than by the construction test, both methods seemed to measure the same variable. The difference between two-dimensional and three-dimensional perceivers was assessed in yet another way. Some Zambian school children were first classified as two- or three-dimensional perceivers by the construction test; they were then asked to copy a drawing of a "two-pronged trident." This drawing confuses many people because it contains depth cues but is impossible to interpret in three-dimensions. As hypothesized, those children classed as three-dimensional perceivers had more difficulty in copying the drawings than those children who did not respond to depth cues.

Do people who can perceive pictorial depth really see depth in a picture or do they merely reason that depth must be present in the depicted scene to account for the symbolic depth cues? An answer to this question was provided by an ingenious device which enables the subject to adjust the distance of a stereoscopically viewed spot of light so that it appears to be at the same depth as an object viewed in a picture. Using this device a Hudson-test picture that embodied both familiar-size and overlap depth cues was shown to a group of unskilled African workers that had previously been classed as two-dimensional perceivers or three-dimensional perceivers. The two-dimensional perceivers, in contrast to the three-dimensional group, set the light at the same depth on all parts of the picture. This result indicates that there is a real perceptual difference between the two groups—not simply a difference in the ability to interpret symbolic depth cues.

Do people who find pictures of the perspective type difficult to interpret prefer pictures that depict the essential characteristics of an object, even if all of these characteristics cannot be seen from a single viewpoint? The answer is yes. African children and adults were shown two pictures of an elephant viewed from above. One view was an accurate perspective drawing; the other was a view with the legs of the elephant unnaturally split to the sides so that both sides of the elephant could be simultaneously viewed. The subjects overwhelmingly perferred the split drawing. Although preference for drawings of the split type has only recently been subjected to systematic study, such preference has long been apparent in the artistic styles of many cultures. What art historians often fail to note, however, is that this particular style is universal. It can be found in the drawings of children in all cultures, even in those cultures where the style is considered manifestly wrong by adults.

II. GLOSSARY

density gradient – change in the size or definition of uniform elements in a picture to produce the impression of depth.
lingua franca – a language which is composed of signs that are comprehensible by people of a wide variety of cultural and linguistic groups.
perspective – the convergence of lines known to be parallel to suggest depth in a drawing.
split drawings – stylized drawings which present both sides of an object on a single, flat surface.

three-dimensional perceivers – subjects who have no problem viewing two-dimensional drawings in three dimensions.
two-dimensional perceivers – subjects who have difficulty viewing depth in two-dimensional drawings.
two-pronged trident – a drawing which confuses many people because it contains powerful depth cues but is ambiguous when viewed in three dimensions.

III. ESSAY STUDY QUESTIONS

1. What is the aim of cross-cultural studies of pictorial perception?
2. Can pictures be the basis of a universal language? Explain.
3. Is the ability to recognize pictures independent of learning?
4. Describe Hudson's test of depth perception. What did he find when he administered this test to African subjects?
5. What findings supported Hudson's initial observation that some African subjects have difficulty perceiving depth in two-dimensional pictures?
6. Describe the experiment which showed that there is a bonafide perceptual difference between "two-dimensional" and "three-dimensional" subjects.
7. Why should people that have difficulty perceiving depth in pictures be less confused by the "two-pronged trident"?
8. What theories have been advanced to account for the split style of art?
9. What evidence is there that individuals who have problems interpreting depth in flat pictures prefer split-style art?

THE ORIGINS OF ALIENATION

Urie Bronfenbrenner   AUGUST 1974

Chapter 39

I. SUMMARY

Profound changes have been taking place in the lives of American young people, and the direction of these changes is one of disorganization rather than constructive development. To a large degree, the problem seems to stem from the failure of young people to integrate into society. This feeling, and fact, of disconnectedness from people and activities has a name that has become familiar: alienation. Bronfenbrenner argues that this alienation has its roots in recent changes in the institutions of society and, in particular, changes in the family unit.

The family of 1974 is strikingly different from that of only 25 years ago. There has been a tremendous increase in the proportion of mothers who work outside the home, and at the same time the number of other adults living in the home who could care for the children in her absence has been declining. There has also been an appreciable increase in the divorce rate over this same period. In 1970, 10 percent of all children under the age of 6 lived in single-parent homes and in most of these cases the income was below the poverty line. This situation is particularly critical for black Americans; a full 44 percent of black children have mothers in the labor force while the figure for whites is 26 percent. Even the children in well-to-do families experience isolation from their parents. The demands of a job that claims evenings and weekends, the trips and the moves, and social and community obligations all produce a situation in which children spend more time with a passive baby sitter than with an active participating parent. It is not only parents, but also people in general, of whom children are deprived. The fragmentation of the extended family, the separation of residential and business areas, the breakdown of neighborhoods, zoning ordinances, occupational mobility, child-labor laws, the abolition of the appren-

tice system, consolidated schools, supermarkets, television, separate patterns of life for separate age groups, and the delegation of child care to specialists are all changes that decrease the opportunity and incentive for meaningful contact between children and others older or younger than themselves.

Social research has pointed to family disorganization as the major source of alienation and has indicated that the major forces of this disorganization come from circumstances outside the family. When outside influences undermine the relationships of trust and emotional security between family members, when they make it difficult for parents to care for, educate, and enjoy their children, and when time spent with one's family means frustration of personal and career goals, then the development of the child is adversely affected.

Can social institutions be modified so that the social context required for the successful development of children can be rebuilt and revitalized? Bronfenbrenner suggests that the following steps could help reduce alienation among the young. (1) So that day care can strengthen the family rather than separating the child from the family and the community, parents and other people in the child's immediate environment must participate actively in day-care programs. (2) If a child is to become a responsible person, his segregation from the world of work must be ended and he must be exposed to adults engaged in demanding tasks. (3) The educational system must be reintegrated into the community and designed so that it prepares the child for his eventual role as an adult. (4) The child's immediate environment, the neighborhood, must be restructured so that it does not preclude the interaction and involvement of children with people who are younger or older than them.

II. GLOSSARY

alienation — the feeling, and fact, of disconnectedness from people and activities.

cognitive crib — a mechanized crib that tends to isolate an infant from its parents.

ecology — the study of the relations between organisms and their environment.

infanticide — murder of children.

III. ESSAY STUDY QUESTIONS

1. In order to scientifically study a phenomenon one must be able to measure it. How have investigators measured alienation?
2. Describe recent changes in the family structure that have contributed to the alienation of the young.
3. Discuss the "scandal" of infant mortality.
4. The study of the amount of time that fathers spend with their one-year-old infants demonstrated the fallibility of questionnaires. Discuss.
5. Describe changes in social structure that have tended to restrict the interaction of children and adults.
6. The author suggests that the increasing proportion of youths arrested for drug abuse is a sign of increasing alienation. Discuss alternative explanations.

7. Some studies have suggested that alienation results from family disorganization; in other cases the degree of family disorganization is used as evidence of alienation. Discuss.
8. Bronfenbrenner suggests that a number of changes could be made in our social institutions that would reverse the recent trend toward alienation. Describe and discuss three of these recommendations.
9. Overcrowded housing is related to poor school performance but this does not necessarily mean that overcrowded housing causes the poor performance. Discuss.

INDEX